Distributed by
Buddhist Books International
P. O. Box 4270
Burbank, Calif. 91503

BUDDHIST MONKS AND MONASTERIES OF INDIA

By the same author

EARLY BUDDHIST MONACHISM

THE BUDDHA AND FIVE AFTER-CENTURIES

BUDDHIST MONKS AND MONASTERIES OF INDIA

THEIR HISTORY AND THEIR CONTRIBUTION TO INDIAN CULTURE

BY

SUKUMAR DUTT
M.A., PH.D.

Illustrated

London
GEORGE ALLEN AND UNWIN LTD
RUSKIN HOUSE MUSEUM STREET

FIRST PUBLISHED IN 1962

PRINTED IN GREAT BRITAIN
in 11 *point Old Style type*
BY C. TINLING & CO. LTD.
LIVERPOOL, LONDON AND PRESCOT

Dedicated to

SAVITRI DUTT

whose love, care and companionship
charmed away all hardships from my
strenuous wanderings in the Buddhist sites of India

PREFACE

The SAṄGHA (Buddhist Monkhood) has received hitherto far less than its due measure of importance in extant studies on Buddhism. The Saṅgha originated in India: its history in this country, where Buddhism is now extinct as an institutional religion, is the history of the growth, progress and organization of a great culture that is interwoven in its historic culture-complex.

A sketch of primitive Saṅgha life and organization was attempted by me in my youth in the book, *Early Buddhist Monachism*, published in Trübner's Oriental Series, so far back as in 1924. In the preface to its recently published Indian edition (Asia Publishing House, Bombay, 1960), I have called attention to its inevitable lack and limitation:

'The book presents a picture in outline of the Buddhist Monastic Order in its growth and development during the first three or four centuries of Buddhism. The need remains yet for a longer dynamic view and more extended historical perspective, for the Buddhist Saṅghas, whose early evolution is the theme of this book, continued to function in this country, especially in the east and the south, for many more after-centuries. The great monastic universities in the east like Nālandā, Vikramśilā, Odantapura and Jagaddala represent the last fine efflorescence of Buddhist monachism, and they were wiped out only towards the close of the twelfth century by the fanatic violence of the Muslim invaders of Bengal and Bihar.'

The object of the present work is to supply this 'longer dynamic view and more extended historical perspective'.

The work has entailed concentrated research work over two and a half years and could not have been undertaken but for the generous encouragement and active support of Dr Malalasekera, renowned Buddhist scholar of Ceylon, recently ambassador for his country in Moscow. It was through his initiative that a Senior Research Fellowship of the University of Delhi was awarded to me enabling me to carry through this work and also making available to me the ripe scholarship of Professor P. V. Bapat, then Head of the Department of Buddhist Studies in the University. His suggestions and corrections, supplemented by Dr V. V. Gokhale's, were very helpful for which I remain grateful.

My source-materials come under two main categories—literary and archaeological.

The literary materials had to be gathered from four languages, Sanskrit, Pali, Chinese and Tibetan. For helping me in the last two, I am indebted to Miss Latika Lahiri of Lady Irwin School, New

Delhi, who studied Chinese for several years in Peking and provided me with translations from Chinese, and to Dr Lokesh Chandra and Lama Chimpa of the International Academy of Indian Culture, New Delhi, for translations from Tibetan.

For the archaeological materials, I had not only to investigate the reports and memoirs of the Archaeological Survey of India, but also to make extensive field-studies of archaeological sites where monastic caves and remains of ancient monasteries still exist. In describing or tracing the history of the monasteries, I have had in several instances to draw upon my own personal knowledge gathered on the spot. I am grateful to the officers of the Archaeological Department, especially to Mr Ghosh, Director-General, and Dr Patil, Deputy Director-General, for providing me with liberal facilities for my field-study as well as for a sheaf of useful photographs. Dr Moreswar Dikshit (now working in the Madhya Pradesh) was kind and generous enough to lend me an unpublished work of his and allow me to draw from it some materials for which acknowledgement has been made in the book in due place.

I am indebted also to my talented daughter, Miss Krishna Dutt, MSc, for the preparation of the Index, a task of great labour willingly shouldered by her, and to Mr Indra Varma for the maps and sketches included.

In writing this book, it was not the scholar and specialist that I had exclusively in view. The subject is likely to interest today the educated public in our country. Curiosity about our ancient Buddhist past is now more widely diffused. Visitors by hundreds who go to see the famous monastic caves of western India, Ajanta, Kanheri, Pandulena, Karle, etc. and the monastic remains of northern India at Nālandā, Sārnāth, Sānchi, Rājgir and other sites will derive a new zest from some knowledge of their historical background and some idea of the part these monasteries played in our ancient life and culture.

A reconstruction of the history of the Buddhist Saṅgha in India has, so far as I am aware, not been attempted yet. I have had to break new ground which seemed at places nearly intractable for the lack of reliable historical data. If those scholars to whose critical judgement I must leave this work be in a position to say that this humble attempt at historical reconstruction has been worthwhile, I shall deem my labours amply repaid.

New Delhi
June 30, 1960 SUKUMAR DUTT

CONTENTS

ILLUSTRATIONS

NOTES ON THE TEXT

In reading the text, the following points should be taken note of:

(i) *Use of Pali and Sanskrit forms of words*
In the present work a number of words will be found either in Pali or in Sanskrit form. The general principle which has been followed in this matter is to take the form which appears in the source drawn upon, Pali or Sanskrit. The language of Theravāda Buddhism is Pali, while that of later Hīnayānist schools (e.g. Sarvāstivāda) and of Mahāyāna Buddhism is Sanskrit. A considerable number of terms, relating to the religion, is common in Pali and Sanskrit variants. 'Buddhist Sanskrit', however, is not exactly 'Classical Sanskrit' and Franklin Edgerton's *Buddhist Hybrid Sanskrit* (Yale University Press, 1953) is a standard work on the subject.

Below are a few examples of variants between Pali and Sanskrit: P. *Ācariya*—S. *Ācārya*; P. *Amata*—S. *Amṛta*; P. *Bhikkhu*—S. *Bhikṣu*; P. *Bhatti*—S. *Bhakti*; P. *Cetiya*—S. *Caitya*; P. *Dhamma*—S. *Dharma*; P. *Hammiya*—S. *Harmya*; P. *Magga*—S. *Mārga*; P. *Paññā*—S. *Prajñā*; P. *Pātimokkha*—S. *Prātimokṣa*; P. *Saṅghakamma*—S. *Saṅghakarma*; P. *Satthā*—S. *Śāstā*; P. *Thūpa*—S. *Stūpa*; etc.

(ii) *References in the Footnotes*
The system of reference in the footnotes is as follows:

(*a*) Original texts in Pali and Sanskrit are referred to by chapter and paragraph (e.g. Mahāvagga, I. 11, 1; Mahāparinibbāna Suttanta, III, 8; Dīpavaṁsa, 5, 52; Chāndogya, 2, 23; Pāṇini III, 2, 97; Mahābhāṣya, III, 1, 26).

(*b*) For published works, excepting well-known and standard ones (like Rhys Davids' *Buddhist India*, Nanjio's *Catalogue of the Chinese Tripitaka*, etc.), the author's name, the name of the publisher and the edition or the year of publication are given in the earlier references, but in later references only the author's name and an abbreviated title, as Beal's *Buddhist Records*, (Nilkanta) Sastri's *Comprehensive History*, Ray Chaudhuri's *Political History*, Lüders' *List*, etc.

(*c*) Cross references are given according to Part and Section of the work (e.g. Part II, sec. 3).

(*d*) In order to avoid repeating myself, I have made some references to my two earlier titles—*Early Buddhist Monachism*, published in 1924 by Kegan Paul, Trench, Trübner and Co. in Trübner's Oriental Series; and *The Buddha and Five After-Centuries*, published by Luzac and Co. in 1957.

NOTES ON THE TEXT

In reading the text the following points should be taken note of.

(i) *Use of Pāli and Sanskrit forms of words*

In the present work a number of words will be found either in Pāli or in Sanskrit form. The general principle which has been followed in this matter is to take the form which appears in the source drawn upon, Pāli or Sanskrit. The language of Theravāda Buddhism is Pāli, while that of later Hīnayānist schools (e.g. Sarvāstivādā) and of Mahāyāna Buddhism is Sanskrit. A considerable number of terms, relating to the religion, is common to Pāli and Sanskrit variants. Buddhist Sanskrit, however, is not exactly 'Classical Sanskrit' and Franklin Edgerton's *Buddhist Hybrid Sanskrit* (Yale University Press, 1953) is a standard work on the subject.

Below are a few examples of variants between Pāli and Sanskrit: P. *Ācariya*—S. *Ācārya*; P. *Attā*—S. *Ātmā*; P. *Bhikkhu*—S. *Bhikṣu*; P. *Bhūmi*—S. *Bhūmi*; P. *Cetiya*—S. *Caitya*; P. *Dhamma*—S. *Dharma*; P. *Nibbāna*—S. *Nirvāṇa*; P. *Paññā*—S. *Prajñā*; P. *Pātimokkha*—S. *Prātimokṣa*; P. *Saddhamma*—S. *Saddharma*; P. *Sutta*—S. *Sūtra*; P. *Thūpa*—S. *Stūpa*, etc.

(ii) *References in the Footnotes*

The system of reference in the footnotes is as follows:

(a) Original texts in Pāli and Sanskrit are referred to by chapter and paragraph (e.g. Mahāvagga, I, 17, 1; Mahāparinibbāna Suttanta, III, 6; Dīpavaṃsa, 5, 54; Udānavarga, 2, 31; Peṭaka, III, 349; Mahāvastu, III, 1, 26).

(b) For published works, excepting well-known and standard ones (like Rhys Davids' *Buddhist India*, Nanjio's *Catalogue of the Chinese Tripiṭaka*, etc.), the author's name, the name of the publisher and the edition or the year of publication are given in the earlier references, but in later references only the author's name and an abbreviated title, as Beal's *Buddhist Records*, Nilkanta Sastri's *Comprehensive History*, Ray Chaudhuri's *Political History*, Eliot's *Eng.*, etc.

(c) Cross-references are given according to Part and Section of the work (e.g. Part IV, sec. 3).

(d) In order to avoid repeating myself, I have made some references to my two earlier titles—*Early Buddhist Monachism*, published in 1924 by Kegan Paul, Trench, Trübner and Co. in Trübner's Oriental Series, and *The Buddha and Five After-Centuries* published by Luzac and Co. in 1957.

'Go forth, O Bhikkhus, on your wanderings, for the good of the Many—for the happiness of the Many, in compassion for the world—for the good, for the welfare, for the happiness of gods and men. Let not two of you go the same way.

O Bhikkhus, proclaim that Dhamma which is gracious at the beginning, at the middle and at the end.'

Caratha bhikkhave cārikaṁ bahujanahitāya bahujanasukhāya lokānukampāya atthāya hitāya sukhāya devamanussānaṁ Mā ekena dve agamittha. Desetha bhikkhave dhammaṁ ādikalyāṇaṁ majjhekalyāṇaṁ pariyosānakalyāṇaṁ.

Mahāvagga, I, II, I.

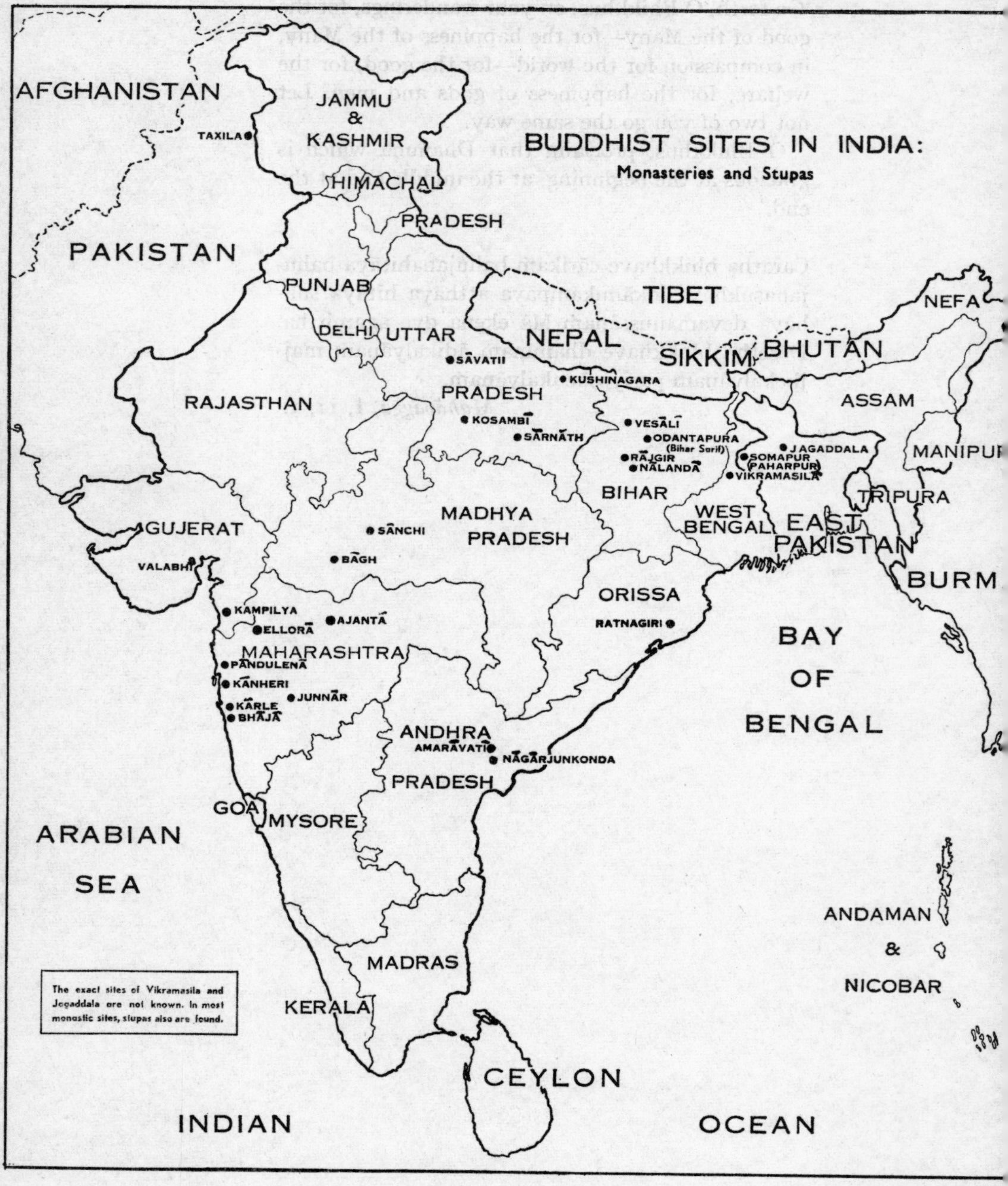
BUDDHIST SITES IN INDIA:
Monasteries and Stupas
AFGHANISTAN
TAXILA
JAMMU
&
KASHMIR
HIMACHAL
PRADESH
PAKISTAN
PUNJAB
TIBET
NEFA
DELHI
UTTAR
PRADESH
NEPAL
SIKKIM
BHUTAN
SĀVATII
KUSHINAGARA
ASSAM
RAJASTHAN
KOSAMBĪ
SĀRNĀTH
VESĀLI
ODANTAPURA
(Bihar Sarif)
RĀJGIR
NĀLANDĀ
SOMAPUR
(PAHARPUR)
VIKRAMASILĀ
JAGADDALA
MANIPUR
TRIPURA
BIHAR
WEST
BENGAL
EAST
PAKISTAN
MADHYA
PRADESH
GUJERAT
SĀNCHI
BĀGH
VALABHI
BURMA
ORISSA
RATNAGIRI
KAMPILYA
AJANTĀ
ELLORĀ
MAHARASHTRA
PĀNDULENĀ
KĀNHERI
JUNNĀR
KĀRLE
BHĀJĀ
BAY
OF
BENGAL
ANDHRA
AMARĀVATĪ
NĀGĀRJUNKONDA
PRADESH
GOA
MYSORE
ARABIAN
SEA
ANDAMAN
&
NICOBAR
MADRAS
The exact sites of Vikramasila and Jagaddala are not known. In most monastic sites, stupas also are found.
KERALA
CEYLON
INDIAN
OCEAN

INTRODUCTION

BUDDHISM, now extinct in India as a formal and institutional religion, has a history in this country spanning nearly seventeen centuries (fifth BC–twelfth AD). It is not the mere history of a faith, though it has been approached too often from this viewpoint only.

Taking Buddhism solely as an '-ism', just a form of faith or system of religion, its history has been sought to be traced through its doctrines and philosophies, its sects and schools, its affinities and inter-connections with other Indian systems of faith or philosophy. This, however, is an introvert view: what it fails to take in is that aspect of the religion which related it most closely to the life of the people—the aspect that is seen in the organization of its monkhood (*Saṅgha*) and the functioning of its monasteries (*Vihāras*). It is the *cultural* aspect of the religion which is perhaps historically and sociologically more significant.

Culture has been defined by scientists in various terms: over a hundred and sixty definitions are listed in a critical review by Kroeber and Kluckhohn. But the simplest, broadest and pithiest one is by the eminent American anthropologist, Henry S. Coon, who identifies culture with the 'sum-total of things people do as a result of having been so taught'.[1]

India had in the past a culture that took its 'teachings' from Buddhism—one extraordinarily long-lived and widespread, that endured over a millennium and a half, spread in its flourishing periods within that wide span of time from end to end of the country. It has left its vestiges scattered all over the land in what are now 'archaeological remains'.

Except for a struggling forlorn existence in a few obscure localities, the Buddhist religion, along with its monk-organization, the *Saṅgha*, was extinct in nearly all parts of India over eight hundred years ago. It had been before that in a state of lingering decline for several centuries. The causes of this decline are complex and obscure and still await exploration. What comes, however, into comparative clearness is that Hinduism in its various forms that displaced Buddhism had amalgamated with itself many of its later developments and finally accepted its divine Founder into its own pantheon.

[1] Carlton S. Coon in *The History of Man* (London, Jonathan Cape, 1955), p. 5. See also *Culture: A Critical Review of Concepts and Definitions*, Peabody Museum, Harvard University, Vol. xlvii, No. 1 (1952).

But the culture Buddhism had 'taught' and the monkhood and monasteries it propagated undoubtedly survived: in fact, it remains to this day a vital functioning part of our cultural heritage.

It was inevitable, however, that with the extinction of Buddhism as an organized institutional religion this Buddhist culture should lose its form and contour—no longer recognizable by its Buddhist affiliation.[1] Yet we are made aware in subtle ways how much of its substance remains as 'crypto-Buddhism' in our cultural complex—for a little delving below the surface reveals it in certain orientations of our philosophy, valuations in our ethics, even in some of the institutes of indigenous law.[2] Less tangibly it inheres and persists in our outlook on life and our attitude towards its problems.

The Buddhist culture cannot be disposed of as a mere historical phenomenon in our culture-history: it has been borne along by the stream of its continuity and is part of its continuum. The history of this culture is bound up with the history of the Saṅgha.

The SAṄGHA has a two-fold meaning in Buddhism—'an entire monk-fraternity' or 'the bond of association among monks', referring in the former to a 'body of persons' and in the latter to the 'confederation which makes them one body'. As we shall presently observe, both concepts of the Saṅgha, concrete and abstract, appear in usage. In the Creed of the Three Jewels (*Tri-ratna*), the parity in which the Saṅgha is placed with the Buddha and the Dhamma is meaningful: it forbids the facile half-baked notion that it represents in Buddhism only the organized missionary agency of a proselytizing faith. The Saṅgha is differently conceived in the system. In fact a comprehension of the triune concept of the creed is essential in our approach to its history. The concept is vitally correlated not merely to the nature of the Saṅgha's functioning, but it sets the course of its evolution and pre-conditions its history.

[1] It is only by very rare flashes that the recognition occurs. A well-known instance is the saying of Ravisena in the *Padmapurāṇa* that the *Māyā-vāda* (Theory of Illusion) of Vedanta philosophy is covert Buddhist doctrine (*Māyāvādamasacchāstraṁ pracchanna-bauddhamucyate*). (*Padmapurāṇa*, uttarakhaṇḍa, ch. 263—Ānandāśrama Sanskrit Series, No. 88, Poona, vol. 4, pp. 1834–5). Usually, however, the Vedantist philosophers are anxious to hide their indebtedness to Buddhism. Thus Gauḍapāda, who was Śaṅkara's 'spiritual grandfather', though in his *Kārikā* he is heavily indebted to Buddhist Mahāyānist philosophers, both in terminology and in illustrations, protests, as says Dr Radhakrishnan, 'rather overmuch that his view is not Buddhism. Towards the end of his book, he says, "This was not spoken by the Buddha"' (see *History of Philosophy, Eastern and Western*, vol. i, p. 273). The words, quoted from Gauḍpāda's *Kārikā* (see *Alātaśānti-prakaraṇa*, iv, 99) have, however, lent themselves to different interpretations. See Mahadevan's *Gauḍapāda—A Study in Early Advaita* (Madras University Philosophical Series, No. 5, 2nd Ed., 1954), pp. 214 ff.

[2] Researches into Hindu Law have revealed various traces of Buddhism in it. See Tagore Law Lectures—K. L. Sarkar's *The Mīmāṁsā Rules of Interpretation as applied to Hindu Law* (pub. by Calcutta University, 1905), pp. 20–24, and K. P. Jayaswal's *Manu and Yājñavalkya* (pub. by *Ibid*, 1930), p. 62. Prof. Sarkar's hypothesis is that both Yājñavalkya and Vijñaneśvara were influenced by Buddhism.

In the very nature of the religion and in the form it first appeared in, was implicit the bond that binds the Buddha, the Dhamma and the Saṅgha together in the creed.

Buddhism has been presented too often in manuals and learned treatises as a system of thought and doctrine. The paradox of it is that it was not as an '-ism' that it was first given to the world: it was conceived not as a *system to be posited* but as a *message to be preached.*[1]

A system has no inner necessity to be propagated, but Buddhism had—and a pointer to this is the well-known scriptural legend that became the nidus of the doctrine, far-reaching in its consequence, of the *Sammā-saṁbuddha* and the *Pacceka-saṁbuddha.*[2]

The legend describes how the Founder, having received in his *Bodhi* (spiritual cognition) the Highest Truth and in virtue of it become the Buddha, passed on to a higher stage of attainment as the *Sammā-saṁbuddha* ('Teacher of all men'). Unique in this attainment among all the 'enlightened ones' of the world, he is singled out under this character by the Buddhist as the object of highest adoration.

Yet, as an *Upaniṣad* says: 'From the bliss of the highest truth (*Brahmānanda*) speech recedes, along with all activities of the mind.'[3] One who has attained to this bliss becomes therefore a *Maunī* ('Silent One'). But the Founder of Buddhism became not a *Maunī*, but a *Satthā* (Teacher). This translation from a Buddha to a *Satthā* is attributed by the ancient maker of the legend to external adventitious causes—the intercession of Brahmā Sahaṁpati, the vision of the miseries of all 'unenlightened' creatures, and the upsurge of compassion (*Karuṇā*) in his heart. Read between the lines, it is a symbolical way of stating that the realization dawned upon the Buddha that the truth received by him had a dynamic quality: it had need to be converted into a message—and that otherwise, in the static form of Knowledge received and kept by the recipient, it

[1] This is how the paradox is presented in the Mahāyāna system in the course of the following dialogue between the Buddha and Subhūti in the famous Mahāyāna *sūtra, Vajra-cchedikā:*

> 'The Lord Buddha addressed Subhūti saying: "What think you—has the Lord Buddha really attained to the supreme spiritual wisdom or has he a system of doctrine which can be specifically formulated?"

'Subhūti replied saying: "As I understand the meaning of Lord Buddha's discourse, he has no system of doctrine which can be specifically formulated; nor can the Lord Buddha express in explicit terms a form of Knowledge which can be described as supreme spiritual wisdom. And why? Because what the Lord Buddha adumbrated in terms of the Law is transcendental and inexpressible. Being a spiritual concept, it is neither consonant with the Law, nor synonymous with anything apart from the Law. This is exemplified by the manner by which wise disciples and holy Buddhas, regarding initiation as the law of their minds, severally attained to different planes of spiritual wisdom" '—(William Gemmell's translation of the *Diamond Sūtra*, Kegan Paul, Trench, Trübner and Co., Ltd., London, 1912, pp. 18–25.)

[2] Mahāvagga, I, 5, and other versions. See *The Buddha and Five After-Centuries* (London, Luzac and Co., 1957), p. 204.

[3] *Taittirīya*, II, 9.1.

was incapable of fruition or fulfilment. What this 'truth' itself was cannot be known by anybody except him who cognized it: 'only the Buddha understood Buddhism'.[1] The 'Deathless' (*Amata*) was the name he gave to it when he turned it into a message and cast it in the form of a *Dhamma* to bring it within average human understanding. The recipient of the truth had to be a *Satthā*: the conviction rings sharp and clear in the trumpet-call of the First Sermon: 'Give ear! The Deathless (*Amata*) has been realized by me; I will instruct—I will teach the *Dhamma*.'[2]

Passages of the early (Theravāda) scripture show that the faith and message delivered to the disciples and the first monk-followers was regarded by them not as a 'system', but as a way of life or form of self-culture: a *Dhamma* whereby one could bring to cessation all sorrows that arise from the life of the world and the flesh.[3] It is described as a Way (*Magga*), and those to whom the Way has been opened—the initiate, the ordained, the 'Knowledgeable'—are enjoined to extend it to the *Bahujana* (Man in the many). This is the apt collective term taken in the scripture to connote men in general or mankind. The Religion must become *Bāhujañña* (adjectival form of *Bahujana*): that was one of the conditions, fulfilment whereof was desiderated by the Buddha before he could think of passing into the 'Great Decease'.[4]

So the credal formula, in the correlated concepts of the Buddha as the Teacher, the Dhamma as the sum and effect of his teachings and the Saṅgha as the instrument by which the Dhamma, becoming *bāhujañña*, fulfils itself, epitomizes and rounds off the whole cycle of the faith.

Some western scholars have expressed the view that Buddhism is a religion 'for the monkhood' and that the laity was 'on its fringes'.[5] The warrant for this view is certain trends in the Theravāda scripture which represent the monk-community as the sole custodian of the religion and draw in respect of participation in the *Dhamma* a dividing line between monks and lay people.[6] But the sequestration of the religion for the ordained receives scant support, as will be

[1] *Per* Christmas Humphreys: *Buddhism* (Pelican Ed.), p. 15.

[2] Mahāvagga, I, 6, 12.

[3] It is described as *Dukkha-nirodha-gāminī*, i.e. what tends to the cessation of Sorrow.

[4] Mahāparinibbāna Suttanta, III, 8.

[5] Kern observes that Buddhism is properly a monastic institution, and the laity is but accessory (*Manual of Indian Buddhism*, p. 72). Dr Archibald Scott finds the broadest distinction between the Christian Church and what he calls the Buddhist Church in the fact that the work of the former lay outside the limits of the Church. Of Buddhism, he says: 'Its lay associates, however numerous, were but the fringes of religious communities' (*Buddhism and Christianity*, p. 272).

[6] If it was the viewpoint of the Theravāda School, it was repudiated early in Buddhist history by the Mahāsāṅghikas (see *The Buddha and Five After-Centuries*, pp. 132–133 and pp. 139–140).

pointed out later, from the Founder's own canon-reported utterances.

Buddhism throve and made headway in India as a *religion of the people*—a religion that was *'bāhujañña'*—not as the cult of a sect or a practice of monkhood.

In its progress and expansion through the long centuries, it continually annexed to itself the culture and art, the traditions and folk-lore, the pieties and emotions of the people. Its history remains incomplete and one-sided unless we bring into integration the two aspects that an exoteric religion must develop in course of its history. 'So far as such religions are systems of belief merely, they constitute what may be called theoretical or speculative systems: so far on the other hand as they are systems of tribal, national, or voluntarily associated life, they may be styled historic or concrete.'[1] The history of the Saṅgha presents this 'historic' or 'concrete' aspect of the religion. Yet the Saṅgha in Buddhism has also an abstract aspect in which it is regarded as a spiritual entity.

'The Saṅgha could not accept gifts, nor sanctify nor enjoy them and gifts made to the Saṅgha could bring no reward': this was the view of an ancient sect of Buddhists, noted in passing in the *Kathāvatthu*.[2] Those who in after times used to make gifts to the Saṅgha, expecting spiritual benefit for themselves, their families and their relatives, recognized in the conventional formula of their donatory inscriptions this abstract character of the Saṅgha.[3] The gift was first dedicated to the ideal Saṅgha and the pecuniary endowment was next put 'in the hand of' the real Saṅgha, the actual beneficiary. In the *Tri-ratna* creed this ideal sense of the Saṅgha is taken: it stands there, not for a particular society or body of persons, but for the great confederation of the faithful.

From the historian's point of view, however, the Saṅgha represents an Institution.[4]

[1] W. F. Warren's *The Religions of the World and World Religion*, p. 2.

[2] The sect is named by the commentator 'Mahāsuññatāvādins'. See *Kathāvatthu*, xvii, 6–8 (Mrs Rhys Davids' *Points of Controversy*, p. 73).

[3] The formula occurs in a large number of donatory inscriptions discovered all over India and also in Ceylon, e.g. Dambulla Temple inscription (*Indian Antiquary*, 1872, p. 139). The dedication to the 'Saṅgha of the Four Quarters' and giving of the endowment in the hand of the resident Saṅgha is found in several inscriptions in the caves of Kanheri, Karle and Nasik given in *Lüders' List*.

[4] 'In anthropological language, an Institution is a group of people. It is organized for some purpose, follows rules and has some structure—in its simplest form that of a leader and a few followers; in its most complicated form a world federation of nations. An individual belongs to several institutions, such as his family, his business organization, church, club, community and nation. If we remember . . . that institution means *people*, not ideas, rules, practices or customs, what follows should be understood without difficulty' (Coon's *The History of Man*, Intro., pp. 1–2). It is in this sense that the term 'Institution' is taken to denote the Saṅgha, i.e. the association of Buddhist monks. Hobhouse prefers the term 'association', as being more distinctive to convey the sense of 'human beings united for a specific purpose' (see L. T. Hobhouse's *Social Development: Its Nature and Conditions*, 1924, pp. 49–50).

The story of the growth, development and functioning of this Institution in India, of which the following pages attempt a broad outline, has a clear beginning, a middle and an end—an integration and unity of interest. A brief recapitulation here of some of its principal aspects and peculiar features may help towards a clearer grasp of the historical perspective.

The *milieu* in which it was founded was the ancient community of India's wandering almsmen. It was this *milieu* that shaped and conditioned it—settled its *ethos* and basic character, the foundation upon which its own system of Vinaya was afterwards built. But we shall see how the Saṅgha separated itself from the parent community by its own modification and specialization of a general custom, *Vassāvāsa* (Rain-retreat), observed by wandering almsmen. This was the starting point from which, outside the wanderers' community, its evolution commenced, leading it through several stages and 'varieties of being'.

The wandering Sect became a settled Order; the unitary Saṅgha became plural; with the spread of Buddhism, the monk-communities, each called a Saṅgha, went on steadily multiplying till they were spread wide over all parts of the country; in their life and organization gradual changes of a transforming character came about through the action of inner and outer forces; and in the final phase of this history, we see a number of monastic establishments functioning as seats and centres of scholarship and learning, and a few as far-famed 'universities'. It is a long and chequered history: yet not the history of a static institution, but one that shows remarkable dynamism and capacity for progress.

The monasteries, from where this Institution functioned, have also a long story of growth by stages. The primitive monk-settlement is represented by the *āvāsa* or the *ārāma*. A typical monastery, called at first a *leṇa*, came into existence when the primitive Saṅgha split up into a number of monk-fraternities (*Saṅghas*). Unlike the *āvāsa* or the *ārāma*, a *leṇa* was not a settlement of monks from all quarters, but accommodated a single fraternity. Originally there were five structural types of *leṇa*, but only two types have survived—the *Vihāra* and the *Guhā*. Taking the Vindhyan range as the 'Great Divide' of India, the *Vihāra* may be said to be the typical monastery to its north and the *Guhā* to its south.

Complete ruin has fallen upon the *Vihāras*. It is only at two or three archaeological sites that standing fragments have been found; elsewhere the excavated foundations are their only remains. But the *Guhās*, in their everlasting inset in the rocks, remain: they bear evidence of the splendid wealth of art and architecture that used to be lavished on monasteries in that spacious age of art and culture known as the 'Gupta Age' in ancient Indian history. To this day the caves of Kārle, Ellorā, Ajantā and Bāgh attract visitors as 'show-places'—treasure-houses of the best and finest specimens of ancient Indian art—but they were built for and inhabited by monks and, as such, have a human, apart from their purely aesthetic, interest.

To those who have visited the caves in their extensive peripheries and the ruined monasteries with their layer upon layer of successive and superimposed construction, it will be a matter for wonder how many monasteries there were in India so long as Buddhism flourished. The first record of an eye-witness is Fa-hsien's who came to India in the early part of the fifth century when Buddhism was already past its hey-day. His record is based on what he saw in northern India where a multitude of monasteries, great and small, were then in ruins. If the Chinese pilgrim could have come to India a couple of centuries earlier and extended his travels as widely as Hsüan-tsang did after him, he would perhaps have described India as a 'land of monasteries'.

Wherever Buddhism spread and the monks came and settled, monasteries were built for them, and both in the flourishing and in the declining periods of Buddhism, the building of monasteries was an industry, motived by piety, that never ceased. Ancient monasteries fell into ruins; on their sites, unrelinquished, new monasteries arose. They were built singly or in clusters and sometimes contiguous monasteries were enclosed within a circuit-wall to form a unitary establishment.

There was an ancient pattern—perhaps going back to the beginning of the Christian era—of monastery construction. This pattern was never abandoned, but many monasteries of the age of the Guptas grew into impressive edifices and some rose to an unexcelled standard of architectural magnificence and artistic beauty. At Nālandā, Gayā and several other sites, these profusely decorated monastic edifices, some several storeys high, were seen by Hsüan-tsang and described by him.

Between Buddhist monk-communities and monasteries and their counterparts in the Christian world, there was an ideological and hence functional difference. Isolation from society was never the cue of Buddhist monachism. It was on the other hand the idea with which the Christian monastic system began. In the first Antonian monasteries in the deserts of Nitria, Celia and Scete, the eremite's aloofness used to be practised in its extreme form. The rule in these establishments was for monks not to see each other except on specified days and the desert was calculated to secure the farthest remove from society. When cenobitism developed under Saint Pachomius and Saint Benedict, isolation from society and the outside world still remained the dominant principle of Christian monachism. Here monastic life is supposed to be a life aloof and inbred; its contacts with the outside world deliberately kept at the minimum, it makes a world of its own and functions within it.

But the Buddhist Saṅgha set out on its historic career from a completely divergent starting point. It was towards the *Bahujana* that its eyes were turned. By their very *raison d'être*, the monasteries had to function differently, and isolation from society was no object of monastic life.[1]

This monk-and-layman intercourse was a feature of Buddhist monastic life from the start. It brought monkhood into such relationship with the life of the laity that it was natural and inevitable that its influence should spread widely into the people's life and culture. It made also inevitable the reaction of lay mentality on monk-mind.

How this intercourse between monks and lay men used to be organized to mark a major Buddhist festival, the *Uposatha*, has been picturesquely described by I-tsing in a section of his 'Record of the Buddhist Religion as practised in India'. It is a picture late in time to which a reference will be made in a different context. The pageantry and ceremonial feasting described by I-tsing is of 'period' interest—the customary form and practice of the *Uposatha* festival of the time of I-tsing's stay in India (AD 671–95). The coming together of monks and lay men to observe and celebrate the *Uposatha* was an institutionalized affair—the ancient tradition and rule of monastic life. It is the socio-religious character of the *Uposatha* festival that is brought into prominent relief in I-tsing's account.

We may presume that intercourse between monks and lay society was by and large of this character—a cordial association and meeting together on a plane that enabled the Saṅgha to 'enter into the social life of bodies of men, constitute a factor in the development of that life, conditioning in a great measure its quality, and being in turn conditioned by it'.[2] There is no doubt that it was interactive in its results, though how far the Saṅgha itself was affected by this kind of intercourse with the laity is not easy to define.

Yet there are unmistakable traces of the trends and the elements of lay mentality impressed in the monks' canonical religion, besides the outstanding example of *Stūpa*-worship which, as we shall see, had been but a lay ritual of *Bhakti*-offering to the Lord in

[1] *Vide* Nāgasena's defence of Monasteries (Trenckner's *Milindapañha*, p. 212)—Vihāre vijjamāne sulabhadassanaṁ dassanakāmānaṁ anikete duddassanaṁ bhavissati. The gist of Nāgasena's argument is that, though monks should live in the depth of a forest, it is necessary for them to live in monasteries, for only then can they be easily visited by those who wish to visit them. Solitude is good for them, but they must make themselves accessible to lay people and so live in monasteries.

[2] Quoted from Warren's *The Religions of the World and World Religion*, p. 3.

the beginning, but was later adopted as a canonical institution.[1]

The geographical distribution of Buddhism over the country varied from age to age. Yet from the first organization of the Saṅgha to its end (fifth century BC–twelfth century AD), its influence over society at large, in smaller or wider areas, was, by the very nature of the Saṅgha's functioning, consistently sustained. It was the achievement of monks to have slowly broadened a cult into a popular culture, a course of doctrines into a way of life for the people. The response on the people's part can be measured by the industry of monastery-building; it never ceased so long as Buddhism in India was a living religion.

It is unhistorical to ascribe any appreciable part of it to the munificence of kings and emperors—not even of those who are known to have patronized Buddhism like Asoka, the Sātavāhanas, the Kuṣāṇas, the Guptas and the Pālas. India never had anything analogous to 'State religion': it is a concept totally foreign to the Indian mind. Not even in the reign of the great Buddhist emperor Asoka did Buddhism enjoy that status. Yet the Buddhist monk-communities were not outside the purview and jurisdiction of the State, and kings, whether Buddhist or Brāhmaṇical, had to do with them in the discharge of their constitutional obligations. The Saṅghas in virtue of their possession of the Vinaya laws were self-governing bodies, and the king's primary and traditionary constitutional duty in ancient India was to protect them in that character and keep them from internal and external disruption.[2] The kings usually respected this function, but the building of a monastery was an act of individual inclination. It does not appear that in any period of Saṅgha history, the Saṅgha throve anywhere merely on royal patronage. Few among the thousands of monasteries that existed in different parts of India, except those of the late Pāla age in Bihar and Bengal, were of royal foundation.

The builders of monasteries were mostly wealthy lay devotees and most of the great monasteries rose by stages from humble beginnings. The munificence of wealthy donors made it possible for monasteries to acquire in later ages their architectural grandeur and decorations of plastic art. The monks themselves were maintained by occasional land-grants or endowments of a permanent kind (sometimes made by a king), but mostly by a continuous stream of 'pious gifts' (*Deya-dharma*) which, in money or in kind, served to alleviate somewhat the rigours of their normal life.

[1] See on this point Part III, Sec. 3, pp. 183–184.
[2] See on this point *The Buddha and Five After-centuries*, pp. 121–122, and Part I, Sec. 5, pp. 81–82 in the present work.

*

In the long history of the Saṅgha in India, there were necessarily flourishing periods and periods of decline. These can be seen but 'darkly, as through a glass'. No period can be chronologically delimited with any approach to precision as representing the 'crest' or the 'trough'.

The peak period of Buddhism in India is identified in the Theravāda legends with the reign of Asoka (*c.* 269–232 BC). In the eyes of the makers of those legends, the era borrowed a certain lustre from the illustrious personality of the emperor himself. In the perspective of Buddhist history, however, it was but the seed-time: the time when Buddhism, till then a regional faith, received the first great impetus that made it known and respected all over Asoka's far-flung empire. The impetus came from a great and widespread missionary movement initiated and organized by Moggaliputta Tissa in Asoka's reign, the historicity of which is not in doubt. But it was the commencement, not the consolidation, for in many regions where the missionaries had introduced the religion in Asoka's reign, Saṅgha life burgeoned only two to three centuries later.

The post-Asokan developments of Buddhism in different parts of the country were neither uniform nor centrally regulated. Buddhism was never a 'church': among the monk-communities, there existed no central authority or central control; even in a single community of monks there was no head or chief—the principle of hegemony or headship having been ruled out by the Founder himself.[1] It was like 'the wind that bloweth where it listeth' that monk-communities spread over the country. In fact, historical information about the state of Buddhism in different regions or localities happens to be so scattered and discontinuous that a whole or integrated picture of any given period of Buddhist history hardly evolves. Throughout, while we see Buddhism flourishing in certain parts, in others it is seen in decline and hence no period can be delimited as marking the commencement of a *general* decline of Buddhism all over India.

But the decline manifests itself. Fa-hsien's account shows it for northern India in the fifth century; Hsüan-tsang's for nearly the whole of India in the seventh. Someway back in the past, the condition of things seen by them must have had its roots—the desertion of many monasteries, their neglected and ruinous condition at many centres once important, the loss of their character as radiating centres of Buddhism, and the dwindling number of inmates. There are some tell-tale statistics of this dwindling to be quoted later, though they are scanty and casual.[2]

[1] See *Early Buddhist Monachism*, pp. 141–145; *The Buddha and Five After-Centuries*, 62–65.
[2] See Part V, Sec. 3, p. 356 and p. 375.

It seems that from the fifth century on, the merely conventual character of a number of monasteries was being cast into the shade by their growth as centres of academic learning and scholarship. The learning was not confined to monks, but was made available to all seekers after knowledge, Buddhist and non-Buddhist alike.

Some of these developed later into large-scale establishments for education and academic culture and Nālandā is the first and foremost of them. And there were others of this type. From the early years of the seventh century right down to the Muslim invasions and conquests, they functioned in the east of northern India—in Bihar and Bengal. Eye-witness accounts of them are fortunately available, from which it appears clearly enough that, by the form and pattern of their organization, these establishments were indisputably entitled to the name of 'Universities'. In mediaeval Europe in the twelfth century, universities grew out of *studia generalia*—seminaries of learning frequented by learners from all quarters.[1] Perhaps several monasteries had, between the fifth and the seventh centuries, developed in India a similar character. Two large monastic establishments visited by Fa-hsien at Pāṭaliputra seem from his description to have resembled these *studia* of mediaeval Europe.

The 'universities' were not flowers of the springtime, but late autumnal blooms of Saṅgha life and its cultural tradition. At the time when they flourished, the Saṅgha had dwindled down to its last resort in a small circumscribed area in the east. Their widespread fame, however, within and outside the borders of India, lends a kind of sunset glory to this troublous end-period of Buddhist decline.

Yet in the monasteries of Nālandā, Odantapura and Vikramaśilā ran the sap of the ancient tradition that associated scholarship and learning with monastic life.

In the early ages (BC centuries) of Saṅgha history, learning had been for the sake of faith; it concerned itself with the canon of the religion, with its interpretation and proper understanding. But monastic learning outgrew this purely inbred cloistered character. It came to be more liberally conceived and construed as learning for the sake of knowledge. But Buddhism, in this phase, had come face to face with the rising strength of Brāhmaṇism and, in order to be able to fight and hold its ground, had to liberalize learning so as to make it more effective in debates and disputations.

The last splendid efflorescence of monastic learning is seen in the 'universities'. But the tradition of it had been long, centuries-old; and the outgrowth of this tradition from century to century was a long line of eminent monk-scholars distinguished in different fields

[1] See *The Shorter Cambridge Mediaeval History* (1952), Vol. I, p. 622.

of scholarship. Their names in their homeland have sunk into near-oblivion: they have to be salvaged from the records of other Asian countries where Buddhism prospered after its decline in India itself.

From Nāgasena of Sākala (second century BC) to Dīpaṅkara Śrījñāna of Vikramaśilā (eleventh century AD), we can trace a galaxy of monk-scholars, each of whom was a shining star, some of the first magnitude. They belong to widely separated periods of Buddhist history: they do not fall into a school, but are individual scholars, each conditioned by the ambience—the state of culture he was born into, the sect or school to which he belonged and the special intellectual interest professed by him.

Out of the BC centuries, only one great name has survived—Nāgasena, preceptor of the Greek king Milinda (Menander). The names multiply in the AD, though a good many of them are transmitted to us wrapped up in legends. The line of monk-scholars of the AD centuries stretches a long way down, beginning from the great *Ācāryas* of Mahāyāna Buddhism. In the means and methods of scholarship and learning, however, there is a dividing line between the BC and the AD: it represents the transition from the spoken to the written word. The 'Scholar-of-the-spoken-word' and the 'Scholar-of-the-written-word' are distinguished by two telling epithets in Pali—the former named '*Bahussuta*' (One who has heard much) and the latter '*Ganthadhura*' (One who bears the burden of books),—very apt expressions no doubt, for books have always been a burden and it is much more pleasant to learn by hearing.

But books, when they came to be written, were eagerly made use of in all the monasteries. Paper, made from fibrous matter, had been in use in China since the second century BC, but became available through the Arabs to the rest of the world long afterwards—in the eighth AD. In India it was not used as writing material until modern times, books (*granthas*) being manuscripts on dried palm-leaves or thin slices of wood tied up in bundles. When scribes took the place of *bhāṇakas* (reciters of texts) in the monasteries, manuscripts were produced in them and preserved, and in the better class of monasteries there were manuscript collections, growing steadily in bulk. With their utility and importance increasing as many of these monasteries became centres of study and learning, more and more care was given to their preservation. There were immense manuscript collections in the 'universities'—what fate befell them will be described in the proper context.[1] The 'library tradition' seems to have been inherited from these universities by Tibet where most of the greater monasteries are store-houses brimful of manuscripts. Out of them have been drawn from time to time stray Buddhist texts now

[1] See for instance Part V, Sec. 3, pp. 357–358.

translated or edited by scholars, but these amount to an infinitesimal part of the whole.

From the fifth century on, China and (later) Tibet had cultural intercourse with the Buddhist world of India. Manuscript-collection from India was the object of many Chinese and Tibetan scholars who came out to this country in these centuries. Manuscripts which found their way into China and Tibet were preserved with care; they were collected to make up standard encyclopaedias of Buddhist literature of those countries. The entire bulk of these encyclopaedic Chinese and Tibetan collections is appalling in its massiveness—they run into some thousands of texts. By far the larger number of them represents the accumulated intellectual products of Indian monk-scholars of successive generations, from the early Mahāyāna *ācāryas* to late writers of Tāntric texts, all of them of the AD centuries.

An interesting side-line of Saṅgha history is concerned with the trans-Indian lives and activities of Indian monks.

When it is recalled that the settled-in monk, living in organized cenobitical society, had yet his prototype in the wandering almsman, it will hardly appear strange that some sort of *wanderlust* stirred in his veins. It impelled monks to migrate from place to place and monastery to monastery within the country. The roving was not always for pilgrimage or for any set or specific purpose for that matter, but perhaps simply to satisfy the urge of a *wanderlust.*

It caused many to wander beyond the confines of India—to Ceylon in the south; to Burma in the east; to Indonesia, China and Korea in the far east; to Nepal and, out of Nepal through the *la*'s (mountain passes) of the eastern Himalayas, to Tibet in the north; wherever in fact they expected welcome as guests from the Buddha's homeland.

We talk lightly nowadays of *visiting* a foreign country, but in the days when travel was a long-term adventure, full of incalculable perils, the traveller to a foreign country, specially one with no home-ties, retained but feebly the *animus revertendi*. Many Indian monks in the course of centuries settled in other Buddhist lands of Asia—wherever in fact their wanderings took them: no memory of them survives. Yet a considerable number of these monk *émigrés* found careers for themselves and rose to fame in the countries of their adoption. Some received great honours there; a few, by virtue of their pre-eminent spiritual and intellectual attainments, achieved such glory that they were worshipped or deified as Bodhidharma was in China, Dīpaṅkara Śrījñāna in Tibet and Dhyānabhadra in Korea.

To this long and varied history of the Saṅgha in India, there was an end—swift and sudden, full of terror and pity, like the *dénouement* of a tragic drama.

The Saṅgha did not survive perhaps more than a decade the storm and violence of Muslim inroads and conquests in northern India. Lapsed into complete quiescence elsewhere in India, its last accents were still being whispered from the monastic towers of Bihar and Bengal, while round the north of the region, the Khiliji hordes were gathering as for a cloudburst. They were fast sweeping down south. These mid-Asian tribesmen had seen no edifices in their desert homeland and knew but little about architectural styles and distinctions. The tall towers of the monasteries, soaring above the circuit-walls, arrested attention; they easily caused the buildings to be mistaken for military fastnesses; so the monasteries became targets of fierce attack. After the razing of the Odantapura monastery in AD 1199 by Ikhtiyar Khiliji's soldiers, it was discovered by the marauders that inside were only heaps of books and no hidden arms or treasures and that the place was merely a *mādrāsā* (educational establishment) and not a fort. But all the monks had been killed and there was no one to explain to the victors what the books were about. Wholesale massacre was the order of the day; monks and monasteries perished together in a terrible holocaust.

Yet a handful of survivors was left in the trail of the general destruction. They dispersed and fled with their cherished treasures—a few bundles of holy texts hugged in the bosom and concealed under the *saṁghāti* (monk's outer robe). They wandered away to remote, secluded monasteries, far out of the invader's track; or to the nearest seaports to take ship and sail away to Arakan or Burma. But most of them wended their way northwards towards the eastern Himalayas. Danger dogged their footsteps until, crossing the Himalayan foothills or stealing farther north along the high wind-swept mountain-passes, the hunted found security at last in the more hospitable countries of Nepal and Tibet.

Thus came about the final dispersal of the Buddhist Saṅgha in India. The Moving Finger wrote *finis* to its history round the turn of the thirteenth century and, having writ, moved on.

I. *Ascent to Gṛdhrakūṭa.* (Photo: Department of Archaeology, Government of India)
Excavated foundations of Jīvakārāma. (Photo: Department of Archaeology, Government of India)

2. *The pit of horse-sacrifice by Cāṁtamūla, founder of Nāgārjunakoṇḍa. The pit, according to ritual requirement, had to be shaped like a turtle.*

The ghāts of Vijayapurī leading down to the Krishnā river. (Photos: Department of Archaeology, N.E. Project, Guntur)

Panoramic view of the Ellora Caves. (*A set of cave-monasteries cut into a mountain-side.*) (Photo: Department of Archaeology, Government of India)

PART I

THE PRIMITIVE SAṄGHA

(500–300 BC)

Origin, Development and Organization

1

'Wandering Almsmen' in the Upaniṣads

POSTULATING 483 BC[1] as the year of the Buddha's 'Great Decease', we arrive by a brief and simple chronological computation at some time near the thirties of the sixth century BC when his ministrations commenced in a small eastern corner of northern India.[2]

Soon there was a group of disciples who had received ordination at his hands and joined the order to which the Master himself belonged—an order that already existed and was even then ancient—the Order of Wandering Almsmen.

In the legends of the Theravāda Canon, we have the story set forth of the early growth of this body of the Buddha's disciples and followers. They formed at the beginning what is defined as a 'cult-group' by anthropologists—of men who recognized the Buddha as their Lord and Master (*Bhagavā* and *Satthā*), accepted his given system of spiritual culture (*Dhamma*) and were devotedly attached to his person. They formed just a *union of faith* under a spiritual guide and master.

Others joined the union and, when it had grown somewhat in numerical strength, the Master charged it with a mission. It was to 'go forth and wander about for the good of the Many (*Bahujana*), the happiness of the Many—in compassion for the world—for the good, the welfare and the happiness of gods and men'.[3]

At the time when they had this message from the Master, the group of disciples was not even a hundred strong and few among them were equal to the given task: the Canon says that there were only sixty-one *arhants* living in the world then.[4] To outsiders this group was known as the 'Ordained Followers of the Sakyaputta' (*Sakyaputtiya Samaṇas*), but the group called itself by the simple name, the 'Union of Bhikkhus' (*Bhikkhu-saṅgha*).[5]

[1] See E. J. Thomas's *Life of the Buddha*, p. xii (Chronology).

[2] The computation is as follows: working backwards from the year 483 BC, accepted by western scholars as the year of his decease at the age of 80, we get these dates—563 BC (Birth); 534 (Renunciation at the age of 29); 528 (Buddhahood after six years' wandering and striving); a couple of months later, the First Sermon and Commencement of ministration.

[3] Mahāvagga, I, II, I.

[4] 'Tena kho pana samayena ekasaṭṭhi loke arahanto honti'—*Mahā*, I, 10, 4.

[5] It will be observed that in the legends of the (Theravāda) Canon, the name by which outsiders designate the *Bhikkhusaṅgha* is always 'Sakyaputtiya Samaṇas'. *Samaṇa* in the expression is just a respectful term for a wandering almsman.

The Bhikkhu-saṅgha of the Buddha's followers represented an organization within a wider community that itself was a dispersed and unorganized one—a community describable only as a horde. As we shall see later, the Bhikkhu-saṅgha, in shaping its own mode of life and form of organization, drew largely upon its heritage from the parent community—ideas and practices, manners and observances, and the 'do's and don'ts' that prevailed in it. This community also was one of *Bhikkhus*, who had different class-wise denominations.

A *Bhikkhu* means an almsman. He is differentiated from an ordinary beggar by the sacramental character of his begging. His beggary is not just a means of subsistence, but an outward token that he has renounced the world and all its goods and thrown himself for bare living on the chances of public charity. A community of men of this type is not found in comparable ancient civilizations, but since remote antiquity they have been a feature of the Indian scene. When the Buddha himself, renouncing the world, became an almsman, the almsmen's community already existed in India: the 'Legend of the Four Signs', from which the story of his 'Great Renunciation' derives, states that the prompting came to him from one of this community.

The 'four signs' (*Nimitte*) are conceived in the legend as four beacons guiding him to the path of Buddhahood, and the first three are said to have been an old man, a sick man and a dead man, seen on three successive occasions for the first time by Prince Siddhārtha on his pleasure-drives in a chariot. The fourth was something different: it was a wandering almsman, a '*Bhikkhu*'. The scrutiny of modern scholarship has challenged the biographical truth of the legend and actuality of the incidents. It has been held to be a 'dramatization' of what other legends report about Prince Siddhārtha's adolescent preoccupation with thoughts of suffering in life, of decay and death.[1] Yet the mention of the 'fourth sign' carries a certain significance: it shows the awareness of the ancient maker of the legend that Prince Siddhārtha's act of renouncing the world was neither original nor without precedent, that he had before him when he left the world (immaterial from this point of view whether a fact or otherwise) the example of a world-forsaker and almsman.

What came to the author of the 'Legend of the Four Signs' by the vague way of tradition is confirmed more definitely by the texts of the *upaniṣads*. The most ancient of them ante-date by at least a century the *abhiniṣkramaṇa* ('going forth') of Prince Siddhārtha, an event assignable by chronological computation to the thirties of the sixth century BC. In the earlier literature of the *Vedas* the 'world-forsaking almsman' is a character unknown, but the *upaniṣads*

[1] See E. J. Thomas's *Life of the Buddha*, pp. 58–59.

describe this condition of life and stress its high ideal significance and purpose.

In our approach to the *upaniṣads*, however, it is essential to distinguish between their different strata. The *upaniṣads* form a group of literature of which the number of texts is traditionally put at 108; they range over long centuries and their chronology is uncertain—the accepted canon being that only those on which Śaṅkarācārya had commented should be counted as genuinely ancient. They are only thirteen (*Īśāvāsya, Kena, Kaṭha, Praśna, Muṇḍaka, Taittirīya, Māṇḍakya, Aitareya, Chāndogya, Bṛhadāraṇyaka, Kauṣītaki, Maitrāyaṇīya* and *Śvetāśvatara*), and these are placed by scholars between 700 and 550 BC, that is, in the pre-Buddhist period.[1] Taken by the orthodox as an appanage to the *Vedas*, the *upaniṣads* really belong to a different world of thought, setting up in its spiritual philosophy the supreme virtue of *Tyāga* (Renunciation) over against the efficacy of Vedic rituals and sacrifices. The knowledge of the Supreme Reality, called *Brahman* or *Ātman*, is conceived as the highest spiritual attainment and *Tyāga* the key to unlock its door.[2]

Of the 108 *upaniṣads*, according to the traditional count, seventeen deal with 'world-renunciation' (*Sannyāsa*) and expatiate on the ideal attributes and approved ways of those who practise it under different names and designations—Bhikṣu, Sannyāsin, Parivrājaka, Avadhuta and Paramahaṁsa.[3] Some of these texts are undoubtedly ancient; others by the evidence of language and style later by many centuries, though conceived in the same cast and tradition of thought. But in the *upaniṣads*, it is not in any human setting or historical context that the figure of the *Bhikṣu* appears: he is presented and glorified as one who typifies in practice the central *Tyāga* doctrine of Upaniṣadic philosophy.

As the highest example and embodiment of this virtue, ancient *upaniṣads* like the *Chāndogya* and *Bṛhadāraṇyaka* point to a class of men who are world-forsakers and almsmen: 'Men, knowing Brahman, give up the desire for sons, wealth and prosperity and become almsmen (*Bhikṣācaryaṁ caranti*)';[4] 'Those who live in the forests purified by austerities, those who know and are learned,

[1] As is done by the German scholar Walter Ruben in *Die Philosophen der Upanishadan* (Bern, 1947). See citation in *History of Philosophy, Eastern and Western* (London, Allen & Unwin, 1952), Vol. I, p. 72 (Note 10).

[2] As said in Kaivalyopaniṣad, 2—*Na karmaṇā na prajayā dhanena tyāgenaiken amṛtatvam anaśuh* (Tr.—Not by work, not by offspring, or wealth; only by Renunciation does one reach life eternal—Dr Radhakrishnan in *The Principal Upaniṣads*, London, Allen & Unwin, 1953, p. 927).

[3] See *The Sannyāsa Upaniṣads* by T. R. C. Dikshit (pub. by the Adyar Library, Madras, 1929).

[4] Bṛhadāraṇyaka, 3.5.1.

become almsmen.'[1] Inset in the *upaniṣads*, such passages seem to anticipate the aims, objectives and customary ways that we find in a later age prevalent among the Bhikkhus, Samaṇas, Yatis, Sannyāsins, etc.—the wandering world-forsaking men of religion who figure in Buddhist and Jaina legends.

They are referred to in the *upaniṣads* as 'knowers of *Brahman*'. *Brahman* is the term for the Supreme Reality, quest for which is termed *Brahmacarya*. The latter expression passed into post-Upaniṣadic religious terminology, but shed its integument of the specific *Brahman*-doctrine of the *upaniṣads*, coming to be employed in the more general sense of striving for the highest spiritual attainment which Upaniṣadic philosophy had conceived as '*Brahman*-knowledge'.

In this freer, more general signification of the term, it appears in the Buddha's message and exhortation to his followers: 'Go along in accordance with what has been enjoined, having realized . . . the Supreme Goal of *Brahmacariya*, for the sake of which family men go forth from home into homelessness.'[2] The concept of '*Brahma*-quest' is identical: the difference relates only to the definition of the Goal—in the *upaniṣads* it is '*Brahman*-knowledge' and in Buddhist concept 'Nibbāna'. Thus a linkage in tradition seems indicated between the almsmen of the *upaniṣads* and the Bhikkhus of the Buddhist legends.

The wholly detached and impersonal descriptions of the *upaniṣads* hardly let us see from what social world or cultural environments men of this persuasion, the world-forsakers and almsmen, used to come: there are no prototypes of them in the *Vedas*. What perhaps is more intriguing is that these men, to whom the earlier *upaniṣads* in their revulsion from the Vedic cults turn as ideals and examples, are so represented in the later *upaniṣads* as to seem alien from the whole orbit of Vedic social and religious culture. A man in this condition of life neither believes in nor performs the sacrifices; wears no token of Vedic social culture like the Sacred Thread (*Upavīta*) nor the symbolical tuft of hair on the head (*Śikhā*). From his habitude he is variously named *Sannyāsin* (one who has 'completely cast off' all things from himself), *Parivrājaka* (a 'wanderer' without home or kindred), or *Bhikṣu* (one without possessions who 'lives on alms'). But his condition of life is applauded and his way of life extolled as the way of *Brahmacarya*.

Later texts go still further in idealizing the wandering almsman, holding up his condition of life as a sort of consummation to which a

[1] Muṇḍaka, 1.2.11.

[2] Mahāvagga, 1, 11, 1 (Horner's translation in the *Book of Discipline*, Vol. IV, p. 23).

man should progress in the course of his life by stages. This 'progress by stages' (called *Āśramas*) was a normative concept of life that took shape and attained to definition only gradually in the *upaniṣads*. It is a clear departure from the Vedic norm of life and the *āśrama*-sequence of Upaniṣadic conception has no roots at all in the *Vedas* which contemplate man's life in one stage only, that of the pious and dutiful householder. The *Vedas* look to no beyond.

But the *Chāndogyopaniṣad* certainly does. 'There are three branches of duty', says the *Chāndogya*, 'first, sacrifice with study of the Vedas and alms-giving; second, asceticism; and the third, the condition of the student who lives always in the house of his teacher. The observance of these will carry one, for meed, to the divine worlds; he, however, who abides steadfast in Brahman wins immortality.'[1] 'The passage names', says Deussen, 'only three *āśramas*, recognizes their value, but contrasts with all three the "abiding steadfast in Brahman"; and this last is subsequently developed into a fourth *āśrama*.'[2] Evidently they who were conceiving life in terms of *āśramas* knew of those who were outside the *āśramas*—whose advance in life was not stage-by-stage, but who, being '*Brahma-saṁstha*' ('firmly grounded in Brahman') were already in a stage transcending all the others.

By the internal evidence of matter and style, the *upaniṣad* called *Jābāla* is posterior to the *Chāndogya*. It is in this *upaniṣad* that the first definite enunciation of the Four *Āśramas* appears, but, what is enunciated as the Fourth *Āśrama*, called that of the wandering almsman (*parivrājaka*), is curiously enough not set in the order of succession: it is said that one may pass on to it from any of the three prior stages and may do so the very day he feels the urge.[3] The *Parivrājaka* stage is felt to be not exactly the culmination of the 'stages', but something apart, not exactly comprehended by the *Āśrama* theory, but a condition of life represented by men who may not have gone at different stages of life through the discipline of graded duties and responsibilities imposed by Vedic culture and its requirements.

More than a millennium after the age of the ancient *upaniṣads*—in what is known as the 'Gupta age' of Indian history—a Brāhmaṇical renaissance and Vedic revival manifested itself. One of its outgrowths was a branch of literature known as the *Dharmaśāstras*. These *śāstras* stem from a late and developed system of social values, ethical concepts, *mores* and ideals of conduct, belonging to a stage of sociological development far more advanced and of more complex

[1] Chāndogya, 2, 23 (translation by Deussen).
[2] Duessen's *The Philosophy of the Upaniṣads*, pp. 60–61.
[3] Jābāla, 3—*Avratī vā vratī vā snātako vā 'snatako vā utpannāgnir' anāgniko vā yadahareva virajet tadahareva pravrajet.*

structure. But the Brāhmaṇical renaissance was traditionalist. Its *Dharmaśāstras* hark back to the ancient Aryan tradition of life of which the *Vedas* are regarded as the depository. They seek to revive it in the life of society and they concern themselves with the exposition and definition of the Aryan tradition.

To the makers of the *Dharmaśāstras*, the Vedic Aryan tradition contemplates only the householder's life: it sanctions and supports only this *āśrama*. The *Parivrājaka*, the wandering almsman, is a recusant from it in his going 'from home into homelessness', a custom bereft of Vedic sanction. The *Gṛhastha* (householder) and the *Parivrājaka* are therefore polar opposites and the householder's *āśrama* is judged to be the highest.[1]

The fundamental conceptual opposition between the two *āśramas* is plain and self-evident. In various contexts in the early Buddhist scripture the contrast between them is brought into prominence: 'the way of *Brahma*-seeking', it is said, is not for householders, but only for the homeless.[2] The standpoint of those who give the call to a higher-than-social life is necessarily different from those to whom the stability of society is the be-all and end-all.

Some of the latter-day authors of *Dharmaśāstras* assail the Upaniṣadic *āśrama* theory of 'life in stages' on the ground that it is not 'seen' in the *Vedas*[3] in which only one stage, viz. that of the householder, is contemplated.

But this antithesis between the householder and the homeless wanderer did not, as it seems, remain in the region of mere theory and speculation. Traces, stray but significant by themselves, occur in Indian legend and literature of its hardening into a class-antagonism. Expressions of it are found fitfully in various contexts and they run through a wide range of centuries.[4]

In the obscurity with which the origin of the custom of world-

[1] See the *Dharmaśāstra* texts on this point quoted in *Early Buddhist Monachism* (Appendix to Chapter II).

[2] The typical passage in the Theravāda canon on this point is in the *Sāmañña-phala Sutta* of the *Dīgha Nikāya* where the way of the householder's life is described as 'full of dust and hindrance' and different from the way of *Brahmacariya* which is pure and free.

[3] e.g. *Baudhāyana-smṛti*, *Praśna* 2, *Adhyāya* 3, 32. It is fabled that an *asura* named Kapila made these differentiations of *āśramas*. But the 'mindful man, inspired by the gods', must disregard them, for they are not 'seen', i.e. in the Vedas.

[4] e.g. (*a*) The story of Aggika (Fire-worshipping) Bharadvāja in the *Vasala Sutta* of the *Sutta-nipāta* (see SBE, Vol. x, p. 20). The Buddha on his begging round went to the house of Brahmaṇa Bharadvāja who was about to commence fire-worship. Bharadvāja, seeing him from a distance, angrily bade him stay where he was, calling him *Muṇḍa* (shaven-headed one) and *Vasala* (casteless one); (*b*) Citation by Patañjali (second century BC) of the expression, *Sramaṇa-Brāhmaṇam*, to illustrate Pāṇini's rule of compound-formation with names of things 'at perpetual enmity'; (*c*) The story of Śaṅkarācārya's encounter with Maṇḍana Miśra, told in Ānandagiri's *Śaṅkara-vijaya* (Jīvānanda Vidyāsāgara's Ed., p. 284) which reproduces the main feature of the story of the Buddha and Aggika Bharadvāja (see *Early Buddhist Monachism*, p. 62).

forsaking and almsmanship is shrouded, one point seems somewhat clearly indicated, viz. that the custom was not of Vedic-Aryan provenance. The mention of the Bhikṣu in some of the older *upaniṣads* is proof of his pre-Upaniṣadic origin. Yet going back beyond the *upaniṣads* into the *Vedas*, we can discover no prototype of him. Neither the 'wandering (*Iyamāna*) Vrātya' of the *Atharva-veda*, nor the 'wind-clad (*Vāta-raśana*) Muni' of the *Rig-veda*, in a state of 'madness proper to his condition' (*unmaditā maunyena*), answers to the Upaniṣadic type.[1] The term, *Muni*, was adopted and used to designate the wandering almsman in Buddhist[2] as well as post-Vedic Brāhmaṇical literature, but not in the tradition of the Rig-vedic Muni, of whom the type is personified in Muni Aitaśeya in the *Aitareya Brāhmaṇa*, vi, 33.[3]

The interesting attempts in some of the later *upaniṣads* at the acculturation in the Vedic Aryan system of the wandering almsman, by glosses and comments on the ritual of *Pravrajyā*, mostly in the nature of 'legal fiction', are tendentious.

A group of *upaniṣads* (*Brahma*, *Sannyāsa*, *Āruṇeya*, *Kaṇṭhaśruti*, *Paramahaṁsa*, *Jābāla* and *Āśrama*) of a later stratum deal specifically, as we have noted, with the Parivrājaka condition of life. In these works an initiatory ritual is prescribed. This is called *Pravrajyā* (Going forth). The details of the ritual vary in different *upaniṣads*. But its pragamatic significance is clear: it is a ceremonial rejection not only of home-life, but of the whole system of Vedic social practice and religious culture and all its signs and symbols. It is therefore called *Sannyāsa*, the 'complete casting off'.

Household, kinship, caste and the external signs of Aryan birth and breeding like the *Śikhā* (sacred tuft of hair on the head) and the *Upavīta* (sacred thread) are ceremonially cast off; the Vedas are consigned by a ritual act to fire or water, and the implements of Vedic sacrifice disposed of. 'He is to stretch his limbs symbolically over the sacrificial utensils, thereby signifying his renunciation of them. He is to throw the wooden utensils into fire, the earthen into water, and to give the metal ones to his teacher.'[4] It is plainly a ritual rejection of Aryanism itself, the going out of the orbit of life that Vedic culture and religion have drawn around him. But to remove the anomaly of it, a gloss of peculiar significance in this context is added—to the effect that the *Sannyāsin*, the 'caster-off',

[1] For a detailed treatment of this point, see *Early Buddhist Monachism*, pp. 52–58.

[2] In *Dhammapada*, 49, in which the Muni is a wanderer; in the *Gāthā* quoted by Milinda in *Milindapañha* (see Trenckner's Ed., p. 211) in which the Muni is homeless; in numerous references to the Muni in the *Sutta-nipāta* (see Index in Vol. x, SBE) where the Muni appears in the same character.

[3] See *Early Buddhist Monachism*, pp. 54–55.

[4] Duessen's *The Philosophy of the Upanishads*, p. 376.

avowed henceforth to lead an unsocial, resourceless and wandering life, symbolically takes the fire he will no longer maintain into himself or into his body. 'The sacrificial fire he takes up into the fire of his belly, the *Gāyatrī* (the Vedic *mantra*, believed by Ragozin to have been a *mantra* for conversion of non-Aryans to Aryan faith[1]) into the fire of his speech.'[2] The gloss looks very much like a subtle attempt to retain within the Vedic Brāhmaṇical fold one who has actually come out of it by his ceremonial renunciation—to affiliate to Vedic Aryan culture a practice felt to be un-Aryan.

The term *Sannyāsin* became denominational in later usage. In the Buddhist and Jaina legends it is usually dropped and the wandering almsman is designated as a *Bhikṣu* or a *Yati*. Only the man who, with a Brāhmaṇical background, betakes himself to the wandering almsman's calling is called a *Sannyāsin*.

For the Parivrājaka Community of India, a deep-rooted many-branched banyan tree, the growth of untold centuries, would perhaps not be an inapt symbol. The Brāhmaṇical *Sannyāsins*, the Buddhist *Bhikṣus*, and the Jaina *Yatis* may be said to represent its longest and most enduring brachiations. Each has its own history of growth and development—its schools, sects and sub-sects and its own contribution to the socio-religious culture-history of the country.[3]

How this unique banyan tree came to be planted in the soil of Indian civilization is a baffling question to which there can be only a theoretic, a speculative approach. A tenable hypothesis can be arrived at by considering a certain sociological aspect of the eastward spread, after 'the age of the *Mantras*',[4] of Aryan culture to the region where Buddhism and Jainism first appeared—the effect of it on people who were touched by this culture, but were imperfectly Aryanized, not possessing yet the characteristic Aryan institutions in their system of social life.[5] Yet the wonder is how a community born so far back in time (seventh century BC?) could survive in the face of all the changes, transformations and revolutions in the practice and conduct of life that had gone on in the track of more than three millennia of history, and exist still. The wandering almsman seen by Prince Siddhārtha in the streets of Kapilavastu is no unfamiliar a figure in the streets of any modern Indian city even today.

[1] See *Vedic India* (Story of the Nations series).

[2] Duessen's *The Philosophy of the Upanishads*, p. 376.

[3] For some account of the Brāhmaṇical and the Jaina branches, see G. S. Ghurye's *Indian Sadhus* (Bombay, 1953) and S. B. Deo's *The History of Jaina Monachism* (Bulletin of the Deccan College Research Institute, Poona, 1956).

[4] By this is meant the age which is represented by the hymns of the Vedas—the primitive stratum of Aryan civilization in India.

[5] The theory is propounded and elaborated in *Early Buddhist Monachism* (Chapter II on the 'Primitive Parivrājakas—A Theory of their Origin').

There have been saints, ascetics and hermits in other countries and civilizations who have 'forsaken the world' at the call of a higher life, but each has acted on his individual urge. In Indian civilization, on the other hand, the act became an institution with the hallmark of a ritual—the ritual of 'Going forth' (*Pravrajyā*)—the passing, as it is concretely phrased in Buddhist scripture, from 'home into homelessness' (*agārasmā anagāriyaṁ*). What is peculiar to Indian civilization is that the 'goers-forth' formed a community that was recognized as such not only by the people, but also by the State. They are so recognized by Emperor Asoka in his edicts in the third century BC.[1]

About six decades prior to Asoka's accession to the throne, the Greeks in the train of Alexander the Great had seen this homeless community in India—to them a strange order of men who were babblers of philosophy, but belonged to no academy—and the Greeks called them by a coined Greek name, *Gymnosophists* (Naked Philosophers). Since then the interest of foreigners in India in these homeless men of religion has never quite ceased,[2] perhaps because a *community* of this kind exists nowhere else.

The secret of such a community persisting continuously down the centuries, over nearly the whole course of the post-Vedic history of Indian civilization, needs must be sought in some sustaining virtue of the civilization itself.

The term 'spiritual' was nearly hackneyed by the first generation of 'orientalists' of the West in characterizing this civilization. The term is neither exact in its connotation nor precise in its application. Yet it has a significance arising from the fact that in all its manifold historic development this civilization has clung to a fixed standard of values in which moral and spiritual values ever have preference over the material. It is because the *Bhikṣu* or the *Sannyāsin* embodies this standard in his own person in the most extreme and striking form, forsaking the world and all its goods for the spiritual quest, *Brahmacarya*, that the Indian mind perceives in him a symbolic relation to the hoary culture it is heir to. To the notion of those who suppose that it presents a phase of ancient Indian mentality that is now outgrown or outmoded, a corrective is supplied by the observation of what is a well-known phenomenon of Indian life even today. One who has need to sway the group-mind—whether a religious preacher, a social reformer or even a political leader—finds it to his purpose to appear in a *Sannyāsin's* likeness in this country,

[1] e.g. Rock Edict 12 in which Emperor Asoka declares his equal regard for all sects whether among householders or among the '*pabbajitas*'.

[2] e.g. Prof John Campbell's volume on *The Mystics, Ascetics and Saints of India* (London, Fisher Unwin, 1903).

for in that semblance he is able to command the highest respect and the readiest following.[1]

In this great 'community of the homeless', already ancient in his time, appeared Gotama Buddha in the thirties of the sixth century BC and he founded within it the organization that styled itself '*Bhikkhu-saṅgha*' and was known to outsiders as the 'Samaṇa-followers of the Sakyaputta'.

[1] If it be not invidious to name an example, we may cite Vinoba Bhave, a disciple of Mahatma Gandhi and now leader of the Grāmadāna Movement in India.

2

THE BHIKKHU-SAṄGHA

as a Sect among the Wanderers

THE Bhikṣu, the wandering almsman, appears in the *Upaniṣads* against no human background and in no social relation. We see him in the abstract as it were—an idealized and isolated figure, type and representative of a doctrine and institution.

Paul Deussen's theory of the origin of the almsman's institution in the teachings of the *upaniṣads*[1] is hardly borne out by the later evidence of Buddhist and Jaina legends. The *upaniṣads* were esoteric learning among the elect and the initiate, but the legends point to almsmanship as something customary among the people—resorted to by those who wanted to renounce household and all social ties. It seems probable that the philosophy of the *upaniṣads* idealized a condition of life that already existed and was in practice, filling it with a spiritual content and idealistic purpose.

As we bring down our vision from the *upaniṣads* to the Buddhist legends, posterior by a whole age to their more ancient texts, we see the wandering almsman emerge as an intelligible human figure: he descends, as it were, from the rarefied heights of Upaniṣadic philosophy to the common earth and the human plane.

As we can see in these legends, world-forsaking does not mean for the world-forsaker a stepping out into solitude or lapse into a social vacuum: in its pragmatical consequence it is a change-over from one condition of life to another—as it is put in the scriptural phrase, 'going from home into homelessness' (*agārasmā anagāriyaṁ pabbajati*). But the 'homelessness' does not necessarily mean a state of aloofness or companionlessness: such a condition for the world-forsaker is optional, as pointed out in *Vanapattha Sutta*[2] where it is said that the almsman 'may dwell in a forest or quit it, or dwell anywhere in a village, a township or a country, according as such dwelling is conducive to his spiritual cultivation or not'.

In the legends themselves, we sight him mostly in the company of

[1] See Deussen's *The Philosophy of the Upanishads*, pp. 411–412; *Early Buddhist Monachism*, p. 49, fn. 3. The institutions of Yoga and Sannyāsa, according to Deussen, were the consequence of 'the clothing of the Doctrine of Emancipation in empirical forms . . . as though it were an event in an empirical sense, from the point of view of causality, as an effect that might be brought about or accelerated by appropriate means'.

[2] In the Majjhima Nikāya, No. 17.

his compeers, in the midst of the 'community of the homeless'. He bears the stamp of the community life; he conforms to the communal pattern in habits and manners, in mental outlook and intellectual interests, and though 'spiritual quest' (*Brahmacariya*) be his professed calling, he has his full share of human weaknesses.

Men of this community are recognized by others by the token of their Begging Bowls. The *Begging Bowl* (*Pātra=Patta* in Pali) has to them a certain sanctity as the visible symbol and token of the almsman's calling. People are aware of their difference in standing from vagabonds and beggars and recognize that their wandering is not wilful vagabondage, but a quest controlled by a purpose and direction: it is *Brahmacariya*, a spiritual quest. Being a professed man of religion, he is supposed to wander about in search of a *Dhamma* most congenial to his own mind and spiritual aptitude.[1] The object may be real or ostensible, but it is the hallmark whereby he is distinguished and known.

When two wanderers meet casually on the wayside, the customary questions asked of one another for mutual recognition are: 'Who, sir, is you Master (*Satthā*)? Whose *Dhamma* (system of spiritual culture) do you find most agreeable to you (*rocesi*)? What is the *Dhamma* you have adopted?'[2] The *Dhamma* is the inner sign of his calling, as the Begging Bowl the outer symbol.

The earliest realistic picture of the community is contained in Buddhist and Jaina scriptural legends, but the picture is not contemporary; it is traditional and needs to be set in relation to place and time. For the purpose, we shall draw upon the legends offered by the scripture of the Buddhist Theravāda canon, the oldest of which, as Rhys Davids believes,[3] were composed out of the traditions of the Lord and his times which the monks found surviving among people within half a century of the 'Great Decease'.

By the evidence of their internal references, ethnical and topographical, these legends were composed in a region in the east of northern India, to which the name, *Puratthima*, is given in the scripture.[4] Here, it seems, was the largest concentration of 'wanderers' and they made a populous community when Buddhism first appeared in the region. At the time of the composition of these legends, a Buddha-cult had already arisen, centring round the Founder's personality, in which he was no longer regarded as an ordinary mortal, but a Superman (*Mahāpurisa*). The legends, once com-

[1] This is implied by the question (see *infra*) which Bhikkhus used to put to one another—'Whose *Dhamma* do you find most congenial to you?'

[2] See *The Buddha and Five After-Centuries*, pp. 34–35.

[3] Rhys Davids' 'Note on the Probable Age of the Dialogues' in *The Dialogues of the Buddha*, Pt. I, p. xix.

[4] See Part II, Sec. 1, p. 101.

menced, were carried on over nearly a couple of centuries more—their purpose being to define and develop this cult. The texts of these legends were afterwards edited, finalized and collected and went to the making up of the oldest canon (Pali Theravāda canon) of Buddhism.[1]

The historical value of these legends, at least those of the earliest stratum, stems from their orientation—their studied, deliberate harking back to the traditions of the Lord and his times. Each legend, early or late, begins with a conventional asseverative formula: 'Thus have I heard' (*Evaṁ me sutaṁ*).[2] The legend itself is supposed to be a continuation of tradition orally transmitted; the formula at the same time is a pointer to the actual origin of the legends.

It is highly probable that the authors of the oldest legends of the scripture were in touch with an actual living tradition, out of the mouths of men, of a great Teacher, a supremely holy man departed not too long from the earth, of his missionary labours over forty-five years, of the tribes, clans and localities of his time, of his admirers, disciples and associates, and the community of wandering religious men in which, after renunciation of the world, he had lived and moved. But this living Buddha-tradition faded away in course of time, while the industry of legend-making remained—only invention took the place of traditions once actually known and reported.

We have no means to draw a line between the 'tradition-reporting' legends and the 'invented' ones. But tradition was the soul of this legendary lore. Among monks of a later generation, there were efforts to keep the dying tradition alive and to imprint it on the minds of new monk generations. Thus in the *Aṅguttara Nikāya* (I, 14), a section of the canon of evidently late compilation, a legend is put into the mouth of the Buddha just to lay down a definitive list of persons who were 'chiefs' among his disciples and lay followers, both male and female, of his own time, in different categories of virtues and attainments. The legend was obviously meant for frequent recitation 'lest they forget': perhaps it used to pass in the form of a catechism between the teacher-monk (*ācariya*) and young monks in the stage of learning.

Transmitted through the medium of these legends, the picture of the wanderers' community when the Bhikkhu-saṅgha was founded within it, is not a contemporaneous one but it achieves a time-relation by its frame and fixture in a tradition. It is a picture little touched up or idealized: in fact some of its realistic details are hardly pleasant to contemplate. In broad outline, it is as follows:

The community had recruits from all ranks of society and from

[1] See Part IV, Sec. 2, pp. 249–250.
[2] See *The Buddha and Five After-Centuries*, pp. 15–16.

widely different cultural and social backgrounds. Of those who passed into its fellowship, it was only perhaps the more serious and more cultured who had a realization or even awareness of the purpose and dignity of the calling. With a good number, the spiritual quest (*Brahmacarya*) must have been just a colourable motive. Among them were those who had left home, not of their own choice, but under compulsion of circumstances—fugitives from justice, bankrupt debtors, vagabonds and idlers, loath to shoulder the responsibilities of a householder's life, disgruntled or frustrated men who had left the world in disgust. All of them were aware, however, that to justify their existence in the community, they had to profess some *dhamma*. Hence the community abounded with men who were mere babblers of doctrines and doxies, often flimsy and of little import—and, as it appears from the picture, unpleasantly quarrelsome and contentious about them.

When some man of wealth in a city wished to earn spiritual merit by organizing a ceremony of alms-distribution to religious mendicants, such men would seize the occasion with greedy eagerness. A ceremony of this kind, held in the city of Sāvatthi, is incidentally described in a legend. Through the city-gates the alms-seekers pour in a swelling crowd—'numerous mendicants, of various denominations, of various views, opinions, inclinations, doctrines and doxies', and quarrels ensue in which they 'wound one another with mouth-javelins (*mukha-sattehi*)', i.e. with sharp words.[1] The vignette is a sketch of the rank and file of the almsmen's community, including also asceties of different orders—hermits with matted hair, self-torturers, fire-worshippers, men who practised in the name of *Tapas* extreme physical mortifications.[2]

In the front rank of the community, however, were those, deemed to be of greater worth and of higher standing, who were designated *Samaṇas* (literally, 'labourers in spiritual life'). The name had within the community itself,[3] as well as outside, an honorific nuance. Among the *Samaṇas*, there were men of superior intellectual attainments who had distinguished themselves as teachers of religion, and, as a class, they seem to have been looked upon with the same honour and reverence as the Brāhmaṇas used to enjoy in society. But the Brāhmaṇas represented a caste and their position was exclusive; on the other hand any one in the casteless wanderers' community could,

[1] *Jaccandhavagga* of the Udāna, 4, 5, 6, and also elsewhere. Specimens of their doctrines and doxies are set forth in the *Brahmajāla Suttanta* of the *Dīgha Nikāya*.

[2] The purpose of *Tapas* is mortification of the flesh with the object of developing extraordinary psychic powers.

[3] In the Mahāvagga there is a reference to the honour paid to a Samaṇa in the Bhikkhu community: he is accompanied by an attendant before and an attendant behind. See Mahāvagga, v, 3, 1 (*Pure-samaṇa* and *Paccā-samaṇa*). Also Cullavagga, II, 1, 2.

as it seems, rise by virtue of his qualities and accomplishments to the status of a Samaṇa, one of equality with a Brāhmaṇa.

The recognized equality of status between a Brāhmaṇa in Brāhmaṇical society and a Samaṇa from the community of almsmen is indicated by the compound designation used in the legends to denote the élite in religious life: it is '*Samaṇa-Brāhmaṇa*'. The origin of the expression is unknown, but we can trace its long currency in usage down to the time of the grammarian Patañjali (second century BC).[1] It appears in the edicts of Asoka, but with the component words reversed. While in both Buddhist and Jaina legends, it is *Samaṇa-Brāhmaṇa*, in Asoka's edicts it appears as *Brāhmaṇa-samaṇa*, a plausible explanation of which is that the legends were composed by those who themselves belonged to the *Samaṇa* class and wished to give it precedence, while the *Brāhmaṇa* is put first in the edicts because the Brāhmaṇical society was perhaps demographically more extensive in Asoka's empire. The accomplishments of this élite, the *Samaṇa-Brāhmaṇa*, are described from the Buddhist point of view in the scripture.[2]

The name *Samaṇa* conveyed honour, and the appellative *Mahā-samaṇa* (the Great Samaṇa)[3] is often applied to the Buddha himself, and his followers in the wanderers' community have from lay people the respectful designation, *Sakyaputtiya Samaṇas*. Besides the Buddha, the *Mahā-samaṇa*, there were in his time six *samaṇas* in the *Puratthima* of outstanding position in the community: their names are well-known from the legends—Pūraṇa Kassapa, Mokkhali Gosāla, Pakudha Kaccāna, Nigaṇṭha Nāṭaputta, Ajita Kesakambalī and Sañjaya Belaṭṭhiputta. Each of them was the propounder of a *dhamma*, and the *Sāmaññaphala Suttanta* of the canon gives *seriatim* an exposé of the *dhammas* of these six great *samaṇa* leaders.

Each of these leading *samaṇas* (and perhaps others whose names do not appear) had his own batch of followers in the community, adherents of the *dhamma* propounded by him. The followers formed sects, but these were more or less fluctuant groups, for it was not uncommon for members of one sect to merge into another, if the latter's *dhamma* found preference in their eyes. The leader tried to prevent disruption, for it meant loss of prestige for him;[4] he also tried to gain strength for his own sect by proselytizing, so that sects waxed and waned, divided or coalesced and remained constantly in a fluctuating state in the community.

A conventional compound name given to the leader of a sect is

[1] See Part I, Sec. 1, footnote 4 on p. 40.
[2] See Aṅguttara Nikāya, I, 173 *et seq.* Also PTS. *Pali Dictionary* under *Samaṇa*.
[3] See PTS. *Pali Dictionary*.
[4] See the story of Sañjaya and the desertion of him by his sect in Mahāvagga, I, 23.

Saṅghī-gaṇī-gaṇācariyo which literally means the instructor (*ācariya*) of a *Saṅgha* or a *Gaṇa*. Both the terms, *Saṅgha* and *Gaṇa*, are of very ancient lineage: they occur in Vedic literature.[1] Originally signifying a 'Collective' or 'Aggregate', the terms take colour from the contexts in which they are used. *Gaṇa* appears in several passages of the *Rig* and *Atharva vedas* in the sense of a tribal or clannish group. Pāṇini equates *Gaṇa* with *Saṅgha*, and Patañjali in his comment on Pāṇini, v, 1, 59, says that a *Saṅgha* was so called because it was one body. But while *Saṅgha* or *Gaṇa* meant in a socio-political sense a type of group life, in the community of 'wanderers' it meant just a Sect.

The name *Gaṇa* was appropriated by the followers of Nigaṇṭha Nāṭaputta and survives in the names *Gaṇadhara* and *Gaccha* in ancient Jaina canon.[2] The name *Saṅgha* was appropriated by the Buddhist monks,[3] who called themselves collectively *Bhikkhu-saṅgha.*

Some light is thrown on the organization of a sect by the story of Sāriputta's conversion told in *Mahāvagga* I, 23. On meeting a fellow-wanderer Assaji on his begging round, Sāriputta was struck by the spiritual radiance of his countenance and enquired of him: 'Under whose guidance have you accepted religious mendicancy? Who is your Master (*Satthā*)? Whose *Dhamma* is agreeable to you?' The same set of questions was put by Upaka to the Buddha himself when the latter, after the 'enlightenment', had just left his seat under Bodhi Tree.[4] The questions are pointed, and their drift shows that it was customary in the wanderers' community for one, specially if he were a neophyte, to attach oneself to a Master (*Satthā*), adopt the *dhamma* propounded by him, and, accepting his leadership, to enlist in the sect, *saṅgha* or *gaṇa*, founded by him. It brings into relief the character of a sect in the community: it is no more than a cult-group delimited by the *dhamma* given to it by the leader and held together by its allegiance to the *Satthā*.

Significantly, however, it is not as a sect-leader that the Buddha figures in the legends: he is always differentiated from other sect-leaders in the community. For this, most probably there was basis in his teachings.

It is re-iteratively stressed in the *Brahmajāla Suttanta* that the Buddha is not the propounder, like the other sect-leaders, of a speculative system: his *dhamma* is something he had, before propounding, 'realized and experienced himself' (*Yaṁ Tathāgato sayaṁ*

[1] See Macdonell and Keith's *Index to the Vedas*.

[2] See J. C. Jain's *Life in Ancient India as depicted in the Jaina Canons*. (New Book Company, Bombay, 1947), p. 25.

[3] Thus *Saṅgha* is distinguished from *Gaṇa* in Cullavagga, VI, 15, 2—'Saṅghena vā gaṇena vā puggalena vā'.

[4] Mahāvagga, I, 6, 7.

abhinnā sacchikatvā pavadeti).[1] It was not given to a sect, but was meant for mankind. Several statements in different contexts and called forth by different occasions are put into his mouth in the legends in which the universality of his character as teacher of religion is emphasized. He is set up not only as *Satthā* to his sect, but as the *Sammā-saṁbuddha* (Universal Teacher). His message, instinct with living truth, self-experienced and self-realized, has come down to us inevitably transformed as a system, as a *Dhamma*.

But in delivering his message, we are told it was not just to a doctrinal system that he pointed. A standing phrase by which the purposiveness of his utterances and their effects on the audience are described is: that he 'gives direction' (*sandeseti*), 'makes them receive' (*samādapeti*), 'excites' (*samuttejeti*) and 'gives satisfaction' (*sampahaṁseti*),[2] and it was to the *Bahujana* ('Many-men') that the message was addressed. If his followers formed a sect, the sect was not to be regarded as an end in itself, but as a means for promotion of the 'welfare and happiness of the Many'. This, as we have seen, was the gist of his exhortation to his monk-followers when they had grown into a body fit to take up his mission.

The universal non-sectarian character of his teachings appears from the legends to have been cherished by the Founder from first to last.

Between the time when the Saṅgha came into existence as a unitary body of disciples and the Buddha's last missionary tour, the Bhikkhu-saṅgha must have grown in strength and cohesion. Yet the Founder refused to the last to recognize it as a circumscribed body or himself as its head or to limit it to sectarian bondage by a system of rules. This is the unmistakable significance of what he declared to Ānanda at Beluva on the last missionary tour. Ānanda had anxiously requested him to 'say something with regard to the Bhikkhu-saṅgha before his decease'. He had obviously meant by the Saṅgha the Master's sect in the wanderers' community. But the Buddha was not concerned about the 'sect': it was the truth he had seen himself and presented in the *Dhamma* that he was anxious to see his followers adopt as their sole refuge.[3] His declaration to Ānanda connects itself with an earlier canon-reported statement of his to Nigrodha: 'Maybe, Nigrodha, you will think: the Samaṇa Gotama said this (i.e. preached his *dhamma*) from a desire to get disciples. But you are not to explain my words thus. Let him who is your teacher (*Satthā*), be your teacher still'.[4]

[1] The asseveration occurs at the end of each recitative section.
[2] See Mahāparinibbāna Suttanta, I, 25 and *passim*.
[3] See *Ibid*, II, 31–32.
[4] Udambarika Sīhanāda Suttanta in *Dīgha Nikāya* (see *Dialogues of the Buddha*, pt. iii, p. 51).

In the canon, while the *Bhikkhu-saṅgha* is the name for the body of his followers, it is as the *Cātuddisa Bhikkhu-saṅgha* (Bhikkhu-saṅgha of the Four Quarters) that the Founder himself calls it. As we have pointed out in the Introduction, the phrase became canonical and in its later use in the formula of donation to a monastery, the Bhikkhu-saṅgha was understood in an ideal sense—as a spiritual entity that transcended the idea of a sect or a body of persons.

The Bhikkhu-saṅgha actually took shape, not conformably to the ideal cherished by the Founder, but to the normal type and configuration of a sect in the wanderers' community. It looked up to the Buddha as the *Satthā*; its bond was the *Dhamma* given to it by the Founder, and the cement of its cohesion common allegiance to the *Satthā*. From the other sects, it was distinguished by its *Dhamma*: the sect rested on the basis of its cult, and there were, as usual, defections from as well as accretions to it.

The real character of the primitive Bhikkhu-saṅgha—as it existed in the Founder's own time—is perhaps well portrayed by the story of Sarabha told in a late legend.[1] Sarabha, who was a wandering almsman (*Paribbājaka*) had joined the Sakyaputtiya sect, but had lost faith in 'the Dhamma of the Sakyaputtiyas'. It is said that, on the intercession of his followers, the Buddha himself appeared before him in person and tried to restore his lost faith. His efforts were unavailing, and the Master, having 'thrice uttered his lion's roar (*sīhanāda*)' in the 'Wanderers' Park (Paribbājakārāma) by the Snake River at Rājagaha', vanished from the spot. The recusant Sarabha was then assailed with a torrent of abuse by the Sakyaputtiyas present there who made great fun of and horse-play with him.

The Sarabha legend is of course not to be taken as historical: it is more likely to be an 'invented' one, just a story with no basis in tradition. But the maker of the legend was evidently trying, with a rude power of realism, to envisage and call up the Saṅgha in the exact 'form and pressure' of the Founder's own time.

This primitive Saṅgha of the Founder's own time—the small body of *Sakyaputtiya Samaṇas* existing as a sect in the wanderers' community—ceased to be a mere Sect, united, like the others, only by a bond of faith and of allegiance to a Master. It emerged out of the parent community in a different character, transforming itself from a wandering sect to a settled Order.

[1] Aṅguttara Nikāya, III, 7.64.3 (see Woodward's *Gradual Sayings*, vol. I, pp. 167 ff.).

3

From Wandering to Settled Life

'Behold ye, how the clouds congregate in the sky and torrents of rain oppress the earth with their fury': thus a Seer (*Ṛṣi*) of the Vedic age describes what is a familiar climatic phenomenon of India, the annual cloud-burst of monsoon.[1]

It ushers in the rainy season over the country. 'The random breezes die, at great altitude a haze covers the sky, and upon tensely expectant people and dessicated plants, the monsoon breaks.'[2]

The countryside gets flooded; the rivers swell and pulsate to the beat of the rain; shrunk streams become unfordable; cross-country tracks are washed away and effaced. This seasonal rainfall occurs round the middle of June, but in some years it is nearly a month late in starting. The season lasts roughly for a period of three months.

Those who were wanderers by their calling had to reckon with the monsoon conditions which made inevitable an annual break in their wanderings. So it became customary for all sects of the wanderers' community to suspend wandering and seek shelter for the season, and the custom was already very old—it had even gained from antiquity the character of a ceremonial observance in the community—when Prince Gotama forsook the world and joined it.

The rule that a wanderer must suspend wandering and remain in retreat during the season of rains occurs among the canonical regulations of different sects: the Buddhists call it *Vassa*, the Jainas *Pajjusaṇa*, and the Brāhmaṇical Sannyāsins are enjoined to be 'of fixed residence' (*Dhruvaśīla*) during the time.[3] This 'rain-retreat' seems to have been a universal customary observance among wanderers of all sects.

The first step in the individuation of the Bhikkhu-saṅgha, differentiating it in character from other sects in the community, was taken when the general custom was specialized by the Buddhists. The Jaina and Brāhmaṇical wanderers had no regulations prescribing 'living together' during rain-retreat. In the Brāhmaṇical texts, it is

[1] Atharva-veda, IV, 153.

[2] Taken from Hart's *New India's Rivers* (Bombay, Orient Longmans, 1956), p. 8.

[3] The texts are: *Āruṇeyopaniṣad*, 3—*Varṣāsu dhruvaśīlo' aṣṭou māsānekākī yatiś-caret dvāveva vā caret* (see *The Samnyāsa Upanishads*, p. 13); *Kaṭharudropaniṣad*, 1 (commentary)—*Caturo māsān vārṣikān grāme vā nagare vāpi vaset* (see *Ibid*, p. 18); *Nārada-parivrājakopaniṣad* 3—*Ekavāsa avāso vā . . . ekadṛṣtir' alolupaḥ: eka eva carennityaṁ varṣāsyekatra saṁvaset* (see *Ibid*, p. 66) and *passim*.

'living at one place' (*ekatra*) or 'at a fixed residence' (*dhruvaśīla*) that is contemplated. In the Jaina rules, no 'specially made' lodgings (like the *āvāsas* of the Buddhists) are allowed and only the teacher (*ācāryopādhyāya*) and his group of pupils (*gaṇavacchedaka*) can lawfully live together.[1] But the Buddhist *Vassa* became an occasion for Bhikkhus to live together in congregation. Thus it is told that when the Buddha on his last missionary tour reached Vesālī, the monsoon had set in and he called upon his followers to spend the *vassa*-period at the village of Beluva, 'each according to the place where his friends, acquaintances and intimate ones might live'.[2]

The Buddhist idea of rain-retreat seems to have been not to live anywhere or alone and companionless or in promiscuous company, but to settle in a congregation of fellow-monks. For that purpose, the settlement needed sequestration within its own boundaries. The demarcation and fixing of boundaries (*sīmā*), therefore, became a matter of some importance in order to allow a body of Bhikkhus to live together by themselves.

This was the character of the Buddhist *vassāvāsa* (rain-retreat) and it seems to have been the practice of no other sect. The story occurs in the Ceylonese chronicle, *Dīpavaṁsa* (*XIV*, 22), that the first Buddhist Ceylonese king who was making a *saṅghārāma* (monastic settlement) for the newly-arrived Buddhist monks from India asked Mahinda whether it had been properly established and was told by the latter that it would not be till the boundaries (*sīmā*) were fixed.[3]

Being professed almsmen, the Bhikkhus would naturally make their *vassa* settlements in localities where alms were available, though a class among them preferred to live in forest-clearings for which they earned the name of *Āraññakas* (Forest-dwellers). Normally these settlements were located in both towns and villages where the Bhikkhus could live in congregations of their own and subsist on alms. The problem of accommodation for the rain-retreat, however, would not be the same in the city as in the countryside.

In the latter, the boundary settlement would be the first task for the monks and the shelters would have to be built by them; in a town or city, on the other hand, there might be found a wealthy lay devotee inclined to donate to the monks as an act of piety, permanently or for use during the *vassa* period, his own private park or pleasure garden. Thus two kinds of settlement for rain-retreat came into existence—(1) the *Āvāsa* in the countryside, staked out, built and maintained by the monks themselves, and (2) the

[1] See Deo's *The History of Jaina Monachism*, pp. 159, 249.
[2] Mahāparinibbāna Suttanta, ii, 22.
[3] See Rahula's *History of Buddhism in Ceylon* (Gunasena & Co., 1956), p. 56, footnote 2.

Ārāma, in or near a town or city, situated within its own private enclosure and looked after by the donor.

It was the rule (still observed by Buddhist monks in all Asian Buddhist countries) to take up *vassa* residence on the day after the full moon of *Āsālha* (Āṣāḍha, i.e. mid-June) or a month later and continue it for the three following months.[1]

The monks during this period were allowed to go out of the settlement only under certain specified conditions when their presence elsewhere was required for good reasons and the absence did not exceed a week.[2] When first instituted, the *Āvāsa* and the *Ārāma* were in the nature of encampments strictly temporary in character: residence in them being limited strictly to the three rainy months.[3] If any residential house was temporarily left by the monks for repairs, it could be reserved for re-occupation, but never beyond the limit of the *Vassa* period.

Even this three months' living together had its effects on the chance-met residents: they developed a collective life which found active expression in institutions, customs and practices of a congregational character. The recital of the *Pātimokkha* became a congregational service; ceremonies like *Pavāraṇā* ('Invitation') and *Kaṭhina* (Distribution of Robes) for the new year commencing after the *vassa* were instituted, and in fact, with donations coming in a liberal measure for the monks' maintenance, the rule of wandering almsmanship lost its urgency and much of its mandatory character. These circumstances formed a background for the transformation that slowly came about of *vassa*-settlements into domiciles. The *āvāsas* and *ārāmas* were nominally for three months' sojourn, but as we shall presently observe, they tended more and more to become establishments at least of a semi-permanent character.

The ancient ideal of a free wandering life, however, was never given up by the Bhikkhus. But they ceased to be wanderers like almsmen of other sects. There are indications of the growth of a custom among them of returning to and occupying the same *āvāsas* and *ārāmas*, on the termination of the wandering period, that they had left after the last rain-retreat—so that those who habitually lived together for the *vassa* in one *āvāsa* (*Samāna-saṁvāsaka*) were distinguished from those who habitually lived together in another (*Nānā-saṁvāsaka*). The 'co-dwellers' were distinguished from others in the matter of allotment of accommodation (*senāsana*) and in the exercise of the rights of Saṅgha life.

[1] Mahāvagga III, 2, 2.
[2] *Ibid*, III, 9, 1–4 and 11 (*vassaccheda*).
[3] Cullavagga, VI, 11, 3—*Anujānāmi Bhikkhave vassānaṁ temāsaṁ paṭibāhituṁ utukālaṁ na paṭibāhitun 'ti.*

As this custom of resorting to the same *āvāsa* for rain-retreat became more and more the use and wont among the Buddhists, the Bhikkhus came to be distinguished from 'wanderers' and they themselves seem to have recognized and accepted the distinction.[1] The idea of a continuing congregation, in spite of its annual regulation break-up after the *vassa*, was responsible for the development of those features of collective life we have mentioned, viz. the *Pātimokkha* recital, the *Pavāraṇā* and the *Kaṭhina*.

The Founder's idea, as we have seen, had been that the Saṅgha should be one entire body, a unitary organization of monks hailing from all quarters irrespective of regional provenance—a *Cātuddisa* (Four-Quarters) *Bhikkhu-saṅgha*. But regional and local distinctions appear in casual references in the *Vinayapiṭaka*, such as to the 'Saṅgha of Sāvatthi', the 'Saṅgha of Jetavana', etc. Evidently the Saṅgha of the Four Quarters was splitting up in actual practice and *āvāsas* and *ārāmas* were becoming units of Saṅgha life. Yet the old idea of the Saṅgha of the Four Quarters persisted and an *āvāsa* or an *ārāma* could not therefore be reserved for any particular company of monks. Each *vassa* period a company, made up of old residents and newcomers would turn up to occupy one of these abodes, but the 'bed-and-sitting accommodation' (*senāsana*) to be supplied to each incoming monk was necessarily limited. Preference then went to the old 'co-dwellers' (*samāna-saṁvāsaka*), and for the delicate task of allotting seats to the incoming company, a monk was appointed *ad hoc* as Chamberlain (*Senāsana-gāhāpaka*).

The rules for the allotment of *senāsanas* throw much light on the growth of *āvāsas* and *ārāmas* from mere rain-retreat shelters to residential units. The rules read thus: 'There are three (times for the assignment of lodgings): the Earlier, the Later and the Intervening. The *earlier* on which they are to be assigned, is the day following the full moon of *Āsāḷha*; the *later* on which they are to be assigned, is the month following the full moon of *Āsāḷha*; the *intervening* on which they are to be assigned, is the day following the Invitation (*Pavāraṇā*) with reference to the next rains-residence'.[2]

The third assignment is called *Antarā-muttaka*, meaning, that which involves giving up claim to a *senāsana* during the non-*vassa* period. But the *āvāsa* was not supposed to be occupied at all during the non-*vassa* period; so a fresh allotment of *senāsanas* on the eve of this period on the closing *Pavāraṇā* day would be meaningless; the

[1] '*Nayyo ete Bhikkhū, Paribbājakā 'ti*' (They are not Bhikkhus, but Paribbājakas)—Cullavagga V, 23, 2. Compare also the Pātimokkha rule—*Yo pana Bhikkhu acelakassa vā paribbājakāya vā sahatthā khādanīyaṁ vā bhojanīyaṁ vā dadeyya pācittiyaṁ* (The Bhikkhu who with his own hand gives food or edibles to an *acelaka* (naked ascetic) or to a *paribbājaka* (wanderer) is guilty of a Pācittiya offence).

[2] Cullavagga, VI, 11, 4 (see Horner's *Book of Discipline*, vol. V, p. 235.)

explanation offered is that it has 'reference to the next rains-residence', but for that there is already provision for allotment on the day following the full moon of *Āsāḷha*. The true explanation is that a fresh allotment of *senāsanas*, when the *vassa*-period had ended with the *Pavāraṇā*, was necessitated by the fact that many monks would choose to remain in the *āvāsa*—that the rule of residence in the *āvāsa only* during the three months of the *vassa* was falling into desuetude. Thus a new unit came to be recognized—'a company of monks belonging to an *āvāsa* (*āvāsika*)'.[1] It is not a fortuitous group of monks out of the Brotherhood of Four Quarters, but a body limited by its habitual occupation of the same *āvāsa*. Hence rose the distinction made in respect both of accommodation and of participation in the affairs of the Saṅgha between the 'co-dwellers' (*samāna-saṁvāsaka*) and the 'separate dwellers' (*nānā-saṁvāsaka*). The *āvāsikas*, dwellers at an *āvāsa*, constituting a unit, called themselves collectively a *Saṅgha*: it was not 'The Saṅgha of the Four Quarters' but a single monk-fraternity.

An *āvāsa* was by no means an organized monastery, but only a colony of monks which constituted the seat of a *saṇgha*. It was so circumscribed by its *sīmā* (limits) as to be completely independent and unitary. The rules for the settlement of *sīmā* are that the limits should generally coincide with natural boundaries such as a mountain, a rock, a wood, a tree, a path, an ant-hill, a river or a sheet of water,[2] but they must not extend beyond three *yojanas*, nor to the opposite bank of a river unless facilities existed for crossing over.[3] Where no such limits could be fixed, the boundaries of the village or of the market-town (*gāmā-sīmā* or *nigama-sīmā*) could serve the purpose.[4] In a forest, the community of residence would extend to a distance of seven *abbhantaras* (a measure of distance). It is further laid down that the boundaries of two *āvāsas* must not overlap: an interstice must be left between.[5]

This process of transition from wandering to settled life was a slow and gradual one, but undoubtedly accomplished early in Saṅgha history—perhaps as early as the fourth century BC. Its consequence was twofold—first, the Saṅgha became an organization independent of the wanderers' community: the Buddhist Bhikkhus were by themselves as well as by others distinguished from 'wanderers'; secondly, it marked the beginning of cenoebium among them. In the *Vinayapiṭaka*, the Bhikkhu-saṅgha appears not as a body of wanderers, but as a settled cenobitical society.

[1] The expression 'āvāsika' occurs several times in the *Vinayapiṭaka* (*vide* Mahāvagga, II, 28 *et seq*; Cullavagga I, 18, 1; VI, 15, 1; VII, 1, 2, etc.) meaning 'a company of Bhikkhus living at an *āvāsa*'. Their 'togetherness' is recognized by the term.

[2] Mahāvagga, II, 6. [3] *Ibid*, II, 7, 1–2. [4] *Ibid*, II, 12.7. [5] *Ibid*, II, 13, 1–2.

4

ĀVĀSAS AND ĀRĀMAS:

Early Monk-settlements

THE legends describe two main types of early monk settlement—*Āvāsa* and *Ārāma*. There is, however, no full-length description of either, but the lack is filled by the abundance of scattered descriptive details. The former was a monks' colony staked out by the monks themselves, while the latter was an enclosed site, usually a donation to monks by a wealthy lay man, in or near a town, looked after by the donor himself.

Within its boundaries an *āvāsa* or an *ārāma* had huts for the monks' dwelling, and *vihāra* was the name originally given to such a hutment,[1] although the term in its later usage came to mean something different. A *vihāra* might be occupied by a single monk or by a small group of monks and, in the latter case, the allotted portion for each monk was called a *Pariveṇa*.[2] The accommodation comprised only what is termed a *senāsana* (bed-and-sitting) and furniture of a simple kind such as a 'board to recline on' (*apassena-phalaka*), a 'spittoon' (*khelamallaka*) and a 'seat' (*piṭha*) with perhaps jointed legs, which seems suggested by the expression, 'lowering the seat' (*piṭham nīcaṁ katvā*). It is difficult to say how the *pariveṇas* were fitted up in a *vihāra*. In the earliest cave-monasteries (second century AD) of Western India, the arrangement is to have in each cave a living-room comparatively large, entered through a narrow porch in front, and dormitory cells round the living-room, opening into it. But in the *vihāras* of the north which were originally of wood and thatch, the *pariveṇas* were probably just partitioned apartments. A common storage room for such articles as were allowable to monks called *Kappiya-kuṭī* was a necessary adjunct.

A whole long section of the *Mahāvagga* (III on *Vassa*) is given to *Āvāsas*, probably because they represented the unaided enterprise of the monks themselves involving the setting up of an entire monks' colony from scratch. It deals with the demarcation of an *āvāsa*, its construction, its maintenance, regulations for communal living

[1] e.g. Mahāvagga, VIII, 15, 4—where the monks of a Saṅghārāma, having gone out into the rain and wetted their bodies, come back and enter each into his own *vihāra*.

[2] e.g. Mahāvagga, VI, 23, 1—where Suppiya, entering a Saṅghārāma goes in search of monks 'from *vihāra* to *vihāra* and from *pariveṇa* to *pariveṇa*'.

within it, and also manners and points of etiquette to be observed. The monk-built *āvāsa* was after all a temporary set-up, liable to be deserted, robbed and dismantled after its evacuation by monks at the end of the *vassa* period. An *ārāma* was more durable and worth-while. It stood within an enclosure, obviating the laborious necessity of *sīmā*-fixation. Perhaps there were also some ready-made structures within. Besides, the charge of looking after and preserving it was the voluntary responsibility of the donor. Even a more important consideration perhaps was that an *ārāma*, by its permanent situation, favoured the continuance from one *vassa*-period to another of those features of collective life that had already emerged in the Saṅgha. While in the legends we find many references by name to those *ārāmas* which became famous Saṅgha centres, none of the *āvāsas* bears a name. The *ārāma* to all seeming was the superior kind of habitat for *vassāvāsa*.

The name, *ārāma*, denotes a pleasure-ground, usually the property within a town or city or in the suburb of a well-to-do citizen laid out as an orchard or flower-garden.[1] When it was given to the monks by the owner, not for temporary use but permanently, it was named a *Saṅghārāma*. The term, meaning originally an *ārāma* owned by the Saṅgha, came later to shed its implication of a donated pleasure-ground and meant simply a campus, and later still a large monastery occupied by a company of monks. The donor of an *ārāma* would not lose inteıest in it even when it had been converted from private property into Saṅgha property. It seems that he would of his own accord continue to look after the property—raise fresh buildings upon it according to the monks' needs and keep it trim and in habitable condition. He might for this purpose employ a special staff of servants (*ārāmika*) and superintendents (*ārāmika-pesaka*) over them, and we are told that when King Bimbisāra obtained the Buddha's permission to employ them on a *saṅghārāma*, there were so many servants employed that they filled an entire village which came to be known as 'Pilinda-gāma'.[2] The *kappiya-kuṭī* of such a *saṅghārāma* would no doubt be always amply stocked with provisions.

Among the structural needs that arose from the institution of congregational rites and activities was the need for a permanent meeting hall. The want of it was keenly felt in connection specially with the *Uposatha* observance. At first the service used to be held in the monks' cells (*pariveṇas*) in succession.[3] But the recital had to

[1] The first donation of an *ārāma* to the Saṅgha is said in Mahāvagga, I, 22, 18, to have been of a garden (*uyyāna*) in Rājagaha, named Veluvana, given to the Buddha and his Saṅgha by King Bimbisāra.

[2] Mahāvagga, VI, 15, 4.

[3] Mahāvagga, II, 15, 1–2.

be abbreviated and the exigency of space also made impossible the presence of all the resident monks. The next device tried was to use for the purpose an entire *vihāra* instead of a *pariveṇa*, but even then the assembly overflowed; so an artificial limit, called *uposatha-pamukha*, was set, making the service valid up to a certain distance—to so far as the assembly within the *vihāra*, together with the overflow audience outside, could hear the *Pātimokkha*-recital.[1] The *vihāra* temporarily arranged for the service was called *Uposathā-gāra* and it was swept and cleansed, appointed and provided with lights for the occasion. A common meeting hall (*Upaṭṭhāna-sālā*) of a suitably large size was a need very much indicated.

The story is told of a Brāhmaṇa, named Ghoṭamukha, who came (some time after the Lord's passing away) to call on a learned monk, Udena by name.[2] Impressed by Udena's sermon, he desired to make an offering of piety to him, setting apart for the monk's personal use a daily allowance out of a grant he enjoyed from the king of the Aṅga country. Udena refused the offer of money. Ghoṭamukha next offered to build a *vihāra* for the monk. This also was refused, but Ghoṭamukha was insistent on making a donation. On this, Udena said to him: 'Well, if your wish is to build, then build a *Upaṭṭhāna-sālā* for the Saṅgha at Pāṭaliputta.' The legend notes that the hall still exists and is called 'even now' by the donor's name (*sa etarahi Ghoṭamukhī 'ti vuccatī'ti*).

To build a meeting hall of suitable dimensions with proper interior decor was a task too difficult for the monks to shoulder by themselves. Help was expected from wealthy lay devotees, like Ghoṭamukha of the legend, who would deem it an act of especial merit to build in a *saṅghārāma* a meeting hall for congregational functions. It would be kept up by the donor for permanent use. So the custom presumably grew up among the monks to return from their wanderings to the same *saṅghārāma* for rain-retreat year by year.

In the legends several *saṅghārāmas* (i.e. *ārāmas* donated by their owners to the Saṅgha) are mentioned by name. Most of these *saṅghārāmas* must have been in existence when legends about them were composed, some already old and famous, and the legends make them contemporaneous with the Lord and describe them as having been sanctified by his visits or temporary residence, viz.:

1. Veḷuvanārāma at Rājagaha
   (said to be the first gift of an *ārāma* to the Buddha and the Saṅgha. It was made by King Bimbisāra).

[1] Mahāvagga, II, 9.
[2] See *Ghoṭamukha Sutta* in the *Majjhima Nikāya*, No. 26 (*Further Dialogues of the Buddha*, vol. II, pp. 92–93.)

2. Jīvakārāma at Rājagaha
(Donated by the renowned physician Jīvaka, contemporary with the Buddha.)
3. Ambapāli-vana at Vesālī
(Donated by Ambapāli, city-courtesan of Vesālī and devotee of the Buddha.)
4. Udambarikārāma near Rājagaha
(This was not a special Buddhist *saṅghārāma*, but for the general use of *paribbājakas*, situated on the bank of a stream named *Sappini*, i.e. the serpentine stream so named from its meandering course. It is also called by the general name *Paribbājakārāma*, i.e. Ārāma for 'wanderers'.
5. Kukkutārāma, Ghositārāma and Pāvārikāmbavana at Kosambī.
6. Jetavanārāma near Sāvatthi.
7. Badarikārāma at some distance from Ghositārāma.
8. Nigrodhārāma at Kapilavatthu—*Et cetera*.

Only three of these ārāmas have been traced by archaeologists, viz. (i) Jīvakārāma, (ii) Jetavanārāma and (iii) Ghositārāma. The sites of these *ārāmas* (except for the first) were occupied by monks for many centuries and monasteries were built on them from age to age. Some of their foundations are still traceable.

JĪVAKĀRĀMA was a great orchard of mango-trees (*ambavana*) on the outskirts of Rājagaha, at a short distance from the foot of the Gṛdhrakūṭa mountain which was the Buddha's favourite resort when he sojourned at Rājagaha. In recent years a flight of steps has been cut in the mountain-side by the Government of Bihar for the ascent of pilgrims to the top where the Buddha used to take his seat.

The wealthiest and most sincerely devoted to the Buddha among his lay followers at Rājagaha was Jīvaka, the leading physician and surgeon of the city. Legends cluster round his name, which, agreeing in the main points, do not tally in details. We have one set of legends about him in Pali in the Theravāda scripture and another in Sanskrit in the Sarvāstivāda. They are legends of a romantic flavour.

According to the Theravāda version,[1] he was a thrown-away child

[1] Mahāvagga, VIII, 1, 3–4. But see *Gilgit Manuscripts* (ed. by N. Dutt), vol. II, pp. 23 (1) ff. and Vol. III (2), pp. 23 (18)–24 (13), where the Sarvāstivāda version of the Jīvaka story will be found. It is somewhat different and more circumstantial. In this version, Jīvaka's mother is not Sālavatī, but the wife of a certain merchant of Rājagaha with whom King Bimbisāra had illicit relations. As a baby, Jīvaka was sent to the king by the merchant's wife in a closed basket which was passed on by the king to his other illegitimate son by Āmrapāli (Ambapāli of Vesālī) named Abhaya. The basket on being opened revealed the child inside it and the king noticed that it was living and said 'Jīvati (he lives)', whence Jīvaka got his name. Abhaya brought up the child who was called Jīvaka Kumārabhṛta (Pali-Kumāravacca), i.e. one brought up by a prince. Both the Pali and the Sanskrit legends, however, agree in saying that his medical knowledge was acquired at Takkasilā, that he became a famous physician and surgeon and that he came later in life under the influence of the Buddha.

of Sālavatī, the city-courtesan of Rājagaha, picked up from a dustbin by a scion of the royal family, brought up by him and educated in the science of medicine at Takkasilā in Gāndhāra, a great centre of learning at the time. His name, Jīvaka (Living One), was given to him by Prince Abhaya who found him still alive when he picked him up from the dustbin. After his medical training at Takkasilā, Jīvaka returned to Rājagaha and legends report stories of his marvellous skill in surgery. He earned great wealth by the practice of his profession and came at some point in his career under the spell of the Buddha's personality. He treated the Buddha himself on a few occasions and gave professional aid to his Bhikkhu-followers free of charge. His crowning act of liberality to the Saṅgha was the gift of his great mango-orchard.

Archaeologists have recently discovered and partially exposed the buried foundations of the *ārāma*.[1] The ground-plan indicates an extensive area, where excavation is still proceeding, and within it have been discovered the foundations of two long elliptical structures parallel to one another, with an extensive open space in between, and of two large halls. Only some iron nails, terracotta balls, animal figurines and pottery of crude red ware have come to light. The walls, it is supposed, were constructed of rubble and mud and the roof was of thatch.

JETAVANĀRĀMA is connected with the name of Anāthapiṇḍada—*clarum et venerabile nomen* in the legends. Perhaps it was the largest and most famous of all *ārāmas* of antiquity and the legends say that the Buddha spent as many as nineteen *vassa*-periods here.

Anāthapiṇḍada, donor of this *ārāma*, was a wealthy banker (*seṭṭhi*) of the city of Sāvatthi and had come to Rājagaha on business during the first year of the Buddha's ministrations. The Lord at that time was staying at Rājagaha with another *seṭṭhi* millionaire who was the husband of Anāthapiṇḍada's sister. When Anāthapiṇḍada came to his relative's house, he found it agog with preparations for a grand feast to the Buddha and his followers. He was naturally curious to see the man in whose honour preparations on so grand a scale were being made. He slept badly at night and in the small hours when the streets were still dark, he started for the place where the Buddha had been put up for the night. Arrived there, he saw for the first time the great and holy man, already up at that hour, walking meditatively up and down a promenade in the cool of early dawn. He approached him and introduced himself and invited him and his followers to a meal on the next day as his guests. The invitation was accepted, and next day after the Buddha with his party had partaken

[1] See *Indian Archaeology*, 1954–55, pp. 16–17. See also sketch given of ground-plan of Jīvaka's 'mango-orchard' *ārāma*.

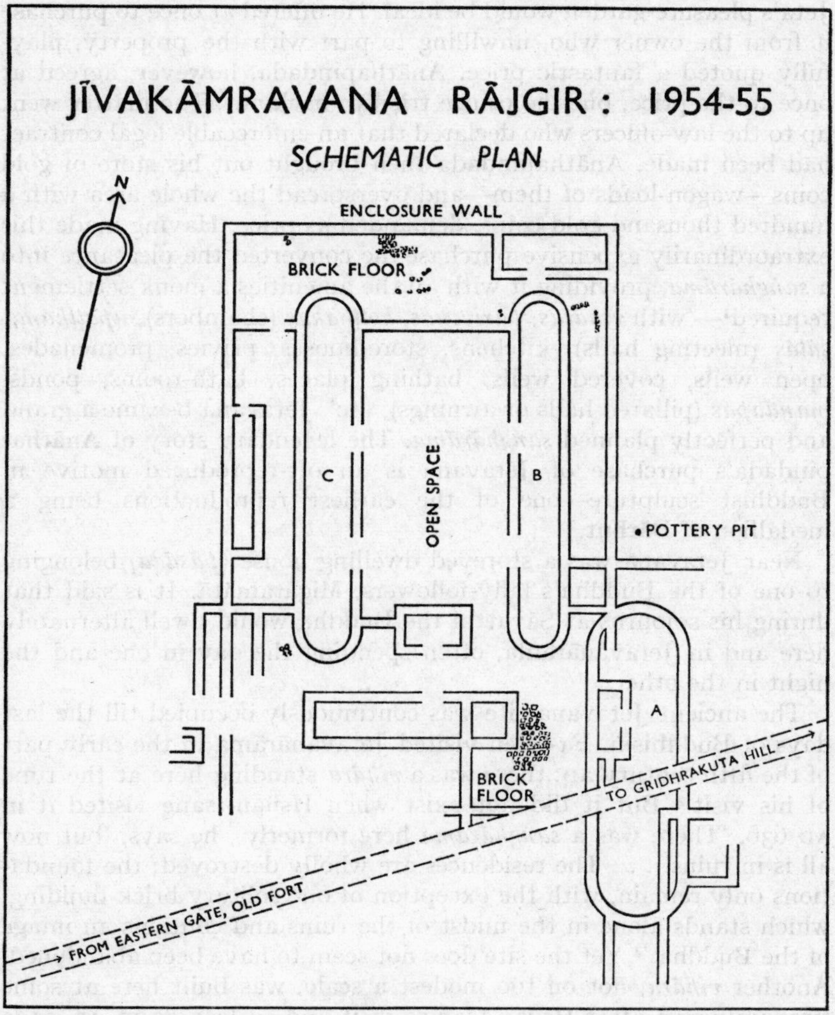

of his hospitality, Anāthpiṇḍada begged him to spend along with his followers the next *vassa* at Sāvatthi. This prayer also was accepted and Anāthapiṇḍada was in high spirits.

On his return journey to Sāvatthi, to all people he met on the way he kept shouting: 'Sirs, prepare *ārāmas*, build *vihāras*, be ready with your gifts. A Buddha has arisen in the world: I have invited him and he will be coming this way.'[1]

Arrived at Sāvatthi, he looked for a place where he could accommodate the Buddha most comfortably, and he thought that Prince

[1] Cullavagga VI, 4, 8.

Jeta's pleasure-garden would be ideal. He offered at once to purchase it from the owner who, unwilling to part with the property, playfully quoted a fantastic price. Anāthapiṇḍada, however, agreed at once to the price, but the prince tried to back out. The matter went up to the law-officers who declared that an enforceable legal contract had been made. Anāthapiṇḍada then brought out his store of gold coins—wagon-loads of them—and overspread the whole area with a hundred thousand gold coins, demanded as price. Having made this extraordinarily expensive purchase, he converted the pleasance into a *saṅghārāma*, providing it with all the amenities a monk-settlement required[1]—'with *vihāras*, *pariveṇas*, *koṭṭhakas* (chambers), *upaṭṭhāna-sālās* (meeting halls), kitchens, store-houses, privies, promenades, open wells, covered wells, bathing places, bath-rooms, ponds, *maṇḍapas* (pillared halls or awnings), etc'. Jetavana became a grand and perfectly planned *saṅghārāma*. The legendary story of Anāthapiṇḍada's purchase of Jetavana is an oft-reproduced motive in Buddhist sculpture—one of the earliest reproductions being a medallion of Bārhut.[2]

Near Jetavana was a storeyed dwelling house (*pāsāda*) belonging to one of the Buddha's lady-followers, Migāramātā. It is said that during his sojourns at Sāvatthi the Buddha would dwell alternately here and in Jetavanārāma, often spending the day in one and the night in the other.

The ancient Jetavana site was continuously occupied till the last days of Buddhism. Fa-hsien visited Jetavanārāma in the early part of the fifth century AD: there was a *vihāra* standing here at the time of his visit.[3] But it did not exist when Hsüan-tsang visited it in AD 636. 'There was a *saṅghārāma* here formerly', he says, 'but now all is in ruins. . . . The residences are wholly destroyed; the foundations only remain, with the exception of one solitary brick building, which stands alone in the midst of the ruins and contains an image of the Buddha.'[4] Yet the site does not seem to have been abandoned. Another *vihāra*, not on too modest a scale, was built here at some time unknown after Hsüan-tsang's visit and as late as in AD 1130 it received a charter sent from Vārāṇasī (Banaras), under the seal of King Govindachandra of Kanouj who had made his capital in that city, recording the gift of six villages to the Saṅgha, 'of whom Buddhabhattāraka is the chief' residing in 'the great convent of Jetavana'. The charter was unearthed at Saheth-Maheth (in Uttar Pradesh) and some of the six villages named in the record are still

[1] They are listed in Mahāvagga, III, 5, 6.
[2] See Barua's *Barhut*, Book III, Plate KLV.
[3] See Beal's *Buddhist Records of the Western World* (Popular Ed.), I, p. xliv.
[4] *Ibid*, II, p. 4.

3. *Two pillars of a gateway of the Mahā-Cetiya at Nāgārjunakoṇḍa.* (Phcto: Department of Archaeology, N.E. Project Guntur)
The remains of the Mahā-Cetiya at Nāgārjunakoṇḍa. (*A relic-stūpa.*) (Photo: Department of Archaeology, N.E. Project, Guntur)

The Nāgārjunakoṇḍa playhouse. (Photo: Department of Archaeology, N.E. Project, Guntur)

4. *Lake for aquatic sports at Nāgārjunakoṇḍa.* (Photo: Department of Archaeology, N.E. Project Guntur)

The Nāgārjunakoṇḍa Stadium. (Photo: Department of Archaeology, N.E. Project, Guntur)

known by their ancient names. The date of the charter is known—June 23, 1130—a time of alarm, when the Muslim invaders were almost at the door of Govindachandra's kingdom.[1] Saheth-Maheth is the ancient city of Sāvatthi, and Jetavanārāma, it appears, was in the 'Maheth' part of the village.

GHOSITĀRĀMA of Kosambī was founded by a *seṭṭhi*, named Ghosita, who had two colleagues or partners in the city named Kukkuṭa and Pāvāriya, and all three of them were interested in entertaining ascetics and wanderers. They had tidings one day that the Buddha was on a visit to Sāvatthi with his company of followers and the *seṭṭhis*, accompanied by the ascetics, went there and listened to a sermon by the Buddha. They became thereafter his followers and invited him and his party to Kosambī where they started building *ārāmas* for the accommodation of the Buddha and his large following. All the three *seṭṭhis* built *ārāmas* of which the one built by Ghosita was probably the largest. On his visits to Kosambī, the Buddha usually stayed at Ghositārāma and numerous incidents are mentioned in the legends in connection with this place—of important religious meetings held here and of sermons delivered by the Buddha and his principal disciples.

The site of this *ārāma* has been definitely located: some inscriptions discovered on the site mention it by the same ancient name, Ghositārāma. There is no doubt about the site being of great antiquity and about its continuous occupation down to the sixth century AD when it seems to have been laid waste by Hūṇa invaders under Toramāna.[2] When Hsüan-tsang visited it in AD 636, it was, as he describes it, 'an old habitation, the ruins only of which exist—the house (i.e. monastery) of Ghosita, the noble man'.[3]

[1] See *Archaeological Survey Report* for 1907–8 (VII in the series), p. 120. For more about Govindachandra and his queen Kumāradevi, see Part III, Sec. 5.

[2] Excavations at Kosambī (Allahabad District) were conducted in 1955–56 by the Allahabad University under G. R. Sharma, of which a report has been published. See *Indian Archaeology* (1955–56) with sketch of the site at p. 21 and plates XXIX-XXXI.

[3] Beal's *Buddhist Records*, i, p. 236.

5

Saṅgha Life and its Organization in Early Settlements

THE legend of Sarabha cited above[1] has perhaps no importance save that it hits off, as though by an unwonted stroke of imagination, the character of the Bhikkhu-saṅgha as we may suppose it to have originally been—that is, when it was no more than a sect in the wanderers' community. The '*Dhamma* of the Sakyaputtiyas' is the name taken to distinguish it from other sects: not '*Dhamma-vinaya*' as the legends usually name and specify it. The faith of the Sakyaputtiyas in this *dhamma* was firm and, if the legend is any indication, almost fanatical. The strength of their union in the faith seems to have become an urge to devise for themselves an outward token for the inner bond, to which the name *Pātimokkha* was given. One must be careful, however, not to equiparate it with the present signification of the term: it did not stand originally for the congregational rite to which the name was later applied.

This original *Pātimokkha* of the Bhikkhus is described in the *Mahāpadāna Suttanta* (Dīgha Nikāya, 13). It is not the recital of a code of offences against the rule and regimen of monastic life, but a congregational chanting by assembled Bhikkhus of a confession of faith; it is not a regularized fortnightly function, but a rite held only once in six years. The confession of faith itself is a summing-up of the fundamental *Sāsana* (Injunctions) of the religion. In this formulated form it must have been current among the Bhikkhus since the early days of the Saṅgha, for it occurs among the verses of the *Dhammapada*:[2]

> *Khantī paramaṁ tapo titikkhā*
> *Nibbānaṁ paramaṁ vadanti Buddhā;*
> *Na hi pabbajito parūpaghāti,*
> *No samaṇo hoti paraṁ viheṭhyanto* (v. 184).
> *Sabba-pāpassa akaraṇaṁ, kusalassa upasaṁpadā*
> *Sacitta-pariyodapanaṁ—etaṁ Buddhāna sāsanaṁ* (v. 183).

(Tr.—Forbearance or Patience is the highest kind of penance—and Nibbāna is declared to be the highest (object) by the Buddhas—for

[1] In Part I, Sec. 2, p. 52.

[2] The accompanying translation is mine. For Maxmüller's translation, see SBE, Vol. X, p. 51.

he is never a mendicant who hurts others and he is not a Samaṇa who molests others.

Abstinence from all evils, accumulation of all that is good, and purification of one's own mind—this is the injunction of the Buddhas.)

If the Bhikkhus used to declare their bond of brotherhood by chanting together this confession of faith, it must have been at a stage when the Bhikkhu-saṅgha was a mere cult-group whose cohesion lay solely in the '*Dhamma* of the Sakyaputtiyas'. It was in fact the archaic *Pātimokkha* of the Buddhists.

In the entire corpus of the Theravāda canon, it is described only once—in the *Mahāpadāna Suttanta*[1] where its antiquity is emphasised in a somewhat curious fashion—by lengthening, as it were, the telescope of time. This *Pātimokkha* is said to have been inaugurated, not by Gotama Buddha, but by Vipassī, the first of his mythical predecessors, who lived many aeons before Gotama Buddha in the city of Bandhumatī. He is said to have sent his disciples in batches on preaching missions, enjoining them to return to and reassemble at Bandhumatī every six years to hold a '*pātimokkha*'.

The object of the injunction seems plain: it is to afford an occasion to the Bhikkhus, after a long period of dispersal, to realize and renew their fellowship and unity as a body, and *this* is called *Pātimokkha*—which directs enquiry to the original meaning of the term.

As Maxmüller observes: 'The etymological meaning of a word is always extremely important both psychologically and historically because it indicates the point from which certain ideas started'.[2] From this point of view the etymology of *Pātimokkha* becomes worthwhile. Though unfortunately we can go by conjecture only, one of its plausible etymological meanings may be 'bond'.[3] The term, however, has undergone semantic developments: it meant one thing when the Buddhists were mere wanderers and another when they were settled in *āvāsas* and *ārāmas*. The rite described in the *Mahāpadāna* symbolizes the 'bond' of the Bhikkhu-saṅgha at the earlier stage; the *Uposatha* service by recital of the *Pātimokkha* described in *Mahāvagga* II is of a much later stage when the Bhikkhu-saṅgha was split up into a number of *saṅghas*, each of which arranged for its own *Uposatha* service. This *Pātimokkha* also was a bond—a symbolical expression of the unity (*samaggatā*) of the *saṅgha*. But its character was fundamentally changed. The '*Pātimokkha*' was no longer a mere affirmation and asseveration of the essential *Dhamma* of a sect, but a list of transgressions against the collective *saṅgha* life, then in process of development in these monk-settlements. With

[1] Mahāpādana Suttanta (Dīgha Nikāya), 3,28.
[2] *The Origin of Religion*, p. 10.
[3] See on this point *Early Buddhist Monachism*, pp. 88–90.

the emergence of this collective life, the *Dhamma* expanded into *Dhamma-vinaya* which is the conventional canonial term for the system of the religion. The recognition of *Vinaya* as collateral with *Dhamma* in the system marks the first step in the transition of the Buddhists from Sect to Order.

a. THE PĀTIMOKKHA

We have touched previously on the insistence in the canon on the universal character of the Buddha's teachings.[1] But, scattered in the body of the canonical legends, are passages in which the Founder speaks exclusively to his monk-followers, giving them in terms of injunction and prohibition directions to the right way of life for them. Thus he speaks of Four Things 'not to be done' (*cattāri akaraṇīyāni*) by one who has been ordained;[2] lays down rules about the settlement of disputes among monks,[3] or discriminates the proprieties of conduct for a monk.[4]

In the general movement among his monk-followers after the Master's decease to define and develop the *Dhamma-vinaya* out of his dispersed teachings and discourses, his 'Thou shalt nots' were enacted as laws for the Saṅgha with penalties attached for their breach. Thus we find the 'Four things not to be done' enacted as *Pārājikā Dhamma* (Acts involving defeat in monastic life); the procedure for the settlement of disputes among monks formulated as the seven *Adhikaraṇa-samathas*; and the broad and general regulations for the monks' conduct of life made into a body of monastic *regula*, classified in different categories, each involving a penalty or act of atonement for its transgression.

The canon assumes that the *Pātimokkha* rules were derived from the Master's teachings.[5] Some of the major ones among them (e.g. *Pārājikā*) were in all likelihood from that source, though the same cannot be claimed for the minor or lesser ones. Many of the Master's discourses, however, must have been retained in the memory of disciples when the drawing up of the *Pātimokkha* code commenced. This fact is curiously betrayed by the form of address, *Bhikkhave* (O Bhikkhus), which occurs twice,[6] presumably through the compiler's inadvertence, in the *Pātimokkha* of the Theravāda school,

[1] In Part I, Sec. 2, pp. 50–51.
[2] Mahāvagga, I, 78.
[3] *Kinti Sutta* (No. 103) and *Samagāma Sutta* (No. 104) in the Majjhima Nikāya.
[4] *Dhammika Sutta* in the *Sutta-nipāta* (see SBE, vol. x, pp. 61 ff.).
[5] Mahāvagga II, 3, 1.
[6] *Pācittiya* 71 and *Nissaggiya Pācittiya* 10. The occurrence of this form of address is noticed by Rhys Davids and Oldenberg in SBE, *Vinaya Texts*, pt. i, p. 23, footnote. But the learned translators, except for raising some pertinent questions, do not attempt any explanation of the anomaly (see *Early Buddhist Monachism*, p. 96, footnote 1).

which represents undoubtedly an early, if not the earliest redaction of the original *Pātimokkha*. The expression is just a 'survival' in the text and we find it expunged in versions which are obviously later than the Theravāda.[1]

If the suggestion be acceptable that *Pātimokkha* etymologically means 'bond' and that it was first applied to the chanting of the confession of faith described in the *Mahāpadāna* (see *supra*), the name *Pātimokkha* given later to a code of monastic *regula* is highly significant. It marks a stage in the evolution of the Saṅgha: the older *Pātimokkha* had been an affirmation of the Dhamma of a Sect; the new *Pātimokkha* was the disciplinary code of an Order.

This new *Pātimokkha* code formulates and defines offences against the regimen of monastic life, beginning with the gravest of them. These, named *Pārājikā*, involve 'defeat', that is, the wrecking of the very fundamentals of monastic life. Next follow offences in several categories, of varying degrees of gravity, till we come to those which are no more serious than mere breaches of etiquette.

The penal consequences of these transgressions are mostly indicated by the category names under which they are arranged—such as, expulsion from the Saṅgha, penance of sequestration from the company of fellow-monks, reproof and warning, solicitation of pardon for the act in the presence of the assembly followed by an appeal for restitution, ending up with minor offences to be atoned for by mere confession. *Exomologesis* or formal confession is the basic operative principle of the code, but in those cases, where confession on the part of the transgressor is not forthcoming, the Saṅgha as a body corporate has to exercise its disciplinary jurisdiction. It is obvious that the form in which the *Pātimokkha* has come down to us reflects different stages in the growth of monastic life: an elastic code in the beginning susceptible of later additions and alterations. The action by the Saṅgha contemplated in several cases of transgression not atoneable by mere confession could not for example have been taken before the Saṅgha had sufficiently advanced in corporate organization with the *Saṅghakamma* as its functioning organ.

It is not known how the code was compiled, who its compilers were or when it was accepted as the basis of the Buddhist Vinaya. But a *Pātimokkha* code must have come into existence not long after the development of cenobitical life in the *āvāsas* and *ārāmas*—perhaps within a century of the Founder's decease.

The rules contained in the *Pātimokkha* are called *Sikkhāpadas* ('clauses to be learnt'), and a *Pātimokkha* text that contained only

[1] Thus in the Mūlasarvāstivāda and Sarvāstivāda versions (see *infra*), there is nothing corresponding to the 'Bhikkhave' of the Theravāda version in any of the rules contained in them.

one hundred and fifty *sikkhāpadas* is often spoken of in the canon. But it is suggested in the canon itself that even this is an enlarged text and that the *sikkhāpadas* accreted gradually, as the Saṅgha grew larger and larger, increasing the need for guarding against a larger number of transgressions.[1]

The original text of the *Pātimokkha* code is untraceable. Three versions of the *Pātimokkha* are available up to date in two languages respectively, Pali and Sanskrit, besides translations and redactions in Chinese and Tibetan. These versions belong to four different schools of Buddhism, viz. Theravāda (in Pali), Mūla-sarvāstivāda (in Sanskrit), Mahāsāṅghika (in Sanskrit) and Sarvāstivāda (in Sanskrit), containing 227, 258, 218 and 263 rules respectively. The rules agree substantially, though differing here and there in wording, arrangement and classification of the listed offences.

The *Prātimokṣa* (Pali—*Pātimokkha*) *Sūtra* of the Mūla-sarvāstivāda school was discovered among the Gilgit Manuscripts and seems to have been current in Kashmir and, outside Indian borders, in China and Tibet since the beginning of the Christian era.[2] It was translated by I-tsing into Chinese in AD 710 (No. 1,110 in Nanjio's *Catalogue*) and perhaps in the same century into Tibetan; it is included in the Tibetan Vinaya works (*Dulva*) under the title *So-sor-thār-pa* (done into English by S. C. Vidyabhusana[3]). The Mahāsāṅghika *Prātimokṣa* has been edited and published by Dr W. Pachow and Ram Kanta Shastri in the *Journal of the Gaṅgānāth Jhā Research Institute* (Allahabad).[4] The Sarvāstivāda version was discovered in China among the Turfan manuscripts by Finot, but is an incomplete text.[5] Only the Pali *Pātimokkha* of the Theravāda School is still current and in use among the monastic orders of Ceylon, Burma, Siam and Cambodia where the Buddhism of that school prevails.

From the viewpoint of the antiquity of the *Pātimokkha* code in Buddhist history and from the evidence of its elasticity, the texts now available, whether in Pali or in Sanskrit, must be held to be developed versions of a lost original—an orally existent text going back perhaps to within a century of the 'Great Decease'. The extant texts combine and consolidate earlier elements with later—elements that passed into it from different stages in the growth of the Saṅgha. The later elements are even capable of being recognized.

Thus one class of transgressions, viz. the *Saṅghādisesas*, are offences that entail suspension from the Saṅgha. They call for a

[1] See *Bhaddali Sutta,* No. 65, in Majjhima Nikāya.

[2] See *Prātimokṣa Sūtram,* edited by Anukul Chandra Banerjee and published by the Calcutta University, 1954.

[3] In *Journal and Proceedings of the Asiatic Society of Bengal,* vol. XI. Also in *Tohoku Imperial University Catalogue,* No. 4107.

[4] See Vol. IX (1951), pp. 239 ff. for Introduction and Vol. X for the Text.

[5] *Journal Asiatique,* 1913 (Nov.–Dec.), pp. 465–567.

form of procedure by the Saṅgha acting as a corporate body and presuppose a certain development of Saṅgha life which must have come about gradually. Again, the seven *Adhikaraṇa-samathas* which are merely enumerated at the end of the text are incapable of being resorted to until the Saṅgha has developed its corporate functioning organ, the *Saṅghakamma*, and its rules of procedure.[1] Besides, the word, *Yathākammaṁ* (According to the procedural rule), which occurs here and there in the text of the *Pātimokkha*, contemplates the pre-existence of these rules. Procedural rules of this character in dealing with transgressions presuppose a stage of development which must have been reached by the Saṅgha much later in time than the compilation of the original *Pātimokkha* code.

The main intent and purpose of the code when it was first taken in hand is abundantly clear. It was to unite the Saṅgha on a new basis—not as of old on *Dhamma* alone and by affirmation and confession of faith in the injunctions (*sāsana*) of the *Dhamma*, but on a recognized and accepted rule and standard of living for monks. This purpose is apparent in the introductory story of the *Gopaka-Moggallāna Sutta*.[2]

It relates an occasion, 'shortly after the Master's decease', when Ānanda was loitering at dawn near the ramparts of Rājagaha, then under repairs. The king's men posted there, on seeing and recognizing Ānanda, were curious to know from him how the Saṅgha was faring now that the leader was no more. The king's minister Vassakāra asked whether the Buddha had nominated anyone as his successor or whether the Bhikkhus had elected a new leader in his place. Being answered for both questions in the negative, Vassakāra asked: 'What was the basis then for unity among them (*Ko hetu samaggiyā*)?' Ānanda explained to him that it existed in the laws of the Order—in the *Pātimokkha* drawn up by the Lord. It was the custom of Bhikkhus who lived in different rural areas to assemble on the sacred days of the *Uposatha* and to have the *Pātimokkha* recited in the assembly. If there had been a transgression on the part of any one of them, it would be confessed and the offender dealt with according to law. It was out of regard for the *Dhamma*, as Ānanda explained, that this was done and the Saṅgha therefore had its refuge in the

[1] *Adhikaraṇa* does not mean any kind of dispute, but one that has been formally brought up before the Saṅgha for adjudication. The meaning of the term in the *Mīmāṁsā* rules of interpretation of Hindu law is similar—Adhikaraṇa is a formal adjudication of a dispute, formally presented, involving five constituents: the subject-matter of the dispute, the issue, the first party's version, the second party's version and the decision:—

'Viṣayo viṣayaścaiva pūrvapakṣa 'stathottaram: Nirṇaya' śceti pañcāṅgaṁ śāstre 'dhikaraṇaṁ smṛtam'—(Kumārila Bhatta cited in Sarkar's *The Mīmāṁsā Rules of Interpretation*, Tagore Law Lecture, 1905, Calcutta University, 1909, p. 62).

[2] In Majjhima Nikāya, No. 3.

Dhamma (*Dhamma-paṭisaraṇa*). The *Gopaka-Moggallāna Sutta* represents a stage when the *Pātimokkha* recital had not yet reached the completely regularized form in which we find it set out in *Mahāvagga*, III. The idea underlying it, as explained by Ānanda, was that the cohesion (*Samaggatā*) of the Saṅgha, snapped by the lapsing of common spiritual allegiance to a Master, was now supplied by the *Pātimokkha*: it was the new bond for the old.

No other sect in the wanderers' community, it seems, developed such a bond of cohesion: nothing analogous to the *Pātimokkha* code evolved in the sect of Nigaṇṭha Nāṭaputta. Its principle of exomologesis obtains among the Jainas too, but transgressions of customary rules for the monks are confessed in private to the spiritual guide (*guru*): it is called *Ālocanā* (Exposure). The confession may be followed by atonement or penance (*prāyaścitta*) of which there are nine kinds. But the confessions are made in private and have no relation to a collective act of discipline.[1]

The *Pātimokkha* was the first clear charter of the Order, the *fons et ergo* of the regimen of monastic life: hence it was regarded as the 'Root of Vinaya' (*Vinaya-mūla*). From this grew the elaborate system of monastic *regula* of which the *Vinayapiṭaka* (of the Theravāda canon) and the *Vinayavastu* (of the Mūla-sarvāstivāda and Sarvāstivāda canons) are depositories. After the Vinaya system had developed to maturity and commanded acceptance as the main source of Saṅgha law and procedure, the original disciplinary application of the *Pātimokkha*, as set forth in the *Gopaka-Moggallāna Sutta*, was completely outgrown. The *Pātimokkha* was thereafter preserved by the Saṅgha only as a holy text; it was treated as liturgical and its recital formed the content of the congregational *Uposatha* service at each monk-settlement. The service itself was given the form of a 'confessional service' to make it accord with the original disciplinary purpose of the *Pātimokkha*. But reality had vanished from it. It was a Vinaya rule that only the 'pure' were entitled to attend the service and any monk who had been actually guilty of any of the offences in the code must 'purify' himself by a preliminary confession in private—the rite being called *Parisuddhi*[2]—before he was eligible to join the service.

This confessional *Uposatha* service, as admitted in the canon[3], was introduced long after the currency among the Bhikkhus of the *Pātimokkha* code. But the incorporation of the *Pātimokkha* with the

[1] See Deo's *The History of Jaina Monachism* (Bulletin of the Deccan College Research Institute, 1956), pp. 152 ff (on *Monastic Jurisprudence*).

[2] Mahāvagga II, 27; Cullavagga IX, 2, 1 and IX, 1, 1.

[3] See Mahāvagga II, 1–2. It gives the original injunction of the Buddha which was for '*Dhamma-rehearsal*', not '*Pātimokkha*-rehearsal' as in *Ibid*, III, 1, viz. ('*Dhammaṁ bhāsituṁ*'). The latter injunction (in *Ibid*, III, 1) was for '*Pātimokkha*-recital'.

Uposatha was the final reaffirmation of the character of the Saṅgha as an Order. The *Uposatha* service of the Buddhist, however, had a strangely composite origin, with successive developments behind it, curiously illustrative of Humbolt's dictum, now the postulate of all sociological studies, that 'man ever connects on from what lies at hand'. The Buddhist *uposatha* evolved in the following sequence.

Among the ritual sacrifices prescribed for householders in the Vedic Age, long before Buddhism was born, were two lunar sacrifices—to the New Moon (*Darśa*) and the Full Moon (*Pourṇamāsa*) respectively. The day preceding a sacrifice was preparatory, observed as a sanctified day with purificatory observances called *Vrata* (meaning literally 'Initiation'), such as fasting, rest from labour, abstinence from sexual pleasure, and retirement at night into the room where the sacrificial fire was kept up all night. It was a 'holy' day on which the auxiliary gods were supposed to dwell with the intending sacrificer. Hence the Vrata day was named *upavasatha* day ('*upa*' near and '*vas*' to dwell). These preparatory *Vrata* or *Upavasatha*-day observances, as well as the lunar sacrifices, were meant for householders. But the *Upavasatha*-day got rubricated as it were—it became a 'holy day', a 'Sunday': it was observed even in the wanderers' community who had no concern with sacrifices and *ex hypothesi* with these observances. At least one sect of wanderers, the *Nigaṇṭhas*, observed the *Vratas* of the *Upavasatha*-day under the name of *Posadha* (Prākrit form of Pali *Uposatha*).[1]

The Vrata-rites had been prescribed for householders; they might be 'purificatory' in the context of a householder's life, but were by and large meaningless in relation to the wanderer's. Instead of these observances, the wanderers' *upavasatha* took a form adapted to the *ethos* of the community: they substituted in place of Vratas '*Dhamma*-rehearsal'. The *upavasatha* days were given by them to the study and rehearsal and public discussion by each sect of its own sacred texts orally preserved. Thus we find the rehearsal of the texts of the *Āraṇyakas* and the *Upaniṣads* prescribed for the Brāhmaṇical *sannyāsins*.[2] The texts for *Dhamma*-rehearsal in the case of Buddhists would consist of the Buddha-legends, *gāthās*, the Lord's sayings, etc., and perhaps their recital existed by custom and convention among the Bhikkhus from the beginning, though the canonical legend speaks of the introduction of '*Dhamma*-rehearsal' among them by the Founder at the instance of King Bimbisāra (*anujānāmi—dhammaṁ bhāsituṁ*).[3] The hymn-chanting at Band-

[1] On the *posadha* observances, see Heornle's *Uvāsagadasāo* (Bibliotheca Indica), note 87.

[2] Āruṇeyopaniṣad, 2—Sarvesu Vedesu āraṇyakamāvartayet' upaniṣadam āvartyaet (see Dikshit's The *Samnyasa Upaniṣhads*, p. 10). *Āvartyayet* means 'should be rehearsed'.

[3] Mahāvagga, II, 1–2.

humatī by the Bhikkhus in the time of Vipassī when they were in their primitive wandering stage seems in line with this custom of '*Dhamma*-rehearsal' on the *upavasatha* (Pali-*Uposatha*) days.

The legends record that, though the Buddha's original injunction to the Bhikkhus had been to observe the *uposatha* days by 'rehearsing the *dhamma*' ('*Dhammaṁ bhāsituṁ*'), it was later that he prescribed a specific text—the *Pātimokkha*—for recital and turned the occasion into a confessional service.[1] It is undoubtedly the legendary version of the fact that, following the change in the character of the Saṅgha from a Sect to an Order, the code of monastic discipline became for the Saṅgha its special *Dhamma*-text—the *Dhamma*-refuge (*Dhamma-paṭisaraṇa*) as Ānanda characterized it in the *Gopaka-Moggallāna Sutta*.

A recurrent descriptive epithet in the canon for a good Bhikkhu is 'controlled by the restraints imposed by the *Pātimokkha*' (*Pāti-mokkha-saṁvara-saṁvuta*). It is a pointer to the original purpose of the *Pātimokkha*—the regulation of the life and conduct of the individual Bhikkhu: the code did not in its original purpose and intent contemplate the collective cenobitical life that developed later in the settlements of monks. At this later stage the Bhikkhu's individual life was taken up and involved in the collective Saṅgha life and the need arose for a more comprehensive and constructive system of discipline than the *Pātimokkha* offered. The *Pātimokkha* was corrective and restrictive—a set of 'Thou shalt nots': the Vinaya on the other hand was constructive and regulative.

The *Pātimokkha* formula is: 'If a Bhikkhu did such-and-such an act, he was guilty of (a named offence)'; the Vinaya formula, positing the Buddha as the law-giver (*Satthā*), is: 'I allow you, Bhikkhus, to do or refrain from doing such-and-such an act.'

b. THE VINAYA

Vinaya is the name given to the system of Saṅgha life that developed in the early monk-settlements. Only a few compendiums of Vinaya are available. They are of different schools of Buddhism and in different languages, but, on the whole, not different in substance. Of them, the *Vinayapiṭaka* of the Theravāda canon, which will be drawn upon in the present section, is the most complete and systematic.

The *Vinayapiṭaka* is not, as the *Pātimokkha* is, in the form of a code nor is it in the form of a body of monastic *regula*. It is a collection of legends, each containing a precept of the Lord that pertains either to the individual life and conduct of the Bhikkhu or to some institution of the collective Saṅgha life. Each gives a rule,

[1] Mahāvagga, II, 3, 1.

either positive or negative in character, e.g. 'I allow you, Bhikkhus, to do this or to refrain from doing that'.

From internal evidence it is clear that these rules do not belong to the same stratum: they accreted gradually, in the process of organization of Saṅgha life in the primitive *āvāsas* and *ārāmas*. Their aim and purpose were evidently organizational. Thus an earlier rule and a later one, altering or modifying it, may be distinguished in many instances; there are also inconsistencies and contradictions; to many of the rules as originally propounded, exceptions and provisos are admitted, and these exceptions and provisos are said to have been necessitated by subsequent experience. There is little doubt about these rules having come into existence piecemeal as the monk-community slowly gravitated from its wandering state to settled cenobitical society and new needs arose for corresponding changes in the conditions of monk-life.

An initial problem posed by the *Vinayapiṭaka* is—why the rules of monastic life of which it consists were not drawn up as a code like the *Pātimokkha* or gathered in a manual like, say, the *Regula Benedicti*? For a key to the problem we have to turn to the intent and purpose of these rules—to their fundamental organizational value. To serve this purpose and realize this value, the rules had to be mandatory—in other words, to be recognized and accepted as the *laws* of collective Saṅgha-life, binding on all members of the Saṅgha. But a rule to become a law needs the backing of authority: sanction and formal promulgation.

Under the constitution the Saṅgha had adopted for itself since the decease of the *Satthā*, no *locus* of authority competent to be a source of law could exist in the Saṅgha: all its members stood in relation to the collective body on a footing of perfect equality. The elders could advise and instruct, but not direct or compel; each member was a 'refuge' unto himself (*atta-saraṇa*). A saṅgha acting as a body could by agreement make a law for itself, but there was otherwise no source of authority within it from which a law could emanate. The whole process, therefore, of converting the rules which existed on a basis of agreement and acquiescence into laws binding on the Saṅgha was inspired by what is known in jurisprudence as 'legal fiction'. The authority that did not actually exist was sought and invoked from the tradition, real or imaginary, of promulgation of these rules by the *Satthā* himself in his lifetime. On the basis of this tradition the industry of framing laws for the Saṅgha must have started fairly early in the development of its collective life. The *Pātimokkha* was still earlier.

It is suggestive and significant that a rule of Vinaya does not stand by itself—it is laid down in a way reminiscent of the mode of law-making that prevailed, according to the theory of Sir Henry Maine, in all primitive society. A Vinaya rule does not answer to our modern concept of a law—as prescription by authority of some regular course of conduct. It almost invariably takes the form of a reported adjudication made by the Buddha as to what is right and what is wrong in a given 'state of facts'.

We may take at haphazard as an example of it the fourteen rules about a Bhikkhu's proper footwear.[1] Each rule is said to have arisen *ex post facto*—each separately promulgated by the Buddha in the form of a pronouncement on certain facts as they arose on some particular occasion. Yet all of them could have been gathered up as in a modern rule of law into one comprehensive formula, laying down the kinds of footwear allowable and the occasions for their use, prescribing a general course of conduct. But this is not done. To each injunction, prohibition or permission, an individual occasion is attributed and a separate story prefixed, describing the occasion.[2]

Yet this equating of a rule of law, not with a command, but with an adjudication as to what was right and what was wrong in a given state of facts used to be the mode of law-making in all primitive society before the idea evolved in history of laws made by State or Church authority. Sir Henry Maine in his classic work on *Ancient Law* illustrates this primitive practice by the Homeric concepts of *Themis* and of *Themistes* 'which were simply adjudications or insulated states of facts'.[3]

Almost all the Vinaya rules, which are meant to be operative as 'laws', are cast in this mould—certain facts come or are brought to the Buddha's notice on a particular occasion and his judgement is given *ex post facto*, and the 'state of facts' on which it is based is presented in the form of a legend. If the 'Themistes' analogy be acceptable, it serves to explain why every Vinaya law has the encasing of a legend, though the legends in many instances are too far-fetched and in others so thin and slight and so loosely adjusted to the rule that their invented character becomes transparent. But

[1] Mahāvagga, V, 1, 29 *et seq.*

[2] See *Early Buddhist Monachism*, pp. 31–32.

[3] *Ancient Law* (ed. by Pollock, 1909), p. 5. Maine's theory, however, is not universally accepted, but it serves nonetheless to explain the form and character of a Vinaya Law. Maine's theory is thus summarized by an American writer who himself does not subscribe to it: 'Maine's basic assumption was the direct opposite of the fundamental principle of regularity in norms that has emerged from the investigations of modern social science. So, when Maine theorized on the nature of law in societies that have gone beyond family atomism into kingship, he saw the early king giving "separate, isolated judgements", not "connected by any thread of principle". The source of these judgements was said to be divine inspiration. The king has a trouble case; the gods gave him the answers. They simply came out of the blue. Such judgements in Homeric Greece were *themistes*, emanating as they did from Themis, the assessor of Zeus'—*The Law of Primitive Man* by E. Adamson Hoebel (Harvard University Press, 1954), p. 259.

the legendary setting was a necessity: it was essential to the process of converting rules existing by convention or general agreement into 'laws' promulgated by authority.

The many provisos, exceptions and modifications, with which we find several rules of the *Vinayapiṭaka* hedged in, leave no doubt of the fact that these rules must have come into existence pragmatically, in a 'trial-and-error' process—that is, as a result of the growing practical experience of the first organizers of the Saṅgha in its primitive establishments.

It is not in the legendary stories that we have the true record of their origin. It would seem, on the other hand, that when a sufficient body of rules, based on agreement and convention, had grown up in the Saṅgha, the task was taken up by the organizers of editing and classifying them and making them up, not as a mere manual of regulations, but as a corpus of laws, taking the *Satthā* as the formal source of each law and setting it forth as an 'adjudication' made by him. All this was in the tradition of primitive law-making on an 'insulated state of facts'. The legends prefacing the rules were, most of them, pre-existing ones: the making of Buddha-legends, as Rhys Davids suggests, commenced in the monk-community within about half a century of the Founder's decease. The doctrines and tenets of the Dhamma would naturally seek for authority in the legends; and the Vinaya also had to seek this authority at a stage when the concept emerged of the Saṅgha as an Order, regulated and governed by its own system. The rules had then to be raised to the status of laws.

When we come to the question, when a complete body of Vinaya laws in this legendary setting came into existence, all the answer that can be given is that it must have been before the rise of any sectarian movement in the Saṅgha, before even the 'Great Schism' (*Mahābheda*) between the Theravāda and the Mahāsāṅghika had taken place. The *Mahābheda* was an early event in Buddhist history, perhaps assignable to some period early or late in the fourth century BC. A complete body of Vinaya laws must have pre-existed the event, for the Mahāsāṅghikas are said to have made many alterations in it.[1] We shall perhaps not be far wrong in holding that round the middle of that century the Saṅgha had a complete corpus of Vinaya laws.

The sects of early (Hīnayāna) Buddhism are traditionally eighteen in number. We are told in the *Dīpavaṁsa* account of the rise of Buddhist sects that each had its own canonical collection, though to what degree of completeness is unknown. The Vinaya works of six sects are available, complete or in fragments, as listed below:

[1] According to the account of the *Mahābheda* in the Ceylonese chronicle *Dīpavaṁsa*, V, 32–38.

1. Theravāda Vinaya .. in Pali *Vinayapiṭaka*.
2. Mahāsāṅghika Vinaya .. in Fa-hsien's Chinese translation; also in Sanskrit in the *Mahāvastu*, which describes itself as the 'initial section' (*Ādi*) of Vinaya of a sect named Supra-mundanists (*Lokottaravādins*) of the Mahāsāṅghika school, though it contains no *regula*, but the legends only.
3. Mūla-sarvāstivāda .. translated into Chinese and into Tibetan most probably from Chinese; also in part in original Sanskrit in Gilgit Manuscripts (see *infra*).
4. Mahīśāsaka-sarvāstivāda in Chinese version.
5. Dharmaguptaka-sarvāstivāda .. .. in Chinese version.
6. Sarvāstivāda .. .. in Chinese version; also in Tibetan renderings included in the Tibetan collection of Vinaya works known as the *Dulva*.

Note—[From the above account, it will appear that, of the Vinaya texts of different schools, the *original* texts of only two schools are available, viz. the *Theravāda* and the *Mūla-sarvāstivāda*. The former constitute the *Vinayapiṭaka* section (published in Roman script in five volumes by Oldenberg in 1879–83) of the Pali *Tipiṭaka*. The latter (in Sanskrit) has been found among the Gilgit manuscripts in four complete chapters (*Cīvara-vastu, Kaṭhina-vastu, Kośāmbaka-vastu* and *Karma-vastu*), five fragmentary chapters (*Bhaiṣajya-vastu, Pravrajyā-vastu, Poṣadha-vastu, Varṣā-vastu* and *Carma-vastu*) and seven miscellaneous chapters (Gilgit Mss., vol. IV, pt. 1). These Mūla-sarvāstivāda texts have been edited by Dr N. Dutt and published under the caption *Gilgit Manuscripts* by the Government of Kashmir. They were discovered round 1930 in the Gilgit pass of Kashmir in a bundle of palm-leaves inscribed in characters of the fifth-seventh centuries—'of the same type', as the editor N. Dutt remarks (*Gilgit Mss.*, vol. I, Intro.), 'as are most of the mss. discovered by Sir Aurel Stein and other explorers in Eastern Turkistan and Central Asia'. The discovery of these mss. was first announced by Sylvain Levi in *Journal Asiatique* (vol. CCXX) in 1932. Besides those in the *Gilgit Manuscripts*, some stray Vinaya works of the Mūla-sarvāstivāda School have also been recovered by Rahula Sankrityayana from Tibet round 1952, written in Sanskrit in old Maithili script, viz. *Upasampadā-jñāpti, Bhikṣu-prakīrṇaka* and

Bhikṣuṇī-prakīrṇaka. These works are not yet edited and published.]

On the similarities and divergences of the Vinayas of the six schools, we may cite the authority of Frauwallner who has made a special study of them:

'. . . We can see at once that the agreement of the texts reaches deep into the particulars. It is strikingly close with four schools above all: Sarvāstivādin, Dharmaguptaka, Mahīśāsaka and the Pali school. Of course, we have to disregard the formal subdivisions appearing in the extant texts. The subdivisions are in contradiction with the inner structure and are probably late, as in the case with the *Mahāvagga* and the *Cullavagga* of the Pali school and the *Śaptadharmaka* and the *Aṣṭadharmaka* of the Sarvāstivādin. Nor must we allow ourselves to be led astray by the fact that the sequence of the several sections appear under different titles in the various schools and that occasionally in this or that school, several sections are joined into one. If we consider the contents only, disregarding all the external features, the result is a complete agreement. . . . The materials are the same, the inserted legends are the same, discrepancies are merely such as are bound to occur when several narrators tell the same story freely from memory.'[1]

This fact of 'complete agreement' among the Vinaya texts of six different schools proves 'the existence of a basic text from which Vinayas of the Sarvāstivādin, Dharmaguptaka, Mahīśāsaka and of the Pali (Theravāda) school were derived'.[2] If the text existed before the rise of the schools—in the fourth century B.C. when sectarianism had not made its appearance yet—it indicates that the Buddhist monk-community even from that early age had its own body of laws by which it governed itself.

It is important to consider the consequences of this fact. With the

[1] The *Earliest Vinaya and the Beginnings of Buddhist Literature* by E. Frauwallner (Serie Orientale Roma, VIII, IsMEO, 1956), pp. 2–4. The monograph propounds a novel theory of the beginnings of Buddhist literature, with which, however, I cannot agree.

The conclusion arrived at by Frauwallner is corroborated by Dr Wieger, the distinguished French sinologist, who says as follows about the Chinese Vinaya versions: 'At the end of the fourth and at the beginning of the fifth century, at the same time as the translations of the *āgamas*, those of the disciplinary *sommes* governing monachism were also made. The *sommes* only differed among themselves in insignificant details, the foundation being approximately the same. They multiplied because each school wished to have its own, through *esprit de corps*, in order not to appear to be tributary to the neighbouring school. All are based on Indian manners and customs, without so much as an attempt at adaptation to Chinese manners and customs (*—which shows their Indian original*). The *somme*, which had in China the greatest influence was that of the school of Dharmagupta, translated in AD 405.' (The italicised words are mine)—*A History of the Religious Beliefs and Philosophical Opinions in China* (translated from French by Edward Chalmers Werner and published by Hsien-hsien Press, Peking, 1927) by Dr Leo Wieger, p. 487.

[2] *Ibid*, p. 53.

development of Vinaya, the monk-community became a self-governing organization and each unit (*saṅgha*) of the community became a body corporate. It resulted in the first place in bringing the community into a certain recognized relation with the State, and, in the second, in giving it a status that guaranteed its right to exist and continue in its own way of life.

The concept of society in the political philosophy of ancient India was that of an aggregate composed of units of diverse kinds—learned bodies, village communities, religious corporations, etc. Each was regarded as subject to its own conventional system of law, called *Samaya* (Conventional Law) in ancient Indian jurisprudence. With regard to these units of society, it was the king's constitutional duty to see that none of them suffered from internal or external disruption and that the established system of conventional law of each was not transgressed.[1] Among these societal units, the Buddhist Saṅgha became one, an 'association group' functioning under a system of law of its own. As such, we find it mentioned by Medhātithi, the ancient commentator on Manu.[2] The duty of the ruler with regard to these unitary bodies was to prevent disruption (*Bheda*) in the group and to uphold its own traditionary laws.[3] Emperor Asoka, implementing this constitutional principle, issued edicts for the 'unfrocking' of schism-mongers in the Buddhist Saṅgha[4] on the basis of the old Vinaya rule—'A schism-monger, if he has not been ordained, should not be ordained; if ordained, is to be expelled' [*Saṅghabhedako bhikkhave anupasaṁpanno na upasaṁpādetabbo upasaṁpanno nāsetabbo*].[5]

If these political theories of immemorial tradition, which Brāhmaṇical legists of ancient India like Yājñavalkya, Manu, Nārada and others enunciate, stemmed from the actual practice of kingship, there can be no doubt that in ancient India a king (unless he were prepared to give the go-by to all recognized traditional principles of constitutional government) would feel bound to extend protection to the Buddhist Saṅgha and prevent infringement of its Vinaya. It would be regarded as a constitutional obligation rather than as service to the faith.

[1] See *The Buddha and Five After-Centuries*, pp. 121–122, where the relevant texts are quoted in the footnotes.

[2] Medhātithi's comment on Manu, VIII, 219: '*Ekadharmānugatānāṁ nānādeśavāsinām nānājātīyānāmapi samūhaḥ: yathā Bhikṣūṇāṁ saṅgho vaṇijāṁ saṅghaścaturvidyānāṁ saṅgha iti.*' (*Saṅgha* is explained by Medhātithi as 'a collection of men who subscribe to the same *Dharma*, of different places and even of different stocks, such as the Saṅgha of the Bhikṣus, the Saṅgha of merchants, the Saṅgha of men learned in the four Vedas.) *Dharma* means in this context 'norm of life'.

[3] '*Bhedaṁ teṣāṁ nṛpo rakṣet pūrvavṛttiñca pālayet*'—Yājñavalkya, ii, 186–192.

[4] There are three pillar edicts on Schism—Allahabad, Sāñchī and Sārnāth. See A. C. Sen's *Asoka's Edicts* (1956), pp. 126–129 (on *Schism Pillar Edicts*).

[5] Mahāvagga I, 67.

Historical illustrations abound to confirm it—they come from the numerous lithic and copperplate records from all parts of India of benefactions made by kings and emperors, not Buddhists themselves, for the maintenance of monks and the upkeep of monasteries. In these dealings, the ruler's personal approval or disapproval of Buddhism was of small account—it was virtually irrelevant: he was bound out of respect for his own constitutional position to say 'let live' to the Saṅgha and its institutions.

The Saṅgha, by virtue of possession of its own system of Vinaya laws, had become a unit in the composition of society with claim to be protected and not disturbed. In fact the only story of persecution of Buddhist monks by an Indian ruler (Mihirakula and the Hūṇas were unaware of the Indian tradition) is that of Puṣyamitra (2nd century BC). We hardly know anything about his real motive. Perhaps it was a very special one dictated by reasons of State—to put down monkish opposition to his institution of Vedic sacrifices with animal slaughter.

Yet through all the after-centuries of ancient Indian history, we find kings of different dynasties in different parts of India—the Sātavāhanas, the Ikṣvākus, the Guptas, the Maitrakas, the Rāṣṭrakūṭas and others, professing different forms of Brāhmaṇical faith—making donations to Buddhist saṅghas and monastic establishments. They made donations to adherents of other religions and other institutions too. This was prompted, not so much by 'religious toleration' as by an awareness of constitutional duty towards organizations which had their places in the overall composition of society. The amount of donation of course varied with the degree of personal inclination. The donations by kings of a Brāhmaṇical faith to non-Brāhmaṇical institutions had undoubtedly popular support, for to the Indian mind, so conditioned by its ancient culture, whatever serves the cause of religion, irrespective of its form or denomination, is worthy of support. We find proofs of this in the donatory inscriptions in the cave-monasteries of western and southern India and in the ruins of *vihāras* and *stūpas* in northern India, in which the names of numerous donors, demonstrably not Buddhist by faith, occur.

Thus, apart from its organizational effect in moulding Saṅgha life, the Vinaya, the great charter of the Order, was also its constitutional guarantee for corporate existence—its claim for protection by powers-that-be from violent hands. A monk-settlement, once established, would continue to exist for many a century unless deserted by monks, decayed to dilapidation or demolished by foreign invaders.

A typical example of the amazing stability and longevity of a monk-settlement is Ghositārāma. Excavations, carried out here in 1955–56, disclosed continuous occupation of the site by Buddhist monks for nearly a thousand years.[1] In course of time, the religion itself had passed from the Hīnayāna to the Mahāyāna stage and the excavated ruins showed structural renovations over centuries carried out to meet the requirements of Mahāyānist worship. Similarly, several *leṇas* of western and southern India hold evidence of long centuries of occupation by monks, of which the Krishnagiri cave-settlement described later[2] is a conspicuous example.

We have so far considered Vinaya in its purely external aspect—*vis-à-vis* State and society at large. In this aspect, the Vinaya is a body of conventional laws (*Samaya*) of a saṅgha or 'association-group'. In its internal aspect, it is law regulating Buddhist monastic life. When we consider the Vinaya in this aspect, it presents not only a picture of primitive saṅgha life, but betrays also the lines on which saṅgha organization proceeded.

We have already referred to the rules about the settlement of *sīmā* of a monks' colony (*Āvāsa*).[3] The effect of the rules is to stake out a self-contained colony—one that must not be a promiscuous settlement, but a site for three months' residence in congregation of a company of Bhikkhus. The rule in particular that the boundaries of two *āvāsas* must not overlap shows that it was intended that each *āvāsa* should be independent and self-contained—a unit by itself. Those who would settle on the site for *vassāvāsa* were expected to form a complete fraternity. They are designated *samāna-saṁvāsakas* (co-residents) and are regarded collectively as a unit of the Order. It is laid down that a Bhikkhu having gone into residence for the *vassa*-period at an *āvāsa* must not stay outside its boundaries unless it were for compelling reasons and the period of absence did not exceed a week. Each fraternity, limited thus by common residence at the *āvāsa*, was regarded as a unit of the Order or a section of the *Cātuddisa Bhikkhu-saṅgha*, and called a *Saṅgha* in a representative sense.

The time-limit of residence seems afterwards to have been regarded as flexible, and though the limit is insisted on in the Vinaya rules, the *āvāsa* shed gradually its original character of a mere rain-retreat shelter. Theoretically it was so, but practice departed from it. It was usual at this stage to identify the *āvāsa* with its habitual body of co-residents—to call a Saṅgha by a local name. This process of making up a saṅgha on residential basis seems to have been complete in effect when the law was made that, on the eve of the *Vassa*, no

[1] On Ghositārāma, see Part I, Sec. 4, and on excavations and finds, *Indian Archaeology*, 1955–56.

[2] In Part II, Sec. 5, pp. 152 ff..

[3] In Part I, Sec. 3, p. 54.

Bhikkhu 'resident outside the boundary of an *āvāsa*' should be allowed lodging (*senāsana*) in it.[1]

At this stage the fortnightly *uposatha* service by the recital of the *Pātimokkha* had become a regular established institution in the monk-community. It was taken as the symbol and expression of the unitary character (*Samaggatā*) of a saṅgha. For this function a *complete* gathering of all the co-residents at an *āvāsa* was required—if the gathering did not include the entire number, the function was not deemed to be valid. It was possible, however, that on a day of *Uposatha*, Bhikkhus from some other *āvāsa* might be present on the spot. The rule was that they were not to be excluded from the assembly, but if they outnumbered the co-residents, the function had to be held afresh.[2] Not only in the rules of the *Uposatha* service, but in several other particulars too, a clear distinction is drawn between the co-residents of one *āvāsa* and those of another.

A Bhikkhu, for instance, who is on *Parivāsa*, i.e. serving the penalty of sequestration for a particular transgression, is not to betake himself to another *āvāsa* (unless the journey there and back takes no more than a day), where there may be Bhikkhus 'not belonging to his own body of co-residents' (*nānāsaṁvāsaka*); but the injunction is relaxed in the case of removal to an *āvāsa* 'occupied by co-residents' (*samānasaṁvāsaka*).[3]

It is plain from such rules that a Bhikkhu, wherever for the time being he chose to stay, was recognized as a monk of that particular *āvāsa* where he actually had to spend the *vassa* (a *senāsana* would not be provided for him elsewhere) and as a member of the collective body resident there. A saṅgha thus became a locally limited brotherhood; membership of a saṅgha was bound up with a domicile and mention is made in the canon of such bodies as 'Sāvatthiya Saṅgha',[4] the 'Vesālika Vijjiputtaka Bhikkhus',[5] etc. When sects arose in Buddhism in a later age, several of them came to be known by place-names, e.g. Jetavaniya, Abhayagirivāsin (Ceylonese), Pubbaseliya and Aparaseliya (of Amarāvatī), etc.

In its later development as a body corporate, it was the unitary character (*Samaggatā*) of each saṅgha that was taken as the basic principle of its constitution. A saṅgha could function only as an entire undivided body. As it was circumscribed by its domicile, two conditions were set down among the twenty-four disqualifications disentitling a Bhikkhu to be regarded as a member of a saṅgha proceeding to perform a *saṅghakamma*. These two conditions are:

[1] Cullavagga, VI, 11, 3—Na Bhikkhave nissīme ṭhitassa senāsanaṁ gāhetabbaṁ.
[2] Mahāvagga, II, 28, 4.
[3] Cullavagga, II, 1, 3.
[4] Mahāvagga, III, 13, 1.
[5] Cullavagga, XII, 1.

(i) 'belonging to a different *āvāsa*' (*nānāsaṁvāsaka*) and (ii) 'staying outside the *āvāsa* boundary (*nānāsīmāya-ṭhita*).[1]

The Vinaya law of 'Schism' (*Saṅghabheda*) also brings into sharp relief the principle of a saṅgha's unitary character (*samaggatā*).

A schism was an act recognized as constitutional in the Vinaya. A whole section of the *Vinayapiṭaka* (*Mahāvagga*, X) is concerned with schisms. Buddhism from its beginning had been anti-authoritarian: there was neither in theory nor in actual functioning any permanent seat of authority within a saṅgha, the result of which was the total absence of any constitutional check on dissent. So a 'division of the saṅgha' (*saṅghabheda*) had to be allowed provided it was grounded on honest differences.

Let us follow what would happen if a schism did actually take place. The law in this respect had been that the schismatic party was to function within the boundary of the *āvāsa* (*anto sīmāya*) as a separate saṅgha, performing by itself all its congregational functions, such as giving ordination, holding the *uposatha* service and carrying out the post-*vassa* ceremony called *Pāvāraṇa*.[2] But as a saṅgha was understood in the sense of a co-resident body of common domicile, the living together of two saṅghas at the same *āvāsa*, which seems to have been allowed at first, became a debatable matter. It is said to have been one of the moot-points (viz. *āvāsa-kappa*) at the 'council of Vesālī' (held, according to canonical tradition, a century after the Founder's decease). Here the old law was rescinded and it was decided that a schismatic party must leave its old āvāsa and settle in a new one.[3]

In this way the evolution of saṅgha life and its progressive organization is gradually unfolded to us in the Vinaya laws. Though the inside story is revealed by glimpses, its main outline integrates.

It was to implement a time-honoured custom of the wanderers' community that the *āvāsas* had been instituted by the Buddhists. But they converted the general communal custom to a special form. The āvāsa developed from a purely temporary shelter to a quasi-permanent abode, and with this transformation the beginning was made of cenoebium in Buddhist monkhood. In course of time the co-residents of an āvāsa came to be recognized as forming a *saṅgha*, a unit of the 'Saṅgha of the Four Quarters'. From this stage, a further stage was reached, when each saṅgha attained to the status of a body corporate functioning through the institution of *Saṅgha-kamma*—each an independent centre of monastic life, with its unitary character (*samaggatā*) as the basic principle of its functioning.

[1] Mahāvagga, IX, 4, 2.
[2] Mahāvagga, X, 1, 9.
[3] Cullavagga, XII, 2, 8.

c. SAṄGHAKAMMA

The *Vinayapiṭaka* insists on the *samaggatta* of a Saṅgha.[1] The term in its literal sense means simply 'unity' or 'wholeness'.[2] What the first organizers of the Saṅgha meant by this 'unity' or 'wholeness'—whether it connoted to their minds the mere negative virtue of avoidance of schism and faction or referred to a positive and active principle of its collective functioning[3]—remains a question. It is raised by certain passages of the canon, especially by the Buddha's great sermon on *Aparihāniyā Dhammā* delivered to monks on the eve of his departure from Rājagaha on the last missionary tour.

In this sermon, the Buddha recommends for emulation by them the customary ways of life followed by the Vajjis. To his mind, these ways constitute conditions for 'insurance against adversity', not merely for the Vajjis but for the monk-community (*Saṅgha*) as well, and the condition placed first and foremost among them is the Vajji custom of holding 'full and frequent assemblies'.[4]

The Vajjis who are held up for emulation were a tribal or clannish group in northern India. Society in that era was in process of evolution to the political stage—to a monarchical pattern—but more primitive societal organizations, referred to as *Gaṇas* or *Saṅghas* in the literature of the Vedas,[5] surrounded the emergent monarchies. They survived long, and are referred to casually in later (Sanskrit) literature on *Arthaśāstra* (Political Philosophy) which contemplates kingship as the ruling institution of society. The emergent kingship was trying to swallow up the primitive organizations of tribe and *gens*. When Buddhism first arose, Magadha was already a kingdom of old standing and the Magadhan king Ajātasatru was trying to 'root out, destroy and bring to utter ruin'[6] the great Vajji-led tribal confederacy on the borders of his kingdom. It was shortly after his

[1] Mahāvagga, IX, 2, 1–4.

[2] *Samagga* is used as correlative of *vagga* which means 'factional'. See *PTS Pali-English Dictionary* under *Samagga*. For example, the expression, *samagga-karanīṁ vācaṁ bhāsitā*, means 'Speaker of words which serve to unite people'.

[3] In the verse quoted at the beginning of Part IV, Śāntideva speaks of '*Saṅgha-sāmagrī*', along with other aspects of Saṅgha life. It hints at this meaning—not merely harmony, but the principle of the Saṅgha's collectively functional life.

[4] *Mahāparinibbāna Suttanta*, I, 6 *et seq* (Yāvakivañ ca bhikkhave bhikkhū abhiṇhaṁ-sannipātā sannipāta-bahulā bhavissanti vuddhi yeva bhikkhūnaṁ pāṭikaṅkhā, no parihāni. Yāvakivañ ca bhikkhave bhikkhū samaggā sannipatissanti samaggā vuṭṭhahissanti samaggā saṅgha-karaṇīyāni karissanti vuddhi yeva bhikkhave bhikkhūnaṁ pāṭikaṅkhā, no parihāni—*Ibid*).

[5] Pāṇini (in iii, 3, 36) makes *Saṅgha* something inclusive in the concept of *Gaṇa*. Both terms mean a 'collective' but there is a controversy among scholars over the kind of 'collective' denoted by these terms in their Vedic usage. See Deviprasad Chattopadhya's *Lokāyata* (People's Publishing House, Delhi, 1959), pp. 152 ff. Professor Chattopadhya's opinion is that *Gaṇa* or *Saṅgha* means a 'tribal collective', the societal organisation in the Vedic age in India being tribal.

[6] *Ucchecchāmi Vajjī vināsessāmi vajjī anayavyasanaṁ āpādessāmi Vajjī ti* (Mahāparinibbāna Suttanta, I, 1.)

declaration of war upon the Vajjis that the Buddha's sermon was preached in the Magadhan capital. His own sympathies were all with the Vajjis—and he set up their tribal life as the model for the Bhikkhu-saṅgha's own group-life.

The *Gaṇas* and *Saṅghas,* in the far later age of the *Arthaśāstras* when the rule of kings was established in society, were still die-hard survivals. The secret of their endurance is exposed by Kauṭilya's recommendation to kings of Machiavellian tactics to subvert their group-unity. 'Saṅghas are invincible by others', says Kauṭilya, 'because of their *Saṁhatatva* i.e. unity or organization.'[1] This seems to have been a current belief, for Ajātasatru's minister Vassakāra, on being told by the Buddha that the king's chances in an armed fight against the Vajjis were in his view slim indeed, agreed with him and left with the remark that there were only two practical alternatives before the king—either to come to terms with the Vajjis or to try to bring about discord among them.[2]

The Bhikkhu-saṅgha represented a form of group-life different from these societal organizations—the *Gaṇas* or the *Saṅghas*—in both aim and purpose, but it aspired to be a firm and united body, and, in pursuance of this objective, the first organizers of the Bhikkhu-saṅgha tried to plant in the Order some of the characteristic institutions in which the vital strength of these group-organizations lay.

The *Gaṇas* and *Saṅghas* knew nothing of personal rule; they deliberated and acted together, were 'communistic' in their property-relationships, republican in the conduct of their affairs and had the tribal council as their organ of Government.

'The Council', says Morgan,[3] 'was the great feature of ancient society—Asiatic, European and American—from the institution of *gens* (clan) in savagery to civilization. It was the instrument of government as well as the supreme authority over the *gens,* the tribe and the confederacy. Ordinary affairs were adjusted by the chiefs; but those of general interest were submitted to the determination of a Council.'

The Pali canon contains several references to the existence of the 'tribal council' among the Sakyas, the Mallas, the Licchavis and the Vajjis.[4] It served as exemplar for the Bhikkhu-saṅgha where its republican note was reproduced.

[1] *Arthaśāstra* Adhikaraṇa xi, Adhyāya 1—Saūghā hi saṁhatatvāddhṛṣyāḥ pareṣāṁ.

[2] *Mahāparinibbāna Suttanta,* I, 5.

[3] *Ancient Society* (Calcutta Ed.), pp. 84–85.

[4] See Rhys Davids' *Buddhist India* (published by Susil Gupta, Calcutta), pp. 13–14; Rhys Davids's *Dialogues of the Buddha,* i. p. 113, Note; Malalasakera's *Dictionary of Pali Proper Names,* Vol. II, p. 970.

But the actual constitution of these primitive 'tribal councils' and the forms of procedure of their joint deliberations are unknown. The 'tribal' analogy, however, has been pressed further to interpret the institution of *Upasampadā* as 'tribal adoption' and the *Pātimokkha* rules about the common use of property in a saṅgha as 'tribal communism'.[1] What impact tribal constitution had on the organization of the Buddhist Bhikkhu-saṅgha is a matter largely of speculation and theory which, however, has been pressed to two formulated propositions, viz.:

(i) That 'the Buddhist Saṅgha was copied from the "political" saṅgha',[2] and

(ii) That in an age when tribal life was becoming obsolete through social evolution, the organizers of the Bhikkhu-saṅgha were trying to perpetuate its features in Saṅgha life and its institutions.[3]

Whatever may be the final evaluation of such theories, the Saṅgha, as we have seen, advanced gradually from its primitive *parivrājaka* (wandering) condition to a stage when each unitary saṅgha could function as a corporate body. It needed at that stage an organ for its functioning. The institution of *Saṅghakamma* became this organ.

Several features of 'democracy', ancient and modern, characterize this institution. The system of joint deliberation, the postulation of equality of all members in decision-making on matters of common concern, the rule of majority, the rejection of personal dictation are its outstanding features. But democracy is a political concept that did not emerge till society had developed a political organization. *Saṅghakamma* does not embody a notion of democracy: it only reproduces into saṅgha life and polity the leading features of the 'tribal council' which in pre-political tribal society was the instrument of government.

The term means literally 'transactions of a Saṅgha'. But it is used in a specialized sense and with a constitutional import: the act of an entire corporate body performed in accordance with set rules and forms of procedure. It is compliance with and accordance to them that confer validity on the act.[4] Even if the basic idea of Saṅghakamma had been the adapted 'tribal council', it was so implanted and naturalized in the Bhikkhu-saṅgha that its growth within it was organic. Its scope and jurisdiction expanded within the Saṅgha till it gradually came to embrace in its purview all matters of common concern. Thus we find the rite of ordination, which had originally

[1] By Debi Prasad Chattopadhyaya, a Bengali scholar who belongs to the Communist School of thought, in his work on *Lokāyata* referred to in footnote 5 on p. 85.
[2] See Jayaswal's *Hindu Polity* (3rd Ed., 1955), p. 86.
[3] See Debi Prasad Chattopadhyaya's *Lokāyata*, p. 483.
[4] See Mahāvagga, ix.

been a personal act, made later on a regular saṅghakamma; certain offences under the *Pātimokkha* code being brought under its jurisdiction and listed as *Saṅghadisesas*;[1] the fortnightly confessional service taking on the character of a formal saṅghakamma.[2] In its mature development, the Saṅghakamma became the normal mode of transaction of all acts to be done by the saṅgha—from the settlement of *sīmā* (the boundary of an *āvāsa*) to the imposing of due penalty under the *Pātimokkha* code on a delinquent Bhikkhu.

The *Samaggatta* (Entirety) of a Saṅgha proceeding to transact a saṅghakamma is jealously guarded, strictly insisted on. One of the safeguards against the degeneration of the Saṅgha is said to be the transaction of all Saṅghakammas in a *valid* manner, that is, in concord and in full assembly.[3] The entire body of qualified inmates of an *āvāsa* or *ārāma* must be assembled—those disqualified being a nun, a novice male or female, and those labouring under any one of the twenty-four disabilities listed in *Mahāvagga*, IX, 4, 2. But, if for any reason one was unable to join, he must remain for the time being outside the *sīmā* or send a proxy to convey his consent (*Chanda*). In order to make a saṅghakamma valid, a certain minimum number was required:[4]

(i) Four for all acts except *Upasampadā*, *Pavāraṇā*, and *Abbhāna*;

(ii) Five for all acts in the 'Middle Country' except *Abbhāna* and *Upasampadā* ('In Border Countries,[5] I allow, O Bhikkhus, the Upasampadā to be held in a meeting of only four Bhikkhus besides the Chairman who must be a Vinayadhara'.—*Mahāvagga*, V, 13, 12);

(iii) Ten for all acts except *Abbhāna*; and

(iv) Twenty and upwards for all acts.

The minimum number was not to be made up by calling in a person under any one of the twenty-four disabilities.

Once a decision was reached with regard to a matter by way of a saṅghakamma, the decision became *res judicata* and an attempt to raise the matter over again would be an offence under the *Pātimokkha* code.[6] The validity of the saṅghakamma itself, however, could be impugned; the impugnment would be treated as a 'formal dispute about the validity of an act' (*kiccādhikaraṇa*) dealt with as *per* rules for a 'disputatious saṅghakamma' (vide *infra*).

Saṅghakammas, as described in the *Vinayapiṭaka*, are of different kinds which can be brought under two categories: (i) *Non-disputatious* and (ii) *Disputatious*, as follows:

[1] See Part I, Sec. 5, pp. 70–71.
[2] See Mahāvagga, II.
[3] *Mahāparinibbāna Suttanta*, I, 6.
[4] Mahāvagga, IX, 4, 1.
[5] That is, countries beyond the *Puratthima*. See Part II, Sec. 1.
[6] It was *Pācittiya*, No. 63.

(i) Acts pertaining to the normal community life and ordinary business of a Saṅgha, for which the consent of all members could be presumed, e.g. settlement of the boundaries of an *āvāsa*; assignment of any part of the monastic establishment to some special utility, such as storage, refectory, kitchen, etc.; appointment of different functionaries to run the establishment; ordination of a monk; settlement of succession to a deceased monk's personal belongings; the holding of the fortnightly *uposatha* service; rehabilitation of a monk who has atoned for an offence committed (*Abbhāna*); arrangement of the *pavāraṇā* ceremony after the *vassa* (rain-retreat); distribution of robes (*Kaṭhina*) to the monks after the *vassa* period, etc.

(ii) Other acts, involving the settlement of a dispute, in which no concensus could be presumed. Under this category would come (*a*) all matters of discipline arising out of breaches of *regula* and amounting to transgression of the *Pātimokkha* code, and (*b*) matters of four kinds arising out of a 'formal dispute' (*adhikaraṇa*), viz. (*a*) a dispute on a point of Dhamma or Vinaya or on the nature of an offence (*Vivādādhikaraṇa*); (*b*) a dispute regarding the state of a Bhikkhu's opinions, morals, character, conduct or manner of life (*Anuvādādhikaraṇa*); (*c*) a dispute regarding the kind or category of offence alleged against a Bhikkhu (*Apattādhikaraṇa*); and (*d*) a dispute regarding the validity of an Act (*Kiccādhikaraṇa*).[1]

In a saṅghakamma of the first category—one that involved no matter of discipline and no dispute—the procedure was simple enough. The matter for decision was placed before the Saṅgha by a Bhikkhu in the form of an Intimation (*Ñatti*) thus: 'Let this (the matter communicated) be done'. Then the proposition on which the saṅgha's decision was sought would be formally placed and declared to the assembly (*Anussāvanā*). Those who were against it were called upon to speak and those in favour to remain silent.

When, in certain cases, this formal declaration (*anussāvanā*) was made once only, it was called *Ñatti-dutiya-kamma* (i.e. an act which required only two stages—one *Ñatti* and one *Anussāvanā*); in other cases it was *Ñatti-catuttha-kamma* (i.e. an act which required four stages—one *Ñatti* and three *Anussāvanās*). The distinction between the two kinds of acts is not found specified in the *Vinayapiṭaka* itself, only in the commentary. Perhaps the real criterion was the degree of gravity or importance of the matter proposed.

When the matter was not disputatious, the assembly remained silent which was the token that the proposition was passed as a Resolution of the Saṅgha. But the intimation to the assembly of the proposal (*Ñatti*) and its formal declaration, once or three times as

[1] See *The Buddha and Five After-Centuries*, pp. 113–114.

required, must follow in order and any violation of this order rendered the Resolution invalid *ab initio*.[1] In the three-*Anussāvanā* act (*Ñatti-catuttha-kamma*), the assembly had more time to deliberate and perhaps to consult each other and arrive at a joint and unanimous decision.

Certain conditions hedged in the validity of the act:[2]

(i) that the assembly must contain the minimum number deemed competent to perform the act. This was a condition precedent. In other words, ratification (*anumati*) by a member, who was not actually present at the saṅghakamma, given after the saṅghakamma had been performed, was not valid. (This is said to have been decided at the Council of Vesāli);[3]

(ii) that consent by proxy of all absentee members residing in the *āvāsa* at the time had been obtained;

(iii) that the Proposal and its Declaration (once or three times) were in due order;

(iv) that there was no dissentient voice.

In a saṅghakamma of the second category—one that involved disciplinary action or the settlement of a dispute (*adhikaraṇa*)—the whole procedure, beginning with the *Ñatti*, was subject to certain preliminary proceedings. The usual procedure could be started only after the preliminaries had been gone through. Evidently the object of these was to clarify the issue and arrive at a definitive form in which the proposal for taking action was placed before the assembly.

The rules governing these proceedings in disputatious saṅgha-kammas are captioned in the concluding section of the *Pātimokkha* under seven heads: (i) Sammukhā-vinaya, (ii) Sati-vinaya, (iii) Paṭin-nāta-karaṇa, (iv) Amūḷha-vinaya, (v) Yebhuyyasikā, (vi) Tassa-pāpiyyasikā, and (vii) Tiṇa-viṭṭhāraka. This section of the *Pāti-mokkha* is entitled *Adhikaraṇa-samatha* (Settlement of Disputes). The term *Adhikaraṇa* seems to be used here in the formal and legal sense of an issue between two contending parties.[4] The rules applic-able to the settlement of such an issue are summed up under the above technical names

Sammukhā-vinaya is a common denominator to them. It signifies the presence at the Saṅghakamma of (*a*) the party concerned, (*b*) the lawfully constituted assembly, (*c*) the *Vinaya* which means in this context the due observance of rules of procedure proper to the case,

[1] This is based on Mahāvagga, ix, 3, 9—Ñattidutiye ca bhikkhave kamme paṭhamaṁ ñattiṁ ṭhāpeti, pacchā ekāya kammavācāya kammaṁ karoti, yāvatikā bhikkhū kammappattā te āgatā honti, chandārahānaṁ chando āhato hoti, sammu-khībhūtā na patikkosanti. The same *mutatis mutandis* for a *Natticatuttha-kamma*.

[2] Compare *Early Buddhist Monachism*, p. 151.

[3] See Part III, Sec. 2, p. 172 (*Anumati-kappo*).

[4] For the legalistic meaning of *Adhikaraṇa*, see Part I, Sec. 5 (c), footnote 1 at p. 71.

and (*d*) the *Dhamma* which means right application of the law. No settlement of a dispute, including an act of discipline, could be performed *in camera*: the settlement or the trial must be open and the law in respect of it, both procedural and substantive, must be meticulously followed and applied.

With *Sammukhā-vinaya*, other forms of proceeding are combined under different sets of circumstances. It is difficult for one, not an expert in Vinaya, to grasp their distinctions and differences. The interested reader is referred to my book *Early Buddhist Monachism*, pp. 156–72, for detailed treatment.

In fact, Formalism is the most striking feature of a saṅghakamma, as appears clearly enough from the ninth section of the *Mahāvagga* on the 'Validity and Invalidity of a Saṅghakamma'. The meticulous observance of the forms and punctilios of procedure is of the essence of its validity. Disregard, omission or dislocation of even an iota lays the act open to impugnment by any member of the Saṅgha and necessitates fresh proceedings *ab initio*. It is well-known to students of jurisprudence that formalism is a feature of all archaic law. As we have pointed out before, the lawfully made decisions of a Saṅgha were recognized by the State and held to be binding on its members as *Samaya* (Conventional Law).[1] The Vinaya in its operation and effect was the positive law of the monk-communities and its administration through Saṅghakamma partakes necessarily of the formalistic character of all archaic law.

[1] See Part I, Sec. 5, p. 80.

6

LEṆAS

The Rise of Monasteries

A WANDERING body of monks whose sole bond of cohesion was ordainment in a common faith—of persons exempt from all social ties, recruited from different regions and unrooted to any local habitation—this was the primitive 'Bhikkhu-saṅgha of the Four Quarters'. It had been a real entity in the prime of Buddhism. But this body, developing and growing in number, did not retain this primitive character. The one body split up into many groups, each with its own group-life, locally delimited and functioning on its own—each of them known as a Saṅgha. At this stage the concept of the 'Saṅgha of the Four Quarters' became only an ideal, but it was, as we have seen, never given up theoretically.

Saṅgha life in the monk-settlements developed in a way that no longer permitted a dispersed mode of living. First, a system of training had been inaugurated among monks and a probationary period instituted between calling and full ordination during which a monk had to go through a period of training called *Nissaya* (Dependence on a Teacher), the period being normally ten years.[1] Secondly, the custom had grown up among monks of holding symposia and debates among themselves called *Abhidhamma-kathā*, out of which evolved the monkish exegetic philosophy, the *Abhidhamma*. Thirdly, collective rites and ceremonies had come into existence like *Uposatha*, *Pavāraṇā* and *Kaṭhina*, regular maintenance of which called for a settled condition of life. These developments took place in the primitive *āvāsas* and *ārāmas*. The *Upaṭṭhāna-sālā* (meeting hall) was the symbol of the collective, congregational life. General dispersal after *vassāvāsa* was hardly favourable for its growth and the custom assumed by degrees a mere token character, no general dispersal actually following the termination of the period.

There arose also the need for ridding the cenobitical society of the violent disturbances and dislocations resulting from the flux of incoming and outgoing Bhikkhus, of which a pretty full picture can be gathered from the regulations in *Cullavagga*, VIII, bearing on

[1] Mahāvagga, i, 32, 1. But see Mahāvagga i, 53, 4, where it is said that an able (*paṭibala*) Bhikkhu may remain in *nissaya* for five years only, but one not so all his life.

proper conduct and mutual relations between old residents (*āvāsikas*) and newcomers. To ensure continuity and progress of Saṅgha life and maintenance of its corporate activities, residence had to be somewhat differently planned. A settled residence for a unitary body was indicated, not a makeshift shelter for Bhikkhus from all quarters. The transition was from the old-type settlement in an *āvāsa* or *ārāma* to a *leṇa*. A *leṇa* was not a monks' colony open to all comers; it was a compact unitary establishment for a settled body of monks, enabling it to function without disturbance as a corporate body—as a Saṅgha by itself.

Etymologically '*leṇa*' means 'private abode' (from Sanskrit form, *layana*, derived from the verb *lī*, to hide). The etymology is indicative of the nature of a *leṇa*. While the old monk-settlement had the character of a *rendezvous*, a sort of monks' caravan-serai, a place of temporary shelter and rest from wandering during the rains, a *leṇa* was a 'private dwelling', i.e. the abode of a limited and specific body of monks. Without barring outsiders, it was meant specially for a single resident saṅgha. Thus a *leṇa* was a Monastery proper, not a shifting and seasonal settlement of monks. Fa-hsien's description of the Hīnayānist monasteries he visited in Udyāna on India's north-western border serves to illustrate the distinction: 'If a strange Bhikṣu arrives here, they give him full entertainment for three days; the three days being over, they bid him seek for himself a place to rest permanently'.[1]

A canonical legend lists five kinds of *leṇas* as fit for monks' dwelling under the names: *Vihāra*, *Aḍḍhayoga*, *Pāsāda*, *Hammiya* and *Guhā*.[2]

The same legend goes on to narrate the story of the construction for the Bhikkhus of the first set of *Vihāras*, sixty in number, in the course of a day by a *Seṭṭhi* (merchant) of Rājagaha. The Vihāra was one kind of *leṇa*, private dwelling-house, the use and utility of which are thus described in the *gāthās* (verses) conveying the Lord's benediction to the donor:

'They (Vihāras) ward off heat and cold, and ward off beasts of prey from there;
Creeping things and gnats and the rainy season's dampness.
When the dreadful heat and wind arise, they are warded off.
For the purpose of residence, for ease, for meditation and gaining insight, the gift of a *vihāra* is the chief gift to the Saṅgha—it is so declared by the Buddha.'[3]

[1] Beal's *Buddhist Records*, p. xxxi.
[2] Cullavagga, VI, 1, 2.
[3] *Ibid*, 5. The translation is mine.

The original purpose of a *vihāra* was apparently to provide shelter from inclemencies of weather and noxious things—they were no more than shelters for monks to dwell in for *vassāvāsa*.

The conversion of a *vihāra* from a dwelling house of private occupation into a communal establishment is traceable from the semantic developments of the word. As Childers says, the word 'in later times almost always was used to designate the whole of a building where many Bhikkhus resided; in older literature the dwelling place, the private apartments, of a single Bhikkhu'.[1] It is in the older sense that '*vihāra*' stands in the canonical legend. When it was developed later into a communal dwelling of more generous proportions, private apartments were constructed within it and they were called *Pariveṇas*. Semantic changes like this in terms relating to monk-settlements and monasteries are found even in their modern usage. Thus in Ceylon the term *Piriveṇa* (from Pali *Pariveṇa*) is now used 'to denote only a monastic college where Buddhism and oriental languages are taught as principal subjects of study; *vihāra* is used only for an image-house; *āvāsa* denotes only a small residence of a few monks without other features of a monastery'.[2]

Vihāra, listed in the legend as *leṇa* of one kind, is a communal (*saṅghika*) dwelling: the *vihāras* built by the *Seṭṭhi* of Rājagaha, on the other hand, were just huts for a Bhikkhu's shelter during rains, each so small and flimsy that sixty could be put up in a day. But from a rain-shelter, the *vihāra* developed into a dwelling-house for a company of monks. The reason why the communal (*saṅghika*) *vihāra* is styled a *leṇa* (a private dwelling) is to distinguish it from an *āvāsa* or *ārāma*. It is 'private' in the sense that it is built to house a single monk-fraternity, with reservations and discriminations made in respect of *senāsana,* and is not intended for the reception of Bhikkhus from all quarters.

It is illuminating to compare the schematic plan of a *vihāra* (which makes one of the five kinds of *leṇas*) with that of an *ārāma*. The comparison is possible only by reference to the foundations of them unearthed by archaeologists. Let us study an example of each. Jīvaka's 'mango-orchard' was an *ārāma* and the Pippala monastery at Taxila a *vihāra*. The foundations of both have been exposed by archaeologists, and the constructional difference indicated by the ground plan is striking. *Jīvakāmravana*, p. 63 and *Pippala*, p. 212.

The two sketches given will help the reader to appreciate the constructional difference.

It will appear from a comparison that, while the developed (*leṇa*)

[1] See Childers' *Pali Dictionary* under *Vihāra*.
[2] Rahula's *History of Buddhism in Ceylon* (1956), p. 132, fn. 5.

vihāra (i.e. *Saṅghika vihāra*) was a compact and unitary building for the accommodation of a single company, a unitary body of monks, meeting the needs of their communal living, the *āvāsa* or *ārāma* occupied a larger area, having the look of an outspread colony, more suitable for seasonal gatherings of monks hailing from all quarters.

The institution of *leṇas* marks the shift of the monk-community from 'monk-settlements' to 'monasteries'. The break-up in the course of time of the 'Saṅgha of the Four Quarters' into unitary groups necessitated a new kind of abode, a *leṇa*, for a single monk-fraternity, which was thus a monastery proper, different in layout and construction from the old-style monk-settlement. Hence in specifying the five kinds of *leṇas*, the canon names each according to its *structural structural peculiarity*. No description of them, however, is given in the canon and we are thus thrown back on the commentator Buddhaghosa's explanations. But in Buddhaghosa's time (fourth–fifth century AD), only two kinds of *leṇas* were in existence, viz. the *Vihāra* and the *Guhā*, the other three having been long obsolete. Hence his descriptive explanations are mostly conjectural, though perhaps they are backed by tradition.

Buddhaghosa explains *Vihāra* as a dwelling-house with a chamber in it, well-protected and containing private lodgings;[1] *Aḍḍhayoga* as a 'gold-coloured Bengal House'; a *Pāsāda* as a 'long-storeyed mansion', i.e. with an upper storey completely covering the lower; a *Hammiya* as a *pāsāda* with an attic on top; a *Guhā* as a 'hutment made of bricks or scooped out of rock or made of wood or laterite (*paṁsu*)'. Other commentators make equally conjectural variations as does Buddhaghosa, specially in respect of his explanation of *Aḍḍhayoga*. It is interpreted by them as a 'Bengali-type house with turned-up eaves looking like the wings of a *suparṇa* (Garuḍa bird)'.[2]

Of the storeyed monasteries called *Pāsāda*, there is mention in the legends of a famous one, owned by a wealthy lady called *Migāramātā* (Mother of Mṛgāra) at Jetavana and it is said that here the Buddha used to stay off and on during his visits to Kosambī. Whether it had ever been dedicated to the Saṅgha or was retained by the owner is

[1] *Vihāro ti antogabbho vā aññaṁ vā sabbaparicchannaṁ gutta-senāsanaṁ.* See *Samantapāsādikā* (Simon Hewavitarne Bequest Series, Colombo), pp. 568–569.

[2] It is likely that Buddhaghosa and the other commentators borrowed the explanation from some Ceylonese *aṭṭhakathā*. But one letter was perhaps ambiguous in the script. In *suvaṇṇa*, was the letter 'v' as Buddhaghosa takes it, or 'p' as the others take? The commentators take it as '*supaṇṇa-vaṅka-geha*' (see PTS *Dictionary*), but Buddhaghosa as '*suvaṇṇa-vaṅga-geha*' (see SBE *Vinaya Texts*, pt. i, p. 173, Note 1). It is explained also as '*Garula-saṁṭhāna-pāsāda*' (see Helmer's *Critical Pali Dictionary*). When these commentaries were written, this type of leṇa had become so obsolete that its structure was unknown.

uncertain. It seems that the name *Pāsāda* (Skt. *Prāsāda*) for a monastery of more than one storey was always in use. So late as in the eighth century AD, we find the name applied to Bālāditya's temple-*cum*-monastery at Nālandā.[1]

Of *Hammiya*, which, according to Buddhaghosa, is a *pāsāda* topped by a single chamber, the only description in the legends is of one in the clearing of a forest called Mahāvana where the Buddha used to stay from time to time on his visits to Vesālī. Buddhaghosa describes, out of his own imagination, the architectonics of this building.[2] Part of it, he says, consisted of a storeyed building with a hall below, surrounded by pillars only. The pillars supported a gabled roof. On this roof was a chamber which was the Buddha's private retiring room and known as *Gandhakuṭī*. The whole *pāsāda* took its name from this sacred top-chamber and was called *Kuṭāgāra-sālā* (the Chamber-topped Mansion). The word *Hammiya,* however, is found on a votive stone to indicate this type of monastic building: it was discovered in January, 1942, on the facade of a cave at Kondane in Western India with an inscription which records: 'This is the *Hamma* of (i.e. donated by) Paraka'. The inscription is dated round 50 BC by the archaeologist Dr Dikshit who discovered it.[3]

Of the *Pañcaleṇāni* (Five *Leṇas*) named in the legend, three structural types seem to have become obsolete; only the *Vihāra* and the *Guhā* survived. The former became the typical monastic building of the north, the latter of the south.

The division of India between the North and the South along the Vindhyan range has been a geographical datum, recognized in the country since immemorial antiquity. The Vindhyan range is a great complex comprising the Sātpurās, the Vindhyas, Mahādeo-hills, Gawaligarh, Maikal range, Hazāribagh range, the Chota-Nāgpur, the Singbhum and the Mānbhum plateaux.[4] The belt runs across India horizontally for about 700 miles touching Sourāshtra in the west and Bihar in the east. It is mentioned in the *Mahābhārata* as marking off the *Dakṣiṇāpatha,* the southern regions of India, from the north. India of the north is plains; of the south it is plateau bounded on two sides by the Eastern Ghats and the Western Ghats. In the plains of northern India and spreading beyond its northern borders, the *Vihāra* became the normal type of monastery; on the western side of the plateau, the *Guhā*. The northernmost *Guhās* are

[1] It is mentioned by Hsüan-tsang (see Watters' *On Yuan Chawng,* vol. 2, pp. 164–165), and described as a *Prāsāda* in Mālāda's *praśasti* discovered at Nālandā in 1925–26.

[2] See *Sumaṅgala-vilāsinī* (PTS ED), p. 310.

[3] Dr Dikshit has described this inscription at p. 461 of his (unpublished) work on *Buddhist Settlements of Western India* (1942) which by his courtesy I was allowed to consult in typescript.

[4] See Subbarao's *Personality of India* (University of Baroda, 1958), p. 14.

5. *A panoramic view of the 'University site' at Nāgārjunakoṇḍa.* (Photo: Government of Andhra)
The 'University site' at Nāgārjunakoṇḍa. (Photo: Department of Archaeology, N.E. Project, Guntur)

6. *View of the dais with the three sockets of Tri-Ratna pillars in front.* (Photo: Department of Archaeology, N.E. Project, Guntur)

Nāgārjunakoṇḍa sculpture. (*Mithuna figures.*) (Photo: Department of Archaeology, N.E. Project, Guntur)

represented by the Bāgh Caves of Gwalior situated on the southern face of the Vindhyan range.[1]

For the plains of the north, the free-standing, brick-or-stone *vihāra* was perhaps more suitable, while the orographic conditions of the south favoured the construction of *Guhās*.

The ancient generic name, *Leṇa*, for a monastic abode, however, became restricted in meaning in later usage. Dropping its ancient generic connotation, it came to denote a *Guhā*-monastery. The *guhās* were structural caves, not natural caverns, but from the use of caves and caverns by hermits for solitary meditation since pre-Buddhistic times, the *guhā* gained a certain association of sanctity. A legend relates the story of an old and venerable Buddhist monk named Pilindavacca trying to make a *leṇa* with his own hands digging in a mountain-side at Rājagaha. It was no easy job for him. King Bimbisāra, who was standing by and watching his unavailing efforts, offered him a helpmate, an *ārāma* servant.[2] Emperor Asoka and Dasaratha, his successor to the throne, dedicated later some caves in the Barābara and the Nāgārjuni hills in Bihar to some *Ājīvaka* hermits. Whether they were lived in or used only for the purpose of secluded meditation is by no means certain. These caves, with elaborate architectural frontage, were artificial caves scooped out of the rocks.

We shall deal later with these two types of monasteries, the *Vihāra* and the *Guhā*, and the story of their development through the ages.

[1] See Part II, Sec. 6.

[2] Mahāvagga, VI, 15, 1, *et seq.*

PART II

THE ASOKA-SĀTAVĀHANA AGE

(250 BC—AD 100)

AND ITS LEGACY

1

Monks of the 'Eastern Tract'

THE *Puratthima* (Eastern Tract) is a geographical expression that occurs only in the legends of the Pali canon. It does not correspond to any known and delimited political or territorial division of ancient India. It is just possible, however, that it was a variant name for the region indicated by Pāṇini as 'Prācya (Eastern) Bhāratavarṣa'.[1]

Those who made these legends were Buddhist monks of an early generation; they belonged to a north-eastern corner of the country, and their geographical ken hardly extended beyond the bounds of what to us is known as Northern India. The great peninsular India of the south, known but vaguely yet, was still known by the more ancient name *Dakṣiṇāpatha* (Way South), a sort of *terra incognita*.

All the places associated in these early legends with the Founder's career and his missionary tours are traceable along a northwest-slanting tongue of land from Rājagaha (in Bihar) in the south to Kushinagara in the north-west (in the northern extreme of the Uttara Pradesh). This portion of northern India would measure hardly two hundred square miles, an extremely small slice of India—yet, hallowed by the tread of the Holy Feet, supremely holy land to the Buddhist. First appearing here, Buddhism spread beyond the limits of this area, probably within only a few decades of the Founder's decease. The entire region where Buddhism was practised by monks and had influence over the people at the time when the legends were composed—those included in the *Mahāvagga* and the *Cullavagga*—was looked upon by the monks as 'Buddhist land' and named by them *Puratthima*.

Magadha was the heartland of the *Puratthima*. It was to Magadha that the Lord had migrated after his 'Great Renunciation', joined the wanderers' community there, and after the 'enlightenment' proceeded from here on his mission. Here the Saṅgha was first planted and here it grew up, spread and burgeoned during the first two centuries of Buddhist history. Emperor Asoka, seeking contact with the monk-community, came to the 'Māgadha Saṅgha' to pay his respects and avow his faith (*prasāda*) in the Buddha, Dhamma and Saṅgha.[2] Magadha had always been under the rule of kings, two of

[1] *Pāṇini*, 8, 3, 75.

[2] The Calcutta-Bairat Rock Edict—*Vidite ve bhaṁte āvatake hamā Budhasi dhaṁmasi saṁghasi ti gālave caṁ prasāde ca* (Tr.—It is known to you, Sirs, how great are my reverence for and my faith in the Buddha, the Dhamma and the Saṅgha). See A. C. Sen's *Asoka's Edicts*, p. 135.

whom, Bimbisāra and Ajātasatru, figure in the legends as having been the Buddha's contemporaries, admirers and supporters.

The history of Buddhism during the first two centuries (from the Founder's decease in *c.* 483 BC to Asoka's accession in *c.* 269 BC or even to the middle of his reign) is confined to the *Puratthima*. To this region we must bring our vision to see saṅgha life in its first burgeoning. Here were the *āvāsas* and *ārāmas* of the monks; here perhaps the largest incidence of lay Buddhists in the population. For the after-career of Buddhism, the rise of Magadha as the seat of Maurya imperial power was a factor of signal importance.

Asoka was the third emperor on the Magadhan throne. He became a convert to Buddhism at a time when it was perhaps little more than a regional faith. His conversion was a matter of inner urge and personal faith, and Rhys Davids' comparison of it with the Roman emperor Constantine's adoption of Christianity is perhaps far-fetched. The position of Buddhism in Asoka's empire at the time of his conversion was by no means analogous to that of Christianity in the Roman empire when Emperor Constantine became a convert.[1] At the time when Asoka embraced the faith, it was a faith current, and perhaps popular, only in the *Puratthima*. Some scholars hold the opinion that the Buddhist Saṅgha itself was then known as the 'Māgadha Saṅgha', having only a regional standing. The boundary landmarks (see *infra*) of the *Puratthima* are mentioned in a legend from which it will appear that it covered an area extending only from the east of Hardwar to the eastern boundary of Bihar.

In this area the Buddhist monk-communities, now settled in their *āvāsas* and *ārāmas*, had built up, within a century of the Founder's decease, a prestige of which we have evidence in the account of the 'Council of Vesālī' (supposed to have been held a hundred years after the 'Great Decease') described in the canonical record (*Cullavagga* XII). This 'council' was an assembly of 700 monks from all parts of northern India, met for the purpose of deciding on ten points of Vinaya over which a prolonged dispute had existed among monks. Contention raged between two parties, one of the west and the other, consisting of Vajji monks, of the east. A monk named Revata was playing a leading role in the settlement of the dispute. Revata was urged by Uttara to lay this before the tribunal chosen to give the verdict: 'Honoured Sirs, it is in the eastern tracts (*puratthimesu janapadesu*) that the Buddhas are born (*perhaps he was*

[1] 'Asoka, as in the parallel case of Constantine, embraced a cause so far successful that it seemed on the verge of victory. And it is not at all unlikely that reasons of State may have had their share in influencing Asoka, just as they certainly did in the case of Constantine'—*Buddhist India*, Ch. XV.

quoting a current proverb); therefore the Bhikkhus of the east are the true spokesmen of the Dhamma'.[1]

On the confines of the *Puratthima Janapada*, deemed, as it were 'the well of Buddhism undefiled', were the Border countries (*paccantima janapada*). Monks were scarce there and monk-settlements few and far between. The bounds of these 'Border Countries' are indicated in a legend by six names of township, village, river and hill[2]—Kajaṅgala (a *nigama*, market town), Mahāsālā (also a *nigama*), Sallavatī (a river), Setakaṇṇika (a *nigama*), Thūṇa (a Brāhmaṇa village) and Usīraddhaja (a mountain). Only two of these boundary marks can be identified—Thūṇa and Usīraddhaja.[3]

In these Border countries, the paucity of Bhikkhus made difficult the due observance of Vinaya laws. The law of Ordination had been that the number competent to confer ordination on a Bhikkhu should be ten, but this minimum number had to be reduced to five in the Border countries,[4] and the relaxation, it is said, was granted by the Lord because a devout Bhikkhu named Soṇa Koṭikaṇṇa had represented to him his own difficulty in getting together ten monks to ordain him. Soṇa Koṭikaṇṇa hailed from Avantī; it was in the south, *Dakṣiṇāpatha,* across the Vindhya range. Avantī seems to have been 'out of bounds' to Buddhist monks of that age.

The state of pre-Asokan Buddhism (of the fifth and fourth centuries BC) may be summed up in a brief *aperçue*. It was a regional faith current within the limits of the *puratthima*; it was chiefly a cult of the monks, still under development in monastic cloisters as 'Dhamma-vinaya', a system of doctrine and practice. But monastic life had developed a feature calculated to bring it out of the cloisters to the people. Monks were dwellers mainly in *āvāsas* and *ārāmas*, but *leṇas* (monasteries), each of which was a communal dwelling for a particular saṅgha, were also cropping up. Though the monk-communities had not outgrown their wandering stage completely yet and many were still wanderers or habitues of forest-clearings (*āraññaka*), cenobitical life had already started and its rules (Vinaya) been put into complete shape. 'Forest-dwellers', when they arrived at the monks' abodes, were required to learn these.[5] The life lived by the monks in these abodes was a life of their own with no ties with the social life outside; yet it could not have been wholly inbred and exclusive—for had not the Founder himself bound up monastic life with the life of the laity by insisting that

[1] Cullavagga, XII, 2, 3.
[2] Mahāvagga, V, 13, 12.
[3] See Cunningham's *Ancient Geography of India* (revised by Majumdar, 1924), Intro., p. XI, iii.
[4] Mahāvagga, v, 13, 12.
[5] See *Gulissāni Sutta* in the *Majjhima Nikāya* (No. 69).

'the good of the Many, the happiness of the Many' must be the aim of a monk's life?

The monk-community therefore kept up not a casual, but a regular intercourse with lay society: the good that they could do to it was by being helpful in its moral uplift and by ministering to its spiritual needs.

On the relations that existed in this early age between monk-community and lay society, before the missionary movement of Asoka's reign brought Buddhism to the doors of the common people, some light is thrown by the legends. They reveal the dawn-time of Buddhism. We hear in these legends of the patronage and benefactions Buddhism attracted from the top ranks of society—from aristocrats and merchant-princes and at times from kings and ministers. But the bulk of those who supported the monks was represented by the middle and lower social ranks—small land-owners, ordinary householders, petty traders, artists and artisans, handicraftsmen and peasantry. Many of them are mentioned in the legends by name. In those ranks of lay society, the monks were looked upon as teachers of morality (*Sīla*) and instructors of religion (*Dhamma*). They were held in especial veneration and were approached for instruction by those interested in the tenets of the faith. Apart from casual and individual occasions, when a learned monk was invited by lay men to give a discourse or the monk did so of his own accord, there was a special ceremonial occasion for the coming together of monks and lay men. It was the *Uposatha*. In this overall picture the legends of the canon assemble, two features come into relief—the laity's support for Buddhism and the monks' ministrations to the laity.

The fortnightly Uposatha day was for the monks a sacred one for the recital of the *Pātimokkha* in an assembly held in the *Uposathāgāra* of an *āvāsa* or in the more commodious *Upaṭṭhāna-sālā* of an *ārāma*; it fell on the fourteenth or the fifteenth of every (lunar) month.[1] Aṣoka by an edict placed these two days in his list of 'auspicious days' (*Sudivasa*) on which a ban was placed by him on the killing or castration of animals.[2]

Lay Buddhists observed the Uposatha days as 'holy days', but their observance was different from the monks', for the *Pātimokkha* was the monks' liturgy in which the laity could not participate. The lay observance of the Uposatha consisted in the acceptance of Eight Precepts of Morality: hence it was called the 'Uposatha of the Eight Parts' (*Aṭṭhaṅgika Uposatha*) and its aim and purpose is stated to be

[1] Mahāvagga, II, 14, 1—Dve me Bhikkave uposathā cātuddasiko ca pannarasiko ca.

[2] Pillar Edict, No. 5 (see A. C. Sen's *Asoka's Edicts*, pp. 154–157).

'purification of a soiled mind by a proper process'.[1] The process was the taking of the vow of abstinence from eight specified disapproved acts. This kind of Uposatha observance by the laity still obtains in countries of Theravāda Buddhism, e.g. Ceylon where the Uposatha day is known as '*Poya*'. On the *Poya* day a Buddhist lay man rests from normal labour, repairs to a monastery, takes the Eight-Abstinence Vow (*Aṭṭhasīla*) and spends the day in the company of monks listening to readings given by them out of the scripture.[2]

One of the six specific duties prescribed for a monk in the *Sigālovāda Sutta* (in the *Dīgha Nikāya*) is to show the laity 'the way to heaven'.

In the *Sutta-piṭaka* of the canon are several sections headed 'Groups of *Suttas* for Householders' (*Gahapativagga*). They embody such canonical legends as the monks were expected to impart to householders. The separate inclusion of them in the canon was necessary, because of the doctrine that prevailed among the earlier monks that those who remain in the world are incapable of the higher reaches of spiritual attainment. On this account the monks were enjoined not to attempt to expound to the unordained *in extenso* all the doctrines of the religion (*Dhamma*).[3] The legends rubricated for householders are those that turn on ethical ideals and practice of morality (*sīla*)—which is the way to the 'goal of heaven', not the 'goal of Arhatship' which is for monks alone. These *Gahapativaggas* of the canon were no doubt delivered on the Uposatha occasion by monks to householders when the latter went to the monastery for the 'purification of a soiled mind' through contact with holy men.

This custom of monks and lay people coming together on the Uposatha day—a custom established since the Saṅgha's early days—helped to popularize the religion and propagate it in the initial stage of its history.

The custom ripened into an institutional observance in the monasteries. Its later history is interesting: the Uposatha became a colourful festival, when the Mahāyāna development introduced the ceremony of image-worship. It lost its ancient simplicity and went back on the original purpose of monk-and-layman intercourse. I-tsing's account in the latter part of the seventh century AD of the ceremonies with which the *Uposatha* was attended in his time[4] shows

[1] See Woodward's *The Book of Gradual Sayings*, Vol. I, p. 187.

[2] See Rahula's *History of Buddhism in Ceylon*, p. 258, fn. 3 and *passim* (ch. XV on *The Lay Life*).

[3] Pātimokkha, *pācittiya* 4—*Yo pana bhikkhu anupasampannaṁ padaso dhammaṁ vāceyya pācittiyaṁ*. '*Padaso*' means 'word by word' and the sense is that of detailed exposition.

[4] See Takakusu, Ch. IX (Rules about the Reception at the Uposatha Day), pp. 35–53.

that they centred mostly on the ritual worship of the Buddha and other deities. The monks were invited by lay men and came to officiate as priests, winding up the worship with offerings of flowers, chanting of hymns and recital of holy legends. 'An offering of music', says I-tsing, 'such as of drum and stringed instruments, accompanied by songs, is made if the host likes it.'[1] This was followed by a sumptuous feast given by the host to the invited monks. I-tsing remarks: 'The ceremony (of feasting monks by a householder) is observed on a scale so grand that all the trays and plates are full of the cakes and rice remaining over; and melted butter and cream can be partaken of to any extent.'[2] The good Chinese pilgrim describes with much gusto the overflowing quantity and excellent quality of food provided and comments on the 'table manners' observed by hosts and guests on the occasion.

[1] *Ibid*, p. 42.
[2] *Ibid*, p. 40.

2

Asoka and Moggaliputta Tissa

a. ASOKA IN BUDDHIST LEGENDS

WITH the concept of a Buddhist India, Rhys Davids' well-known monograph, first published in 1903, but still a *vade mecum* for students of early Buddhism, has made us familiar. But, if the expression, 'Buddhist India', connotes an India with Buddhism as a widespread or prevailing faith in it, its application to the country before Asoka's time would perhaps be unhistorical.

From the region called *Puratthima*, the spread of Buddhism was due mainly to two events of history—first, the rise of Magadha from a petty kingdom to the seat of Maurya imperial power, and secondly, the adoption of the Buddhist faith by a great Maurya emperor.

The Maurya capital at Pāṭaliputra in Magadha rose at a time when Buddhism was a Magadhan religion, scarcely two centuries old and known but little outside the *Puratthima*. It is said that the Buddha had already prophesied its rise from a petty village to a 'Chief Town' (*Agga-nagara*).[1] Ruling from here, the Maurya dynasts acquired a far-flung empire in three generations, stretching north-to-south from Gāndhāra (now merged in Afganistan) to Mysore, and east-to-west from Bihar to Sourāshtra. It was the largest empire ever established in India, including the British.

Candragupta, the founder of the dynasty, had seen India's north-west shaken to fragments by Alexander's abortive invasion in 325 BC. Integrating small territories under one rule, sometimes by conquest, but mainly by diplomacy, he built upon the wreckage a sizable and integrated empire. It was added to by further conquests by his son Bindusāra whose suggestive nickname, 'Slayer of Foes', has been handed down to us by Greek historians and the Sanskrit grammarian, Puṣyamitra's priest (second century BC), Patañjali.[2] Asoka, the next heir to the throne, made only a single conquest by force of arms—of the Kaliṅga country on the eastern seaboard—extending thereby the empire from sea to sea.

The terrible massacre, the ruthless displacement of population and the widespread suffering of survivors, involved in this war, drove him

[1] Mahāparinibbāna Suttanta, I, 28.

[2] See Hultzseh's *Inscriptions of Asoka* (*Corpus Inscriptionum Indicarum*, Vol. I), p. xxxiv, and Patañjali on Pāṇini, III, 2, 97.

into a poignant psychological crisis.[1] He could pull himself out of it only by embracing the faith then flourishing in Magadha—the religion of humanity and of peace and goodwill to men that the Buddha had preached and the Saṅgha was diligently propagating. No more in his empire throbbed the 'sound of Drum' (*Bherighosa*) for the following thirty-seven years of his reign, but a sound of a different evocation—what the emperor calls *Dhammaghosa* (The Sound of Religion).

Asoka was the first Indian emperor to become a convert to Buddhism and his reign saw the religion spread far and wide by the missionaries of Moggaliputta Tissa.[2] Naturally those, who in the after-ages when Buddhism was a good many centuries old in India, looked back on its early growth and development, were struck by the towering imperial figure in the far background. They were monk-historians interested only in recalling the great story of Buddhism. Tradition was perhaps not completely silent yet about the first Buddhist emperor; and monks made legends about him on the basis of stray traditional tales, completely ignorant that contemporary evidence of him lay scattered in the country in indelible epigraphs on pillars and rocks. The script and language of these epigraphs had long passed into oblivion: the pillars and rocks were at deserted inaccessible spots.

Into their retrospect the figure of Asoka came in the light of a great Buddhist emperor of India of the far past in whose illustrious reign Buddhism flourished and spread wide over the vast country. It was natural for them to attribute the spread and prosperity of the religion in his reign to his personal initiative, leadership and patronage—to give him credit for acts and measures that were hardly open to him as the constitutional ruler of a country of diverse and often contending faiths. They looked upon Asoka in one aspect only—as a *Buddhist* emperor.

In the eyes of the modern historian, however, the figure of Asoka stands cross-lit from two sources—the Buddhist legends on one hand and his edicts and rescripts on the other. But the cross-lighting, curiously enough, does not reveal the same picture.

'*Dhammika Dhammarāja*' (The Pious King who rules according to Dhamma) is the conventional expression in Buddhist literature to describe an ideal ruler. It is said that the memory of such a ruler should be enshrined by erecting a *stūpa* to his memory.[3] Asoka was taken by the chroniclers and makers of legends as the *beau idéal* of

[1] Rock Edict 13. See Sen's *Asoka' Edicts*, p. 98.

[2] See *infra*, Sec. (b).

[3] Among those specified in the *Mahāparinibbāna Suttanta* as 'thūpāraha', i.e. worthy of commemoration by a Thūpa, is an emperor (Cakkavatti rājā) who is remembered as a 'dhammika dhammarāja' (see V. 31).

such a ruler and at the same time his 'piety' was interpreted as single-minded devotion to Buddhism and its cause.

The Buddha himself, it is said, had prophesied his advent.[1] Asoka, according to this prophecy, would be ruler from sea to sea, ruling 'without oppression, without enforcing penalties, without the force of arms, but according to Dhamma and customary law'; his piety would reach its consummation when late in life, 'giving up his empire, he would shear off his hair and beard, don the yellow robe, go from home into homelessness, and ultimately attain to the status of a Pratyeka Buddha'. Other legends supply fringes to this idealized picture—legends about his zeal in propagating Buddhism within his empire and outside, occurring chiefly in the Ceylonese chronicles, and specially his feat of covering the whole of India (*Jambudvīpa*) with *stūpas*, *stambhas* (Pillars) and *vihāras*, for which, it is fabled, he had supernatural agencies in his employ. Hsüan-tsang, who heard the legend in India, speaks of almost every *stūpa* he saw in this country and on its western borders as having been built by 'Asoka-rājā' and refers also to the supernatural agents engaged by him. Later on we find this legend of elfin architecture recorded with fantastic embellishments in the *Mañjuśrī-Mūlakalpa* (*c.* AD 800).[2] And, lastly, the legend of Asoka's having held a great council in order to purify the Saṅgha by purging heretics in it under Moggaliputta Tissa's guidance is current in Theravāda literature. The result of the work of this Council was, it is said, the expulsion of 80,000 heretics who were recognized by their failure to subscribe to the Analytic Method of Scriptural Exegesis (*Vibhajjavāda*) favoured by the Theravāda school.[3]

The legends are mostly of the Theravāda School, and in them, specially in the story of the 'Council', the emperor is represented as an earnest adherent and active patron of that school. But in the picture framed in these legends the bias of those who painted it in these colours is all too apparent. Much of the picture melts away as soon as we turn upon it searchlight from the edicts

The edicts issued by the emperor are described by himself in his thirteenth regnal year (*c.* 256 BC) in the following terms:[4]

'(These rescripts) are (written) in brief, (or) in medium (length or) elaborately.

'Not all occur everywhere—(for) large indeed is (my) dominion and

[1] See *Asokavarṇāvadāna* (XI) of the *Divyāvadāna*. Cowell and Neil's Edition, pp. 140–141.

[2] See Jayaswal's *Imperial History of India*, p. 12, and Text, p. 24 (vv. 369 ff.).

[3] The tradition of this 'council' is of Theravāda provenance. It occurs in Buddhaghosa's *Samantapāsādikā*, the Ceylonese chronicles, *Dīpavaṁsa* and *Mahāvaṁsa*, and the *Kathāvatthu* commentary.

[4] This is the Girnir version of Rock Edict 14. See Sen's *Asoka's Edicts*, p. 106.

much has been written, and I shall cause yet more to be written.
'And there are here some (matters which have been) spoken of again and again—because of the interest of their respective subjects, in order that the people may act accordingly.
'If some thereof are written incompletely—it is so because of the locality, or in consideration of the object or by the fault of the engraver.'

The edicts of Asoka are not a closed chapter yet; discoveries are still being made—the latest being one, not in Prākrit, but in bilingual Greek-Aramaic,[1] discovered in Kandahar (Gāndhāra in Asoka's time, now in southern Afghanistan) by an Italian archaeological mission early in 1958.[2]

But from all these edicts discovered so far the figure of Emperor Asoka as an enthusiast and propagandist for Buddhism scarcely emerges. All that appears is—that the emperor was a Buddhist himself; that he had some personal contacts with the monk-community and visited at least one of its centres (in Magadha); and that, in his capacity as a ruler whose constitutional duty obliged him to see that corporate bodies like the Buddhist *saṅghas* did not come to shipwreck through internal dissensions, he revived and proclaimed the Vinaya rule of 'unfrocking' and expelling schism-mongers.

Perhaps in his private life, apart from his imperial office, he was a pious Buddhist himself; meaningless rites and ceremonies as well as animal slaughter were repugnant to him; he held faith (*prasāda*) in the creed of the Three-fold Refuge and was to some extent conversant with the scripture; went on pilgrimage to Buddhist holy places, and had in fact so imbibed the inner spirit of Buddhism—its charity and human-heartedness, its sensitiveness to suffering, whether of men or of animals, its message of peace and goodwill to all—that it breathes ineffably through the phraseology of his multi-purpose edicts. Only they do not confirm what the legends say about his actual service to the cause of Buddhism, unless one were to identify thoughtlessly the term *Dhamma* occurring in nearly all the important edicts with the Buddhist religion. From reasons *pro* and *con* discussed threadbare by scholars, this identification is far from established except in the one edict (Calcutta–Bairat), addressed to monks, where the word *Dhamma* stands in its scriptural connotation as *Buddhavacana* (the sayings of the Buddha).

The question has been often debated what this *Dhamma*, so

[1] Aramaic is a dead language which belonged to the northern branch—Hebrew being its modern representative—of the Semitic linguistic group.
[2] Reported in the *East and West* (organ of the IsMeo of Rome) in its March–June, 1958, number. See also *Un editto bilingue greco-aramico di Asoka* by G. Tucci and others (Serie Orientale Roma, xxi, 1958).

untiringly repeated in the edicts, is. It undoubtedly stands for some ideal cherished by the emperor in his own mind, but it is nowhere associated with the specific values given to it in the scripture, nor is it anywhere defined or put into positive terms. Asoka professes to follow Dhamma himself; he wishes to teach it to his subjects; he exhorts them to understand it and act up to it; all his acts and measures, he declares, are in pursuance of Dhamma and have the object of promoting it. But judging by the emperor's own elucidation, it means not the promoting of the Buddhist religion as formulated in the scripture or any of the specific values inculcated by it, but the culture of fundamental social and ethical virtues. Yet there is no doubt that the ideal of Dhamma he holds up to his people is tinged by the Buddhist faith personally held by him. The emperor says in one of the edicts: '(The practice of Dhamma) is commendable—but what constitutes the Dhamma? (These constitute the Dhamma, viz.)—little sin, many good deeds, mercifulness, charity, truthfulness and purity. The gift of the eye too, of many kinds (*meaning perhaps practical demonstrations so that people can see what such deeds and virtues are*) has been bestowed by me. On bipeds and quadrupeds, on birds and aquatic animals, various benefits have been conferred by me, (even) as far as the grant of life. And many other good deeds too have been performed by me. For this purpose has this Dhamma-rescript (*Dhamma-lipi*) been caused to be written by me, (viz.) that (the people) may follow (it) as instructed and that (it) may be of long duration. And who will thus follow it properly will perform a good deed'.[1]

Perhaps it is possible to account for the deliberate stressing and endless iteration of *Dhamma* in the edicts. The emperor took his cue from the scripture. The edicts show that Asoka knew something of its contents as they existed in his time. In the phraseology of the edicts there are echoes from the *Dhammapada*,[2] quotation of a saying from the *Aṅguttara Nikāya*, and citation also of a number of *Suttas*, some identifiable in the Pali Theravāda canon, recommended by him in an edict (Calcutta-Bairat) addressed to monks, though the selection seems to be at haphazard. One part of the scripture, he seems to have been well acquainted with, was the *Aṅguttara*. In the opinion of some scholars, one of Asoka's recommended texts, *Aliya-vasāni*, corresponds to the fourth *nipāta* (section) of the *Aṅguttara*.[3] In that edict occurs also a saying taken from the same text.[4]

[1] Pillar Edict 2. See Sen's *Asoka's Edicts*, p. 146.

[2] See Hultzsch's *Inscriptions of Asoka* (Corpus Indicarum Inscriptioum), Intro., pp. li–liv.

[3] It is so held by Kosambi and Lanman. See *Indian Antiquary*, Feb. 1912, pp. 37–40.

[4] 'Whatever, sirs, has been spoken by the Blessed Buddha, all that is well-spoken'—Woodwards' *The Book of Gradual Sayings*, Vol. IV, p. 112 and *Aṅguttara Nikāya*, PTS, Vol. IV, p. 164.

It is intriguing to find in the *Aṅguttara Nikāya* a *sutta* which describes what the relation of a pious emperor (*Cakkavatti rājā*) to *Dhamma* should be:[1]

'Herein a *rājā* who is a *cakkavatti* and *Dhammika Dhammarājā* is in dependence on Dhamma, honouring Dhamma, respectful and deferential to Dhamma, with Dhamma as his banner, with Dhamma as his standard, with Dhamma as his overlord, keeps watch and ward among his folk.

'Then again, a *rājā* (who is, etc. etc.) keeps constant watch and ward among the warriors who follow in his host, among Brāhmaṇas and householders and dwellers in outlying parts, among Sramaṇas and Brāhmaṇas, beasts and birds alike.

'(Such a one) rolls the wheel of sovereignty not to be upset by any human being whatever, by any foe that lives.'

It was perhaps Asoka's aspiration to fill the role of the *Dhammika Dhammarājā* as described in this *sutta*. It is not too far-fetched to assume that the passage suggested to him the place he assigns to Dhamma in the edicts. It rationalizes the remarkably frequent iteration of Dhamma in the edicts as being the objective of his imperial acts and measures.

Whatever may have been Asoka's actual service to the cause of Buddhism, his reign of thirty-seven years came to be regarded in later ages as the 'first glad confident morning' of Buddhism in India. Says the author of the *Dīpavaṁsa* (early years of the fourth century AD):[2]

'Two hundred and eighty years after the Great Decease, Piyadassi was crowned. After his coronation in Jambudvīpa (India), the Holy Flame (*Puṇṇateja*) glowed and waxed and prevailed high and low, and for leagues (*Yojana*) around in the great empire under his dominion.'

If it points to Asoka as the feeder and sustainer of that Holy Flame, his edicts hardly bear out that credit. They show decidedly greater concern on the emperor's part with the Dhamma of his own conception than with the Dhamma founded by the Buddha and postulated by monks in scripture. The one was by no means co-extensive or conterminous with the other.

For example, in one edict, the emperor, after disparaging *maṅgala* (auspicious) ceremonies, current in India even today among the

[1] *Aṅguttara Nikāya*, III, 2, 4; *The Book of Gradual Sayings*, Vol. I, pp. 94–95.
[2] *Dīpavaṁsa*, 6, 1–2.

populace during illness or at a wedding or the birth of a child or the commencement of a journey, goes on to comment:[1]

'Now, auspicious ceremonies should certainly be performed, but of little fruit indeed are auspicious ceremonies such as these. But of great fruit is this auspicious ceremony, viz. the auspicious ceremony of Dhamma. In it, these (are comprised)—proper behaviour towards slaves and servants; commendable deference towards elders; commendable gentleness towards animals; commendable gifts to Brāhmaṇas and Samaṇas—these and similar other (acts) are called the auspicious ceremonies of Dhamma.'

If the spread of Buddhism had been any object in the emperor's mind, it is reasonable to suppose that among these items of 'Dhamma-maṅgala', he would have included paying reverence to the *Stūpa* and taking the eight vows of morality (*Aṭṭhaṅga-uposatha*). Dhamma evidently was to his mind a concept of culture, of the cultivation of social and ethical virtues, rather than of religious faith or observances.

It was the propagation of this Dhamma that was nearest to the emperor's heart and, as we are told in another edict, he took a keen personal interest in it. When he went out of the capital on a pilgrimage, he used to invite personal contact with different classes of people among his subjects and it was his practice to give them informal and friendly talks on *Dhamma*:[2]

'(On a pilgrimage) these things take place—meeting and making gifts to Brāhmaṇas and Samaṇas, seeing aged people and bestowing on them money for their maintenance, visiting different regions and seeing the people there, giving instruction to them on Dhamma, catechising them on Dhamma such as is suitable for them. This is another kind of revenue gathered by Piyadassi (Emperor Asoka), because it brings much pleasure to the Devānaṁpiya (i.e. His Majesty).'

In the edicts, there is nowhere the remotest allusion to the 'Council'; the object of veneration by people is always named 'Brāhmaṇa-samaṇa'; the 'Dhamma-mahāmātās' are enjoined to see that sects do not foment quarrels among themselves, and, as regards the *stūpa*-building legends, it is suggestive that, except for the find of a pillar outside the outer railing of the 'Great Tope' at Sanchi

[1] Rock Edict, No. IX. See Sen's *Asoka's Edicts*, p. 87.
[2] Rock Edict, No. 8. See Sen's *Asoka's Edicts*, p. 85. The translation is slightly altered.

inscribed with the '*Saṅgha-bhedaka*' edict, but containing no reference to locality, there is no archaeological find connecting Asoka with any *stūpa*, except that of Koṇāgamana which he renovated at Nigālī-sāgara. The *Saṅgha-bhedaka* edict was in discharge of his constitutional duty as a ruler to prevent disruption of a recognized 'association', i.e. the Saṅgha of Buddhist monks (*vide* Medhātithi's comment on Manu cited on p. 80 *supra*).

b. MOGGALIPUTTA TISSA'S MISSIONARIES

Whatever the part played by Asoka in the propagation of Buddhism, his own conversion to the religion would by itself be likely to give an impetus to the spread and progress of the religion—giving it a certain prestige and place of honour among the diverse contending faiths that, as we know from his edicts, prevailed in his own time among the people.[1] His conversion actually opened the door for a movement to carry the 'Holy Flame' beyond the limits of the 'Eastern Region' far and wide over his vast empire. But this movement, as all the legends indicate, was initiated and organized not by the emperor, but by a great and powerful religious leader, his contemporary and perhaps his friend, Moggaliputta Tissa.

In the Buddhist world of Asoka's time he was perhaps the most outstanding figure: the pre-eminent leader of the Theravāda school of Buddhism. Naturally in the traditions of that school, Tissa's name is associated with the emperor's and what was accomplished by him is supposed to have had the latter's consent, support and active patronage. The Theravāda legends relating to him leave no doubt about his intellectual greatness and pre-eminent position. The mantle of Upāli—the disciple who is said to have rehearsed to the 'Council', held at Rājagaha after the Great Decease, the Vinaya propounded by the Master—fell, the legends say, upon Moggaliputta Tissa; he is said to have presided over the 'Council' held by Asoka at his capital, and expelled 80,000 heretics from the Saṅgha; after this, he composed the great work, *Kathāvatthu*, incorporated in the *Abhidhamma* section of the Theravāda canon, refuting current heresies from the Theravāda standpoint.

Most of these legends about him may be apocryphal. But in support of one, there is historical confirmation, namely, that he organized a widespread missionary movement for propagation of Buddhism within Asoka's empire.

In the Ceylonese chronicles, as well as in Buddhaghosa's *Samanta-pāsādikā*, the credit for sending out the missionaries is given to

[1] See Rupnāth, Māski, Gujarra and other minor rock edicts, in which the divergent creeds and sects are referred to.

Moggaliputta Tissa himself. The *Dīpavaṁsa* (Chapter VIII) mentions the missionaries by their names and records somewhat briefly their achievements, and the whole of chapter XII of the *Mahāvaṁsa*, headed the 'Conversion of Different Countries', describes in verses 1–52 how the missionaries named in the earlier chronicle converted people to Buddhism by thousands, and in verses 29–38 specifies what *suttas* they preached in Mahiṣamaṇḍala (Mysore), Vanavāsi (North Kanara), Aparāntaka (Western border province of the empire), and Mahāraṭṭha (Mahārāshtra), and adds that they bestowed ordination on thousands. Buddhaghosa bases his account in the *Samanta-pāsādikā* on the *Dīpavaṁsa* chronicle. From these Ceylonese sources, we get the names of the missionaries and the countries to which they were deputed:

1. Majjhantika	to Kashmir and Gāndhāra.
2. Yona Dhammarakkhita .. (a monk of Greek origin)	to Aparāntaka.
3. Majjhima	to Himalayan Region.
4. Mahārakkhita	to the country of the Yonas (perhaps to the Bactrian kingdom to the north-west).
5. Mahā-dhammarakkhita ..	to Mahārāshtra.
6. Rakkhita	to Vanavāsi (North Kanara).
7. Mahādeva	to Mahiṣamaṇḍala (Mysore).
8. Soṇa and Uttara	to Suvarnabhūmi (Burma?).
9. Mahinda and, Moggaliputta's own disciples, Iṭṭhiya, Uttiya, Saṁbala and Bhaddasāla ..	to Ceylon.

Archaeology has confirmed the historicity of Tissa's missions. In a *stūpa* (No. 2) at Sanchi were found two relic-caskets, probably deposited there in the second or first century BC, on which some of the names of the missionaries are inscribed—Majjhima (the missionary to the Himalayan region) and two of his associates, Kassapagota and Dundubhissara, out of the four mentioned in the *Samanta-pāsādikā* as having been associated with him on the mission, viz. Kassapagota, Alakadeva, Dundubhissara and Sahadeva.

We have no further trace of these missionaries and no subsequent record of their achievements save in respect of those who worked in Ceylon. There is no doubt that these missions met with a measure of success. We may set no store by the legendary report in the *Dīpavaṁsa* of their resounding success—of thousands of men converted and monks ordained. But what is strongly plausible is that the propagation of Buddhism in Asoka's reign in those areas which later fell largely within the Sātavāhana empire prepared the ground for the rise, south of the Vindhyas, of Saṅgha life and the *leṇas* in the following century. The *leṇas*, a good many of which had started in the second century BC, proliferated in hundreds along the hills of the Western Ghats from Sourāshtra to Mysore.

In spreading among the people, Buddhism developed to some extent a popular aspect: its impress is indelibly left on the *stūpa*-sculpture of Sanchi, Bhilsa and Barhut. It is striking in its difference from the religion of the canon as monks understood and interpreted it.[1] Folk-elements abound. The *Jātaka* stories were popular and abundant use is made of them in the sculpture; Yakṣas and Yakṣiṇis, minor gods, and semi-celestial beings of folk-cults are freely introduced—it was not from Buddhism that they came; rites of piety and devotion, quite alien from monastic practice, are shown—and what is most significant is that this sculpture, in its overall impression, is suffused with the spirit of *Bhakti*, with an emotive feeling that transcended the mere 'taking of Refuge'. It shows a faith visibly merging into worship in its delineations of the symbolical forms of the faith. We shall deal later[2] with the evolution of *Stūpa*-worship, of which a chief determinant seems to have been the impact and stress of the Buddhist lay mind. From the lay mind the *Bhakti* movement spread into the monk mind. Its ferment is seen in the growing concept of the Lord as Saviour rather than as instructor (*satthā*) or pathfinder on which emphasis waxes from earlier to later passages of the scripture, while his Superman (*Mahāpurisa*) aspect advances more and more to a docetic one, also in *Stūpa*-worship becoming a rite of monastic life, and monks like Upagupta of Mathura of the *Divyāvadāna* legend becoming apostles of *Bhakti*.[3] The *Bhakti*-movement in Buddhism first manifests itself round the stūpas of Sanchi, Bhilsa and Barhut.

The impetus Buddhism had received in Asoka's glorious reign was not spent with the downfall of the Mauryas. It started an age in Buddhist history, the integrity of which is betokened by several features. Political history does not record it as an *age*, but only a long period, much distracted and broken up, of changing dynasties, foreign inroads and conquests and repeated reshufflings of territories in northern India. Yet the Buddhist culture that had spread among the people of the north was steadily expanding—spreading uninterrupted through the reigns of the Śuṅgas, the Kāṇvas and the Kuṣāṇas into the midland Sātavāhana empire. It received no setback from the disturbed political conditions, except that it lost much of

[1] See Part II, Sec. 3 [2] See Part III, Sec. 3 (a).

[3] See the Māra-Upagupta legend (No. XXVI) in Cowell and Neil's *Divyāvadāna*, pp. 348 ff. Cf. Upagupta's advice to Māra: 'In this matter a little Bhakti leads to the fruit of Nirvāṇa' (Svalpā hi atra bhaktir' bhavati matimatāṁ nirvāṇaphaladā). See *Ibid*, p. 360.

its hold under the Śuṅga king Puṣyamitra in Magadha. How well integrated this expanding culture was is evident from many signs—the palaeography of all inscriptions of this age is in the Brāhmī script of Asoka's edicts; the architectural modes and decorative motifs are all interlinked with northern (Maurya) traditions,[1] and the aspect of Buddhism that prevailed both north and south of the Vindhyas is one and undifferentiable. The age coheres.

In the history of Buddhism we may not inappropriately call it an *age*—the 'Asoka-Sātavāhana Age'—though for lack of political unity and integration, it may not be counted as such in political history.

[1] See Part II, Sec. 5, pp. 140–141.

3

Early Buddhist Culture and its Trans-Vindhyan Expansion

THE introduction of Buddhism by Tissa's missionaries into various regions of India in Asoka's reign is known to us from legends as also from historical evidence. But how the religion fared thereafter in these far-flung parts of the empire is not so evident. In northern India, it may be presumed, Buddhism during the remainder of Maurya rule made headway and the monk-settlements spread gradually from the ancient *Puratthima* in the east as far westwards as Ujjayinī.

The Maurya dynasty came to an end round 184 BC. The wreckage of its northern empire was divided among three ruling powers—the Śuṅgas in the east ruling from Pāṭaliputra, the old Maurya capital, the Yavanas (Bactrian Greeks) in the north, and the Sātavāhanas in the west and south, with their old capital at Amarāvatī shifted north to Pratisthāna.

Till the extinction of Maurya power, Magadha had been the head-quarters of Buddhism and ancient stronghold of the Saṅgha. It does not seem to have flourished as such afterwards. Only after the lapse of four to five centuries when the Guptas ruled once again from the ancient imperial seat of the Mauryas, did Buddhism reassert its influence in this region. Its setback here followed close on the set-up of the successor dynasty.

The Śuṅgas were Brāhmaṇas of the Sāma-Veda school, wedded to Vedic rites which required animal sacrifice.[1] A long way back in the past Emperor Asoka had forbidden by an edict animal-sacrifice at Pāṭaliputra.[2] Perhaps during the remainder of Maurya rule, the ancient edict was more or less respected. But, with inauguration of Vedic rites since the first Śuṅga king Puṣyamitra seized the throne, the blood of sacrifice began to flow in the capital and the Buddhist monks must have resented and opposed the innovation. Whether the opposition had taken any active form is not known from history or legend, but bitter enmity sprang up between Puṣyamitra and the

[1] See Hara Prasad Sastri's article, *Chips from a Buddhist Workshop*, in *Buddhistic Studies*, ed. by B. C. Law (Thacker Spink, Calcutta, 1931).

[2] Rock Edict No. I—'Here no living things whatever are to be killed and offered in sacrifice' (*Idha na kiṁci jīvaṁ ārabhitpā prajūhitavyaṁ*). 'Idha' means at Pāṭaliputra. Sen's *Asoka's Edicts*, p. 65.

monks, and the king's relentless persecution of them is a gruesome theme of Buddhist legends.[1]

But over against the story of the Śuṅga king's persecution of monks, we have the legend of the patronage of Buddhism by the contemporary Yavana king Menander who ruled an extensive empire from his capital Sakala (Sialkot in the West Punjab).[2] The Yavana kings appear to have been generally friendly and favourable to Buddhism; so were the Sātavāhanas.

But it is idle to follow these legends of persecution or patronage of the religion by local or regional kings and dynasts. They become increasingly unimportant in Buddhist history as Buddhism, diffused among the people in Asoka's reign, gives birth to a popular culture from its teachings. It was bound in the nature of things to grow of itself and strengthen its roots in the mass-mind, quite apart from acts of persecution or patronage by rulers. It is exemplified by the flourishing of *Stūpa*-worship in that age in localities over which the Śuṅgas then held sway.

We have referred already in a different context to the decorative art of the *stūpas* of Sanchi, Bhilsa (modern Vidiśā) and Barhut. Perhaps the beginnings of these *stūpas* were in the late Maurya period, but the decorative slabs on them were the work of later times when this part of northern India was under Śuṅga rule. Worship at these *stūpas* was undoubtedly held on a grand ceremonial scale and it was the lay Buddhists who were most zealous in *stūpa*-worship and *stūpa*-decoration. Their sculpture has been studied minutely by competent scholars in its immensely varied themes and breath-taking profusion.

This *stūpa*-art has also an interest and significance from a different viewpoint—as the first tangible expression of Buddhist culture that had grown up since Asoka's reign among common people in Northern India. Its accents are different from the culture of the monasteries; it is to all appearance neither monk-moulded nor monk-directed; it is just a reflection of the popular mind under the impact and influence of Buddhist faith.

This first efflorescence of a Buddhist culture among the people is in stone, not in texts. Monks only had the ability to compose texts; lay men could write their faith only in pictures and symbols on stone. This lithic expression of lay Buddhist culture in northern India during the closing decades of the BC centuries is revelatory of its free and spontaneous folk-character.

[1] See *Divyāvadāna* (ed. by Cowell and Neil), pp. 429–434; *Mañjuśrī-Mūlakalpa* (ed. by K. P. Jayaswal) 1934, under the title *An Imperial History of India*), V. 532.

[2] The fame of Menander, Puṣyamitra's contemporary, and his keen interest in Buddhist scripture are perpetuated in the *Milindapañha*.

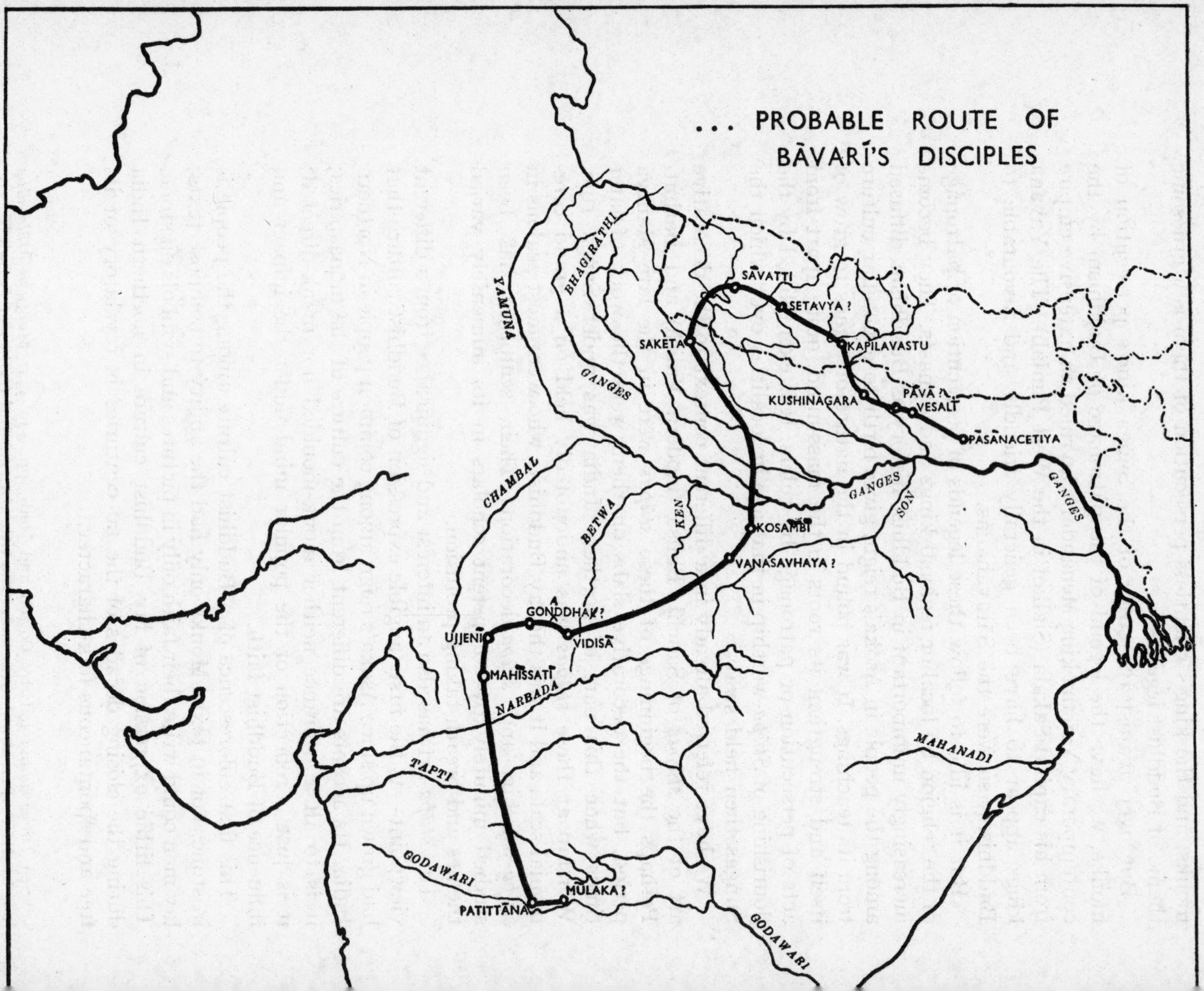

... PROBABLE ROUTE OF
BĀVARĪ'S DISCIPLES
SĀVATTI
SETAVYA ?
SAKETA
KAPILAVASTU
KUSHINAGARA
PĀVĀ ?
VESALĪ
PĀSĀNACETIYA
GANGES
SON
KOSAMBI
VANASAVHAYA ?
KEN
BETWA
CHAMBAL
YAMUNA
BHAGIRATHI
GONDDHA ?
UJJENI
VIDISĀ
MAHISSATI
NARBADA
TAPTI
MAHANADI
GODAWARI
MULAKA ?
PATITTĀNA

The *stūpa*-decorators evidently knew the main legends of the Lord, a number of Jātaka stories, the sacred symbols and their significance. But their work is untouched by the influence of monkish learning; it gives no hint of the special interpretations and doctrinal matters developed in the monks' *Abhidhamma* philosophy. Evidently their faith was intimate with life, forming one complex—the sacred unsifted from the profane, and the ideal elements of Buddhism promiscuously blent with folk-cults, folk-superstitions and concepts alien from canonical teachings. It was a faith that had stirred their hearts, activized their imagination and evoked the emotion of *Bhakti*—an emotion that lies near the surface of untutored folk-mind. Their concept of Him who gave this faith to the world was not the canonical concept of a Teacher (*Satthā*) or even of a Superman (*Mahāpurisa*), but of one who transcended all earthly relations and could not therefore be represented in art by a human figure, however idealized.[1] To the *stūpa* which since the days of Asoka had become the grand visible emblem of the faith, they flocked to avow and articulate their faith in the Three Refuges (*Ti-saraṇa*), and the *stūpa* stood to them not, as the canon contemplated it, as a memorial monument to the Lord, but as a symbol of Divine Presence.

This popular Buddhist culture of the north migrated south of the Vindhyas into the empire of the Sātavāhanas. It was in the wonted way of all culture-migrations in ancient history—that is, by the existing routes of travel and communication. With the tramp of merchants and men on business went in softer tempo along these routes the unhurried tread of migratory parties of Buddhist monks.

Pāṭaliputra, ancient Maurya capital in the east, and Ujjayinī, headquarters of Maurya imperial government in the west, were connected by a long trunk-route, the main artery of traffic in northern India. It had branch-routes to several cities in between its termini, some of which are still dots on the map of the Uttar Pradesh and Bihar. When the old empire was falling to pieces in the north and the empire of the Sātavāhanas rising in the west, with its capital shifted to Pratisthāna, Ujjayinī lapsed into Sātavāhana territories. The ancient trunk-route of northern India was extended to the new Sātavāhana capital and this link-road is still faintly visible in patches of crumbled masonry. From Pratisthāna the route continued southwards, bifurcating in both eastern and western directions.

Thus was established a continuous communication between northern India and southern (ancient *Dakṣiṇāpatha*), the spread and

[1] The absence of the Buddha-figure from the *stūpa*-art of Sanchi, Bhilsa and Barhut is related to this supramundane concept as I have tried to explain in *The Buddha and Five After-Centuries*, pp. 184–188.

extent of which northwards from the bank of the Godāvarī is illustrated by the story of Bāvarī in the *Sutta-nipāta.*[1]

Bāvarī was an old ascetic living in his hermitage on the bank of the Godāvarī river and he happened to incur the curse of an irate Brāhmaṇa. At the instance of the Deity of the place, he sent sixteen disciples to the Buddha to know what the curse would mean to him. So these delegates of Bāvarī went from Mūlaka[2] on the Godāvarī far up north, visiting different places in northern India, in search of the Buddha. This was their itinerary:

'To Paṭiṭṭhāna (Pratisthāna) from Mūlaka (*name of the place of starting, a township unidentified on the Godāvarī*) first—then to Mahīssatī (*Mahīsmatī is an ancient town now represented by the village Mahāsar in the Madhya Pradesh, one of the earliest settlements of the Aryans in the Dakṣiṇāpatha and one-time capital of Avantī*) and also to Ujjenī (Ujjayinī),[3] Gonaddha (unidentified), Vedisā (*Bhilsā, now renamed Vidisā, in the Madhya Pradesh*), Vanasavhaya (unidentified):

'And also to Kosambī (in the Uttar Pradesh), Saketa (in the Uttar Pradesh) and Sāvatthi (Muzaffarpur in Bihar), the most excellent cities, to Setavya (unidentified), Kapilavatthu (Kapilavastu in the *tarai* region between northern boundary of the Uttar Pradesh and Nepal) and the city of Kusinārā (Kushinagara—on the northern boundary of the Uttar Pradesh):

'And to Pāvā (near Kushinagar, identified with a village named Padaon), the city of wealth, to Vesālī (the ancient capital of the Licchavis in Magadha, now represented by the village of Besarh in Bihar) to Pāsāṇaka Cetiya, the lovely, the charming.'

A sketch is supplied of the route covered by Bāvarī's disciples.

From the upper reaches of the Godāvarī, the route dipped downwards across the Krishnā river and extended far south to Kāñchī (Conjeevaram in Madras) and Madurai (in Madras). 'Thus early in the Christian era developed a network of roads linking all the important cities of the peninsula.'[4]

During the age when the extensive midland empire of the Sātavāhanas was expanding, these communication facilities allowed men and women to visit and place their offerings at *Stūpas* and in

[1] *Sutta-nipāta,* 1011-1013 (SBE, Vol. X, pt. II, p. 180).

[2] The name appears as *Alaka* in the Singhalese texts and as such in SBE translation of the *Sutta-nipāta*. But in Burmese texts it is *Mūlaka*. The place seems to have taken its name from the Mūlaka tribe settled here. About the *Mūlakas,* see B. C. Law's *Tribes in Ancient India* (Bhandarkar Oriental Series, No. 4, 1943), pp. 184–185.

[3] The shortness of the route between Mahīsmatī and Ujjayinī is indicated by a reference in Patañjali's *Mahābhāsya*, III, 1, 26—'Start from Ujjayinī for Mahīsmatī when the sun is about to rise, the sun rises (at Mahīsmatī)'.

[4] See Basham's *The Wonder that was India* (London: Sidgwick and Jackson, 1954), p. 224.

monasteries in different parts of the country.[1] These travels and pilgrimages and visits to sacred spots were no doubt a potent means of cultural diffusion. 'Benefactions of persons residing in Vaijayantī or Vanavāsi and Sorparaka or Supara are recorded in the cave at Kārle; of a Nasik merchant at Beddsā; of some inhabitants of Bharukachcha and Kalyan at Junnar; of natives of northern India and Dattamitri (in Lower Sindh) at Nasik; and of an ironmonger of Karahakada or Karhad are recorded on the *stūpa* at Barhut which lies midway between Jabbalpur and Allahabad. Unless there were frequent communications between these places, it is not possible that the natives of one should make religious endowments at another.'[2]

The nucleus of the Sātavāhana empire had formed even before the final break-up of the Maurya and the empire lasted in unbroken continuity for more than three centuries (*c.* 78 BC–AD 218). In the north there were several dynastic changes during this period (the Mauryas, the Śuṅgas, the Kāṇvas and the Kuṣāṇas); the Sātavāhana empire, on the other hand—extending at one time from sea to sea, but with shifting marches in the reigns of different dynasts—maintained its integrity. People within this empire enjoyed, so long as South India's commerce with the Roman and western world lasted, the twin blessings of prosperity and peace. It achieved, like the Maurya empire, not only a political, but also a cultural unity; it brought within a single cultural as well as political bond diverse regional tribes on both sides of the Vindhyas—the Mālavas, the Bhojas, the Peṭenikas, the Raṭhikas, the Āndhras, the Pārindas and the Drāviḍas. The 'peace of the Sātavāhanas' guaranteed progress and consolidation of culture in the empire: it was a culture that was by and large a continuation from the north. In more senses than one, the empire was heir in the Deccan to the Maurya empire in the north.[3] In the words of a contemporary writer: the 'historic mission' of the Sātavāhana dynasty was 'to integrate the north and the south', and the geographical position of the empire was favourable to it. 'The basic tradition in middle India is the Sātavāhana empire, as in the north it is the Maurya.'[4]

None of the thirty and odd Sātavāhana kings was a professed

[1] The evidence for it is inscriptional. At Barhut in Central India have been discovered several inscriptions of donors from Karhalaka (see *infra* in the quotation from Bhandarkar's *Early History of the Deccan*), given in Lüders' *List*, Nos. 705, 763, 767 and 809). Pratisthāna is mentioned four times in the Sanchi inscriptions (see Majumdar's *Monuments of Sanchi*, Nos. 214, 229, 546 and 717). In the caves of Kārle, Salarwadi and Kanheri, there are several inscriptions of donors from Dhanakaṭaka. (See Lüders' *List*).

[2] See Bhandarkar's *Early History of the Deccan* (Sec. VIII on *Religious, Social and Economic Conditions of the Maharashtra under the Andhrabhṛityas or Sātavāhanas*): Sushil Gupta's Ed. (Calcutta, 1957), p. 54.

[3] See *Comprehensive History of India* (Orient Longmans, 1957), ed. by Nilkanta Sastri, Vol. II (*The Mauryas and Sātavāhanas*), p. 293.

[4] See K. M. Panikkar's *Survey of Indian History* (Bombay, 1947), pp. 79–80.

Buddhist. They belonged to different branches of Brāhmaṇical faith. But while several of them were active patrons of Buddhism, none seems to have been inimical.

The kings are listed in the *Purāṇas* as *Andhrabhṛtyas*. The significance of the designation is obscure and has lent itself to different interpretations.[1] It seems that the region between the lower reaches of the Godāvarī and the Krishnā rivers, now comprised in the Andhra Pradesh, was the heartland of the empire. It is rich in sites which have yielded Buddhist finds of different descriptions to archaeologists—Amarāvatī, Bhattiprolu, Nāgārjunakoṇḍa and Goli (in District Guntur); Ghanṭāsālā, Jaggayyapeta, Godivāda and Pedda Ganjam (in District Krishnā); Salihunḍam (in District Srikakulam); Sankaram Hill (in District Visakhapatnam); Gunṭupalli (in District West Godāvarī); Kapavaram (in District East Godāvarī), etc. In this area can be traced a series of ruined *stūpas* and monastic remains at different localities—at Bhattiprolu, Amarāvatī, Goli, Ghanṭāsālā, Gummaḍiḍurru and Nāgārjunakoṇḍa—some so ancient as to date back undoubtedly to the Sātavāhana age.

In that age, it seems, the movement for *stūpa*-building had passed from north of the Vindhyas far into the southern parts of the country. The models and exemplars already existed at Sanchi, Bhilsa and Barhut. The builders of the southern *stūpas* made some small architectural variations, e.g. the projecting platforms at the base, which will be described in a later context. Amarāvatī became, even in that age, a great trans-Vindhyan centre of Buddhism and remained so for well-nigh a thousand years. Round the *stūpa* of Amarāvatī and, later, round the Mahā-cetiya of Nāgārjunakoṇḍa,[2] grew up a cluster of monasteries which in the after-centuries were added to, rebuilt and from time to time renovated. During the reign of the Sātavāhana king Pulumāyi II (*c.* AD 96–119), the Amarāvatī *stūpa* was enlarged, surrounded with a stone-railing and encased in sculptured limestone slabs. In the post-Sātavāhana times, the Mahā-cetiya of Nāgārjunakoṇḍa was similarly treated during the reign of an Ikṣvāku king, Vīrapurisa-data, of the third century AD.

The Andhra region is comprised in the lower eastern basins of the Godāvarī and the Krishnā; in the upper western basins of the rivers is Mahārāshtra. Both Andhra and Mahārāshtra were under the Sātavāhanas, but the *leṇa* (cave) represented in the Mahārāshtra section the typical monastic building. In that age, several *leṇas* had already sprung up here in the complex of the Western Ghats and a few inscriptions show that some of them received attention and

[1] See Sastri's *Comprehensive History*, pp. 298–299.

[2] Some coins of Pulumāyi II have been discovered in the monastic site (marked No. 11) opposite to the Mahā-cetiya, which indicate its existence in the Sātavāhana times.

donations from Sātavāhana kings or their feudatories and officials.[1]

But no empire in India has lasted too long, and the great empire built up and consolidated by the Sātavāhanas crumbled and fell after three centuries of existence. This was in the first half of the AD third century The *Purāṇas*, presenting historical chronicle in the form of prophecies, record: 'When the kingdom of the Āndhras (that is the *Andhrabhṛtyas* or Sātavāhanas) has come to an end, there will be kings belonging to the lineage of their servants: 7 Āndhras and 10 Ābhīra kings; also 7 Gardhabhins and 18 Śakas. . . . The Śrīpārvatīya Āndhras will endure 52 years, the 10 Ābhīra kings 67 years, the 7 Gardhabhins will enjoy the earth for 72 years, the 18 Śakas for 187 years.'[2]

Of these successor dynasties named in the *Purāṇas*, the 'Śrīpārvatīya Āndhras' are represented by five kings whose names appear in these forms in the inscriptions: (1) Cāṁtamūla, the founder (*c*. AD 223–240), (2) Vīrapurisa-data (*c*. AD 240–265), (3) Ehuvala Cāṁtamūla (*c*. AD 265–275), (4) Rudra Vīrapurisa-data and (5) Vīrapurisa-data II, both sons of Ehuvala Cāṁtamūla. The regnal periods of the first three kings add up to almost exactly the number of years delimited for the 'Śrīpārvatīya Āndhras' in the *Purāṇa*, but the kingdom must have existed at least a decade beyond that period, till, as it seems, it fell between two stools—the Pallava power pressing it on one side and the Bṛhat-phalāyana on the other.[2] Its ancient *locale* is now known by the name Nāgārjunakoṇḍa.[3]

These 'Śrīpārvatīya Āndhra' kings all belonged to a dynasty called *Ikṣvāku*, which claimed, as it appears from the inscriptions, affinity with the ancient Ikṣvāku dynasty of Ayodhyā in northern India, of the *Rāmāyaṇa* fame. One inscription speaks of this dynasty as '*Ṛṣi-pravara*', i.e. descended from the *Ṛṣis*.[4] But the Dravidian origin of the dynasty is betrayed by the facts that the kings bear matronymic designations in the inscriptions and that cross-cousin marriage was permissible among them: three of Vīrapurisa-data's queens were daughters of his father's sisters. Such marriage is a custom never practised in the north, but is allowed for 'southerners alone' by the ancient Brāhamaṇical legist, Baudhāyana. It is prevalent to this day only in the south.

[1] See Part II, Sec. 5 (c) and (d).

[2] Pargiter's *Dynasties of the Kali Age*, p. 72; *Comprehensive History*, p. 325.

[3] See *Successors of the Sātavāhanas* by D. C. Sircar (Calcutta University, 1939). The name of the last one of these five kings, which Sircar does not mention, was discovered in an inscription in 1956–57 recording the erection of a temple to the Mahādeva under the name of Puṣpabhadra-svāmī (see *Indian Archaeology*, 1956–57, pp. 36 and 39).

[4] Bodhisiri's inscription at the 'Singhalese monastery' on Śrīparvata (Nāgārjunakoṇḍa), cited in the following section.

4

NĀGĀRJUNAKOṆḌA

An Aftermath of Sātavāhana Culture

THIS small Āndhra kingdom put forth a belated flower, sprung from the Buddhist culture that had been seeping down from its northern pool and fertilizing for a space of three centuries the trans-Vindhyan parts of Sātavāhana empire.

Nāgārjunakoṇḍa was born out of the ribs of the old empire; it had been carved in a fold of the Eastern Ghats, known locally as the Nallamalai Range, and covered an area of a little over eight square miles. Set in a valley and girt by tall hills on the east and the south, it is flanked by the river Krishnā on the west and partly on the north. Its stream, rock-strewn here, could allow only of a traffic of country-boats. Thus Nāgārjunakoṇḍa had a natural strategic situation—for which reason it seems to have been selected by Cāṁtamūla, the founder. Asserting independent sovereignty, he celebrated it by performing a Horse-sacrifice (*Aśvamedha*), the site of which may be seen even today at Nāgārjunakoṇḍa. The capital of the territory was named Vijayapurī (City of Victory), located in the western section of the valley on the right bank of the Krishnā. In the east and north of Vijayapurī was an extensive outlying plateau called Śrī-parvata. It is by the Śrī-parvata area that the Ikṣvākus are denominated in the *Purāṇas*. Evidently the city was carved out of it by Cāṁtamūla.

Sometime after the extinction of the kingdom and devastation of its capital, its name Vijayapurī passed into oblivion: the entire site of the Ikṣvāku kingdom acquired a new name, Nāgārjunakoṇḍa (Hill of Nāgārjuna). The identity of this Nāgārjuna after whom it was named cannot be ascertained. But the story is put across in Tibetan legends that the great Ācārya Nāgārjuna, founder of the Mādhyamika school of Mahāyāna Buddhism, shifted his seat from Amarāvatī to Śrī-parvata and spent his last days here.[1] The record of these Nāgārjuna legends is not older than the thirteenth century AD and they stand on their own merits in the absence of corroborative evidence of any kind. The name Nāgārjuna does not occur in any of the epigraphs recovered here so far.

[1] For instance, see the Tibetan Nāgārjuna legend given in Part IV, Sec. 5, pp. 278–279, in which it is said that Nāgārjuna lived for 171 years at Śrī-parvata out of his lifetime of over 500 years.

The modern discovery of Nāgārjunakoṇḍa dates back to the year 1926. The importance of the site in Buddhist history, a tiny nook of India as it is, derives from the fact that the archaeological finds obtained here since 1927 afford us a sample and measure of the development of Buddhism and monastic life south of the Vindhyas in a definite chronological period—the third century AD. The finds include a fairly large number of *Prākrit* inscriptions, indited in a modified form of Brāhmī script, throwing much light on the history of the kingdom as well as on the character of the relics. The site, however, is destined to pass out of view once again—its complete submergence under deep backwaters from a river-valley project nearby is almost imminent.

The Ikṣvāku kings who ruled here were not Buddhists themselves.

It was they who built and set up on the bank of the Krishnā the citadel town of Vijayapurī, carved out of Śrī-parvata, with a *ghāt* (landing stage) on the river. This *ghāt* is an arrangement of broad stone platforms joined by short flights of steps balustraded on the sides, so modern in its plan of construction that nothing like it appears on any other holy river of India. The *ghāt* leads up from the river to a temple which, from an epigraph found here, was called *Sarvadeva Temple* (Temple of all Gods). From the riverside the city was entered through the premises of this temple. On the eastern side of the city was a moat; the other three sides were enclosed by a bow-shaped stretch of ramparts. Perhaps the capital extended to the other bank of the river where stray ruins have been found.

Within Vijayapurī itself are remains only of secular buildings—one of which is a set of military barracks and another a theatre—but on the outskirts stood sizable temples to the Brāhmaṇical deities, Mahādeva and Kārtikeya (*Skanda*). Undoubtedly the Ikṣvāku kings were of Brāhmaṇical faith—no Buddhist relics have been found within the city-limits, except an ancient monastery, recognizable by its sunk monks' cells, which evidently had gone to ruin and then been converted to other uses.

Outside the city was the extensive Śrī-parvata area. There are remains here of about twenty-seven monasteries and twenty *stūpas* of which the largest is the most ancient, called the *Mahā-cetiya*. In the inscriptions it is referred to as 'holding the holiest relics' (*Dhātuvara-parigahita*). On excavation, this *Stūpa* yielded a buried casket of Buddha-relics which are now enshrined in the Ceylonese temple Mūlagandhakūṭi Vihāra at Sārnāth. This *Stūpa*, perhaps in a crumbling condition already in the time of the Ikṣvākus, was renovated under the supervision of a monk named Ānanda round AD 246 (in the reign of Vīrapurisa-data) by his aunt and mother-in-law Cāṁti-siri.[1] It seems also that several ladies pooled their donations for this pious undertaking.

The Sātavāhana *stūpas* of Andhra had a structural peculiarity absent from the *stūpas* of northern India. Round the base were platforms called *Āyakas* projecting towards the four directions, on which worshippers going round laid their offerings. The platforms were set round with tall pillars of stone, sculptured and decorated, called *Āyaka-stambhas*; they had no structural functions, but were intended to bear sculptured Buddhist signs and emblems. These *Āyaka* pillars were utilized for dedicatory inscriptions. There are seventeen pillars, none *in situ*, belonging to the Mahā-cetiya, all inscribed, and in thirteen of them the inscriptions appear completely. They are records of gifts and benefactions by female members and relatives of the royal family. Besides these *Āyaka* pillar inscriptions which run to considerable length, shorter inscriptions have been discovered at different sites within the Śrī-parvata area.

In all these inscriptions no name of a royal donor occurs, but they introduce us to the names of several ladies of the royal family—a queen-mother, queens and princesses of the Ikṣvāku house. Evidently while the kings were of Brāhmaṇical faith, their mothers, wives and daughters were pious Buddhists. Their multifarious donations and benefactions are recorded on the *Āyaka* pillars. It seems that some of the wealthy merchants of Nāgārjunakoṇḍa also were not behindhand. Their epigraphic records are few, but stray inscriptions have been found containing the names of merchant donors, e.g. Kumāranandin, a *seṭṭhi* who installed a Buddha-image in a *cetiyaghara*,[2] and Vardhamāna, a *seṭṭhivara* ('great merchant') who made some gift to a *stūpa* (archaeological number nine).

The following list shows how the royal ladies of Nāgārjunakoṇḍa helped to maintain Saṅgha life and its monastic establishments in the Śrī-parvata area and kept up Buddhist worship by their donations of various kinds:[3]

Name	*Relationship*	*Benefactions*
CĀṀTI-SIRI	Sister of CĀṀTAMŪLA, founder of the kingdom; paternal aunt and later mother-in-law by cross-cousin marriage of Vīrapurisa-data.	Setting up some *Āyaka* pillars; repair and renovation of the Mahā-cetiya, as 'accepted' by the 'noble and learned company of Aparaseliya monks', under the supervision of learned Ānanda; *Cetiyaghara* at the

[1] Āyaka Pillar Inscriptions—B4, B5, C2, C4, C5 (see *Epigraphia Indica*, XX, pp. 18–21).

[2] See *Indian Archaeology* (1956–57), pp. 36 and 39.

[3] The list is based on Vogel's *Prakrit Inscriptions from a Buddhist Site in Nāgārjunakoṇḍa* in *Epigraphia Indica*, Vol. XX.

7. *The great Amarāvatī Stūpa* (*of which only the foundations remain*). (Photo: Department of Archaeology, N.E. Project, Guntur)

An Amarāvatī slab showing how the stūpa looked before ruin

8. *Front view of the Kārle Caitya.* (Photo: Department of Archaeology, Government of India)

Inside the Kārle Caitya. (Photo: Department of Archaeology, Government of India)

Name	*Relationship*	*Benefactions*
		foot of the Mahā-cetiya with a square stone pavilion (*catu-sālā*) for 'acceptance of the Mahāseliya monks' and use of Bhikrus 'from all quarters assembled', wishing long life and victory for her son-in-law Vīrapurisa-data.
AḌAVĪ CĀTISIRI	Daughter of CĀṀTAMŪLA and sister of his son and successor Vīrapurisa-data.	*Āyaka*-pillar at Mahācetiya.
CULA-CĀTISIRIṆIKĀ	Daughter of the Kulahas and wife of Khamidacali-Kiremmaṇaka of the Hiramñakas—perhaps a lady of some aristocratic family. Relationship with the royal family not set out.	*Āyaka*-pillars at Mahācetiya.
MAHĀDEVĪ RUDRADHARA-BHAṬĀRIKĀ	Daughter of the Mahārājā of Ujjayinī.	A stone-pillar at the Mahāvihāra (near Mahā-cetiya). It was erected by her while CĀṀTISIRI and others were renovating the Mahācetiya. (Her inscription further records that '. . . this Mahā-vihara of the Mahācetiya was being raised by the ladies, Matalavani, Cāṁtisiriṇikā of the Pukiyas and others'.
BĀPI-SIRIṆIKĀ	Daughter of Hamma-siri who was a sister of CĀṀTMŪLA; became wife of his son and successor Vīrapurisa-data.	A stone-pillar; renovation of the Mahā-cetiya 'for the benefit of the monks of the Aparaseliya sect' under the supervision of Thera Ānanda.
MAHĀDEVĪ CĀṀTHISIRI	Another daughter of Hammasiri—later wife of Virapurisa-data. (It appears that Vīrapurisa-data married one daughter of one of his paternal aunts Cāṁti-siri and two daughters of another paternal aunt Hammasiri. There is mention of another queen of his, Bhaṭidevā, but whe-	An *Āyaka*-pillar.

Name	*Relationship*	*Benefactions*
	ther she was the same as Cāṁti-siri's daughter or someone else does not appear. This Bhaṭidevā was perhaps his principal queen, for she became the mother of his successor Ehubala Cāṁtamūla. The cross-cousin marriages of Vīrapurisa-data show the southern origin of Ikṣvākus of Nāgārjunakoṇḍa.	
BODHI-SIRI	Wife of Budhimnaka, son of Revata, a householder of Govagāma. Describes herself as a *Upāsikā*. Her maternal uncle was Bhada, a Koṣṭāgārika (probably, Treasurer) in the king's employ.	Her donations were many and of various sorts: (i) a *cetiyaghara*, with a *cetiya* (*stūpa*) in it, in the monastery of Culla-Dhammagiri at Śrī-parvata 'to the east of Vijayapurī' for the benefit of monks from Ceylon; (ii) a *cetiyaghara* at Kulaha Vihāra; (iii) a shelter for the Bodhi Tree maintained in the Ceylonese Culla-Dhammagiri monastery; (iv) a monk's cell at Mahā-Dhammagiri; (v) a *maṇḍapa* pillar at Mahā-vihāra near the Mahā-cetiya; (vi) a *Padhāna-sālā* (Hall of Meditation) at Devagiri; (vii) a tank, a verandah (*alinda*) and a pillared hall (*maṇḍapa*) at Pūrva-saila; (viii) a *maṇḍapa* of stone at the eastern gate of the 'Great Cetiya' at Kaṇṭaka-śaila (Ghantāśilā or some spot in Nāgārjunakoṇḍa?); (ix) three monks' cells at Hirumuṭhuve; (x) seven cells at Papila; (xi) a stone *maṇḍapa* at Puṣpagiri; (xii) a stone *maṇḍapa* at (illegible) Dham(ma)-Vihāra. NB. It is not possible to trace most of the topographical names. 'All these new works described'—so runs the inscription—'were done for the endless welfare

Name	*Relationship*	*Benefactions*
		and happiness of men of religion and of all men, under three superintendents of works, the three Theras Candamukha, Dhammanandi and Nāga. It is the work of the mason Vidhika'. With regard to the Ceylonese monks, to whom gifts (i) and (iii) were dedicated, it is said in the inscription that the monks of 'Taṁbapaṁna' (Ceylon) have converted Kashmir, Gāndhāra, China, Kirāta, Tosāli, Aparānta, Vaṅga, Vanavāsi, Yavana and Tamil country, Paluva (Dantapura in Orissa?) and the island of Ceylon.
BHAṬI-DEVĀ	Wife of Vīrapurisa-data and mother of Ehuvala Cāṁtamūla, his son and successor.	A monastery for the 'Masters of the Bahu-śrutīya Sect'.
KOḌABALI-SIRĪ	Daughter of Vīrapurisa-data and sister of Ehuvala Cāṁtamola; wife of the Mahārāja of Vanavāsaka (North Kanara).	A monastery for the 'Masters of the Mahiśāsaka Sect', built under the direction of a *Thera* and dedicated to 'Bhikṣus of all Quarters' and under the supervision of Dhammaghosa, 'the great preacher of the Law'. Also a stone pillar to commemorate the donation.

At Nāgārjunakoṇḍa in the third century AD Saṅgha life and organization must have reached a highly prosperous state: an index to it is the number of monasteries (twenty-seven) unearthed so far (January 1958) within the five to six miles' periphery of the Śrīparvata area. Some of these show traces of having been re-built on old sites or renovated and enlarged later, but most of these monasteries appear to have been newly constructed during the Ikṣvāku period—that is in the course of five to six decades only. This is clear evidence of the influence of the monk communities in the Ikṣvāku kingdom and also of the munificent patronage enjoyed by them from royal ladies and wealthy merchants. Unlike the monasteries of northern India, the Nāgārjunakoṇḍa monasteries do not seem to have had land-grants—there is no mention of any in the inscriptions. In this mountain-valley there was perhaps not much surplus land to give and what there was was not very productive. In all the donatory inscriptions discovered here, there is one solitary record of a grant of land, presumably made by the State, to a Mahādeva temple at Vijaypurī called Puṣpabhadra-svāmī Temple.[1]

Things necessary for maintaining monks at the monasteries and conducting ritual worship at the *stūpas* seem to have been supplied from two sources: donations from ladies of royal and aristocratic families, of which there are many epigraphic records, and gifts of piety chiefly from the merchant (*Seṭṭhi*) class, of which the records are few. The *seṭṭhi* class had an ancient tradition of supporting monk-communities; there is no reason to suppose any departure from the tradition here. And among the *seṭṭhis* of Nāgārjunakoṇḍa during the Ikṣvāku regime there must have been several merchant-princes.

Wealth came into the kingdom from commerce. Not too far by river-route from Nāgārjunakoṇḍa was Masulipatam, then a very important commercial port on the east coast of India near the estuary of the Krishnā. Its current name is reminiscent of the name, *Maisolia*, given to this part of the coast in the classical sailors' guide-book of the first century AD, the *Periplus of the Eurythrean Seas*.[2]

The chief merchandise of Maisolia, eagerly sought for by merchants from the Roman world, was *muslin*—so favourite a wear with fashionable Roman ladies of that age that a Roman legend has it that an ounce of muslin used to sell in Rome for an ounce of gold. Roman gold coins poured into 'Maisolia' (which is the eastern section of modern Andhra Pradesh), and, among those unearthed, two have been found at Nāgārjunakoṇḍa—a gold coin of Emperor Tiberius and another of Empress Faustina.

No doubt Nāgārjunakoṇḍa had a share in Andhra's commerce with the Roman world.

The many stately buildings, secular and religious, of whose one-time external magnificence no idea can now be had, for they are all

[1] See *Indian Archaeology* (1956–57), pp. 56–57.

[2] 'The increase of trade with India created the demand for a guide-book which was produced in the form of the "Periplus of the Eurythrean Seas" by an anonymous author (first century AD) who evidently had sailed in person round the coast of India. It contains the best account of the commerce carried on from the Red Sea and the coast of Africa to the East Indies during the time Egypt was a Roman province. It mentions river-mouths, ports, etc., with distances from one another, exports, imports, and such other details as a merchant must most value'—McCrindle's *Ancient India as described by Ptolemy* (ed. by S. Majumdar, pub. from Calcutta, 1927), p. XVII. 'Maisolia is the name of the coast between the Krishnā and the Godāvarī. It is the Maisolia of the *Periplus* which describes it as the seaboard of a country extending far inland and noted for the manufacture, in immense quantities, of the finer kinds of cotton fabrics. The name is preserved in Masulipatam.'—*Ibid*, pp. 67–68.

levelled to the ground, constitute a monument to the phenomenal prosperity of this small Ikṣvāku kingdom and its population.

The wealth that poured from commerce into the hands of the people enabled them to organize and indulge in pleasures and gaieties which in that age must have been hardly available elsewhere in India and in a city comparatively so short-lived.

Thus the remains of a pillared building have been unearthed which was very likely a sumptuous playhouse with all the complements of a green room, a fixed stage and a large auditorium. In its background is a tall hill: it probably eked out the acoustics of the building. A seal has been found here inscribed with a feminine name, Śaśīkalā (Digit of the Moon), perhaps an actress or a dancing girl whose name her admirers wanted to advertise. A Stadium also has been discovered at Nāgārjunakoṇḍa with ascending rows of galleries cut in stone around a temple-topped hill, with acoustics so skilfully set that the normal voice of a speaker or singer from the central pit is more and more distinctly heard higher and higher up in the galleries. Nowhere else in India has a comparable structure of ancient times been discovered. A Stadium is a Roman idea and the likelihood is that it was borrowed by Nāgārjunakoṇḍa merchants from some Roman traders, or their agents or factors, whom they had contacted at the ports of 'Maisolia'. There are proofs of such contacts. From several sites in Andhra have been recovered relics of Indo-Roman intercourse—coins, amphora, sprinklers of a fine variety, pictorial reproductions of wine-glasses. Aquatic sports also seem to have had their attraction for the citizens of Nāgārjunakoṇḍa, and a sheet of what was once water, but is now a stretch of marsh, has been discovered here, enclosed by ranges of steps in galleries where spectators congregated to watch the water-sports. Nāgārjunakoṇḍa was a 'city-state', i.e. a state comprised in and conterminous with a city, but it seems that it was not shut-in and isolated; there were cross-country roads, now effaced, and fine stone-built pavilions (only the foundations now remaining) are scattered here and there in the valley to indicate their ancient alignment. They were rest-houses of improved and costly pattern such as would be built for travellers only where money was no object.

All these were on the city-side. Out in the Śrī-parvati plateau, there was a different air. The whole area was dedicated to Buddhism and its religious pursuits.

The existence of such a large number (twenty-seven) of monasteries, most of them of considerable size, within a square area of about five miles, is proof that here at Nāgārjunakoṇḍa Buddhism had no lack of support or patronage. The monasteries seem, judging from the traceable ground plan, to have been not only large but well-built.

Laid out on the standardized pre-Gupta pattern with shrine, quadrangle and monks' cells arranged along the sides, the improvements on this pattern which came about later are already in evidence: the quadrangle is often roofed and converted into a pillared *maṇḍapa* and the shrine so placed as to face and dominate it. We shall have occasion later to refer to a peculiarity of the monastic shrines, seen nowhere else in India—the provision of double shrines in a single monastery, one enshrining a *stūpa* (*Cetiya-ghara*) and the other a Buddha-image (*Buddha-ghara*)—symbolical of the transition, which will be described later, from ancient symbol-worship to image-worship in Buddhism.[1]

The largest and presumably the central monastic establishment of Nāgārjunakoṇḍa is represented by a great structure (traceable now only by its ground plan) with two extensive wings, set within a circuit-wall. It is of noble proportions and is unique in that it combines in one establishment a monastery and a nunnery (*Bhikṣuṇī-vihāra*). The nunnery part is recognizable by its privacy arrangements—two narrow doorways for entrance and exit and a set of private bathrooms. Here also we have double shrines set in a line, one housing a *stūpa* and the other a Buddha-image, both opening on one spacious *maṇḍapa*.

The establishment has other features of interest. Part seems to have been used as a hospital as appears from an inscription on one of the walls, viz. *Mukhya Jvarālaya* (Main Room for sufferers from fever). Adjoining this, is a spacious chamber, remarkable for its interior construction, the purpose and utility of which, however, is not so apparent, though it has been surmised that the whole establishment was designed to house a monastic 'university'.

This chamber is remarkable for the arrangement of its interior. Within there was a raised dais: at a little distance in front of it were three separate pillars, obviously not tall enough to support any part of the roof. They were seemingly of some symbolical import. Local archaeologists have tentatively given this chamber the name of 'Convocation Hall', where degrees and diplomas were ceremonially conferred and received. The three pillars (now fallen and in a ruined state) are supposed to have symbolized originally, when they stood decorated with sculptured slabs, the *Tri-ratna* of the creed. But the idea of a monastic establishment functioning on a 'university' pattern does not seem to have emerged in monastic history before the fifth century AD. It is true that Amarāvatī was an ancient centre of learning and Nāgārjunakoṇḍa may have imbibed something of its turn for learning and scholarship, but the existence of a monastic university here as early as in the third century AD is hard to

[1] See Part III, Sec. 3, pp. 191–192.

believe on available evidence. Perhaps the hall was an 'Ordination Hall', though there is no other instance of a hall set apart for this purpose in a Buddhist monastery discovered so far.

The influence on Nāgārjunakoṇḍa of Amarāvatī, however, is evident. Both are on the Krishnā, and, as the crow flies, the distance between them is about sixty miles, though a little more than double by river-route. The influence is obvious in the Buddhist sculpture of Nāgārjunakoṇḍa—less obvious, yet perceptible, in the composition of its Saṅgha life.

Nāgārjunakoṇḍa developed its own sculpture. It is of fine quality. The hills round about are of granite, but, within measurable distance at Palnad, were stone-quarries that supplied softer, more workable, materials. These were used by the Nāgārjunakoṇḍa sculptors and their workmanship is distinctly imitative of the more famous sculpture of Amarāvatī.[1] The fineness of the chiselling and the forms of *Jātaka* and Buddha-life stories are in Amarāvatī style with its somewhat primitive 'frontality'. As in Amarāvatī sculpture, the Buddha-figure sometimes appears in the episodes and sometimes is absent.

Amarāvatī was the ancient Dhanakaṭaka; the identification has been confirmed by the name Dhanakaṭaka appearing in two inscriptions found at Amarāvatī.[2] Round the great *Stūpa* built here in the Sātavāhana times, a community of monks had settled and made Amarāvatī in course of time a famous seat of monastic culture.

The community had originally consisted mostly of monks of the Mahāsāṅghika school. But at the time of Hsüan-tsang's visit (A.D. 639), Amarāvatī had developed as a Mahāyānist centre. 'The people', says Hsüan-tsang, 'greatly esteem learning. The saṅghārāmas are numerous, but are mostly deserted and ruined; of those preserved, there are about twenty, with 1,000 or so priests. They all study the law of the Great Vehicle.'[3] Perhaps the Mahāyānism was a late transformed development of Mahāsāṅghika faith and its doctrines of which Amarāvatī had been anciently a stronghold. But Hsüan-tsang's Amarāvatī was of the thirties of the seventh century. Four centuries earlier it must have presented a different aspect. It was not then in its decline and the monks' studies were not confined to Mahāyānist scripture.

When Nāgārjunakoṇḍa arose, Amarāvatī's fame was already ancient and was being preserved there by a number of monk-settle-

[1] 'The sculpture of Nāgārjunakoṇḍa on the same light-green sandstone was a sequel to the earlier Amarāvatī school and had its beginnings contemporary with the third period of Amarāvatī art.'—See Sastri's *Comprehensive History*, Vol. II, p. 754.

[2] Lüders' *List*, 1,225 and 1,271.

[3] Beal's *Buddhist Records*, ii, p. 221.

ments not exclusively Mahāyānist as in Hsüan-tsang's time. Here developed two leading Mahāsāṅghika schools. Their adherents occupied at Amarāvatī two separate establishments situated on two cliffs—one in the east and the other in the west—and were known as East-cliffers (*Pūrvaśailika*) and West-cliffers (*Aparaśailīyas* or *Aparaśailakas*) respectively. Perhaps a considerable number of West-cliffers migrated to Nāgārjunakoṇḍa when the kingdom had been newly founded. They are mentioned more than once in the Nāgārjunakoṇḍa inscriptions as settled in Śrī-parvata.

The queen-mother Cāṁti-siri, as we have seen, donated a monastery 'for the acceptance of monks of the Aparaśaila School (*apara-mahāvinyaseliyanaṁ parigahe*). Mention is made in queen Bāpisiriṇikā's inscription also of monks of the Aparaśailaka sect, for whose benefit something (a monastery or a *cetiya-ghara*) was constructed by her in the proximity of the Mahā-cetiya. Evidently the West-cliffers formed a considerable and influential section of the monk-community of Śrīparvata.

This small kingdom of the Ikṣvākus stands, in respect of the monastic life that developed here, in the main line of Buddhist development, in process since early Sātavāhana times in trans-Vindhyan regions—in Andhra, Vanavāsi (Kanara), Mahārāshtra and other regions farther south included within the Sātavāhana territories. A complete picture of this development in its maturity is presented to us by Nāgārjunakoṇḍa and gains importance from the fact that it is of an assignable period—third century AD.

Mahāyāna Buddhism had by then emerged on the other side of the Vindhyas from northern India, but seems not to have gained a foothold yet in the south. There are no traces of it in the sculpture or the inscriptions of Nāgārjunakoṇḍa. It was only four centuries later, near the end of the third decade of the seventh century, that (on Hsüan-tsang's evidence) Amarāvatī became a centre of Mahāyānist studies. All the schools of which mention is found in the Nāgārjunakoṇḍa inscriptions are Hīnayānist schools—the Aparaśailakas, the Bahuśrutīyas, the Mahīśāsakas and the Theravādins from Ceylon. Yet certain developments in the religion, as practised here, seem clearly tendentious: they foreshadow, in their obvious significance, the transition from the Hīnayāna to the Mahāyāna.

Congregational and ritualistic worship has become part and parcel of monastic life. The circumambulation (*pradakṣiṇā*) of the sanctuary is as much a ritual act as the offering of flowers, lights and incense. In fact we can spot in the monastic remains shrines or *stūpas* in which the circumambulatory path is too narrow to be traversed, but is kept as a token of the ritual observance. The worship of the Buddha-image has come into vogue, but the ancient canonical worship of symbols still continues: a compromise, however, is effected by having two kinds of shrine in a monastery—the *Buddha-ghara* for image-worship and the *Cetiya-ghara* for symbol-worship. The monasteries also show improvement in layout, and are of more solid build, showing considerable advance on the primitive type of monastery-construction. In some monasteries, as those near the Mahā-cetiya, there are three or four wings; and the central Nāgārjunakoṇḍa monastery, in which a Bhikṣuṇī-vihāra is combined with a Bhikṣu-vihāra, is constructed on an extensive plan—with two wings spreading out on two sides, spacious *maṇḍapas*, a private hospital and what seems to be a studio for sculpture. But the ancient traditional pattern is kept—only the open quadrangle is most often converted into a roofed and pillared hall, a *maṇḍapa*.

Except for an interim of a little over half a century (*c.* 90–35 BC)—the period of Sātavāhana-khatrapa struggle—the Sātavāhana empire touched both the Eastern and the Western Ghats: its territorial expansion was wide in the Deccan. The monasteries on the eastern side were in the traditional style of the vihāras of the north—the style that was followed in the post-Sātavāhana Ikṣvāku kingdom of Nāgārjunakoṇḍa.

Here the rocks were granite, difficult to excavate and scoop out; the Western Ghats, however, lent themselves more easily to the construction of cave-monasteries. Soon the western side of India developed from early Sātavāhana times a long chain of cave-monasteries, which were extended, enlarged and added to from era to era and enriched in later times with the finest decorations of plastic art. Several of these cave-monasteries functioned till the very last days of Buddhism in India.

5

LEṆAS

The Cave-Monasteries of Western India

a. BEGINNINGS

FACTUAL data are scarce on the migration of Buddhism from the north into the Sātavāhana empire. It was probably sometime after the fall of the Maurya dynasty that the movement commenced. In the very prime of the Sātavāhana times, *Guhā*-monasteries were sprouting up on the flank of the Western Ghats. A fact of much significance in this southward spread of Buddhism must have been the shifting of the Sātavāhana capital to Pratisthāna.

We have described elsewhere the ancient trunk-route that had existed in northern India in the age of the Mauryas connecting Pāṭaliputra with Ujjainī.[1] It was linked afterwards with Pratisthāna and extended by many branches far into the south. The passage from north to south was by way of the west, the east being largely blocked, hardly passable.

For a few centuries since the beginning of the Christian era, the country was at peace. There are no records of foreign invasions or internecine wars. Routes of communication were comparatively safe and trade could prosper. Between the north and the south, the goings-on of trade seem to have been brisk and uninterrupted and large in volume. From peninsular seaboards, both eastern and western, commerce with the outer world was also beginning to grow into a great source of wealth for the whole country. The main evidence of the existence and extent of this commerce is afforded by a work of the first century AD to which we have already made a reference—the *Periplus*.[2] All this activity of trade and commerce must have been a great stimulant to inland traffic.

We may be allowed to indulge a little in imagination to call up the variegated colourful traffic that flowed in that age in a steady stream from the north round Pratisthāna into the south and *vice versa*. Its tempo promoted travelling companionship. Leisurely, unhurried, with frequent stoppages at rest-houses and caravan-serais, it afforded opportunity to fellow-travellers to cultivate each other's acquaint-

[1] See Part II, Sec. 4, p. 121. [2] See Part II, Sec. 6, p. 132 and footnote 2.

ance and also time to discuss matters of mutual interest—all that the quick high-speed journeys of our machine-age inhibit.

In the traffic's southward drift, going along with the merchants and traders, there must have been wandering Buddhist Bhikkhus: perhaps among them were small groups, weary of long wandering, who wished to settle down to saṅgha life. For their settlement, we may presume they preferred seclusion. Wandering among the hills of the Deccan tableland, they discovered spots where it would be possible for them to live in secluded monasteries of the *guhā*-type—for was not the *Guhā* one of the five kinds of *leṇa* that the scripture sanctioned as a fit dwelling place for monks? The monks did not lack devotees among fellow-travellers of the *Vaiśya* (merchant) class: the *Vaiśyas*, since Buddhism's early days, had been supporters of the faith and benefactors of monkhood. These men blessed with wealth were perhaps ready, even eager, to oblige the monks and earn at the same time spiritual merit for themselves and their families by settling them according to their desire. Such an act of piety was calculated also to draw down divine favour on the business enterprises they had on hand.

The Deccan trap is comparatively soft. If the monks preferred settlements on the mountain-sides, wealthy merchants would not be wanting to build them. There were winding passes among the heights for the flow of internal trade and traffic. Places, not too distant from these routes, yet at a suitable remove to secure secluded life, were naturally favoured. In this wise perhaps was the first beginning of the famous *leṇas* of western India, which count, so far as discoveries have been made up to date, about a thousand in number. They are scattered along the length of the Western Ghats from Sourāshtra to Mysore. Once a settlement had been established on a mountain-side, it would attract further donations and benefactions. There would be no question of abandoning it, and cave by cave the settlement would go on expanding. A lifetime of a thousand years can be traced in some of these cave-settlements. In their architecture and art which grew by degrees—each age contributing something to the embellishment—the cultural link forged in the Sātavāhana age between the north and the south shows itself in several technical particulars, though the *Guhā* represented a pattern of construction different from that of a *Vihāra*.

In the history of *guhā*-construction, two main stages may be distinguished. First built was a set of residential caves—(i) '*Bhikṣu-gharas*', as they are labelled by archaeologists; next, when they were occupied and a Saṅgha started, adjuncts necessary for the collective functioning of saṅgha life were added bit by bit—these adjuncts, as named by archaeologists, are (ii) *Cetiya-gharas*, where congregational prayer and worship were conducted before a *stūpa* or a Buddha-image, and (iii) *Maṇḍapas*, pillared assembly-halls. Artistically the most sumptuous, as functionally the most important, part of a cave-settlement was the *Cetiya-ghara*.

The finest, loveliest and most exquisitely artistic *cetiya-ghara* among all the *leṇas* of western India is the one at Karle. We shall presently observe how some features of its architecture and sculpture give clear evidence of migration of northern traditions into the south.

Its hall is 124 feet long, 45½ feet broad, with an average height of 246 feet. The façade covers a massive vestibule with an arcaded screen behind. Two pillars, each with a pair of lions on top, stood in front of the vestibule, of which only one remains, the other replaced now by a small Hindu shrine of modern construction to the goddess Durgā. The shrine has destroyed the façade's original grandeur, but the interior which is intact is a marvel of the sculptor's art. No photograph can bring out the exquisite proportioning of its details nor the sense of complete and finished harmony it evokes.

The main part of the cost of its construction was probably stood by a wealthy merchant named Bhūtapāla of Vejayantī (in Mahārāshtra: ancient seaport) and he has left for posterity his own name and that of his home-town in an inscription in the vestibule: 'Rock-mansion established by Bhūtapāla, *seṭṭhi* from Vejayantī, the best in Jambudvīpa (*Vejaṁtito seṭhina Bhūtapālena selagharaṁ pariniṭhāpitaṁ, etc.*).[1] The date of the inscription is a matter of guess, but the sculpture in the hall, in its impeccable neatness, fineness and delicacy, is a far cry from the somewhat primitive art of Sanchi and Barhut.

Gazing at the sculpture inside the Karle *cetiyaghara*, one would fain believe that its original conception and archetype could not have been taken from tradition, but was born fresh in the architect's mind. Yet with the tradition of northern Maurya or Asokan architecture, it keeps up an obvious link:

(i) The bell-shaped capitals of the sixteen octagonal pillars, separating on each side the nave from the aisle, copy the Persepolitan motives of the Maurya pillars of the third and second centuries, BC.

(ii) The pair of lion-pillars (*Siṁha-stambhas*) in front of the *cetiya-ghara*, one now broken, have capitals of purely Maurya tradition—a lotiform ball-capital surmounted by two lions crossing each other.

But Karle is not the only instance of transmittance of northern art-tradition into the south. It appears in a number of caves and shows the artists' harking back to northern models and motifs: gateways (*toraṇas*) of Sanchi pattern appear in Ajanta painting; the

[1] See *Archaeological Survey of Western India*, Vol. IV (*Report on the Buddhist Cave-temples and their Inscriptions*), p. 90.

stūpa balustrade, made in imitation of wooden models of uprights and horizontals, is copied in ornamental engravings at the entrance to a *Cetiyaghara* or on the pediment of a *Bhikṣughara* porch; the Buddhist symbols carved in the caves reproduce the designs of Sanchi and Barhut; perhaps the arch in the sun-window of a *cetiyaghara* recalls the architectural fashion, now untraceable—for all *vihāras* are completely ruined—that used to mark the entrance to a *vihāra*. The *leṇa* art in fact draws most of its models and motifs from the north. They came with the flow of the north-south stream of culture-migration of the Sātavāhana times.

Monastic centres came into existence in the south in the wake of the monastic tradition that was already centuries-old in northern India. It was a continuation of the tradition with an inevitable time-lag. The saṅgha life that developed in the south was patterned on that of the north with all its sectarianism, its rites and ceremonies, its forms of worship. Afterwards when the Sātavāhana empire ended, but the *leṇas* continued, Mahāyāna Buddhism also came in (perhaps in the fifth century) from the north and the Mahāyānists imparted to many a cave a new look, a fresh splendour of art that was of the Gupta-age renaissance.

b. REGIONAL DISTRIBUTION: ART AND ARCHITECTURE

The story of the *leṇas* is different from that of the *vihāras*. In their mountain inset they have escaped the devastation that befell the latter in the northern plains, and it is even possible to place the *leṇas* in a rough chronometric series.

Cleared of debris since the forties of the last century and placed under the care and supervision of official archaeologists, the distribution of the *leṇas* by regional groups is as follows:[1]

Group		*Sites*
A. Bombay	..	Kalyan, Sopara, Broach, Kanheri, Magathan, Karanja, Elephanta, Kondivte, Nasik.
B. Poona ..	..	Karle, Bhaja, Bedsa, Patan, Selarwadi, Nenauli, Kondane, Ambivle, Junnar, Ayara.
C. Deccan	..	Karad, Sirwal, Lohari (Wai), Patan (Satara), Kolhapur.
D. Konkan	..	Chaul, Kol, Mahad, Kuda, Ratnagiri, Dabhol, Khed, Chiplun, Owle, Nadsur, Karsambla, Gomashi.
E. Hyderabad	..	Ajanta, Pitalkhora, Ghatotkach, Aurangabad, Ellora, Paithan (ancient Pratisthana), Kondapur.
F. Kathiwad	..	Sana, Talaja, Junagad, Jhinjhurijhara, Dhank, Valabhi.

(The total number of caves at all these sites is near one thousand.)

[1] I am indebted for this list to Dr Moreswar Dikshit whose work in typescript on 'Buddhist Settlements in Western India' was made available to me by the Central Archaeological Department in New Delhi through the author's courtesy.

Of these *leṇa*-groups, a number of caves in (A), (B) and (E) have acquired celebrity and are eagerly sought by visitors for their incomparable art-treasures. Their sculpture and mural paintings have now a world-wide fame.

The exploration of these caves, commenced in the 1820's under Fergusson and Burgess, has revealed some of the highest reaches of Indian art in sculpture and painting. In their classic excellence,

Design of a Caitya window (Ellora)

they at their best may challenge the Greek Periclean marbles. Yet the discovery of this excellence is by no means modern. After-generations of artists in India took their models from these *guhās* and some features of their sculpture and specially the Ajanta style of painting passed into the later art-history of India.

There is a standard design for the frontage of a *cetiyaghara*—the contour of a *peepul* (ficus religiosa) leaf topped by a sun-window of varied pattern. The *peepul-leaf* motif had a certain sanctity to the Buddhist from its association with the legendary Bodhi-tree. Applied in the front of the prayer-hall, it formed a beautiful pointed arch. It was a Buddhist design, which, after passing through some plastic varieties, became a pure and simple art-motif and was adopted for all sacred buildings. It is endlessly repeated in the Hindu temple architecture of the south—on the gateways (*gopuram*), on the temple superstructure (*vimāna*) and on decorative slabs of sculpture.

The Ajanta style of painting similarly spread in India and even overflowed her boundaries and is traceable in specimens of temple and monastery decoration in China. Its classic quality found early recognition in India, an interesting instance of which has been recently discovered in the Drāvidian temple of Bṛhadīśvara at Tanjore, one of the grandest of Hindu temples in India.

The temple dates back to the time of the Chola king Rāja-Rājā (AD 985–1018). In its sanctuary is a huge phallic symbol of Śiva and on the walls of the ill-lit circumbulatory passage round the sanctuary there is a number of murals badly time-worn and blackened with soot. Among them have been discovered some early Chola works and they show unmistakably that painters of these murals were trying to follow, though at a long distance, the figures of Ajanta. The poses of the figures and the combination of pigments leave no doubt about their being attempts to imitate the Ajanta style and its distinctive peculiarities. And these early Chola artists were forerunners by several centuries of a school of painting, called the 'Ajanta School', initiated in Bengal round 1905 by Abanindra Nath Tagore and Havell, importing the classic Ajanta idiom into modern Indian art.

Among all the art-treasures of these caves, the murals of Ajanta have received the widest attention in India and abroad. They are popularly called 'frescos', though it is open to doubt whether the name is technically applicable to them.[1] The Ajanta murals have been studied minutely by experts and connoisseurs, appraised by art-critics, and so many times reproduced in print and lithograph that there is now a whole illustrated literature on them. But what this literature must fail to capture is a magical quality—something so ineffable that it lends itself only to actual visual experience.

In several respects, the art of Ajanta murals falls short of technical perfection. Anatomical symmetry in the figures is not studied; the sense of perspective is not firm; the disposition of parts in a panoramic presentation is often at haphazard. There is no formal lifelikeness. Yet life and movement are so evoked by a rhythm, a measure, a subtle quality of expression, a subdued blend and harmony of colours—so insinuatingly indeed that they recall the words D. H. Lawrence used in describing a Mexican tribal dance: 'Everything is

[1] All the murals of Ajanta are on plaster ground. A true fresco is a method of painting on plaster while it is still wet so that the colours become incorporated. Whether this was the method followed in Ajanta murals or the pigments were laid on when the plaster was dry is doubtful, for there are patches in them where the plaster remains but the pigmentation has got largely effaced or is fading.

very soft, subtle, delicate. There is none of the hardness of representation. It is a soft, subtle *being* something'.[1]

Stepping out of the spell, as we pause to take stock of the mere themes of this art, there is enchantment for us of a different kind.

The themes are uninhibited in their mixture of sacred and profane: with the idealistic elements of Buddhism are interwoven things purely mundane that seem to have slipped into the artist's vision out of real life—of today, yesterday and of yore. The form and colour of things, receded now into the antique, leap to a living thrilling presence—customs and manners; deportment and sartorial fashions; feminine charms and masculine strength; palaces, monasteries and hutments, their façade and interior decor. Their quaint 'otherness' enchants. Among the real-life murals, two fine paintings of historical interest invite special notice—Vijaya's victorious landing in Ceylon, taken from tradition, and the Sātavāhana king Pulakesin's reception of a Persian envoy, taken from historical reminiscence perhaps not far distant.

Yet all this art, choice and exquisite as it is, was lavished not to decorate a palace or a banquet-hall or an arch of triumph, but only a settlement of monks. The monastic life itself has been extinct for several centuries now; but not the art, and in the silence of these forsaken caves one may fancy whisperings in many voices of what the Grecian urn said to the poet—on life timed and art timeless.

Glimpses into that defunct monastic life, which, while it lasted in these caves, counted for so much with the people, but has lapsed now into a subsidiary interest with the modern visitor, are afforded by the comparatively large number of epigraphic records discovered in them. Most of these are donatory: they record the gifts of piety of men and women of several generations. Among them are kings and officers of State, potentates and wealthy merchants, men and women of middle-class society, monks and nuns, people of different castes, occupations and racial stocks—Vaiśyas and Brāhmaṇas, Śakas and Yavanas.[2] The beautiful architecture and artistic decorations of these caves were wholly financed out of their voluntary donations.

The Deccan plateau is hilly on its edges and the topography of the caves was mainly determined by the orography.

Many of the caves are situated in deep ravines between mountain-chains or hill-ranges, but accessible from passes which were then known and charted routes of inland communication and trade. They were traversed by parties of merchants and traders, and donations

[1] D. H. Lawrence's *Mornings in Mexico*.

[2] Dr Moreswar Dikshit has given a classified list of all the donors to the caves of western India from Lüders' *List* in his (unpublished) work on 'Buddhist settlements in Western India'.

came chiefly from this class. Trekking along the passes, the travellers would alight at a convenient stopping place, walk up to the mountain-base or hill-side and clamber up to the monasteries. Their rites of worship performed under the direction of monks, they would leave there the offering called *Deya-dhamma* (Gift of Piety) and return to resume the journey. The offering was in kind or in money, usually earmarked for some specific purpose of the monastery—adding a *leṇa*, digging a water-reservoir, setting up a ruined pillar, supplying some furniture, effecting some repairs, etc. A wealthy merchant like Bhūtapāla might pay the cost of an entire *cetiyaghara* or of a series of sculptural decorations or of a large-sized Buddha or Bodhisatva image. The merchants engaged in overseas commerce were naturally the wealthiest and the prosperity of Kanheri (Krishnagiri Settlement, described *infra*), the largest monk-settlement in western India, was probably due to its comparatively easy access from commercial seaports like Sopara, Kalyan and Chaul on the western seaboard.

None of the monk-settlements was built to a blueprint; there was no pre-planning; each grew up bit by bit as donations came in and a whole set of caves took perhaps a good many decades to complete. Many caves may be seen commenced, but left unfinished, for neither the cost of construction nor of maintenance came out of a common pool.

Among the Vinaya rules we find mention among the office-bearers of a Saṅgha of a functionary named *Navakammika* (Supervisor of New Works).[1] Each saṅgha, it seems, had one *Navakammika* or several ones—monks who had some knowledge of monastery building and its requirements. When a wealthy devotee produced a substantial building grant, the constructional operations would be directed by a *Navakammika* or a group of *Navakammikas* appointed *ad hoc* out of its own body by the saṅgha.

In the entire ensemble of a *guhā*-settlement, three main parts may be distinguished:

(i) Residential caves with monks' dormitory cells in them, called by different names in the inscriptions, viz. *Garbha*, *Vihāra*, *Leṇa* and *Ovaraka*;

(ii) Assembly halls, called *Sālās* or *Maṇḍapas*;

(iii) Prayer halls, called *Cetiyagharas*, with the far end of apsidal shape where a *Stūpa* or a Buddha-image was installed.

Of these, No. (iii), the *Cetiyaghara*, may be described as the hub of congregational life in the monk-settlement. It was here that the Saṅgha assembled and performed jointly the rites of the religion. Hence the *cetiyagharas* of these monk-settlements bear marks in

[1] See *Nava* (*-kammika*) in PTS *Pali-English Dictionary*.

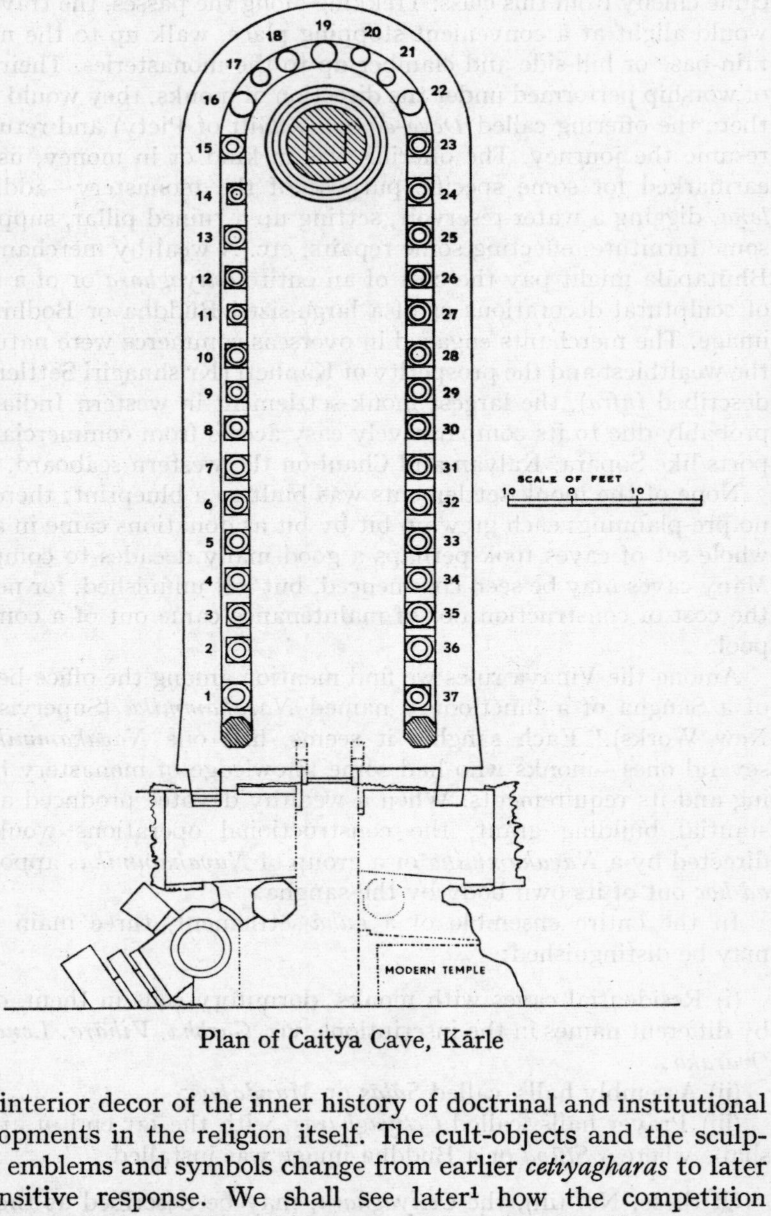

Plan of Caitya Cave, Kārle

their interior decor of the inner history of doctrinal and institutional developments in the religion itself. The cult-objects and the sculptured emblems and symbols change from earlier *cetiyagharas* to later in sensitive response. We shall see later[1] how the competition between symbol-worship and image-worship reflects itself in the cult-objects and symbols of the interiors.

The prayer halls are of two types of construction—earlier and

[1] See Part III, Sec. 3, pp. 190 ff.

San Lorenzo Fuori le Mura, Rome

later. The earlier type has a fixed pattern consisting of (i) the nave, (ii) the aisle, on each side of the nave, separated from it by a row of pillars, and (iii) the apsidal end holding the cult-object. In the later type, instead of a nave, there is a pillared pavilion (*maṇḍapa*) of considerable size through which the sanctuary is approached across a vestibule.

The earlier pattern with the aisles and the nave and the rounded and apsidal end was not of Buddhist invention. The apsidal end of a sanctuary, where the image used to be installed, is still to be seen in the ruined Puṣpabhadra-swāmī Temple (Brāhmaṇical) of the third century AD at Nāgārjunakoṇḍa. What is more intriguing is the exact resemblance of the interior of such a *cetiyaghara* to that of a Christian cathedral—for example, the cathedral of San Lorenzo Fuori le Mura in Rome, built by Emperor Constantine. There is the same arrangement of nave, pillars, side-aisles and the consecrated apsidal end.[1] As the *vihāras* of northern India show almost nothing but their foundations, it is difficult to say what their prayer-hall

[1] See picture of Constantine's Cathedral facing page 65 in *A History of Religious Architecture* by Ernest H. Short (new and revised ed. pub. by Philip Allen and Co., London, 1936).

pattern was. But the ruins of a huge *cetiyaghara*, with flanking *maṇḍapas* and shattered remains of two rows of pillars, an edifice of the Gupta age, may be seen at Sanchi, facing the 'Great Tope'. The end of the nave is apsidal and the pedestal on which the image once stood is still *in situ*.

Some archaeologists speculate that the 'nave' and the 'consecrated apsidal end' are part of a general shrine-pattern invented in far antiquity by the Phoenicians and diffused from Western Asia.

c. SAṄGHA LIFE IN THE LEṆAS

In several of these cave-settlements, it is possible to place the *leṇas* in a rough chronometrical series, distinguishing between earlier work and later. The indications lie in the style of construction and plastic decoration, concept of the cult-object, either a *stūpa* or an image, accessory emblems and symbols, and the comparative roughness or fineness of workmanship.

By these indications, it appears that the first settlers who came, perhaps early in the second century BC or late in the first, were monks of Hīnayānist faith, Theravādins or Mahāsāṅghikas. The Mahāyāna had not developed yet in northern India. But, according to the archaeologists' reading, at some time in the fifth century AD, Mahāyānist monks occupied these settlements in considerable numbers and introduced several alterations in the caves to suit their special ritual requirements.

The donatory inscriptions discovered in these caves,[1] of which only a few can be dated, are illustrative of the initial Hīnayānist tradition of the early occupants of the caves. The idea of the 'Saṅgha of the Four Quarters' still lingered. The canonical phrase appears in many a donatory formula in Karle, Nasik and Kanheri caves. But the phrase of course did not express any reality then, for the Saṅgha of the Four Quarters had split up long before into unitary saṅghas. The donors, therefore, while directing and dedicating the donation to the former, make the actual endowment on a particular saṅgha named after the locality.

A few examples may be cited. Ṛsabhadatta, of whom more will be said later, makes the gift of the revenue of a village to the monks of Karle (Velūraka). Its object is stated to be to enable them to 'spend the time' ('*Japanatha*') which alludes probably to *vassāvāsa*.[2] But

[1] Almost all of them are catalogued and translated in Lüders' *List of Brāhmī Inscriptions from the Earliest Times to about* 400 *AD* (Calcutta, 1910).

[2] See *Archaeological Survey of Western India*, Vol. IV, p. 101—*Japayita (-ta) valūrakesu lenavāsa(si)na pavajitānaṁ cātudisasa saṅghasa yapanatha gāmo Karajiko dato* (The village of Karajika is given to enable the wandering saṅgha of the four quarters to spend the *vassa* in *leṇas* at Valūraka).

these *leṇas* were regular monk-dwellings. Ṛṣabhadatta belongs to a period between the last quarter of the first and the first quarter of the second century.[1] The formula of the donation suggests that the Karle caves were then occupied by Hīnayānist monks. In later inscriptions the fiction of the wandering 'Saṅgha of the Four Quarters' and use of the *leṇas* for *vassāvāsa* is dropped. Monks are taken to be permanent residents as they actually were, forming a *saṅgha* bearing the local name of the settlement. Thus the donation of a village to the same company of monks at Karle by the Sātavāhana king, Pulumāyi II (Vāsaṭhīputra) in his seventh regnal year (*c.* AD 103), is made to the 'Valūraka Saṅgha', earmarking it for repairs of the *leṇas*.[2] No formular reference is made to the 'Saṅgha of the Four Quarters'. After the Sātavāhana age, the ancient formula of donation to the 'Saṅgha of the Four Quarters' becomes in these donatory inscriptions fewer and rarer: in the Gupta-age inscriptions it does not occur at all.

Saṅgha life in the *leṇas* did not depart from its norm in the *vihāras* of the north. Several terms of ancient usage, that occur in the *Vinayapiṭaka* in reference to saṅgha life, appear in the earlier cave-inscriptions, e.g. *Kappiyabhūmi* (Store-room for allowable provisions; Lüders' No. 988), *Caṅkama* (Promenade: Lüders' No. 998) and *Navakammika* (Superintendent for new constructions).[3] But certain officers with new functions, unknown in the *Vinayapiṭaka*, are also mentioned, e.g. *Upa-rakṣita* (Lüders, No. 1,100 at Karle) whose duty was to look after the repairs, and *Gandhakūṭi-bhārika* who was in charge of the sanctuary (Lüders, No. 989 at Kanheri) and probably had to keep it clean and make arrangements for the daily worship. Scripture was in oral texts, not reduced to writing till the first century BC or AD. The contents used to be imparted by word of mouth and the reciters formed an important functional class in a saṅgha.[4] We are told that there were six schools of reciters.[5] A Bhikṣu of Soparaka who donated a pillar, 'containing a relic', to the monk-community at Karle describes himself as a '*Bhāṇaka* of the Dharmottarīya sect' (Lüders, No. 1,095).

In the monk-communities who first settled in the *leṇas*, there were adherents of different sects. They were all Hīnayānist sects—the Mahāyānist monks did not come in before the fifth century AD. The two principal sects of early Buddhism were Theravāda and Mahāsāṅghika. Monks of the Mahāsāṅghika sect are named as beneficiaries

[1] See Sastri's *Comprehensive History*, p. 278.
[2] Lüders' *List*, No. 1,100.
[3] Mentioned in Cullavagga, I, 18, 1 and VI, 5, 2–3. This officer is also mentioned in Lüders' No. 1250 at Amarāvatī, No. 154 at Sanchi, No. 773 at Barhut.
[4] See Part IV, Sec. 1, p. 249.
[5] See B. C. Law's *History of Pali Literature*, Vol. II, p. 382.

in a number of donatory inscriptions (Lüders, Nos. 1,105, 1,106, etc.). Minor sects of later origin also appear, e.g. Bhadarāyanas (Lüders, Nos. 987, 1,018, 1,123, 1,124 at Nasik and Kanheri)—a sect which seems to have been held in much esteem in the first and second centuries AD; Dharmottorīyas (Lüders, Nos. 1,094–95, 1,152); Cetikas (Lüders, 1,130, 1,171) which had a wide following in the lower Krishnā valley.

A 'residential cave' (see p. 145 on 'ensemble of a monk-settlement') had normally (except in the most primitive ones) two parts: (i) a 'living room' behind a narrow porch or verandah and (ii) narrow dormitory cells which opened only into the living room. In *leṇas*, as well as in *vihāras*, the monks' cells (called in the *guhā*-settlements by various names, e.g. *Garbha*, *Ovaraka*, etc., and in the *vihāra*-settlements by the name *Pariveṇa*), were designed for sleeping in only; the living room into which they opened was designed for the inmates' meeting together. The dormitory cells in the *leṇas* were normally cut into the rocks; the living room was a square rock-cut chamber with a ledge running along three sides, leaving the front open. Out of it one could pass into the porch and descend below by a short and narrow staircase.

The number of monks' cells in a 'residential cave' varied from two to twenty—the gift of a nine-celled cave ('*nava-garbha*') is on record in a Karle inscription (Lüders, No. 1,106).

The oldest cells are mere 'hermit-cells', each with one fixed rock-bed or two (never more than three) and, in most instances, with a rock-pillow at the head, the bed occupying almost the whole of the floor-space. The cell was semi-dark inside—rarely was there a window, for it must have been a matter of practical difficulty to cut through the rocks behind and the only aperture was the door. But some small amenities were provided—a niche in the longer side of the rock-bed to keep clothes in, a niche in the wall for a lamp, a rod to hang clothes on, as seems indicated by existing mortice-holes. The door was a pair of wooden planks, of which the hinge-holes can still be seen in several caves. It seems that in a later age the construction of these cells was improved, and the doors were provided with some sort of ornamental work on the outside, of which faint traces remain at Nasik and Ajanta. Some inscriptions refer, among articles donated for the use of monks, to items of furniture, such as seats (*Satta*—Lüders, No. 985, 988), straight-backed chairs (*Piṭhas*—Lüders, No. 998), stools to sit on (*Āsana-peṭhikas*—Lüders, No. 998). Perhaps they found place in the 'living room'. The *Vinayapiṭaka* allows the use of such simple furniture to monks.[1]

[1] See *Early Buddhist Monachism*, p. 182, and *The Buddha and Five After-Centuries*, p. 80–81.

The 'hermit-cells', probably the work of the first century BC or AD, came in afterwards for considerable improvement. They were made larger and gradually provided with several structural amenities. An open stone-built courtyard was laid in front of a residential cave to which one could descend by a stairway from a comparatively spacious verandah on a higher level. The ceiling of the verandah was supported by two pillars in the centre and two pilasters at the two ends and stone-benches were placed in the verandah facing its rear walls. The backs of these stone-benches, usually decorated with carved floral and other designs, served as a parapet. The approach to a residential cave was thus made more spectacular. It is the verandah that is probably meant when the inscriptions refer to *Caṅkama* (promenade).

The 'living room' also expanded into a spacious chamber. In later times, its walls were sculptured and small Buddha-images were placed in niches. Over the doorway of the chamber was cut a latticed window (*vedikā-vātāyana*) which admitted air and mellowed light within.

Other developments came still later, perhaps after the fourth century AD. What had been used as a 'living room' was converted into a pillared hall (*Maṇḍapa*) and in its back-wall was recessed a chamber, serving for a sanctuary, sometimes with a vestibule in front of it. In the sanctuary was installed a large Buddha-image. Ultimately the bareness and simplicity of the old residential cave gave place to an appearance of grandeur with the 'living room' converted into a great hall with many pillars. The pillars, richly covered with sculpture, are of different shapes from cave to cave—octagonal, fluted, 'pot-and-foliage', capitalled, reeded and corbelled. They contain some very fine specimens of Gupta-age workmanship.

The water-supply of these hill-side settlements was obtained either from natural springs bursting through crevices in rocks or from cachements. The cachements, called *Poḍhis* in the inscriptions, were open reservoirs, often gifts of donors, some of them open caches of rainwater and some fed with oozings from rocks or hidden springs. They were scattered here and there, enough for constant overall water-supply. There were also common kitchens, and some caves at Karle and Bhaja, with patches of petrified soot in the ceiling, seem from their general appearance to have been used as such. At Bhaja is to be seen a hall, adjoining what was presumably the kitchen. Here a low but extensive platform exists, where perhaps monks squatted to take their meals. Dining halls (*Bhojanasāḷā*) are referred to in some donatory inscriptions at Kanheri (Lüders, No. 998) and Junnar (Lüders, No. 1182). The Dining hall was a later improvement on the primitive monk-refectory in an *āvāsa* or *ārāma* of which a representation appears in a piece of Mathura sculpture of the second century BC. These improvements indicate a little rise, within narrow limits, in the living standard of monks, *pari passu* with its general rise in contemporary society. There are several references also to reception rooms (*Upaṭṭhāna-sālā*) (Lüders, No. 988, 998 and 1,151) and pillared halls (*Maṇḍapa*) (Lüders, No. 1,000, 1,174 and 1,182).

Primitive Āvāsa Refectory (from Mathura Sculpture).

d. THE KRISHNAGIRI (KANHERI) CAVE-SETTLEMENT

The most extensive monk-settlement in western India was at Kanheri about twenty-five miles from Bombay—a great belt of caves, of earlier and later construction in different architectural styles, from rudely primitive to elegantly mature, round the waist of a tall height of the Western Ghats.

Its current name Kanheri is a corruption of (Sanskrit) Kṛṣṇagiri (Black Hill). In its Prākrit form, Kaṇhasela (Sanskrit-Kṛṣṇasaila), it occurs in a donatory inscription in which mention is made of Gotamiputra Yajñaśrī Sātakarṇi as the regnant Sātavāhana king (AD 150–189) (Lüders, No. 1,024). It is the oldest inscription discovered here. But the settlement must have been in existence at least a century before Sātakarṇi's reign.

From the ancient west-coast seaports of Sopara, Kalyan and Chaul, it was not too far off. From the middle height of Kṛṣṇagiri, there is a fine view, beyond the wooded hills girding it, of a shimmering stretch of the sea in the distance. One of the caves is given an apt name in the donatory inscription—the Sea-view (*Sāgara-pralokana*). Probably marine traders of the seaports had a large hand in the construction of the earliest caves, if it was not actually they who had started the settlement. Almost all the donatory inscriptions in these caves record names of persons who had come to the settlement from the seaboard. The caves discovered up to date at Kānheri number 112, of which 107 are residential containing monks' cells.

The first comers to this settlement, as to others in western India, were Hīnayānist monks. Cave No. 1 (Archaeological Survey number) shows the kind of rough-hewn residential caves with which the settlement started. They are distinguishable by the absence of any Buddha-image and are without sculptural decorations, of small size and rough pattern. Apparently there was a steady increase in the strength of the monk-community here and more and more *leṇas* were subsequently constructed. The *leṇas* of later construction are superior in architecture. There is also evidence of several primitive caves having been enlarged and decorated afterwards with sculpture and images.

Of the earlier residential caves, the architectural pattern was a standardized one—a short flight of steps leading to a narrow verandah with rock-cut benches at its two ends, a 'living room' inside with a projecting rock-cut ledge running along three sides, and, opening into this room, small dormitory cells recessed into the rocks with one rock-bed or two.

As more and more monks joined in course of time and saṅgha life commenced, caves were required for community purposes, for holding assemblies and for congregational worship, and donors came forward to fulfil these requirements too. The emplacement of the prayer halls (*Cetiyagharas*) was not central, but was determined by the contour of the mountain-side. But they were built to pattern—rectangular shape with apsidal end, side-aisles separated from the nave by two rows of pillars and the *stūpa* or the image set up in the apse at the nave's far end. At first, the old Hīnayāna symbol-worship was conducted in these halls, with flowers and lights and processional circumambulation of the *stūpa*. Much later, the cult-object was changed to an image and it was the normal object of worship of the Mahāyānists who came late to the *leṇas* of Kanheri, not perhaps before the fifth or even the sixth century AD.

They caused Buddha-images to be installed in profusion. At first the images seem to have been introduced only as sacred symbols, rather than for the purpose of ritual worship: they were placed in niches in the walls with no altar in front to lay offerings on. A sanctuary with an image installed in it, as we see at Ajanta or Ellora, became the place of congregational worship in the *leṇas* later, but it seems that at Kanheri this stage was scarcely reached. There is no evidence of image-worship conducted *within a sanctuary*.

The settlement was apparently in its prime and flourishing in the reign of Gotamiputra Yajñaśrī Sātakarṇi (AD 150–189); as many as seven donatory inscriptions can be assigned on palaeographic grounds to his reign (Lüders, Nos. 987, 998, 999, 1,006, 1,007, 1,020, 1,024). With the influx later of monks of Mahāyānist faith, the art of the Gupta age came in, renovating piecemeal a number of caves. Sizable Assembly Halls (*Maṇḍapas*)—one of them of great dimensions—were also constructed in these after-centuries. In the history of this settlement, there seems to have been a sort of water-shed between its Hīnayānist past and its later Mahāyānist renovation.

What this process of Mahāyānist renovation at Kanheri was like is illustrated by the history of one of the caves—No. lxvi (Archaeological Survey number). This cave had been originally constructed, as the palaeography of an inscription in its verandah suggests, in the latter half of the second century AD—perhaps in the reign of Gotamiputra Yajñaśrī Sātakarṇi.

It consisted then of a verandah, a 'living room' and the monks' dormitory cells. When the earliest batch of Mahāyānists joined the settlement, they had the walls of the cave decorated with several sculptured panels, representing the 'Srāvasti miracle' and the symbols of their faith, Dhyānī Buddhas and Avalokiteśvaras. Other batches of Mahāyānists followed who made further additions to these decorations. They carved out a sanctuary at the back of the interior 'living room' and placed there a seated Buddha-image and inserted several panels of larger size again showing the 'Śrāvasti Miracle'. Then came still other batches of the school. They covered with small *stūpa*-panels the undecorated gaps left on the walls by the earlier decorators. These panels by their style of sculpture belong to the seventh century. Later on two more panels were inserted in the vestibule of the newly constructed sanctuary.

This piecemeal decoration and renovation of the cave went on for years—perhaps for more than a century—and this sort of activity can be traced in most cave-settlements of western India. Differences in sculptural style and constructional technique in different parts of one and the same settlement always strike the eye. In outline the history of the Krishnagiri settlement is typical of other monk-settlements of western India. Most of them have an earlier 'Hīnayānist' period and a later 'Mahāyānist' one.

Most of the cave-settlements of western India were long-lived, and Krishnagiri, commencing from the first century BC or AD, continued to be a monk-settlement even beyond the time when Buddhism as an organized religion was extinct in this part of India.

In cave No. XXXIX, which is a *Cetiyaghara*, an inscription was discovered on the *stūpa* inside showing its occupation by monks in the Śaka year 913 (i.e. AD 991).[1] In another *stūpa* in cave No. XIII was found a lot of Bāhmani coins—evidence that even after the Muslim invasion of the Deccan in the thirteenth and fourteenth centuries, the caves were not altogether deserted.[2] In many of them ascetics (*sādhus* and *yogis*) had made their haunts after the Buddhist monks had left.

[1] See *Journal of Bombay Branch of Royal Asiatic Society*, VII, No. 54, Appendix B.
[2] See *Ibid*, VI, p. 157, and plate (West's *Excavation in a Cave at Kanheri*).

Dr Moreswar Dikshit has drawn up a very interesting chart based on a survey of all the cave-settlements of western India showing for each the number of (i) Caves, (ii) *Stūpas* (named *Chaityas*), (iii) *Cetiyagharas*, (iv) Residential Caves (named *Vihāras*) and (v) Years of Occupation (i.e. when first started, when flourished most and when nothing about it is known).

The following excerpt from the chart relates to the most popularly known of these cave-settlements:[1]

Place	*No. of caves*	*Chaityas*	*Cetiyagharas* (with cells in them)	*Vihāras*	*Years of occupation in centuries* (commencement, peak period, unknown period)
1. Kanheri	112	1	4	107	I–II–XI
2. Junnar	140	5	4	131	I–II–V
3. Karle	7	1	nil	6	I–II–VI
4. Bedsa	4	1	nil	(not given)	I–II
5. Karad	63	nil	nil	nil	II–IV
6. Nasik	27	1	2	24	I BC–AD II–VI
7. Kondivle	18	1	2	16	I–II–VI
8. Aurangabad	12	1	nil	11	IV–VI–VIII
9. Ellora	12	1	nil	11	IV–VI–VIII
10. Sana	62	1	nil	61	II–IV
11. Talaja	30	1	nil	29	II
12. Pithalkhora	8	1	4	2	II BC–AD II–VIII
13. Ajanta	30	4	24	2	II BC–AD V–IX

By the standard of our modern economic age, the maintenance of these numerous cave-settlements, involving the cost not only of excavations, buildings and repairs, but also of providing necessaries of life for the large community each cave-settlement represented, would seem a task beyond the scope of private benefactions. About the *vihāras* of northern India, we have it from the Chinese pilgrims that it was a long-standing practice to endow them with land-grants, either from kings or landowners. But for the monk-settlements of western India (except perhaps in Saurāshtra under the Maitraka kings), there are few records of land-grant: their main stand-by was casual donations. At Kanheri and Karle, there are a few epigraphic records of donations by Sātavāhana kings, not by any means on an extensive scale—in fact very small. For the most part, the occasional gifts of chance donors defrayed the costs of excavation, of the construction of monks' cells, and, later, of the sumptuous *Cetiya-*

[1] This chart is given in Dr Dikshit's (unpublished) work on 'Buddhist Settlements in Western India'.

gharas and spacious *Maṇḍapas*, as well as of the maintenance of the monk-community settled there. Not all the donors were Buddhists.

Any gift, in money or in kind, however large or small—of a water-cistern (*Poḍhi*), a set of furniture, a pillar or a door, and, for the matter of that, any thing for use or decoration—would be received by the monk-community.

The gift was called *Deya-dhamma*; the term has a nuance; it implies something more than a mere gift (*Dāna*). It is '*deya*' (to be given), suggesting obligatoriness—the discharge on the part of those who are in secular life of the duty of meeting the earthly needs of those in the higher, holier life. It was a sort of 'must'. To keep going an extensive establishment like Kanheri, the gifts to it, large and small, by lay people must have been continuous and countless. Only an infinitesimal portion of the total is known from epigraphic records.

In these records, the name of one wealthy donor figures prominently. He was a Śaka, not Buddhist by faith, son-in-law of a Śaka ruler who is known to have been ousted by Gotamiputra Sātakarṇi in AD 124[1]—Ṛṣabhadata or Uṣabhadata by name. He is outstanding among the donors to Karle, Pandulena and Kanheri. He seems to have been a generous-minded open-handed patron, during the early Sātavāhana times, of Buddhist monks in his own part of the country where Śaka satraps ruled. Not much is known about him save what appears from his donatory inscriptions. They reveal, however, a very interesting personality.

He describes himself as a Śaka (Indo-Scythian). His father was one Dinika and his father-in-law was the Śaka governor (*Kṣatrapa*) Nahapāna, described as 'King of Kṣaharata', of whom Ṛṣabhadata seems to have been somewhat snobbishly proud. Fathers-in-law are rarely named in donatory inscriptions, but Ṛṣabhadata makes it a point to mention his own in every inscription he has left. Unquestionably Ṛṣabhadata was a man of wealth and he was an army officer under Nahapāna.

At the same time he was a person of philanthropic bent, but he did not believe in doing good by stealth. So he takes occasion always—as in the following inscription purporting to commemorate the gift of a cave and a water-cistern to monks residing in one of the caves excavated by him on the Tri-raśmi Mountain ('Pandulena caves' at Nasik)—to announce his manifold public benefactions and no less famous heroic deeds:[2]

'The son-in-law of the Kṣaharata king Kṣatrapa Nahapāna, Dinika's son, Ṛṣabhadata (or Uṣabhadata) who has given three hundred

[1] See Sastri's *Comprehensive History*, p. 276.
[2] See *Report of Archaeological Survey of Western India*, Vol. IV, pp. 99–100.

thousand cows—who gave gold to establish a *tīrtha* (holy bathing place) on the river Bārāṇasa—who gave sixteen villages to gods and Brāhmaṇas—who annually causes to be fed one hundred thousand Brāhmaṇa—who has given wives to eight Brāhmaṇas at the holy *tīrtha* of Prabhāsa—who has built quadrangular rest-houses at different places (named) and who has made gardens, tanks and drinking fountains—who has established for the sake of spiritual merit ferries with boats on the rivers (named) and has erected on both banks of these rivers rest-houses and places for the distribution of water—who has given in the village (named) one thousand as the price of 32 cocoanut trees for the benefit of Caraka (?) congregations at (places named)—has caused this cave and these cisterns to be made on Mount Tri-raśmi (i.e. where the Pandulena caves of Nasik are located). And he (i.e. Ṛsabhadata himself) went in the rainy season to liberate a chief (named) who was besieged by the Malayas and they fled before the roar (of his army). . . . Afterwards he proceeded to Puṣkara and bathed there and gave three thousand calves and a village. He bought a field for 4,000 (*Kahāpaṇas*) that lay to the north-west of the boundaries of the town belonging to his father. Out of this the Saṅgha of the Four Quarters, dwelling in the *leṇa* of his gift, will obtain their provisions.'

The hyperbole of self-advertisement could scarcely go farther! Ṛṣabhadata's wife Dakṣamitrā, daughter of the great father-in-law Nahapāna, also donated a monks' cell.[1]

The inscription also describes how dispositions of pecuniary gifts by him to the monks dwelling in the *leṇa* constructed by him, have been made:[2] 3,000 *Kārṣāpaṇas*[3] for provision of clothes and *kaṣana*[4] were deposited in two parts with two merchant-guilds of the neighbouring town of Govardhana—2,000 with one weavers' guild at an interest of 100 *Kārṣāpanas,* and 1,000 with another weavers' guild at an interest of 75 *Kārṣāpaṇas;* the capital was not to be repaid, but the interest was to be remitted regularly to the twenty monks who were then occupants of the cave on Tri-raśmi mountain. The sums to be paid thus out of the interest on the deposits were allocated under two heads—*civara* (clothing) and *kaṣana.* Besides, he paid 8,000 for the purchase of a plantation of cocoanut trees for the monks' benefit, perhaps for their food-supply. 'And all of this', declares Ṛṣabhadata, 'has been proclaimed in the guild-hall ('*Nigama-*

[1] *Ibid,* p. 103. [2] *Ibid,* p. 102.

[3] *Kārṣāpaṇa* was the basic punch-marked silver coin of 57.8 grains which was current from the fourth century BC to the fourth century AD and perhaps later in ancient India. We find mention of it in Pali Buddhist legends as *Kahāpaṇa* and in inscriptions up to the end of the Sātavāhanas.

[4] The meaning of this word is uncertain. 'Beads for rosaries' has been suggested.

sabhāya') and written on a large board ('*phalakavare*') in accordance with custom ('*caritraiaḥ*').[1]

It throws light on the customary manner of making substantial pecuniary endowments to monasteries in that age.

For the gift of landed property to the monks of Tri-raśmi Mountain, ratification by the reigning king Gotamiputra Sātakarṇi had to be obtained and his ratification is recorded in another inscription in the cave.[2] It says that the king grants immunity (from interference and taxation) for the field given by Ṛṣabhadata to the monks and that 'it shall not be entered (by royal officers), nor meddled with (by them) and possess immunities of all kinds'. It records further that, in respect of this field and the immunity conferred by the king upon it, a charter has been drawn up and deposited among records relating to contracts.

From the ranks of aristocracy, to which Nahapāna's much-advertised son-in-law belonged, there were perhaps other liberal donors whose names are unknown. But a large part of the donations must have come from wealthy merchants who were proverbial patrons of monk-communities. They abounded in western and southern India so long as India's commerce with the Roman world lasted. Yet few have left, like Bhūtapāla of Vejayantī at Karle, a record of their benefactions. Perhaps the bulk of the donations consisted of pecuniary endowments and, Ṛṣabhadata's apart, the land-grants are few, while they are many for the *vihāras* of the north.

The *leṇas* have been carefully surveyed by archaeologists and their art-treasures by connoisseurs and historians of Indian art.[3] Yet the sort of life that was lived in these *leṇas* by long generations of monks calls for a word of appraisal. In evaluating this monastic life, we have to shed at the outset the *à priori* notion that life in a monk settlement must have been like a stagnant pool where one day was like another and where no impact of the outside world was ever felt.

*

Down below the caves of Kanheri at a turn of the mountain there is a cemetery where generations of monks have left their ashes. The question must haunt one standing in this cemetery: were the lives that ended here spent collectively in a dead round of rites and rituals, individually in the inaction of introvert meditation?

[1] *Ibid*, p. 103. [2] *Ibid*., p. 105.

[3] The two standard archaeological works are: Fergusson and Burgess's *Cave Temples of India* (1880) and Burgess' *Report on the Buddhist Cave-temples and their Inscriptions* (1883) in the *Archaeological Survey of Western India*, Vol. IV. The two best art-histories are: Percy Brown's *Indian Architecture* (1942) and Rowland's *The Art and Architecture of India* (1953).

Yet life in a Buddhist monk-settlement, circumscribed as it was within the sphere of its own preoccupations and interests, was never perhaps of this listless, stagnant and vegetative kind.

We may imagine the animated scenes in the assembly halls, of which no report has come down to us, when doctrines were discussed and debated, for in these settlements were monks of different sects. When the Mahāyānist monks first appeared in the saṅghas, which had originally consisted of monks of Hīnayānist faith, and demanded renovation of the caves to suit their different mode of worship, there must have been a profound stir and acute heart-searching. The ritual worship of the Buddha-image in a sanctuary was perhaps not established without some articulate protest from those long accustomed to *stūpa*-worship. The facts are not known, but indications remain—notably in the architectural attempts seen in some *cetiyagharas* to effect a compromise by inserting an image in a *stūpa*.[1]

Construction, decoration, renovation and repair-work were, as several inscriptions attest, carried on under the supervision of a single monk (*Navakammika*) or a committee of monks. The monk-authority laid down the requirements generally, leaving the actual construction and craftsmanship to the workmen—masons, sculptors and decorators. In this work the monk mind and the lay mind had to come together, but the lay mind, it seems, had its way.

The series of sculptured figures on the door-jambs of *cetiyagharas* and *maṇḍapas* of a male and a female in love-making pose (*Mithuna*) were just a traditional art-motif followed by the *leṇa*-decorators. But the monks, one may be sure, would not like to have them so. In fact the art of the caves shows many a feature, both secular and sacred, that emerged independently and spontaneously out of the artist's untutored mind.

To turn for a moment to the murals of Ajanta. Their predominant note is not monkish. The stories taken from the *Jātakas* and other popular sources had no need to be dictated by monks. But in the dramatic drift and sweep of the story in the painter's rendering, its moral is apt to get submerged: the monks would perhaps not have liked the paintings done so. But the artists were evidently not concerned with 'moralizing' their art. And all the points of purely artistic, but exclusively secular, interest—women's hair-do, men's headgear and dress ensemble, poses and gestures and flow of action—were just the independent imprint of the lay mind in a monks' abode. No doubt in the construction, decoration and maintenance of the caves the monk mind and the lay mind came actively together—yet from what different planes!

A fine sculptural composition, seen at Aurangabad, Kanheri,

[1] See Part III, Sec. 3, p. 192.

Avalokiteśvara Litany in Sculpture (Ajanta).

Ajanta and Ellora, left amidst the Mahāyānist renovation of the caves, is named the 'Avalokiteśvara Litany'[1] by archaeologists.

It sets forth Avalokiteśvara as saviour from all deadly dangers—and the dangers are graphically represented: arson, murder, captivity and slavery, forest-fire, enraged animal, striking snake, shipwreck, disease and death. The 'Litany', which has counterparts in late Mahāyāna texts like the *Śragdharā Stotra*,[2] appears to have been

[1] The best specimen of this sculptural composition is in Aurangabad Cave, No. VII.

[2] Pub. in *Bibliotheca Indica*.

Apsidal end of the Sanctuary. (Photo: Department of Archaeology, N.E. Project, Guntur)

Kanherī cave, No. 1. (showing type of early construction.) (Photo: Department of Archaeology, Government of India)

A primitive residential cave at Kanherī (enlarged and decorated with sculpture by Mahāyānists). (Photo: Department of Archaeology, Government of India)

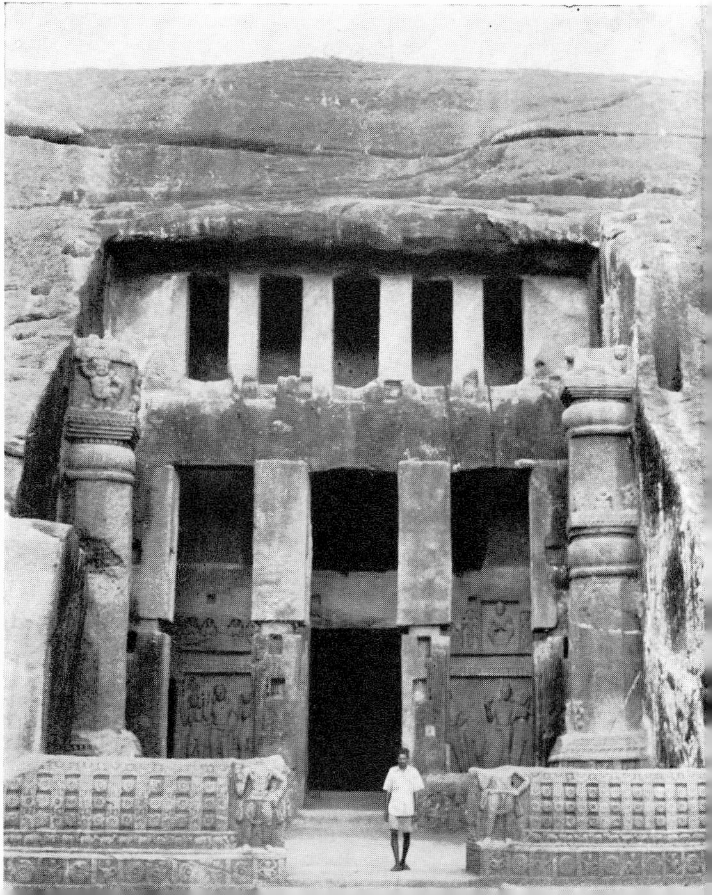

10. *Sculptural decorations made by Mahāyānist monks at Kanherī*. (Photo: Department of Archaeology, Government of India)

evolved from the minds of the workmen themselves—those who had to face such deadly dangers in the game of life from which the Lord alone could save them.

It would seem that other interests than those of worship and meditation also sprouted up in the *leṇas* in course of time as they did in the *vihāras* of northern India. One was the interest in knowledge and learning for their own sake, organizedly pursued.

Several caves at different centres raise a suspicion in the visitor's mind of their having been set apart to serve this interest—used for study, discussion and teaching. At Kanheri, cave No. 11, called the 'Durbar Hall', which has twenty monks' cells cut into its walls and a somewhat peculiar seating arrangement, certainly gives such an impression. Opposite to it is a cave (No. 12) which seems to have been the *Ācārya's* (Instructor's) residence—an ordinary *vihāra*, but more spacious in lay-out, with a single cell adorned with a Buddha-image. Again at Ellora, the fine three-storeyed *leṇa* called *Tin-Tal* ('Three-storeyed'), with an extensive courtyard in front and two tall columns set up at its outer edge, has decidedly the ensemble of a college. Its top storey is a hall; its first floor has a number of residential cells; the ground floor a set of chambers. A most curious, most significant, detail in it, overlooked by visitors, is the existence at one end of the verandah of the first floor of a small projecting platform; access is had to it by a narrow staircase from the ground, and, just above the platform and within easy reach of a stretched hand, there appears a fairly large and perfectly rectangular patch of scrubbing. Looking at this patch, one would wonder if written announcements used to be put up here for monks living in the cells of that storey—time-tables for lectures and meetings, just as on the notice-board of an up-to-date college. The 'Tin-Tal' edifice is late in time—perhaps it is of the eighth century AD. But was it, one wonders, a regular monastic college in that establishment?

At no time in its history was Buddhist monastic life meant to be a self-chosen process of world-forgetting and being by the world forgot. It was not, as we have observed, the purpose of a monastery to shut out the world, but only its distracting evils. One class of monks shunned the world—those called *Āraññakas* (Forest-dwellers) in the *Vinayapiṭaka*—and they are not regarded in it as necessarily the best specimens of monkhood.

F

6

The Bāgh Caves

THE *Leṇas*, described so far, are situated on the western side of peninsular India. Many of them go back in their beginnings to the early Sātavāhana times—to the second or first century BC—and their lifetime as monk-settlements covers many after-centuries. Some of them possibly functioned even to the end of the eighth when Buddhism, save at certain localities in the east of northern India, was in the last stage of decline.

The tradition of *guhā*-monasteries was strangely persistent south of the Vindhyas. Even in the late decline of Buddhism, a splendid set of caves was constructed on the southern face of the Vindhyan hills in a part of the Madhya Pradesh now called Gwalior. These are known as 'Bāgh Caves' from a nearby village of that name. About thirty feet below them, a small stream known locally as Bāghinī meanders down from its source somewhere up in the hills and, flowing through a channel called Kukshi, discharges itself into the Narmadā river. Among the *guhā*-monasteries of India, these caves are the most northerly. In their time, they must have been of striking spectacular magnificence. The approach to them from the plains is somewhat difficult—through several folds of the Vindhyan range.

These caves have not yielded a single epigraph to give a clue to their history. It is not known who started them or who their patrons or benefactors were or when they were deserted. But they are set in a region where Buddhism evidently had a great hold at the time of their construction. The region was anciently named Malwā (Mālava), in the extreme west of the Madhya Pradesh. At several sites in Malwā have been discovered stray remains of monasteries of the *guhā*-type,[1] but the Bāgh Caves represent a whole great range of them planned on a large scale. Archaeologists have cleared these caves of debris and brought nine to view, and in the entire complex there are probably several more still out of sight. Archaeological excavation is still on.

The Bāgh Caves have suffered some natural vicissitudes which caves of western India were happily exempt from. They were carved out of sandstone rocks, but these rocks happened to be topped by a deep band of clay-stone. The weight and pressure of this top-layer

[1] For these sites, see the 'Sketch-map of Malwā' in Marshall's *The Bāgh Caves* (pub. by India Society, London, 1927).

and the seepage of water through it have ruined most of the caves and their porticos and largely demolished their sculptured façades. But the remains still indicate what an amazing wealth of decoration, both sculpture and painting, they possessed in their time. Except at Ajanta, these caves are the only ones in India which contain large pieces of mural painting. They are, however, in a much worse state of preservation here, with sequence and continuity lost through effacement of large portions.

The complete absence of lithic inscription in any of the caves is sought to be explained by the surmise that the practice here may have been to set up inscriptions in paint instead of etching them in stone, with the regrettable result that they have all got effaced by weathering and drippings from the top.

Lending a slight colour to the surmise, a solitary letter, *ka*, initial consonant of the alphabet, has been discovered standing oddly under a scene depicted on the back-wall of the portico joining caves Nos. 4 and 5 (Archaeological Survey number).[1] The solitary letter has been submitted to palaeographic test: expert opinion is that it is a Gupta character referable to the sixth or seventh century, when the 'later Guptas' were still reigning after the break-up of the empire. This palaeographic indication is borne out and amplified by the existing sculpture and painting. Especially the painting, in its general idiom and in all particulars of pigmentation, posture and pose, is unmistakably in the style of Ajanta.

But there is a little difference in the selection of themes. As Cousins says: 'The Bāgh frescos are taken by competent authorities to be contemporaneous with the later Ajanta frescos. In craftsmanship they are similar. Their mastery over spontaneous technique of mural painting is no less. They have the same mood of reserve in the midst of joy. . . . But, while the Ajanta frescos are more religious in theme, depicting incidents from the previous lives of the Buddha with their human associations, the Bāgh frescos are more human, depicting the life of the time with its religious associations.'[2]

The impress of the Gupta age in these caves is unmistakable—they are characterized by a largeness of structural dimensions and correspond in their artistic decorations, though mostly spoiled now and mutilated, to Gupta traditions in their maturity.

There are earlier caves and later. The differences between them in respect of craftsmanship have been collated with similar differences at Ajanta. 'Cave No. 1 with its simple four-pillared hall is probably the earliest. Caves Nos. 2 and 3, which come next with their clumsy pillars are perhaps to be ranked with the twenty-pillared cave No. 12 at Ajanta. Cave No. 4 may be contemporary with the cave bearing

[1] See Marshall's *The Bāgh Caves*, p. 22. [2] *Ibid*, p. 73.

the same number at Ajanta, although the paintings on the former are allied to those of caves Nos. 16 and 17 at Ajanta. Caves Nos. 4, 5 and 6, connected as they are, externally or internally, through a passage to caves Nos. 5 and 6, would appear to be contemporary and chronologically the last of the surviving caves in this group.'[1]

It does not appear, as in so many West Indian caves, that the settlement was first started by Hīnayānist monks and had a later influx of Mahāyānists. There are no signs of later Mahāyānist renovation or later Mahāyānist iconographic decorations. The entire group of caves at Bāgh must have been from the beginning in the occupation of Mahāyānist monks and all the Buddha-images here, sculpted or painted, are accompanied by Bodhisattva figures or are flanked on each side with the figures respectively of Avalokiteśvara and Mañjuśrī.

But it seems strange that in the chapels and sanctuaries discovered so far, the object of worship is nowhere a Buddha-image, but a *stūpa*—the Buddha and Bodhisattva images occupying only the niches, in one of which a big Buddha-image has been replaced by a Hindu Gaṇeśa of the same size. The *Stūpa* installed as the only cult-object here points to the long survival of symbol-worship in the monasteries—over several centuries after the image had been invented and accepted for ritual worship by the Hīnayānist and the Mahāyānist monks alike.

The monks' cells are mostly square in shape—not rectangular as in the *leṇas* of western India. There are some with an antechamber at a lower level reached from the cell by a very narrow doorway in a side wall. Perhaps it represents a 'meditation chamber', of which there are several examples in the monasteries of Nālandā. In none of these monk-cells is to be seen the usual rock-bed. Cave No. 5 is a very capacious pillared hall without any monk's cell and was evidently used as the central assembly hall of the establishment. On all sides of it runs a broad ledge cut into the rock and the pillars also are joined at their bases, apparently to provide seats.

Nothing is known as to why and when these caves were deserted. Probably the desertion was due not so much to the decline of Buddhism in this part as to the unsafe condition of the caves sagging under the heavy top-layer of water-logged clay-stone. Absolutely nothing is known as to who built, decorated or maintained them. But from their size and the profusion of artistic decorations, they must have enjoyed the munificence of royal or of wealthy patrons.

The Gupta emperors were builders of Buddhist temples and monasteries at Nālandā, patrons of Buddhist saṅghas. Perhaps the tradition they had set did not die out when the imperial Guptas

[1] *Ibid.*, p. 22.

were succeeded by local and regional kings, the Gupta branch line whose rule, even round AD 600, extended to 'Mālava' (Mālwa).

'Mālava was graced by the presence of the Guptas as early as in the fifth century. . . . In the latter part of the sixth and the commencement of the seventh century, it seems to have been under the direct rule of a line of Guptas whose precise connection with the great Guptas is not clear. . . . The precise location and extent of "Mālava" of the later Guptas cannot be determined.'[1] Perhaps the Bāgh Caves, when they were commenced, were within the territory of these later Guptas. Except that they hold evidence of Gupta art and were planned in the larger style, characteristic of Gupta construction, we have no clue to their actual builders.

It is impossible of course in the general ruin and dilapidation that has befallen the caves to form an adequate idea of their one-time magnificence: the ensemble is wholly lost.

Yet some parts of the ruins still show the large scale on which the caves had been originally planned and designed and to what magnificent spectacular effect. Caves Nos. 3 and 4—largest in the range—are joined by a continuous portico of considerable width with a length of 220 feet, borne on as many as twenty-two pillars. The roof has fallen down, but some decorative slabs that originally stood between the tops of the pillars and the roof have been recovered with remains on them of fine Ajanta-style sculpture and painting.

In the painting the secular motives outnumber the sacred more pronouncedly than at Ajanta; scenes from life appear more frequently—from gorgeous cavalcade and full-dress processions with horses and elephants to intimate domestic incidents like an irate husband catching the hair of a seemingly cantankerous wife and threatening her with an upraised stick.

Yet in the context of the magnitude and magnificence of these caves, the paucity of monks' cells is striking. The settlement had been started evidently in the late decline of Buddhism and its saṅgha life was by no means commensurate with its architectural proportions.

[1] Ray Chaudhuri's *Political History*, 6th Ed., p. 582, footnote 5.

were succeeded by local and regional kings, the Gupta branch line whose rule, even round AD 600, extended to 'Malava' (Malwa).

'Malava was graced by the presence of the Guptas as early as in the fifth century. . . . In the latter part of the sixth and the commencement of the seventh century, it seems to have been under the direct rule of a line of Guptas whose precise connection with the great Guptas is not clear. . . . The precise location and extent of "Mālava" of the later Guptas cannot be determined.'[1] Perhaps the Bagh Caves, when they were commenced, were within the territory of these later Guptas. Except that they hold evidence of Gupta art and were planned in the larger style, characteristic of Gupta construction, we have no clue to their actual builders.

It is impossible of course in the general ruin and dilapidation that has befallen the caves to form an adequate idea of their one-time magnificence: the ensemble is wholly lost.

Yet some parts of the ruins still show the large scale on which the caves had been originally planned and designed and to what magnificently spectacular effect. Caves Nos. 5 and 4—largest in the range—are joined by a continuous portico of considerable width with a length of 220 feet, borne on as many as twenty-two pillars. The roof has fallen down, but some decorative slabs that originally stood between the tops of the pillars and the roof have been recovered with remains on them of fine Ajanta-style sculpture and painting.

In the painting the secular motives outnumber the sacred more pronouncedly than at Ajanta; scenes from life appear more frequently—from gorgeous cavalcade and full-dress processions with horses and elephants to intimate domestic incidents like an irate husband catching the hair of a seemingly cantankerous wife and threatening her with an upraised stick.

Yet in the context of the magnitude and magnificence of these caves, the paucity of monks' cells is striking. The settlement had been started evidently in the late decline of Buddhism and its sangha life was by no means commensurate with its architectural proportions.

[1] See Chaudhuri's *Political History of Ancient India*, p. 582, footnote.

PART III

IN THE GUPTA AGE

(AD 300—550)

AND AFTER

1

Saṅgha Life in Transition

FROM a founder's inspired teachings to a system of doctrinal interpretations made by disciples and followers seems to be a law of the historical development of a religion. When the religion has been reduced to a system, the system itself launches on its own career of development. The history of Buddhism is no exception and here it was not one system that developed but two—the earlier Hīnayāna and the later Mahāyāna.

Both systems were traditionalist, built on *Buddhavacana* (Words of the Buddha), though approached by two different ways.[1] In respect of Saṅgha life, the outstanding difference between the two systems lay in the relative importance assigned to Ordination—entering the Order and observance of Vinaya. In the Mahāyānist view, the potentiality exists in all men and women for attainment of the *summum bonum,* Buddahood. It is attainable by all, whether monks or lay men, who cultivate the *Bodhicitta* (Direction of the heart towards *Bodhi*) and everyone who does so is a 'potential Buddha' (*Bodhisattva*). Hence monkhood to the Mahāyānist is not a necessary pre-condition for the spiritual career, but only an aid.

The older system was called *Dhamma-vinaya* by its adherents;[2] the new system was designated *Mahāyāna* (Great Vehicle) by its followers who later invented for the older system (*Dhamma-vinaya*) the disparaging correlative name Hīnayāna (Small Vehicle).

The origin of the Mahāyāna is obscure; it must have been in the making for two or three centuries BC, but emerged, individuated as a system, only in the first or second century AD. In the after-history of the Saṅgha in India, there were both Hīnayānist and Mahāyānist monks in its fold, though even in the seventh century AD, when Hsüan-tsang was in India, the former considerably outnumbered the latter.[3]

So far as the general character and constitution of saṅgha life was concerned, the existence of Mahāyānist monks in the Saṅgha—

[1] See Part IV, Sec. 3 (a). [2] See Part I, Sec. 5, p. 68.

[3] 'Some writers speak as if, after our era, Mahāyānism was predominant in India and Hīnayāna banished to its extreme confines such as Ceylon and Kashmir. Yet about AD 640, the zealous Mahāyānist (Hsüan-tsang) states that half the monks of India were definitely Hīnayānist, while less than a fifth had equally definite Mahāyānist convictions'—Eliot's *Hinduism and Buddhism*, Vol. II, p. 101.

monks to whom monkhood itself was not so essential or important—was neither disruptive nor productive of any revolutionary change. But the *Dhamma-vinaya* itself, on the basis of which the Saṅgha had been originally built up and on which it rested, did not remain immutably fixed. No discerning student of early Buddhist development can fail to be struck by the fact that the *Dhamma-vinaya* of the Buddhist was peculiarly liable to changes from within as well as responsive to influences from without.

We have expatiated in the introductory part of this work on the integral place of the Saṅgha in the Buddhist system. In consequence of this relation, developments that took place in the religion (*Dhamma-vinaya*) itself would translate themselves, sooner or later, into concrete forms within Saṅgha life and organization. The Saṅgha could not have stayed at its old moorings while the concept of the Vinaya shifted and the Dhamma put forth new trends. The Vinaya was its outer life and organization and the Dhamma its inner life and spirit, and in respect of both the Vinaya and the Dhamma, changes, profound and of a transforming character, set in early and came about in the course of five centuries of its previous history. Saṅgha life in passing through these centuries and emerging into the Christian era was so transformed that the Saṅgha in the AD cannot be regarded as a mere continuation of the Saṅgha of the BC: to conjugate them in a single tense would certainly be unhistorical.

In our approach to the later Saṅgha life, it has to be borne in mind that historic changes in the religion first started in the field of speculative and doctrinal differences, which the anti-authoritarian principle of Buddhism left free and unrestricted; that they took all the foregoing centuries to grow, articulate and affirm themselves, and that they finally took form and substance and became established in the institutional practices of monastic life.

The transition of the Saṅgha from the BC to the AD is the result of these changes that came about, first, in the attitude towards the Vinaya and, secondly, through the *Bhakti*-movement in the Dhamma. They are foreshadowed in the contentious views and controversies of its early history to which it is necessary to advert.

2

THE VINAYA:
Its After-history

THE Vinaya laws constituted, as we have seen, the charter of primitive Saṅgha life: they evolved completely in the *āvāsas* and *ārāmas*. The initial aim and object of these laws had been organizational—their main purpose to form a settled Order out of a wandering Sect.[1]

By regulating not merely the monk's personal life, but also his relations to others and his rights and duties as member of a corporate body, the Vinaya aimed to establish a new pattern of collective and organized life for the Bhikkhus. A saṅgha was to function within the scope of these laws; of its existence as an Order the Vinaya was the bond. It is possible therefore to frame in the setting of the Vinaya laws a picture of Saṅgha organization as it had existed in the early centuries of Buddhism. But in the centuries that followed the picture did not remain the same. When the Order had attained to a norm and pattern, the Vinaya laws outgrew their original purpose: no longer was there a need for the pressure of the mould in which it had been brought already into a consistent shape.

Whether Saṅgha life was coincident and conterminous with the system of Vinaya as it had developed became a debatable matter very early in the monk-community.

The Vinaya, as we have seen, stemmed from the *Pātimokkha* code, and so long as the *Pātimokkha* did not become a fixed-word liturgy, it was elastic in its contents. It admitted additions and alterations to its *Sikkhāpadas*,[2] so that a number of these accreted which were of minor importance (e.g. the *Sekhiyas*) and for breach of which mere admission sufficed for atonement. With this state of things the question cropped up naturally whether all the *Sikkhāpadas* in the code would be binding. In the Theravāda canon there is implicit evidence of a contention over the question and a bifurcation of views that persisted for a whole century after the Founder's decease (down to the Vesālī 'council').

The *Mahāparinibbāna Suttanta*, VI, 3, records that before his expiry at Kusinārā, the Buddha had given permission to the monks to dispense, if they liked, with the 'minor and very minor precepts'

[1] Part I, Sec. 5 (b). [2] See Part I, Sec. 5, pp. 69–70.

(*khuddānukkhuddāni sikkhāpadāni*). This matter, it is further reported, came up before the first monks' conference at Rājagaha after the Lord's decease and was duly debated. But as nobody could specify for certain which were of the minor category, it was decided that *all* of them must be retained and deemed equally binding.[1]

This is the Theravāda tradition. Read between the lines, the account suggests that, already among the early Buddhists, there had sprung up two views regarding Vinaya grounded on the question whether it was to be carried out to the letter or observed only in substance.

Between the two sections of monks—the thorough-going Vinaya-ists and the liberal interpreters—differences broke out which came up before the Vesālī 'council' a hundred years, as the canonical tradition is, after the 'Great Decease'. We are told that there was a prolonged trial of strength between the two sections; that the differences were reduced to ten moot-points at the council; that they were considered and adjudicated upon in favour of the 'thorough-goers' with clause-by-clause reference to the letter of the law.[2]

The moot-points placed before the 'council' appear a little differently in the canons of different sects;[3] none has any bearing on the *ethos* or *mores* of Saṅgha life. In the Theravāda enumeration, they are as follows:[4]

WHETHER IT IS ALLOWABLE TO—

(i) Preserve salt in a horn (*Siṅgiloṇakappo*)

(ii) Take food after noontide (*Dvaṅgulakappo*)

(iii) Take food after taking a meal at a different village (*Gāmantara-kappo*)

(iv) Perform *saṅghakamma* by two schismatic parties at the same *āvāsa* (*Āvāsakappo*)

(v) Hold a *saṅghakamma* and obtain the Bhikkhus' consent afterwards to ratify (*Anumatikappo*)

(vi) Do an act simply because it is the practice of the *Upajjhāya* (*Āciṇṇakappo*)

(vii) Eat curds after a meal (*Amathitakappo*)

(viii) Drink toddy (*Jalogipātakappo*)

(ix) Use a borderless rug or mat to sit upon (*Adasaka-nisīdana-kappo*)

(x) Receive gold and silver (*Jātarūpa-rajata-kappo*)

[1] Cullavagga, XI, 1, 9. [2] *Ibid*, XII, 2, 8–9.

[3] See W. Pachow's *A Comparative Study of the Prātimokṣa* (Santineketan, 1955), pp. 24–25.

[4] Cullavagga, XII, 1, 10, and 2, 7–8.

These points shot up into prodigies, because, in the view of a section of the primitive monk-community, they were matters of Vinaya, and Vinaya was the very rock-bed of Saṅgha life and must be preserved whole and entire; the least whittling down of it would weaken the foundation of the Saṅgha. Perhaps there were others who were not of this view: at any rate we are told in the Ceylonese chronicles that the old controversy was not set at rest by the decision of the Vesālī council, but was followed by the first 'Great Schism' (*Mahābheda*) which split the order into the two principal schools, *Theravāda* and *Mahāsāṅghika.*

The Theravāda was undoubtedly the inheritor of the view that insisted on the letter of the law, recognized no discrimination between major rules and minor, and even today wherever Theravāda Buddhism prevails, Ceylon, Thailand, Cambodia or Burma, the same sacrosanct view of the Vinaya prevails. In the Theravāda canon, the *regula* are preserved with more particular and meticulous care than in the canons of other sects or schools.

The Vinaya, as we have seen, belongs to 'basic Buddhism', that is Buddhism anterior to the rise of sects among Buddhists.[1] It was from this 'basic Buddhism', as is held by some scholars, that different streams of tradition emanated and passed into the canons of different sects and schools. The Theravāda tradition was that every one of the Vinaya rules was obligatory, but the great ancient Mahāsāṅghika work, *Mahāvastu,* which survives in the original and describes itself in the title as the initial section (*ādi*) of the Vinaya of the Lokottaravādins, a Mahāsāṅghika sect, contains, strangely enough, no monastic *regula* at all.[2]

The Vinaya, representing an essential part of 'Basic Buddhism', has naturally a place in the canons of all sects.

The Mahāsāṅghikas had the Vinaya in their canon, some texts of which were taken from Pāṭaliputra to China by Fa-hsien and are found in Chinese in Fa-hsien's own translation.[3] It does not vary substantially, so far as the rules are concerned, from the Theravāda Vinaya. The Vinaya works of the Sarvāstivādins (a school of much later growth than the ancient Mahāsāṅghika) are preserved in Tibetan. 'All the *Vinayadharas* of Tibet belong to the school of the Sarvāstivādins', says a Tibetan historiographer.[4] Large parts of Mūla-sarvāstivāda Vinaya in original Sanskrit have been discovered among the Gilgit Manuscripts. So far as the actual Vinaya rules,

[1] Part I, Sec. 5, p. 77.
[2] On the difference in contents between the *Vinayapiṭaka* and the *Mahāvastu,* see *The Buddha and Five After-Centuries,* pp. 146–147.
[3] Jointly with Buddhabhadra. See Nanjio, No. 1,119.
[4] See *Blue Annals,* Vol. II, p. 1064. It is the translation of the work of a fifteenth-century Tibetan historiographer, 'Gos lo-tsa-ba.

apart from their legendary settings, are concerned, there is substantial agreement among the texts of different sects.

The study of Vinaya as *canonical text* or part of the canon, never fell into desuetude; it was kept up by all sects, and the generation of ancient *Vinayadharas* was never extinct. Even the Mahāyānists studied the Vinaya, and Guṇaprabha, a Mahāyānist and pupil of Vasubandhu, is said to have been a consummate scholar in that section of canonical lore.[1]

But the preservation by different sects of the Vinaya rules in their respective canons does not mean that the rules in their actual bearing on Saṅgha life or, in other words, in their practical and operative aspect, were taken by all sects in the same way as by the Theravādin. The fundamental institutions of monastic life like Ordination, Rain-retreat, *Pavāraṇā*, *Kaṭhina*, etc., were governed by the canonical rules, but it is doubtful whether, except among the Theravādins, the *Uposatha* and the system of *Saṅghakamma* followed in actual practice the ancient Vinaya pattern. In minor and personal matters, relating to food, robes, footwear, bedding, etiquette, etc. there was a large latitude.

The dissent of the Mahāsāṅghikas from the Theravādin's strict and literal interpretation of the Vinaya may be traced from the very inception of that dissident school—from the *Mahābheda* itself. The Lokottaravādins among them, as we have seen, were not particular about inserting the *regula* in their Vinaya work. We have it on the authority of Paramārtha that a sect called the Kaulikas held the extreme view that the real teachings of the Buddha were not the Vinaya,[2] but Abhidhamma, and that 'a Bhikkhu may or may not have three robes for covering his body; may or may not reside in a monastery; and may or may not take his meal within the time-limit'.[3] This sect is mentioned by Vasumitra as a Mahāsāṅghika sect.[4]

Some scholars believe that the Mahāsāṅghika school was the nidus of Mahāyāna Buddhism.[5] Mahāyānist works like *Śūraṅgama Sūtra*, *Upāli-paripṛcchā*, *Bodhicaryāvatāra*, etc., contemplate Vinaya as cultivation of certain attitudes of mind and qualities of heart rather

[1] See for Guṇaprabha, Part IV, Sec. 6, p. 292.

[2] This is quite consistent with the docetic view of the Buddha entertained by the Mahāsāṅghika school. He could not have been in the Mahāsāṅghika concept a *Satthā*, i.e. a Law-giver.

[3] See Paul Demiéville's *L'origine des Sects Bouddhiques* (Melanges Chinois et Bouddique, Vol. I, 1931–32, pp. 19, 46).

[4] See Thomas's *History of Buddhist Thought*, p. 288. It is perhaps the same sect as is called 'Kaura Kullaka', one of the eighteen early schools of Buddhism, named in *Pag-sam-jon-zang* (Q.V.—Part IV, Sec. 1), a Tibetan history, p. 44 (S.C. Das's Ed.).

[5] 'The Mahāsāṅghikas became the starting point of the development of the Mahāyāna by their more liberal attitude and by some of their special theories'—Conze in *Buddhism: Its Essence and Development* (Oxford, 1951), p. 121.

than as observance of a set of rules.[1] Yet even if the Mahāyānists regarded it more as mental and moral discipline than as a system of rules and regulations, they did not go so far as to discard the rules—only they did not recognize them as 'categorical imperatives'. From the testimony of Hsüan-tsang and I-tsing it appears that in the seventh century AD there existed Mahāyānist saṅghas or groups of Mahāyānist monks who were meticulous in their observance of Vinaya rules.

In the great Mahābodhi Saṅghārāma at Gaya, says Hsüan-tsang, one thousand monks resided, 'all Mahāyānists of the Sthavira School, all perfect in Vinaya observances'.[2] In Kaliṅga (ancient Orissa) he reports the existence of ten *saṅghārāmas* with about 500 inmates 'who study the Great Vehicle according to the teaching of the Sthavira School'.[3] He speaks also of 100 monasteries in Ceylon where the monks 'follow the teachings of the Buddha according to the *dharma* of the Sthavira School of the Mahāyāna'.[4] There is no 'Sthavira School' in Mahāyāna Buddhism, and Hsüan-tsang's meaning must have been that all the monks he refers to were of Mahāyānist faith and yet were as particular about the observance of Vinaya rules as monks of the Theravāda school. Another instance of Hīnayānist Vinaya subsisting among a group of Mahāyānist monks is cited by him from Udyāna, then a small state on the Indian border on the Swat river to the north of Peshawar. Here was only a small handful of monks: 'they studied the Great Vehicle', but prohibited 'the use of charms' (i.e. they were not Tāntrics). Hsüan-tsang says about them that they had 'traditional knowledge' of the Vinaya of five Hīnayānist schools, viz. of the Sarvāstivādins, the Dharmaguptīyas, the Mahīśāsakas, the Kāśyapīyas, and the Mahāsāṅghikas.[5] I-tsing, coming to northern India three decades later than Hsüan-tsang, did not notice any outstanding difference in respect of Vinaya between the Mahāyānists and the Hīnayānists, who, in his opinion, differed only in the matter of the holy texts they studied and the cult-objects they worshipped.[6]

[1] (i) *Śuraṅgama Sūtra* is a great work of Mahāyāna philosophy, held in great esteem by Chinese Buddhist scholars. It was translated from its original (no longer found) into Chinese in Canton by Paramārtha with the help of a Chinese scholar in AD 705. *Re* Paramārtha, see Part IV, sec. 7. (ii) *Upāli-paripṛcchā* forms the ninth book of the Chinese *Daśādhyāya-Vinaya*. It purports to be a discourse given by the Buddha to Upāli about the Vinaya to be observed by followers of the Mahāyāna. See Anukul Chandra Banerji's *Sarvāstivāda Literature* (Calcutta, 1957), pp. 32–36. (iii) *Bodhicaryāvatāra* is a work by Śāntideva extant in original Sanskrit, describing the all-compassionate mind which a Bodhisattva must cultivate and the attributes of such a mind. He calls *this* the 'Vinaya of a Bodhisattva'. *Re* Śāntideva and *Bodhicaryāvatāra*, see Part IV, Sec. 5, p. 287.

[2] Beal's *Buddhist Records*, ii, p. 133. [3] *Ibid*, ii, p. 208.

[4] *Ibid*, ii, p. 247. [5] Beal's *Buddhist Records*, i, 121.

[6] Takakusu's *A Record of the Buddhist Religion*, etc. p. 15: 'Those who worship the Bodhisattva and read the Mahāyāna Sūtras are called Mahāyānists, while those who do not perform these are called Hīnayānists. There are two kinds of the so-called Mahāyāna, first, the Mādhyamika: second, the Yoga'.

Thus in the AD centuries, in those monasteries that were not exclusive to any particular sect and where both Hīnayānist and Mahāyānist monks lived together, the overall monastic discipline was uninterrupted. No 'vinaya', in the sense of *monastic regula*, was developed in Mahāyāna Buddhism, but the ancient 'Hīnayānist' Vinaya, no longer observed in each and every particular, sufficed as a basis for discipline in a monastery. The *modus vivendi* may be described in the words of a Buddhist English scholar of the Mahāyānist School: 'A Mahāyānist Bhikṣu is not one who belongs to a Mahāyāna Order in the sense of a separate religious corporation, but simply one who, observing in fundamentals the same monastic discipline as his Hīnayāna brother, devotes himself to the study and practice of the Mahāyāna *sūtras*. Similarly a Hīnayāna monk is simply one who follows the Hīnayāna *sūtras*. No Buddhist country, regardless of the school to which it belongs, has a monopoly of the Vinaya.'[1]

Of the sects that emerged in early Buddhism—eighteen being their traditional count, though the actual number as it seems, far exceeded it and also varied from age to age, the formation of a sect being easy under the 'Schism (*Saṅghabheda*) rules'[2]—the orthodox Theravāda insisted on one view of Vinaya, while the Mahāsāṅghika held a somewhat different one and perhaps the other sects and sub-sects wavered between the two.

The Mahāyāna movement started in the early centuries of the Christian era. It introduced and established a 'neo-Buddhism' with a system of new concepts and a new outlook on the aim and purpose of spiritual life. It did not produce sects, but schools of philosophy in which there was a complete re-orientation of interest from outward observances to the inner contemplative life. Out of its emphasis on *Bhakti* (Devotion) as fundamental in the religion, the Mahāyāna evolved an elaborate ritualism of *Pūjā* (Worship), but by-passed the ancient Vinaya. To Mahāyānist thinking, the Vinaya had a use and significance different from what the Theravāda conceived: its *raison d'être* was to lead the devotee's mind to a state most favourable to cultivation of the Higher Wisdom.

'In explaining to you the rules of the Vinaya', says the Buddha to his assembled disciples in the *Śūraṅgama Sūtra*, 'I have frequently emphasised three good lessons, namely, (i) the only way to keep the Precepts is first to be able to concentrate the mind; (ii) by keeping the Precepts you will be able to attain *samādhi*; (iii) by means of

[1] *Survey of Buddhism* by Bhikṣu Sangharakṣita (Bangalore, 1957), pp. 147–148.
[2] About the rise of sects through schisms, see *The Buddha and Five After-Centuries*, pp. 123–139.

samādhi one develops intelligence and wisdom'.[1] The Vinaya was thus not an object in itself—its importance or significance was little unless it were helpful in making the mind receptive to 'intelligence and wisdom'.

This relaxed emphasis on the Vinaya *regula* makes a difference in the picture of saṅgha life in the AD centuries.

A Saṅgha is no longer an organization founded on and sustained by the Vinaya: it is not the regimen that holds it together. We have seen that the '*Āvāsakappo*' had been one of the moot-points at the 'council' of Vesālī: it turned on the question whether it was allowable for two schismatic parties to hold *Uposatha* and perform *Saṅghakamma* in the same *āvāsa*. But it ceased to be an issue; sect was no longer a separatist principle in saṅgha life: monks of different sects could live in the same saṅgha. For this there is evidence both from epigraphs discovered in the monastic ruins and the eye-witness accounts of the Chinese pilgrims. Although there were monasteries exclusively occupied by Mahāyānist or by Hīnayānist monks, or by monks of a particular sect, co-existence of different sects in a saṅgha seems to have been the normal practice.[2] While monks of different Hīnayāna sects and both Hīnayānists and Mahāyānists lived in common residence in the same monastic establishment, their views on the obligatory character of the Vinaya rules could not have been the same. Perhaps, with the changed outlook on Vinaya in the later centuries, established ancient institutions like *Uposatha* and *Saṅghakamma* ceased also at some stage (except among monks of the Theravāda school) to conform in practice to the ancient canonical rules.

Saṅghakamma had been a most important function of the Saṅgha. The Vinaya rules define its strictly 'republican' character, precluding all personal control or dictatorial interference. But in the AD centuries, both epigraphs and the Chinese accounts make us aware of the existence in the monasteries of 'Chiefs' or 'Abbots' or 'Principals'.[3] What their exact functions were is not specifically known, but it seems that the appointment of a 'Chief' in a monastery became customary even in Theravāda establishments: the custom prevails to this day in the Asian countries of Theravāda Buddhism.[4] None of the Chinese pilgrims from Fa-hsien to I-tsing whose object in coming

[1] In Goddard's translation quoted in Lin Yutang's *Wisdom of India* (1944—Original Edition), p. 505.

[2] See for instance the names of different sects appearing in Sārnāth inscriptions—Part III, Sec. 6, p. 216.

[3] A controlling personal authority of this kind never existed in a primitive Saṅgha. It is inconsistent with Vinaya rules. See *Early Buddhist Monachism*, pp. 145–146.

[4] In Ceylon, Burma, Thailand and Cambodia, there is always a chief or an abbot, called by different names or designations in different countries, as the head of a monastic establishment.

out to India was to observe the Vinaya practices of Indian monks seems to have seen the holding of a *Saṅghakamma*. We look in vain in their *Ki*'s for an allusion to this fundamental Saṅgha institution.[1] It must have taken some form not prescribed in the Vinaya.

[1] The question whether Saṅghakamma was practised according to the ancient rules in Indian monasteries (specially in non-Theravāda ones) in the seventh century AD must be left to negative evidence. The nearest approach to a *saṅghakamma* found in the Chinese records is had from the Korean monk Prajñāvarman's description of what he observed at Nālandā: 'If something happened in the monastery, all the monks of the monastery got together to discuss the matter. The monks, one by one, with folded hands, reported the matter. If one of the monks objected, nothing could be done. If any one did anything without the consent of all the monks of the monastery, he would be forced to leave the establishment. If there were differences of opinion, they would try to convince the other group with reasons. No force was used to convince.' (See Part IV, Appendix). This is but faintly reminiscent of the ancient saṅghakamma with its elaborate rules of procedure.

3

BHAKTI

in Later Buddhism

BASED on the Vinaya and with the Saṅghakamma as its functioning organ, the primitive Saṅgha took as a directive the Lord's dictum that so long as Bhikkhus 'assembled unitedly and assembled frequently' ('*abhinnhaṁ sannipātā sannipāta-bahulā*'),[1] they would prosper and not decline. The meeting hall (*Upaṭṭhāna-sālā*) was, therefore, the hub of saṅgha life, and we have elsewhere referred to its importance in a primitive monk-settlement.[2] Yet when we pass on to monastic remains of later times, we observe that there the *Cetiyaghara* takes the place of central importance.

The functional importance of the *Upaṭṭhāna-sālā* was in connection with the Vinaya and the implementation of its rules; the *Cetiyaghara* was a place of congregational worship. The emphasis in saṅgha life had evidently shifted in these centuries from Vinaya to the cultivation of *Bhakti* and its ritual expression in worship of the *Stūpa* or the Buddha-image. It is an index to a deeper change in the spirit of the religion.

Bhakti has encroached largely on the system of spiritual training and self-culture deemed essential to the *Dhamma* enunciated in the canon. 'Only a little *Bhakti*', says Upagupta to Māra in the *Divyāvadāna* legend, 'becomes for the wise fruitful of *Nirvāṇa*.'[3] But it is decidedly not in this line that *Nibbāna* is led up to in the system of the early (Theravāda) scripture.

A school of religious thought, which may have been more ancient than Buddhism or at least as ancient, had existed in India which, deriving from Vedic and Upaniṣadic doctrines and speculations, turned away, like Buddhism, from Vedic sacrificial rituals: it insisted on single-minded devotion to the object of adoration as the only way of salvation.[4] This was the school of *Bhakti*: its fundamental tenets

[1] Mahāparinibbāna Suttanta, I, 6. [2] Part I, Sec. 4, p. 60.

[3] '*Svalpā hi atra bhaktir'bhavati matimatāṁ nirvāṇa-phaladā*'—Cowell and Neil's *Divyāvadāna*, p. 360. The words of Upagupta recall Śāṇḍilya's *Bhakti-sūtra*, II, 76: *Laghvapi bhaktādhikāre mahatkṣepakamaparasarva hānāt* (Tr.: In the path of the devotee, an act of *Bhakti*, ever so slight, is destructive of great sins, because of its doing away with all other things)—See Vol. VII (*Bhakti-Śāstra*) of the Sacred Books of the Hindus Series, Panini Office, Allahabad, 1912.

[4] See R. G. Bhandarkar's article on the Origin of the Bhakti School in *Indian Antiquary*, January, 1912.

are collected in two Sanskrit works in *sūtra* form—Śāṇḍilya's (earlier) and Nārada's.[1]

The influence of this school permeated religious thought in India; it persists to our day in various forms, and in both Brāhmaṇism and Buddhism, its ferment is unmistakably felt.

The term *Bhakti* is used in Indian religious terminology in a connotation hardly covered by its current English equivalent 'Devotion'. The term has a specific significance: it has also a range of nuances. It implies a subjective state—an attitude and condition of heart and mind in which the devotee turns from the ethical and other aspects of religion to prayer and adoration and complete self-surrender to the adored. To one who is settled in this attitude and condition of mind, it is, as Śāṇḍilya in his *Bhakti-sūtra* puts it, the 'idea of the Lord', rather than his ordainments or teachings, that occupies the forefront of mind and heart and its 'fruits' appear 'in reverence and worship paid to the adored, the casting out of all unclean thoughts and passions, the celebration of the praise of the Lord and the wish to continue to live in his service and for his sake alone'.[2]

Thus interpreted and understood, *Bhakti* is a *sine qua non* in all religions that are 'religions of grace'. Religions of this type are soteriological: they postulate a Saviour. To him it is left to grant the fruits of a man's work and endeavour—to bestow on the devotee the ultimate salvation. The Saviour must be propitiated, not by holy living alone, but by refuge (*Śaraṇa*) being sought in him, by adoration (*Vandanā*), prayer and supplication (*Stava* and *Stuti*) and by ritual worship (*Pūjā*).

Over against these 'religions of grace', there are faiths and creeds in which a Saviour has no place. The salvation, the goal of religious life, however it may be conceived or in whatever term expressed, is, in their view, not a gift but an attainment: to be reached by steadily progressing stage-to-stage along a Way (*Magga*). Hence the man of faith must rouse volition and self-effort—regard religion as primarily 'practical' and concerned with the proper direction and control of the will. Basic in this view, is the 'Moralist' theory of religion of which Kant was the most influential exponent in Europe in the eighteenth century.

In the early Buddhist (Theravāda) scripture, two terms, which belong to what is called the 'psychology of religion'[3] appear, viz.

[1] These two *Sūtras* (with commentary and translation) are included in the *Sacred Books of the Hindus*, Panini Office, Allahabad, Vol. VII (*Bhakti-śāstra*).

[2] See article on *Bhakti* in the *Encyclopaedia of Religion and Ethics*. This is the gist of the aphorisms of Śāṇḍilya, as given in the article.

[3] See Ch. I on 'The Psychological Approach to Religion' in Dr W. B. Selbie's *Psychology of Religion* (Oxford: Clarendon Press, 1926).

Saddhā (Sans. *Śraddhā*) and *Bhatti* (Sans. *Bhakti*).[1] The former implies in this scripture a firm faith and conviction that the Way of Dhamma (the *Magga*) must lead one assuredly to the goal of *Nibbāna*. The term *Bhakti* is of rare occurrence in it and has nowhere the implications and nuances that belong to its use in Mahāyānist as well as in non-Buddhist scripture. Yet the two trends in the 'psychology of religion' that are typified by *Śraddhā* and *Bhakti* appear side by side even in Theravāda Buddhism. Along with the idea of volitional self-effort appears also the idea of a Saviour who has to be propitiated and in whom refuge (*Saraṇa*) is sought.[2]

Where the main emphasis lay in the Founder's original teachings cannot be known except inferentially from the system that stemmed from them and is presented in the scripture of the Theravāda.

In this system, the religion is significantly described as the Way (*Magga*): it is specified as the 'Noble Eightfold Path' (*Ariya aṭṭhaṅgika magga*), and no system, it is affirmed, can claim to be a religion in which the 'eightfold path' is not laid down; progress along this path is by stages and at its end is the goal of *Nibbāna*. The stages are indicated by key-terms:

'*Sīla, Samādhi, Paññā, Vimutti*—these were realized by the Lord; knowing them, he proclaimed them to his followers and entered into Parinibbāna.'[3]

What these terms technically formulate amounts to a system purely psycho-ethical in its character; *saddhā* is essential to one who wants to follow it, as several *suttas* (especially the *Cetokhila Sutta*[4]) inculcate. But from the system thus formulated, *Bhakti*, as conceived in a 'religion of grace', must seem alien. Central in it, is the 'practical' concept[5]—that of self-effort towards a goal and its attainment, which has no implication with 'the grace of a Saviour' or the need to invoke his grace or for the associated acts of prayer and worship.

Its most succinct exposition is in Buddhaghosa's manual *Visuddhimagga*.[6] While it takes as basic the concepts of *Sīla, Samādhi* and *Paññā*, it is absolutely untouched by any *Bhakti* concept and gives the go-by entirely in its scheme of religious practice to acts like

[1] Śāṇḍilya distinguished *Bhakti* which is a specific concept from *Śraddhā* which is a general concept (*Naiva śraddhā tu sādhāraṇyāt*—Śāṇḍilya's *Bhakti-sūtra*, II, 24).
[2] Mahāparinibbāna Suttanta, V, 62.
[3] *Ibid*, IV, 3 (*Gāthā*—partly translated here).
[4] In the *Majjhima Nikāya*.
[5] *Tumhehi kiccaṁ ātappaṁ akhātāro Tathāgatā* (Tr: You yourself must put forth exertion, for the Tathāgatas are but Signposts)—*Dhammapada*, 276.
[6] *Re* Buddhaghosa and the *Visuddhimagga*, see Part IV, Sec. 2.

'taking refuge', singing lauds and offering worship. This authentic manual of Theravāda Buddhism thus contrasts sharply with what may be regarded as its counterpart in Mahāyāna Buddhism, Śāntideva's *Śikṣā-samuccaya*, in which the place of 'prayer and worship' is pronounced.[1]

Yet the concepts of *Bhakti* appear in Theravāda Buddhism as well. The formula of *Ti-saraṇa*, first invented for use in the ceremony of Ordination,[2] ripens into a credo; the compassionate (*Kāruṇika*) aspect of the Lord is iteratively stressed; the poetical manuals which form a group in the *Suttapiṭaka* of the scripture—*Thera-therī-gāthā*, *Apadāna*, *Petavatthu* and *Vimāna-vatthu*—abound in passages that refer to the efficacy of worship-offering to the Buddha (though no image of him had been invented yet) and the ritual worship of the *Stūpa* and the *Dhātu* (Holy Relics). The *Pūjā*, which in the *Dhammapada*[3] is a mental act or attitude, becomes in these later canonical works a ritual performance.

These notes in Theravāda Buddhism are indicative of a strengthening and upsurge of the *Bhakti* element in the religion. It eventuated in trends that slowly materialized in institutions, which Buddhism in its primitive form knows nothing of. Perhaps it was through the lay mind that these trends came to maturity. While for the monks the discipline and doctrine of the Way was of primary importance, for the mass of lay Buddhists, *Bhakti*-offering in the form of prayer and worship became the essence of the faith. We have touched upon the interactive effects of intercourse that existed in Buddhism between monkhood and laity[4] and no wonder these institutions were accepted, canonized and adopted by the Saṅgha. In course of time they were incorporated in Saṅgha life.

a. STŪPA-WORSHIP: PHASES OF DEVELOPMENT

The origin of *stūpa*-worship in Buddhism is obscure, nor is it lighted by the *stūpa*-legend elaborately woven into the *Mahāparinibbāna Suttanta*. Whether Buddhism inherited it from some practice of folk religion of higher antiquity, or itself initiated it, is a question that research has not tackled yet. But *stūpa*-worship goes back to the early days of Buddhism: it is one of its fundamental institutions.

Besides its mention in later texts of Theravāda scripture, the practice of *stūpa*-worship prior to Asoka is proved by his Nigālīsāgara

[1] *Re* Śāntideva and the *Śikṣāsamuccaya*, see Part IV, Sec. 5.
[2] Mahāvagga, I, 12, 4.
[3] See *Dhammapada*, 195–196, where '*pūjā*' means obviously the simple paying of honour and reverence. *Pūjā* is not conceived there as a ritual, but as a mental act.
[4] See Introduction.

pillar inscription.[1] If the Asoka legends are any indication, it was during his reign that large-sized *stūpas* were constructed at several centres in his empire for ceremonial public worship and *stūpa*-worship spread as a popular institution. The exhortation of Soṇa, the Brāhmaṇa who is said to have distributed the body-relics of the Lord from his funeral pyre, '*Vittharikā hontu disāsu thūpā*' (Let *stūpas* spread in all directions), reflects perhaps the popular enthusiasm for *stūpa*-worship in Asoka's reign.[2]

An initial problem posed by Buddhist *stūpa*-worship is: whether it was monks or lay men who introduced it into Buddhism?

Out of the training and discipline of monks, concerned for the most part with doctrines and their exegesis in *Abhidhamma* philosophy, *stūpa-pūjā* could hardly have taken rise. Regarded from any angle, a rite of this character can hardly be said to have any root in the formulated doctrines or in the fundamentals, defined as *Sīla*, *Samādhi*, *Paññā* or *Vimutti*, of the faith. None of these can have any relation to or be said to be advanced by *stūpa*-worship. With regard to the rite itself, significantly enough, the monk mind and the lay mind were never at one.

The rite, however, was invested with the sanctity of the canon: set down as an ordainment of the Lord in the *Mahāparinibbāna Suttanta*, but is converted there into worship of holy relics—the holy mound being regarded as a reliquary. *Stūpa-pūjā* is identified with *Sarīra-pūjā*. On the other hand we find the Buddha himself enjoining the disciples not to occupy themselves with *sarīra-pūjā*, but leave it to the laity.[3] Nāgasena in a later age comments in his reply to Milinda that *Sarīra-pūjā* was meant for the laity, while for monks (*Jinaputtas*) the things that mattered were the doctrines and the discipline.[4] It seems that for a long time after *stūpa*-worship had received canonical sanction and been accepted as a rite and institution of the religion, the monkish mind was averse to it, though a time came when it became the practice in every monastery to have a *stūpa* installed in the prayer hall.

Before this form of worship became universally prevalent among all Buddhists, both lay men and monks, it had to go through two phases—first, a lay ritual found place in the monk-made canon and was invested with a sacramental character, and next, the canonical

[1] In the village of Nīglīvā in the Nepalese *tarai* existed a stūpa dedicated to one of the Buddha's mythical predecessors Koṇāgamana. Asoka visited it some time before his visit to Lumbinī and enlarged it to double its former size. '*Konākamanasa thūbe dutiyaṁ vaḍhite*, etc.'—A. C. Sen's *Asoka's Edicts*, p. 125.

[2] I have discussed the probable date of the *Mahāparinabbāna Suttanta* in its enlarged version in the Theravāda scripture in *The Buddha and Five After-Centuries*, p. 47. The *gāthā*, in which Soṇa's exhortation finds place, occurs in the *Mahāparinibbāna Suttanta*, VI, 59.

[3] Mahāparinibbāna Suttanta, V, 24.

[4] *Milindapañha*, IV, 3, 24–27.

concept of the *stūpa* as a memorial was converted into a symbol or representation of Divine Presence.

In the engravings of Sanchi sculpture, there are several representations of *stūpa*-worship.[1] It is shown as a congregational and ceremonial worship with music and floral offerings. But in most representations there are just half a dozen worshippers—in others the worshippers are only a pair, male and female. This last, the private and individualistic worship, seems to have been the primitive form. What is remarkable, however, is that no monk appears and the worshippers by their habiliments are all lay men and women. They are apparently making the offering of *Bhakti* to a recognized holy symbol.

How the monks interpreted *stūpa*-worship in the canon appears from chapter V (26–31) and chapter VI (50–61) of the *Mahāparinibbāna Suttanta*. This monk-made manifesto of the *stūpa*-cult explains why and to whom a *stūpa* should be erected and why it is worthy of worship. It touches also on its origin in the Lord's own ordainment and gives an account of the building of the first ten *stūpas* over the relics of his body.

The *Suttanta* text undoubtedly belongs to a time when to this kind of worship, having already become a widespread popular practice, the monks desired to impart the canonical sanction. The text explains and authorizes. On its genesis, the following observation by Professor James throws light: 'Everywhere it seems that ritual as a product of unreflected habit normally has preceded the development of specific ideas concerning the how and why of what has been done when the activity has been of a purely practical nature; the ritual enjoined by custom has in the process of time required justification and explanation in terms of a supernatural sanction'[2]—which in the present case is ordainment by the Lord himself.

The *Stūpa* is regarded as only a memorial in the canonical text—a memorial of the noblest kind reserved for specified classes of mortals who deserve such commemoration (*Thūpāraha*: Sans. *Stūpārha*). They are not exclusively those pre-eminent in the field of religion: a righteous ruler (*Dhammika dhammarājā*) also is among the *Thūpārahas*. It is said that the ritual worship of a *stūpa* 'with garlands or incense or paint' redounds to what is called '*cittapasāda*', i.e. a tranquil and blissful state of mind, induced by contemplation

[1] See *The Monuments of Sanchi* by Sir John Marshall and Alfred Foucher, Vol. II, Plates 12, 15, 26, 32, 33, 36, 41, 43, 45, 47, 48, 60, 62, 63. Of these, Plate 36 shows public worship with many worshippers and a band of musicians; Plates 41, 43, 62 and 63 show six worshippers; Plates 45, 47, 48 and 60 show only a pair, male and female.

[2] *Myth and Ritual in the Ancient Near East* by Dr E. O. James (London: Thames and Hudson, 1958), p. 294.

of the memory of a person of supreme holiness or greatness.[1] It is not suggested that any specific spiritual benefit accrues from it.

While this was originally the monkish view of the *stūpa* and the efficacy of *stūpa*-worship, the popular conception seems to have been widely at variance. It was not the limited benefit of canonical definition, 'tranquillity of mind', that was sought by the lay *stūpa*-worshipper, nor did the *stūpa* stand in his eyes as no more than a sacred memorial.

The *stūpa* was regarded by him not as embodying the 'memory' of the Lord, but the 'idea' of him. In other words, it stood as a symbol of the divine presence: the Lord himself supposed to be symbolically present in the sacred mound enshrining his *dhātu* (Body-relics). Prayers were offered to the *stūpa* itself; rites of worship performed; boons of all sorts, both spiritual and secular, solicited—a complete tergiversation from the idea of a Lord deceased to that of a living Lord with boons to dispense. To worship and circumambulate it was not a mere emotional satisfaction, but a spiritual gain—a gain so great and enduring that it availed the worshipper till his final *nirvāṇa*.[2]

It was the popular, as distinguished from the canonical or monkish conception of the *stūpa* and *stūpa*-worship. It prevailed in the long run. The *stūpa* became a symbol of divine presence as manifestly as a Buddha-image.

The evidence of this comes from an ancient text, an *Avalokana* (or *Avalokita*) *Sūtra*, which does not exist separately, but is found incorporated with the Mahāsāṅghika Vinaya work, *Mahāvastu*, and from a version of this ancient *sūtra* long extracts are given in the seventeenth chapter (on Prayer and Worship) of Śāntideva's *Śikṣā-samuccaya*.[3] Evidently this ancient *sūtra* gives the popular view of *stūpa* and *stūpa*-worship, while the monkish view appears in the text of the *Mahāparinibbāna Suttanta*.

Here the sacred mound is not regarded as a memorial, nor are the fruits of its worship confined to '*Cittapasāda*'. The worship is not a simple token offering of 'garlands, incense or paint', but is attended with all the ritualism of image-worship—circumambulation (*Pradakṣiṇā*); obeisance with folded palms; miscellaneous offerings of flowers, garlands, incense, buntings, clothes (spread round the mound), blankets and fabrics (*Cīvara*) of cotton and silk; placing of lights

[1] Mahāparinibbāna Suttanta, V, 26.

[2] *Tathāgatasya yaḥ satkāraṁ kuryāt puṣpa-mālya-gandha-dvajapatākehi vā'th'anulepanehi na tasya puṇyasya śakyaṁ paryantamadhigantuṁ' . . . yāvanna parinirvāṇaṁ na tasya paryantaḥ*.—Senart's *Mahāvastu*, II, p. 362.

[3] See *Ibid*, pp. 363 ff. See also Bendall's *Śikṣā-samuccaya* (1957), pp. 297 ff. 'Senart's hypothesis', says Bendall, 'that the *sūtra* is an interpolation in the *Mahāvastu* is rendered probable by Śāntideva's citations from it as a separate work and by the independence of the Tibetan version.'—*Ibid*, p. 297, footnote 6.

(*Dīpa*) and striking up of instrumental music (*Vādya*); cleansing and spreading perfumed paste; collecting offered flowers (*Nirmālya*) save those offered by the worshipper himself; and, as a special offering, the donation of a *Chatra* (umbrella to serve as top-covering for the *stūpa*). The boons expected by the worshipper are not of mere spiritual benefit, but are also those calculated for advancement in wordly life. 'He becomes rich and wealthy with an abundant treasury who bows with folded palms at the *stūpa* of the Buddha.'[1]

Stūpa-worship spread with the spread of Buddhism all over the country. Historical reminiscence of a time when the whole of India was dotted with *stūpas* appears not only in Buddhist legends, but also from an opposite angle in the *Mahābhārata* epic.

The *stūpa* was an outstanding emblem of Buddhist faith and the adherents of Brāhmaṇism regarded its popularity with a jaundiced eye. They gave it a contemptuous name, *Eḍūka*, a structure of rubbish.[2] In a section of the *Mahābhārata*, the degeneracy of the *Kaliyuga* (Iron Age) is described in a prophetic vein. One of the marks of this degeneracy is said to be that 'the earth shall be covered with *Eḍūkas* instead of with temples to the gods'.[3]

In the Buddhist Asokan legends, as we have seen, the time when the whole land was dotted with them is taken to be in Asoka's reign. The tradition is recorded in the Ceylonese chronicles. 'From the offerings made on behalf of the Buddha in various ways and in various cities', says the author of the *Mahāvaṁsa* in reference to Asoka's reign, 'various festivals are constantly celebrated in honour of *Thūpas*.'[4] Hsüan-tsang, relying on this ancient tradition, describes almost every *stūpa* seen by him as 'built by Asoka-rājā'.

But the golden age of *stūpa*-building was not conterminous with Asoka's reign: it covered the reigns of the post-Maurya dynasties of northern India and also of the early Sātavāhana dynasts. The greatest *stūpas* seem to have been post-Mauryan.

Extremely few, however, of the thousands which once dotted the land, both north and south of the Vindhyas, remain above ground. Of those, sunken or still standing, four kinds may be distinguished:

(I) A *Stūpa* set up for public worship, round which Buddhist festivals used to be celebrated.

Such *stūpas* are found as far north as Taxila down to the banks of

[1] '*Āḍḍyo dhanī bhoti prabhūta-kośaḥ yo añjalibhir' namati buddha-stūpam.*'—Bendall's *Sikṣā-samuccaya*, p. 308. Cf. also Senart's *Mahāvastu*, II, pp. 362–364.

[2] See *St Petersberg Dictionary* under *Eḍūka*. A Pali variant of this word, *Eḷuka*, also is found. It has been suggested that the word is of Dravidian origin. See article on *Sanskrit Eḍūka-Pali Eluka* by F. R. Allchin in *Bulletin of the School of Oriental and African Studies*, London University, Vol. XX (1957), pp. 1–4.

[3] See *Mahābhārata* (Asiatic Society's Ed.), Vanaparva, vv. 13074–13076, or the Poona Ed., Araṇyaparva, III, 188, vv. 64–66.

[4] Turnour's *Mahāwaṁso* (1889), p. 19.

the Krishnā river. Those at Sanchi and Bhilsa in northern India and at Amarāvatī and Nāgārjunakoṇḍa in the south were of great dimensions, with surrounding balustrade and tall gateways (*toraṇas*). Some of them are distinguished by the name *Mahā* (*Great*)-*cetiya*. The reliquary *cetiyas* of Amarāvatī and Nāgārjunakoṇḍa have now fallen to ground-level. There is no doubt that from time to time they were enlarged in size, and also grew richer and richer with sculptural decorations contributed by lay worshippers, as *stūpa*-worship flourished among them. *Stūpas* for public worship existed in Asoka's time—their worship had become by then a canonical institution. Curiously, however, though Asoka himself is described as a zealous '*stūpa*-builder', only a single legend relates the foundation of a *stūpa* by him—the 'Great Tope' of Sanchi. The story has to be taken on its own merits.

It is said that Asoka, posted at Ujjainī as a provincial governor under his father Bindusāra, had an occasion to visit Vidiśā, where he fell in love with and married the daughter of a local merchant. Later at the instance of his mother-in-law, who seems to have been a Buddhist, he erected a *stūpa* at Sanchi just to gratify her. Asoka was not a Buddhist then. The 'Great Tope' was built up piecemeal; it has a very ancient brick-core, a later encasing of stone and mortar, and, under the Śuṅga kings, it was enlarged and its balustrade sculptured, and perhaps still later was provided with its magnificent gateways.[1]

(II) A miniature *Stūpa* in a monastery chapel (*cetiyaghara*). The *cetiyaghara*, which was originally unknown and is not mentioned in the scripture among the requirements of a monk-settlement, became afterwards a necessary adjunct.

The *Vinayapiṭaka* knows only of the *Upaṭṭhāna-sālā* (meeting hall) where congregational services were held. In the more primitive among the *guhā*-monasteries of western India, the *cetiyaghara* is not seen. At Bhājā, a collection of *stūpas*, most of them probably votive offerings, is found stowed away in one chamber, and at other places a *stūpa* may be seen standing outside a set of caves. The ancient *upaṭṭhāna-sālā*, it seems, gave place in course of time to the *cetiya-ghara*, which in its turn developed into a *maṇḍapa*, a roofed and pillared pavilion. At the far end of it was recessed a *stūpa* sanctuary.

A custom of high antiquity in India is to pass round a person of reverence or a holy object, keeping him or the object on the right hand. It is called *Pradakṣiṇā*—'to go round keeping the object of reverence on the right'. In the scriptural legends a visitor always

[1] For the legend of Asoka's building a stūpa at Sanchi, see Geiger's *Mahāvaṁsa* (Pali Text Society), pp. 100–101, and also *Dīpavaṁsa* (ed. by Oldenberg), pp. 42, 63, 147, 168 and 370.

behaves thus when about to take leave of the Buddha. The custom became a ceremonial rite in *stūpa*-worship and a path for circumambulation was usually provided in a *cetiyaghara* for the *pradakṣiṇā*. Passage along this path was through the pillared aisles. There are several unfinished circumambulatory paths seen in the *cetiyagharas* of the cave-settlements, the rocks behind the *stūpa* having been found to be intractable. *Pradakṣiṇā* was so necessary a ritual observance that at the Nāgārjunakoṇḍa monastic sites, it is seen as a sort of conventional requirement in sanctuary construction. The circumambulatory path is seen merely aligned to symbolize the observance, but is actually too narrow to be traversed.

(III) Ex-voto *Stūpa*: A custom grew up among lay Buddhists to donate a miniature *stūpa* to a saṅgha as votive offering.

When such an offering was received, it was the practice to install it outside but in close proximity to the *cetiyaghara* or in the precincts of a temple when (in the Gupta Age) Buddha-temples were built separately and outside the monastery building. A large number of these votive *stūpas*, both large and small in size, may be seen at Nālandā, Boddhgaya, Ratnagiri and several other sites. Many of them are so alike in size and shape as to suggest that they could be obtained ready-made. Perhaps they were put up in stone-cutters' and sculptors' shops for sale. They are beautifully executed and not too large to be portable.

(IV) According to the canon, a *stūpa* is a reliquary memorial, a *Dagoba* as its name is in Ceylon, meaning *Dhātugarbha*, i.e. 'with relics in its womb'. Yet the *dhātu*-content was often supposititious and few *stūpas* in India have yielded relics. The actual relic-containing *stūpas* were some of the *Mahā-cetiyas*. But whether a *dagoba* or not, the Holy Mound was a symbol of divine presence and continued till the last days of Buddhism in India to receive adoration from monks in their monasteries and from lay people in public places.

This symbol-worship seems never to have been wholly replaced by image-worship, and between the two forms, as we shall presently see, there was a long competition or contention, intriguing signs and indications of which may be read in the monastic remains.

b. WORSHIP OF THE BUDDHA-IMAGE

Symbol-worship preceded image-worship by several centuries in Buddhist history.

There is a controversy of long standing among experts in iconography about the origin of the Buddha-image. The issue lies between the rival claims of two ancient schools of sculpture—Gāndhāra in the far north-west of India and Mathura in the east. It is reasonably certain, however, that the Buddha-image came into existence in the first century, either BC or AD.

In a frieze of Mathura sculpture, conjecturally dated in the first century BC, an image of the Buddha appears along with other worshipped symbols. It is one of the earliest specimens of a Buddha-image, figuring the Superman (*Mahāpurisa*) with the characteristic physiognomical marks, as the Buddha is conceived in ancient scriptural legends.

Here at Mathura, it seems, the cult of *Bhakti*, of which the nascent expressions appear in the later passages of the Theravāda canon, had already come to birth before the image was thought of or designed. But the mind has to make a conscious effort to associate a symbol like the Bodhi tree, the Wheel or the Mound with the idea of the Lord. The devotee would still yearn to have before him something more directly evocative, concretely expressive, and immediately representative of his Lord. To supply this spiritual need seems to have been the urge and motive for designing an image.

That this yearning and this need actually existed when worship was confined in Buddhism to symbols, there are indications in *stūpa*-sculpture itself as well as in literary texts.

Early Buddhist sculpture never represents the figure of the Buddha, though a Bodhisattva (i.e. a previous incarnation of the Buddha in a *Jātaka*) is represented. Whatever the reason for this reticence, the suppressed desire for a Buddha-image seems conveyed by several features of the sculpture of Sanchi, Bhilsa and Barhut. Footprints are shown; the descent of the Lord from Heaven to earth is shown by a footprint on the lowest rung of a ladder and another on the topmost one and, as Stella Kramrisch has pointed out, in one Sanchi panel footprints, tree-motif, wheel and umbrella are combined in a vertical succession, 'alluding in a childish way to the bodily appearance of a man'.[1]

The Māra-Upagupta legend in the *Divyāvadāna*, the legend of a great apostle of *Bhakti* who lived in Mathura once upon a time and converted Māra, is the clearest expression of the yearning for a Buddha-image of one inspired with *Bhakti*. The internal evidence of the legend points to a time when the Buddha-image had not been invented; yet so strong was Upagupta's yearning for it that he had recourse to Māra's magic to conjure it up before his eyes.[2] It is a legend of Mathura, and it is in a sculptured frieze of Mathura, as already noted, that one of the earliest of Buddha-images in the figure of a *Mahāpurisa* appears.

The impulse or the plastic motive behind the images of Gāndhāra

[1] *Indian Sculpture* (Heritage of India Series), p. 24.

[2] The legend is given and these points are brought out in *The Buddha and Five After-Centuries*, pp. 234–239.

seems on the other hand to have emanated from a different source—from the anthropomorphism of Greek mythology. Gāndhāra had received Hellenistic culture from Bactria, and there can be no doubt that there were Buddhists in Gāndhāra who had come under the influence of that culture and desired to see the Lord in an image of idealized human likeness. Right from the earliest specimens, Greek traits are kept up in Gāndhāran images—in the halo and the toga-like drapery.

The question whether Mathura or Gāndhāra gave the Buddha-image to the devotee is a somewhat academic one. The really significant fact is that, round the beginning of the Christian era, the devotee had something that could evoke and satisfy his emotion of *Bhakti* more immediately and completely than a purely symbolic cult-object could do. Whether in the *Mahāpurisa* style of Mathura or the 'Indian Apollo' style of Gāndhāra, the image, irrespective of its technical points of iconography, attracted *Bhakti* and demanded worship.

Yet, after the invention of the image, a somewhat disturbing question became unavoidable: whether to retain the traditional symbol-worship or to adopt the image. The question was of some importance with worshippers, both monks and lay men.

In the remote past—long, long before the image had been invented—the question, it seems, had been anticipated. A legend reports that the monks of Jetavana once wished to install in their monastery something by way of remembrancer (*cetiya*) of the Lord.[1] The form of it was discussed. At the time it must have been a moot-point of a purely hypothetical nature, for there was no Buddha-image available yet. But three kinds of remembrancer were considered and preference went to an 'associative' and symbolical one (*Paribhogika*, something associated with the Lord—in this case a seed of the Bodhi Tree), while a physically representative one (*Uddesika*, which the commentator explains as a 'Buddha-image') was rejected as being 'unreal and imaginary' (*avatthuka manamattaka*).

When an *'uddesika'* form of *cetiya* actually came into existence, it had to be evaluated for the purpose of worship and the question was hypothetical no longer, but had a practical bearing. The issue was whether (i) to replace the symbol by the image, or (ii) to keep both, or (iii) to reject the image and perpetuate the symbol. On the vexed question, monks had to make up their minds.

For two following centuries, it seems the issue remained more or less unsettled. Perhaps there were debates in monk circles, but we have no literary source of information, except an obscure *sūtra* that exists only in its Chinese version. It was translated into Chinese by a

[1] *Kaliṅga-bodhi Jātaka* (No. 479): Fausböll's *The Jātaka*, Vol. IV, pp. 228 ff.

Parthian monk who joined the White Horse Monastery at Loyang in AD 148.[1] This *sūtra* recommends daily worship of the Buddha-image in ritual form. It is said that 'a true disciple of the Buddha venerates his image evening and morning; often lights a lamp before it to honour it; observes the abstinences and precepts; is always resigned to his lot. It is him that the good *devas* protect'.[2]

Buddha-image inset in a Stūpa. (Ellora, Cave No. 10).

Archaeological evidence, however, exists to show that in the third century AD a latitudinarian attitude developed, both forms of worship being recognized and choice between them left to the worshipper. The evidence comes from the monastic ruins of Nāgārjunakoṇḍa and also from some of the West Indian cave-monasteries.

The Nāgārjunakoṇḍa monasteries were of the third century AD. As already noticed,[3] a curious feature of some of them is the con-

[1] About the Parthian monk, see Part IV, Sec. 7, p. 299.
[2] See Wieger's *A History of the Religious Beliefs and Philosophical Opinions in China* (tr. by Werner and pub. by Hsien-hsien, Peking, 1927), p. 357.
[3] See Part II, Sec. 4, p. 134.

struction of *double* shrines—a shrine with a *stūpa* in it and another with a Buddha-image. The shrines stood side by side. Evidently the worshipper was free to offer worship, according to his inclination, either to the *stūpa* (*Cetiya*) or to the Image (*Paṭimā*).

In several *guhās*—at Ajanta, Ellora, Nasik, etc.—we see a sort of compromise effected by engraving an image on the *stūpa* itself or recessing the image into it,[1] so that the worship becomes a combined

Mahādeva icon inset in a Linga (Udaigiri, Cave No. 4).

worship of both symbol and image. The combination of symbol and icon was not felt to be incongruous: the practice seems to have been not unknown among the adherents of Brāhmaṇical cults too. In the Udayagiri caves of Vidiśā, built by Vīrasena Śāba in the first decade of the fifth century,[2] one cave-temple houses a huge *liṅga* (phallic emblem) combined and conjunct with a Mahādeva icon in stone. This sort of combination may be seen elsewhere too in a Brāhmaṇical temple.

Among different Buddhist sects, the attitude towards image-worship seems to have varied.

The Theravāda was conservative. Even long after image-worship had come into vogue, the exponents of Theravāda gave to this form of worship a grudging and reluctant recognition. At the turn of the

[1] At Kanheri, Cave IV, and at Ajanta in the façade of Cave XIX.
[2] See Part III, Sec. 6, p. 221.

11. *A residential cave at Kanherī before Mahāyānist renovation.* (Photo: Archaeological Department, Government of India)

Avalokiteśvara Litany in sculpture. (*Ellora.*) (Photo: Department of Archaeology, Government of India)

Sculptured figures of two donor couples at Kanherī. (Photo: Department of Archaeology, Government of India)

12. *The 'Durbar Hall' at Kanh*
(outside view
Photo:
Department o
Archaeology,
Government
of India)

The interior
the Durbar H
and the seati
arrangement.
(Photo:
Department
Archaeology,
Government
of India)

A section of t
Tin-tal at Ell
(Photo:
Department o
Archaeology,
Government
of India)

fifth century AD, when Buddhaghosa wrote his great commentaries on the Theravāda scripture in Ceylon, image-worship had become an established custom in that island. An image-shrine (*paṭimāghara*) had already become an usual adjunct in a monastic establishment. But it is curious that among the Theravādin monks of Ceylon an opinion prevailed that sacrosanctity had to be imparted to an image by placing *Dhātu* (Holy Relics) inside it: evidently they stood by the canonical *sarīra-pūjā* (Relic-worship) and the image had had to be aligned to it before it was thought worthy of worship.

'According to the (Theravāda) Commentaries, an image was important only if the relics of the Buddha were enshrined in it. At the time the Pali commentaries were written in the fifth century AD, on the occasion of alms-giving to the Saṅgha, 'wise men' (*paṇḍita-manussā*) used to place an image or a casket with relics (*sadhātukaṁ paṭimaṁ vā cetiyaṁ vā*) and offer food and drink first to the image or the casket. In the discussion as to when it was lawful to cut a branch of a Bo-tree it is said that it should be cut only if it interferes with ('*bādhayamanaṁ*') a ***thūpa*** or an ***image with relics***'.[1]

In the Ceylonese commentaries on the scripture, there is no mention of an image-shrine (*paṭimā-ghara*) though it actually existed, and Buddhaghosa, mentioning the different parts and adjuncts of a monastery, ignores the image-shrine altogether. 'It is surprising', says Rahula, 'that the Buddha-image, though in existence at the time, was not given a place in the scheme of worship by the Pali commentaries. Instructions are given to meditating monks that they should go and worship the *cetiya* and the *bodhi*, and then set out for the alms-round, but the image is completely ignored. Even in other places where worshipping is casually referred to, only the *cetiya* and the *bodhi* are mentioned, and no image or image-house at all.'[2]

What the attitudes of other sects were—the Mahāsāṅghikas for example—cannot be ascertained, for only scraps remain out of their scriptures. But it may be presumed that among all those sects in whose systems of faith *Bhakti* was expressly recommended, image-worship became a concomitant of *Bhakti*.

In the centuries immediately following the adoption of the Buddha-image, the Mahāyāna appeared. The Mahāyānists represented in respect of prayer and worship a pole opposite to the Theravādins. They stressed *Bhakti* as a cardinal virtue. From the Mahāyānists, image-worship received a premium which the Theravādins were loth to give. We have seen how the appearance of Mahāyānist monks in the *leṇas* of western India led to large-scale renovations of their

[1] Rahula's *History of Buddhism in Ceylon* (Colombo: Gunasena and Co., 1956), p. 125. The authorities are cited in the footnotes. The italics are mine.
[2] *Ibid*, p. 126. The authorities are cited in the footnotes.

decorative designs and the profuse introduction of images, large and small, into their interior. The central image to which daily ritual *pūjā* was offered was the largest one, placed in the 'holy of holies'—in a sanctuary separated from the prayer hall and marked off from it by a vestibule.

At a later stage, a temple housed the image: it seems to have become the customary and prevalent practice in the Gupta age and later. The 'Buddha-temple' was perhaps an innovation of this age, and at Sanchi, Nālandā, Kushinagara and elsewhere we see Buddha-temples of Gupta age that are separate and free-standing buildings and not sanctuaries within the monasteries.

A new feature is noticed in both sculpture and painting in the *guhā*-monasteries as Mahāyāna develops towards the Tāntric phase. While the new deities of the Mahāyāna pantheon are introduced, the central image in the sanctuary, executed now in grander proportions, is invariably attended on by Bodhisattvas. The image with the Bodhisattva attendants becomes definitely the object of worship; the ancient cult-object, the *stūpa*, is reduced either to an art-motif or to a mark of distinction on the attendant Bodhisattva's forehead or headgear.

Stūpa-worship does not seem to have been ever abandoned even after the introduction of image-worship. At Amarāvatī an ancient school of Buddhism developed. It is virtually known only by its obscure, yet significant, name—*Cetiyavāda*. One wonders whether the name could relate to one aspect of the creed of this school, viz. its affirmation of the superior merit of *stūpa*-worship. Long after the invention of the Buddha-image, the sculpture of Amarāvatī invariably uses the *stūpa* instead of the recumbent Buddha figure to typify the 'Great Decease'. In the later (eighth century AD) *guhā*-monasteries of Bāgh, which were all along in the occupation of Mahāyānist monks, one is surprised to find *stūpas* installed instead of Buddha-images in all the sanctuaries discovered so far.[1]

[1] See Part II, Sec. 6, p. 164.

4

Monasteries under the Gupta Kings

To a certain period of European history, historians assign the label: 'the age of Renaissance and Reformation'. Interpreted in the context of ancient Indian history, the phrase may perhaps serve to indicate the quality and character of the two and a half centuries (*c.* AD 300–550) known as the Gupta Age. Culture flourished, and side by side was a movement for remodelling society on fresh ideological foundations.

A phenomenal broadening and enrichment of literature in its chosen linguistic medium Sanskrit—a many-sided development in scholarship and learning—a flowering of the Fine Arts, specially sculpture and painting, out of tentative beginnings to such finished perfection that later ages looked to its achievements as classic examples and models—represent its cultural side. It was also the golden age of Sanskrit literature.

While this literature reflects the opulence of its aesthetic culture and its abounding curiosity of mind, it mirrors also a process of transformation of society, of a rethinking and re-laying of the bases of social life and a transvaluation of values accompanied with the formulation of new theological concepts and new forms of practice in religion. The movement finds literary expression in different types of literature. The final redactions of the sacred epics, a good many of the *Purāṇas*, the *Dharmaśāstras* and the *Arthaśāstras*, the fundamental texts of both Brāhmaṇical philosophy and Mahāyāna Buddhism—all belong to this age.

The Gupta-age 'reformation' was traditionalist: it sought to derive its basic ideas and governing principles from a source of higher antiquity than Buddhism—the *Vedas*. But Buddhism was neither suppressed nor regarded as a cross-current or counter-force in the rising tide of this reformation. On the other hand the Mahāyāna development gave the religion a congenial form—even, one might say, a kind of family likeness.

In the Mahāyānic emphasis on *Bhakti*, in the form and ceremony of image-worship that had become prevalent in Buddhism, in the enlarged Mahāyānist pantheon, which, like the Brāhmaṇical, admitted deities, both male and female, both principal and attendant, and even in the speculative trends of Mahāyāna philosophy, Buddhism showed an obvious likeness that made it seem not to belong to another house. Only in the adoration paid to the Buddha and the Bodhisattvas was the specific hallmark retained, but as we shall presently observe, the sharpness of its distinction was about to wear off.

The Buddhist (Mahāyānist) rites of worship are described in Canto II, vv. 10 ff., of the *Bodhicaryāvatāra* of Śāntideva (eighth century AD).[1] They are practically the same as those performed in Brāhmaṇical image-worship—bathing the image with scented water, vocal and instrumental music, offering of flowers, food and clothes, swinging censers and burning incense, etc.[2] Only the images represent the deities of the Buddhist Mahāyāna pantheon and some (e.g. *Tārā*) found place later on in the Brāhamaṇical pantheon too.

The hypothesis is not groundless that it was towards the end of the Gupta age (round the middle of the sixth century AD), that the psychological background was set for the emergence of that arresting phenomenon in India's religious history—the acceptance of the Buddha as a deity of the Hindu pantheon. It did not take place in the Gupta age itself, but not very long afterwards.

Several *purāṇas* (of unknown date) enumerate ten incarnations (*avatāras*) of Godhead; some of them place the Buddha among the incarnations, while others substitute some other name.[3] The *Śrīmad-bhāgavata*, a leading scripture of the Vaiṣṇava cult, mentions the Buddha as one of the *avatāras*.[4] We find in one of the *purāṇas* a certain date in the calendar assigned as sacred to ceremonial worship of a Buddha-image—a clear indication of the adoption of *Buddha-pūjā* by the Hindus.[5] In the opinion of Dr Kane, 'the Buddha became in popular view an *avatāra* of Viṣṇu'—though as he adds, 'he was not universally so treated'—about the seventh century AD.[6]

The great Śaivite Bṛhadīśvara Temple at Tanjore was built in the reign of the Chola king Rāja-rājā (985–1018). Here on the right hand of the main *gopuram* a large seated Buddha-image is installed, and among the mythological figures carved on a broad belt of sculpture round the sanctuary is a Buddha-figure under a Bodhi Tree, so stylized as to be nearly beyond recognition. In the Kashmirian poet and polymath Kṣemendra's *Daśāvatāra-caritam* (Canto IX) written

[1] On Śāntideva, see Part IV, Sec. 5, pp. 286 ff.

[2] See Śāntibhikṣu Śāstri's Ed. of *Bodhicaryāvatāra* (Lucknow: Buddha vihāra, 1955), pp. 8–9 of the Text.

[3] See Kane's *History of the Dharmaśāstras* (Poona: Bhandarkar Oriental Research Institute, 1941), Vol. II, Pt. II, p. 720.

[4] *Tataḥ kalau sampravṛtte sammohāya śūradviṣām Buddha-nāmnā jina-sutaḥ kīkaṭeṣu bhaviṣyati* (Tr.: Then, when the Kaliyuga has commenced, in order to drive into confusion the enemies of the gods, a son of *jina* or conqueror named the Buddha will appear in Kīkaṭa).—*Śrīmad-bhāgavata*, I, 3, 24.

[5] Kane's *History*, etc., Vol. II, Pt. II, p. 721.

[6] *Ibid*, p. 721.

in 1065–66,[1] the Buddha figures as one of 'the Ten Avatāras'. Kṣemendra, though not a Buddhist, was under the spell of Buddhism, as evidenced by his long labour of rendering *Jātaka* stories in the *Avadāna-kalpalatā*.[2] And in the twelfth century the devout Vaiṣṇava poet of Bengal Jayadeva described the Buddha in a verse (*aṣṭapadī* I, 9) of his *Gīta-Govindam* as the ninth incarnation of Keśava (Viṣṇu).

A trend towards assimilation between Brāhmaṇism and Buddhism seems to have started sometime in this spacious age. From the point of view of Buddhist history, the Gupta Age cannot be described with any precision as a flourishing one for Buddhism, although it was one in which monasteries grew bigger and richer in artistic decorations and large monastic establishments flourished with plentiful provision for their inmates. At the same time a power was rising against Buddhism which was finally to engulf and submerge it: it was the renovated and transformed Brāhmaṇism of the age. While professing a theoretic affiliation to the Vedas, it was a far cry from the Vedic. But it was shaping for the people a complete system of thought and philosophy—of sociology, ethics, theology and religious practice—represented by the law-codes (*Smṛti*) and the *Purāṇas* and the sacred epics, the practice of temple-worship and its rituals, and the premium in religion on *Bhakti* as a form of emotional culture indispensable for a devotee.

In several royal seals, the Gupta rulers style themselves as '*parama-bhāgavata*' (Devout followers of the Bhāgavata cult). None of them was a professed Buddhist. Only one of the Guptas is said to have been brought up in his youth under Buddhist influence—Bālāditya who as a prince had the famous Buddhist scholar Vasubandhu as his tutor and afterwards built a great Buddhist temple at Nālandā.[3] It is evident, however, that the attitude of the Gupta rulers towards Buddhism far exceeded the tradition of kingly liberality to religious institutions. They themselves founded Buddhist monasteries and helped in building them and maintained monk-communities with land-grants, and we have it on the statements of Chinese pilgrims, based undoubtedly on local information, that the great establishment at Nālandā was the achievement of the Gupta kings. None of the archaeological remains and relics at Nālandā points to pre-Gupta times.

For this zealous patronage and support of Buddhism and its monkhood, two plausible reasons suggest themselves—first, that the

[1] See *Kṣemendra Studies* by Dr Suryakanta (Poona Oriental Series, No. 91, 1954), p. 8.

[2] This work was presented by the author to a Tibetan lama in AD 1202. Seventy years later it was translated into Tibetan. The Tibetan version was discovered by Sarat Chandra Das and collated with the Sanskrit and edited and published for the first time in the *Bibliotheca Indica* series.

[3] On Bālāditya and Vasubandhu, see Part IV, Sec 5, p. 282.

Guptas did not look upon the Buddhist religion as antagonistic to their professed Brāhmaṇical faith; and, secondly, that Buddhist monasteries of that age were not the same in character and function as in earlier ages: no longer 'radiating centres' of Buddhism, but developing at Nālandā and elsewhere as efficient academies and seats of learning. They were Buddhist monasteries still, but the learning they conserved and also dispensed was not canonical in spite of its necessarily Buddhist bias.[1]

The age is distinguished by a great efflorescence of the Fine Arts. The artistic tradition was a unified one, neither Brāhmaṇical nor Buddhist. For the sake of art alone, it was applied in all its forms—sculpture, iconography and painting—according to its own set standards, to uses both Brāhmaṇical and Buddhist. 'In the Gupta period', as observes Rowland, 'no distinction of style can be made between works of art produced for various religions. A typical Brāhmaṇical fragment from the Mathura workshops of the fifth century reveals the same tradition and stylistic idiom as the Buddha-images from the same site.'[2] The standards of this art have never been excelled in India.

At its best, it ranks as purely classic as the art of Periclean Athens in the West. It supplied the prototypes not for the religious art of India alone, but of all Buddhist Asia (e.g. the Tun-huang caves of mid-Asia).[3] It thus occupies a position in Asia, as observes Rowland, 'corresponding to Greek and Roman art in the West'.[4]

Buddhist monasteries of the Gupta age received a new look from this art. The severely utilitarian appearance of monasteries of the Kuṣāṇa-age pattern was modified and enriched; structural measurements were enlarged; both the insides and the outsides of the buildings were beautified with sculpture and painting, and the compactness and simplicity of the old pattern was replaced by a new splendour. Monasteries were not constructed or decorated by the monks themselves, but their attitude towards the appropriation of art in monastery construction and decoration was by no means unfavourable.

The scheme of monastic life made no room for the practice of art; yet art by its evocative power could be an ally of religion. The orthodox Hīnayānist attitude in this matter is well illustrated by a

[1] See Part V, Sec. 1, p. 324.

[2] Rowland's *The Art and Archietcture of India* 1953), p. 140.

[3] These caves were first discovered by the great explorer, Aurel Stein. The discovery is described in Ch. xii (*The Cave Shrines of the Thousand Buddhas*) in his book *On Ancient Central-Asian Tracks*. The mural art of these caves which ranges from the third to the tenth century includes several Ajanta-style paintings distinctly Indian and bearing the stamp of the Gupta age. The murals are described in Gray and Vincent's *Buddhist Cave Paintings at Tun-huang* (London: Faber & Faber, 1959).

[4] Rowland's *The Art and Architecture of India* (1953), p. 150.

story told by Buddhaghosa of a certain monastery of Ceylon and of an old and venerable monk named Cittagutta who dwelt there.[1] There was a very fine piece of painting in the monastery, either on the ceiling or on a side-wall, showing seven Buddhas, each in the act of renouncing the world. This painting was an object of admiration in the locality. A party of monk visitors who had much appreciated its art spoke of it admiringly to the aged Cittagutta. But the *Thera* who had been for sixty years an inmate of that monastery had no inkling of it: his eyes, always downcast in meditation, had never during these long years been once lifted to the picture. 'Friends', said Cittagutta to the visiting monks, 'I have lived here for over sixty years. But I did not know there were paintings. Today I learn about them, through the help of those who have eyes (*Ajja dāni cakkhumante nissāya jātan 'ti*).'

Towards beauty perceived by the eyes Cittagutta's attitude was quite opposite to that of Saint Bernard who, as a legend has it, covered his eyes from the sight of the beautiful lakes of Switzerland 'lest they take too sensual a delight'. The attitude of Mahāyānist monks was far in advance of mere passive appreciation. We have described the activities of Mahāyānist monks in decorating the *leṇas* of Kanheri and other cave-monasteries of western India;[2] in the Vinaya literature of Tibet (*Dulva*) there are texts on the scheme of monastery-decoration.[3]

The art-renaissance of the Gupta age was not confined to the north: it was diffused all over the country. We cannot trace its impress on the *vihāras* because of their complete state of ruin. But in the *leṇas* we can see how the achievements of the mature art of the age were uninhibitedly appropriated by monks.

At Aurangabad, Ellora and Ajanta, even a casual visitor making a round will be struck by the abrupt advance—a leap forward, as it were—visible in several caves in their architecture and interior decoration. A new fineness of composition, a new creativeness of design, an unwonted mastery of execution are evident in them. Where this is seen, the inscriptions show that the caves are of the age of the Guptas or of the Vākāṭakas, their successors in the Deccan. They are impressed with the tradition of the 'classic age'—early Gupta or late or its aftermath. Sculpture has lasted, but mural decorations have peeled off and disappeared from most of the caves except at Ajanta, or remain in scraps as at Bāgh, or in traces only as at Aurangabad, Kanheri, Badami and elsewhere.

It would be unreasonable to suppose that only the *Guhās* were

[1] *Visuddhimagga* (*Sīlaniddeso*, 105). See Kosambi's Ed., p. 25.

[2] See Part II, Sec. 5, p. 153.

[3] See Grünwedel's *Buddhist Art in India* (English translation), revised and enlarged by Burgess, London, 1901, p. 46.

adorned and the *Vihāras* left without adornment. The *vihāras* as well as the *guhās* must have received this artistic dower. But the art in the monasteries of northern India must have been stylistically different. A subtle quality of the cave-art is its meticulous adaptation to the physical contour and configuration of the caves. Much of the exquisiteness of effect is due to this fitting of the art to its physical medium. In the free-standing stone-or-brick-built *vihāras* of the north a somewhat different artistic composition and art-idiom must have been employed.

In this splendidly flowering age of art and culture Fa-hsien came to this country and visited the monasteries of northern India: in the reign of Chandragupta II (*c.* 375–415 AD),[1] perhaps the peak period of the imperial Gupta age.

Fa-hsien notes the 'prosperous condition' of the monasteries and of the considerable real property and assets held by them in 'Madhya-deśa' (Middle Country) by which he means the whole of northern India south of Mathura. 'Down from the Buddha's *nirvāṇa*', says Fa-hsien, 'the kings of these countries, the chief men and householders, have raised *vihāras* for the priests (i.e. monks) and provided for their support by bestowing on them fields (i.e. agricultural lands), houses and gardens with men and oxen. Engraved title-deeds were prepared and handed down from one reign to another; no one has ventured to withdraw them, so that till now there has been no interruption. All the resident priests having chambers (in these *vihāras*) have their beds, mats, food, drink and clothes provided without stint; in all places this is the case.'[2]

The custom of maintaining monasteries with land-grants which Fa-hsien noticed in the '*Madhya-deśa*' was in fact the general custom all over northern India. Near upon three centuries later than Fa-hsien, I-tsing who visited the monasteries of northern India records that the 'Indian monasteries possess special allotment of lands'.[3] Out of the income from landed property, supplemented by casual donations, the needs of resident monks used to be supplied 'without stint'. I-tsing seems even to have noticed a tendency to hoarding in these monasteries which prompted him to strike a somewhat censorious note: 'It is unseemly for a monastery to have great wealth, granaries full of rotten corn, many servants, male and female, money and treasures hoarded in the treasury, without using any of these things, while all the members are suffering from poverty.'[4] It shows at the

[1] 'For the reign of Chandragupta II, we possess a number of dated inscriptions so that its limits may be fixed with more accuracy than those of his predecessors. His accession should be placed before AD 381 and his death in or about AD 413–414'—Ray Choudhry's *Political History*, p. 554.

[2] Beal's *Buddhist Records*, i, p. XXXVIII.

[3] Takakusu's *A Record of the Buddhist Religion, etc.*, p. 193. [4] *Ibid*, p. 194.

same time the extent of the prosperity enjoyed by the monasteries.

It was not always kings or members of the aristocracy who made these land-grants. Well-to-do lay Buddhists who had lands to give would donate them to a saṅgha to earn spiritual merit. It has even been suggested that the theory of 'joint ownership' or co-parcenery was evolved by the Brāhmaṇical legists, Yājñavalkya and Viṣṇu, chiefly to prevent a Buddhist member of a joint family of landed proprietors from alienating family property in this way. It had perhaps become at the time a widespread practice.[1]

Though Fa-hsien had an eye for the grand and spectacular in Buddhist rites and ceremonies witnessed by him, he was not enough of an art-connoisseur to describe architecture and sculpture. Beyond saying that he had seen 'great *vihāras*', he does not give descriptive particulars of any of them. But he describes in detail some public Buddhist ceremonies seen by him in the '*Madhya-deśa*', like the grand 'Procession of Images' held annually on 'the eighth day of the second month'.[2] Too intent on his purpose which was to see the customary ways of monks ('*Vinaya*') in India, he had no eye for mere externalities—the architecture of *vihāras* or their sculpture or pictorial decorations.

Over a couple of centuries separates Fa-hsien and Hsüan-tsang. In the two intervening centuries, the predatory Hūṇa incursions and the relentless vandalism of Mihirakula had reduced to ruins many great *vihāras* in Gāndhāra, Kashmir, and western Uttar Pradesh. Besides, the neo-Brāhmaṇism of the Gupta Age was gaining definitely on Buddhism, reducing the number of *vihāras* and increasing Brāhmaṇical establishments. Many once-famous monasteries were deserted or left in melancholy ruins. Fa-hsien in his time had seen many ruined or deserted monasteries, and in Hsüan-tsang's time they were prominently in evidence. In northern India it was only in Magadha that the latter saw monasteries that still retained something of their old-time magnificence. The Gupta empire was then a memory, though a touch of its afterglow lingered in Harṣavardhana's smaller empire in the east. In the west, Buddhism showed only in shreds and patches.

The Tilodaka Saṅghārāma, the Mahābodhi Saṅghārāma and the Nālandā Mahāvihāra were the three grandest monastic establishments of Magadha still functioning, described by Hsüan-tsang. They were not at a great distance from one another, all situated in a cross-section of the modern Bihar State.

The Tilodaka Saṅghārāma which provided residence for 1,000

[1] See *Hindu Law of Inheritance* by Dr. Bhupendra Nath Datta (Calcutta: Nababharata Publishers, 1957), p. 194.

[2] See Beal's *Buddhist Records*, i, pp. lvi–lvii.

monks was visited later by I-tsing also.[1] It was a very large establishment, about twenty-one miles west of Nālandā. But grander and more sumptuous was the many-storeyed Mahābodhi Saṅghārāma at Gayā. It was visited by both Hsüan-tsang and I-tsing, but not by Fa-hsien though he had been to the Bodhi Tree near it. A Ceylonese king, Meghavaṇṇa (AD 362–409), as recorded in the *Mahāvaṁsa*,[2]

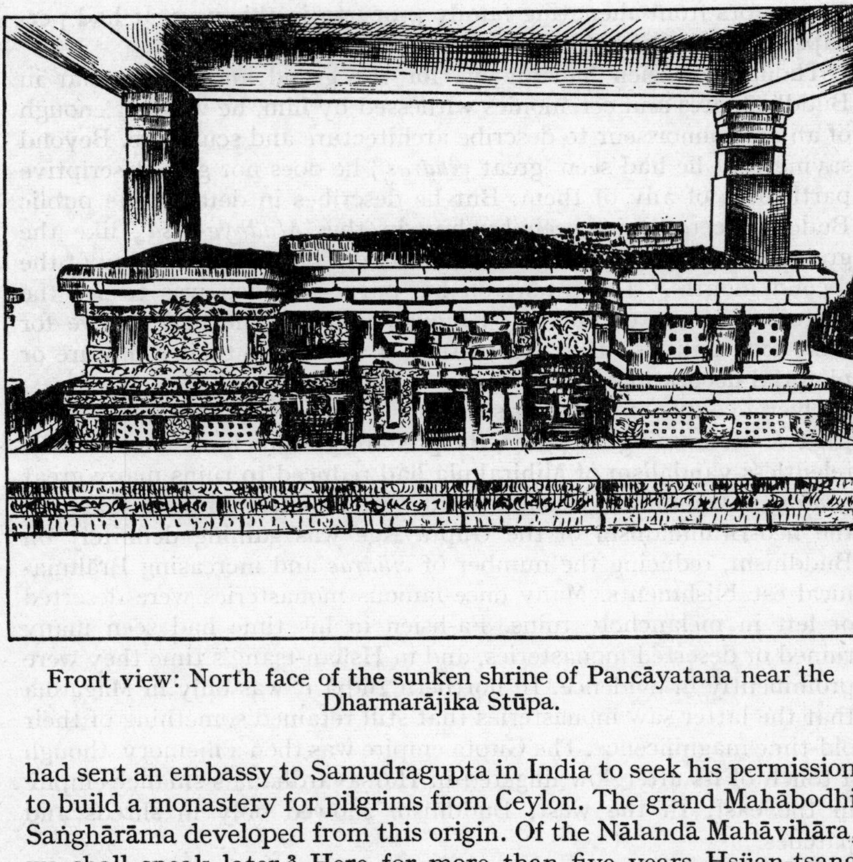

Front view: North face of the sunken shrine of Pancāyatana near the Dharmarājika Stūpa.

had sent an embassy to Samudragupta in India to seek his permission to build a monastery for pilgrims from Ceylon. The grand Mahābodhi Saṅghārāma developed from this origin. Of the Nālandā Mahāvihāra, we shall speak later.[3] Here for more than five years Hsüan-tsang studied *Yogācāra* philosophy. The magnificence of all these establishments in Magadha must have been the heritage of the Gupta age, over and gone and a memory only when Hsüan-tsang saw them with such admiration and wonder.

Hsüan-tsang opens the second book of his 'Record' with a general and summary account of his observations of Indian life during his

[1] See Takakusu's *A Record of the Buddhist Religion*, p. 184.
[2] See Geiger's Translation, Intro., p. XXXIX. [3] See Part V, Sec. 2.

stay in the country. It contains a short section on *Saṅghārāmas*.[1] The Chinese pilgrims use the term *Saṅghārāma* not in any specific sense, but to indicate a monastic establishment of any type. 'The places where the priests stop and lodge, they call "Saṅghārāms" ', says Fa-hsien.[2] Hsüan-tsang uses the terms *Saṅghārāma* and *Vihāra* interchangeably.

About Saṅghārāma architecture, then a legacy of the Gupta age, the following points are noted by Hsüan-tsang:

(i) Skilful construction.
(ii) Four Angles.
(iii) A three-storeyed tower at each side.
(iv) Doors, windows and low walls, profusely painted.
(v) Monks' cells, plain outside, but ornamental inside.
(vi) Assembly halls (*Maṇḍapas*), high and wide and in the middle of the building.
(vii) Storeyed chambers and turrets of different height.
(viii) Doors, eastward facing.

We find reproduced here two characteristic features of Gupta architecture—the *Śikhara* (Tower) and the *Pañcāyatana* (Four-square temple with a shrine or a turret at each angle, best exemplified by the Daśāvatāra Temple at Deogarh in the Jhansi district of the Madhya Pradesh[3]).

Hsüan-tsang saw several large monasteries with towers on top. These towers were a Gupta-age speciality[4]—an architectural feature absent from the basic and traditional pattern of a monastery. One of the grandest of these towered monasteries, of which his description is given later,[5] was seen by him at Sārnāth. Its ruins cannot be located, but Hsüan-tsang speaks of its 'lofty towers mingling with the clouds'.[6]

It seems that the turreted monastic architecture reached its apogee at Nālandā. Here was an aggregation of monasteries—several built by Gupta kings—enclosed later, as we are told by Hsüan-tsang, by a boundary wall with a single gate, thus converting them into a Mahāvihāra. 'A long succession of kings', says the Chinese pilgrim,

[1] See Beal's *Buddhist Records*, ii, p. 74.
[2] *Ibid*, pp. XXX–XXXI.
[3] It is described in the *Memoir of the Archaeological Survey of India*, No. 70 (*The Gupta Temple at Deogarh* by Vats). A shrine exactly of this architectural type is discernable among the excavated Gupta-age monastic ruins at Sārnāth to the south of the Dharmarājika Stūpa. It is in a sunken condition (see sketch).
[4] 'The *Śikhara*, which some writers see as a specially north Indian development, becomes more and more prominent in the architecture of the Gupta and later period'—Rowland's *The Art and Architecture of India* (1953), p. 133.
[5] See Part III, Sec. 6, pp. 216–217.
[6] Beal's *Buddhist Records*, ii, pp. 98–99.

'continued the work of building (Nālandā's monasteries) using all the skill of the sculptor till the whole is marvellous to behold.'[1] The most striking and spectacular feature of the ensemble was the row of tall towers. About a hundred years after Hsüan-tsang's first visit to Nālandā, one Mālāda, son of a minister of Yaśodharma Deva, came to Nālandā, made some offerings to the resident monks and donated for their use an abode (*layana*) on the bank of a stream. These gifts are commemorated by him in a long inscription in high-flown Sanskrit. It mentions Nālandā's 'row of monasteries with towers licking the clouds (*Ambudharāvalehi-śikharaśrenī-vihārāvali*)'.[2] Master architects who had the genius to:

'write their Euclidean music, standing with a hand on a cornice of cloud, themselves set fast earth-square',

must have been at work uprearing those 'cloud-licking' towers.

*

All these *vihāras* are now rubble and dust; yet it is a surprise that we can see a sort of 'shadow-play' of them far away in the south, at Mahābalipuram near Madras.

In the earlier half of the seventh century, Narasiṁhavarman of the Pallava dynasty was ruling in Drāviḍa over tracts on the east coast of India. He shifted the old Pallava capital from Kañcī (Conjeevaram) to a seaport built by him near the mouth of the Palar river about thirty-five miles south of Madras. It was called after him Mahāmallapuram, corrupted later into Mahābalipuram.

The king wished to decorate the new seaside capital with works of architecture. In his time there was not much tradition of architecture in the south. But the Pallava king seems to have been keen on architectural decoration of the capital. So he set up different kinds of architectural construction on the city's water-front—cave-shrines, free-standing temples on the sea-beach (of which only one now remains) and a few monolithic storeyed structures of which the main purpose seems to have been to assemble rock-cut models of architecture. European sailors who came cruising near the coast seven to eight centuries later, when the city of Mahāmalla was no more, descried the landmarks from the sea and named them 'Seven Pagodas', though they are only five. Local people called them '*Raths*'. They are not whole structural temples, but only the top parts (called *Vimāna*) of temple superstructure. The Pallavas were

[1] *Ibid*, ii, p. 170.

[2] See *Epigraphia Indica*, Vol. XX (Hirananda Sastri's *Nalanda Stone-inscription of the Reign of Yasodharma-deva*), pp. 37 ff.

Brāhmaṇical in faith, and there is no Buddhist symbol anywhere on any of the *Raths*.

Yet it seems that, lacking a traditional style of temple architecture in that part of the country at the time, the architects of Mahāmalla copied in the offsets of the *raths* and of the shore-temples the models of northern Buddhist monastic architecture.

Even a cursory survey reveals how carefully the Buddhist architecture has been reproduced in them in miniature forms. One of these structures which are all in granite, now called 'Ganesh Rath', is thus described by Fergusson and Burgess: 'The temple diminishes upwards in a pyramidal form, the offsets being marked by ranges of small simulated cells, such as no doubt existed in the Buddhist *vihāras* on a large scale and were thus practically the cells in which the monks resided. In this instance they are much more subdued than was originally the case, but throughout the whole range of Drāviḍian architecture to the present day, they form the most universal and most characteristic feature of the style'.[1]

The porch of a *vihāra* with twin pillars, the attic (*vimāna*) of a storeyed *vihāra*, the long vaulted roof of a prayer hall (*cetiyaghara*) and specially its 'sun-window' shaped like the leaf of a *Peepul* tree, have all become with the Mahāmallapura architects and sculptors models and art-motifs. They passed into the southern Pallava (Brāhmaṇical) architecture that developed in the after-centuries into a distinct school known as the 'Drāviḍa School'.

The great historical value of these offset forms on the shore-temple and the *raths* of Mahābalipura lies in the fact, as Fergusson and Burgess point out, 'that they are the only known specimens of a form of Buddhist architecture which prevailed in the north . . . and that they are the incunabula of thousands of Hindu temples which were erected in the south of India during one thousand years that have elapsed since they were undertaken.'[2]

[1] Fergusson and Burgess's *Cave Temples of India* (1880), p. 115.
[2] *Ibid*, p. 128.

5

The Devastation

HISTORY holds record of two devastations on an extensive scale of the *vihāras* of northern India—once by Mihirakula in the western sector in the early part of the sixth century, and again, several centuries later, by Muslim invaders in the eastern sector round the turn of the thirteenth.

A branch of the Hūṇas, called Epthalite or White Hūṇas, had entered India between AD 500 and 520 and seized ruling power over the border provinces of Gāndhāra and Kashmir. A Chinese pilgrim, Sung-yun, sent on an official mission to India by an empress of the Wei dynasty, arrived in Gāndhāra in AD 520. He found the country devastated by the Hūṇas and a puppet of the Hūṇa ruler cruelly exercising power.[1] The Hūṇas gradually penetrated into the interior, carved out a kingdom and over it the Hūṇa king Mihirakula held sway in *c.* 518–529. The kingdom included Gāndhāra and Kashmir and perhaps extended farther east, embracing parts of the West Punjab even as far east as Kośāmbī.[2]

From all accounts, this Hūṇa king was a Śaiva by faith and a sworn enemy of Buddhism. Though he had adopted an Indian faith he had imbibed little of Indian culture. The barbarian lust for destruction and vandalism ran in his veins. The Gupta kings fought off and on against the power of the Hūṇa, but it was not till some time before AD 533 that Mihirakula was subjugated by Yaśodharman of Mandasor.[3]

Nearly a hundred years later—in AD 630–631—Hsüan-tsang, passing through Gāndhāra and Kashmir, heard about Mihirakula's devastations. They were then traditional tales in these parts; they are reported by the Chinese pilgrim as he heard them. In Gāndhāra alone Mihirakula, says Hsüan-tsang, 'overthrew *stūpas* and destroyed *saṅghārāmas*, altogether one thousand and six hundred foundations'.[4] Perhaps the work of destruction spread as far as Kośāmbī, though it affected especially Gāndhāra and Kashmir. But in that age Buddhism had enough vitality to bind up the wounds inflicted by

[1] See Beal's *Buddhist Records*, Intro., pp. XV–XVI.
[2] See *Indian Archaeology* for 1955–56 in which finds showing Hūṇa penetration to Kośāmbī are reported.
[3] See Raj Chaudhuri's *Political History* (6th Ed., 1953), p. 596.
[4] Beal's *Buddhist Records*, i, p. 171.

the Hūṇa depradations lasting just over a decade. Saṅgha life picked up, at least partially, its broken threads; it went on in new monasteries that rose on the ruins of the demolished ones.

Next, in the early part of the twelfth century there was a foregathering in the northern regions of the country of Muslim tribesmen from Afghanistan. They were fanatical Muslims, bent on conquest and predatory excursions, and their advance posed a tremendous threat to all monasteries and temples of northern India. Buddhism had slowly shifted eastwards in the intervening period and was flourishing once again in Magadha under the Pāla kings. But its vital strength was at an ebb; it was becoming more and more regional, more and more dependant on outside protection, when the Moslem fanatics were descending southwards in short swift rushes.

In spite of this perilous state of Buddhism in the twelfth century, there were efforts at revival; new monasteries were being built and old ones endowed afresh to keep up saṅgha life and the monks' ministrations.

The most noteworthy of these revivalist efforts is associated with King Govindachandra (AD 1114–1154) of the Gahadvala dynasty and his pious Buddhist queen Kumāradevī. Govindachandra had inherited the throne of Kanouj, shifting his capital to Banaras. Perhaps he wished to revive the tradition of patronage to Buddhism set by Harṣavardhana, his illustrious predecessor on the Kanouj throne.

The invaders moving down from the north, who were then known by the blanket name of *Turaṣka* or *Turk*,[1] were already knocking at the gates of his kingdom and one of Govindachandra's several grants, dated in AD 1120, mentions the levy of a special tax called 'Turaṣka daṇḍa' to meet the cost of warding off the invaders.[2] He was not a Buddhist himself, but his queen Kumāradevī, who had some distant blood-relationship with Rāmapāla, a Buddhist Pāla king of Bengal, was a devout Buddhist. Both the king and the queen, even in those troubled fear-haunted years with crisis just ahead, were zealously trying to revive monastic life in the kingdom.

In a village Saheth-Maheth (in eastern Uttar Pradesh), anciently Jetavana, a charter of Govindachandra has been found recording the gift of six villages to 'the Saṅgha, of whom Buddha-Bhaṭṭāraka is the chief and foremost, residing in the Mahāvihāra of Holy Jetavana'.[3]

[1] They were in fact Khalijis of Turkish origin. 'Khalj is the name given to the land lying on either side of the river Helmand in Afganistan. Various nomadic tribes had settled in Khalj from very remote times, and under such circumstances it is impossible to assert with absolute certainty that the Khalijis belonged to a particular tribe or race.'—*History of the Khalijis* by K. S. Lal (Allahabad: Indian Press, 1950), p. 14.

[2] See Smith's *Early History of India*, 4th Ed., p. 400, footnote 1.

[3] *Archaeological Survey Report for* 1907–1908, p. 120.

Its date, given according to the Śaka era, is June 23, 1130. Another inscription found in the same locality records the establishment of a monastery by one Vidyādhara, counsellor of Madana, 'king of Gadhipura', most probably a feudatory of Govindachandra. It dates in AD 1219—nearly two decades after the site had been devastated by Muhammad Ghori at the end of the twelfth century.[1]

Kumāradevī wanted to revive ancient Sārnāth, near Banaras which was then the Gahadvala capital, and she added the very last monastery to the immense complex that had grown up there from age to age.[2] But nearly all of them were then in almost complete ruin.

Kumāradevī's in fact was the biggest single construction in that monastic complex—an immense rectangular structure which was partly built over the ruins of, and partly encompassed, several pre-existing Gupta monasteries and shrines. In this monastery, also in ruins now, a *praśasti* on a stone-slab has been discovered—a lengthy poem in Sanskrit in eulogy of the queen Kumāradevī, composed by a poet named Kunda of Bengal 'versed in six languages', and inscribed on stone by Vāmana, an artist.[3]

It gives us a personal glimpse of the queen, though the description is couched in the conventional hyperbolic felicities: 'Her mind was set on religion alone; her desire was bent on virtue; she had undertaken to lay in a store of merit; she found a noble satisfaction in bestowing gifts' (verse 13). Nor is a reference to the attractive graces of her person omitted: 'Her gait was that of an elephant; her appearance charming to the eye; she bowed down to the Buddha and people sang her praise.' The *vihāra*, built by her, is described as an 'ornament to the earth' and consisting of nine segments (*Navakhaṇḍa-maṇḍala-mahāvihāra*)', expected to last 'as long as the moon and the sun'. Her husband King Govindachandra is spoken of in the *praśasti* as descended from God Hari—one who was 'commissioned by Hara to protect Vārāṇasī (i.e. the capital city, Banaras) from the wicked Turaṣka warriors'. Evidently the terror of Turaṣka invasion was looming ahead: its shadow lay heavy on the minds of all then dwelling in Banaras.

The remains of Kumāradevī's imposing monastery, which, as it appears from inscriptions, bore the name of Dharmacakrajina-vihāra, measure 760 feet from east to west (on the longer side of the rectangle) and has a central block of buildings. It encompasses several ruined *vihāras*. There is an open paved court on the west with rows of monks' cells on three sides. There were two gateways to the

[1] See *Journal of the Asiatic Society of Bengal* (1925—Vol. XXI, New Series).
[2] See also Part III, Sec. 4, p. 217.
[3] It is given in the *Archaeological Survey Report for* 1907–1908.

monastery towards the east, 290 feet apart from each other. The basement of the monastery, eight feet in height, is built of neatly chiselled bricks, decorated with various elegant mouldings on both the outer and the inner faces. But all the halls and apartments have long since crumbled to dust.

The efforts of Govindachandra and Kumāradevī to resurrect saṅgha life at Sārnāth on the eve of Muslim conquest were most remarkable, but it seems that both before and after the event, other attempts were made with the same aim and object here and there in Bihar (Magadha).

Jayachandra (*c.* AD 1170), a king of the same Gahadvala dynasty, has left an inscription at Bodhgaya, 'which opens with an invocation to the Buddha, the Bodhisattvas and the king's own religious preceptor, a monk named Śrīmitra' and records the construction at a place called Jayapura of a *guhā* (cave-monastery).[1] In a hill-region, anciently known as Saptadalākṣa near Gayā, a later inscription was discovered, of the reign of a 'king' named Asokacalla, recording the erection of a *vihāra* by Bhaṭṭa Dāmodara at the request of a number of the king's officers who evidently were Buddhists.[2] Such sporadic and strictly localized attempts at revival were made for some years even after the Muslim invaders had overrun nearly the whole of northern India.

Perhaps the strangest story of a monastic establishment outliving the Muslim depradations, is that of Nālandā. Here, even in 1235, when the University was but a sprawling mass of ruins, a solitary nonogenarian monk-teacher with a class of seventy students 'still rang the bell', like President Ewell of the ill-fated College of William and Mary.[3]

The question, whether saṅgha life and its traditions of so many centuries were entirely uprooted after the establishment of Muslim rule, admits only of a speculative answer. History bears witness in many odd ways that an institution, religious or cultural in character, does not die off even when all its vital organs have been crushed. It retains yet a ghostly sort of life. After the annihilation of monasteries, the old saṅgha life, as some scholars are inclined to believe, persisted,

[1] Cited in R. C. Mitra's *Decline of Buddhism in India* (Visva-Bharati, 1954), p. 42.
[2] *Ibid*, p. 43.
[3] This is from the eye-witness account of the Tibetan Lāmā, Dharmasvāmī who visited Nālandā in 1235. See Part V, Sec. 2, pp. 347–378.

The story of President Ewell, preserved by the Yale University Corporation, is as follows. In 1881, this college had to close its doors for seven years during the Civil War in America. The college was deserted and fell into ruins. It was finally overcome by financial catastrophe. 'But every morning during these seven years, President Ewell used to ring the chapel bell. There were no students; the faculty had disappeared; and the rain seeped through the leaky roofs of the desolate buildings. But President Ewell still rang the bell. It was an act of faith; it was a gesture of defiance. It was a symbol of determination that the intellectual and cultural tradition must be kept alive even in a bankrupt world.'

only it went underground. But out of its seed sprouted new cults and new monastic orders, of which one, the Mahimā-dharma, which sprang up in the eighteenth century at Mayurbhanj in Orissa, offers a most curious, most remarkable and significant instance.[1]

[1] Mahimā-dharma was a cult that grew up in Orissa and had a large following. Its adherents created a monastic order, the rules and regulations of which are formulated and set down in its Oriyan scripture. The discovery of this cult and its monastic order was made by an eminent Bengali scholar, Nagendra Nath Vasu, in the opening years of this century, and an account of it is given in his monograph, *Modern Buddhism and its Followers in Orissa* (pub. in Calcutta, 1911). 'Of the twelve or thirteen ascetic rules,' says Mr Vasu at pp. 174–175 of the monograph, 'mentioned in the Buddhistic scriptures, the Mahimā-dharmin monk has even up till now been observing the rules of Piṇḍapātika, Sapadāna-cārika, Ekāsanika, Paṭṭapiṇḍika and Khalu-pacchādbhaktika. But these are never found to be observed by Vaiṣṇava monks or ascetics or those of any other sect.'

Some scholars hold the opinion that the Buddhist Saṅgha tradition was followed by Śaṅkarācārya in the institution of 'Maths' and that the tradition survives to this day in the still vigorously functioning *āśramas* set up by Swāmī Vivekānanda in India in the last century. These *āśramas* function under a central *āśrama* at Belur in Bengal and have many establishments all over India.

6

Survey of Monastic Remains of Northern India

IN India, north of the Vindhyas, such a clean sweep has been made of vihāras by time's ravages and men's that no monastery ruins remain standing except at two places, Nālandā and Somapura (Paharpur). A good many of them, however, sunk to their earth-buried foundations, have disclosed their lost identities under the archaeologist's spade and shovel.

Excavations over more than a century at different archaeological sites in northern India have shown that a monastery site was rarely abandoned. When the first structure got totally ruined or destroyed, it was replaced by a new one *in situ*, so that the original foundations went deeper and deeper under layers of successive construction. The monastic remains already brought to view, except at Taxila, are mostly of the Gupta or post-Gupta age, but from under the excavated foundations peep out vestiges of more ancient Kuṣāṇa-age structures. They are distinguishable by the special shape and size of bricks used in Kuṣāṇa constructions.

The remains of the Taxilan monasteries are the most ancient hitherto discovered. Before the Hūṇa invaders laid it waste in the fifth century AD, the Taxila region under the Kuṣāṇa kings (first-third centuries AD) had been a flourishing seat of Buddhism. It covered three city-states, now known as Bhir Mound, Sirkap and Sirsukh, where saṅgha life appears to have flourished in a number of large monastic establishments. Their foundations have been unearthed; they form an extensive complex. Their age is indicated by the archaeological finds in the debris. Among them are sundry specimens of Gāndhāra art, but no find of post-Kuṣāṇa period. Back of the Kuṣāṇa age, no trace of monastic ruins of the BC centuries has been discovered so far.

Among these ruins of Taxila are the remains of the Pippala Monastery, so called from the name of the mound on which it was situated. Judged by the layout it was a unitary construction. It is thus described by Marshall.[1]

'Of the Buddhist monuments (at Taxila), the most interesting was that unearthed in a mound called Pippala. . . . The remains brought

[1] (Annual) *Archaeological Survey Report*, 1923–24, pp. 61–62.

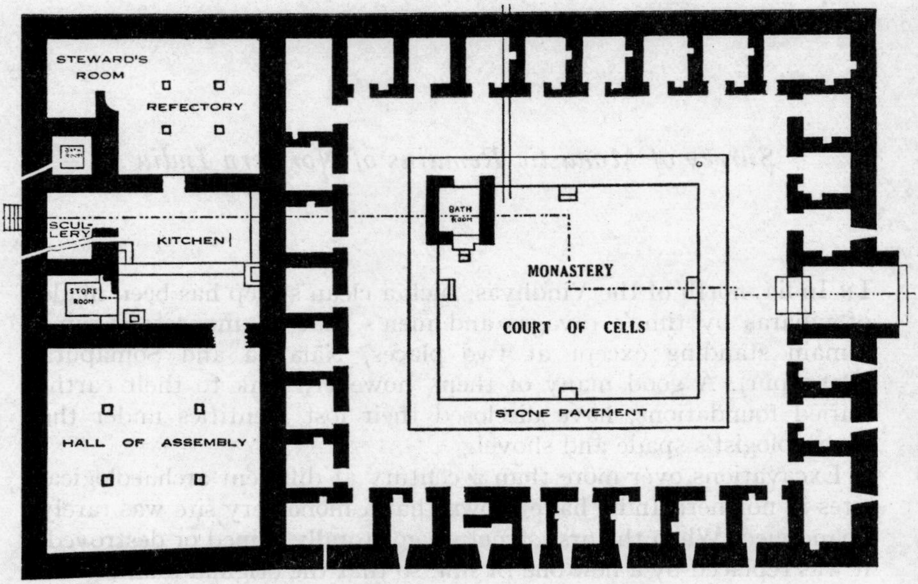

Plan of Pippala Monastery, Taxila.

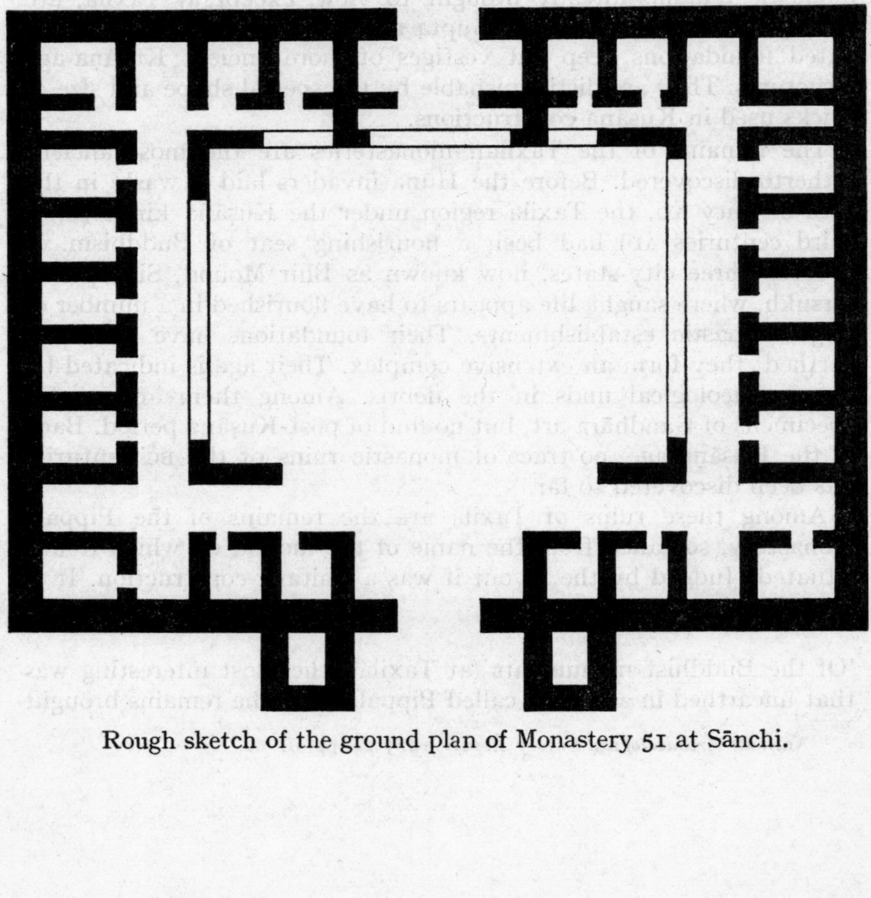

Rough sketch of the ground plan of Monastery 51 at Sānchi.

to light are of two distinct periods. To the east is the courtyard of a monastery dating from the Kuṣāṇa times and consisting of an open quadrangle in the centre with ranges of cells on its four sides. In the middle of the courtyard is the basement of a square *stūpa* facing north, and close beside it the ruins of three other *stūpas*. This early monastery, which is constructed of diaper masonry of the typical Kuṣāṇa pattern, must have fallen to ruin before the fourth century of our era: for at that time a second monastery was erected over the western side of it, completely burying beneath its foundations all that remained of the old cells and verandah on this side. At the same time also the rest of the early monastery was converted into a *stūpa*-court by dismantling and levelling with the ground everything except the *stūpas* in the open quadrangle and the back walls of the cells which were now to serve as an enclosure wall, probably five or six feet in height, for the new courtyard.'

What Marshall calls the 'typical Kuṣāṇa pattern' was perhaps older than the Kuṣāṇa age. It was the pattern on which the *leṇa*-type monasteries of the BC centuries used to be built for the accommodation of a single monk-fraternity in each. We find this ancient pattern adopted not only in the Taxilan monasteries, but prevalent all over northern India, though the Gupta age made, without scrapping the pattern, diverse architectural variations upon it.

Its basic character appears from the fact that it is reproduced in *all* regions of northern India. This can be visualized by taking for comparison monastery foundations unencumbered by later constructions upon them, allowing us thereby to form a general idea of the original structure. For the purpose of such comparison, let us take two monastery-foundations from two widely separated zones—Taxila in Gāndhāra and Sanchi in the Madhya Pradesh. Their exact similarity of pattern shows that they conformed to a general tradition in monastery construction, rather than to a local or regional architectural mode.

Compare the two sketches of the Pippala Monastery of Taxila and Monastery No. 51 discovered at Sanchi in 1936.[1] Their similarities indicate that by the first or second century AD a type and pattern of *vihāra* construction had emerged and become fixed all over northern India from Taxila down to Sanchi.

A monastery thus built was a compact building designed to fit exactly the living needs of a single saṅgha, of just one congregational unit. But, within this pattern, the open quadrangle developed afterwards into a roofed and pillared hall (*Maṇḍapa*) and the cult-object (*Stūpa* or Buddha-image), originally installed in the quadrangle itself,

[1] About this monastery, see Part III, Sec. 6, p. 222.

was afterwards shifted to a sanctuary with facility for circumambulation (*pradakṣiṇā*).

'The best gift to the Saṅgha is the gift of a *vihāra*', is the Lord's saying reported in the canon,[1] and *vihāras* were built over all the early centuries of Buddhism by lay devotees for the accommodation of monk-communities (*saṅghas*). The original purpose of the gift, as we have seen,[2] was to provide shelter for the *vassa* (rain-retreat) for wandering monks; later on when the monks ceased to be wanderers and the *vihāra* became more or less the permanent abode of a saṅgha, the purpose was to house a monk-fraternity at a population centre.

These *vihāras* in the early age of Buddhist history, that is, through all the BC centuries, were the nerve-centres of Buddhism. They were not mere convents to shelter monks from contact with the world—to facilitate exclusive pursuit, away from the world, of the round of their rites and meditations. As Nāgasena points out,[3] the chief use of a *vihāra* was not for the monks themselves, but for the facilities it provided for contacts between monks and laity. This, in Nāgasena's view, was the sole justification for the institution of monasteries; otherwise the monks might find it more congenial to spiritual exercise to live in the depths of a forest. It was in recognition of this use and utility of a *vihāra*—as a radiating centre of Buddhism—that lay Buddhists were zealous to build monasteries and see them prosper and multiply.

In northern India there were favoured sites for monastery building: these were places which provided occasions and opportunities for the coming together of monks and lay people—first, the four pre-eminent places of Buddhist pilgrimage, viz. Lumbinī, Gayā, Sārnāth and Kushinagara; secondly, those celebrated in the Buddha-legends and associated with the Buddha's earthly career; and thirdly, the vicinity of the great *Stūpas*.

a. IN THE FOUR PLACES OF PILGRIMAGE

In the *Mahāparinibbāna Suttanta* are listed the four holiest places of pilgrimage for a Buddhist—the sites respectively of the Lord's nativity, his 'enlightenment', his first sermon and his great passing away.[4]

Lumbinī, the holy birthplace, had been known to Buddhists from the Buddha-legends, though it would seem that to the legend-makers themselves its exact location was not known. Its geographical bearing is mentioned vaguely: 'in the Sakya territory beside the

[1] Cullavagga, VI, 5—*Vihāradānaṁ saṅghassa aggaṁ Buddhena vaṇṇitaṁ.*
[2] Part I, Sec. 6, p. 94. [3] See Introduction, p. 26, footnote. 1.
[4] Mahāparinibbāna Suttanta, V, 16–22.

Himālayas'.[1] From Magadha, where the legends were being made, to the Himalayan foothills, the trek by no means was easy; the way was long and difficult—across rivers and forest-lands—and few could venture on the pilgrimage. He who brought Lumbinī out of the mist of legends into the light of topography was no other than Emperor Asoka himself. A legend, drawn from distant historical reminiscence, about Asoka's pilgrimage to Lumbinī undertaken in his twentieth regnal year (*c.* 249 BC) is given in the *Divyāvadāna*:[2] it is now confirmed by the discovery of Asoka's commemorative pillar at the site.

The history of Lumbinī is a blank for nearly seven hundred years after that, until we hear of it again from Fa-hsien who did not, however, find it possible to visit it: it had been swallowed up by the *tarai* (forest overspreading the Himalayan foothills). Hsüan-tsang did visit Kapilavastu in the same terrain, but found it likewise in the jungle's death-grip. It seems from his account that he was able to gather some information about Lumbinī, which he does not seem to have visited, from contact with a company of thirty monks who still clung to the ruins of the holy Sākya capital—particulars about Asoka's pillar and the 'oil-river' running nearby. These are the two landmarks of Lumbinī today, besides an ancient shrine of unknown age containing a defaced image of Māyā.

Perhaps between the time of Asoka's visit and its disappearance in the *tarai* forest—the span probably of a century or two—some monasteries did spring up at Lumbinī. Archaeological exploration, however, has not been too diligent here and no ruins identifiable as monastic remains have been discovered. When in the nineties of the last century the Asoka Pillar was discovered, it stood in the midst of an extensive wilderness of *Sāla* (*shorea robusta*) trees.

At Gayā, the venue of the 'enlightenment', no traces of ancient monasteries have been discovered, although some remains of Kuṣāṇa sculpture have been found. The great monasteries seen here by Hsüan-tsang were none of them earlier than the Gupta age.

The story of Sārnāth where the Wheel of Law was first set rolling is different. Here were set up two great *stūpas* for ceremonial public worship called respectively *Dhāmekh* (*Dharmekṣa*? or *Dhamaka*?) and *Dharmarājika*. What their ancient names were or when they had been first built is not known. Dhamekh is still *in situ*, but Dharmarājika was pulled down in the eighteenth century by Jagat Singh of Banaras who was then prospecting for quarries of building materials. He found a casket within the *stūpa*, encasing some relics, which was consigned by him to the Ganges. Near it stands an Asoka Pillar.

[1] See *Pabbajjā Sutta* in the *Sutta-nipāta*, vv. 18–19 (SBE, vol. X, pp. 68–69).
[2] *Divyāvadāna* (Ed. by Cowell and Neil), pp. 389–390.

Probably it had been planted here by command of the emperor himself, with the emperor's '*Saṅghabhedaka*' edict inscribed upon it.

If the pillar has been, as it seems, all along *in situ*, the inscription suggests that even in Asoka's reign there was a monk-community of recognized standing settled at Sārnāth. A great complex of ruined monasteries lies round about covering an extensive area to the north of the two great *stūpas*. Further excavations may reveal more monasteries; those unearthed belong to the Gupta age. But under their foundations are remains of older Kuṣāṇa buildings and, out of their debris, a number of finds of Kuṣāṇa age have been obtained.

It is not known when this great monastery cluster at Sārnāth first began—certainly it was long before the commencement of the Gupta age and, probably even before that of the Kuṣāṇas. The first beginnings might have been in BC centuries—perhaps in the second or the first; and, if the existence of the Asoka Pillar with the inscription, which concerns the monk-community in particular, can be taken as an indication, the time may be pushed still farther back to Asoka's reign in the third BC. There are ruins upon ruins and, as depths are excavated, stray artefacts and bits of brick-work come to light. The finds of greatest antiquity at Sārnāth, save the Asoka Pillar, are some railings of uprights assignable to the Śuṅga era.

It seems that at Sārnāth, from the beginning to the end of its history, monks from all quarters, of different sects and schools, used to congregate, with the result that fissiparous tendencies were apt to set in and widen, which may be taken as the reason why Asoka's '*Saṅghabhedaka*' edict had to be promulgated here. Maybe it was considered only fit and proper that the saṅgha should be at union at least on the supremely holy spot which saw the first turning of the Wheel of Law. At any rate, we can trace in the Kuṣāṇa and Gupta inscriptions the existence at Sārnāth of three sects and schools, viz. Vātsīputrika, Sarvāstivāda and Sāmmitīya.[1] The settlement of Mahāyānist monks too, as we shall presently see, is traceable and images of the Mahāyānist pantheon like Bodhisattvas, Tārā (in several varieties) and Hārukā (Tāntric) have ben found at Sārnāth.

A great monastic establishment flourished at Sārnāth at the time of Hsüan-tsang's visit in *c.* AD 637. It is difficult to say whether the present ruins indicate any part of it. It was, as described by Hsüan-tsang,[2] 'in eight divisions all enclosed within one wall', that is, a monastery of the *Mahāvihāra* type—'with tiers of balconies and rows

[1] (*a*) *Vātsīputrika*—mentioned in an early Gupta inscription on the Asoka Pillar; (*b*) *Sarvāstivāda*—mentioned in an inscription on some construction round the ruined Dharmarājika Stūpa (*Ācāryānāṁ Sarvāstivādināṁ parigrahe*) and in two other places; (*c*) *Sāmmitīya*—mentioned in another inscription on the Asoka Pillar and also in other inscriptions (seventh century AD?).

[2] Beal's *Buddhist Records*, ii, pp. 45–46.

of halls, extremely artistic'—which suggests Gupta-age construction—'inhabited by 1,500 monks of the Sāmmitīya school'. 'Within the great enclosing wall was a temple above 200 feet high, surmounted by an embossed gilt *āmra* (mango fruit); the base and the steps were of stone; in the brick portion above were more than 100 rows of niches each containing a gilt image of the Buddha; inside the temple was a bell-metal image of the Buddha in the attitude of preaching, as large as life.'

The Sāmmitīya monks were Hīnayānists, but a number of Mahāyānists too occupied the monasteries of Sārnāth. A stone-inscription in six fragments has been found in the ruins to the east of the Dhāmekh Stūpa, which records that a copy of the holy Mahāyāna text, *Aṣṭasāhasrikā*, was prepared by a monk in AD 1058 and presented along with other offerings to the monks of the establishment called 'Saddharmacakra-pravartana-Mahāvihāra', which is now untraceable.

If monasteries had started growing up at Sārnāth in Asoka's reign, monastery-building here must have had a history of over thirteen hundred years. All kinds of monasteries, great and small, must have gone up during this span of centuries and been occupied by monks of various sects—how many in all it is impossible to say. The last monastery built here, enclosing a number of ruined shrines and monks' cells and covering the ruins of an earlier establishment, was in the reign of Govindachandra (AD 1114–1154) of Kanouj who ruled from the nearby city of Banaras. It was built by his devout Buddhist queen Kumāradevī. It has been already described.[1] The *praśasti* (Poetic Eulogium) in Sanskrit discovered in its ruins, which has been already referred to, says that the site has been kept by her '*as it was in the time of Asoka*'—only she has restored it and made it 'more wonderful'.[2]

Kushinagara, the scene of the 'Great Decease', ancient Kusinārā, which at the time of the memorable event was a mere 'wattle and daub (*Kuḍya*)' township of the Mallas, 'set in the midst of jungles', as described in the legend,[3] has only been partially explored. But the foundations of at least ten ancient monasteries have been revealed.

The most conspicuous landmark of Kushinagara is a huge *stūpa* called Mukuṭabandhana which, according to the scriptural legend, was consecrated by the Mallas to the Buddha's body-relics after his cremation.[4] About half a mile to its west stands a smaller *stūpa* flanked by a shrine (now renovated) which houses a huge recumbent

[1] Part III, Sec. 5, pp. 208–209.

[2] '*Dharmāśoka-narādhipasya samaye Śrī-dharmacakrajina-mahāvihāra yādṛk tannyāya rakṣitaḥ punarāyana-cakre tato'pyadbhutam*'—v. 23. (The text of the *Praśasti* will be found in *Archaeological Survey Report* for 1907–1908.)

[3] Mahāparinibbāna Suttanta, v. 41.

[4] Mahāparinibbāna Suttanta, VI, 62.

stone-image of the Buddha. The image, made at Mathura, had been installed at Kushinagara by a monk named Haribala sometime in the reign of the Gupta king Kumāragupta (AD 413–455). This image was seen by Hsüan-tsang on his visit to Kushinagara in AD 637. It seems to have got shattered to fragments since, but has been restored now. The large area, now empty, between the Mukuṭabandhana Stūpa and the stūpa close by the shrine was probably covered with monasteries, now sunk underground. Near the image-shrine, the existence of an ancient Mahāvihāra is indicated by the discovery of a number of clay-seals with the legend in Gupta characters, 'Śrī Mahāparinirvāna-Mahāvihārīya-ārya-bhikṣusaṅghasya' (belonging to the Bhikṣu-saṅgha of the Mahāparinirvāṇa-Mahāvihāra, which was the name of this monastic establishment).[1]

Fa-hsien, Hsüan-tsang and I-tsing all visited Kushinagara, and Hsüan-tsang describes it as a desolate town. The township is full of ruins of which no precise chronometric account is possible. Round the smaller stūpa near the Mahāparinirvāṇa shrine, where the great image of the recumbent Buddha rests, there are large remains of brick-structures, once monasteries. They have yielded on excavation archaeological finds which date them earlier than the fourth century, proving their pre-Gupta construction. To the west of them is another extensive block of ruins, covering a length of 150 feet, remains of two monasteries of two different periods, the second built on the ruins of the first. The second monastery seems to have been of several storeys from the thickness and massiveness of the walls. The archaeological finds point to its having been 'constructed in about the eighth century and deserted after AD 900'. There are later monuments also datable in the tenth and eleventh centuries.

b. ON SITES OF LEGENDARY FAME

Over the area called *Puratthima* in the ancient legends were places of legendary fame associated with the Lord's earthly career.

The Chinese pilgrims knew of them, and, as they descended from the border provinces of Gāndhāra and Kashmir into the interior of northern India, their pilgrim-steps turned naturally to these localities. They saw functioning there monastic establishments, both old and new, great and small.

Fa-hsien 'did' only a section of northern India in AD 399–414 during reign of the Gupta emperor Kumāragupta and, as he left India at Tāmralipti, taking ship at that eastern port for Ceylon, his travels in India did not extend farther. More than two centuries later came Hsüan-tsang, when the Gupta empire had passed away

[1] *Annual Report of Archaeological Survey*, 1911–1912.

with all its glory, leaving but a little after-glow in Harṣavardhana's comparatively small eastern empire. Hsüan-tsang in AD 630–643 travelled over most parts of India, both north and south, and his travel-record, supplemented by his biographer Hwui-li, is a mine of information on the monasteries of northern India then existing at the famous ancient seats of Buddhism. The state of monastic life and the condition of monastic establishments observed by him are, however, of 'period interest': of a period set in the very penultimate chapter of Buddhist history.

Yet the high antiquity of many of the monasteries, visited by both Fa-hsien and Hsüan-tsang, is pointed by the legends heard by them on the spot and reported in their records. These monasteries of ancient foundation must have been many times re-built on the original sites, and there was also a large number of monasteries seen by them deserted or in the last stages of decay.

Others, however, were not so ancient: among them were monasteries, built not to the simple square or rectangular pattern of old, seen at Taxila or at Sanchi (Monastery No. 51), but grand, multi-storeyed, turreted, with spacious *maṇḍapas* and large well-made *stūpas* or large-size Buddha-images in their sanctuaries, works of fine architecture and craftsmanship. We find also examples of the type of monastery called *Mahāvihāra* ('Great Monastery'), an aggregation of several monasteries, forming a single establishment within an enclosing circuit-wall. This type of grouped monasteries seems to have been a late development of the Gupta age.

Fa-hsien's *Fo-kwo-ki* and Hsüan-tsang's *Si-yu-ki* are no picturesque travelogues: they are *Ki*'s ('Records'), composed from an objective viewpoint and in the realistic trend of the Chinese mind. The pilgrims were interested mainly in observing monastic life as it was led in India in their own times—Fa-hsien declares that he made up his mind 'to go to India for the purpose of seeking the rules and regulations (*Vinaya*)'—also in collecting manuscripts, picking up legends and traditions of the holy places visited by them and, in the case of Hsüan-tsang, in studying Indian thought and philosophy.

On monastic art and architecture, Hsüan-tsang alone gives us some general observations. Occasionally, when something grand or spectacular strikes his eyes, he vouchsafes a short descriptive sketch. Only of Nālandā, his beloved *alma mater* in India, he speaks at large, with admiration as soulful as Matthew Arnold's in referring to his own *alma mater* Oxford—'that sweet city of dreaming spires', as Nālandā also was in Hsüan-tsang's time.

Since their translation into French and English by eminent sinologists of the last generation, Julien, Legge, Beal, Watters and Takakusu, the travel-records of the pilgrim trio, Fa-hsien, Hsüan-tsang and I-tsing, have been indispensable source-books for ancient Indian history. The routes followed by the first two have been carefully charted by Cunningham (in the *Ancient Geography of India*) and by other scholars after him.

On these routes lay the capital cities of several kingdoms and principalities. But to the visiting pilgrims more attractive and worthwhile in northern India were the places known to them from the Buddha-legends—Rājgir, Nālandā, Kosambī, Srāvasti, Vesālī and a host of others. Some of these were difficult of access or entailed wide detours, but the pilgrims were undeterred. At most of these ancient places they found not only monastic establishments, large and small, still functioning, but also ruins of monasteries that had existed centuries before their own time. They rehearse in their records legends heard by them about these ruined ancient monasteries and describe those they actually saw existing on the spot.

They found monastic life not exactly flourishing in northern India; at many places establishments of other religions were more numerous, perhaps more influential; only in Magadha the Saṅgha still maintained its hold.

c. ROUND THE STŪPAS

A series of *stūpas*, evidently for popular and ceremonial worship, sprang up since Asoka's reign in different parts of northern India. The best known are at Taxila, Sanchi and Sārnāth. The history of their construction is more or less a matter of guess or of legend. They are now silent sentinels of antiquity. Yet in the flourishing periods of Buddhism, they were centres of abounding life and activity, alive and agog with worshippers in hundreds congregating round them to celebrate, on a more or less grand scale, Buddhist religious festivals.

Round these *stūpas*, *vihāras* naturally grew up in clusters—not of mushroom growth, but settled monk-establishments traversing a centuries-old history of decay, renovation, structural additions and alterations.

At Taxila, near the Dharmarājika Stūpa and other smaller *stūpas*, the foundations of an extensive complex of monasteries have been revealed by several years' archaeological field-work under the late Sir John Marshall.[1] Among them the most clearly traceable is the monastery 'Pippala', already described. These monasteries in all likelihood came into existence in the early centuries of the Christian era when the Kuṣāṇa kings ruled here and perhaps all of them were

[1] See Marshall's *Taxila* and *The Stūpas and Monasteries of Jaulian* (Memoir No. 9 of *Archaeological Survey Report*, 1921). See also *Archaeology in India* (Publication No. 66 of Bureau of Education, India, 1950).

devastated in the fifth century AD when Taxila fell to the Hūṇas.[1] In the debris of these monasteries the archaeological finds are wholly of the Kuṣāṇa period; they consist of Kuṣāṇa coins and Gāndhāran artefacts. But they represent the only monastic complex discovered in India that goes so far back in time, with perhaps the sole exception of Sanchi Monastery, No. 51.

The story of the Sanchi monasteries is decidedly more historical, fuller and more varied, and may be told at greater length.

Here at Sanchi, saṅgha life began early. The place was anciently known as Cetiyagiri, and the legend is that it was here that Mahādeva—a name that seems ghostly, but is great in the history of the rise of sects in Buddhism, as one whose attack on the presumptions of Arhats blasted the way for the emergence of the Mahāsāṅghika sect—settled down and established a new school of Buddhism called Cetiyavāda. It flourished later at Amarāvatī.

Sanchi was a sort of satellite to the Maurya city of Vidiśā and traces still remain of an ancient highway from Vidiśā to Cetiyagiri (Sanchi). But the city seems to have lost its importance in the early centuries of the Christian era when the Kuṣāṇa kings ruled in this part. Although they are known to have been patrons of Buddhism, no traces of their benefactions have been found at Sanchi. By-passed for several centuries, Vidiśā regained importance early in the fifth century when Chandragupta II (of the Gupta dynasty), campaigning against Kuṣāṇa satraps, came there in person with an entourage of ministers, generals and feudatories and annexed the Kuṣāṇa territory.[2] Among his ministers was one Vīrasena Śāba of Pāṭaliputra, who, perhaps as a monument to the Gupta victory, made a series of cave-temples in the neighbouring mountain of Udayagiri (in the Sātpurā range, a branch of the Vindhyas) and left inscriptions there.

Thus Sanchi came under Gupta dominion in the first decade of the fifth century and became at once the headquarters of saṅgha life in the region. But oblivion had fallen on its old name Cetiyagiri: it acquired a new name, Kākanāda, probably from the small village at the foot of the hill from which it is attained from the Vidiśā side. The village now bears the somewhat altered name Kānakheḍā.

On the balustrade of the 'Great Tope' of Sanchi, inscriptions of the Gupta age point to the existence round the *stūpa* of some great monasteries, one of which is called the 'Mahāvihāra of Kākanādabhoṭa'. To this monastery, one Āmrakāradeva, son of Undāna, made a donation of 25 *dinars* in cash and the revenue of a whole village purchased by him for the purpose of donation; the modern name of

[1] Taxila is now in West Pakistan. The name is the Graecized form of Sanskrit *Takṣaśilā*.
[2] See Ray Chaudhuri's *Political History*, pp. 555–556.

this village tallies with that given in the inscription. This donation is dated in the ninety-third year of the Gupta era, i.e. AD 412–413, which is round the time when Sanchi came under Gupta rule.[1] The other donation to the same 'Mahāvihāra' was made a few years later by a lady named Harisvāminī. Consisting of 12 *dinars* in perpetuity (*akṣayanivi*), it is dated AD 450–451, in the reign of a later Gupta king Kumāragupta I.[2]

The record of these donations indicates that, as Sanchi came under Gupta dominion, a new chapter opened in the monastic life of this centre. All the monastic ruins excavated here are of the Gupta age, though there is reason to think that one pre-Gupta monastery also has been discovered—Monastery No. 51.

Its priority in time is suggested by two facts. The remains are on a lower level than the foundations of the Gupta monasteries and they lie outside a circuit wall which sometime, probably, according to archaeological evidence, in the eleventh century, was constructed to mark out the main *stūpa*-and-monastery area on the hill, encompassing the 'Great Tope' and the smaller one near it and including all the scattered outlying ruins of monasteries and temples. At the time of erection of this boundary wall, Monastery No. 51 was perhaps not visible at all, having disappeared underground. It was excavated as late as in 1936.

The Gupta-age monastic remains of Sanchi are in two great complexes—one to the east and the other to the south of the 'Great Tope'. How many edifices were comprised in these two groups it is impossible to compute, as they present successive layers of construction. They are deposits of succeeding centuries. Neither can it be ascertained whether some of these ruins represent the 'Mahāvihāra' referred to in the two inscriptions of Āmrakāradeva and Harisvāminī.

A tall towering temple of late construction (tenth or eleventh century), built on the ruins of an older one, destroyed by fire, dominates the eastern group.

Adjacent to the temple are ruins of monasteries, built and rebuilt, with numerous monks' cells in them. In the confused heap of ruins, structures, dating by archaeological evidence so late as the tenth or the eleventh century, are traceable.

To the south also of the 'Great Tope' is a complex of buildings, all in ruins, comprising monasteries, *maṇḍapas*, shrines and chambers.

This group directly faces the 'Great Tope'. In the front line are two Gupta-age temples. One of these is comparatively small, but in a good state of preservation; the other is a vast one, in ruins, sprawling

[1] Lüders' *List*, No. 35.

[2] See Radha Govinda Basak's *History of North-eastern India* (Calcutta, 1934), pp. 58–59.

over a large area. This latter temple, rectangular in shape, shows an apsidal end with an inset platform where a great Buddha-image, of which no trace has been found, perhaps used to stand. Broken shafts of pillars still stand, their arrangement suggesting that the temple had a nave with apsidal end, flanked by aisles on both sides for circumambulation and separated from the nave by two rows of pillars. The temple is of great dimensions with many-pillared *maṇḍapas* adjunct to it, and is of special interest as being the only example in northern India of the *cetiyaghara* pattern of West Indian *leṇas*.

Both the monastery-groups are dominated by the 'Great Tope'. They appear to have been built in the Gupta age on the ruins of older monasteries. It is likely that one of them comprised the 'Kākanāda Mahāvihāra' of early Gupta times.

Sanchi was first discovered in 1818 by a party of British soldiers who were passing along the valley down below.[1] They descried the 'Great Tope' on the hill-top and reported the discovery to the Calcutta headquarters of the East India Company then ruling in India. At that time its ancient name *Kākanādabhoṭa* was not known, and it acquired a new one from a hamlet, a tiny cluster of hutments, named Sanchi, clinging still to the hill-side.

[1] See *Journal of the Asiatic Society of Bengal*, vol. III (1834), p. 489, and vol. IV (1835), p. 172.

7

The Maitraka Monasteries of Valabhī

On the break-up of the Gupta empire round the middle of the sixth century AD, the political history of India repeated itself. It became once again a string of regional histories—of small kingdoms with shifting boundaries, leaping up to power by just a *pronunciamento*, whose commencement or continuity is in most cases indeterminate.

Among these kingdoms, however, the Maitraka kingdom in Sourāshtra (Gujerat) with its capital at Valabhī has more spotlight from history. This off-shoot kingdom seems to have inherited the Gupta tradition of royal patronage to monasteries, and Buddhism flourished at its capital Valabhī which rose to widespread fame as a centre alike of learning and commerce under a dynasty of kings styling themselves 'Maitrakas' in their royal seals.

Valabhī, now a petty township of about 7,000 inhabitants and hardly three square miles in extent, is about three to four miles inland, eastward of the Bay of Cambay. Local tradition has it that many centuries ago it spread right down to the coast. Then the sea gained upon it on one side, giving it the 'semblance of a human ear', and swallowed up the great harbour and wharf and all the edifices of the hinterland.

On one side of Valabhī flows a stream called Ghālā. It was anciently a river of considerable width and the main artery of outward merchant traffic. It is now a short and narrow inland channel, yet with a knack of going into spate during the rains. When the water is low, the ruined foundations of many a building, washed away centuries ago by its strong current, can still be glimpsed in its bed.

From bordering fields on the north-west of the Ghālā stream have been dug out an assortment of broken pieces of red polished ware of non-Indian make, imports from Persia or Rome with which Valabhī was in commercial intercourse in ancient times. Along with these antiquities has also been found a number of scattered Buddhist antiques—small images and Buddha-heads and tiny terra-cotta tablets called *Dharmagutikās* with the formula of the Buddhist creed, *Ye dharmā hetu-prabhavā, etc.*, inscribed on them.[1] But other finds of

[1] The formula itself is very ancient. It is found in the Theravāda Pali canon (Mahāvagga, I, 23, 5) where it is called '*Dhamma-pariyāya* (*Formula of Dhamma*) *for a Paribbājaka*'. It is found inscribed on votive stūpas and clay tablets all over India from Taxila and Kushinagara in the north to Ajanta and Kanheri in the south, mostly in its Sanskrit version. Perhaps its use as a credal formula commenced not

13. *The Bāgh Caves*

Panoramic view of Bāgh caves, showing the debris clearance between caves No. 3 and 4. (Photo: Department of Archaeology, Government of India)

14. *Prayer hall* (*Cetiyaghara*) *in a monastic establishme*[nt] *showing the façade.* (*Developed style from Pāndulenā.*) (Photo: Department of Archaeology, Governmen[t] of India)

Prayer hall (*Cetiyaghara*) *showing the façade.* (*Primitive style from Bhājā*)

greater historical value and interest have been yielded by archaeological excavation—a number of copperplate grants, neatly inscribed, of the ancient Maitraka rulers who had their capital at Valabhī from *c.* AD 490 to 770.[1]

The history of the rise of this kingdom is brief. At the time when the Gupta empire was tottering to its fall, an army-officer (*Senāpati*) of the Guptas name Bhaṭṭārka carved out of the dissolving empire a feudatory State for himself in Sourāshtra. He made Valabhī its capital and founded the dynasty named Maitraka. The third descendant in the line, Droṇasiṁha, became an independent sovereign and took the title of Mahārājā.[2] In the dynasty there were about twenty kings in all, and it seems that they were enlightened rulers under whom their capital became as far-famed a centre of learning in the west as Nālandā was then in the east.

The Maitraka kings professed the Brāhmaṇical Śaiva faith; the royal seals on their copperplate grants bear the sign of Nandī (Śiva's Bull) above the name of the founder of the dynasty, Bhaṭṭārka. Yet all of them appear to have been patrons of Buddhism and made several money-grants and land-grants to the Buddhist monasteries that sprang up in the capital and its vicinity.

At some time unknown, perhaps not long after Valabhī's rise as the Maitraka capital, here had come two distinguished Mahāyāna masters who were disciples of Vasubandhu—Sthiramati and Guṇamati—and they settled in a monastery with a view to pursuing uninterruptedly their philosophical studies and literary labours.[3] Hsüan-tsang visited the ruins of this monastery near Valabhī. He says that it was not far from the capital—was a large monastery which had been originally founded by an *arhat*, named Acala. At Valabhī it was known by the reverential name, Bappāpādiya Monastery (Monastery of the Father). The name occurs in a grant to this monastery made by King Dhruvasena II in *c.* AD 588, in which he makes mention of 'Ācārya Bhadanta Sthiramati who

much earlier than the commencement of the Gupta age. The formula stands thus in translation: 'Of all phenomena that proceed from a cause, the Tathāgata has told the cause; he has also told about their ending (*nirodha*). Thus has spoken the Mahā-Sramaṇa (i.e. the Buddha)'.

The formula sets up the Buddha as the master exponent of the Law of Causality and it was accepted by both the Hīnayānists and the Mahāyānists. There is a brief commentary upon it in Buddhaghosa's *Samantapāsādikā* and a longer one in the Tibetan version of a Sanskrit text entitled *Āryadharma-dhātugarbha-vivaraṇa*, fathered on Nāgārjuna (see *Gautama Buddha—25th Centenary Volume*, 1956, ed. by B. C. Law, pp. 246–249).

'The practice of imbedding such seals in stūpas and even on statues has been illustrated by many Buddhist monuments both in India and in Burma'—*Archaeological Survey Report*, 1914–1915, pp. 506.

[1] All these inscriptions discovered at Valabhī and at other places in Sourāshtra will be found collected in Girija Sanker Vallabhaji's *Historical Inscriptions of Gujerat* (two volumes, pub. from Bombay, 1935).

[2] See Rai Chaudhury's *Political History*, pp. 629–630.

[3] See Part IV, Sec. 6, pp. 291–292.

founded the *vihāra* of Śrī Bappāpāda at Valabhī'. Sthiramati and Guṇamati were eminent Mahāyānist scholars whose works, genuine and apocryphal, are extant in Chinese and Tibetan.[1] Their monastery must have become at that time a seat of Mahāyānist learning.

But at Valabhī, Mahāyāna Buddhism, to all seeming, did not make much headway. From the Maitraka copperplate grants and the statement of Hsüan-tsang, who visited the city in AD 640 when Dhruvasena II was on the throne, it appears that it was Hīnayāna Buddhism that flourished at the capital. 'There are some hundred saṅghārāmas', says Hsüan-tsang, 'with about 6,000 priests. Most of them study the Little Vehicle according to the Sāmmitīya school. There are several hundred Deva temples, with very many sectarians of different sorts.'[2]

The growth of Valabhī as a centre of Hīnayāna Buddhism seems to have started contemporaneously with the foundation of the Maitraka dynasty itself. Bhaṭṭārka was not a Buddhist himself, but a Śaiva. Yet an old monastery, associated with his name, is referred to as 'Bhaṭṭāraka Monastery' in one of the grants (*c.* AD 567) of Guhasena, suggesting its foundation by Bhaṭṭārka himself. It had stood for nearly three quarters of a century, was probably in ruins in Guhasena's time and was given (*'prasādīkṛta'*) to one of the king's officers (designated *Rājasthānīya Śūra*)—whether for renovation or for demolition is anybody's guess. Close by, another monastery called Abhyantarika, built by a lady named Mimmā, had sprung up and Guhasena's grant was made to this monastery.

Moreover, a great central monastic establishment, which seems to have grown afterwards into a sort of Maitraka State-institution, had already commenced at Valabhī with the foundation of a monastery by a grand-daughter of Bhaṭṭārka and sister's daughter (*Bhāgineyī*) of Dhruvasena I. The name of this noble lady was Duḍḍā. Nothing further is known of her personal life. The first royal endowment on her single, original monastery was made in AD 535 by her uncle Dhruvasena I, Bhaṭṭārka's son and successor. It consisted of the revenue of a village. Her monastery then became the nucleus of an extensive monastic group known as the 'Duḍḍā group of monasteries' (*Duḍḍā Vihāra-maṇḍala*) and was looked after by the State. Later royal grants refer to it by this name or call it a *Mahā-vihāra*, which means a number of monasteries aggregated as one establishment.

Of these monasteries in the Duḍḍā circle, the following are known from the grants: (i) Buddhadāsa Vihāra named after Ācārya

[1] See *Indian Antiquary*, Vol. VI, p. 9. Also Nanjio, No. 372 (C). Only one of Sthiramati's original works, a Sanskrit commentary on Vasubandhu's *Triṁśatikā*, is available. It has been edited by Syvain Levi.

[2] Beal's *Buddhist Records*, ii, pp. 266–267.

Bhadanta Buddhadāsa, (ii) Abhyantarika Vihāra built by Mimmā, (iii) Kākā Vihāra built by a merchant named Kākā, (iv) Gohaka Vihāra built by Gohaka, (v) Vimalagupta Vihāra built by Ācārya Vimalagupta, and (vi) Sthiramati Vihāra built by Sthiramati (probably not the Sthiramati who was Vasubandhu's disciple). Wealthy citizens chose the site to build monasteries upon because it was regarded as 'classic ground'. The following table of grants made to the monasteries by successive generations of Maitraka kings will show that those within the Duḍḍā circle were under royal care and protection: they formed, as it were, a State establishment.

From Dhruvasena I, son and heir to the founder Bhaṭṭārka, to the last-known king Śīlāditya III, nearly all the kings deemed it a matter of royal concern to see the Duḍḍā group of *vihāras* properly maintained:

Grants to Monasteries by Maitraka Kings:

Kings		*Grants made to*
1. Dhruvasena I (AD 519–549) (Varāhadāsa, a feudatory, also dedicated a *vihāra* to Ajita in AD 549)	(i)	Original Duḍḍā Monastery (AD 535)
	(ii)	Buddhadāsa Monastery in 'Duḍḍā circle' (A.D. 536)
2. Guhasena (AD 553–569)	(i)	Duḍḍā Monastery (AD 559)
	(ii)	Another grant to *ibid* (AD 565)
	(iii)	Mimmā Vihāra in 'Duḍḍā circle' (AD 567)
3. Dharasena II (AD 569–589 or 590)	(i)	Bappāpādiya Monastery, founded by Sthiramati (AD 588)
	(ii)	Kākā Monastery in the 'Duḍḍā Circle' (AD 589)
	(iii)	Duḍḍā Monastery (undated)
4. Śīlāditya I (AD 590–615)	(i)	Some monastery in the 'Duḍḍā Circle' (AD 605)
	(ii)	Duḍḍā Monastery (AD 605)
	(iii)	Vaṁsakata Monastery in village of the same name (AD 605)
	(iv)	Yakṣaśora Monastery (AD 608)
	(v)	*Ibid* (AD 609)
	(vi)	Vaṁsakata Monastery (undated)
5. Dhruvasena II (AD 627–641)	(i)	Purmmabhaṭṭi's Monastery, near Yakṣaśora Monastery (AD 629)
	(ii)	Yodhāvaka Monastery (AD 645)
6. Dhruvasena III (AD 650–654 or 650)	(i)	Duḍḍā Monastery (date gone)
7. Śīlāditya II (AD 658–685)	(i)	Gohaka Monastery in 'Duḍḍā Circle'
8. Śīlāditya III (AD 690–710)	(i)	Vimalagupta Monastery in 'Duḍḍā Circle' (undated)
	(ii)	*Ibid*
	(iii)	Some Monastery in 'Duḍḍā Circle' (date gone)

NOTE—The regnal years of the Maitraka kings, of whom only the principal donors to monasteries are named here, are approximate. They are set down as given in Dr Vriji's *Ancient History of Sourāshtra* (1952). The Maitrakas used the Gupta era and, as more than a hundred Maitraka inscriptions have been discovered, in almost all of which the year of the inscription appears according to Gupta era, it is quite possible to reconstruct an approximate chronology of the dynasty. The year of the Christian era is arrived at by adding 319 to that of the Gupta. The Maitrakas were succeeded by the Rāshṭrakūṭas and some Rāshṭrakūṭa kings also made grants to the Kampilya Monastery (see *infra*).

The *Duḍḍā Maṇḍala* of monasteries was for the use of monks only. But there was another *maṇḍala*, founded by one Yakṣaśrī, which was intended for nuns. The names of these nunneries too appear from the grants: (i) Yakṣaśūra Vihāra built by Yakṣaśūra, (ii) Pūrṇānnabhaṭṭa Vihāra built by Pūrṇānnabhaṭṭa and (iii) Ajita Vihāra built by a merchant named Ajita. Both Śīlāditya I and Dhruvasena II made grants to some of these nunneries.

The name of Duḍḍā is memorable in the history of Maitraka monasteries. Dhruvasena I, in giving the first royal donation to the monastery she founded, ensured its perpetual maintenance by the gift of the revenue of the village Pippalaruṅkari, to be applied to the specified normal purposes of these royal grants, viz. (i) repair of buildings, (ii) supply of requisites for regular maintenance of worship, and (iii) provision of victuals for the monks.[1] He mentions Duḍḍā in the grant as 'my own sister's daughter (*sva-bhāgineyī*)' and describes her as a 'most pious lay devotee (*paramopāsikā*)'. Prestige gathered round her name with the passing of time. To kings of later generations (as Guhasena) she was the 'worshipful (*pujyā*) Duḍḍā'—one of venerable memory.[2]

An interesting and perhaps significant point in Guhasena's grant of AD 565 to the Duḍḍā monasteries is the mention, in addition to the normal purposes conventionally listed in almost all Maitraka grants, of the acquisition of 'books on Buddhism' (*saddharmasya pustakapakra*. . . .). The addition of this item perhaps indicates that by Guhasena's time the monasteries were either organized or were in process of organization as seats of study and learning and were building up libraries.

It was Hīnayānist monks mainly who occupied these monasteries, for we find that the grants refer to the resident monk-community as 'Ārya Bhikṣu-saṅgha' or, as in Guhasena's grant, as 'Sākyārya

[1] *Vihārasya patita-viśīrṇa-pratisaṁskaraṇārthaṁ dhūpa-dīpa-taila-puṣpopoyogi ca sarvaṁ dravyaṁ valabhyāṁ svabhāgineyī paramopāsikā Duḍḍā-kārita-vihāra-pratiṣṭhā-pitānāṁ; Bhagavatāṁ samyak-saṁbuddhānāṁ-(ā)rya-bhikṣu-saṅghasya ca piṇḍapātāya*, etc.—See *Indian Antiquary*, Vol. IV, p. 106.

[2] See Guhasena's grant: '(*Valabhī*) *pure pujyā-Duḍḍā-kṛta* (*vi*) *hāra* (*sya*)'.—*Indian Antiquary*, vol. VII (Bühler's *Additional Valabhi Grants*), p. 67.

Bhikṣu-saṅgha of eighteen schools (*nikāyas*)'—the traditional number of schools in Hīnayāna Buddhism. The monks are described as 'coming from different directions (*nānādigabhyāgata*)' which is only a version of the ancient canonical phrase descriptive of the Bhikṣu-saṅgha as being of 'Four Quarters'. Though Hīnayāna Buddhism seems to have prevailed in these monasteries, we find traces also of the existence side by side of Mahāyāna Buddhism. Dhruvasena II made a grant to a monastery at the village of Yodhāvaka, built by one Skandabhaṭṭa, the resident saṅgha of which is described in the grant as '*Mahā-nikāya Ārya Bhikṣu-saṅgha*', where the expression, *mahā-nikāya*, most probably means Mahāyānist.[1]

Yet in the Hīnayānist monasteries of Valabhī, Buddha-pūjā, the ritual image-worship, seems to have been a major activity of the monks, attended with due rites and ceremonies. The kings in their grants provide for it: they include in the items of expenditure 'the cost of incense, lamps, oil and flowers (*dhūpa-dīpa-taila-puṣpa*)'.

Not a trace of the Maitraka monasteries of ancient Valabhī now remains in that township. Of their ensemble, it is impossible to form an idea. There is no eye-witness description, although Hsüan-tsang and probably I-tsing visited Valabhī in the seventh century AD. These monasteries must have been built in the Gupta style of turreted architecture and decorated with sculpture and painting.

The author of *Mañjuśrī-mūlakalpa*, writing at Gaura (in North Bengal) near the turn of the ninth century,[2] seems to have known from tradition something about the artistic appearance of the Maitraka monasteries. But as Gaura lay at a distance of over 1,000 miles to the east from Valabhī, he could have had no direct personal knowledge. In the conventional form of prophecy, adopted by him in the work, he speaks of the Valabhī king Śīla (Śīlāditya)—probably the same as Dhruvasena II (AD 627–641) of whom Hsüan-tsang speaks in the *Si-yu-ki*—as one who will make 'artistic (*citrān*) monasteries . . . and beautiful Buddha-images and various worshipable things.'[3]

After the reign of Śīlāditya III (AD 690–710), the Maitraka kingdom went into dissolution. But the Rāshṭrakūṭas, who wrested away

[1] See Bhandarkar's *A Valabhi Grant* in *Indian Antiquary*, Vol. I, p. 14. Also Vriji's *Ancient History of Sourashtra*, p. 176, footnote 5. Dr Vriji is of opinion on grounds which seem to me insufficient that 'in the sixth and seventh centuries, the chief form of religion must have been Mahāyānism' in Valabhī. It is contradicted by Hsüan-tsang's statement.

[2] See Jayaswal's *Imperial History of India*, Intro., p. 3.

[3] See *Mañjuśrī-Mūlakalpa*, vv. 587–589 (Jayaswal's *Imperial History of India*, Text, p. 24). 'In the country of the Lāḍas, there will be King Śīla, a Buddha. At Valabhī he will be Dharma-rājā. He will make attractive (*citrān*) monasteries with relics for public good, and beautiful Buddha-images, and various worships (vv. 586–589). He will be in the dynasty of Dhara and Kings of the Lāḍas. He rules for thirty years (vv. 59–98).'—Jayaswal's translation.

the major part of Maitraka territory, do not seem to have laid hands on the monasteries maintained by their predecessors. On the other hand two Rāshṭrakūṭa kings made grants at Kampilya for the usual purposes of a monastery as we find listed in Maitraka grants. They were: Dantivarman and Dhārāvarṣa.[1] Kampilya was a township in Sourāshtra, on the outskirts of modern Surat. In the latter's grant (*c.* AD 884) it is said that 500 monks were staying at that monastery at the time. It seems to have been the last stronghold of Buddhism in ancient Sourashtra.

When the Maitraka kings were still on the throne of Valabhī, I-tsing was on tour in northern India. He records the contemporary reputation of Valabhī as a famous educational centre to which students used to resort for higher education. In I-tsing's time there were two pre-eminent centres of learning in India—Nālandā in the east and Valabhī in the west. Speaking of the 'Method of learning in the West (i.e. India)', I-tsing says that it was usual for learners, after preliminary training, to resort to Nālandā or to Valabhī for further studies:

'Thus instructed by their teachers and instructing others they pass two or three years, generally in the Nālandā monastery in central India, or in the country of Valabhī in western India. These two places are like Chin-ma, Shi-chii, Lung-men and Chue-li in China, and there eminent and accomplished men assemble in crowds, discuss possible and impossible doctrines, and, after having been assured of the excellence of their opinions by wise men, become far-famed in their wisdom. To try the sharpness of their wit, they proceed to the king's court to lay down before it the sharp weapon (i.e. of their intelligence); there they present their schemes and show their (political) talent, seeking to be appointed in practical government. . . . They receive grants of land and are advanced to high rank; their famous names are, as a reward, written in white on lofty gates. After this, they can follow whatever occupation they like.'[2]

One may well wonder whether I-tsing was speaking of the Maitraka court at Valabhī in his reference to learned men seeking and finding careers in the government. The Maitraka kings, if the epithets describing them in the inscriptions be not purely conventional hyperbole, were men of learning and patrons of learning.[3] It was but natural

[1] See *Epigraphia Indica*, vol. VI (Bhandarkar on *The Plates of Dantivarman of Guzarat*), p. 286; *Ibid*, Vol. XXII (Altekar on *A New Copperplate of Dhruva II*), pp. 66–67.
[2] See Takakusu's *A Record of the Buddhist Religion*, p. 177.
[3] See Virji's *Ancient History of Sourashtra*, pp. 206–207.

that the royal court at Valabhī would be sought by men who had achieved success and done brilliantly in their academic curricula.

The existence of Jaina as well as Brāhmaṇical institutions for learners at Valabhī under the Maitraka régime is based on historical evidence. The Buddhist monasteries did not enjoy a monopoly in this matter. But the royal endowments were made mostly on the '*Duḍḍā-vihāra-maṇḍala*', and, as already said, in at least one of these grants a library of books on *Saddharma* (Buddhism) is envisaged.

Buddhist vihāras of the age, as we gather from Chinese records, were open to all learners, *māṇavakas* (ordinary pupils) as well as monks;[1] it was not necessary to be ordained to take advantage of the learning dispensed by them. The Śaivite Maitrakas would not be concerned with the propagation of Buddhism. But when we recall their partiality for culture and scholarship, it is legitimate to suppose that, aside from the desire to perpetuate Duḍḍā's memory and maintain monastic life in the Duḍḍā Mahāvihāra, the royal liberality towards it was motived by some such consideration. And the Mahāvihāra had already become a seat of learning or was growing to be one in AD 565 when Guhasena's grant was made.

What I-tsing says in his *Record*, made in 690,[2] represents the full maturity and consummation of Valabhī's tradition of learning. He speaks of Nālandā and Valabhī in the same breath as the two most distinguished seats of higher learning in India in his time. It is somewhat far-fetched to infer from this that they were parallel in their system and organization, or that one was a replica of the other. Almost nothing is known of the centres of learning in China with which I-tsing compares Nālandā and Valabhī. Though as seminaries both of them must have had certain common features, the fact that the Nālandā monasteries were Mahāyānist and the Duḍḍā monasteries at Valabhī Hīnayānist, must have made an appreciable difference in the syllabi and courses of instruction at the two centres. We know something of the organization of teaching at Nālandā, but the character of the organization at Valabhī is unknown. How far it conformed, as Nālandā did, to the university-type is, in the present state of our knowledge, a matter of pure conjecture.

The death-blow to Valabhī came not from the Rāshṭrakūṭas, but from the Tajjika (Arab) invaders—perhaps at some time in the eighties of the eighth century AD. They reduced all its edifices to rubble and dust including the Maitraka monasteries. We have no historical account of the final demolition of Valabhī, only a few fantastic legends from different sources.[3] But the vanished Maitraka

[1] See Part V, Sec. 1, p. 326.
[2] See Takakusu's *A Record of the Buddhist Religion*, Intro., p. lii.
[3] See Virji's *History of Ancient Sourashtra*, pp. 103–105.

capital left behind a trail of after-fame, fragments of which are caught in legends and stories of after-times.

Inset in the *Kathāsarit-sāgara* (a collection of stories in Sanskrit verse, composed by the Kashmirian poet Somadeva between AD 1063 and 1081) are a few references to Valabhī. Once famous for its wealth and culture, by then it had become only a city of legend.

We are told of the great merchants of Valabhī—of one named Vidyādhara and another named Devasena who had come all the way from Pāṭaliputra to Valabhī to make a fortune by trade.[1] Perhaps the legend is an echo of the city's one-time fame for commercial prosperity which is referred to in a story of Daṇḍin's *Daśakumāra-carita* (*c.* AD 700—when Valabhī was still the Maitraka capital) about a shipowner of Valabhī named Gṛhagupta said to have been so wealthy as to vie with Kuvera, god of wealth.[2]

In Gṛhagupta's days, Valabhī, now an inland town, was a busy seaport. Perhaps there were other cities on India's sea coasts as prosperous from commerce, but Valabhī's reputation was chiefly as a centre of learning. It is recalled two centuries after Valabhī's downfall in Somadeva's story of Viṣṇudatta, who, when he had completed his sixteenth year, prepared to go to Valabhī for education.[3] Coming of a family settled in the east where seats of learning like Banaras were available, he was yet sent to Valabhī far away to the west, perhaps because of its superior renown.

[1] *Kathāsarit-sāgara* (Taraṅgas 22 and 29). See D. P. Pandit's Ed. (1924), pp. 85 and 130.

[2] *Daśakumāra-caritam* (Kale's Ed., Bombay, 1925), p. 225.

[3] *Sa viṣṇudatto vayasā soḍaśa-vatsaraḥ; Gantuṁ pravavṛtte vidyāprāptaye Valabhī-purīṁ—Kathāsarit-sāgara, Taraṅga* 32.

PART IV

EMINENT MONK-SCHOLARS OF INDIA

1

Sources of Information

Śāntideva (eighth century AD) concludes the *Bodhicaryāvatāra* with a canticle, sublime and soulful, in which he prays that ideal conditions may supervene in all spheres of human life. For the monasteries, the conditions he desires as these:

'Let the Vihāras remain well established, humming with teaching and recitation (of lessons); let the unity of the Saṅgha be perennial and the work of the Saṅgha successfully carried out; let the Bhikṣus find solitude and also be desirous of learning, and meditate with minds, pliable and energetic, casting off all distractions.'[1]

In associating earnest study and learning with monastic life, Śāntideva was adverting to a traditional aspect of it—one that had become most pronounced in the monasteries of his own time.

The tradition had started far back in the early days of the Saṅgha. The Vinaya prescribed for a monk newly ordained a period of several years during which he had to be *in statu pupilari* under an *Upajjhāya* and an *Ācariya*. This period was called *Nissaya* (Dependence on a teacher).[2] The learning was at first conceived as a grounding in canonical lore, but at a certain stage this cloistral learning was liberalized and its scope extended.[3] The object in view evidently was that the Saṅgha should consist of men who were learned, who could effectively explain the doctrines of the religion to lay men and defend and uphold them in disputation.[4]

This tradition of learning and scholarship was continuous in the monasteries: it was incorporated with saṅgha life. Hence from century to century monastic learning produced a long line of monk-scholars, in the BC as well as in the AD centuries, but only a comparatively few outstanding names are known. Of its products in

[1] *Pāṭhasvādhyāya-kalilā vihārāḥ santu susthitāḥ Nityaṁ syāt saṅgha-sāmagrī saṅghakāryañca siddhyatu; Vivekalābhinaḥ santu śikṣākāmāśca bhikṣavaḥ Karmaṇya-cittā dhyāyantu sarvavikṣepavarjitāḥ.—Bodhicaryāvatāra*, Pariccheda 10, vv. 42–43. *Re* Śāntideva and *Bodhicaryāvatāra*, see Part IV, sec. 5 (b). The translation is mine.

[2] See Part I, Sec. 6, p. 92.

[3] See Part V, Sec. 1 (b).

[4] Compare the Buddha's declaration to Māra (in *Mahāparinibbāna Suttanta*, III, 7) that he would not pass away until his followers, 'having themselves learnt the doctrine, shall be able to tell others of it, preach it, make it known, establish it, open it, minutely explain it and make it clear—until they, when others start vain doctrine, shall be able by their truth to vanquish and refute it, and so to spread the wonder-working truth abroad'. (See SBE, Vol. X, p. 43.)

the BC centuries, we know little besides what is conveyed by their legendary after-fame. Writing had not come into use then; a scholar was one 'who had heard much' (*Bahussuta*) and the fruits of his scholarship, treasured in memory and orally dispensed, were liable to be dissipated by time—eventually lost to the world.

The transition from oral texts to written manuscripts to be perused and preserved is a crucial event in the history of a country's culture. Ceylonese chronicles record the time when it took place in Ceylon—between 43 BC and 17 BC in the reign of Vattagāmaṇi.[1] There is no comparable record for India. Yet a legend in the *Divyāvadāna* describes women reading the *Buddhavacana* by lamplight after the day's household chores were done, and taking notes on birch-bark leaves with pen and ink.[2] The legend is undated,[3] but by the third century AD the practice of writing was in vogue of which evidence comes from a slab of sculpture found at Nāgārjunakoṇḍa. This depicts the court of Suddhodana where priests interpret the Buddha's horoscope to the king, while a clerk standing at the foot of the throne makes a record of it with a stylus on a palm-leaf or thin slice of wood.[4]

When, however, from the early AD on, the function of *Bhāṇakas* (Reciters) was taken over by scribes, there were monk-scribes and monk-authors perhaps in every monastery of a better sort. Thus oral texts were replaced by an ever-growing manuscript literature which accumulated from century to century. This literature was almost wholly in Sanskrit, for when manuscript-writing commenced in India, Sanskrit was the established language of culture and scholarship. The Buddhist part of Sanskrit literature, however, disappeared almost wholly from the country through centuries of attrition, neglect and mass destruction.

A holy book is a precious gift worthy to be offered to a learned visiting monk at a monastery: perhaps the presentation was also deemed to be an act of merit on the donor's part. Advantage was taken of it by scholarly Buddhist monks who came out to India from other countries, specially from China and Tibet, both on pilgrimage and for collection of texts to supplement the literature of Buddhism in their own homelands. Manuscripts thus vanished lot by lot from India and found place in the stacks of Chinese and Tibetan monasteries.

[1] Oldenberg's *Dīpavaṁsa*, 20–21, and Turnour's *Mahāvaṁso*, Ch. xxxiii, vv. 100–101; Geiger's *Mahāvaṁsa*, (Trans., 1912), p. 237.

[2] Cowell and Neil's *Divyāvadāna*, p. 532—Rātrau pradīpena Buddhavacanaṁ paṭhanti; tatra bhūrjeṇa prayojanaṁ tailena masinā kalamāya tulena.

[3] The first century BC is a probable conjecture.

[4] This sculptured slab may be seen in the improvised museum at Nāgārjunakoṇḍa. Writing for certain purposes was not unknown in India even in the fifth century BC. There are references in Pali legends to writing and 'composition of letters' (see Oldenberg's *Vinayapiṭakam*, Vol. II, Index, p. 359, *Brahmajāla-suttanta*, 1, 14, etc.). But it seems to have been a special aptitude, rather than a general practice.

How many defies count. Fa-hsien took away a good number; later Hsüan-tsang and I-tsing in the seventh century a larger collection—the former '520 *fasciculi*, comprising 657 distinct volumes, carried upon twenty horses',[1] and the latter 400 in round number.[2] This manuscript collection from India by Buddhist pilgrims from abroad

Hsüan-tsang returning to China with a load of Sūtras on his back, a lamp hanging in front and a chowrie in the right hand. From a Chinese stone engraving.

became a customary practice. We are told in a Tibetan history that even so late as in the twelfth century a learned monk-scholar of Tibet who died in 1190 visited India with this object and took away 'many man-loads of Indian books', many of which, says the historian, 'are still preserved in the Monastery of Nor'.[3] On the other hand, Indian monks too who emigrated to and settled in China, Tibet,

[1] Beal's *Life of Hiuen-tsiang*, p. 214.
[2] Takakusu's *A Record of the Buddhist Religion*, p. xvii.
[3] See *Blue Annals*, Vol. II, p. 1053.

Burma and other countries must have taken large assortments of books with them. Thus India's cultural intercourse over several centuries with other Buddhist countries of Asia was attended with a steady loss of her wealth of Buddhist manuscripts.

The relieving feature of this process was that books that went out of India were looked after; they were preserved with pious care in the monasteries of China and Tibet, each find regarded as holy—as the 'precious life-blood of a master-spirit, embalmed and treasured on purpose to a life beyond life'. In the ancient 'Celestial Empire', the copying, translation and classification of these books was an organized industry carried on through several imperial régimes and often under imperial patronage; in the 'Land of Snow', as Tibet is named by her historians—a country less advanced culturally—the lāmās also preserved and translated the Indian books that passed across its borders, but this was done in several monasteries without a State-sponsored organization as in China.

These works were afterwards included in two encyclopaedic canonical collections: (i) the Chinese *Tripiṭaka* and (ii) the Tibetan *Kanjur* and *Tanjur* respectively. The Chinese and Tibetan collections together number in all about 6,753 works[1]—some of appalling length, others comparatively short. But the total number of Indian works in them represents only part of the whole.

When Buddhism went into decline, Buddhist literature fell into neglect in this country. The whole of it had been in Sanskrit, but the Sanskrit literature India has preserved as her classic heritage is non-Buddhist: we have to look to China and Tibet for the Buddhist supplement, and even literary works like those of Aśvaghoṣa and Śāntideva, fit to take at least a middling rank in Sanskrit literature, have been recovered from outside India.

Yet in this expurgated classical Sanskrit literature, there are scattered vestiges of the Buddhist part that has disappeared—citations in works of philosophy of the views of Buddhist scholars mentioned by name,[2] a few original texts on logic and metaphysics, a few text-books (like Candragomin's) on grammar.[3] They amount, however, to extraordinarily little.

[1] *Kanjur* and *Tanjur* contain 4,569 texts (according to *Tohoku Imperial University Catalogue*); the Taisho Edition of the Chinese *Tripiṭaka* 2,184 texts (according to *Hobogirin Catalogue*); but the Taisho edition is a syncretic one and the figure is therefore inconclusive.

[2] As Mādhavācārya does in the chapter on *Bauddha-darśana* in his compendium of Indian philosophy, *Sarva-darśana-saṁgraha*.

[3] Candragomin's work known as '*Candra-vyākaraṇa*' exists in original Sanskrit and is rival to Pāṇini's *Aṣṭādhyāyi*. It takes a high rank in the literature of Sanskrit grammar and Bopadeva in his grammar known as *Mugdhabodha* (latter half of thirteenth century?) names him among the 'eight great philologists' of India. Many works of Mahāyānist Buddhism in Tibetan are ascribed to Candragomin. S. C. Vidyabhusan assigns him to the early part of the eighth century (see Vidyabhusan's *Indian Logic*: *Mediaeval School*, pp. 121–123).

They are supplemented by stray Sanskrit manuscripts recovered from private collections in different parts of India, some of which have now been edited and published. To mention a few of the chance finds: a copy of *Tattva-saṁgraha* by Śāntarakṣita of Nālandā was discovered by Dr Bühler in Jasalmir Palm-leaf Collection;[1] a commentary on this work, entitled *Tattva-saṁgraha-pañjikā* by Kamalaśīla (also of Nālandā) was found in a section of the Jaina manuscript collection known as Pattan Bhandar at Pattan in Sourāshtra; from this collection were also recovered a copy of Vinītadeva's *Hetubindu-ṭīkā* (all these previously known only from Tibetan versions) and a copy of *Tarkabhāṣā* by Mokṣākaragupta of Jagaddala Mahāvihāra.[2] Perhaps other stray discoveries will be forthcoming in the future.

The Hūṇa and the Muslim destruction of monasteries in northern India has been referred to in Part III (Sec. 5). It made a clean sweep of Buddhist literature stocked in the better class of monasteries where works by eminent monk-scholars used to be preserved and studied, while the monastic universities of latter days had huge manuscript libraries. But in the ruthless wholesale destruction by fire and sword, these libraries were not spared.

The net result to us of this concatenation of historical circumstances is that, for the Buddhist literature that originated and developed in India, we have to look outside Indian borders, to Ceylon, China and Tibet.

The earliest and most ancient literature of Buddhism was recovered from Ceylon well over a hundred years from now. It is the literature of the original Buddhist school, Theravāda, composed in Pali. Of the works of other (Hīnayāna) schools, only remnants have come to light.

The Pali literature includes the complete canon of the Theravāda, a number of original works and a mass of exegetic and commentarial works upon the texts of the canon, among which those of Buddhaghosa are outstanding. For nearly a century now this literature has been explored by scholars of the East and of the West; most of it is now available in printed editions and translations. But the huge bulk of Buddhist (Mahāyānist) works of Chinese and Tibetan provenance is still for the most part unexplored. What stores remain inaccessible and out of sight in the lamaseries of Tibet are unguessed. Tibet is at present politically under a power that has forsworn religion and will give no quarter to its religious establishments. The ultimate fate of their stores of manuscripts is in the lap of the gods at the moment.

[1] It has since been published in Gaekwad Oriental Series, 30–31, and translated with Kamalaśīla's commentary by Ganganath Jha into English.

[2] See *A Descriptive Catalogue of Mss. in the Jaina Bhandars at Pattan* (Baroda), Vol. I, pp. 42–43. For Mokṣākaragupta, see Part V, Sec. 3 (d).

*

a. PALI, CHINESE AND TIBETAN SOURCES OF INFORMATION

In tracing the monk-scholars of India who built up this vast Buddhist literature, we have to resort mainly to three sources of information described in outline below:

A. MONK-SCHOLARS OF THERAVĀDA BUDDHISM

(Outstanding names—Nāgasena, Buddhaghosa, Buddhadatta and Dhammapāla)

Source—*Pali Literature*

(i) *Milindapañha* ..	.. It gives in Book I some information derived from traditional legend about Nāgasena's life and career.
(ii) Works of Buddhaghosa	.. His is the most outstanding name in Pali literature.[1] In the course of his voluminous works, Buddhaghosa names a number of monk-scholars whom he contacted in different monasteries in South India and who acted as friends, advisers or inspirers of his literary labours.
(iii) Commentarial Works of Buddhadatta and Dhammapāla	Buddhadatta was probably the oldest among the successors of Buddhaghosa. In the wake of Buddhaghosa came several commentators on Theravāda canonical works who all wrote in the 'sacred language', Pali.

B. MONK-SCHOLARS OF MAHĀYĀNA BUDDHISM

(A long line starting from the Mahāyānist *Ācaryas*)

Source—*Chinese*

(i) *Tripiṭaka* Catalogues	.. *Note*—Since Buddhism started from the 'White Horse Monastery' at Loyang, ancient capital of China, in the first century AD, Chinese redactions or translations of Indian Buddhist texts in Sanskrit had multiplied in a few centuries to encyclopaedic proportions.[2] Need was felt for the compilation of *catalogue raisonné*. Under several imperial dynasties such catalogues of Buddhist works collectively entitled '*Tripiṭaka*', were drawn up and printed. They were known as 'Imperial Catalogues'. The last was under the Ming Dynasty (fourteenth–fifteenth century), put into print a couple of centuries later (seventeenth century). This 'Ming' catalogue is best known in Nanjio's English edition published in 1883. The 'Tripiṭaka Catalogues' contain, under assorted heads, titles of canonical

[1] See Part IV, Sec. 2.

[2] See Part IV, Sec. 7.

works, of which the Sanskrit equivalents can be reconstructed in almost all cases, together with the names of their authors. Among the authors is a large number of Indian monks who had migrated from India and settled in China. There is also included a 'Miscellaneous section' in Nanjio's Englished Ming-dynasty catalogue listing 147 works all written by Indian monk-scholars.

(ii) *Tripiṭaka* Collections .. *Note*—The collections themselves, thus catalogued, were made separately in different centuries under different imperial dynasties. Three Tripiṭaka collections are extant in three editions: (i) Sung Edition (*c.* AD 1239), (ii) Yuan Edition (*c.* AD 1290) and (iii) Ming Edition (*c.* AD 1601). The last collection, catalogued under the Mings, has in modern times been followed up by one of a syncretic character, issued from Japan in 1924–29, under the title 'Taistro Issaikyo' in fifty-five volumes, containing in all 2,184 'sūtras'. A catalogue also of this collection has been published under the title 'Tables of Taisho' in a Fascicule annexed to the *Hobogirin*, Tokyo, 1931.

(iii) Dynastic Annals (*Shu*), Lists of Patriarchs, Collected Lives and Individual Lives. *Note*—The recorded 'Annals' of several imperial dynasties of China are extant, but they have been little explored yet except by Chinese scholars. Buddhism enjoyed imperial patronage and flourished greatly in China during the rule of some of these dynasties. In these flourishing periods of Buddhism, there were Indian monks of eminence in Buddhist centres of China, whose names or careers may be traced in these 'Annals'.

There are also lists (not always identical) of 'Patriarchs' of Chinese Buddhism. In these lists are included the names of several Mahāyāna masters of India like Aśvaghoṣa, Vasubandhu, Nāgārjuna and others.

In the 'Tripiṭaka' are found several serial biographies, entitled *Kao-seng-chuan* ('Biographies of Eminent Monks'), which are collected in Vol. 50 of the Taisho Edition. These 'biographies' are by Hui Chao (Text No. 2059), Tao Hsuan (No. 2060), Tsanning of the Sung Dynasty (No. 2061), Jushing of the Ming Dynasty (No. 2062), Paoch'eng (No. 2063, which is a collection of lives of Bhikṣuṇīs) and another with the title 'Shen-seng-chuan' (No. 2064) which may be rendered as the 'Lives of Supernatural (perhaps *Tāntric*) Monks'. Among the eminent monks mentioned in these biographies, appears a good number of Indian monks who went to China from India and were settled there.

(iv) The *Ki*'s (Records) of Hsüan-tsang and I-tsing.

Note—In their references to the monk-scholars of India, the records of these two learned Chinese pilgrims are of especial importance on two counts: (*a*) they report the legends they heard in India about the great *ācāryas* of the past, and (*b*) they give their own impressions of contemporary or near-contemporary scholars, contacted or known from reports by them in India.

Source—*Tibetan*

(i) The *Kanjur* and the *Tanjur*

Note—Known popularly by these titles, these two are encyclopaedic Tibetan collections of standard Buddhist works. They contain between them 4,569 texts, all Tibetan translations from Sanskrit and original works in Tibetan.[1] They represent the productions of both Indian and Tibetan monk-scholars of different centuries—from works of the great Indian Mahāyānist *ācāryas* to late Tāntric texts. Among them, a large number is concerned with *Hetuvidyā* (Logic). These treatises on Logic were first explored, mostly from xylographic reproductions obtained from the India Office, London, by Dr S. C. Vidyabhusan of Calcutta who was the first to discover that they represented the 'Mediaeval School' of Indian logic. The school was developed wholly by Buddhist and Jaina scholars.[2]

(ii) Tibetan Historiography . .

Note—Six works of this category have been discovered up till now. They are as follows in sequence of chronology:

(*a*) 'History of Buddhism (Chos-hbyung) in two parts by Bu-ston Rin-po-che (AD 1290–1364): translated into English by Dr Obermiller (Heidelberg, 1931–32). The work was composed in AD 1322—perhaps the earliest Tibetan history so far discovered.

(*b*) The 'Blue Annals' (Deb-thar snon-po) in fifteen books by 'Gos lo-tsa-ba (1392–1481), completed in 1478: translated in two

[1] See Preface to *Tohoku Imperial University Catalogue* (1934).

[2] See S. C. Vidyabhushan's *Mediaeval School of Indian Logic* (Calcutta University, 1909).

parts by George N. Roerich and published by the Asiatic Society of Bengal (Calcutta, 1949).

(*c*) 'History of Buddhism' (Rgyagar chos hbyun) by Lāmā Tāranātha (b. 1573), completed in 1607: translated into German by Schiefner.

(*d*) 'History of Buddhism: Its Rise, Decline and Downfall' (Pag-sam-jon-zang) by Sumpa khanpo Yese Pal Jor, completed in 1747: edited with a List of Contents and an Analytical Index by Sarat Chandra Das (Calcutta, 1908).

These four works ((*a*)–(*d*)) have been published. Two others are still under preparation by the IsMEo (Istituto Italiano per il Medio ed Estremo Oriente) of Rome:

(*e*) The Chronicle of Tibet by the Fifth Dalai Lama surnamed 'the Great' (1615–80) who became overlord of all Tibet in 1640: to be edited and translated by Professor Tucci.

(*f*) The 'History of Tibet' by Dp'ao-gtsug-pr'en-ba: to be edited and translated by Professor Tucci.

Tibet, being a theocratic State, where the Dalai Lama is the Head of both Church and State, Tibetan historiography is mainly 'church history'. The treatment by the Tibetan historiographers is genetic: as a rule, the writers trace the development of Mahāyāna Buddhism in India prior to its introduction into Tibet and link it up with their own 'church history'. Indian Mahāyānist teachers and their works as well as the legends of their lives receive detailed treatment at their hands. Bu-ston's 'History', for example, presents a whole series of life-sketches, though mostly legendary, of Nāgārjuna, Āryadeva, Nāgabodhi, Candragomin, Candrakīrtti, Asaṅga, Vasubandhu, Sthiramati, Dinnāga, Dharmakīrtti, Guṇaprabha, Śāntideva and a few Tāntric teachers.[1]

(iii) Biographies of Atīśa (Dīpaṅkara Śrījñāna of Vikramaśilā, A.D. 980–1054).

Note—In Tibetan 'church history', Atīśa is a pre-eminent figure. The lamaism of Tibet is said to have been established by him on an organized basis. Hence in all Tibetan historiographical works, a sketch of his life and his work in Tibet is given. But there are besides separate biographies of Atīśa in

[1] See Obermiller, Pt. II, pp. 122–166.

Tibetan, which are outside the *Kanjur* and the *Tanjur*, e.g. 'The Book of the Father of Bkah-gdams-pa Sect', 'Rgyas-pa' which is a more detailed biography, 'A Biography of Atiśa describing his missionary activities in India and how he became a disciple of Gser-glin-pa', and lastly, a 'Biography of Atiśa' supposed to have been written by his chief Tibetan disciple Bromton.[1]

While the Pali, Chinese and Tibetan works remain the main sources of our knowledge of Buddhist literature, as well as of the generations of devoted monk-scholars by whom it was built up, there are also some minor sources of information, such as the colophons of manuscripts, recovered from time to time from Nepal or Tibet. Several of these colophons show that the manuscripts were works of Indian monk-scholars of Nālandā, Vikramaśilā, Odantapura and other centres of monastic learning. They found their way into those countries mostly along with their authors who had fled away northwards from the terror of the Khiliji invasion.

Other possibilities remain. In other parts of Asia where Buddhism now prevails such as Burma, Thailand and Cambodia or did in the long past as in Indonesia, there may be untapped sources of information on monks from India who had gone there and worked for the cause of Buddhism.

b. EVALUATING THE LEGENDS

From these sources, so dispersed and so various in character, what we derive by way of information about the eminent monk-scholars and their works is a vast mass of legendary stories, purporting to conserve the fame of some of the most illustrious figures of Buddhist history.

In the front rank are men styled 'Bodhisattvas' or 'Ācāryas' or, as in Chinese, 'Patriarchs'. It would seem that most of the recorded legendary tales about them originated in India itself and were transplanted into Chinese and Tibetan from Indian books.

In their growth and transmission, three stages may be presumed. They originated at first with 'Somebody'; next, they went through a period of oral transmission; and, finally, they were gathered up and conserved by Indian monk-scholars at different times in written biographies.

[1] For information about the first three Tibetan biographies of Atiśa, I am indebted to Dr Lokesh Chandra of the International Academy of Indian Culture, Delhi. Bromton's biography, however, is well-known, and a running summary of it is given in S. C. Das's *Indian Pandits in the Land of Snow* (Calcutta, 1893). But in the work itself the author is referred to as an incarnation of Avalokiteśvara which casts doubt on its putative authorship (see Waddell's *Buddhism in Tibet*, p. 35, footnote 4).

These original Indian works of biography are irretrievably lost, but we can detect their vestiges in three Chinese 'lives', viz. of Aśvaghoṣa, of Nāgārjuna and of Vasubandhu.

The 'Life of Aśvaghoṣa' in Chinese is a short treatise translated by Kumārajīva from a Sanskrit original, now untraceable. 'The original Sanskrit text', says Suzuki, 'is stated in the Cheng Yuan Catalogue to have been existing at that time (i.e. when the catalogue was made).'[1] The 'Life of Nāgārjuna' by the same author is also a version of an untraced Sanskrit original. Similarly Paramārtha's 'Life of Vasubandhu' is partly based on traditions about Vasubandhu brought by Paramārtha with him from India and partly on some original text. We are informed by I-tsing of a serial biography of ten great Mahāyāna masters written by an Indian monk not long before I-tsing's own time. He refers to this work in his 'Record' in naming the successive generations of Mahāyāna masters of India:

'*Nāgārjuna, Deva, Aśvaghoṣa*—of an early age; *Vasubandhu, Asaṅga, Saṅghabhadra, Bhāvaviveka*—of the middle age; *Jina, Dharmapāla, Dharmakīrtti, Śīlabhadra, Siṁhabhadra, Sthiramati, Guṇamati, Prajñāgupta, Guṇabhadra and Jinaprabha*—of late years.'

And he adds a note to say: 'Their lives are fully described in the "Biography of the Ten *Bhadantas* (Venerable Ones)", written by Jina'. This biographer Jina may be the same as the Jina mentioned by him among 'those of late years', but the work itself has never been discovered.[2]

For one who would care for the truth of history or biography, these tales set a delicately difficult task—that of winnowing inventions from facts. It is a task calling not only for an apparatus of scientific scholarship, but also for a knowledge of the subtle and intricate ways by which mythology and legend grow up and proliferate all the world over.[3]

A prominent feature of these tales is circumstantiality.

To take an example at random: in the Tibetan *Pog-sam-jon-zang* (eighteenth century) it is stated that the father of Aśvaghoṣa (i.e. the poet, the sage and the philosopher who are rolled into one person in the legends) was one Saṅghaguhya who was a Brāhmaṇa belonging to a place named Khorta in the Prācya (Eastern Region) who married the daughter of a merchant of Khorta and that Aśvaghoṣa was the offspring of this marriage (see S. C. Das's Ed., Index, p. cxxvi). It is typical of the general trend of these tales; the particulars are

[1] See Suzuki's *Awakening of Faith, etc.*, p. 12, footnote 2.

[2] See Takakusu's *A Record of the Buddhist Religion*, p. 181.

[3] See on this point Chaps. VIII, IX and X of Tylor's *Primitive Culture* (3rd Ed., 1891), Vol. I.

prolific, but they cannot be verified.[1] The Tibetan historiographers exceed the Chinese writers in this sort of circumstantiality of narrative.

But one is put on one's guard by Tylor's pregnant observation:

'All men feel how wanting in sense of reality is a story with no personal name to hang it to. This want is thus graphically expressed by Sprenger the historian in his life of Mohammad: "It makes on me at least quite a different impression when it is related that 'The Prophet said to Alkama', even if I knew nothing whatever else of this Alkama than if it were merely stated that 'he said to somebody'." This feeling has, from the earliest times and in the minds of men, troubled with no such nice historic conscience, germinated to the production of much mythic fruit. Thus it has come to pass that one of the leading personages to be met with in the traditions of the world is really no more than—*Somebody*. There is nothing that this wondrous creature cannot achieve. . . . So rife in our own day is this manufacture of personal history, often fitted up with details of place and date, into the very semblance of real chronicle, that it may be guessed how vast its working must have been in days of old.'[2]

We cannot track this elusive Protean 'Somebody' through the wilderness of the legendary stories, but evidently in the eyes of those who represent Tylor's 'Somebody' in them, the greatest were repositories of all spiritual lore; they could not have been ordinary mortals, for their wisdom was divinely inspired; their capacities were more than human and there were miraculous events and supernatural interventions in their lives. Out of the magnifying mists of legend, they hardly emerge as intelligible human figures.

A few examples will suffice to illustrate how the legends 'glamorize' their subjects.

The Pali work *Buddhaghosuppatti* is a digest of Ceylonese legends about the great Theravāda scholar, Buddhaghosa. It is stated in this work that the original manuscript of his *magnum opus*, *Visuddhimagga*, was thrice purloined from his cell at night by the jealous god Indra. But so prodigious was his power of memory that he succeeded in making a fresh and complete transcript of the stolen work each time, without change of a single word.

Again, in Paramārtha's 'Life of Vasubandhu' we are told that Asaṅga, who converted his younger brother Vasubandhu to Mahāyāna faith, had gone up to Heaven and received his learning in

[1] Compare with it the Nāgārjuna legend in the same work, given in Part IV, Sec. 5, pp. 278–279, which is parallel in its circumstantiality.
[2] See *Primitive Culture* (1893 Ed.), Vol. I, p. 394.

Mahāyānist doctrines from no other than the divine Maitreya himself and that Maitreya Bodhisattva, on Asaṅga's intercession, came down himself to the earth to deliver to mortal men the work *Yogācāra-bhūmi śāstra*.[1]

This great Mahāyānist work has both Chinese and Tibetan versions[2]—the Chinese one by Hsüan-tsang (Nanjio—No. 1170). This version ascribes it to Maitreyanātha, but the Tibetan to Asaṅga. The name *Asaṅga* means 'unattached' i.e. 'unattached to any human teacher': this sense is to be understood, for Asaṅga's wisdom was gained from the divine Maitreya himself.

The Asaṅga story belongs to an aspect of myth-making touched upon by Tylor—the transfiguration of reality to a supernatural semblance. The heavenly teacher of Asaṅga has been completely tracked down to earth by modern scholarship and identified with Maitreyanātha who, according to Chinese tradition, was Vasubandhu's preceptor and the real author of the *Yogācārabhūmi-śāstra*.[3] Similarly the story of Indra's purloining of Buddhaghosa's work may only be the mythical version of a fact, viz. that its original was somehow lost and it was afterwards re-written by the author.

There are subtler and more deeply intriguing examples, however, of this kind of 'supernaturalizing' in the prolific Nāgārjuna legends. The compound form of Nāgārjuna's name is broken up to mean that the great philosopher was born under an *arjuna* tree (*terminalia arjuna*), and that his wisdom was derived, not from Heaven as Asaṅga's was, but from the underworld of *Nāgas* (Serpents).[4] The legend is an extraordinary one, for such a source of enlightenment is not imagined for any other Mahāyānist *ācārya* and we are left wondering over the factual basis on which a legend like this could have arisen. It teases thought by its cryptic brevity: it sets us wondering in any case whether it is implied that Nāgārjuna's doctrine of *Śūṇyatā* was taken by him from the secret cultus of a nameless sect, to which the name *Nāgas* is a covert allusion. Again the fact that Nāgārjuna ended his life by suicide is disguised in the form of a supernatural tale, current in both Chinese and Tibetan legends, which Hsüan-tsang also has recorded.[5]

Most of the legends are thus steeped in the supernatural and miraculous; these elements, however, are not always just frills or

[1] See Thomas's *History of Buddhist Thought*, p. 237, footnote.

[2] The original Sanskrit *Yogācārabhūmi-śāstra* also has been recovered from Tibet by Rahula Sankrityayana. Pundit Vidhu Sekhar Sastri has edited the Sanskrit text collating it with the Tibetan version (*The Yogācārabhūmi-śāstra* of Ācārya Asaṅga by V. S. Sastri, Calcutta University, 1957).

[3] See Tucci's *Doctrines of Maitreya* (*nātha*) *and Asaṅga* (Calcutta University, 1930).

[4] This legend of Nāgārjuna in its Tibetan version is given *infra*, Sec. 5, under Nāgārjuna.

[5] See Beal's *Buddhist Records*, ii, p. 214.

excrescences. In fact-finding from the legends, they cannot be ignored or excised: they are too much in the grain. Taken all in all, the task of discrimination calls for a skilled technique more delicately difficult than the mere rough and ready application of common-sense tests. It is a technique not evolved yet, but much needed. Yet it is through these unsifted and mixed-up tales that the approach lies to the lives and works of the long line of monk-scholars whose contributions built up the vast literature of Buddhism.

Their scholarship is articulated to two widely different traditions—the Theravāda tradition and the Mahāyāna. The former was the older tradition of monk-scholarship going back to the beginnings of the Saṅgha; the latter originated out of the Mahāyāna form of Buddhism. The two were not successive; for Hīnayānist and Mahāyānist monk-scholars worked, each in his own tradition of scholarship, side by side in the monasteries of India, but their works were resultantly different in form as well as in kind and quality.

The older Theravāda tradition of 'textual' scholarship was concerned mainly with the exegesis and elucidation of existing canonical texts, oral or in script. This tradition is represented by all monk-scholars of the conservative Theravāda school—Buddhaghosa, Buddhadatta, Dhammapāla, Ānanda, Upasena and others. Pali, identified by the Theravādins with 'Māgadhī', the ancient language of Magadha and hence preferred as a sort of sacred language, is their chosen linguistic medium. Mahāyāna Buddhism also started—if we can trust the legends about its origin—with a rearrangement of the canonical texts of one school, viz. the Sarvāstivāda, and the composition of commentaries.[1]

From this start, it evolved a new system of faith and philosophy that developed in the hands of the great *ācāryas* whom I-tsing, as we have seen, names in order of priority. The monk-scholars of the Mahāyāna were not exegetists or commentators: they were principally concerned with the scholastic phase of Mahāyāna development. Their works therefore took the form of philosophical discourses, treatises and dissertations. The period during which the Mahāyānist monk-scholars flourished in India may be roughly delimited between the third and the ninth centuries AD. Sanskrit, their literary medium, was throughout India the language of scholarship and culture in this age.

[1] These legends come from both Chinese and Tibetan sources. The Tibetan 'histories' record the legend of Kaniṣka's council where the re-arrangement of the canonical texts and the composition of commentaries was done. The Chinese legend to the same effect is given by Hsüan-tsang (see Beal's *Buddhist Records*, ii, pp. 151 ff.; also *The Buddha and Five After-Centuries*, pp. 246–247).

2

The Hīnayāna (Theravāda) Tradition of Textual Scholarship

FOR the growth of the tradition of textual scholarship in Buddhism, we have to turn to Saṅgha history of the earliest chapter, when the monks, settled in their *āvāsas*, were trying to systematize and conserve a literary heritage they much cherished—the current Buddha-legends. These had begun to be composed perhaps within half a century of the Founder's decease and were indefinitely continued, purporting to recall traditions of the Founder and his teachings.

An industry of editing these legends and making texts out of them seems to have grown up in the primitive monk-settlements—captioning, classifying, grouping all their diverse contents into discourses, formularies, moral precepts, rules for monks, etc. Out of this effort stemmed the earliest scripture of Buddhism to be adopted by the Theravāda School. Out of it, also resulted the standardized division of a Buddhist canon into *Sutta*, *Vinaya* and *Abhidhamma* and of its contents into nine literary forms (*Navaṅga*).

In the larger monk-settlements there were small specialist-groups of recognized status concerned with different division of this work—the *Vinayadharas* dealing with the Vinaya, the *Suttantikas* with the 'longer discourses' and the *Mātikādharas* with the formularies. Thus came into existence a considerable body of definitive texts, intended to be learnt, understood and memorized. Out of these in later times different sects made their respective canonical recensions. To prevent the faith from falling into confusion, it was deemed necessary *to preserve the purity of the texts*.

All this industry was prior to the practice of writing: the texts, thus edited and settled, were imparted by word of mouth and were to be retained in memory. They contain different kinds of aid to memory—set word-orders, conventional and repetitive epithets, stereotyped fixed-worded descriptions, *memoria technica*, etc. The texts used to be delivered sometimes in solo recitation[1] and occasionally in joint congregational recital called *Saṅgīti* (chanting together).[2] A class of professional reciters called *Bhāṇakas* arose from this practice.

[1] e.g. Soṇa's solo recitation of the *Aṭṭhakavagga*. See Mahāvagga, V, 13, 9.

[2] e.g. the congregational recital led by Sāriputta described in the *Saṅgīti Suttanta* of the Dīgha Nikāya.

The texts were regarded as all important in settling the authenticity of any rule or doctrine. If doubt arose, it could be set at rest by textual reference.[1]

Hence correct knowledge, proper understanding and true interpretation of the texts were deemed to be of vital importance: without them the purity of the religion itself would stand in jeopardy. Therefore the course of training called *Nissaya* was made obligatory for every monk newly ordained before he could acquire the full status of a qualified member of a Saṅgha. It was the texts that constituted a safeguard for the religion—was its rock of ages and its guarantee for continuance.

The question is mooted in a legend[2]—what conduces to the confusion or vanishing away of the True Religion (*Saddhamma*)? Four conditions are specified—first, when 'monks get by heart a text that is wrongly taken, with words and sense wrongly arranged'; second, when monks are not amenable to training; third, when monks, who are widely learned, versed in traditionary lore (*āgatāgama*), who know the Dhamma by heart, who know the formularies (*mātikās*) by heart, do not dutifully hand on a text to another—'thus when they pass away, the text is cut down at the root and it has nothing to stand on'—and, fourth, when the elders (*theras*) in a saṅgha are ease-loving and lax.

'The text is cut down at the root' means that with the death of the monk from whose memory it spread among others, the text ceases to exist. It was exactly for this reason that the Theras of Ceylon in the reign of Vaṭṭagāmaṇi thought of reducing the texts of the canon to writing. It was a time when the vihāras were deserted and oral transmission of texts was difficult. Their object in resorting to the writing down of the canon is expressed by the phrase, 'for the eternal existence of the Dhamma (*ciraṭṭhitiṁ dhammassa*)'.[3]

The tradition of scholarship in the texts of the religion passed from the earlier stage of oral training and transmission to the stage of writing and the making of manuscripts. This was sometime perhaps in the first century BC.

The most distinguished representative of the 'oral' stage was Nāgasena. He is said to have been a contemporary of the Greek king Menander (second century BC), ruler of an extensive territory in northern India. Only a single Pali work, *Milindapañha*, tells us about Nāgasena and Menander (Pali, *Milinda*)—several of whose coins have been discovered—and their mutual relations. It is not a con-

[1] '*Sutte otaretabbāni vinaye sandassetabbāni*' (literally, 'to be brought down to the Sutta or shown in the Vinaya')—*Mahāparinibbāna Suttanta*, IV, 8, *et seq*.
[2] Aṅguttara Nikāya, IV, xvi, 160.
[3] See Rahula's *Buddhism in Ceylon*, pp. 83–84.

temporary work, but made perhaps a couple of centuries after Milinda's time.

The king is represented here as having been earnestly inclined to Buddhism, but his acute Greek mind discovered in it dilemmas, for the solution of which he put himself under the instruction of Nāgasena. The 'subtle questionings' of the Greek king and the 'profound solutions' of Nāgasena are given *in extenso* in the work. Book I describes Nāgasena's scholastic career. We are told that Nāgasena, who became a 'world-famous sage', had betaken himself to Asokārāma Monastery where he garnered his phenomenal store of knowledge from a monk named Dhammarakkhita, and that he possessed a memory so quick and capacious that he got by heart the whole canon (*Buddhavacana*) by having it recited to him once and mastered its meaning at the second recital. But Nāgasena is about the only great monk-scholar of towering eminence who comes out of the BC centuries.

The 'textual' tradition was strongest in the Theravāda school. The school was conservative—perhaps most so of all schools of Buddhism. In the AD centuries, the Theravāda monk-scholar, who represented the tradition most fully and with a lifelong and unremitting devotion, was one who belonged to the end of the fourth and the early years of the fifth century AD—Buddhaghosa.

BUDDHAGHOSA—TYPICAL THERAVĀDA MONK-SCHOLAR

Buddhaghosa belonged to the Theravāda school, and in those Buddhist countries of Asia where Theravāda Buddhism prevails there is no name held in greater veneration. The Ceylonese legends pun on his name which means 'the voice of the Buddha': 'The Buddha laid down the religion, but it has found voice in Buddhaghosa'; 'His voice had the solemnity of the Buddha's voice; so he was named Buddhaghosa; he was like the Buddha on earth', says Dhammakītti in the *Cuḷavaṁsa*.[1]

He was the great exponent and interpreter of the doctrines and scriptural texts of the Theravāda school and his exegesis of the scripture is deemed to this day as the master-key to its meaning. The bulk of Buddhaghosa's life-work was on the scripture—its interpretation, explanation and exegesis, and his scholia and commentaries have become an indispensable appanage to the scripture.

A scholar of profound and varied learning and writer of almost indefatigable diligence, his fame rests on his original as well as commentarial works—his recognized masterpiece being an original

[1] Buddhassa viya gambhīraghosattā naṁ viyākaruṁ; Buddhaghoso ti so sobhi Buddho viya mahītale—*Culavaṁsa*.

work, *Visuddhimagga*, a standard compendium of Theravāda Buddhism, a guide and *vade mecum* to the Buddhist wherever Theravāda Buddhism prevails. In Buddhaghosa, the learning of the school put forth its one grand full-blown flower.

An intriguing phenomenon to which we shall have occasion to refer in dealing with the Mahāyānist *ācāryas* is 'the merger of personalities' which occurred in the cases of at least three of them, Aśvaghoṣa, Vasubandhu and Nāgārjuna. In the case of Buddhaghosa too it has sometimes been suggested that the author of the *Visuddhimagga* was a different person from the writer of the commentaries, even though both bore the same name.[1] But this seems hardly tenable, as in some commentarial works the *Visuddhimagga* is mentioned as his own work.[2]

There are two streams of Buddhaghosa tradition—one of Ceylon and the other of Burma. They are widely divergent in respect of his birthplace and antecedents as well as of the incidents of his career. But about his date the traditions agree: he belonged to the end of the fourth and the beginning of the fifth century AD and was in Ceylon in the reign of the Ceylonese king Mahānāma (AD 409–413).

Attempts have been made to salvage out of the welter of Ceylonese and Burmese legends a consistent life-story.

The Ceylonese source is mainly represented by two Pali works: (i) *Cuḷavaṁsa* (a supplement contributed by Dhammakītti, a great *thera* of Ceylon of the thirteenth century, to the ancient Ceylonese chronicle *Mahāvaṁsa*),[3] and (ii) *Buddhaghosuppatti* (a digest of Ceylonese legends about Buddhaghosa).[4] The Burmese source is represented by the so-called 'Great and Middle Chronicles' of the country. But apart from these legends, there exists internal evidence in Buddhaghosa's works by which the degree of trustworthiness of the legends may be tested.

The Ceylonese legends relate (i) Buddhaghosa's antecedents and family relations, (ii) his life and work in Ceylon, (iii) his return home, and (iv) his end at Gayā. But not a word is said about his connection with Burma. The narrative is heavily spiced with supernatural and miraculous elements.

Cleared of these spicy elements, the story stands thus:

Buddhaghosa was born in a Brāhmaṇa family of Magadha and his father was a renowned Vedic scholar. Buddhaghosa, even as a boy,

[1] See B. C. Law's *Buddhaghosa* (Memoir of the Royal Asiatic Society), pp. 71 ff., and Nihar Ranjan Ray's *Theravāda Buddhism in Burma*, p. 28.

[2] *Vide* passages quoted at pp. xvii–xviii of Kosambi's Ed. of the *Visuddhimagga* (Bharatiya Vidyabhavan, Bombay, 1940).

[3] Verses 215–246 of Chapter xxxvii of the *Mahāvaṁsa* are Dhammakītti's contribution.

[4] This work was edited and translated by James Gray in 1892 under the title 'The Advent of Buddhaghosa'.

became under his father's tutelege a precocious scholar in Vedic lore. The father, whose name is given as Keśī (Long-haired), happened to be on friendly terms with an eminent and learned Buddhist monk, a *Mahā-thera* named Revata. The boy Buddhaghosa and the *Mahā-thera* met at a dinner at Keśī's house. Ignorant of the guest's learning, Buddhaghosa tried to test his knowledge of the Vedas, whereupon the guest recited to him all the Vedic texts. He was next questioned by the boy about the faith he himself held. When he was thus questioned, he recited the *Abhidhamma* and explained its more difficult points. This made so profound an impression on Buddhaghosa's juvenile mind that he sought his father's leave to be ordained as a Buddhist monk. It was not easily given, and so, as it is said, Buddhaghosa coerced his father to turn a Buddhist by locking him up in a room and wresting from him the permission sought for.

We are next told of Buddhaghosa's migrating to Ceylon where at first he was not received kindly. People supposed him to be only a merchant from India. But he was afterwards greatly honoured, when, going to Anurādhapura (ancient capital of Ceylon), he allowed himself to be tested by the learned Ceylonese monks there. It was a severe test of his knowledge of the Buddhist religion and its scriptural texts. Having passed it with credit, he was settled by the monks in the Mahāvihāra of Anurādhapura.

Here he pursued with single-minded devotion and unshaken concentration the literary labours he had begun in India. He composed the *Visuddhimagga* and translated into Pali the Ceylonese commentaries on the *Tipiṭaka*. The whole canon, it is also said though the statement is hardly credible, was done by him from the Ceylonese language into Pali, and we are further told that, after his translation of the canon into Pali, the scripts of the original canon in the native language of the island were collected and burnt. After finishing his prolonged literary labours at Anurādhapura, which were committed to a huge pile of palm-leaves supplied *gratis* from day to day to him by an admiring toddy-seller, he left Ceylon for his Magadhan home and died at Gayā.

There are two considerations, however, which throw doubt on the veracity of the story.

First, the internal evidence of his works shows that he could not have been a native of Magadha: it is hardly credible that a Magadhan would describe its capital city Pāṭaliputra as a seaport. Yet Buddhaghosa in the *Visuddhimagga* (ix, 64–69) tells the story of a *Thera* named Visākha who, intending to go to Ceylon, spent a month on the seaside at Pāṭaliputra looking for a ship, maintaining himself meanwhile by doing some petty business there. This Visākha is said in the story to have at last been able to embark at Pāṭaliputra on his voyage to Ceylon and, on arrival there, to have received ordination at the Mahāvihāra of Anurādhapura.[1] Secondly, the incidents related about Buddhaghosa's birth, early life and conversion to Buddhism in the Ceylonese legends are suspiciously like those related of Nāgasena in Book I of *Milindapañha*.[2]

The Burmese legends tell a quite different story. The tradition in Burma is that Buddhaghosa introduced the *Visuddhimagga* and the sacred books (in Pali) of the Theravāda canon into Burma from Ceylon. The Burmese count a new era in their religion from the time of his arrival in Burma with these books. But, except for agreeing that Buddhaghosa had been in Ceylon round AD 400 in the reign of Mahānāma (to whom he is said in the Burmese legends to have given a white elephant as a present[3]), the Ceylonese and Burmese legends have few points of contact.

The latter claim Buddhaghosa as a native of Burma—of the 'Telaing country' in Lower Burma. The Telaings were Indian immigrants from the east-coastal regions of India who had in ancient times migrated to and settled along the lower reaches of the Irrawady, becoming in course of time Burmese to all intents and purposes. This great 'Ashin' (Burmese equivalent of *Thera*), who was a Teliang, went from his native country Burma to Ceylon and returned with the sacred books to Burma. The event was an epoch-making one in the history of Burmese Buddhism. His arrival with the books at Thaton, the Burmese capital of the time, is described colourfully in the chronicles.

It is said that when he was on his way to Thaton, vast multitudes went forth to receive him with offerings and festive celebrations; on his arrival at the city, a pavilion was erected in front of the royal palace and all the sacred books brought by him from Ceylon were put on show there. He was liberally patronized by the reigning king Dhammapāla who, himself a devout Buddhist, gave Buddhaghosa 'four nobles as attendants and many gifts including an elephant'.

The works of Buddhaghosa are more completely preserved in Burmese script in Burma than in Ceylon and it was from Burma that Thailand and Cambodia obtained his works. He himself is nowhere spoken of in the legends as having visited these countries. Yet in Cambodia an ancient monastery stands in its own ruins which, called 'Buddhaghosa Vihāra', is sanctified by the legend that it was here that Buddhaghosa spent his last days.

[1] '*Nikkhamitvā samuddatīre nāvaṁ udikkhamāno ekamāsaṁ vasi . . . tenevantaramāsena sahassaṁ abhisaṁharīti—anupubbenna mahāvihāraṁ āgantvā pabbajjaṁ yāci*'—(Kosambi's Ed. p. 212).

[2] See B. C. Law's *Buddhaghosa*, p. 14.

[3] See Nihar Ranjan Ray's *Theravāda Buddhism in Burma*, citing an extract from a late Burmese chronicle, *Hmannan Yazawin*.

There is no doubt that the works of Buddhaghosa when they were studied and taught in Burma gave a great impetus to Buddhism in that country. This was in the early part of the fifth century AD, and the renaissance of Buddhism that resulted from the study of his works is perhaps symbolized by the legendary story that Buddhaghosa himself had brought it about.

But the ascription to him of Telaing-Burmese nationality and the story of his voyage from Burma to Ceylon in the interest of Burmese Buddhism are cast into grave doubt by an important though negative piece of evidence. This evidence comes from certain inscriptions known as 'Kalyāni Inscriptions'. Their texts have been fully edited and translated.[1]

These inscriptions were caused to be made by king Dhammaceti who ruled at Pegu in Lower Burma round AD 1476. The legend about them is as follows: Dhammaceti had sent a mission of twenty monks to Ceylon all of whom had fresh ordination at the Mahāvihāra of Ceylon in a *sīmā* (monastic site) on a river named Kalyānī. Thereafter, the Burmese king staked out a *sīmā* at Pegu for performance of ordination rites for intending monks, naming it 'Kalyānī Sīmā'. Here he set up a number of inscriptions on stone recording in an abridged form from all available sources, archives and chronicles, the history of the rise and progress of Buddhism in Burma. But Buddhaghosa, strangely enough, is nowhere mentioned in the inscriptions.[2]

Leaving all the legends, both Ceylonese and Burmese, on one side, we may turn more profitably to the internal evidence of his works. This leaves little room for doubt (i) that Buddhaghosa was an Indian, a native of Andhra, (ii) that he stayed from time to time at several monasteries (e.g. at Kāñcīpura) and Buddhist centres in South India, (iii) that he knew well the topography as well as the social life of the south, while his knowledge of northern India was remarkably sketchy, and (iv) that most of his literary works (all in Pali) were actually undertaken and completed at Anurādhapura in Ceylon.

The *Visuddhimagga* ends with a colophon in which the author describes himself as having his home (*vattabba*) at a place called Moraṇḍakheṭaka.[3] The place-name, which means the 'District of Peahen's Eggs', is likely to be the Pali version of the name of his native village.

In 1952, two officers of the Archaeological Survey of India (South-

[1] See *Ibid*, p. 91, footnote 1. [2] See *Ibid*, p. 90.

[3] *Buddhaghoso ti garuhi gahitanāmadheyyena therena moraṇḍakheṭakavattabbena kato visuddhimaggo nāma* (Tr. 'By Buddhaghosa, known reverently by this adopted name, a *thera* who has his home at Moraṇḍakheṭaka, this work named *Visuddhimagga* is done').—See Kosambi's Ed., p. 506. The translation is mine.

western Circle) touring in the Guntur District of the Andhra State, chanced upon a locality where two villages, lying side by side, bore Telagu names which meant respectively 'the place of *Nemalis*', Telagu equivalent for *Morā*, peacock, and 'the place of *Gundla*', Telagu for *Aṇḍa*, egg. In the site of these two villages, now deserted, were numerous ancient Buddhist remains. It was here, according to their highly plausible suggestion, that Moraṇḍakheṭaka must have anciently stood. It is at a distance as the crow flies of fifty-one miles from Nāgārjunakoṇḍa and fifty-eight miles from Amarāvatī.[1] The discovery establishes Buddhaghosa's Andhra origin and internal evidence from his works confirms it. They show fairly accurate knowledge on his part of the land and the peoples of trans-Vindhyan India.

The details of customs and usages, of weights and measures, of current coins, etc., of the Andhra country of his time are mentioned *passim* in his works. The names of his contemporaries and associates, among whom Jyotipāla of Kāñcīpura has honourable mention, as well as the places and monasteries visited or lived in by him, are all of southern India. He seems to have spent a few years, before going to Ceylon, in the 'country of Cola'—that is Drāviḍa in the Deccan. Perhaps he took a course of study at Kāñcīpura, one of the most famous centres of learning in the south in his time. It was here at Kāñcīpura that Jyotipāla suggested to Buddhaghosa the undertaking of some of his commentarial works. Other works were suggested by another monk-scholar at Mayūrasutta-pattana, probably modern Māyāvaram in the Madras State. It was perhaps at Nagapattinam at the mouth of the lower distributary of the Kāverī that he embarked for Ceylon.

Buddhaghosa had a fair idea of the non-Aryan ethnic character of Drāvidian peoples. He speaks of Andhakas (men of Andhra) and Damilas (Drāvidians) as *Mleccha* (non-Aryan). He makes the interesting statement that the spoken dialects current in India in his time were 'one hundred and one', which, however, must not be taken as an exact count, and he distinguishes Māgadhī (Pali) as an Aryan form of speech from the eighteen principal non-Aryan languages then spoken in India, such as Oḍḍa (language of Orissa), Kirāta, Andhaka (modern Telagu), Yavana (literally, the language of Yavanas meaning foreigners domiciled in India), Dāmila (Drāvidian or Tamil), etc. He characterizes the Kirāta, Yavana and Dāmila languages as abounding in consonants.[2] Buddhaghosa had also an eye for the striking features of South Indian landscape. The island

[1] See *Journal of Oriental Research*, Madras, Vol. XIX, pt. IV (1952)—article on *Buddhaghosa: His Place of Birth*. '*Kheṭaka* is Sanskrit for village and remains in the modern South Indian vernacular as Kheḍā'—Kosambi's *Visuddhimagga*, p. xv.

[2] See B. C. Law's *Buddhaghosa* (1946 Ed.), p. 35.

15. *An ancient Buddha-image from Mathura modified by Indo-Hellenistic art-mode as shown by the halo and drapery in folds*

Buddha-image inset in a stūpa. (*Ellora, cave No. 10*). (Photo: Department of Archaeology, Government of India)

16. *Image of a standing Buddha in a sanctuary at Kanherī.* (Photo: Department of Archaeology, Government of India)

The Buddha under the Bodhi-tree. (*In a belt of sculptured slabs round the sanctuary of the Bṛhadīsvara-siva temple of Tanjore.*) (Photo, Archaeological Survey of India, Southern circle)

in the midst of the great South Indian river, the Godāvarī, which divides its current for three *Yojanas,* must have been observed by him with interest and made an impression on his mind, for he presses it into the service of a metaphor.[1]

The Ceylonese legends make Buddhaghosa a Brāhmaṇa by birth: his pronounced partiality, however, for the farmer class suggests his origin in a farmer's family. 'Why does the Buddha mention the farmer caste first?' says Buddhaghosa, 'Because farmers have the least pride and they are largest in number. Often the monks from a Kṣatriya family are proud of their learning; those from the low castes . . . are unable to continue long in the Order. But the young farmers plough their land while all their bodies are running with sweat. . . . Therefore they are not proud. . . . From the other families not very many become monks; from the farmer's many.'[2]

Buddhaghosa's extant works—some like his first work *Ñānodaya* written by him before he left India for Ceylon are untraceable (though it is supposed that a copy of *Ñānodaya* may exist in Thailand)—are voluminous. Among them, *Visuddhimagga,* which is comparatively short and compendious, is admittedly the brightest gem.

Its title which means the 'Path of Purity' has a nuance: for *Nibbāna* (literally, Extinction) is a negative concept, for which Buddhaghosa substitutes a positive one, *Visuddhi.* Both stand for the same goal or ideal—the absolute release from the bonds of grossness that bind men down to the earth.[2] He proceeds to show, with the scripture as his guide, how the way (*magga*) to this ideal condition lies through *Sīla* (Morals), *Samādhi* (Concentration) and *Paññā* (Wisdom). The work is divided into twenty-three sections, each called a *Niddesa* (Analytical Explanation), and covers the whole field of mental and moral discipline which forms the practical core of Theravāda Buddhism.

The rest of Buddhaghosa's extant works are exegetic and commentarial. They deal with different sections and texts of the Theravāda canon. Buddhaghosa's *Samanta-pāsādikā* has a general introduction in which he states that in these other works he translated the Ceylonese commentaries on the canon (*Aṭṭhakathās*),

[1] See *Suttanipāta Commentary,* Pt. II (PTS Ed.), pp. 580–581: Yathā Godhāvarī dividhā bhijjitvā tiyayojanappamānaṁ antaradīpaṁ akāsi.

[2] Cited from the *Aṭṭhakathās* of Dīgha and Majjhima Nikāyas by Kosambi in his edition of the *Visuddhimagga,* pp. xvi.

[3] See Sīlaniddeso, V—'*Tattha visuddho ti sabbamala-virahitaṁ accanta-parisuddhaṁ nibbānaṁ veditabbaṁ; tassa visuddhiyā maggo ti visuddhimaggo. Maggo ti adhigamupāyo vuccati; taṁ visuddhimaggaṁ bhāsissāmi 'ti attho*' (Tr.: Here by Purity is meant Nibbāna which is free from all taints and is exceedingly pure. The way to that Purity is Visuddhimagga. The 'way' connotes the means of attainment. I shall call that 'visuddhimagga' in this work). The translation is mine.

only leaving out unnecessary details, repetitions and irrelevant matters.

The *Aṭṭhakathās* and *Tīkās* made a branch of Theravāda learning in Ceylon that had kept growing there among learned monk-scholars over five centuries or more and in Buddhaghosa's time they were redacted into three great works containing exegesis on all texts of the Theravāda canon, viz. the *Mūla-(Mahā)-aṭṭhakathā*, the *Mahā-paccarī* and the *Kuruṇḍī*. Not a fragment of these Ceylonese works is now extant. How much matter out of them was really taken over by Buddhaghosa in his commentaries does not admit of precise assessment. The Ceylonese tradition is that Buddhaghosa translated them all and incorporated them in his works:

> '*Parivattesi sabbā pi sīhalaṭṭhakathā tadā*
> *Sabbesaṁ mūlabhāsāya māgadhāya niruttiyā.*'

(Tr.: He translated all the Singhalese *aṭṭhakathās* and restored them to the original language, the speech form of Magadha)—*Cuḷavaṁsa*. No doubt Buddhaghosa had access to these ancient commentarial works in the Ceylonese language in the Mahāvihāra of Anurādhapura and his own commentaries were largely based on them.

The commentarial works of Buddhaghosa have now been published almost wholly by the Pali Text Society of London and they run into several sizable volumes. But, except to the devoted and painstaking student, they are rather dreary reading—yet refreshingly relieved here and there by interesting legends, episodes and personal reminiscences, introduced by way of explanation or illustration. The style of the commentaries is different from the rigid and somewhat pedantic style of the *Visuddhimagga*—easier, clearer and more discursive and hence more profuse. The titles Buddhaghosa gives to his works are delightfully informal—just fancy-names without any relation or reference to their subject-matter, e.g.

Sumaṅgala-vilāsinī	.. The Book that displays things auspicious (Commentary on the *Dīgha Nikāya*).
Papañca-sūdanī	.. The Book that consumes all worldly troubles (Commentary on *Majjima Nikāya*).
Sārattha-ppakāsinī	.. The Book that illuminates the essential meaning (Commentary on the *Samyutta Nikāya*).
Manoratha-pūraṇī	.. The Book that fulfils the object of desire (Commentary on the *Aṅguttara Nikāya*).

These four commentarial works on the first four *nikāyas* of the *Suttapiṭaka* are undoubtedly of Buddhaghosa's authorship, as we find at the end of each some verses in which the author refers back by name to his own work *Visuddhimagga*.[1] Whether other commentarial works fathered on Buddhaghosa (e.g. *Kaṅkhā-vitaraṇī*, 'That which transcends all doubts'—a commentary on the *Pātimokkha*)[2] are in fact his is doubtful. It has been suggested that the title of his commentary on the *Aṅguttara Nikāya*, *Manoratha-pūraṇī*, carries an innuendo: it was the object of Buddhaghosa's desire to write commentaries on the *Nikāyas* only and the title signifies the finis to his labours—the 'fulfilment of his desire'.

The achievement of Buddhaghosa was to develop the Theravāda from a mere body of doctrines into a school of philosophy. The Theravāda standpoints in doctrine became those established by Buddhaghosa in his works, so completely indeed that Theravāda is practically identified with his system of thought and scriptural interpretation. But the system was not his own nor even largely original; it followed closely the line of tradition current in the monkish circles of Anurādhapura, and, as he himself admitted, must have been moulded and shaped by and large for him by the ancient Singhalese *aṭṭhakathās*.

The legends given in the *Buddhaghosuppatti* afford interesting glimpses of his life and labours in Ceylon. His was the completely dedicated life of a typical monk-scholar—one 'scorning delights and living laborious days'.

Buddhaghosa had lived a strenuous life, perhaps a hard life, until the Ceylonese *theras* came to appreciate his worth and settle him at Anurādhapura enabling him to pursue his labours in comparative ease. Yet from the tone of the personal reminiscences interspersed in his works, it would appear that he never lost his freshness of mind or interest in men and things.

Nothing is known about the date of his birth or the span of his life, but he must have been old when he migrated to Ceylon, for the legend is that he returned to his homeland only to die. In the midst of the small comforts of his monastic cell in the Anurādhapura Mahā-vihāra, going out every morning on his begging round, with an eye askance for a fallen palm-leaf he could pick up and write upon, we may suppose that Buddhaghosa was:

> 'Still happy as a child with its small toys,
> Over his ink-pot and his bits and pieces—
> Life's arduous, fragile and ingenuous joys,
> Whose charm faileth never—nay, it ever increases!'

Working all day till daylight failed, we may call up in imagination the figure of the old scholar reluctant still to quit his books:

[1] See verses quoted at pp. xvii-xviii of Kosambi's ed. of the *Visuddhimagga*.
[2] Published by the Pali Text Society in 1956.

'. . . his bedtime nigh,
Who still at western window stays to win
A transient respite from the latening sky,
And scarce can bear it when the sun goes in.'[1]

*

Buddhaghosa is unquestionably the most towering figure in the field of Theravāda scholarship. In his shadow are two eminent monk-scholars in the same field, his senior or junior contemporaries, who also are great names in Pali literature—Buddhadatta and Dhammapāla. Their works, among others, are listed in the old Pali book, entitled *Gandhavaṁsa*, which gives a brief outline of Pali literature.[2]

These two monk-scholars stood near to Buddhaghosa—Buddhadatta being actually associated with him in his labours. The story in Buddhadatta's own work, *Vinaya-viniccaya,* is that he met Buddhaghosa on the sea-journey from India to Ceylon and, coming to know from him of his project to engage himself in Ceylon in writing commentaries on the canonical works, the former expressed a wish to produce summaries of them. Buddhaghosa's consent was obtained, and this became the genesis of Buddhadatta's two outstanding works, *Vinaya-viniccaya* and *Abhidhammāvatāra*. In these he excelled his original. 'The psychology and philosophy are presented through the prism of a second vigorous intellect, under fresh aspects, in a style, often less discursive and more graphic than that of the great commentator (Buddhaghosa) and with a strikingly rich vocabulary.'[3]

Dhammapāla's canonical commentaries are on the same exegetic lines as Buddhaghosa's and, on the basis of their similarities, the conclusion is most probable that Buddhaghosa and Dhammapāla came under the same system of training in Ceylon.

Both Buddhadatta and Dhammapāla hailed from South India. The former belonged to Ugrapura in the Kāveri region, then under the Chola (Kadamba) kings; the latter to Kāñci (Conjeeveram in the Madras State).

[1] Walter de la Mare's *A Portrait.*
[2] Ed. by Minayeff.
[3] *Per* Mrs Rhys Davids in *Buddhist Psychology*, 2nd Ed., p. 174.

3

The Mahāyāna and its Scholastic Tradition

a. EARLY EXPONENTS OF THE MAHĀYĀNA

WITH the monk-scholars of the Mahāyāna, we enter upon another phase and a divergent tradition of monk-scholarship.

The sects of Hīnayāna Buddhism are known to have made 'canons' in which the traditions of the Lord and his teachings were enshrined, although only one of these has come down to us in a complete collection, that of the Theravāda. The Theravāda, as we have seen, regarded its canon as the 'Bible' of the religion, the accepted standard of reference for the faithful in all matters of doctrine and rule.[1] We may presume the same regard on the part of other sects for their own respective canons.

Their texts were closed; Hīnayānist scholarship was spent on their exegesis and amplification or on original works grounded in them. Their works amounted almost wholly to analysis or synthesis of the rules and doctrines. Speculative philosophy was not the cue of this scholarship. Mahāyānist tradition was different—separated from the Hīnayānist by a Great Divide as it were.

The Mahāyāna movement started with the *Sūtras*: like the Hīnayānist *suttas*, they claimed to be the *ipsisimma verba* of the Lord (*Buddhavacana*). Asaṅga in the *Mahāyāna-sūtrālaṅkāra* is at pains to affirm and establish this authentic character of Mahāyāna *sūtras*: '(Some say) the Mahāyāna is not *Buddhavacana*—how then can it be admired? To meet this doubt, this initial *śloka* (verse), by way of an analysis of the reason, is put forth, in order to raise perfect credence that the Mahāyāna is really *Buddhavacana*.'[2]

But in Mahāyāna thought the Buddha was an essentially dissimilar concept, different in essence and attributes. While the Theravāda is oriented to a personal tradition of him, which it seeks to keep alive by recalling in its legends the great names associated with the tradition,[3] the Mahāyānist Buddha-concept is extra-traditional. Without actually denying the personal and temporal tradition, the position taken up by it is that, if the Lord had lived on earth and in a parti-

[1] See Part IV, Sec. 2, p. 250.

[2] *Naivedaṁ Mahāyānaṁ Buddhavacanaṁ: Kutas-tasyāyaṁ anuśaṁso bhaviṣyaty-atra vipratipannās-tasya Buddhavacanatva-prasādhanārthaṁ kāraṇavibhājyam ārambha-ślokaḥ—Mahāyāna-sūtrālaṅkāra* (Levi's Ed.), p. 3.

[3] See Part I, Sec. 2, p. 47.

cular span of time, it was in a 'body self-created (*Nirmāṇa-kāya*)' by a Being who was cosmic and eternal. His teachings as recorded in the Hīnayānist canons were either symbolical in meaning or were adapted to the various mental capacities of his hearers.[1] Besides these teachings delivered to hearers of an inferior calibre, there were others confided to men of superior understanding which came down recorded in the great Mahāyāna *sūtras*. They related not to what Hīnayānists called *Dhamma-vinaya*, but to a transcendental wisdom termed *Prajñā*.

In the history of Buddhist thought, the problem how this transition came about from the *Dhamma-vinaya* of the Hīnayānist to the *Prajñā* of the Mahāyānist as being the substance and purport of the Lord's teachings, is still an unsolved one. Behind it there must have been a complexity of psychological urges of which little is known; also the impact of the speculative philosophies of western Asia extending to the Indian border provinces of Gāndhara and Kashmir and infiltrating from that quarter into Indian thought. Keith calls *Prajñā* the 'twin-sister of Sophia or Gnosis of Asiatic Greece'[2] and Sylvain Lévi suggests an element of Manichaean and Neo-Platonic thought in Asaṅga's *Mahāyāna-sūtrālaṅkāra*.[3]

The earliest group of Mahāyāna *sūtras* are entitled *Prajñā-pāramitās* (Perfections of *Prajñā*), of which there are five large recensions in 100,000, 25,000, 18,000, 10,000 and 8,000 verses respectively. How far these great volumes of the supposed records of the Buddha's profounder teachings go back in time, how they were preserved and transmitted, how much of them was developed out of the more ancient forms of Buddhist thought and how far they were conditioned by contacts of Buddhist thought with non-Buddhist philosophies of both India and 'Asiatic Greece' are problems that are still obscure.

The *sūtras*, as well as the Mahāyānist literature that developed on their basis, are in Sanskrit; and it is believed that the earliest of them like the *Prajñā-pāramitās*, *Saddharma-puṇḍarīka*, *Laṅkāvatāra* and *Gaṇḍavyūha* were probably products of the first two centuries of the Christian era.[4] There is little doubt, however, that in the beginning both Hīnayāna and Mahāyāna were involved in one system of thought and remained so for a few centuries.

Although in several early Mahāyāna *sūtras*, the old cult of Buddhism is referred to as an inferior one—as the 'way of Beginners' (*Śrāvaka-yāna*) or the 'way of those who aim at salvation for self

[1] See Sec. 5, *infra*, under 'Re-interpretation of the Hīnayāna'.
[2] *Buddhist Philosophy*, p. 216.
[3] See Sylvain Levi's edition and translation of *Mahāyāna-sūtrālaṅkāra* (Paris, 1907–11), ii, Intro., p. 18.
[4] See N. Dutt's *Aspects of Mahāyāna*, p. 43.

only' (*Pratyeka-yāna*)—a bifurcation between the two ways is not contemplated in them yet: on the other hand the *Saddharma-puṇḍarīka* and the *Laṅkāvatāra* insist that the way is always one.[1] The idea of '*two yānas*' (ways or vehicles), and the studied contrast and contradiction between the Hīnayāna and the Mahāyāna, emerged only when scholars, basing themselves on pre-existing Mahāyāna *sūtras*, started building up a system, expounding, developing and carrying to their logical and speculative conclusions the various concepts dispersed in these *sūtras*—such as, the Buddha's 'threefold body' (*Tṛkāya*), the Transcendental Wisdom (*Prajñā*), the Perfections (*Pāramitās*), the Avowed Aspirant to Buddhahood (*Bodhisattva*), the Psychological Potential for Buddhahood (*Bodhicitta*), the stages to attainment of Buddhahood (*Bhūmis*), the Theory of Void (*Śūṇyatā*),[2] etc. Some of these very concepts, however, are foreshadowed in the texts of different sects of early Buddhism—what was named Hīnayāna by the Mahāyānists.[3]

It was not a fixed-worded canon that the Mahāyānist scholars had to deal with exegetically—they were drawing out of the *sūtras* concepts of metaphysics, ontology, epistemology, etc., and formulating doctrines on the basis of these concepts. These scholars were creative thinkers and philosophers, and the most striking advances in Mahāyānic thought were made through individuals like Aśvaghoṣa, Nāgārjuna, Asaṅga, Vasubandhu and others. Naturally their speculative philosophies gave rise not to 'sects' (as in earlier Buddhism) but to 'schools': they stemmed from fundamental differences of intellectual standpoint, emphasis and outlook.

At an early stage in the evolution of the Mahāyāna, its two main schools of thought emerged—the MĀDHYAMIKA and the YOGĀCĀRA. In the general history of Indian philosophy, the early Mahāyānist schoolmen take a high rank. The neo-Vedantic philosophy that was initiated by Gouḍapāda and developed by Śaṅkara takes over and develops several of their fundamental concepts. It

[1] Both these great Mahāyāna scriptures speak of 'one way', not 'two ways', a higher one and a lower. '*Ekaṁ hi yānam dvitīyaṁ na vidyate*: *Tṛtīyaṁ naivāsti kadāci loke*'—*Saddharma-puṇḍarika* (see *Lotus of the Good Law*, SBE, Vol. 21, p. 6). On *Ekayāna* in the *Laṅkāvatāra*, see Suzuki's *Studies in the Laṅkāvatāra Sūtra* (Reprint, 1957), pp. 358–361. The 'one way' is identified with the Mahāyāna.

[2] *Śūṇyatā*, though popularly translated as 'Void', has a special connotation in Mahāyāna philosophy. It is derived from the fundamental Buddhist doctrine of *Pratītya-samutpāda* (Dependent Origination). In Nāgārjuna's *Mūla-madhyamaka-kārikā* (xxiv, 18), *Śūṇyatā* is identified with this doctrine (*yaḥ pratītya-samutpādaḥ śūnyatāṁ tāṁ pracakṣmahe*).

[3] For example: 'The formation of the Ten Pāramitās of Mahāyāna sūtras,' as Kimura points out, 'is almost identical with the Ten *Pāramitās* of the *Cariyāpiṭaka*'. (Kimura's *A Historical Study of the terms Hinayāna and Mahāyāna, Calcutta University*, 1927, *p*. 134). The *Cariyāpiṭaka* is a collection of 35 *Jātaka* tales and is included in the *Khuddaka-nikāya* of the *Suttapiṭaka* section of Theravāda canon. But it gives *seven* Pāramitās, not ten.

was in this 'school' period that the parting of ways between the old Hīnayāna and the new Mahāyāna really took place, that is, when Mahāyāna had come to a self-conscious stage in its evolution.[1]

b. DEVELOPMENT OF DIALECTICS AND LOGIC

The *Sūtras* come early in the history of Mahāyāna development and are anonymous; they were followed by the *Śāstras* of schoolmen who rank as Masters (*Ācāryas*) in Mahāyāna history. In these *śāstras* we see monk-scholarship shifting into the line of scholasticism.

Ratiocination is not a feature of the works of the Theravāda monk-scholars: their works are mainly expository, analytical, amplifacatory. In Mahāyānist literature this old exegesis is replaced by what is called *Alaṅkāra*.

An *Alaṅkāra* is 'an exegetical work which may be called a commentary in so far as it explains either a particular book, as in the case of *Abhisamayālaṅkāra*, or a class of books, as in *Sūtrālaṅkāra*, but it is not a commentary in the usual sense of the word, because it does not explain any particular passage separately taken, but all the *sūtra* or the *sūtras* as a whole'.[2] The *Alaṅkāras* are in verse and they enumerate and classify the topics in a *sūtra* or in the *sūtras*. 'It is evident', as says Professor Tucci, 'that the chief aim of the authors was to bring some systematical arrangement out of the clumsy and bulky Mahāyāna treatises and, while formulating a new system, to support their claim that the new ideas were all concealed in these venerable texts.'[3]

Thus the exegesis of *Sūtras*, in the hands of the *ācāryas*, turned from the mere development of particular concepts to the work of inter-relating and systematizing them. The work necessarily called for a high premium on ratiocination.

A lofty monument to the ratiocinative power of Mahāyānist scholarship is the *Śūraṅgama Sūtra*. Though in the form of a *sūtra*, with the Buddha as spokesman as in all *sūtras*, it is really a *śāstra*. The tradition is that it was composed by Dharmapāla at Nālandā, found its way into China and was translated into Chinese in AD 705.[4] It is highly esteemed by Chinese and Japanese Buddhist scholars. A well-known Chinese scholar and writer of our day describes it 'as a kind of *Essay on Human Understanding* and the *Gospel*

[1] On this point, see *Ibid*, Part II, Chap. 2 (on *Application of the terms Hinayāna and Mahāyāna among founders of Mahāyāna School and their followers*).

[2] G. Tucci's *On some aspects of the Doctrines of Maitreya* (*nātha*) *and Asaṅga* (Calcutta University Readership Lectures, Calcutta University, 1930), pp. 11–12.

[3] *Ibid*, pp. 10–11

[4] See Beal's *Buddhist Records*, ii, p. 110, footnote 55. It has been translated into English by Dwight Goddard in *A Buddhist Bible* (revised and enlarged ed., New York, 1952).

of St. John combined, with the intellectual force of the one and the religious spirit of the other'.[1]

Alongside of ratiocination, what is termed Dialectics developed—the holding in balance of two viewpoints (*Dṛṣtis*), opposed diametrically to one another as thesis and anti-thesis, and posing the problem in the form of a *quaestio* exactly in the manner of mediaeval Christian theologians.[2]

In its most pronounced and pointed form it appears in the *Madhymaka-kārikās* of Nāgārjuna, e.g. the following *kārikās* (verses) on *Nirvāṇa*:[3]

Nirvāṇa, first of all is not a kind of Ens (i.e. *Sat*);
It would then have decay and death.
There altogether is no Ens
Which is not subject to decay and death.

If Nirvāṇa is Ens,
It is produced by causes,—
Nowhere and none the entity exists
Which would not be produced by causes.

If Nirvāṇa is Ens,
How can it lack substratum?
There whatever is no Ens,
Without any substratum.

If Nirvāṇa is not an Ens,
Will it then be a non-Ens?
Wherever there is found no Ens,
There neither is a (corresponding) non-Ens.

Now, if Nirvāṇa is a non-Ens,
How can it then be independent?
For sure, an independent non-Ens
Is nowhere to be found.

The uninitiated are apt to be baffled and mystified by dialetic of this kind; yet it is the soul of Mādhyamika philosophy—a pronounced note also of the Yogācāra.

From dialectics stemmed Logic, a widespread and flourishing branch of Mahāyānist learning. The Yogācāra School was the nursery of Logic. Perhaps its growth in Buddhist learning and scholarship was stimulated by the fact that it was a potent intellectual instrument in public debates and disputations.

Maitreyanātha, preceptor of Asaṅga and putative founder of the

[1] Lin Yutang in *The Wisdom of India* (original ed., 1944), p. 459.
[2] See Gordon Leff's *Mediaeval Thought* (Pelican Book, 1958), p. 93.
[3] The English translation is by Stcherbatsky, taken from quotation in Sangharaksita's *Survey of Buddhism* (1957), pp. 342 ff.

Yogācāra School, was the first Buddhist scholar to bring into relief and stress the importance of the observance of the rules of ratiocination in Debate (*Vāda*). Among works ascribed to him is the voluminous *Yogācāra bhūmi-śāstra* (Nanjio No. 1170 under the title *Sapta-daśa-bhūmi-śāstra*) which, however, is assigned to Asaṅga in Tibetan tradition.[1] About this work, Professor Tucci says: 'We find here a full chapter dedicated to *Vāda* and divided into eight different items—*Vāda* in itself; the place where the speech is made, *vādādhikaraṇa*; the points of discussion, *vādasthāna*; the adornment of the speech, *vādālaṅkāra*; fallacy, *vacanadoṣa*; defeat, *vādanigraha*; the starting point of the speech, *vādaniḥsaraṇa*; and characteristics by which a speech is appreciated, *vāde bahukāradharmaḥ*'.[2] According to Professor Tucci, this portion of the work belongs to the 'pre-history' of Logic. Maitreyanātha was followed by Vasubandhu who, regarding Logic as the chief instrument in *Vāda*, wrote the triology, (i) *Vādahṛdaya* (Heart of Dispute), *Vādavidhi* (Method of Dispute) and *Vādavidhāna* (Rule of Dispute).[3]

It was Vasubandhu's illustrious pupil Dinnāga, however, who developed Logic from a set of rules of *Vāda*, from mere *elenchoi*, to a purely formal science and gave it the name *Nyāya*.

Perhaps the development of *Nyāya* as a science was not a purely academic one. Behind it was a practical urge—the stress of an exigency. This emanated from an ancient institution, evolved by the genius of Indian civilization to ease social tensions which were apt to arise from the clash of diverse faiths, sectarian rivalries and contending philosophies. It served to lift such differences from cantankerous quarrels and faction-fights to a calmer academic and intellectual sphere.

Many of the foremost Buddhist teachers and scholars are said in the Chinese and Tibetan legends about them to have won eminence by defeating *tīrthikas* (adherents of non-Buddhist faiths) or sectarian opponents in public disputation.

This kind of intellectual tournament among spokesmen of contending faiths had in fact been a long-established 'institutionalized' affair in India, evoking widespread popular interest. Sometimes these tournaments were arranged under royal patronage. Hsüan-tsang has given a full description of one such occasion. King Harṣa, who became Hsüan-tsang's friend and patron in India, used to hold annually what was known as a *Mokṣa* (Salvation) Festival. Part of this consisted in holding a religious convention at which several rounds of religious disputations took place. Invitations were sent out

[1] See Part IV, sec. 5 (under *Asaṅga*).
[2] Tucci's *On Some Aspects of the Doctrines, etc.*, p. 46.
[3] See *Ibid*, p. 70.

to scholars all over the country to participate and notices issued to the public to attend. The last of King Harṣa's convocations was held when Hsüan-tsang was with him in India and the Chinese scholar-guest was invited to preside. The pomp and circumstance that attended the occasion are colourfully described by Hsüan-tsang and his biographer Hwui-li.[1]

Harṣa's religious convocation was not an innovation; it was in the line of old Indian tradition. One can see at a glance how it was that the high propaganda value of these public disputations, in which the Buddhists had to hold their ground among adherents of different faiths and sects, served as the seed-bed from which sprouted Maitreyanātha's and Vasubandhu's *vāda*-manuals.

[1] See Beal's *Buddhist Records, etc.*, i, pp. 214–221. Also Beal's *Life of Hiuen-tsiang*, pp. 176 ff.

4

The Ācaryas and Mahāyānist Literature

THOSE who were the master-architects of Mahāyāna Buddhism had long passed away when Hsüan-tsang visited India. Already in AD 630 when the Chinese pilgrim was on tour in Gāndhāra and Kashmir, where the stronghold of Mahāyānism had once been, their identities had grown dim and their figures somewhat distant. The time was one of decline for Buddhism in these parts of India; the monasteries, where old traditions about the eminent Mahāyāna masters of the past might be expected to linger, were untenanted and in ruins.

Loitering among these ruins, Hsüan-tsang recalls with a touch of nostalgic sadness the legends about the 'many authors of *Śāstras*' who were natives of Gāndhāra:

'From old time till now this borderland of India has produced many authors of Śāstras, for examples, Nārāyaṇadeva, Asaṅga Bodhisattva, Vasubandhu Bodhisattva, Dharmātrāta, Manohṛta, Pārśva the noble, and so forth. There are about 1,000 *saṅghārāmas* which are deserted and in ruins. They are filled with wild shrubs and solitary to the last degree. The *stūpas* are mostly decayed. The heretical temples to the number of about 100 are occupied pell-mell by the heretics.'[1]

To Hsüan-tsang the Mahāyāna masters of Gāndhāra were splendid luminaries of a great age, then receded into a storied past. He views them together from the distance of time as a constellation—not as separate stars. He makes no distinction in their relative positions to one another nor in their temporal succession. For instance, in referring to Kumāralabdha, founder of the Sautrāntika School, Hsüan-tsang says:[2] 'At this time in the east was Aśvaghoṣa; in the south Deva; in the west Nāgārjuna; in the north Kumāralabdha. These four were called the Four Suns that illumined the world.' Perhaps he was quoting a Chinese byword current among Buddhist scholars of China of his own time.[3]

[1] Beal's *Buddhist Records*, i, p. 98.

[2] *Ibid*, ii, pp. 302–303.

[3] This saying about the 'Four Suns' occurs, as Suzuki tells us, in the preface of Śikṣānanda's Chinese translation of Aśvaghoṣa's *Mahāyāna-śraddhotpāda*: 'Aśvaghoṣa was numbered among the Four Suns.' The writer of the Preface was most likely a contemporary of Śikṣānanda who died in AD 710 (see Suzuki's *Awakening of Faith, etc.*, pp. 3–4).

Hsüan-tsang does not trouble over the question, debated by modern scholarship, of their contemporaneity: to him they were just charmed names that emblazoned a glorious golden past of Buddhism. The vagueness of his reference to the '*śāstra*-masters' reflects only the state of historical knowledge about them that existed in India in the early decades of the seventh century AD.

The Mahāyāna *śāstra*-masters' may be generally assigned to the period between the fourth and the sixth centuries AD. But their priorities are difficult to settle nor is a closer chronological approximation possible. The philosophy of the Mahāyāna, of both Mādhyamika and Yogācāra schools, was developed by them on the basis of *sūtras* of which the authorship is unknown, but which had undoubtedly appeared before their time during the first three centuries of the Christian era.

They came to be regarded in their after-fame as the true Fathers of the Mahāyāna Faith. Bu-ston, the Tibetan historiographer of the fourteenth century, for example, quotes from Mahāyāna *sūtras* a number of passages prophetic of the advent of saints and apostles to transmit the Buddha's teachings to posterity. He lists the '*Śāstra*-masters' as first and foremost among them.[1]

The vagueness of Hsüan-tsang's reference, however, contrasts oddly with the profusion of personal details about them in Chinese and Tibetan legends.

These legends offer a considerable number of biographical particulars about their subjects which we have no means of testing—native place, parentage, family, connections with different localities—Nālandā having grown into a great seat of monastic learning is most often mentioned[2]—achievements, disciples, etc. If in the six-thirties traditions about them had been already bedimmed by time, it seems unbelievable that circumstances, so precise and particular about their personal lives and careers, should have been remembered so late unless set down in archives. What seems to have happened is that, to let light into the obscurity into which the early 'saints and apostles' of Mahāyāna Buddhism had lapsed, legendary stories were invented by Mahāyānists of later times. But the 'say-so' of legend has no claim to rank as biography. Its uncritical reproduction serves only to obscure, rather than clarify, historical and biographical perspective.

Identities got mixed up in these stories—separate streams of tradi-

[1] See Obermiller's *History of Buddhism by Bu-ston* (Heidelberg, 1931–32), Part II, pp. 108–122.

[2] Nāgārjuna, Āryadeva, Vasubandhu and Asaṅga are said by Tāranātha to have been connected with Nālandā (see A. Ghosh's *A Guide to Nalanda* (2nd Ed., 1946), p. 40, where the references are given. See also *Pag-sam-jon-zang* (S. C. Das's Ed.), pp. 94–107.

tion mingling under one name borne by different persons. Thus three holders of the name Aśvaghoṣa, two of Vasubandhu and two of Nāgārjuna seem to have been rolled into one. We shall presently advert to this curious feature of the stories—the merger of personalities that came about through coalescence under one name of traditions originally relating to different individuals.

It also led to the jumbling up in the Chinese *Tripiṭaka* and in the Tibetan *Kanjur* and *Tanjur* of the genuine and the apocryphal among works ostensibly by the same author. The greatest names among the '*śāstra*-masters' became 'prestige names': it would boost the authority of a *śāstra* and enhance its sanctity to pass it under the name of any one of them. 'The names of men like Aśvaghoṣa, Nāgārjuna and Vasubandhu often attracted to themselves so many works that pious tradition sometimes extended the lifetime of the holders over many centuries, while modern historical criticism has had the greatest difficulties in distinguishing the different persons behind the one name.'[1] The result is that the task of sorting out the genuine works of an author from the apocryphal demands a considerably more than ordinary apparatus of technical and philological scholarship.

Mahāyānist religious literature preserved in Chinese and Tibetan collections may be classified in three broad categories: (i) *Sūtras*, (ii) *Śāstras*, and (iii) *Vibhāṣās*.

A text is called a *Sūtra* when it claims to have been spoken by the Lord himself—by the Buddha or any of the divine Bodhisattvas. Such a *sūtra* echoes the ancient formula of introduction with which every *sutta* in the Pali Theravāda canon begins—'So have I heard'—and adds also the *nidāna* (statement of time and occasion): 'At one time when the Lord was staying at such and such place, etc.' The *Prajñāpāramitā Sūtras*, which fill many volumes, pass as records of the Lord's sayings. Their anonymous authorship must have extended over more than a century. A *Śāstra* is a treatise written by an individual author or by joint authors, known by name, which quotes the *sūtras* as authority and formulates or systematizes the profound mystical truths contained in them, either in verse (*Kārikā*) or in prose. It is usually metaphysical and epistemological in the staple of its subject-matter. A *Vibhāṣā* (or *Vibhaṅga* or *Alaṅkāra*) is an exegetic and commentarial work, but different from Hīnayānist exegesis in its form and mode, not being 'textual', but aiming at critical examination or exposition of the dogmas and doctrines of the *sūtras*.

Besides these three, there are two subsidiary categories: (i) *Lekha* and (ii) *Stotra*.

[1] *per* Edward Conze in *Buddhism: Its Essence and Development* (Oxford, 1951), p. 31.

A *Lekha* is an Epistle (or an Essay, in its eighteenth-century connotation in English poetry like Pope's *Essay on Man*), of which there are several specimens in the Tibetan *Tanjur*, the best known being Nāgārjuna's Epistle, entitled *Suhṛllekha*, to Udāyibhadra, a Sātavāhana king.[1] There are three Chinese translations of this work listed in Nanjio's *Catalogue* as Nos. 1,440, 1,441 and 1,464. A *Stotra* is a hymnology, always in verse and meant to be chanted.

These categories, however, do not cover the large number of Tāntric works of later growth which abound in both Chinese and Tibetan collections. They are more plentiful in Tibetan, but they cannot be ranked as works of scholarship by any stretch of definition of the term.[2] They relate mostly to the practice of a mystic and esoteric cult called *Guhya-samāja*.[3] In Book VII of the 'Blue Annals', entitled 'The preaching of the *Tantras*', is described how, under Indian instructors, this cult grew up and flourished in Tibet.[4]

RE-INTERPRETATION OF THE HĪNAYĀNA

Mahāyānist schools, as we have pointed out, made no canons, although some texts were regarded by them as fundamental and some as more authoritative than others. With this lack of canon, the Mahāyāna strikes us, as Eliot puts it, as 'not a single vehicle, but rather a train comprising many carriages of different classes'.[5]

In the making of *śāstras* out of the *sūtras*, the endeavour of the *ācāryas* was both synthetic and creative. They aimed to establish a

[1] This epistolary form seems to have become a recognized one in Buddhist literature, and in a much later century (eighth AD?), it is adopted by Candragomin in his *Śiṣyalekhā-dharmakāvya* (see Keith's *History of Sanskrit Literature*, Reprint 1953, pp. 71–72). Nāgārjuna's work is ostensibly addressed to Udāyibhadra, mentioned as a Sātavāhana king. Historians have puzzled over the name. It occurs neither in the Purāṇic lists nor in any coin or inscription (see *A Comprehensive History of India*, ed. by N. Sastri, Vol. II, p. 323). A late work on the line of *Suhrillekha* is one listed among the works of Dīpaṅkara Śrijñāna ('Atīśa'), named *Vimala-ratna-lekhana*, an epistle by the author to Nyāyapāla, the Pāla king, on his departure for Tibet round AD 1030 (see Waddell's *Buddhism of Tibet*, 2nd Ed., p. 36, footnote 2; Nos. 4,188 and 4,566 in the *Tohoku Imperial University Catalogue*).

[2] These works of purely Tāntric Buddhism are thus characterized by Dr S. K. De: 'They were meant for a limited sectarian purpose and possess little that is of general or literary interest. Apart from their technical or esoteric terminology, they are often written with an entire disregard of grammatical or elegant expression. They never pretend to be academic. . . . Most of these works consist either of *Stotras* of varying lengths to Tārā, Avalokiteśvara, Mañjuśrī and other personages of later Buddhist pantheon, or of theurgic texts, called *Sādhanās* or *Vidhis*, of esoteric devotion, doctrine and practice. Some of them are also texts of magical ritual or completely dedicated to magic, even to black magic.'—Majumdar's *History of Bengal*, Vol. I, p. 328.

[3] See Part V, Sec. 3, p. 349.

[4] See *Blue Annals*, Vol. I, pp. 351 ff.

[5] Eliot in *Hinduism and Buddhism*, Vol. II, p. 4.

new system of faith within Buddhism—one that was by no means a continuation of the old. Both in spirit and in form, its differences were fundamental.

It was permeated by a new spirit of altruistic idealism that is typified by the doctrines of 'transferring one's own merit to all creatures (*pariṇāmanā*)' and of refraining from self-salvation until all creatures were saved.[1] Its doctrines were derived from the metaphysical, epistemological and ontological concepts of the *sūtras*, unknown in earlier Buddhism. Although the Mahāyāna system constituted so definite a break with the old cult—with the Hīnayānist *Dhamma-vinaya*—yet the break is not recognized. Hīnayāna is not put out of court nor given the go-by. Without breaking the old bottle, they pour into it the new wine.

The Hīnayāna cult is re-interpreted in the light of the Mahāyāna, of which an outstanding example may be cited from a work by Bhāvaviveka, extant in Chinese (Nanjio, No. 1,237) entitled *Karatala-ratna* ('Jewel in the Palm of the Hand').

The old cult described itself as the 'Aryan Eightfold Path' (*Ārya Aṣṭāṅgika Mārga*)—the *Ariyo Aṭṭhaṅgiko Maggo* of the Pali Theravāda canon. Its eight *aṅgas* (parts) are: (i) Right View (*Sammādiṭṭhi*), (ii) Right Aspiration (*Sammāsaṅkappo*), (iii) Right Speech (*Sammāvācā*), (iv) Right Conduct (*Sammākammanto*), (v) Right Livelihood (*Sammā-ājīva*), (vi) Right Effort (*Sammāvāyamo*), (vii) Right Mindfulness (*Sammāsati*) and (viii) Right Contemplation (*Sammāsamādhi*). While retaining these, Bhāvaviveka gives to each one of them a new interpretation from the Mahāyānist point of view, so that the ethical or 'practical' content of each is transmuted into an attribute or attitude of the inner life of contemplation. According to Bhāvaviveka:[2]

(i) Right View *means*	Complete Insight into the Dharmakāya of the Tathāgata.
(ii) Right Aspiration *means*	Suppression of all discursive thought (*parikalpana*).
(iii) Right Speech *means*	Realization of the non-reality of all objective categories and resolution of all disputes.
(iv) Right Conduct *means*	To refrain from acting physically, verbally or mentally on realizing the emptiness of all *Dharmas* (Physical Existences).
(v) Right Livelihood *means*	To live on the principle that all things are without origination or destruction and have no reality.

[1] See Part IV, Sec. 5, under Aśvaghoṣa and Śāntideva, p. 283 and p. 288.

[2] See *Karatala-ratna* (translated from Chinese into Sanskrit by Aiyaswami Sastri), Visvabharati Studies, No. 9 (Visvabharati, 1949), p. 98. The work is ascribed to Bhāvaviveka, about whom see Part IV, Sec. 5, p. 286.

(vi)	Right Effort *means*	Not to commit oneself to any physical act realizing that strength or skill does not avail.[1]
(vii)	Right Mindfulness *means*	Not to brood over *ens* and *non-ens*, realizing that all things, to true intellectual perception, lack objectivity.
(viii)	Right Contemplation *means*	Not to embrace any conclusion without arriving at certainty which follows the seeing and realizing of the end of all *Dharmas* (Physical Existences).

Bhāvaviveka adds that the significance of all these is shown *loco citato* in the 'Bodhisattva-piṭaka', by which is meant the Mahāyāna *Sūtras*.

This is only a typical example to show how Mahāyānist *ācāryas*, without discarding as false the system of the Hīnayāna, tried to raise its ethical and psychological categories to a rarefied metaphysical significance, opening thereby the perspective on what they believed to be a higher spiritual goal, viz. Buddhahood which, in Mahāyānic concept, was loftier than the goal of Arhatship pointed to by the Hīnayānist 'eightfold path'. It was loftier in the sense of being a goal open to all men—all who could develop the psychological capacity for progress towards it—and not exclusively to those ordained.

The makers of the Mahāyāna *śāstras* derive authority from the same formal source as the Hīnayānists—the *ipsisimma verba* of the Lord as recorded in the *Sūtras* (Pali-*Suttas*). But the 'sayings' the former relied upon were not those accepted and incorporated in the Hīnayāna canons.

This difference regarding the provenance of *Buddhavacana*, dividing the two systems so sharply, was at the same time reconciled by a Mahāyānist dogma.

This posited a concept of the 'Lord in Threefold Body' (*Tṛkāya*). What the Hīnayānist accepted as the Lord's sayings was, according to this dogma, delivered in one 'body'—that assumed by him in his earthly manifestation—the 'built-up body' (*Nirmāṇa-kāya*); the Lord's sayings in this 'body' had been adapted to the varying levels of intelligence of people who heard him. There were other sayings of his delivered on earth to men of superior wisdom and capability, traditions of which were preserved by them, or they had been delivered in Heaven in his 'celestial body' (*Sambhoga-kāya*). It was

[1] cf. Taoist doctrine of inaction:
'He who acts, spoils;
He who grasps, lets slip.
Because the sage does not act, he does not spoil;
Because he does not grasp, he does not let slip;
The affairs of men are often spoiled within an ace of completion;
By being careful at the end as at the beginning
Failure is averted . . .'
Lin Yutang's *Wisdom of China* (London: Michael Joseph, 1948), p. 58.

believed that in the Mahāyāna *Sūtras* like *Saddharma-puṇḍarīka, Laṅkāvatāra-sūtra,* the *Pāramitā-sūtras* and others of the same sanctity and standing, these higher teachings were extant.

The *Sūtras* are mystical, unsystematic and asymmetrical, and record the teachings of one who transcended the Hīnayānist's temporal concept of him—not the Buddha as the Hīnayāna conceives him, one fixed to time and space.[1]

This conflict between the Hīnayānist concept of a Buddha in time and space and the Mahāyānist concept of a Being eternal and supramundane is presented in the *Saddharma-puṇḍarīka* in the form of an apocalypse.

Before the eyes of Maitreya is conjured up a wonderful vision of unnumbered Bodhisattvas coming out of the earth's womb, each of whom is a disciple of the Lord. Maitreya in this *sūtra* stands forth as spokesman of the Hīnayānist Buddha-concept. He asks in all innocence how all these Bodhisattvas could possibly be the Buddha's disciples and worshippers, seeing that the Buddha had left Kapilavastu as a young prince and attained enlightenment at Gayā just a little over forty years ago. The impossibility of it, as Maitreya puts it, would be like that of a young man claiming centenarians as his sons. But Maitreya's doubts are resolved by the Tathāgata: he explains to Maitreya that for countless aeons he has been an omniscient Buddha, though human creatures in their ignorance hold that Śākyamuni went forth from the Śākya clan and obtained the supreme enlightenment in the 'Bodhi circle' (*Bodhimaṇḍa*) at Gayā only in recent times. *Naivaṁ draṣṭavyam*—'it must not be so regarded'—asserts the Tathāgata, and proceeds to explain to Maitreya how that illusion arises from his own *Upāya-Kauśala* (Skilfulness of Device).[2]

The grand achievement of the *Ācāryas* lies in the elucidation and systematization of the inset mystical or transcendental concepts of the *Sūtras* and in bringing out their implicit interrelations. The prevailing tone is more or less polemical, for the *sāstras* are a call to stragglers in the strait or the lower way, *Hīnayāna,* to the broad or the higher way, *Mahāyāna*. This is conceived as the Broad Way because it is open to all and is not reserved only for the ordained. The Sanskrit word *Yāna* means both a 'way' and a 'vehicle' and it is

[1] *Vide* the argument put forward by the Theravāda protagonist in the *Kathāvatthu* (xvii) in reply to the dogma that 'the Buddha never lived on earth': 'Was he not born at Lumbinī? Did he not receive perfect enlightenment under the Bodhi tree? Was not the Wheel of *Dhamma* set rolling by him at Banaras? Did he not renounce the will to live at Cāpāla Cetiya? Did he not complete existence at Kusinārā?' (see *Points of Controversy,* PTS., p. 323). Yet the supramundane concept of the Buddha existed several centuries before the emergence of the Mahāyāna.

[2] See Chs. XIV and XV of the *Saddharma-puṇḍarīka*. The theme of the eternity of the Buddha's existence is taken up also in the *Suvarṇa-prabhāsa,* Ch. II.

in the latter sense that it is employed in the *sāstras*. In the *Sūtras* it is used in contexts which suggest that the word may have been originally a Sanskrit equivalent for Pali *Magga*.[1]

This *śāstra*-literature is vast in volume; a large part of it is preserved in the Chinese and Tibetan collections, but for most of these works, chronology is uncertain and authorship confused.

The *Ācāryas* who were the authors of these texts are great names in Indian philosophy. Yet they were not philosophers in the ordinary sense—not intellectualists or academicians. With them, as with the ancient Greek philosophers, philosophy meant a way of life, a means to man's highest self-fulfilment. They linked philosophy with man's spiritual aspiration and endeavour and the end of philosophy in their view was the ultimate realization of spiritual possibilities latent in every 'aspirant' (*Bodhisattva*) after *Bodhi* (Supreme Knowledge). For the Vedanta philosophy, propounded by Gouḍapāda and developed by Śaṅkara, which still rules largely Indian thought and colours Indian outlook on life, the speculations of the Buddhist *ācāryas* undoubtedly laid the basis.[2]

Mahāyāna philosophy had schools and sub-schools. The two principal schools, as we have noted, were the *Mādhyamika* (founded by Nāgārjuna) and the *Yogācāra* (founded by Maitreyanātha). Under the second school were two sub-schools, viz. (i) *Svātantrika* led by Bhāvaviveka, and (ii) *Prāsaṅgika* founded by Buddhapālita and developed by Candrakīrtti. The sub-schools, however, do not make any fundamental change in the philosophy, but differ only in the methodology of exposition. Bhāvaviveka's *Svātantrika* school goes in for 'direct reasoning', while Buddhapālita's *Prāsaṅgika* school for the method of '*reductio ad absurdum*'.

The uncertain chronology and the confused authorship which beset

[1] e.g. 'Mahāyāna is nothing but a Broad Way (*Yāna*) laid through the worlds of gods and men, wide as the sky—hence called Mahāyāna'—*Aṣṭa-sāhasrikā-prajñā-pāramitā* (Bibliotheca Indica Ed., p. 24). 'There is only one Way (*Yāna*); no second way exists, and certainly not a third ever in this world.'—*Saddharma-puṇḍarīka* (see *Lotus of the Good Law*, SBE, Vol. XXI, p. 6). The idea seems to be that the Mahāyāna is not a new way struck out, but the old one so widened as to be a broad thoroughfare for all.

[2] Of all schools of Indian philosophy, the Vedanta has been most influential in the life and thought of India. Gouḍapāda, founder of the school, lived in the age in which the great Mahāyānist *ācāryas* flourished. His work, called *Āgamaśāstra* or *Gouḍapāda-kārikā*, has been edited, translated and annotated by Pandit V. S. Bhattacarya and published under the title of *Āgamaśāstra of Gouḍapāda* by the University of Calcutta in 1943. In his Introduction, the learned editor and translator has made a detailed examination of Gouḍapāda's indebtedness to the Mahāyānist philosophers. His conclusion is that Gouḍapāda 'has quoted almost fully or partially or substantially, from the works of some celebrated Buddhist teachers who flourished between AD 200 and AD 400' (*Ibid*, pp. lxxvi–lxxvii). 'Nāgārjuna, Aryadeva, Maitreyanātha or Asaṅga, and possibly Yaśomitra, would seem not only to have supplied Gouḍapāda with philosophic thoughts to adopt, but also with model verses to follow in his composition of the *Kārikā*'—says Dr Mahadevan (*Gouḍapāda—A Study in Early Advaita*, 2nd Ed., p. 185), although in his opinion the source of his philosophy was the *Upaniṣads*.

Mahāyāna *śāstras* certainly lends colour to Eliot's somewhat caustic characterization of the Mahāyāna:

'Although the record of the Mahāyāna . . . is clear and even brilliant, it is not easy either to trace its rise or connect its development with other events in India. Its annals are an interminable list of names and doctrines, but bring before us few living personalities and hence are dull. They are like a record of the Christian Church's fight against Arians, Monophysites and Nestorians with all the great figures of Byzantine history omitted or called in question.'[1]

We shall presently see how three towering figures among the *ācāryas* have been 'called in question' by modern critical scholarship.

[1] *Hinduism and Buddhism,* Vol. II, p. 5.

5

The Ācāryas

a. MERGER OF PERSONALITIES: AŚVAGHOSA, NĀGĀRJUNA AND VASUBANDHU

IN the roll of the first generation of Mahāyānist schoolmen and philosophers who are known as *Ācāryas* or '*Śāstra*-masters', the outstanding names are: Aśvaghoṣa, the two brothers Asaṅga and Vasubandhu, Dinnāga, Nāgārjuna, Kumāralabdha, Buddhapālita and Bhāvaviveka (or Bhāvya). In respect of at least three of them, of pre-eminent position, the phenomenon we have referred to as 'merger of personalities' is evident.

AŚVAGHOSA is perhaps the most venerable name among the *ācāryas*. The legend about him (both Chinese and Tibetan) is that he played a most important part in the 'council' convened by Kaniṣka, which, according to Tibetan legend, was the first great gathering in Buddhist history of Bodhisattvas—the first Mahāyānist council. Aśvaghoṣa was among the assembled Bodhisattvas and his literary genius was availed of for precise and effective formulation of the doctrines arrived at by the council. The legend thus points to the reign of Kaniṣka (first or second century AD) as the time of his advent, though there are other legends that assign him to a later period.[1]

His name became a 'prestige name': in the Chinese and Tibetan canonical collections a large number of Mahāyānist works, different in kind and diverse in character, are fathered on him. They are highly esteemed by Mahāyānists:

1. *Treatises on the Mahāyāna:*
   (a) Mahāyāna-śraddhotpāda
   (b) Sūtrālaṅkara-śāstra
   (c) Gaṇḍīstotra, and a large number of minor works.

2. *Epic poems:*
   (d) Buddha-caritam
   (e) Saundarānanda-Kāvya

3. *Dramatic work:*
   (f) Śāriputra-prakaraṇa

[1] The Chinese and Tibetan legends of Aśvaghosa are summarised in Suzuki's *Awakening of Faith, etc.*, pp. 2–32. One of these legends (Chinese) speaks of six Aśvaghoṣas (*Ibid*, p. 6) who flourished at different times.

But on a critical examination of these works from the points of view of style, manner and contents, the putative single author splits up into three: (i) Aśvaghoṣa, author of the *Sūtrālaṅkara-śāstra*, who flourished 'three hundred or three hundred and seventy years after the *Nirvāṇa*', (ii) Aśvaghoṣa, better known as Sthavira Aśvaghoṣa, a Hīnayānist monk, who lived 'four hundred years after the *Nirvāṇa*' and was disciple either of Sthavira Pārśva or of the latter's pupil Puṇyayaśa, and (iii) Bodhisattva Aśvaghoṣa, author of the *Mahāyāna-śraddhotpāda*, who appeared 'five or six hundred years after the *Nirvāṇa*'. "Anesaki does not find 'enough evidence' either to affirm or to deny the identity of any of the Aśvaghoṣas with the author of the *Buddha-caritam*. The same epithet may have been applied to many authors in different periods." (ERE, ii, p. 160).[1]

In the Chinese 'Life of Aśvaghoṣa'[2] and in several accounts of him in other Chinese works, sharp discrepancies arise from a coalescence of traditions about three distinct personalities under one name.[3]

NĀGĀRJUNA appears in the legends as an incompatible double personality—as an idealist philosopher who was author of the *Madhyamaka-kārikā*, and as a magician and alchemist, author of *Rasaratnākara*.

The following is the Tibetan legend about him.[4] As is usual in Tibetan legends, it is full of unverifiable personal details:

'Ācārya Nāgārjuna was born in the south, in Vidarbha, in a Brāhmaṇa family. At the time of his birth an astrologer told his parents that they should feast, according to rites, one hundred Brāhmaṇas for days and months so that the child should have at least seven years of life. When the seven years were about to expire, his parents, not bearing to see their son dead, sent him to another land. He (the son Nāgārjuna) reached Nālendra,[5] and saw Saraha who gave him the consecration of Amitāyu and made him recite *mantras* for longevity. Having obtained the *pravrajyā* from Rāhula, the Grand Abbot (of Nālandā or Nālendra), at an age a little over eight, he acquired learning in *Sarvāstivāda*. He got instructions from Saraha in *Kālacakra*. At the age of nineteen, from the aforesaid Grand

[1] *Per* Dr B. C. Law in the article on Aśvaghoṣa in the Volume of Specimen Articles (1957) of the *Encyclopaedia of Buddhism*, ed. by Dr Malalasekera.

[2] See Part IV, Sec. 1, p. 245.

[3] The discrepancies are pointed out by Suzuki in the Introduction to the *Awakening of Faith*, etc.

[4] The legend is taken from *Pag-sam-jon-zang* (ed. by S. C. Das—see Part IV, sec. 1 (a) under Tibetan), p. 85. I am indebted to Dr Lokesh Chandra of the International Academy of Indian Culture, Delhi, for translation of the passage. See also Bu-ston (Obermiller, ii, pp. 112–130).

[5] In Tibetan legends Nālandā is often referred to by this name, in accordance with a Tibetan tradition that it was built by a *Rājā* (see Roerich's *Biography of Dharmasvāmin*, pub. by Jayaswal Research Institute, Patna, 1959, p. 90.)

Abbot he obtained his ordination and his name, Nāgārjuna (Tibetan Dpal-ldan-blo-hohan). He attained *siddhi* (mastery) in Mahāmāyūrī, Kurukulle (?) and several other (magic) cults and arts, and specially in *Rasāyana* (Alchemistry) and became "thunder-bodied" (*vajrakāya*). He got instruction from Bhalava, obtained the "touch-stone" from Dvīpāntara. But unable to use it, he listened to an exposition by a female wine-merchant, and with the perfected touch-stone, he fed, during the term of his superintendence, the Mahāyāna *saṅgha* of Nālendra when a famine was raging. He continued to do so (i.e. perform such miracles), having attained *siddhi* from Caṇḍikā Devī. A sermon of his was attended by two daughters of Nāga Takṣaka who invited him to Nāgaloka (Serpent World) to hear the Doctrine. He went there and brought back the *Śatasāhasrikā*, a little incomplete, and several *dhāraṇīs* (spells) and hence on, he came to be known as Nāgārjuna. In Puṇḍravardhana he produced gold with his touch-stone and offered *dāna* (gifts). He heard the *Tārātantra* from Hayaghoṣa. From Dhanyakaṭaka Vihāra, he brought the *Mahākālaratna*, *Kulukulle-tantra* and other *tantras*. Hereafter no new Mahāyāna *sūtras* came out in India.'

The legend goes on to describe the many miracles performed by him and asserts that he 'showed the profound path of *Mādhyamika*' by composing the *Madhyamaka-kārikās* (referred to under a Tibetan name) and lived for 500 years.

In combining the philosopher with the alchemist, the legend is a fair sample of all Nāgārjuna legends. It is difficult, however, to believe that he who founded the Mādhyamika school of Mahāyāna Buddhism could have been the same person as the Tāntric scholar, magician, miracle-monger and possessor of the philosopher's stone.

Traditions undoubtedly existed about an ancient alchemist bearing the name Nāgārjuna, to whom several works on *suvarṇatantra* (Alchemy) are ascribed—*Rasaratnākara* being the best known among them.[1] He is believed to have flourished so late as in the eighth century AD, but the time should be shifted a couple of centuries back, for Hsüan-tsang knew the traditions about the alchemist and, as in all Nāgārjuna legends, mixed them up with those of the Mādhyamika philosopher.

Nāgārjuna Bodhisattva, according to Hsüan-tsang, was not only a great teacher and philosopher, but also a maker of the 'elixir of life' and an alchemist who could turn stone into gold. 'Nāgārjuna Bodhisattva was well practised in the art of compounding medicines;

[1] The alchemist Nāgārjuna's works are noticed in Dr P. C. Ray's *History of Chemistry in Ancient and Mediaeval India* (pub. by Indian Chemical Society, 1956), p. 118.

by taking a preparation (pill or cake), he nourished the years of life for many hundreds of years, so that neither the mind nor the appearance decayed.' Hsüan-tsang narrates a miracle performed by him: 'moistening great stones with a divine and superior decoction (medicine or mixture), he changed them into gold'.[1] Evidently this alchemist must have flourished a considerable time, maybe two centuries, before the Chinese pilgrim.

Between the nihilistic idealism of Mādhyamika philosophy and the crude empiricism of Suvarṇatantra (Alchemy), it is difficult to conceive any possible relation. Two streams of tradition about a philosopher and an alchemist must somehow have got interfused—certainly long before Hsüan-tsang's time (first half of the seventh century).[2]

VASUBANDHU is the putative author of a number of works—thirty-six in the Chinese collection and eight in the Tibetan. His *magnum opus* is the *Abhidharma-Kośa* with an auto-commentary entitled *Kośabhāṣya*.

It is said in the legends that Vasubandhu was in the beginning a Hīnayānist of the Sarvāstivāda school and it is to this period of his life that the work belongs. It is a classic work of Abhidharma philosophy, summarizing all its topics under eight captions (*Kośa-sthānas*). It is in verse and in the concluding couplet Vasubandhu states that his work is mostly according to the system of the 'Vaibhāṣikas of Kashmir'.[3]

Its one-time currency among learned Buddhists all over India is hinted at by a passage in the Sanskrit poet Bāṇa's *Harṣa-caritam* in which the poet describes parrots (*śukas*) chirping scraps of the work.[4] It was studied as a text-book by students of metaphysics in I-tsing's time.[5] In the Tibetan *Tanjur*, there are five commentarial works upon it written by the famous scholars, Yaśomitra, Puṇyavardhana, Śāntisthiradeva, Dinnāga and Sthiramati. Twice translated into Chinese by Paramārtha and Hsüan-tsang respectively, Vasubandhu's *Abhidharma-Kośa* in its Chinese translation is the basic work of one of the traditional Ten Schools, called the *Kośa* School, of Chinese Buddhism.

[1] Beal's *Buddhist Records* (Popular Ed.), ii, p. 212.

[2] The philosopher Nāgārjuna was probably earlier in time than the alchemist Nāgārjuna. A Japanese scholar, Hikata, has tried to arrive at the time of Nāgārjuna the philosopher on the basis of mention of him by Dharmarakṣa, in Kumārajīva's biography and in Nāgārjuna's *Suhṛllekha*. Hikata's conclusion is that 'Nāgārjuna was a man living from the latter half of the second century to the first half of the third century'. See Hikata's *Prajñāpāramitā-sūtra*, pub. by Kyushu University, Fukuoka, Japan, 1958), Intro., p. liii, footnote.

[3] '*Kāśmīra-vaibhāṣika-nītisiddhaḥ; Prāyo mayāyaṁ kathitobhidharma*'—VIII, 40.—See Rahula Sankrityayana's *Abhidharma-Kośa* (Sanskritized) (Kashi Vidyapitha Publication, 1931), p. 235.

[4] See *Ibid.*, Intro., p. 18, where the Sanskrit verse is quoted.

[5] Takakusu's *A Record of the Buddhist Religion*, etc., p. 176.

The legends relate that Vasubandhu was converted by his elder brother Asaṅga from the Hīnayāna to the Mahāyāna faith and thereafter made valuable contributions to Mahāyānist philosophy.

The principal source of our knowledge about this leading exponent and scholar of Mahāyāna Buddhism is his life in Chinese composed by Paramārtha in the sixth century.[1] According to the biographer's chronology, he flourished in the fifth century which is corroborated by Hsüan-tsang.[2]

But in the opinion of Takakusu, Paramārtha's biography 'represents a sort of mosaic, composed of materials which he (Paramārtha) took from different books and also from the memory of events with which he became acquainted when he was still living in India'.[3] This heterogeneous character of the work has raised a doubt whether Paramārtha did not actually mix up traditions pertaining to two different persons. As a matter of fact one '*vṛddhācārya* Vasubandhu' (Elder Vasubandhu) is referred to in Yośomitra's *Sphuṭārthā*, a commentarial work, extant in Sanskrit and in Tibetan translation, on Vasubandhu's *Abhidharma-Kośa.*[4]

Vasubandhu's life-story is thus sketched by Paramārtha:[5]

'The biography begins with a legend on the name of Vasubandhu's native city Puruṣapura and goes on telling of his family, of his father, the Brāhmaṇa Kauśika, of his three sons, Asaṅga, Vasubandhu and Viriñcivatsa. Then follows a new section, which could be called the story of the antecedents of the compilation of the *Abhidharmakośa*. The text gives an account of the great "council" of Kashmir. . . . Then the narrative passes on to Vasubandhu. We read of the Sāṅkhya teacher Vindhyavāsin, his victory over Vasubandhu's teacher Buddhamitra during Vasubandhu's absence, of Vasubandhu's return and of the composition of the *Paramārtha-saptati-ṭīkā* in which he confuted Vindhyavāsin. Then follows the composition of the *Abhidharma-Kośa*, Vasubandhu's dispute with the grammarian Vaheerata and the appearance of Saṅghabhadra who polemizes against Vasubandhu's *Abhidharma-Kośa* and challenges its author to a disputation, but meets with a refusal by Vasubandhu who alleges his own very old age. Now enters Asaṅga and converts to Mahāyāna his brother Vasubandhu, who, after this, develops a

[1] *Re* Paramārtha, see Part IV, Sec. 7, pp. 306–307. Paramārtha's 'Life of Vasubandhu' has been translated into English by Takakusu (in 1904) in *T'oung Pao*, Serie II, Vol. V, pp. 269–296.

[2] Frauwallner's *On the Date of the Buddhist Master of Law Vasubandhu*. IsMEO, Rome, Serie Orientale, III (1951), pp. 8–10.

[3] Cited by Frauwallner in *Ibid*, p. 17.

[4] See Jaini's article *On the Theory of Two Vasubandhus* in the *Bulletin of the School of Oriental and African Studies*, University of London, Part I, Vol. xxi, 1958.

[5] See Frauwallner's *On the Date of Vasubandhu*, pp. 14–15.

great literary activity in favour of Mahāyāna. The account closes with a list of the Mahāyāna works of Vasubandhu and a short mention of his death.'

The legend about Vasubandhu given by Hsüan-tsang in the *Si-yu-ki* follows the version of Paramārtha's 'Life', speaking of Vasubandhu's conversion to Mahāyāna and his later authorship of 'a hundred and more *śāstras* in agreement with the Great Vehicle'.[1]

On a critical analysis of the narrative, from different points of view, Frauwallner comes to the conclusion that the Hīnayānist author of the *Abhidharma-Kośa* and the Mahāyānist scholar who was the younger brother of Asaṅga and was converted by him were two different persons.

Traditions about the two got telescoped and the 'Life' was a reconstruction—a piecing together of stories by one of Paramārtha's disciples on the basis of information hailing from his master.[2] The mistake was possibly Paramārtha's own. It seems that he knew of an earlier Vasubandhu (the *Vṛddhācārya* of Yaśomitra's *Sphutārthā*?) and also of a later Mahāyānist scholar of the same name who had composed many Mahāyānist works. It was, according to Frauwallner, this later Vasubandhu who enjoyed the patronage and favour of Skandagupta (surnamed Vikramāditya—AD 455–467) and was entrusted by him with the education of the heir-apparent Bālāditya. This Vasubandhu lived at the capital city of Ayodhyā, expiring there at the age of eighty. Traditions about two illustrious monk-scholars, one a Hīnayānist and the other a Mahāyānist of two different periods, were dovetailed by the story of the conversion.[3]

b. LIVES AND WORKS

We have named eight out of the roll of Mahāyānist *ācāryas* and seen how three leading names are wrapped in a confusion of legends. To these eight may be added the name of one, who flourished much later in time, but may be placed by the side of the greater *ācāryas* of old—Śāntideva.

It is beside our purpose to deal with the Mahāyāna philosophy that

[1] See Beal's *Buddhist Records*, ii, pp. 228–229.

[2] See Frauwallner's *On the Date of Vasubandhu*, p. 18.

[3] The theory of 'two Vasubandhus', worked out by Frauwallner, is not fully established yet. Some manuscripts recovered from Tibet by Rahul Sankrityayana in 1937 have been found to contain two works—a fragmentary one containing a *Kārikā* text on the lines of Vasubandhu's *Abhidharma-kośa* and the other a prose commentary on it. In the commentary there are several references to the 'Kośakāra' and his views, challenged by the commentator as Mahāyānist. If the 'Kośakāra' betrayed these leanings to the Mahāyāna, the story of his conversion becomes at least plausible. See Jaini's article on *The Theory of Two Vasubandhus* in the *Bulletin of the School of O. and A. Studies*, London University, Part I, Vol. xxi.

was developed by them, except to touch cursorily upon some of their individual contributions.

There are eight works ascribed in the Chinese *Tripiṭaka* to AŚVAGHOṢA including the *Buddha-caritam*.[1] Who this Buddhist poet was whose great epic (*kāvya*) bears clear stylistic resemblance to the poetry of Kālidāsa, the foremost Sanskrit poet, poses a problem. But the poet Aśvaghoṣa is to be distinguished from the eminent Mahāyānist scholar who wrote the *Mahāyāna-śraddhotpāda* and other works of Mahāyānist philosophy.

The *Mahāyāna-śraddhotpāda* (translated by Suzuki under the title *The Awakening of Faith in the Mahāyāna*) is a syncretized and integrated presentation in a brief and compact form of both Mādhyamika and Yogācāra thought. Its chief title to distinction is that it gives the first explicit formulation of the *Tṛkāya* doctrine of Mahāyānist philosophy. The work does not exist in its Sanskrit original, but only in Chinese translations of which the first was made in AD 405.

Tṛkāya is the basic doctrine of the Mahāyāna: a dogma that forms, as it were, the keystone of its arch—for the presumed authenticity of the whole Mahāyānist system of faith, as we have explained, depends upon it. It imparts to its fundamental texts, the *sūtras*, the character of *Buddhavacana*. As usual in Mahāyānist *śāstras*, the work is a call from lower forms of faith to a higher one, from other *yānas* to the sublime Mahāyāna. The essential spirit of Mahāyānism bespeaks itself in the *Pariṇāmanā* (Transference of Merit) with which the work concludes:[2]

'I have now finished elucidating the deepest and greatest significance (of the Dharma). May its merit be distributed among all creatures, and make them understand the Doctrine of Suchness (*Bhūta-tathatā*, i.e. the oneness of the totality of things).'

It is usual with Mahāyānist writers to articulate such a formula at the end of their work.[3] *Pariṇāmanā* rises to a crescendo in the tenth canto of Śāntideva's *Bodhicaryāvatāra*.[4]

Regarding the two brothers ASAṄGA and VASUBANDHU, we

[1] Suzuki's *Awakening of Faith*, etc., pp. 36–38.
[2] See Suzuki's *The Awakening of Faith, etc.*, p. 149.
[3] cf. *Bodhicaryāvatarā*, III, 6: Evaṁ sarvamidaṁ kṛtvā yanmayāsāditaṁ śubhaṁ; Tena syāt sarvasattvānāṁ sarvaduḥkha-praśāntikṛt.
[4] The term *Pariṇāmanā* is a technical term in Mahāyāna Buddhism meaning, as Suzuki explains it, 'transference, especially of one's merit, to another or towards the realization of supreme wisdom' (*Studies in Laṅkāvatāra Sūtra*, p. 418). 'It may be said', adds Suzuki, 'that the object of gaining an insight into the inner truth of things (. . . which is *Bodhi*) is really to qualify oneself for social work' (*Ibid*, p. 214). See also under Śāntideva *infra*.

have already referred to the legends which seem to point to two different scholars bearing the same name Vasubandhu.

The author of the *Abhidharma-Kośa*, in spite of his intellectual leanings to Mahāyānism, was not a Mahāyānist, but a 'Vaibhāṣika' of Kashmirian school and cannot therefore be counted among the Mahāyānist *ācāryas*. The *śāstras* in the Chinese and Tibetan collections that pass under his name will then have to be assigned to the other Vasubandhu of the fifth century, tutor of prince Bālāditya, a monk of great learning, who had the Gupta king Skandagupta as his patron and lived at Ayodhyā, the imperial capital of the time. It was perhaps this Vasubandhu who was actually the author of the treatises in the Chinese collection, *Vāda-hṛdaya*, *Vāda-vidhi* and *Vāda-vidhāna* to which we referred in speaking of the development of Logic.

Asaṅga himself belonged to the Yogācāra school and is the putative author of the three great works of Mahāyāna philosophy, besides others of lesser note—*Mahāyāna-saṁparigrāha*, *Mahāyāna-sūtrālaṅkāra* and, according to Tibetan tradition, *Yogācāra-bhūmi-śāstra*. In the different Chinese and Tibetan versions, however, the titles of these works do not tally.

His greatest work undoubtedly was the third title, but Chinese tradition attributes it to Maitreyanātha. Hsüan tsang translated it into Chinese (Nanjio, No. 1,170) under the title *Saptadaśa-bhūmi-śāstra*. Its original has been recovered from Tibet. It is a monumental work in five divisions of which a brief summary appears in the work of the Tibetan historiographer Bu-ston.[1]

The subject-matter of the *Yogācāra-bhūmi-śāstra* is an exposition, in categories, of the seventeen fundamental intellectual and spiritual attainments which together constitute the basis of the Yogācāra discipline (*Ityete saptadaśa-bhūmayaḥ samāsato yogācāra-bhūmi' rityucyate*—tr: 'These seventeen *bhūmis* taken together are called Yogācāra-bhūmi)'.[2] *Bhūmi* is a technical term in Mahāyānist philosophy, meaning a stage in the upward grading of a Bodhisattva's spiritual progress which culminates in Buddhahood.[3] This work has been published in parts only;[4] it is couched in highly technical language. The *Mahāyāna-sūtrālaṅkāra* of Asaṅga has been edited and translated into French by Syvain Lévi.

A legend (both Chinese and Tibetan) about Vasubandhu, pointing

[1] See Obermiller, Part I, p. 55.

[2] See Vidhu Shekhara Sastri's *The Yogācāra-bhūmi of Ācārya Asaṅga* (Calcutta University, 1957), p. 3.

[3] See for the meaning of *Bhūmi*, Suzuki's *Studies in the Laṅkāvatāra Sūtra*, pp. 429–30.

[4] By J. Rahder (only two sections); by Unrai Wogihara, Tokyo, 1930 (only the fifteenth chapter), and by Vidhusekhara Bhattacarya, Calcutta University, 1957 (only the first division on *Bahu-bhūmika-vastu*).

probably to the later Vasubandhu, tutor of Bālāditya, is that he was for some time the head of Nālandā Mahāvihāra and had a number of disciples and pupils—Guṇamati, Sthiramati, Dinnāga, Dharmapāla and others, each of whom won fame in the field of Mahāyānist philosophy as a scholar and writer of eminence.

Of them, perhaps the most brilliant was DINNĀGA. We may place him at the end of the fifth or the beginning of the sixth century. Reference has already been made to him as the founder of Buddhist Logic (*Nyāya*). His main treatise on the subject, preserved in Tibetan in its original, is *Pramāṇa-samuccaya*.[1] Two other works on *Nyāya* ascribed to him are *Nyāyamukha* (extant in Chinese and Tibetan versions) and *Nyāyapraveśa* (extant in Sanskrit), but the authorship of the last work is assigned by some scholars to a disciple of Dinnāga, named Saṅkarasvāmī. Some of the *Nyāya* works of Dinnāga were studied, as we are told by I-tsing,[2] as text-books by students of Logic in India in I-tsing's time, though it seems from his statement that the works of Jina were more popular. Perhaps Dinnāga's only Buddhist rival in the science of Logic was Dharmakīrtti—he must have belonged to the seventh century, as he is mentioned by I-tsing as one of 'late years'—who, dissatisfied with Dinnāga's *Pramāṇa-samuccaya*, wrote from a fresh angle a number of treatises on Logic, of which *Nyāyabindu* is the only one surviving in the original Sanskrit.

The masterpiece of NĀGĀRJUNA is the fundamental text of Mādhyamika philosophy, *Mūla-madhyamaka-kārikā*, a set of verses in dialectical style, on which the standard commentary is a work entitled *Prasanna-padā* by Candrakīrtti.

ĀRYADEVA (or DEVA), one of Hsüan-tsang's 'Four Suns',[3] who was a southerner, is said in the legends to have been a disciple of Nāgārjuna. He is the author of *Catuḥśataka* which exists in Tibetan version[4] and of two classic texts on *Prajñāpāramitā*, of which the originals have disappeared.

KUMĀRALABDHA, a northerner, was another of the 'Four Suns'. But, though leaning very near to the Mahāyāna, he was not a professed Mahāyānist, but the founder of the Hīnayānist *Sautrāntika* school. The school was the rival of the *Vaibhāṣika*, differing from it in several matters of doctrine. Vasubandhu in the *Abhidharma-Kośa* makes a few references to Sautrāntika doctrines, showing occasionally

[1] A brief sketch of this work will be found in S. C. Vidyabhushan's *Mediaeval School of Indian Logic* (Calcutta University, 1909). The first chapter of this work was retranslated from Tibetan into Sanskrit in 1930 by K. R. R. Aiyangar of Mysore.

[2] See Takakusu's *A Record of the Buddhist Religion, etc.*, p. 186.

[3] See Part IV, Sec. 4, p. 268.

[4] It has been reconstructed and edited by V. S. Bhattacharya in *The Catuḥśataka of Āryadeva* in the Visvabharati Series, April, 1931.

his own preference for some of them.[1] The great exponent and champion of the school was ŚRĪLABDHA, an eminent monk-scholar of Ayodhyā. The ruins of the monastery at Ayodhyā where Śrīlabdha wrote his exposition (*vibhāṣā*) of Sautrāntika doctrines were seen by Hsüan-tsang on his visit to the city in AD 643.[2]

BUDDHAPĀLITA and BHĀVAVIVEKA (or BHĀVYA) were two most powerful and systematic exponents of the Mādhyamika school founded by Nāgārjuna. The former wrote a commentary on Nāgārjuna's *Mūla-madhyamaka-kārikā* and the latter an expository treatise. Besides a number of works turning on Mādhyamika philosophy extant in the Chinese *Tripiṭaka*,[3] Bhāvaviveka is the author of *Karatalaratna* we have previously cited. The works of Mādhyamika philosophy fathered on him are *Mādhyamika-hṛdaya-kārikā*, *Mādhyamika-ratna-pradīpa*, *Karatalaratna*, etc., all existing only in Chinese versions.

Bhāvaviveka, according to Hsüan-tsang, was a contemporary of Dharmapāla.[4] If so, he must have flourished at the end of the sixth and the early part of the seventh century.[5] 'This master of *Śāstra*', says Hsüan-tsang of Bhāvaviveka, 'was widely renowned for his elegant scholarship and for the depth of his vast attainments. Externally he was a disciple of Kapila (i.e. was a Sāṅkhya philosopher), but inwardly he was fully possessed of the learning of Nāgārjuna (i.e. Mādhyamika philosophy).'[6]

Somewhat apart from this line of creative philosophers and profound schoolmen, regarded as 'masters of Śāstras', though their extant original works in contrast to the number of Chinese and Tibetan translations make only a handful, stands ŚĀNTIDEVA. He flourished much later and was an inheritor rather than originator of Mahāyāna philosophy.

About his time, Bendall says: 'In any case AD 800 will be admitted as the latest possible *terminus ad quem*. The *terminus ad quo* is somewhat difficult to determine'.[7] Neither Hsüan-tsang nor I-tsing knew of him, and it will perhaps not be far amiss to place him somewhere in the eighth century. What we know of him is almost wholly from Tibetan sources and of somewhat doubtful biographical value.

Tāranātha states that he was the son of a king of Saurāshtra 'in

1 Vasubandhu's references to the Sautrāntika doctrines are specified by Poussin in the Introduction to his French translation of *Abhidharma-kośa*.

2 Beal's *Buddhist Records*, i, p. 226.

3 They are cited at p. xiii of Ayaswami Sastri's Sanskrit version of *Karatalaratna* published by the Visvabharati in 1949.

4 See Beal's *Buddhist Records*, ii, p. 223.

5 The time-calculation is on the basis of I-tsing's statement that the grammarian Bhartṛhari, who died in AD 651–652, was a contemporary of Dharmapāla.

6 Beal's *Buddhist Records*, ii, p. 223.

7 *Śikṣāsamuccaya*, ed. by Bendall (The Hague: Indo-Iranian Reprint, No. 1, Moutan and Co., 1957), Intro., p. 5.

the days when Śrī-Harṣa's son Śīla reigned'. But this Śīla is wholly unknown to ancient Indian history. It appears from Chinese records that Śrī-Harṣa's immediate successor was a usurper, probably a minister of his court.[1] Bu-ston speaks of Śāntideva's ordination at Nālandā, the miracles performed by him there and his famous victories in disputations.[2] But such legends are the common stock-in-trade of Tibetan historiographers.

Three works are ascribed to him in the Tibetan accounts: (i) *Sūtra-samuccaya*, (ii) *Śikṣā-samuccaya* and (iii) *Bodhicaryāvatāra*. The last one, according to Tāranātha, was written after the other two. Of these three works, the first has entirely disappeared, but the other two are extant in their Sanskrit originals. It seems that the three works together formed a sort of triology to make up a brief compendium of the Mahāyāna system.

Śāntideva belonged to the Yogācāra school which combines in the career of a Bodhisattva both *Yoga* (Meditation) and *Ācāra* (Practice of Self-culture). *Ācāra* is designated by Śāntideva as the '*vinaya*' of a Bodhisattva. But it consists not in external observances, but in the cultivation of the spirit of worship and prayer, of self-purification and self-abnegation, and, above all, of universal compassion. In the two surviving works of Śāntideva, the theme of *Ācāra*, understood in this sense, predominates.

Śāntideva may be characterized more aptly as a poet, rather than as a philosopher of Mahāyānism.

Śikṣā-samuccaya opens with a set of twenty-seven verses (*Kārikās*), followed by nineteen chapters (*paricchedas*) in which the themes of these verses are amplified with illustrative citations from a large number of *sūtras*. Most of these *sūtras* are now untraceable. The work is rounded off with verses in salutation to god Mañjuśrī, with a finis recapitulating its subject-matter: 'Concluded is the *Śikṣā-samuccaya*, a work on the Vinaya of a Bodhisattva, compiled from many *sūtrāntas*' (*Samāptaś-cayaṁ bodhisattvavinayo'nekasūtrāntoddhṛtaḥ*).

Bodhicaryāvatāra is one sustained poem in ten books (*paricchedas*) which Keith characterizes as 'a strange blend of passionate devotion to the aim of aiding men to achieve freedom from the miseries of life coupled with the utter negativism of Mahāyāna philosophy'.[3] In the whole range of Buddhist devotional poetry, it is a gem of the purest lustre.

Buddhist literature is rich in the poetry of devotion. It goes back

[1] For a brief discussion of these Chinese records which relate to the state of affairs in Harṣa's realm after his death, see Dr Sudhakara Chattopadhyaya's *Early History of Northern India, 300 BC–AD 650* (Calcutta, 1958), pp. 274–275.

[2] See Obermiller, Part II, pp. 161 ff. (Śāntideva among life-sketches of Mahāyāna masters).

[3] Keith's *History of Sanskrit Literature* (Oxford University Press, 1953), p. 72.

to the early days of Buddhism. It is the response to the inner repercussions of the faith on the emotional side of the lives of monks and nuns. The earliest examples occur in the poetical anthologies—*Apadāna* and *Thera-therī-gāthā*—in the *Khuddaka Nikāya* of the Pali Theravāda canon. Of such poetry, art is no object; its spontaneity is clear of all artistic sophistications.

The recurrent notes in the early poetry of devotion are of *Bhakti* articulated in *vandanā* (laud), *stuti* (prayer and propitiation) and *pūjā* (worship). But a note which rose to a higher pitch of lyricism was introduced into it by the grand altruistic idealism of the Mahāyāna. The Mahāyānist doctrine of *Pariṇāmanā*—the conversion by a Bodhisattva of his own personal good into the good of all creatures—inspired in Buddhist devotional poetry a new, an impassioned note.

The strain is taken up in the very first book of Śāntideva's *Śikṣāsamuccaya* on *Dāna-pāramitā* (Perfection in Giving), e.g. 'For the release (from misery) of all creatures, turn your heart to Bodhi' (*Sarvasattva-vimokṣāya cittaṁ bodhāya nāmayet*),[1] and it swells into a full-throated crescendo, to a sublime canticle, in the tenth chapter (*pariccheda*) of the *Bodhicaryāvatāra* which has the title '*Bodhi-pariṇāmana*:[2]

'As Mañjuśrī ranges in order to secure the welfare of all creatures, in all the ten directions, even up to Heaven, so (wide) be my range; so long as the sky lasts and the earth remains, let me live to bring to an end the miseries of the world. Whatever misery there is in the world, let all of that settle on me: let the world be happy through all the Bodhisattvas' welfare-work; let the *Śāsana* (Buddhist Religion), which is the medicine for the world's ills and the cause of all happiness and prosperity, live for ever with honour and advancement.'

[1] See *Śikṣāsamuccaya* (Bendall's Ed.), I, 1.17, p. 5.
[2] See vv. 54–57 in the 10th *Pariccheda*. The translation is mine.

17. *The great temple on the sea shore at Mahābalipura.* (Photo: Archaeological survey of India, Southern circle)

The 'Raths' of Mahābalipura. (Photo: Archaeological survey of India, Southern circle)

18. *Sculptured panegyric composed by Kunda on Queen Kumāradevī.* (Photo: Department of Archaeology, Government of India)

View of a portion of the decorated brickwork plinth of Kumāradevī's monastery. (Photo: Department of Archaeology, Government of India)

6

Contemporaries and Near-Contemporaries of Hsüan-tsang and I-tsing

IN the seventh century, when Hsüan-tsang and I-tsing visited India, the age of the '*Ācārya śāstra*-masters', Fathers of the Mahāyāna, as we have said already, had long passed away. The legends about them recorded by the pilgrims were stories gleaned from fading tradition.

But in the train of the *ācāryas* came later many monk-scholars of different orders and of various accomplishments. They stand, however, in a separate rank; they were philosophers, logicians, grammarians, commentators and schoolmen, who were more systematizers of learning than original or creative thinkers. But about this generation of scholars, the legends are neither so bedimmed by time nor so vague in content as those of their precursors, the earlier *ācāryas*. Several of them were not too far back in time from the Chinese pilgrims of the seventh century: some were their senior contemporaries.

The names of monk-scholars that occur in the record of I-tsing have been carefully listed by Takakusu in the Introduction to his English translation of the work.[1] Takakusu has placed under two chronological divisions the successors of the *ācāryas* who find mention in I-tsing's record as being: (i) those of 'late years', and (ii) those referred to as contemporaries or personal acquaintances, of whom some are mentioned by Hsüan-tsang also.

AD 550–670

Among the monk-scholars of this period, JINA was a famous logician. He must have belonged to the early part of this period—probably his rise to fame was at its beginning. The elders among the scholars are designated 'Bodhisattvas' by the Chinese pilgrims and Jina has that designation.

He was probably a man of Andhra, and a legend about him was heard by Hsüan-tsang at a monastery near Ajanta with which Jina's name was associated and is recorded by him. In this legend it is said that he received direction from the heavenly Maitreya to specialize in Yogācāra philosophy. 'Then having given himself to profound study, he developed the teaching of the *Hetuvāda Śāstra*

[1] Takakusu's *A Record of Buddhist Religion*, Intro., p. lviii.

(Logic).' It was in the Yogācāra system, as we have noted, that Logic developed. But fearing that students of logic would be deterred by the subtle reasoning and precise style insisted on in this branch of learning, he composed the *Hetuvidyā Śāstra*, 'exemplifying the great principles and explaining the subtle language in order to guide the learners'.[1] His pre-eminence in Logic is undoubted, though his aim was to popularize the subject: I-tsing cites several works of Jina which were used as text-books by students of logic in India in his time.[2]

Another great logician who flourished in this period was DHARMAKĪRTTI. A Tibetan account of him makes him contemporary with the Tibetan king Sron-tsang-gan-po (AD 629–98). His high standing in the field of scholarship is testified to by the mention of him in the well-known Sanskrit work *Sarva-darśana-saṁgraha* ('Conspectus of All Systems of Philosophy') by Mādhavācārya.[3]

BHARTTṚHARI was the author of a learned commentary on Pāṇini's grammar, which used to be studied as a *locus classicus* by all students of the system of Sanskrit grammar and was, according to I-tsing, 'famous throughout the five parts of India'.[4] I-tsing cites the legend about him that he found the austerities of a monk's life too oppressive and, alternating as many as seven times between monkhood and the easier lay life, he at last decided to stay in a monastery, but as a lay man exempt from its strict discipline. Happily the year of his death is known. Takakusu fixes it at AD 651–52 from I-tsing's statement: 'It is forty years since his death.'

DHARMAPĀLA is said to have been a contemporary of Bharttṛhari; he was a great philosopher and academician to whom several Mahāyānist works are ascribed. He belonged no doubt to an older generation, for Hsüan-tsang calls him a Bodhisattva.

According to Hsüan-tsang, Dharmapāla's native place was Kāñcīpura. We have some details about his early life and conversion, though it is difficult to say how far they are really biographical, for Hsüan-tsang reproduces them from a legend heard by him. It is reported in the legend that Dharmapāla happened in his boyhood to witness a grand marriage feast given by the king, but the pomp and circumstance of it prompted in him only the thought of the world's 'vanity of vanities'. The thought preyed upon his mind; it drove him to seek seclusion from the world in a mountain-convent where he was afterwards ordained as a monk. While yet a young man, he won great renown by defeating a *tīrthika* (non-Buddhist) opponent

[1] Beal's *Buddhist Records*, ii, p. 220.
[2] Takakusu's *A Record of the Buddhist Religion, etc.*, p. 186.
[3] See Cowell's Translation (in Trübner's Oriental Series), p. 24.
[4] Takakusu's *A Record of the Buddhist Religion*, p. 179.

in a disputation organized at Kośāmbi by the king.[1] We have it from Hsüan-tsang, which makes the statement somewhat credible, that he acted for some time as head of the Nālandā University, where, as the tradition is, he wrote the larger *Śūraṅgama Sūtra*,[2] to which we have already referred.[3]

Dharmapāla's most distinguished pupil at Nālandā was ŚĪLABHADRA, who stepped into the shoes of Dharmapāla, succeeding him as head of the University. Hsüan-tsang himself studied over five years at Nālandā under Śīlabhadra and what he says about his master may, therefore, have some claim to authenticity.

Śīlabhadra, according to Hsüan-tsang, belonged to the family of the king of Samtata and was of Brāhmaṇa caste. Having travelled widely in India, improving his store of learning, he came at last to Nālandā where he met Dharmapāla and expressed to him a wish to be his disciple. About that time Dharmapāla had received a challenge to a disputation with a heretic of South India and the king had asked him to accept it. He proceeded to the venue along with his disciples, Śīlabhadra being among them. Śīlabhadra asked his master to allow him to hold the disputation himself and his request was granted. At the time he was only thirty years of age. The heretic was defeated and the king pressed on him a substantial reward for his scholarship which the latter at first refused, but finally accepted on the king's insistence. With the money awarded, he built a monastery near Nālandā.[4]

Hsüan-tsang who studied Yogācāra philosophy under Śīlabhadra held him in the highest esteem. On his return to China, Hsüan-tsang founded one of the traditional ten schools of Chinese Buddhism called the *Fa-hsiang* (Dharmalakṣaṇa) school. He based it on the teachings of Śīlabhadra who is recognized by the school as its real founder.[5]

Two other renowned scholars of this period were GUṆAMATI and STHIRAMATI, both disciples of Vasubandhu. They were senior contemporaries of Hsüan-tsang. They are said to have acquired their learning at Nālandā. Their works are found in the Chinese collection. Guṇamati is said by Hsüan-tsang to have been a man of South India, 'who in his youth had displayed great talents and acquired early in life a brilliant reputation'.[6] He is also described as having won renown by victories in several religious disputations. Both Guṇamati and Sthiramati settled finally at Valabhī. In the Bappāpāda

[1] See Beal's *Buddhist Records*, ii, pp. 229–230 and pp. 237–239.

[2] *Ibid*, ii, p. 110, footnote 55. For *Śūraṅgama Sūtra*, see Part IV, Sec. 3 (b), pp. 264–265.

[3] Part IV, Sec. 3 (b). (See also p. 337.)

[4] Beal's *Buddhist Records*, ii, pp. 110–112.

[5] See *History of Philosophy, Eastern and Western* (London: George Allen & Unwin, 1952), Vol. 1, p. 593.

[6] Beal's *Buddhist Records*, ii, p. 105.

Monastery at Valabhī, these two monk-scholars carried on over the remainder of their days their philosophical studies and literary activities.[1]

Another of Vasubandhu's disciples was GUṆAPRABHA. He seems from his works preserved in Chinese to have specialized in Vinaya. Of him, the Tibetan historiographer Bu-ston says that, though a pupil of Vasubandhu, he excelled his master in knowledge of Vinaya, wrote several works on it, and was the pre-eminent authority on the Vinaya of the Mūla-sarvāstivāda school.[2] Hsüan-tsang says that he composed 'hundreds of *Śāstras*' and had a wide reputation; also that he was originally a Mahāyānist, but became later a convert to the Hīnayāna and wrote several treatises attacking his former Mahāyānist faith.

About JINAPRABHA, another distinguished monk-scholar whose name appears in I-tsing's record, little is known except that he was teacher of the Chinese pilgrim Hiuen Chao who was in Nālandā round AD 649.[3]

AD 670–700

We have glimpses in the record of I-tsing of a few other distinguished monk-scholars who were all living during the last three decades of the seventh century.

'The following', says I-tsing, 'are the (most distinguished) teachers who now live in the West (i.e. India and Indonesia).'[4] They are: Jñānacandra, who is mentioned by Hsüan-tsang also as one of the famous scholars of Nālandā[5] and described by I-tsing as a 'Master of the Law' of the Tilodha monastery (in Magadha); Ratnasiṁha of the Nālandā Monastery; Divākaramitra of eastern India; and Tathāgatagarbha of the 'southernmost district'. At Śrībhoja (in Sumatra) resided Sākyakīrtti in I-tsing's time. He had travelled through all the 'five countries' of India and was settled there.

How the traditional learning was kept up by these famous teachers, zealously emulating the *ācāryas* of old, is thus described by I-tsing:[6]

'All these men are equally renowned for their brilliant character, equal to the ancients and anxious to follow in the steps of the sages. When they have understood the arguments of *Hetuvidyā* (Logic), they aspire to be like Jina; while testing the doctrine of Yogācāra,

[1] About Bappāpāda Monastery, see Part III, Sec. 7, pp. 225–226.
[2] See Obermiller, Part II, pp. 160 ff. (under Guṇaprabha).
[3] He is referred to in Chavannes' *Memoirs*, p. 17.
[4] Takakusu's *A Record of the Buddhist Religion*, p. 184.
[5] Beal's *Buddhist Records, etc.*, ii, p. 171.
[6] Takakusu's *A Record of the Buddhist Religion*, p. 184.

they zealously search into the theory of Asaṅga. When they discourse on "non-existence", they cleverly imitate Nāgārjuna; whilst, when treating of "existence", they thoroughly fathom the teaching of Saṅghabhadra.'

I-tsing concludes his account of contemporary teachers, whose instruction he was privileged, as he says, to receive in India, on a note of sincere and deep-felt gratitude:

'I, I-tsing, used to converse with these teachers so intimately that I was able to receive invaluable instruction personally from them (literally, "I came closely to their seats and desks and received and enjoyed their admirable words"). I have always been glad that I had the opportunity of acquiring knowledge from them personally which I should otherwise never have possessed, and that I could refresh my memory of past study by comparing old notes with new ones.'

And this devoted Chinese scholar who had braved all the perils of a journey to India to collect original texts of Vinaya was veritably like the grammarian described by Browning—one 'who decided not to live but know':[1]

'It is my only desire', declares I-tsing, 'to receive the light handed down from time to time, and my satisfaction is in the fact that, having learned the Law in the morning, my wish is to dispel my hundred doubts rising as dust; and, if in the morning my wish be fulfilled, I shall not regret dying at eventide.'

I-tsing speaks of individual teachers. But from the fifth century on, there had been growing up organized seats of learning in India—monastic *studia* and some institutions of the stature of universities with schools of study and teaching staffs and well-stocked libraries treasuring the accumulated manuscript records of this learning. We shall see later what became of these treasure-houses of learning when towards the end of the twelfth century massacring Muslim hordes swooped down on them with Khalif Omar's famous slogan at the seige of Alexandria ringing in their hearts—'Burn all the libraries, for their value is in one book'.

[1] *Ibid*, p. 185.

7

Indian Monk-scholars in China

THE roll of Indian monk-scholars cannot be closed without a glance at those who migrated to and settled in China and whose names are interwoven with the history of Buddhism in that country. The largest number of them appears in a definite chapter of the history of Sino-Indian relationship. It covers roughly a period of five centuries from the third to the eighth AD, but overflows into later times.

Sino-Indian relations during these centuries were founded upon Buddhism. It was a common ground of spiritual and intellectual interest between India and China. The relations that arose from this ground were purely cultural in character, carried on by Buddhist monks in the cause of Buddhism.

The cultural intercourse of these five centuries actually stemmed from China and put forth two spreading branches. On one hand, a stream of Chinese monks came out to India during these centuries, and on the other a large number of Indian monks emigrated to and settled in China. The object of the former was a twofold one—to earn spiritual merit by pilgrimage and to study Buddhism in its homeland and collect authentic Buddhist texts. Very few of them settled in India. The Indian monks on the other hand who went out to China were not transients. Moved solely by the desire to promote Buddhism in that country, they made China the land of their adoption and lived and worked there continuously over long years. Very few are known to have come back from China to India.

As this intercourse was initiated and developed by the Chinese, the source-materials of its history are in the Chinese language. The materials have not been fully explored yet, though modern scholars of China have been engaged in the task for several years now.

The carrying on of this Sino-Indian cultural intercourse was a vast and difficult enterprise. It was attended with hardships and perils that seem legendary in modern times when science has made nothing of distance and foreign travel a luxury.

The routes along which passage and communication between China and India lay were both overland and by sea. They were long and perilous, hardly possible to negotiate in less than a couple of years; often considerably more time was needed. The overland route was more ancient; and the sea-route became slightly less difficult with China's progress during these centuries in shipbuilding and seamanship.

The earlier Chinese travellers used to start on the adventurous journey to India from China's western border. In the first stage, the trekking was to one of the caravan-towns like Tun-huang scattered outside the Great Wall on the edge of the Gobi Desert. Here the necessary preparation were made for the desert-crossing on the back of camel, pony or mule and the plunge into the perilous 'Moving Sands' sprawling hundreds of miles over mid-Asia.

Across the desert were two miles-and-miles long tracks; they stretched so far that their mileage defied count: first, the 'silk-way', used by silk-merchants since remote antiquity, trailing westwards to Parthia and still farther west; secondly a track, ill-defined and winding, in the south-west direction through a number of small mid-Asian States in uneven stages of civilization, where Buddhism of some sort prevailed. This track continued through the difficult crests and up-and-down gorges of the sand-blast-eroded Karakorum and Kohibaba into north Afghanistan or into Ladhak on the Tibetan border. South of Kapiśa, then a small State to the north of the modern city of Kabul, India commenced with the kingdom of Gāndhāra, lying alongside the stretch of the Kabul river between the Kunar and the Indus. Gāndhāra has now merged wholly in southern Afghanistan.

The terrible hardships of the whole journey, described in the records of the Chinese travellers, were relieved only by the welcome and accommodation received by them from the Buddhist populations of the intervening states.

The sea route was available from one of the ancient seaports in the south-eastern provinces of China. The route was through the South China Sea into the Indian Ocean and via the Indonesian islands and Ceylon to some port on India's eastern seaboard. Tāmralipti (in Bengal) was a well-established port of disembarkation for voyagers from the Far East and there were others down south.

Navigation in those times was under mast and sail without modern scientific aids except the mariner's compass, an ancient Chinese invention in common use by navigators of the Tang period sailing off from the South China Sea.

The ships were either cargo-bearing junks or tall floundering vessels of three tiers into which one clambered by a tall ladder. They were made of timber and so apt to spring a leak. The occurrence of typhoons between China and the Indonesian islands was a dreaded danger. The sea-goers were mostly merchants among whom the travelling monks had to find their berths. From the pen of Fa-hsien we have an animated description how the merchantman he sailed in on his voyage from Ceylon to China sprang a leak, was swept out of course by a fierce typhoon and how, when cargo was being thrown overboard for reasons of safety, he kept fervently praying to Avalokiteśvara that he might not be compelled to jettison the invaluable relics and manuscripts collected by him in India.[1] Even I-tsing, coming to India by sea two and a half centuries later from Sumatra, wrote a short poem on the eve of his embarkation to fortify his spirit for the great adventure ahead.[2]

Over such routes were the comings and goings of the hardy, intrepid and resolute monks who built up Sino-Indian cultural intercourse during these centuries. It was usual for Chinese monks to set out for India in parties, but the journey took its toll. On the long, long trek many died from sheer physical exhaustion or disease; some returned half-way; some had to leave their bones in desert-sands or somewhere out in India.

Many of these Chinese monks, as it appears, had put on record their experiences of the journey and their observations on India. Most of these records perished; some are known only by their titles, while brief extracts or stray passages from them appear in obscure nooks and corners of China's vast ancient literature.[3] Only three records, found complete, have come down to us: (i) Fa-hsien's *Fo-kwo-ki* ('Buddhist-Country-Record'—for AD 319–414), (ii) Hsüan-tsang's *Si-yu-ki* ('Western-Country-or-Travel-Record'—for AD 630–43) and I-tsing's *Nan-hai-ki-kuei-nai-fa-chuan* ('Record of Inner Law sent home from the Southern Sea'—for AD 671–95).

I-tsing 'sent home' to Changan through a friend of his, along with his *Nan-hai-ki*, another work written by him in which he had given brief accounts of fifty-one pilgrims including himself who had gone out to India for study and pilgrimage since the commencement of the Tang dynasty. They are mostly Chinese, but with a sprinkling of Koreans and Indonesians.[4] I-tsing met several of them himself in India and all were his contemporaries, senior or junior. The work, not translated yet,[5] is a mine of information and a few extracts are given in the Appendix to this section. Besides the names I-tsing records in this work, there are some others to be found in the consecutive series of *Kao-seng-chuan* (Biographies of Eminent Monks),

[1] See Beal's *Buddhist Records*, p. lxxx.

[2] Quoted in Takakusu's *A Record of the Buddhist Religion*, p. xxvii:

'A good general can obstruct a hostile army,
But the resolution of a man is difficult to move.'

[3] See Dr Lo's *Chinese Sources for Indian History* in *Indian Archives* (published by the National Archives of India, New Delhi), January–December 1949 (Vol. III, Nos. 1–4), pp. 84 ff.

[4] The Chinese title is: *Ta-Tang-shi-ku-fa-kao-sung-chuan* (Monks of the Buddhist faith who went to western countries under the Tang Dynasty). See Takakusu's *A Record of the Buddhist Religion, etc.*, p. xxxvi. See also Appendix to this section.

[5] There is an abstract of this work in French by Chavannes published in Paris in 1894, entitled *Mémoire Composé à l'époque de la grande dynastie T'ang sur les Réligieux Eminents qui allerent chercher la loi dans les pays d'occident, par I-tsing.*

written by several hands in different centuries and included in the Chinese *Tripiṭaka*.[1]

Counting from I-tsing's work and some of these biographical works, the number of pilgrims comes up to sixty-seven. But Professor Liang Chi-chao, rummaging also in other parts of Chinese literature, was able to trace for this period round 180 names. His researches are embodied in any essay in Chinese on 'Chinese students going abroad 1,500 years ago and afterwards'[2] and his findings are thus tabulated by Dr Lo:

'In the latter part of the third century—2; fourth century—5; fifth century—61; sixth century—14; seventh century—56; and eighth century—31.'[3] The conditions of their journey to and sojourn in India could be traced in respect of most of them as follows:[4]

42	Studied in India and returned to China.
16	Known to have gone as far as Western Sinkiang, but not certain whether they could proceed to India.
unknown number ..	Could not reach India, and returned.
2	Returned shortly after starting for India.
31	Died on the way.
31	Died in India.
5	Died on way back to China after completing studies in India.
6	Made a second pilgrimage to India; one died mid-way on return trip.
7	Stayed in India indefinitely.
unknown number ..	Not known whether they stayed on in India or returned to China or where they died.

The findings of Professor Liang assemble a picture of the terrible uncertainties that attended the efforts of the Tang-dynasty Chinese pilgrims, who were sustained and heartened only by the conviction held by the Chinese Buddhists of the age that the practice of Buddhism in Indian monasteries was the standard one and Indian Buddhist texts the authentic ones. Hence they longed to see for themselves how Buddhism was practised in India and what authentic texts were available. Hence also arose the demand for scholarly monks from India chiefly to translate the Indian texts or help in their translation into Chinese. We have abundant record in the Chinese *Tripiṭaka* catalogues to show how the Chinese need was sought to be met by Indian monks.

Some went out of India on private invitation; some were brought

[1] The entire series will be found in the 50th volume of Taisho Ed. See Part IV, sec. 1 (B iii).

[2] See Dr Lo's *Chinese Sources, etc.*, p. 83. [3] *Ibid.* [4] *Ibid.*

to China by official envoys; but many perhaps went on their own to promote Buddhism in a country, so eager to receive its blessings, and of them much less is known than of the Chinese pilgrims. The Chinese mind is of a realistic turn interested in objective observation: the stamp of it is borne by the known records left by the pilgrims. Perhaps the Indian mind is of a different make-up—and not one of the numerous Indian monks who went to China and settled there has left a scrap of record about his journey to and experiences in China. There can be no doubt, however, that, since the beginning of Buddhism in China, especially under the Tang and Sung dynasties, the number of Indian monks settled there was large. Their antecedents are mostly unknown.

In their forefront are three illustrious monks of unquestioned preeminence, held by the Chinese Buddhists in the highest veneration—Kumārajīva (early fifth century), Paramārtha (sixth century) and Bodhidharma (sixth century), of whom the first two were undoubtedly highly accomplished scholars. Behind them in the rank and file were many who enjoyed local or regional fame and are mentioned in Chinese 'Dynastic Records' (*Shu*). Yet a whole host of others unknown to fame were absorbed in the organized industry of translating Sanskrit texts, working singly or jointly with Chinese scholars.

In the *Tripiṭaka* catalogues, their names are recorded. Nanjio has listed the *Tripiṭaka* translators, both Chinese and foreign, whose names occur in the Ming-dynasty catalogue done into English by him. These translators worked under successive as well as contemporaneous imperial dynasties from the first century on. Among Nanjio's names are several said simply to have come from the 'western region' and there is no doubt that among them were monks from India. Leaving out those of unknown *patrie*, there are 173 names in all and fifty-one of them are of Indians.[1]

It was two Indian monks who had initiated this great industry of Translation in the White Horse Monastery at Loyang; afterwards it was carried on over several centuries by Chinese and Indian collaborators. To these translators, of whom the Indian monks settled in China formed a large section, we owe the great wealth of Buddhist literature that disappeared from India, but is available in translated versions in Chinese.

The significance of the work of the translators is highlighted against the chequered historical background of Buddhism in the 'celestial empire' where it gained its first foothold in the first century AD.

In that century China held her indigenuous faiths, Confucianism and Taoism, and Buddhism was regarded as a foreign faith—a sort

[1] See Nanjio's Catalogue, Appendix II, pp. 381–458. Compare also P. C. Bagchi's *Le canon Bouddhique en Chine* (Paris, 1938).

of exotic or fancy article imported through the whim of the Han emperor, Ming-ti. We need not recapitulate the Chinese legends about its miraculous introduction into the country, but the Han emperor vouchsafed for it a local habitation in AD 67 when he built a monastery (of which the remains may still be seen) in his capital Loyang (in modern Honan, four hundred and odd miles to Peking's southwest). It was named the 'White Horse Monastery', and during the first few centuries of Buddhism in China it played a most important part in transforming the 'court religion' into a popular one.

Two Indian monks joined this monastery shortly after its foundation. The Chinese name of the first equates to Kāśyapa-mātaṅga; of the second to Dharmāraṇya.[1] They both died shortly after at Loyang. But their achievement was to give the start to what developed later into a sort of main industry in Chinese Buddhist establishments, viz. the supply on an extensive scale to the people of written texts on Buddhism. They were mostly translated and summarized versions of Indian texts. These texts kept coming through different channels into China.

From these two pioneer Indian monks, 'there remain a single pamphlet and four titles of lost works'.[2] They were not issued to the public, but were meant for the emperor's own notice and were 'shut up in the fourteenth stone-chest of the imperial library'.[3] But the pamphlet entitled the 'Sūtra of the 42 Articles' remains, piously preserved by Chinese Buddhists, as 'the first ray of the Law' in their country.[4]

More than seventy years elapsed after the death of the two Indian pioneers before a famous Parthian monk appeared at Loyang and settled in the White Horse Monastery in AD 148. He gave a fresh spurt to the literary activity they had initiated. 'The Buddhist catalogues attribute to him 176 works, of which fifty-five still exist.'[5]

The emphasis placed by the missionaries on the supply of texts was motivated by the proverbial Chinese reverence for the written word, a tradition of Chinese civilization of almost immemorial antiquity.

Between the first century and the fourth the White Horse Monastery grew into a regular beehive of this industry. At least till AD 317,

[1] This is the name given by Wieger. Others give it as Dharmaratna.

[2] See Dr Leo Wieger's *A History of Religious Beliefs and Philosophical Opinions in China,* translated from French into English by E. E. Werner (pub. by Hsien-hsien Press, Peking, 1927), p. 343.

[3] *Ibid,* p. 343.

[4] This *Sūtra,* which is more Hīnayānist than Mahāyānist in its purport, will be found in translation in Beal's *Catena of Buddhist Scriptures* (Kegan Paul, London, 1871) and summarized in Wieger's book, pp. 345–350. A modern translation is Chu Chan's *The Sūtra of the 42 Sections* (pub. by the Buddhist Society, London, 1947).

[5] See Wieger, p. 353.

it maintained that character, and among those who took part in it were monks, besides the Chinese, from India, Parthia and other parts of Central Asia. Loyang was abandoned as capital in AD 317, but the White Horse Monastery went on functioning. From 317 to 419, Chien-king (modern Nanking) flourished, a new capital in 'China of the Three Kingdoms'.

'In spite of continual wars, the Buddhist missionaries—monks and lay men—continued to arrive in China, bringing their books, translating them, and gaining native adepts. Through force of circumstances, they divided themselves into two groups, one in each capital.'[1]

They were the Loyang group and the Nanking group. Among both groups were Indian monk-scholars, e.g. Dharmakāla in the former and Vighna, a *Jaṭilaka* (fire-worshipper) convert to Buddhism, in the latter. Vighna made a popular Chinese adaptation of a manual of Buddhism, entitled *Dharmapada*, attributed to the Mahāyānist *ācārya* Dharmatrāta.[2]

By AD 280, the 'Three Kingdoms', into which China had split up, were remelted into a single empire governed by the Chin dynasty, and under this dynasty, Buddhism was no longer a 'court religion'; it had already begun vigorously to spread among the people.

All through these early centuries, the spread of Buddhism in China was mainly through the agency of Chinese Buddhist texts. From the fourth to the fifth, Buddhism, outliving Confucian and Taoist opposition, inundated China. China became practically a Buddhist country. 'The empire, being then reduced to almost nothing, the Literati could not oppose. . . . Then, the Indian monks were extremely pleasing to the barbarian kinglets who had divided amongst themselves the whole north of China, because, besides Buddhism, they had brought to them something of Indian civilization. Finally, at the time there were, among the Buddhist monks, very clever fellows (*sic*). Some knew how to choose, among the incongruous practices grouped under the rubric *Buddhism*, those which suited the taste of the Chinese people. Others used the personal favour they enjoyed in the development of the indigenous monachism, and, in consequence, in the propaganda among the people. Finally the Chinese monks . . . ill-content with the incomplete instruction and training they received in China, went at their own risk as far as India, passed there some years in the great Buddhist convents, learnt Sanskrit, chose the texts, and then returned, bringing to the conventss of China both the theoretical doctrine and the practical experiences of asceticism. There followed a great impetus.'[3]

[1] Wieger, p. 380.
[2] *Ibid*, p. 380. A Summary of this work is given in pp. 381 ff.
[3] *Ibid*, p. 407.

It was this impetus that started the exodus to India of monk-scholars from China.

Meanwhile, the White Horse Monastery was functioning. It was the resort of monk-scholars, translators and writers from different parts of Asia including among them Indian monks. In AD 266, Dharmarakṣa, a Getian monk, arrived from Tun-huang and settled in the monastery and died there round 317 at the age of eighty-seven. He made 175 translations of which ninety remain. 'Besides the Getian, an Indian of Khọtan, the citadel of Buddhism in the Tarim,[1] a Parthian, two Chinese monks and two Chinese lay men, distinguished themselves by the number and importance of their translations.'[2] A distinguished figure in the White Horse Monastery in the last years of Loyang was one whose name has been equated by Wieger to Buddhajaṅgha and he is said in the Chin official annals to have been born in India and arrived at Loyang in 310, declaring himself to be a centenarian. He seems to have been a Tāntrika and miracle-worker and he died at Loyang.[3]

After the Chin dynasty, pushed further south by the Huns, had made its capital at Changan, here came from Kuchā a famous monk-scholar, a half-blooded Indian, whose fame had already spread to China. He was Kumārajīva, son of a Kashmirian *pandit* settled in Kuchā. His is one of the greatest names in Chinese Buddhism: we shall deal with his career later. Fifty works of large size translated by him are in the Chinese *Tripiṭaka* and he became in his time the most influential figure in the Buddhist world of China.[4]

Following is a summary account of the state of Buddhism in China in the fourth and fifth centuries:[5]

'In the fourth and fifth centuries, there was an immense expansion of Buddhism in northern China. This area being in contact with the Central Asian trade-routes, by which communications with India were made, it was naturally the region to which the Indian missionaries of Buddhism paid the greatest attention. The petty kingdoms of northern China under their short-lived Tungus and Hun dynasties were distinguished by the richness and productivity of their Buddhist Schools, by which alone they are remembered. At Changan in AD 401–12, then the capital of a small State of Later Chin, the celebrated

[1] The Tarim river, China's biggest inland river, skirts the northern fringe of the vast mid-Asian desert-land before entering the Lop Nor and Taitehma Lake in the east. The basin of the Tarim was then famous as a seat of Buddhist culture.

[2] *Ibid*, p. 407.

[3] *Ibid*, p. 413. Wieger's equation of the name is somewhat doubtful. Could it be Bodhiśānta?

[4] See Nanjio's *Catalogue*, Appendix II, 59.

[5] Fitzgerald's *China—A Short Cultural History* (London: The Cresset Press, 1942), pp. 275–276.

Kumārajīva . . . worked and taught, spreading the doctrines of the new schools of Buddhism, hitherto unknown in China. (*There were also several persecutions of Buddhism in this part of China.*) These ineffective and intermittent persecutions failed to arrest the progress of the new religion. In AD 405 the historians confess that nine out of every ten families in the northern empire had embraced the Buddhist faith.[1] . . . A hundred years later, in AD 500, it is admitted that the whole of China, north and south alike, was Buddhist.'

Fitzgerald qualifies the last statement by adding: 'That is to say, Buddhist rites and ceremonies were everywhere practised; temples and monasteries had arisen in every district; priests and nuns were numerous and highly respected'. This is corroborated by an official census made between 512 and 545 which states that 'in the kingdom of Wei' (i.e. North China), there existed 13,000 Buddhist temples and convents and there lived in the capital 3,000 foreign monks, without counting the far more numerous indigenous monks scattered throughout the country.[2] We may presume that among these three thousand was a goodly number of Indians. In this century both northern China under the Wei dynasty and southern China under the Liang had staunch imperial patrons of Buddhism in the persons of Queen Hu (Regent for the boy emperor) in the north and Emperor Wu of the Liang dynasty in the south.

But a most intriguing feature of the situation was that the Buddhism that was spreading in the country and taking shape in 'schools' was not Indian, but 'Chinese Buddhism', hybridized by makers of texts hailing from different races, regions and countries.

The proof of it lies in the *Tripiṭaka* texts themselves. They are supposed to be renderings of Sanskrit texts with a few drawn from Hīnayānist sources, Pali or Sanskrit. The texts are known in Chinese Buddhism as *Āgamas* and are so many and so voluminous that it is the work of a lifetime for a competent sinologist to explore their contents. But some of the texts may be sampled in the summaries given in the French sinologist Wieger's learned work. They show at a glance that what these texts aimed at was not exact fidelity to the original, but a presentation of the subject-matter (both legends and doctrines) in such a way as to be acceptable to the Chinese mind. They were more adaptations than translations and had on that account a greater measure of propaganda value.

The result was a seepage into them of a good many Taoist elements that had a certain affinity to Mahāyānism. Kumārajīva's works, for

[1] Cf. 'The official history informs us that, in the year AD 405 in China, of ten families, nine practised Buddhism.'—Wieger, p. 509.

[2] See Wieger's *A History of Religious Beliefs, etc., in China*, p. 521.

example, show a strong admixture of these elements; the 'Amidism' that developed in China colours much of his presentation of Buddhism. It was out of this 'Chinese Buddhism' that there developed in later times the Ten Traditional Buddhist Schools of China.[1] They do not correspond to any of the 'sects' or 'schools' of Indian Buddhism, though some take as their scripture Indian works as found in their Chinese rendering. This tendency of Buddhism in China to depart from its standard in India was noticed early by Chinese monk-scholars. They came to realize that to preserve the purity of the religion in their land it was necessary to study it in its homeland, India. The movement by Chinese monk-scholars for the purification of Chinese Buddhism lasted from Fa-hsien's time to I-tsing's, arising out of the felt need for knowledge of true Buddhism through close and sustained cultural intercourse with India.

At the same time the methods of translation kept on improving in scholarly circles and the association and collaboration in translation work between an Indian monk-scholar and a Chinese, as it appears from the paired names in the *Tripiṭaka* catalogues, was deemed essential. The loss of the originals of most of the works, however, renders it impossible to assess how far accuracy was actually achieved in the Chinese translations.

KUMĀRAJĪVA, PARAMĀRTHA AND BODHIDHARMA

Among the numerous monk-scholars from India in China during the five centuries and more of Sino-Indian cultural intercourse, the names of these three stand indisputably highest in Chinese estimation. Their influence in different centuries was epoch-making in the history of Chinese Buddhism, and Bodhidharma (called also Dharmabodhi[2]), the last in time among them, has been deified by Chinese Buddhists. The school of Buddhism founded by him is still alive in the Far East, specially in Japan where it has its headquarters at Kyoto. A good deal of fable has naturally accreted round the lives and careers of this illustrious trio, but the Chinese traditions about them are on the whole not too discrepant.[3]

KUMĀRAJĪVA (*c.* AD 343–413) was not a full-blooded Indian, but

[1] A succinct account of the Ten Traditional Schools of Chinese Buddhism, written by myself, will be found in the *History of Philosophy, Eastern and Western* (London: George Allen & Unwin, 1952), Vol. I, Ch. xxiv.

[2] The name is equated from the Chinese 'Ta-mu-phu-thi'.

[3] Traditions about these three are scattered in a number of works in Chinese historical and Buddhist literature. The accounts here given are drawn mainly from Wieger's *History of Religious Beliefs and Philosophical Opinions in China* and Chou's *Indo-Chinese Relations* (*A History of Chinese Buddhism*), pub. by Indo-Chinese Literature Publications, Allahabad, 1955. Both these works are based on original Chinese materials and the sources are cited.

was regarded as an Indian by the Chinese who, when he died at Changan, cremated his body according to Indian custom.

His father, Kumārāyaṇa, who became a Buddhist, was a Kashmirian scholar. He migrated to a mid-Asian township named Kiue-tsa near the Tsunling Mountains.

The township was in the State of Kuchā—one of the small oasis-states on the edge of the Gobi Desert, described by ancient Chinese historians as the most advanced among them, in both material wealth and culture.[1] Its situation was such as to keep it open to both Indian and Iranian influences. 'Kuchā from the literary and religious points of view formed an integral part of "Outer India"; from the point of view of material civilization, it was at the same time a province of "Outer Iran".'[2] Hsüan-tsang, who on his way to India passed across the Tsunling Mountains through Kuchā some time in AD 629–30, gives a glowing account of the State and of its Buddhist culture. Kumārāyaṇa settled down here, but, eschewing Iranian modes current in the land, used to live in Indian style. He married a Kuchān woman, daughter of a local chieftain, whose name was Jīvā. Kumārajīva was the offspring of this union and it is said that his name was made up from the names of his Indian father and Kuchān mother.

The family, however, did not lose its link with Kashmir. When Kumārajīva was only nine years old, his mother took him from Kiue-tsa to Kashmir for education, his father having expired in the meantime. On their way back, they stayed for some time at Kashgar where the boy's studies were continued. It is said that, as a result of these studies, the boy Kumārajīva, while staying at Kashgar, became a convert from Hīnayānist faith to Mahāyānist. From Kashgar the mother and the son went back to and settled once again at Kiue-tsa. As Kumārajīva grew up, he acquired a great reputation among people for scholarship and learning which overflowed to all parts of Kuchā from the little town where he had his home.

In AD 384 Kuchā was invaded and annexed by the Chinese. Kumārajīva was then forty-one years of age. His fame as a scholar had spread already from Kuchā to China and his name happened to be known to the Chinese emperor. It is said that the emperor had given a directive to the general who conquered Kiue-tsa to bring Kumārajīva to China. So, after Kuchā had fallen to the Chinese, he was taken under military escort to the Chinese town of Liang-how round AD 401 and subsequently to the capital city Changan where the emperor himself received him. He was accommodated in a

[1] See Grousset's *In the Footsteps of the Buddha* (London: George Routledge & Sons, 1932), p. 53.

[2] *Ibid*, p. 57.

monastery known as the 'Great (*Mahā-*) Monastery' of the city, where he lived continuously for twelve years. Here, at the Great Monastery of Changan, the emperor himself, it is said, used to come and hold discussions with him and listen to his sermons.

When Kumārajīva was working in the cause of Buddhism at Changan, the activity of translating Buddhist texts into Chinese, started at the northern White Horse Monastery way back over three centuries, had increased in vigour, volume and organization. This industry was under imperial patronage at Changan and Kumārajīva was put in charge of it.

He was not satisfied with the current Chinese renderings; their language had grown archaic and, to his mind, needed revision. With the assistance of a number of Chinese collaborators, he made a fresh translation of the voluminous work (*Mahā*) *Prajñāpāramitā Sūtra*. It is said that more than five hundred clerks assisted him in this exacting job. Next, other Buddhist texts were taken up by him, and from one to two thousand Chinese scholars were employed as his assistants. Thus his monastery at Changan outrivalled in this industry the old White Horse Monastery of the north. When he had reached sixty years of age, he was still hard at work translating or composing Buddhist texts and he carried it on to his dying day. The total number of these texts is put at 300, of which many were included in the *Tripiṭaka*. He was, besides, the author of a few original works in Chinese which include the 'Life of Aśvaghoṣa' from a Sanskrit source now untraceable.[1] The successors of the emperor who had him brought to Changan were also Buddhists and Kumārajīva enjoyed their patronage too.

In the official history (*Shu*) of the Chin dynasty, there is a life-sketch of Kumārajīva.[2] It hints, as do other legends, at some weakness in his moral fibre. One legend is that an imperial patron of his tempted him to marry, and, for that purpose, sent from his court ten glamorous ladies for him to choose a bride from. He yielded to the charms of one, doffed his monk's robe, married her and settled down to worldly life. He soon came, however, to repent of his lapse. It is reported that thereafter he always used to start his preachings with the apologetic exordium: 'Follow my work, but not my life which is far from ideal. But the lotus grows out of mud. Love the lotus; do not love the mud'.

He left, when he died at Changan in some year after AD 412, a

[1] See reference to this work in Part IV, Sec. 1, p. 245.

[2] It occurs in the 95th chapter and Wieger has given a summary of it in his work (*History of Religious Beliefs and Philosophical Opinions in China* at pp. 416–417). Some particulars in it vary from the sketch given above, but the main outline is the same.

whole host of disciples and pupils by whom his literary work was carried forward into the next era.

PARAMĀRTHA (*c.* AD 498–569) hailed from Ujjainī and enjoyed in his time a widespread reputation in India as a distinguished monk-scholar. In AD 539, the Chinese emperor Wu-ti of the Liang dynasty sent a goodwill mission to India with a charge to search for Indian Buddhist manuscripts and acquire them for China. This mission in the course of its duty came to Magadha where a king of the Gupta dynasty (Kumāragupta or Jīvitagupta) was then reigning. The wishes of the Chinese emperor were made known to the Gupta king who decided to send Paramārtha with the Chinese envoy along with an assortment of Buddhist works.

Under Chinese escort Paramārtha reached Canton at the middle of August AD 546. From there he hastened to Nanking where he was cordially received by the emperor who offered him a fine residence in one of his palaces, called the 'Palace of Treasury Clouds'.

But at that time there were grave disturbances in the capital; a rebellion was on, led by the general of the emperor's army. So Paramārtha left Nanking for a safer and quieter place, Fuchung in the Chunking province. Here he settled down to the work of translating Buddhist texts, starting with the *Sapta-daśa-bhūmi Śāstra*.[1] He returned to Nanking in AD 552 when the trouble was over and, in the monastery of Chin Kuan where he settled, he continued his translation work. Later he visited Chunking, and, returning again to Nanking, lived in the 'Monastery of Treasury Field' where he completed the translation of another Buddhist Mahāyānist classic *Vajracchedikā Prajñāpāramitā*. He moved afterwards to Hsin-wu where he took up residence at the monastery of Mei-tu and completed a few original works, among them his 'Life of Vasubandhu'.[2] His next move was to Canton where he made a Chinese version of one of the works of Guṇamati.[3] We find him later settled single-mindedly at Nanking to his work of translation, but visiting from time to time different towns in southern China and sojourning in local monasteries.

When Paramārtha was sixty-three years old in AD 561, he was seized with a longing to return to India. Making up his mind, he took a small boat and sailed to a port in the south-east of China. But he stopped there at the intercession of the local magistrate and betook himself to a local monastery called the 'Monastery of Construction'. After a brief sojourn, he left the place and was back again at Canton. He made no further move thereafter to return to his homeland.

[1] About this work, see Part IV, Sec. 5, p. 284. It has a later Chinese translation by Hsüan-tsang.

[2] About this work, see Part IV, Sec. 5, pp. 281–282.

[3] *Re* Guṇamati, see Part IV, Sec. 6, p. 291.

After continuing his literary labours over all these years, he died in January, AD 569, at the age of seventy-one. He had lived and worked in China for about twenty-three years.

A large number of works by Paramārtha, both original and translations, are included in the Chinese *Tripiṭaka*, among them his version of Aśvaghoṣa's *Mahāyāna-śraddhotpāda*.[1] A commentary on this version was written some time between AD 634 and 712 by a famous Chinese scholar Fa-tsang to serve as a key to the work of Aśvaghoṣa. The commentarial work in its turn became one of the basic texts of two Chinese schools of Buddhism, Tien-tai and Hsien-shu.

We have seen how the main agency for the propagation of Buddhism in China and for the foundation of the Ten Schools (called *Tsung*) of Chinese Buddhism, all of which arose between the fifth and the eighth centuries, was Chinese translation of Indian Buddhist works. The Indian monk-scholars who went to China were not only scholars in Sanskrit, but most of them mastered Chinese and worked jointly with Chinese scholars: some acquired high proficiency in the language. Seeing that in vocabulary and system of expression it is so completely different from Sanskrit or any of the Indian languages, this must be deemed a remarkable feat of scholarship, especially when undertaken without the aid of any philological apparatus.

Kumārajīva and Paramārtha stand at the head of a whole host of Indian monk-scholars, translators of Indian Sanskrit texts into Chinese. Most of them are unknown except by their names: there is no tradition about any of them in India. Only of those who rose to the height of fame are there biographical notices in the Chinese records; the others are just names. To mention a few of these little-known scholars—Buddhabhadra of Kapilavastu (AD 389–421), translator of the *Avataṁśaka Sūtra* (Nanjio, No. 88); Buddhayaśas of Kashmir (fourth century AD) who was Kumārajīva's teacher in Kashmir and followed him to China and joined him there in the work of translation; Bodhiruci of southern India (AD 727) who devoted the largest part of his phenomenally long life—he is said to have died in his 156th year—to translation work in China. The Chinese *tsung* (Buddhist Schools) took their stand on different texts (*Sūtras* and *Śāstras*) which had been made available to them through the joint work and literary collaboration of Chinese and Indian monk-scholars.

But among all Indian monks in China, he, who stands highest in prestige not only in that country, but in all the Buddhist world of the Far East, was one who contemned all texts, preached the supreme spiritual efficacy of *Dhyāna* (Meditation) and was an out-and-out follower of the philosophy of *Sūnyatāvāda* (Emptiness) initiated in

[1] See Part IV, Sec. 5, p. 283.

India by Nāgārjuna. 'Chinese Buddhism', as a Chinese scholar has put it, 'reached its climax not in the Tien-tai and Hua-yen schools, but in the Meditation School, the *Chān* (Japanese Zen)'.[1] The founder of this school was Bodhidharma. Its rapid growth and wide propagation in China was due perhaps in a large measure to its close affinity, on the side of practice, to China's native Tao cult.

BODHIDHARMA (arrived in China by sea in *c.* AD 527), being the founder of a leading school of Chinese Buddhism, has his life more heavily draped in legends than Kumārajīva or Parmārtha.

About his antecedents, the legends are somewhat contradictory; one makes him not an Indian, but an Iranian.[2] Others say that he was the son of a king of South India and that he left India and sailed for China at the behest of his teacher Prajñāratna, the voyage taking as long as three years. He arrived at a port in southern China and, after a period of sojourn there, went north to Nanking. Here he had a famous interview with Emperor Wu-ti of the Liang dynasty which is reported in the narratives of both the two *shus* (Dynastic Histories) of the Wei and the Liang.[3]

Bodhidharma is said to have declared his faith in *Sūṇyatāvāda* to the Chinese emperor and refused to give him any credit for his distinguished services to Buddhism—his building so many temples, patronizing monk-communities and helping in the compilation of Buddhist canons. 'Where all is emptiness, nothing can be called holy', said Bodhidharma. Amazed at the statement, the emperor asked: 'Who is he who speaks to me thus?' 'I don't know', was Bodhidharma's cryptic reply. After this interview with the emperor, Bodhidharma left Nanking and went north to Loyang.

On the outskirts of that ancient city, which had been the cradle of Buddhism in China, he saw the monastery of Shao-lin on the Sung mountain. It cast a spell over him. It had been founded in the first quarter of the fifth century and its ruins may still be seen near Loyang in Honan. It was here that he died, wrapped in lonely meditation, with his face constantly to a wall, but he left behind him a host of disciples and admirers. He used to tell people that he was a century and a half old.

Bodhidharma wrote no books and went on no missionary tours. But he used to recommend the *Laṅkāvatāra Sūtra* and is said to have handed over a copy of it to his principal Chinese disciple Hui-ke. This *sūtra* is said to have been first introduced by Bodhidharma into Chinese Buddhism and Hui-ke's successors went by the name of '*Laṅkāvatāra* masters'.

[1] See *China* (ed. by MacNair, University of California Press, 1946), p. 256.
[2] See Chou's *Sino-Indian Relations*, p. 91.
[3] See Wieger's *A History of Religious Beliefs, etc.*, p. 532.

It was the missionary work of Hui-ke and his followers that laid the foundation of the great *Chān* (Skt. *Dyāna*) school. The school cared little for theology or metaphysics and avoided written texts, relying on personal oral teaching transmitted from master to disciple. It became in later times the most flourishing school of Chinese Buddhism.

From China the cult of Bodhidharma was taken over by Japan under the name of Zen and is still practised in the country at its centre in Kyoto.

During the great Muromachi period of Japanese history (AD 1334–1573), the influence of Zennism on Japanese culture was deep and many-sided. During this efflorescent epoch of Japanese art and aesthetic culture, Bodhidharma was nearly idolized by the Japanese people. His swarthy, bearded face, staring eyes and gnarled limbs became a popular motive in Muromachi art, from the *kakemonos* of tea-houses and temples to the sword-hilts of the Samurai. 'Indeed there is in Japan hardly a form of thought or activity', remarks Anesaki, 'that Zen has not touched and inspired with its ideal of simple beauty.' The impact of Zennism on the life of old Japan may be studied in the classic work of Suzuki on *Zen Buddhism and its Influence on Japanese Culture* (1938).

*

The long vista of time through which the story of Indian monk-scholars and their works transports us may well occupy our thought for a moment. Scholarship and learning grew into an essential part of Saṅgha life and activity; it went on expanding through all the BC centuries of Buddhist history and continued to expand in the AD.

Those who were known as *Theras* in the primitive saṅgha and who, according to Theravāda tradition, settled the Theravāda canon;[1] those called *Ācariyas* through whom the Vinaya is said to have been transmitted;[2] those non-conformists again—Mahādeva for example—who attacked the presumptions of the Arhats;[3] those who led movements of thought which resulted in the formation of sects but who remain anonymous; those like Moggaliputta Tissa who were great in polemics; and scholars of the type of Nāgasena who were profound in canonical learning; exegists of later AD centuries whose works are outstanding in Pali literature; cannot be classed as mere saints and religious leaders: their achievements were such as

[1] They were Kassapa, Ānanda, Upāli, Anuruddha, Vaṅgīsa, Kumāra-Kassapa, Kaccāna, Koṭṭhika and others (see *Dīpavaṁsa*, 5. 2, 7–9).

[2] The succession of *ācariyas* (Ācariya-paraṁparā) from Upāli to Tissa, viz, Upāli, Dāsaka, Sonaka and Tissa mentioned in Buddhaghosa's *Samanta-pāsādikā* (see Oldenberg's *Vinayapiṭakam*, Vol. III, p. 313)).

[3] See Malalasekera's *Dictionary of Pali Proper Names* under Mahādeva and de la Vallée Poussin's article on *The Five Points of Mahādeva* in JRAS, 1910, p. 414.

called for scholarly accomplishments and intellectual greatness.

With the emergence of the Mahāyāna in the AD centuries, a long line of creative thinkers and philosophers ensued—those, 'the great unknown', who composed the fundamental *sūtras* of Mahāyāna Buddhism, and the profound philosophers who made the Mahāyāna *śāstras* on their basis. The first 'masters of *Śāstras*' have come down to us in the trappings of legend, but others followed in their train whose figures are more familiar.

Through notices by the Chinese pilgrims, through references to them in Chinese and Tibetan literature, through their surviving works—genuine mixed up with apocrypha—preserved in Chinese and Tibetan collections, and also through some of their stray works in original discovered in India, we can see how the ancient tradition of monk-scholarship passed on from age to age until the time when Buddhism in India was extinct. It did not remain confined to India; monks in other Asian countries, especially China and Tibet, promoted the cause of Buddhism by their dedicated lives and works.

It would hardly be correct to think of these generations of Indian monk-scholars purely in terms of their individual distinctions and achievements: they were an institution incorporated with Saṅgha life. Yet how few are the individuals that emerge! We see them glimpse-wise in the sweeping river of time and lapse into the meditation of Marcus Aurelius: 'Time is a sort of river of passing events and strong in its current; no sooner is a thing brought to light than it is swept by and another takes its place and this too will be swept away.'

APPENDIX

(to Part IV, Sec. 7)

(*On I-tsing's 'Account of Fifty-one Monks'*)

A PASSING reference has been made to this important work by I-tsing. It throws a flood of light on the immense hardships and privations borne by pilgrims from the Far East to India, their varied experiences in the country, their indomitable spirit and insatiable desire for learning and also their acute longings to return to their homeland to give compatriots the benefit of their Indian learning and experiences.

The title of the work, rendered in English, is: 'Monks of the Buddhist Faith who went to the Western Country under the Tang Dynasty'. It is included in the fifty-first volume of the Taisho *Tripiṭaka* (No. 2,066).

The Tang dynasty was founded by Li Shih-min and lasted from AD 618 to AD 907, with its capital at Changan. The Dowager Empress Wu was ruling in the time of I-tsing. 'In 684 she assumed actual control of the government, and in 690, as substantive empress, she changed the name of the dynasty from Tang to Chou.'[1] I-tsing was in India during AD 671–95.

The practice of adopting a Sanskrit name on ordination prevailed, as the record shows, among the monks of the Far East.

From I-tsing's account it will appear that in his time Nālandā was the most flourishing centre of Buddhist learning in India. Most of those who visited India from China and the Far East, except those who had already learnt the language in their own country or outside, used to spend some time on arrival in India in studying Sanskrit. Those who went in for advanced learning would spend a few years at Nālandā. Several monasteries, mentioned by the monks, however, cannot be exactly located or identified. The distances in *Yojanas* are computed from Chinese *li*.[2]

The following is I-tsing's epilogue to the work:

'I, Shamana I-tsing, returned to Śrī-vijaya in South Sea from the Western Country (i.e. India), and from there, carrying the map of Nālandā, came back to China. There were previously many noble monks, who, without caring for their lives, had gone to the Western Country in search of the Law. Fa-hsien went forth on the difficult and perilous route to the Western Country and Hsüan-tsang also, following his footsteps, went there. Some monks went by the South Sea route. The monks, while journeying by land or by sea route, remembered all along the traces of the Buddha and prostrated themselves before the law of the Buddha.

'Arriving in the Western Country, they always desired to go back to their motherland to report their experiences to the Emperor.

'Though it is a great fortune and luck to go out to the Western Country in search of the Law, it is an extremely difficult and perilous undertaking. . . . It

[1] *China*, edited by MacNair (University of California Press, 1946), p. 85.

[2] The following translations are more or less free. They have been supplied to me by Miss Latika Lahiri of Lady Irwin School, New Delhi. Miss Lahiri spent several years in China and made a special study of I-tsing's work under her Chinese teacher in Peking.

is only with the help of elephants, etc. that the desert can be crossed. Nothing can be seen there except the sun. The sea route also is dangerous with the surging waves cast up by whales (?). I alone went outside the Iron Gate, and passing through many dangerous mountain-peaks, reached the Iron Pillars.[1]

'Many days I have passed without food and even without a drop of water. I was always worried and no spirit was left in me. Due to this perilous journey and its hardships, the colour of my face was changed. When I left China I had fifty companions with me, but when I reached the Western Country only two or three were left. There was not a single Chinese monastery there. Because there was no fixed place (for us), we had to move from place to place like grass swept by wind. Under such difficult circumstances, to study Buddhism and the Law is really a very great effort.

'I wish to fulfil my desire (to write about these things) so that the next generation may know all this. I have myself heard with my own ears and seen with my own eyes the difficulties that other monks have undergone. So I intended to write this book on the basis of the lives of the present monks and those of the past, of those who are living and those who are dead.'

Among the fifty-one pilgrims, including I-tsing himself, from China and the Far East were the following:[2]

PRAJÑĀVARMAN (a native of Korea). He renounced the world when he was in his own country. He desired to pay respect to the relics of the Buddha. So he sailed from his own country to Fukien in China and travelled a long distance to reach Changan. The emperor ordered a certain Chinese monk to accompany him to the Western Country (i.e. India).

Thus they left for India. (On the journey) they lived in the 'Monastery of Great Faith' for about ten years.[3] This monastery had been built for the use of Buddhist pilgrims from Tokhara. It was a rich monastery; the food served was excellent. Here Prajñāvarman learnt Sanskrit and studied the *Kośa*. Monks from the north usually stayed in this monastery.

There was a monastery known as Kapiśa Monastery to the west of the Monastery of Great Enlightenment. It was rich in wealth and knowledge and the monks were well-versed in the Hīnayāna. To the north-east of the Monastery of Great Enlightenment was another monastery which had been built by Chalukya kings of the south (i.e. Sourāshtra). Though not very rich, it was famous for its magnanimity. Another monastery near this old monastery had been built by Bhāshkara-sena (of the Maitraka dynasty of Valabhī in Sourāshtra?) which Buddhist monks coming from the south stayed in. For the

[1] The 'Iron Gates' was the name of a mountain-pass about ninety miles south-south-east from Samarkand. 'The pass so called,' says Hsüan-tsang, 'is bordered on the right and the left by mountains. These mountains are of prodigious height. The road is narrow which adds to the difficulty and danger. On each side there is a rocky wall of iron colour. Here are set up double wooden doors, strengthened with iron and furnished with many pendent bells. Because of protection afforded to the pass by these doors when closed, the name of "Iron Gates" is given.'—Beal's *Buddhist Records*, i, p. 36. The Turks controlled by this means the trade between Mid-Asia and India.

[2] The 'Life and Travels' of I-tsing himself are given more at large than in this work in Takakusu's *A Record of the Buddhist Religion*, pp. xxv-xxxviii.

[3] This monastery is spoken of by other pilgrims too. Where it was located is not exactly known. Likely to have been not very distant from the State of Kapiśa (in northern Afghanistan), it seems to have been a centre of Sanskrit learning, as several monks say that they stayed there for a number of years learning Sanskrit before they entered India.

Chinese monks no such monastery had been built by the rulers of China and so they had to face many difficulties. . . .

The Mrigadāva Monastery is about forty *yojanas* to the east of Nālandā. Not far from it is another monastery whose remnants only are left. This was known as 'China Monastery'. It is said that the great king Śīlāditya (Harṣavardhana) established this saṅghārāma for the Chinese monks. There were about twenty (Chinese) Buddhist monks here. (These monks) had taken the land route from Szeichwan and arrived at the Mahābodhi Saṅghārāma. The king had welcomed them with great respect and they had stayed at the Saṅghārāma. The king (afterwards) donated to this monastery twenty-four villages. Later on, the Chinese monks died; there was a fight over the possession of these lands. Only three villages now belong to it.

(At Gaya) the Great Enlightenment Monastery had been built by a king of Ceylon.[1] Pilgrim monks from Ceylon used to stay in this monastery.

About seven *yojanas* to the north-east of the Mahābodhi Monastery was the Nālandā Monastery.

In olden times King Śakrāditya had built (a monastery at Nālandā) for Bhikṣus from northern India.[2] The foundation was laid, but for some time work was stopped. After that the rulers of the country, descendants of the former king (i.e. kings of the Gupta dynasty) completed successively the vast buildings of Nālandā. It is beyond one's power to describe the workmanship, but let me give a general description.

The shape of (each) saṅghārāma is square. There is a big (internal) corridor running along the four sides, all made of brick. The rafters are wooden. All the rooms in a saṅghārāma are interconnected. The floor-area of each room is not more than ten square feet (according to Chinese measure). The windows in the back-wall face the cornice (i.e. are very high up) and only the high door is set in the wall. But no screens are used so that one can see from one door through all others. At the four corners (of the establishment) are four halls (auditoria) made of bricks. It is said that the Buddha once lived at Nālandā.[3]

All the walls are skilfully and marvellously carved. Every time during meal-hours the doors are closed so that books and other things may not be stolen. The floors and the caves are mosaic, made of bricks large and small—some as small as dates or peaches. They are plastered with a paste which is a mixture of finely powdered lime, earth, jute-fibres, oil and jute fluff.

This paste is kept for days together to soak and mix. (The process of manufacturing this paste is described). When dry this paste is polished with soapstone and brushed over with a vermilion colour. Finally it is rubbed and polished with oil, and when spread, it gives to the brickwork the look of a mirror. The stairs also are polished (like this) and no crack appears in ten to twenty years' time. Right in the foreground are the Buddha-images before which valuable lustrous ornaments of gold are laid (Note: *The images were housed at Nālandā in temples*).

Both monks and lay men have to observe the rules and ceremonies of monastic life. . . . The oldest man of the monastery is regarded as the Director. It is the rule to hand over the keys of the doors to the Director when the doors are put under lock and key. There is a sub-director known as *Karmadāna*. The founder of a saṅghārāma is known as *Vihārasvāmī*. The person in charge of announcing time and reporting it to the inmates is known as *Vihārapāla*. The person in charge of the kitchens is also known as *Karmadāna*.

[1] By Meghavaṇṇa. See Part III, Sec. 4, at p. 202.
[2] This is said by Hsüan-tsang also in his 'Record'.
[3] The Buddha's sojourns at Nālandā are referred to in several legends.

If something happened in the monastery, all the monks of the monastery got together to discuss the matter. The monks, one by one, with folded hands reported the matter. If one of the monks objected, nothing could be done. If anyone did anything without the consent of all the monks of the monastery, he would be forced to leave the establishment. If there were differences of opinion, they would try to convince the other group with reasons. No force was used to convince.

There were some monks who were in charge of the treasury of the monastery. If a monk wanted some money, he would go to two or three officers in charge and with folded hands request for money. If he got it he could spend it, but if anyone used the money without the permission of the officers-in-charge, even if it were for a quantity of rice in husks, he would be expelled. Only the *Kulapati* was allowed to do so.

PAÑCASUMATI (a native of Senshi in China). He left China and passed through 'the countries of the barbarians' in mid-Asia, crossed Turfan and reached Tibet, and was helped by the Queen of Tibet to go on his journey to northern India.

He entered India by a completely new route, by the Shipki Pass to Jalandhar. But before he could enter the city, he fell into the hands of thieves. There was no place where merchants and travellers could go and report the crime or get help. Despairing of human help, he prayed to the Buddha for help. He had a dream that the Buddha had come to release him. Waking up, he saw that all the thieves were fast asleep and he stealthily left the place and fled away and the danger was passed.

He lived for four years at Jalandhar. He was warmly received by the king and all arrangements for his food and stay were made. There (at Jalandhar) he studied the Buddhist *sūtras* and *vinaya* and practised the Sanskrit language. He acquired much knowledge.

After that, he went southwards and reached the Mahābodhi Saṅghārāma. He again stayed for four years there. He could not see the sacred traces of the Buddha, but he saw the images of Maitreyanātha. . . . He studied the *Kośa* and *Abhidharma Śāstra*.

Next he went to Nālandā where he spent three years. There he studied a hundred *śāstras* with a monk. He learnt also from a great and virtuous preceptor the *Yogācāra-bhūmi-śāstra*. . . . He realized the inner meaning and significance of Buddhism and completed the study of almost all the Buddhist *śāstras*.

Thence he proceeded north along the bank of the Ganges. He received hospitality from the kings. He lived in the Monastery of Great Faith and other monasteries.

The envoy from the Tang emperor gave, on return to China, a very good report about him to the emperor. (On receiving this report) the emperor sent men to western India to search for him and escort him back to the Chinese capital. On their way back (taking the monk with them), they came to Nepal. The King of Nepal helped the monk to proceed to Tibet. There he met the Queen of Tibet, who had helped him before, with money needed for the journey from Tibet to China. So after travelling a long distance, he reached China. (In the Chinese capital) the emperor gave him a long audience and commanded him to go to Kashmir to escort (to China) an old Brāhmaṇa named Lokāditya.

Next he went to Loyang and took a hand in translation work, but after some time he proceeded again towards northern India in obedience to the emperor's command. After various misadventures on the way, he met a

Chinese envoy sent by the emperor who had Lokāditya already under his escort. Lokāditya directed Pañcasumati to take the company of some people who were going to the Lāṭa country (i.e. Sourāshtra) in western India to collect medicinal herbs for longevity. (He went there and then proceeded on a tour of the country in the course of which he came to Bodhimaṇḍa, i.e. Buddhagayā where he stayed for some time and then shifted to Nālandā).

In the famous Nālandā Saṅghārāma, he met the Chinese monk I-tsing who advised him to go back to China. But the road from Nepal to Tibet and the road through Kapiśa were blocked. So he took shelter in the Venuvana (bamboo-grove at Rājgir), stayed on there and enjoyed the sight of the waving bamboo-leaves. But he was always thinking of return to China after learning Buddhism to spread the religion (in his own country). But, alas, his desire was not fulfilled. (He died in India) and his bones were cast into the big rivers of India. But his name is famous in China. (He was about sixty years old when he died in India).

'VINAYA MASTER OF VAST WISDOM'—(equated from the Chinese name Chih-hung-lu-shih—Sanskrit name not given) was a native of Loyang. . . . He left China and went first to Java and thence to Sumatra. He, along with his companions, reached the Monastery of Great Enlightenment (perhaps somewhere in mid-Asia) where they stayed for two years. There he practised the recitation of Sanskrit *śāstras* and learnt the Sanskrit language. He studied *śabdavidyā* (i.e. Sanskrit grammar) completely and learnt fully to understand Sanskrit. He studied also *Vinaya śāstra* and *Abhidharma*, mastered the *Kośa* and also became proficient in *Hetuvidyā-śāstra* (Logic).

He studied Mahāyāna philosophy at Nālandā, and at the Monastery of Faith at Bodhimaṇḍa (perhaps the Mahābodhi Saṅghārāma at Bodhgayā or some other monastery at the place), he studied especially Hīnayāna philosophy and also other subjects. He was very hard-working. He studied the *Vinaya-sūtra* written by Guṇaprabha. He maintained perfect self-restraint in life and very seldom slept. For most of the time he studied and carried on self-examination. . . . He visited Gṛdhrakūta at Rājagṛha, Mṛgadāva, the Jetavana Monastery, the Mango-grove of Āmrapālī and other (holy) places. (He observed) at Nālandā the custom of offering food first to the image of the Buddha (and then to others). Precious articles also were offered (to the image). These (offered) articles were stored in the city of Rājagṛha (for safe-keeping).

He lived in Central India for about eight years and later went to Kashmir which was like his homeland to him. It is said that he and another Chinese monk (named) lived together in Kashmir, but nobody knows where they went afterwards. These monks translated many Sanskrit texts into Chinese.

PRAJÑĀDEVA was a native of Chiang-ling in the province of Chiang in China. (He was one of those who accompanied Chih-hung-lu-shih to India). He sailed north-east from Ceylon and, after a fortnight's sailing, reached the port of Harikela on the eastern shore of India.[1] He stayed there for one year and then moved into the hinterland. He and Chih-hung-lu-shih were always together. After staying for some time at Nālandā, Prajñādeva went to the Monastery of the Great Enlightenment (Mahābodhi Saṅghārāma at Bodhgayā). He was welcomed by the king and allowed to become the head of that monas-

[1] It was probably a port situated in what is now East Pakistan. It is referred to by slightly variant names in several ancient Sanskrit works, e.g. *Mañjuśrī-mūlakalpa* c. eighth century). See Nihar Ranjan Ray's *Bāṅgālīr Itihāsa* (in Bengali), pp. 139–140, where all the references are cited.

tery. It is not easy to become an abbot or head of a monastery in the Western Country (i.e. India).

Later on Prajñādeva went to Nālandā where he attended lectures on *Yoga* and learnt *Chung-kuan* (*Mādhyamika Darśana*) and made a thorough study of *Kośa* and the *Vinaya* canon.

From Nālandā he went to the Tilodhaka Monastery.[1] It was about two *yojanas* from the Monastery of the Great Enlightenment (Mahābodhi). In the Tilodhaka Monastery was a monk who had great mastery of *Hetuvidyā* (Logic). In the discussions and meetings, this (learned) monk used to cite the works of Jina and Dharmayaśa. In his leisure hours Prajñādeva used to translate the *Āgama Sūtras* in three volumes. Before his return to China, he made a complete translation of the Sarvāstivāda Vinaya . . . Prajñādeva wished to stay in India, but all the time he remembered China longingly.

On one occasion I-tsing along with Prajñādeva was on a visit to Gṛdhrakūṭa. They offered worship there and, then ascending to the mountain-top, (they cast their glances afar) and seemed to see China (on the horizon). Both were sorrowful at heart and I-tsing composed a poem expressing his feelings of the moment. Its concluding lines were: 'You go out to India not for worldly happiness, but for the Life Eternal.'

On his way back to China, Prajñādeva proceeded to the north of India and next day I-tsing from Nālandā turned up there to bid him farewell. (They went some way together), and, when they parted, it was a moving scene . . . Prajñādeva was about fifty-six years old at the time.

[1] See Hsüan-tsang's description of this great monastery in Part III, Sec. 4, at pp. 201–202.

PART V

MONASTIC UNIVERSITIES

(AD 500—1200)

1

From 'Study for Faith' to 'Study for Knowledge'

A PHENOMENON, increasingly evident in the decline of Buddhism, is the gradual modification of the purely conventual character of the monasteries. From being seats of monk-life and monk-culture, they grew into centres of general learning and liberal scholarship. It was the late fruition of the ancient tradition of saṅgha life which we have seen carried on by a long line of monk-scholars whose lives and careers have been noticed in the previous part.

The type of monastery organization called *Mahāvihāra* commenced probably sometime in the Gupta age—an aggregation of several monasteries combined in a unitary organization. In these Mahāvihāras, a re-orientation took place of the old traditional monk-culture, redounding to the loss in a large measure of its exclusively monkish preoccupation. This liberalized culture was the Indian 'Buddhist Culture' of that age. The Mahāvihāras were both its depositories and purveyors during the decline of Buddhism in India. It spread in the country from the Mahāvihāras; it was there that foreign monks resorted to imbibe it.

Nissaya was an ancient rule of Vinaya—dependence on a teacher for a space of years which varied with the trainee's ability to learn.[1] It was part of the *regula* and regimen, but it served at the same time to create a new value in monastic life, a tradition of learning and scholarship. It continued unbroken in the monasteries and grew, as we have observed, into an inalienable aspect of Saṅgha life. We have seen how the ideal monastery Śāntideva contemplates in the eighth century AD is conceived by him as a place 'humming with reading and recitation of lessons'.[2]

This traditional learning of the monasteries had been at its beginning a cloistered pursuit—learning in canonical lore for the benefit and use of monkhood. But it was progressively liberalized—extended and enlarged in its scope and contents and made available not to monks alone, but to all seekers after knowledge. It was a new development of monastic life and activity and one involved in the complex of conditions and circumstances Buddhism had passed through since the beginning of the Gupta era in its long and historic process of decline. It is an obscure chapter of Buddhist history, but the Chinese pilgrims' accounts afford us glimpses into it.

[1] See Part IV, Sec. 1, p. 235.
[2] See verse from Śāntideva's *Bodhicaryāvatāra* quoted at the beginning of Part IV.

Signs and indications appear in the record of Fa-hsien. Buddhism, once prospering all over northern India, has become regional in his time, uneven in its incidence and distribution, languishing in some parts, while flourishing in others. The decline must have been general and continuous, for, a little over two centuries later it is more clearly, more sharply articulated by Hsüan-tsang. He notes it, not only in statistical form for several ancient seats of Buddhism visited by him, but also with a poignant sense and awareness of the religion being already in the sere and yellow leaf, hastening to its fall. The dire event is foreseen by him in omens and portents.

At the time of his visit to Bodhgayā, the 'Bodhimaṇḍa' (consecrated area round the Bodhi-tree) had two boundary-marks—two statues of Avalokiteśvara, about which a local legend had it that the 'law of the Buddha' would come to an end as soon as the statues sank into the ground and disappeared. The pilgrim saw with alarm the statue at the southern end already sunk up to the breast.[1]

Nālandā was then at the zenith of prosperity and fame. Yet, residing here in a chamber of Bālāditya's great temple, Hsüan-tsang had a depressing nightmare and a warning vision.[2] In a dream he saw all the magnificent courts and chambers of Nālandā deserted and befouled and 'there was nought but water-buffaloes fastened in them—no priests or their followers'. While trying to climb to the top of the temple, he had a sudden vision of god Mañjuśrī. The visionary figure pointed from the temple's pinnacle to a conflagration raging round Nālandā and, prophesying a period of confusion and anarchy in India after King Harṣa's death, warned him to leave the country. The dream and the vision must have been prompted by Hsüan-tsang's own haunting thoughts of a dark future—a time when Buddhism would fall into eclipse and Buddhist culture into neglect.

Hsüan-tsang watched the process of decline at only one of its stages: he saw it objectively, on its external side—in the dwindling of the adherents of Buddhism, the strengthening of rival faiths, the decline in the number of monastic establishments and their inmates. What was not apparent to him was a subtler, inner side of this decline. It related to the condition and status of Buddhism itself as it stood *vis à vis* other faiths then gaining ground.

Buddhism had been born as a religion distinct and apart from current Brāhmaṇical faiths and philosophies.

The half-baked theory that it was an 'off-shoot from the ancient faith of the Hindus, perhaps a schism or heresy' and that the Buddha's 'main object was to bring about a reformation in religious practices

[1] Beal's *Buddhist Records*, ii, p. 116. Watters' comment (*On Yuan Chawng*, Vol. II, p. 115)—'The two images here mentioned apparently did not exist at the time of Fa-hsien's visit and they are not in other treatises.'

[2] Beal's *Life of Hiuen Tsiang*, p. 155.

19. *Remains of monasteries at Kushinagar.* (*The modern temple which houses the great image of the recumbent Buddha brought by Haribala is in the background.*) (Photo: Department of Archaeology, Government of India)

Ruins of monasteries to the south of the 'Great Tope' of Sanchi. (Photo: Department of Archaeology, Government of India)

20. *The pre-Gupta monastery at Sanchi.* (*Monastery, No. 51, excavated in 1936.*) (Photo: Department of Archaeology, Government of India)

A temple dominating a number of monasteries to the east of the 'Great Tope' at Sanchi. (Photo: Department of Archaeology, Government of India)

21. *Monastery remains to the south of the 'Great Tope' of Sanchi.* (Photo: Department of Archaeology, Government of India)

The Temple of many pillars at Sanchi. (*Only the broken shafts remain.*) (Photo: Department of Archaeology, Government of India)

22. *View of a courtyard (with inset oven) which served as a classroom at Nālandā.* (Photo: Department of Archaeology, Government of India)

View of a courtyard (with inset oven and well) with monks' cells at the sides at Nālandā. (Photo: Department of Archaeology, Government of India)

and return to the basic principles'[1] rests mainly on certain key-terms (e.g. *Brahmacarya*) which it borrowed from the *Upaniṣads*; yet used in what widely different connotations![2] In the earliest formulation of the religion, as we find it in the Theravāda canon, the body of doctrines and practices presented is unrelated to the more ancient Brāhmaṇical faith. Nor were their after-developments towards that faith or philosophy. Buddhism may be described more rightly as a tree with its own organic growth rather than as an 'offshoot'.

The Mahāyāna, as one of the two main branches of this tree, appeared in the early AD centuries. Its growth, stimulated and conditioned by factors and circumstances of which no synthetic estimate has been made yet, still poses a problem in Buddhist history. One peculiar consequence of its emergence was to make dubious the trenchant distinction of Buddhism, so obvious in its early history, as a non-Brāhmaṇical faith. Mahāyāna, as it developed in its *śāstras*, drifted into certain channels of speculative thinking in which it mingled freely with Brāhmaṇical philosophy; it raised, as in Brāhmaṇical religions, a pantheon of deities, some of them invested with symbolisms of Brāhmaṇical faith; its ritual practices came increasingly into the Brāhmaṇical pattern of worship.[3] A palpable outward likeness thus developed between Mahāyānist Buddhism and the normal type of a Brāhmaṇical religion.

While the decline of Buddhism is marked by its gradual loss of ground to the revived Brāhmaṇism, this likeness of its Mahāyānist form to a Brāhmaṇical religion was a factor that served also to make its difference from the latter seem hardly of greater consequence than a sectarian difference.

It is difficult to point to the time when this outlook originated, but in the Gupta age (AD 300–550) it seems to have been prevalent. One indication of it is the attitude taken up by the Gupta kings towards the Buddhist religion. They lived in the high noon of the Brāhmaṇical revival and professed Brāhmaṇical faith themselves. Yet their active patronage of Buddhist monasteries and monkhood was of a kind that went much farther than warranted by the mere spirit of 'toleration'. This liberal outlook went on broadening till in after-centuries it reached a consummation in the acceptance of the founder of Buddhism as a deity of the Brāhmaṇical pantheon.[4]

Set in this outlook the monasteries ceased to be regarded as organs and institutions of a faith opposed to or even isolated from currently

[1] See Dr Radhakrishnan's Foreword to 2,500 *Years of Buddhism* (pub. by the Publications Division, Government of India, 1956), pp. xiii-xiv.

[2] In the *Upaniṣads*, the term means 'quest after the Supreme Reality' conceived as Brahman or Ātman; in the *Buddhavacana* its end is conceived as *Nibbāna*—a subjective state in which the ego is completely dissolved. The two concepts are essentially dissimilar and different.

[3] See Part III, Sec. 4, p. 196. [4] See Part III, Sec. 4, pp. 196–197.

prevailing forms of faith. In fact, since Buddhism had begun to ebb, monasteries had ceased to be propaganda-centres of the religion as in the past. They had been enlarging one aspect of monastic life that was rooted in their ancient tradition of monk-scholarship.

The process is marked by a re-orientation of monastic learning, whereby it outgrew its cloistered inbred character and turned into a learning that was liberal and many-sided.

In the monasteries the ancient principle of learning had been 'study for faith'. Its aim was to produce the 'perfect monk'. Within the monastic regimen the immemorial custom of education in India, the *Gurukula*—taking lessons from a master who presides over a small circle of resident pupils—was reproduced. *Nissaya* was, *mutatis mutandis*, its counterpart in monastic life. A few passages of the Theravāda canon throw light on the education of a monk under *nissaya*—its approved mode, its prescribed contents and its standard of attainment.

In *Aṅguttara Nikāya*, vi, 51, Ānanda explains 'how a monk may learn new and unheard things (i.e. matters in which he had had hitherto no oral instruction) relating to the Dhamma, without getting confused'. For this, as Ānanda says, the first condition is the teacher's own ability and range of knowledge. The teacher himself should have mastered the Dhamma as set forth in the Nine *Aṅgas* (Parts) of the canon:[1] 'as learnt, as mastered (by himself), he teaches others the Dhamma in detail; as learnt, as mastered, he makes others repeat it in detail; as learnt, as mastered, he ever reflects, he ever ponders it in his heart, mindfully he pores over it, etc. etc.' Thus is the instruction carried on by the teacher, himself accomplished in canonical lore, taking the monk-learner through the whole of the canon until the trainee becomes 'much-heard' (*bahussuta*) or 'learned' (*paṇḍita*).

In *Majjhima Nikāya* (No. 115—*Bahu-dhātuka Sutta*), the question is put by Ānanda to the Buddha—At what stage may a Bhikkhu be rightly described as a *Paṇḍita*? The answer is: 'When the Bhikkhu has mastered (i) the Elements, (ii) the Senses, (iii) the Chain of Causation, together with (iv) the Rationally Possible and the Rationally Impossible.' The gist and effect of this Sutta is that the learning becomes complete when the monk has mastered the whole of the canonical lore and grasped the fundamental doctrines and basic ideas on which the practice of the Dhamma rests.

Under the ancient *Nissaya* system, it seems that monastic learning was confined to the canon and its philosophy (*Abhidhamma*): its object being to turn out the perfect (*bahussuta* or *paṇḍita*) monk.

[1] The Nine *Aṅgas* are the nine forms of composition of which the canon is made up, viz., *Sutta, Geyya, Veyyākaraṇa, Gāthā, Udāna, Itivuttaka, Jātaka, Abbhutadhamma, Vedalla*. They are mentioned as subjects of study in other passages of the same *nikāya*: see iv, 1, 6; iv, 11, 102, and iv, xix, 186 and 191, etc.

establishments in China. Hence for the special benefit of those engaged in this line of work, I-tsing gives a more detailed review of *Śabdavidyā* (Grammar and Philology) as practised in India, reproducing both the curriculum of studies and the syllabus on the subject followed by academicians in the country.

Students, after acquiring proficiency in language, says I-tsing, 'began to learn composition in prose and verse and devote themselves to Logic (*Hetuvidyā*) and Metaphysics (*Abhidharma-kośa*)'.[1] The *Abhidharma* in Buddhist learning took the place of metaphysical works (*Adhyātma-vidyā*) current in non-Buddhist systems. 'Thus instructed and instructing others, they pass two or three years in the Nālandā monastery in Central India or in the country of Valabhī in Western India.'[2] I-tsing states also that works on different subjects, as listed by him, are studied by 'both priests and lay men; if not, they cannot gain the fame of being *Bahuśruta* (i.e. learned)'.[3] Besides subjects of a secular character, monks had to learn 'all the Vinaya works and investigate the *sūtras* and *śāstras* as well'.[4] These works evidently represented the specially Buddhist part of the curriculum.

By virtue of this liberal learning, the learned among the monks, says I-tsing, were able 'to oppose the heretics as they would drive beasts . . . and explain away disputations as boiling water melts frost'.[5] But 'of such persons in every generation only one or two appear'. The great Mahāyāna masters—those who flourished in the early Christian centuries—and their followers of later times are pointed to by I-tsing as the highest specimens of the class.

The monasteries, having grown up as seats of liberal learning, did not, however, change their character as monastic establishments, even though from the early decades of the fifth century several of them used to be resorted to by learners from different parts of the country. They seem to have partaken of the character of *studia generalia*. Such undoubtedly were two monastic establishments visited by Fa-hsien at Pāṭaliputra which are thus described: 'By the side of the tower of King Ashoka is built a *saṅghārāma* belonging to the Great Vehicle, very imposing and elegant. There is also a temple belonging to the Little Vehicle. Together they contain about 600 or 700 priests; their behaviour is decorous and orderly. Here you may see eminent priests from every quarter of the world; *shramaṇas* and scholars who seek for instruction all flock to this temple. The Brāhmaṇa teacher is called Mañjuśrī. The great *shramaṇas* of the country and all the Bhikṣus attached to the Great Vehicle esteem and reverence him; moreover, he resides in this *saṅghārāma*'.[6]

[1] Takakusu's *Record*, pp. 176–177. [2] *Ibid*, p. 177.
[3] *Ibid*, p. 180–181. [4] *Ibid*, p. 181. [5] *Ibid*, p. 181.
[6] Beal's *Buddhist Records*, etc. p. lvi.

Mañjuśrī (with the Buddhist name) is described as a Brāhmaṇa, but there is no further information to show whether he was a learned Buddhist monk or only a highly reputed and learned lay teacher who chose to reside in the saṅghārāma. Fa-hsien's description, however, clearly points to this monastic establishment as having been of the nature of a *studium*.

During the two centuries and odd between Fa-hsien and Hsüan-tsang, the *studium-generale* character of a number of monasteries must have so developed that their strictly conventual outlook had to be somewhat modified. Though they remained monastic establishments, run and administered by the monks and functioning under monk-made regulations, there were besides the monks many lay students, interested in studying either Buddhist literature or purely secular subjects, who had come to reside there just for the sake of learning.

These lay men in a monastery are divided by I-tsing into two categories, *Māṇavas* and *Brahmacārins*, between whom the monk authorities used to make some distinction:[1]

'Those white-robed (i.e. lay men) who come to the residence of a priest and read chiefly Buddhist scriptures with the intention that they may one day become tonsured and black-robed(?) are called "children"(?), *Māṇava*. Those who (coming to a priest) want to learn secular literature only, without having any intention to quit the world, are called "students", *Brahmacārin*.[2] Those two groups of persons (though residing in a monastery) have to subsist at their own expense.

(Note by I-tsing): In the monasteries of India there are many "students" who are entrusted to the Bhikṣus and instructed by them in secular literature.'

Between these two classes of resident lay students—the *Māṇavas* who studied the scripture intending to qualify for monkhood and the *Brahmacārins* who only studied secular subjects—the former were treated more liberally. The latter used to render personal services to the teacher as was the immemorial custom of India, but the cost of their maintenance was not defrayed out of the monastery funds. 'The "students" (i.e. the *Brahmacārins*)', says I-tsing, 'must not be fed from the permanent property of the Saṅgha, for this is prohibited

[1] Takakusu's *A Record of the Buddhist Religion*, pp. 105–106.

[2] Both the terms, *Māṇava* and *Brahmacārin*, are of ancient usage, denoting *a* pupil or learner. The term *Māṇavaka* in this sense appears in Patañjali's *Mahābhāsya* (second century BC). See *India in the time of Patañjali* by B. M. Puri (pub. by Bharatiya Vidyabhavan, Bombay, 1957), pp. 148–149. The distinction, made by Fa-hsien, betwe.n *Māṇava* and *Brahmacārin*, was evidently just a custom of the monasteries.

in the teaching of Buddha;[1] but, if they have done some laborious work for the Saṅgha, they are to be fed by the monastery, according to their merit.[2] Food made for ordinary purposes or presented by a giver to be used by the "students" (*Brahmacārins*) can be given to them without wrongdoing.'[3]

It seems from this that learning at a monastery by a lay man was not a costly proposition: there is no mention of fees in I-tsing's account and the cost of living could be met by serving the saṅgha. I-tsing speaks of 'many students' being instructed in secular subjects by monk-teachers in Indian monasteries, but it is not known what proportion the lay students bore to the number of monk inmates. In any case it could not have been negligible, as these monasteries attracted general students presumably by their superior efficiency of instruction.

Some of the monasteries which had grown into seminaries of learning, perhaps between the fifth century and the seventh, developed an organization entitling them to be classed as 'universities'. What we know of this organization is only in respect of two of them, Nālandā and Vikramaśilā. There were five of these monastic universities, so far known. They were all located in Bihar and Bengal, all of them in the east of northern India within the territories of Buddhist Pāla kings.[4] But the possibility of some organized monastic universities, functioning in the south during Buddhist decline, cannot be ruled out. In the *leṇas* of southern India, there are indications pointing towards this development.[5] Yet, if they did in fact exist there, they have left not a wrack behind.

[1] By this I-tsing probably means that it was illegitimate to use Saṅgha property except for the upkeep of the monks.

[2] That is, they could pay their way by the custom of sizarship, such as formerly obtained in the Universities of Cambridge and Dublin in Great Britain.

[3] Takakusu's *A Record of the Buddhist Religion*, p. 106.

[4] A great Buddhist establishment of the Mahāvihāra type has been recently discovered on a hill called Ratnagiri, about thirty-nine miles from Cuttack in Orissa. Archaeological exploration of it is still going on. From the evidence of the ruins now unearthed, it appears to have been an enormous quadrangle surrounded by monks' cells, two storeys high. A sizable portion of the upper floor with a grand stone staircase leading up to it has been unearthed. It has been supposed to be the remains of the *saṅghārāma* called Pushpagiri in Udra (Orissa) described by Hsüan-tsang (Beal's *Buddhist Records*, ii, p. 205). Perhaps this establishment in the Pāla age functioned as a *mahāvihāra* of the university type. But we have to await the results of further exploration.

[5] See Part II, Sec. 6, p. 161.

2

Mahāvihāras that functioned as Universities

THE UNIVERSITY OF NĀLANDĀ

(i) *The Antiquity of Nālandā*

A TRADE-ROUTE from north-west to south-east, between Upper India and the kingdom of Magadha, seems to have existed in the far past—in the age (fifth–fourth century BC) when the ancient canonical legends of Buddhism and Jainism took shape.

Among the many localities mentioned in them, Nālandā is one. Though the location of Nālandā on the trade-route is not expressly mentioned, it may be inferred. It seems to have been a distributing centre; within a few miles of the Magadhan capital, Rājagaha, and within easy reach of Gangetic riverine traffic. From its importance as a trade-centre, it grew from a village to a township, described in a legend as 'influential, prosperous and full of folk'.[1]

This well-populated township naturally attracted the great religious leaders of the time when they came here on and off on their preaching missions—the Buddha himself, Nigaṇṭha Nāṭaputta and Mokkhali Gosāla. Here was held, according to Jaina tradition, the historic controversy between Gosāla and Mahāvīrā which resulted in a schism and the foundation of Jainism as a separate form of faith. Nālandā is on this account a sacred place (*tīrtha*) to the Jainas.[2] The town was not without its beauty-spots: the legends give us glimpses of two—a park called Hastiyāma[3] and a mango-grove owned by a wealthy citizen Pāvārika which was the Buddha's favourite resort on his visits to Nālandā.

In later times Nālandā must have been regarded by Buddhists as a holy place on account of its association with the Buddha in the legends. But this seems to have been about its only title to distinction. It never rose to fame either as a great city or as a prominent centre of Buddhism. Some monasteries may have sprung up here in the after-centuries, but its coming into limelight was long after—not earlier than the fifth century AD when a Gupta king, wishing to build a monastery, 'selected by augury' Nālandā as a 'lucky spot'. A Jaina soothsayer is said to have confirmed the choice with a prophecy

[1] *Kevaddha Sutta* in the *Dīgha Nikāya* (see *Dialogues of the Buddha*, pt. i, p. 276).
[2] The legend occurs in the *Bhagavatī Sutta* in the *Uvāsagadasāo*—see *Jaina Sūtras*, SBE, Pt. II, Appendix, for Hoernle's translation.
[3] See *Jaina Sūtras*, SBE, II, pp. 419 ff.

about the future growth of the royal monastery as a far-famed and model seat of learning. The sceptic is free to doubt if the prophecy was not a fiction invented *ex post facto*, but the monastery founded by the king actually became the nucleus of a great *Mahāvihāra*.

(ii) *Nālandā of the Guptas*

The story of the foundation of the *Mahāvihāra* is told by Hsüan-tsang.[1] It reproduces no doubt the local tradition about it: repeated by a Korean monk Prajñāvarman also, who visited Nālandā about four decades after Hsüan-tsang.[2]

The name of the royal founder of Nālandā is given as Śakrāditya by both Hsüan-tsang and Prajñāvarman. It occurs in a seal discovered at Nālandā.[3]

The Gupta kings were known by variant names and, following this clue, Śakrāditya has been identified with Kumāragupta I who reigned in *c.* 415–55.[4] He was known also synonymously as Mahendrāditya.[5] Fa-hsien toured northern India in AD 400–11 and visited both Pāṭaliputra and Gayā from neither of which places Nālandā is far away.[6] But he mentions only a village named Nāla in Nālandā's neighbourhood which was celebrated as the birthplace of Śāriputra.[7] If the foundation of Nālandā had been in Kumāragupta I's reign, it would explain why it is not mentioned by Fa-hsien.

It seems that with the establishment of Śakrāditya's monastery, the site of Nālandā acquired a new interest for the Gupta rulers. Prajñāvarman says that 'the foundation was laid, but the work for some time was stopped'. The monastery of Śakrāditya was afterwards added to by several kings of the Gupta dynasty who built monasteries of their own on different sides of the original structure. Four of these kings are mentioned by Hsüan-tsang—Buddhagupta, Tathāgatagupta, Bālāditya and Vajra.

Buddhagupta (son or grandson of Śakrāditya)[8] built a monastery to the south of the original one; Tathāgatagupta another to the east of Buddhagupta's; Bālāditya built a three-storeyed pavilion (temple and monastery combined) and signalized the occasion by a religious convocation to which some Chinese monks were invited who, how-

[1] See Beal's *Buddhist Records*, ii, pp. 168–170.
[2] See Part IV, Appendix (under *Prajñāvarman*) (p. 312).
[3] See *Memoir of Archaeological Survey of India* (by H. Sastri), No. 66, p. 38.
[4] 'The earliest date of his reign, AD 415, is known from his Bilsad inscription, while his silver coins give his last date, AD 455.'—Sudhakara Chattopadhya's *Early History of North India* (Calcutta, 1958), p. 175.
[5] See Ray Chaudhuri's *Political History of Ancient India*, 6th Ed., pp. 570–571.
[6] From modern Patna, about fifty-six miles; from Gayā forty-nine miles.
[7] Mr Ghosh, however, is of opinion that Nāla, Nālaka, Nālakagrāma and Nālandā are all variants of the same place-name. See Ghosh's *A Guide to Nālandā*, 2nd Ed., p. 39.
[8] See Ray Chaudhuri's *Political History*, p. 517, footnote, about Buddhagupta's relationship to Mahendrāditya.

ever, failed to attend; Vajra, his son, built a monastery to the west of Bālāditya's.

This gives five monasteries of Gupta foundation in a space of time which may roughly be computed as a century and a decade. Whether other monasteries of private foundation had gone up during this period is not known. But we have it from Hsüan-tsang that, after Vajra's time, a certain 'king of central India' built another monastery to the north of Vajra's and that 'he built round these edifices a high wall with one gate'. Thus the separate monasteries which had gone up one by one were brought into aggregation. The whole was converted into a *Mahāvihāra*, a unitary establishment, and started to function as such. Several specimens of the later official seal of the establishment, a device of the 'Pāla age', bear the inscription: 'Of the venerable Monk-community of Nālandā Mahāvihāra (*Nālandā-mahāvihārīya-ārya-bhikṣu-saṅghasya*)', setting forth its unitary corporate character.[1]

The builder of the enclosing wall 'with a single gate' is not named by Hsüan-tsang, but only described as a 'king of Central India'. Yaśodharmadeva, whose exploits are described in the Mandasor Pillar Inscriptions, set himself up between AD 530 and 535 as ruler over an area which certainly included 'central India'. 'It is not improbable', says Ray Chaudhuri, 'that he defeated and killed Vajra, the son of Bālāditya.'[2] If it was Yaśodharman who had walled in the monasteries, Nālandā as a *Mahāvihāra* was a little over a century old when Hsüan-tsang visited it.

In Gupta coins and epigraphic records, no Buddhist sign or symbol appears. Kings of this dynasty professed Brāhmaṇical faith. Of Nālandā's royal patrons among them, Bālāditya only is said to have received training in his youth under the great Mahāyānist philosopher, Vasubandhu.[3] His son and successor Vajra is said by Hsüan-tsang to have been 'firm in faith'. The coins of the other two Gupta kings, each the builder of a monastery at Nālandā, do not show any Buddhist sign or symbol. Nālandā's founder, Śakrāditya (assuming his identity with Kumāragupta I), himself performed the Horse Sacrifice and had the image either of Kārtikeya (God of war in Hindu mythology) or of a peacock (Kārtikeya's bird-mount) imprinted on several of his coins.[4]

[1] See Ghosh's *A Guide to Nālandā*, 2nd Ed., p. 37. See pp. 352–353, for official seals of *Mahāvihāras* under Pāla regime.

[2] Ray Chaudhuri's *Political History*, etc., p. 597. 'Yaśodharman must have come to power after AD 529, for Yuan Chwang speaks of a king of central India as the successor of Vajra, the son of Bālāditya, and this king of Central India has been rightly identified with Yaśodharman.'—Sudhakara Chattopadhyaya's *Early History of North India*, p. 199.

[3] See Part IV, Sec. 5, p. 284.

[4] See Ray Chaudhuri's *Political History*, p. 568.

The question must suggest itself—why a Gupta king of Brāhmaṇical faith and in an age when Brāhmaṇism was in the ascendant should deliberately choose a Buddhist site and build a Buddhist monastery there? A liberal attitude towards Buddhism is hardly sufficient to explain the active patronage and promotion by these Gupta kings of Buddhist monastic life and its activities. I-tsing reports that the lands in possession of the Nālandā establishment contained more than 200 villages and that 'they had been bestowed (upon Nālandā) by kings of many generations'.[1] The motive for all this liberality and generous assistance is perhaps to be found in the fact that, by the time of Śakrāditya, Buddhist monasteries had developed as seats and centres of learning. To build monasteries and provide for their upkeep was regarded more as a service rendered to the cause of learning and culture than to the cause of Buddhism.

The Gupta monasteries at Nālandā, one may legitimately assume, were following the academic tradition of monasteries, functioning as seminaries of learning for about a century, when their conversion in the third or fourth decade of the sixth century into a unitary establishment facilitated an overall organization of teaching and learning in them.

(iii) *The University: its Academic and Social Life*

Nālandā developed into a monastic university. Functioning as such over a century or so, the fame it acquired is evident from the eagerness of foreign monk-scholars, coming to India from abroad, to resort to Nālandā for higher studies.

Chinese monk-scholars had already begun to travel to India in the footsteps of Fa-hsien. They were attracted by its fame and, about the time when Hsüan-tsang was at Nālandā, Tibetans also had started on a cultural intercourse with India and come to know of the Nālandā Mahārihāra as India's premier Buddhist seat of learning.

The academic life and activities that prevailed here at the peak of its fame in the seventh century are known to us almost exclusively from Chinese sources. These give, however, no full-length description; scraps of information have to be pieced together, out of which a complete picture hardly appears. Yet is is clear that Nālandā in that century was regarded as a seat and seminary of *higher learning*—to put it in modern terms, as an institution of university grade. This is indicated by its insistence on entrance qualifications.

In that century it was customary in Indian monasteries of a better sort to maintain a register of inmates. I-tsing came to know of this custom at the Varāha Monastery of Tāmralipti on setting foot in

[1] Takakusu's *A Record of the Buddhist Religion*, p. 65. But Hwui-li gives the number as 100 besides large donations in kind (*Life*, p. 112).

India.[1] One who violated the rules and regulations of the monastery was 'expelled without sounding the *ghantā* (bell)'. The precise significance of the expression is not clear, but probably it meant 'secretly'. I-tsing found, on going to Nālandā, that its 'rites' (i.e. rules and regulations) were 'still more strict'. For this extra strictness, a special reason probably existed, for we are told by Hwui-li that in the whole history of Nālandā no case of 'guilty rebellion against the rules', and presumably the consequent expulsion, ever happened.[2]

The reason seems to have been that Nālandā had to cope with a rush for admission to its schools of study. To have taken a course here was a matter of prestige and many 'usurped the name of Nālandā students'.[3] Hence registration and admission was tightened up: it was made conditional on success in a severe intellectual test, thus described by Hsüan-tsang: 'If men of other quarters desire to enter and take part in the discussions, the keeper of the gate proposes some hard questions; many are unable to answer, and retire. One must have studied deeply both old and new (books) before getting admission. Those students, therefore, who come here as strangers (i.e. intending entrants), have to show their ability by hard discussion; those who fail compared with those who succeed are as seven or eight to ten.'[4]

The designation of the officer in charge of this 'screening examination' is given as *'men-che'* in Chinese which is translated as janitor or porter, but he must have been a responsible officer of considerable learning with sufficient ability to pronounce on the merits of candidates for admission.

It does not appear that any fixed period of residence was prescribed. It was determined perhaps by the time taken by the learner to complete his study of the subject selected. The conferment of a degree or diploma at the end of the course does not appear to have been the custom at Nālandā. Hsüan-tsang who studied Yogācāra philosophy with Śīlabhadra was in residence for about six years and I-tsing for ten. Both had had a solid grounding of scholarship before they joined.

The traditionary 'Five *Vidyās*' constituted liberal learning in that age.[5] The studies obtainable at Nālandā are described generally by Hwui-li thus:[6]

'The priests, belonging to the convent, or strangers (residing therein) (i.e. *who came from outside and joined it*) . . . all study the Great

[1] Takakusu's *A Record of the Buddhist Religion*, p. 65.
[2] Beal's *Life of Hiuen-Tsiang*, p. 112.
[3] Beal's *Buddhist Records*, ii, p. 170.
[4] *Ibid*, pp. 170–171.
[5] See Part V, Sec. 1, p. 323.
[6] Beal's *Life of Hiuen-tsiang*, p. 112.

Vehicle, and also the works belonging to the eighteen (*Hīnayāna*) sects, and not only so, but even ordinary (i.e. secular) works, such as the Vedas and other books, the *Hetuvidyā* (Logic), *Śabdavidyā* (Grammar and Philology), *Cikitsāvidyā* (Medicine), the works on Magic (*Atharva-veda*), Sāṅkhya (system of philosophy); besides these, they thoroughly investigate the miscellaneous works (*by which is probably meant works of literature and general knowledge*).'

Nālandā, being a seat of higher learning, had a system of specialization. There were 'schools of studies'. They are significantly described as 'schools of discussion', implying that, besides formal instruction given by teachers, it was the regular practice to throw open the subject taught for discussion and investigation from different angles and standpoints. Hsüan-tsang describes these discussions as 'hard', i.e. making a high demand on intellectual ability and acquired learning. Those who passed the preliminary test and joined a 'school', says Hsüan-tsang, 'are sure to be humbled and to forfeit their renown', if they are of moderate talent, 'when they come to discuss in turn in the assembly.'[1]

'But', continues Hsüan-tsang, 'those of conspicuous talent and solid learning, great ability, illustrious virtue—distinguished men—these connect (their high names) with the succession (of celebrities) belonging to Nālandā such as Dharmapāla and others (whom Hsüan-tsang names as the most distinguished products of the university) and still others whose names are lost.'[2]

Legend ekes out the names listed by Hsüan-tsang with those of some great Mahāyānist *ācāryas* who certainly had flourished earlier than the sixth century, before Nālandā became a *Mahāvihāra* and full-fledged university—*ācāryas* like Nāgārjuna and others.[3]

Much as we may wish one of the learned Chinese monks who visited Nālandā had left a sketch of a 'discussion' held in one of the schools to illustrate the high intellectual level of these discussions they speak of, no such sketch exists. But some light is thrown by Hwui-li on the arrangement of teaching.

We are told by him that about 100 pulpits used to be arranged daily for the delivery of discourses, evidently in different 'schools', and that 'the students attended them without any fail even for a minute'.[4] Counting their total number, as given by I-tsing, at round 3,000, each discourse must have been attended by a class of about thirty students. Irrespective of their special subjects, they all had to study Mahāyāna philosophy.

[1] Beal's *Buddhist Records*, ii, p. 171. [2] *Ibid.*
[3] See Part IV, Sec. 5. [4] Beal's *Life of Hiuen-tsiang*, p. 112.

This philosophy was really the *forte* of Nālandā learning; it gives point to Vincent Smith's remark that 'a detailed history of Nālandā would be a history of Mahāyānist Buddhism'.[1] Almost all the names listed by Hsüan-tsang as Nālandā's finest products are names of those who developed Mahāyānist philosophy. 'Each of them composed some tens of treatises and commentaries which were widely diffused and which for their perspicuity are passed down to the present time.'[2] The name of Nālandā stood for this philosophy.

But by Hīnayānists it was scoffed at as 'sky-flower philosophy'. The story is told by Hwui-li that when King Harṣavardhana had constructed near Nālandā a magnificent monastery about a hundred feet in height and covered with plates of brass, Hīnayānist monks of Orissa approached him on his arrival in their country, and the following passage took place between the monks and the king:[3]

Monks: We hear that the king has built by the side of the Nālandā convent a *vihāra* of brass, a work magnificent and admirable. But why did not your majesty construct a *Kāpālika* temple, or some other building of that sort?
The King: What mean you by these words of reproach?
Monks; The Monastery of Nālandā with its 'sky-flower doctrine' is not different from that of a *Kāpālika* sect—this is our meaning.

The *Śūraṅgama Sūtra*, composed by Dharmapāla at Nālandā,[4] contains a brilliant exposition of the illusory, 'sky-flower' character of all objective phenomena.[5]

The normal tempo of Nālandā's academic and intellectual life is indicated by Hsüan-tsang's eloquent words of praise:[6]

'The day is not sufficient for the asking and answering of profound questions. From morning till night they engage in discussion; the old and the young mutually help one another. Those who cannot discuss

[1] *Encyclopaedia of Religion and Ethics*, Vol. IX (under Nālandā), p. 127.
[2] Beal's *Buddhist Records*, ii, pp. 171–172.
[3] Beal's *Life of Hiuen-tsiang*, p. 159. [4] See Part IV, Sec. 3, pp. 264–265.
[5] Compare the following two passages from the translation of the *Śūraṅgama-sūtra* in Goddard's *A Buddhist Bible*:
'In comparison with the Mind-Essence, all conditioned things are as empty as space. Existing as they do under conditions, they are false and fantastic; unconditioned things, having neither appearance nor disappearance, are as imaginary as blossoms seen in the air' (p. 255). 'Ānanda! As you return to the phenomenal world, it will seem like a vision in a dream. And your experience with the maiden Pchiti will seem like a dream, and your own body will lose its solidity and permanency. It will seem as though every human being, male or female, was simply a manifestation by some skilful magician of a manikin all of whose activities were under his control. Or each human being will seem like an automatic machine that once started goes on by itself, but as soon as the automatic machine loses its motive power, all its activities not only cease but their very existence disappears' (p. 259).
[6] Beal's *Buddhist Records*, ii, p. 170.

questions out of the *Tripiṭaka* are little esteemed and are obliged to hide themselves for shame. Learned men from different cities, on this account, who desire to acquire quickly a renown in discussion, come here in multitudes to settle their doubts, and then the streams (of their wisdom) spread far and wide.'

It is a testimony at the same time to the manner in which the culture of Nālandā gained currency among India's intelligentsia of that age.

The routine of daily life was mainly divided between two occupations—study and religious rites. Time was regulated by a clepsydra. I-tsing speaks of clepsydrae (water-clocks) being much used in the great monasteries of India.[1] 'These, together with some boys who watch them, are gifts from kings of many generations, for the purpose of announcing hours to the monasteries.'

The clepsydra was a contraption consisting of a small perforated copper bowl floating in a larger one filled with water, time being noted by each immersion of the smaller bowl and announced regularly. I-tsing describes at some length how it used to be done:[2]

'Commencing from the morning, at the first immersion of the bowl, one stroke of a drum is announced, and at the second immersion, two strokes; at the third immersion, besides four strokes of a drum, two blasts of a conch-shell, and one more beat of a drum are added. This is called the first hour, that is when the sun is in the east between the zenith and the horizon. When the second turn of four immersions of the bowl is done, four strokes (of a drum) are sounded as before, and a conch-shell is also blown, which is followed by two more strokes (of a drum). This is called the second hour, that is the exact (beginning of the) horse-hour (i.e. noon). If the last two strokes are already sounded, priests do not eat (*Note*—This was an ancient Vinaya rule), and, if anyone is found eating, he is to be expelled according to the monastic rites. There are also two hours in the afternoon which are announced in the same way as in the forenoon. There are four hours at night which are similar to those of day. Thus the division of one day and one night together makes eight hours. When the first hour at night ends, the *Karmadāna*[3] announces it to all, by striking a drum in a loft of the monastery. This is the regulation of the clepsydra in the Nālandā monastery. At sunset and at dawn, a drum is beaten ("one round") at the outside of the gate. These unimportant affairs are done by the servants and porters. After sunset till dawn, the priests have never the service of striking the *Ghantā* (Bell), nor is it the business of those servants; but of the

[1] Takakusu's *A Record of the Buddhist Religion*, p. 144.
[2] *Ibid*, p. 145. [3] See *infra*, p. 338.

Karmadāna (*Note*—That is, perfect silence is maintained at night unless, for any special reason, the *Karmadāna* wants to awaken the sleeping inmates).'

The hours of worship and the holding of 'classes' were no doubt fixed with reference to regulation time on the clepsydra.

In Nālandā's excavated ruins a row of monasteries and a row of temples run parallel with a stretch of bare ground in between. Presumably the inmates crossed this ground to go from monastery to temple. The rites performed, the rest of the day was given to studies and discussion, the inmates meeting at stated hours for lectures and discourses in separate groups in the different 'schools'.

There was, however, no united congregational worship; it was held in different halls. 'In the Nālandā Monastery', says I-tsing,[1] 'the number of priests (i.e. monks) is immense, and exceeds three thousand; it is difficult to assemble so many together. There are eight halls and three hundred apartments (i.e. blocks of monks' cells) in this monastery. The worship can only take place separately, as most convenient to each member. Thus it is customary to send out every day one precentor to go round from place to place chanting hymns,[2] preceded by monastic lay servants and children bearing incense and flowers. The precentor goes from hall to hall, and in each he chants the service—three or five *ślokas* (verses) in a high tone, and the sound is heard all around. At twilight he finishes this duty. (For this service, I-tsing adds, the precentor receives a special gift.) In addition, there are some who, sitting alone and facing the shrine, "praise the Buddha in their hearts". There are others "who, going to the temple (in a small party), kneel side by side with their bodies upright, and, putting their hands on the ground, touch it with their heads, and thus perform the Threefold Salutation".'

The Gupta monasteries of Nālandā were built in the old traditional Kuṣāṇa-age pattern—a spacious square courtyard flanked on all sides with a running verandah with the monks' cells at the back. Some of these courtyards and their verandahs with rows of supporting pillars (of which only the sockets show now), and the monks' cells behind, are still to be seen among the ruins.

In some of them a shrine with a dais in front on a lower level appears. It was in these courtyards, it seems, that lectures and discourses used to be delivered—the preceptor standing or sitting on the dais with a pulpit in front of him to spread his manuscripts upon, while the students squatted round him. A well and a small set of

[1] Takakusu's *A Record of the Buddhist Religion*, pp. 154–55.

[2] Takakusu's note on this is that the Chinese expression here means 'To send out one teacher who takes the lead in chanting'.

open ovens also are seen in some of these courtyards: perhaps they were meant to meet the occasional physical needs of students during the prolonged lecture-hours.

One may pause for a moment to consider how this simple seating arrangement served to call up the proper atmosphere. Within the shrine stood the holy image—Avalokiteśvara or Tārā. With eyes that never winked seeming to watch the proceedings, it dominated the

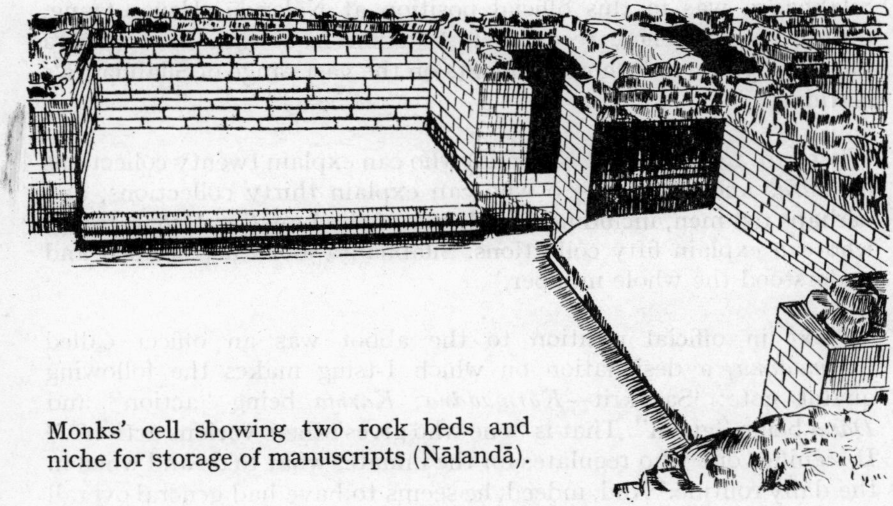

Monks' cell showing two rock beds and niche for storage of manuscripts (Nālandā).

scene. During the discourse and the following discussion, nothing false or frivolous, rude or unholy might be uttered. The oneness of learning and religion could hardly find a more emphatic or impressive articulation.

Studies did not end with these lectures and discussions. In several monks' cells, more spacious and better arranged at Nālandā than is usual in the monastic ruins, an adjacent cell too small to live in is occasionally provided. Perhaps it was intended for the safe keeping of manuscripts borrowed for private study.

A Saṅgha in that age had place for a chief or abbot, though the ancient Vinaya rules make no provision for it.[1] It recognized a head. Perhaps such an institution developed late in Saṅgha history; it continues to this day in all Asian Buddhist countries where it is an old established custom to have a functionary, called by different names, acting as the chief of a monastic establishment.

It was the rule at Nālandā. In its history and legends names occur of learned monks of the highest eminence—some among them

[1] See *Early Buddhist Monachism*, pp. 143–44.

ācāryas and makers of *śāstras*—who are said to have held the headship of the establishment. Though Nālandā may have had a succession of abbots from its beginning as a Mahāvihāra, the genuine historical names appear only in the Chinese pilgrims' records. Little definite is known about the powers and functions of the head or of his official designation—*Adhyakṣa* (as he was called at Vikramaśilā) or something else. It seems, however, from the Chinese and Tibetan accounts, that he was expected to be the most erudite man in the Saṅgha. Śīlabhadra was in this official position at Nālandā. Hsüan-tsang, during his residence, received instruction from him in Yogācāra philosophy. Hwui-li thus comments on the vast range of Śīlabhadra's learning:[1]

'There are 1,000 men (at Nālandā) who can explain twenty collections of *Sūtras* and *Śāstras*; 500 who can explain thirty collections, and perhaps ten men, including the Master of the Law (i.e. Hsüan-tsang) who can explain fifty collections. Śīlabhadra alone has studied and understood the whole number.'

Next in official position to the abbot was an officer called *Karmadāna*, a designation on which I-tsing makes the following quaint note: 'Sanskrit—*Karmadāna*; *Karma* being "action" and *Dāna* being "given". That is "one who gives others various action".'[2] It signifies one who regulates for the inmates what to do and when in the daily routine.[3] And, indeed, he seems to have had general overall charge of management—superintending the buildings,[4] regulating time,[5] arranging the order of precedence at a congregational feast,[6] etc.—in short, preserving regularity and order in the establishment.

We have referred already to another important officer—the 'Doorkeeper' who used to hold the 'screening examination' of candidates seeking admission to one of the 'schools' of Nālandā.

Towards the northern end of its excavated row of monasteries, the ruins of a grand staircase leading into rooms on an upper level is to be seen.[7] It may have been the way of entrance to the offices of the university. It would hardly be practicable to run efficiently an establishment of that size without several office rooms for administrative officers.

The amenities of life for the inmates seem, from the evidence of

[1] Beal's *Life of Hiuen-tsaing*, p. 112.
[2] Takakusu's *A Record of the Buddhist Religion*, p. 148.
[3] The form of the name would be hardly correct in Sanskrit etymology. But I-tsing not only gives it thus, but shows its derivation in a note which will appear a little absurd to a Sanskrit grammarian. See also reference to *Karmadāna* by the Korean monk Prajñāvarman in Part IV, Appendix.
[4] *Ibid*, p. 84. [5] *Ibid*, pp. 145, 146. [6] *Ibid*, p. 102.
[7] It is in Monastery Site, No. 1—See Ghosh's *Guide to Nalanda*, p. 9.

existing remains, to have been a little superior to those provided in ordinary monasteries. The cells have more space and the stone beds therein more breadth; an extra cell is sometimes added for storage of books and personal belongings. The lighting arrangements cannot be traced. Bathrooms were not provided, though for laundering clothes, an arrangement is seen at one place among the ruins where there is a set of cells with a central water-reservoir and a stone slab at the opening of each cell for thrashing dirt out of wet clothes. A time in the forenoon was appointed for all residents to go out for a bath and was announced by striking a bell. There were ten great ponds on the campus. All inmates would move out of their rooms, each with a bathing suit, for the open-air bath. 'Sometimes a hundred, sometimes a thousand, leave the monastery and proceed in all directions to these ponds, where all of them take a bath.'[1]

No community kitchen or common dining-room can be traced among the ruins; there are only a few open ovens scattered here and there in the courtyards where snacks or merely small quantities of food could be cooked. This has often surprised visitors to the Nālandā ruins. But an explanation of this lack comes from I-tsing:[2]

'What we call a monastery', says I-tsing, 'is a general designation for the place of residence (for the Saṅgha), the whole of which may be regarded as a monastic kitchen. In every apartment, raw and cooked food may be kept. (But), if sleeping in the monastery is not allowed, all the priests then residing must go out and lodge somewhere (else); . . . the keeping of provisions in a monastery is allowable (according to Vinaya). . . . The traditional custom of India is to consecrate the whole monastery as a "kitchen", but to take a part of it to be used as a kitchen is also allowed by the Buddha.'

It seems that food used to be prepared in a closet or compartment within the monastery and taken by the inmates to their own cells and eaten there. Toilet arrangements also are conspicuous by their absence and the lack seems to suggest either that the Indian practice of defecation at a secluded spot out in the fields obtained or that there were trench-latrines now untraceable.

What the numerical strength and size of the University was at the time when the Chinese pilgrims visited or came to reside in it is an interesting question. The institution had then been growing for over a century; it was under royal patronage; the revenues of 200 villages had been earmarked for its upkeep;[3] people came here from different

[1] Takakusu's *A Record of the Buddhist Religion*, pp. 108–9. [2] *Ibid*, p. 84.

[3] See Takakusu's *A Record of the Buddhist Religion*, p. 65. But, according to Hwui-li, it was a hundred, *plus* contributions in kind of rice, butter and milk (*Life of Hiuen-tsiang*, p. 122).

quarters to reside and receive its benefits. The number of inmates, says Hwui-li, 'always reach the number of 10,000'.[1] This, however, looks like a gross exaggeration, for I-tsing who came to Nālandā only about three decades after Hsüan-tsang puts the number at 'upwards of 3,000' in his Record and as 3,500 in his Memoirs.[2] I-tsing's count is perhaps more reliable, though, judging from the size of the ruins, so far excavated, even this appears to be an overstatement. From the Chinese evidence, Nālandā does not seem to have been far ahead in numerical strength of the other great monastic establishments of the time. But it was probably the consequence of the strictness of its rule of admission.

Monks of Nālandā enjoyed prestige in society. They, as a body, are characterized as 'dignified and grave',[3] and the 'venerable and learned' among them used to ride in sedan-chairs when going out, with attendants to carry their baggage. This was probably a mark of dignity and rank, for we are told that those of the 'Mahārājā Monastery' also did the same.[4]

(iv) *The Campus and its Ruins*

The campus caught and ravished the eye by its grandeur and magnificence. There are three impressionist sketches of it of three different centuries—the first, Hsüan-tsang's of AD 637, the second, Mālāda's of a century later in a dedicatory inscription, and the third, Dharmasvāmī's who came to Nālandā in 1235 when it lay sprawled amidst its widespread ruins.

Hsüan-tsang's description comes through the summarized version of Hwui-li.[5] It is a totalist impression, presented in a dazzle of colour and splendour, of Nālandā's 'richly adorned towers and fairy-like turrets, the four-storeyed outside courts, their dragon-like projections and coloured eaves, carved and ornamented pearl-red pillars, richly adorned balustrades and roofs covered with tiles that reflect the light in a thousand shades'.[6] One misses what is of more value to an historian—realistic particulars; only a few appear in Prajñāvarman's later account[7] and in I-tsing's reference to 'Nālandā's eight halls and three hundred apartments'.[8] All this superlative wealth of architecture and sculpture Hwui-li so ecstatically describes must have been Nālandā's heritage from the sumptuous Gupta age.

The same lack of significant details, the same generality of impression, is characteristic also of the description of Nālandā in Mālāda's

[1] *Ibid*, p. 112.
[2] Takakusu's *A Record of the Buddhist Religion*, p. 154, and footnote 2 on the page.
[3] Beal's *Life of Hiuen-tsiang*, p. 112.
[4] Takakusu's *A Record of the Buddhist Religion*, p. 30.
[5] The words quoted below do not occur in the *Si-yu-ki*.
[6] *Life of Hiuen-tsiang*, pp. 111–12. [7] See Part IV, Appendix (pp. 312–314).
[8] Takakusu's *A Record of the Buddhist Religion*, p. 154.

inscription. It is couched in the usual high-faluting rhetoric of these lithic records:[1]

'Nālandā has scholars well known for (their knowledge of) sacred texts. . . . She has a row of vihāras whose spires lick the clouds. That (row of vihāras) seems to have been built by the Creator himself like a garland hanging up high. Nālandā has temples which are brilliant with the network of rays from various jewels set in them and it is the pleasant abode of a learned and virtuous Saṅgha; and resembles Sumeru, the charming residence of the noble Vidyādharas.'

The Towers, tall and stately, were the most spectacular landmark of the campus. They stood magnificently arow, topping the monastic buildings and soaring above the encompassing wall. When the Tibetan monk Dharmasvāmī visited Nālandā in AD 1235, a good many of these towers were still erect, sentinels then over a scene of utter ruin and desolation.[2] Reduced to dust with the passing of centuries, nothing of them now remains.

New monastery-constructions and alterations of old structures at different periods of Nālandā's history are referred to in legends as well as in lithic records.[3] They must have changed considerably the look of the campus as it had appeared to the eyes of Hsüan-tsang, I-tsing and other pilgrims from the Far East in the seventh century, the peak-period in its annals.

Even when Hsüan-tsang first visited Nālandā, the original monastery of Śakrāditya's foundation was in ruins. It was then about three hundred years old, and 'forty monks were sent from another vihāra to eat their breakfast at it, to keep up the memory of its founder. At I-tsing's time there were only the foundations of this monastery visible'.[4] No trace of Yaśodharmadeva's circuit wall is now extant. Many monasteries in the long history of Nālandā must have been worn down by time and treated in the same way as monasteries elsewhere—the old site not abandoned and new constructions made on the debris of the old.

[1] Hirananda Sastri's translation as given in his article on *Nalanda Stone Inscription in the Reign of Yasodharmadeva* in *Epigraphia Indica*, Vol. XX, p. 45. Slightly modified. A fresh translation (abbreviated) will be found in Ghosh's *Guide to Nalanda*, pp. 34–35.

[2] See *infra*, p. 347.

[3] King Bālaputradeva of Suvarṇadvīpa (Sumatra) built a monastery to which King Devapāla (*c.* 815–54) granted five villages (*Epigraphia Indica*, Vol. xvii, pp. 310 ff.). Muditabhadra, a Buddhist sage, is said to have built a large number of temples and monasteries at Nālandā after Turaṣka ravages according to a Tibetan legend (see Index in S. C. Das's *Pag-jam-jon-zang*). Vipulaśrīmitra built a vihāra (Monastery Site No. 7—See Ghosh's *Guide to Nalanda*, p. 35). Vīradeva in the reign of Devapāla (*c.* 815–54) made reconstructions and repairs (see Devapāla's inscription in *Epigraphia Indica*, Vol. xvii, pp. 310 ff.).

[4] Watters, *On Yuan Chawng*, Vol. II, p. 167.

Its present ruins are a complex of *stūpas*, temples and monasteries. While they give us no idea of what the campus was like originally, we can trace from them some of the features noted in the descriptions of the ancient eye-witnesses. But the most spectacular feature, the towers, which seemed from a distance like a 'garland of architecture hung up in the sky'—some visible even so late as in the third decade of the thirteenth century—has completely disappeared.

In the block of monasteries (eleven of them have been exposed by archaeological excavation) there are passages between one mass of monastic ruins and another, indicating that the original structures were built separately, as tradition reports, and did not adjoin one another. The different storeys of a monastery can hardly be distinguished, but the arrangements for drainage and the outflow of water from storey to storey are still visible. Traces of damage caused by outbreaks of fire are seen on the bricks, but they show at the same time that conflagrations, of which there are legends in Tibetan histories and mention in one inscription of the eleventh year of Mahīpāla's reign (*c.* 988–1026),[1] were localized and did not spread over or destroy the whole campus. It is evident from the ruins that all the architectural constructions were solid and substantial and, though not fireproof, could not be wholly destroyed by fire. The only part of the campus that entirely perished in a conflagration, if we can rely upon a Tibetan legend, was Dharmagañja where the library buildings were, providing huge combustible materials to feed the fire on for hours.

Curiously enough, there is no mention of these library buildings in the Chinese records.

Tibetans, however, had started coming to Nālandā at the time Hsüan-tsang was in residence there. Sron-btsan (born in AD 617), the Tibetan king, had sent to Nālandā a scholar who had been in his own country a minister to him. He was Thonmi Sambhota. Commissioned by the king who, under the influence of his Chinese Buddhist wife, had a leaning to Buddhism, Thonmi Sambhota left Tibet to study the religion at its source in India. He returned after a course of study at Nālandā to report on what he had learnt. The king was converted and Buddhism was for the first time declared the State religion of Tibet.[2] Thonmi Sambhota is credited with having remodelled the Tibetan language on the principles of Sanskrit grammar. It is not

[1] This inscription was found at Nālandā in 1863, before the commencement of systematic excavation of the site by the Archaeological Department. It speaks of the restoration of a door-jamb after a fire ('*Agnidāhoddhāre*'). See Broadley's *Ruins of the Nalanda Monasteries at Burgaon* (1872).

[2] See Waddell's *Buddhism of Tibet* (2nd Ed., 1934), pp. 21–22. Almost all the histories of Tibet mention this event and trace from it the beginnings of culture and religion in the country, e.g. *Blue Annals*, vol. I, p. 39.

known who came from Tibet in the footsteps of this pioneer, but they evidently carried home reports of what they had seen at India's premier monastic university. Nālandā became in the eyes of later generations of Tibetans the name and symbol for a monastic establishment that concerned itself with study and learning and philosophy. In 1351, a monastery named *Nālandā* was founded in Tibet and maintained a 'school of philosophy'. 'This great monastery was a place filled with monks of different sects, where preaching and study continued without interruption. . . . It was a self-refuge for preachers who wandered about the country.'[1] The Tibetan monastery, it appears, was modelled on Nālandā's liberal traditions of culture. So it proudly bore Nālandā's name.

Tibetan legends supplement to some extent the Chinese accounts. It is in these legends that mention is found of Nālandā's great library buildings. They were huge many-storeyed edifices located in a part of the campus known as Dharmagañja, and three of them bore the fancy names—*Ratnodadhi* (Sea of jewels), *Ratnasāgara* (Ocean of jewels) and *Ratnarañjaka* (Jewel-adorned). A legend occurs in a Tibetan history written in the eighteenth century, though by its quaint supernatural flavour seems to have been of ancient tradition. These libraries, as it reports, perished in flames kindled by an incendiary.[2] When the event happened is unknown.

We can only surmise that Nālandā came into possession in the course of its centuries-old history of a huge wealth of manuscript literature—both original works written at Nālandā and copies of *sūtras* and *śāstras*. To a monastery which had been built here by a king of Sumatra, King Devapāla (*c.* 810–50) donated the revenue of five villages for the maintenance of monks and *the copying of manuscripts.*[3] During the Pāla age, numerous manuscripts must have been written and copies of old manuscripts made in Nālandā's monasteries. But few have survived. Three copies made in the Pāla age of

[1] *Blue Annals*, Vol. II, pp. 1081–84.

[2] The story is that Kukutasiddha, who was a minister to the reigning king, erected a temple at Nālandā. 'At its inauguration ceremony two heretic beggars came. These two naughty *śramaṇeras* threw dirty water on the workmen, pressed them between two doors (and caused them other troubles), at which they became angry. One of them helped the other who entered a deep hole and in twelve years propitiated the sun-god. After performing a *Yajña*, they threw ashes in eighty-four Buddhist temples and all were on fire, especially *Dharmagañja* of Nālandā and the three great temples containing the scriptures. When all of them were ablaze, streams of water gushed forth (i.e. miraculously) from the *Guhyasamāja* (manuscript of a Tāntric work) and the *Prajñāpāramitā* (manuscript of the great Mahāyānist Sūtra) from the ninth storey of the Ratnodadhi temple and many *punthis* (manuscripts) were saved. Afterwards the two heretics out of fear of the king tried to run away to Hasam(?) in the north, but they perished in the fire they themselves had kindled' (see S. C. Das's ed. of *Pag-sam-jon-zang*, p. 92. I am indebted to Dr Lokesh Chandra for the translation).

[3] For the copperplate inscription of this grant discovered in the site of the vihāra, see *Epigraphia Indica*, Vol. xvii, pp. 310 ff.

Nālandā of the voluminous text of the *Aṣṭasāhasrikā-prajñāpāramitā* are known.[1] Stray copies of other works, e.g. *Arthaviniścaya Sūtra* and its commentary (dated AD 1199—*Samvat* 319 of the Nepalese era), in the colophon of which Nālandā Mahāvihāra is mentioned as the place where the author was living, have been discovered outside Indian borders.[2]

(v) *Nālandā in the Pāla Age*

Nālandā was perhaps the longest-lived of the *Mahāvihāras* of India. Its history falls into two main divisions—the first, one of growth, development and fruition from the sixth century to the ninth, when it was dominated by the liberal cultural traditions inherited from the Gupta age; the second, one of gradual decline and final dissolution from the ninth century to the thirteenth—a period during which the Tāntric developments of Buddhism became most pronounced in eastern India under the Pālas and laid their killing influence on Nālandā's culture.[3] We may label the first as the 'Gupta Period' of Nālandā and the second as the 'Pāla Period'. There is also a pre-history of over a century when Nālandā was in the making by Gupta kings from Śakrāditya to Vajra.

The 'Gupta period' of Nālandā closed with the rise of the Pāla dynasty. Its founder Gopāla is said in the Tibetan legends to have founded a *mahāvihāra* of grand proportions in the newly built city of Odantapura, only about six miles from Nālandā. Its name was known to the Arabs as Adwand-Bihār;[4] its modern name is Bihār-Sharif. At the time of its foundation by Gopāla, Nālandā was still functioning and was perhaps not in decline. The Pāla kings were Buddhist, and it may be supposed that Gopāla and his descendants were keen on developing the Odantapura monastery as a parallel, if not a rival, seat of Buddhist learning. In course of time, other seats of learning, for which Nālandā was the most obvious and ready-to-hand exemplar, were established by other kings of the dynasty.

The Pāla establishments must have drawn away a number of learned monks from Nālandā when all of them, including Nālandā itself, came under the aegis of the Pālas. There is evidence in the

[1] (i) Copy made in the sixth year of King Mahīpāla's reign, recovered from Nepal.
(ii) Copy made in the reign of Rāmapāla (*c.* 1084–1126) (see *Catalogue of Sanskrit Buddhist Manuscripts in the Bodlein Library*, Vol. II, p. 250).
(iii) Copy made in the reign of Govindapāla in the later half of twelfth century (*Journal of the Royal Asiatic Society, New Series*, 1876, p. 3).

[2] The library of the University of Delhi is in possession of a copy of the *Arthaviniścaya Sūtra* and its commentary (photostatic), discovered in a monastery of Tibet.

[3] See *infra*, p. 345.

[4] Hodiwala's *Studies in Indo-Muslim History* (Bombay, 1939), p. 89.

Tibetan legends that there used to be migration of scholars from one to another.[1] Nālandā's pride of place must have been largely impaired by these adventitious circumstances. Also, from the eighth century on, Buddhism was shrinking in northern India: it was only in the eastern areas over which the Buddhist Pāla kings ruled that its waning influence lingered and the kings sought to consolidate it by the establishment of new monastic centres.[2] Its once widespread fame in the country that had extended in the seventh century beyond its borders into the Far East and Tibet dwindled to a regional or local reputation.

What is more important and significant is that during the 'Pāla Period' of its history Buddhism itself was already in a phase wherein it was heavily adulterated by the Tāntric cult and its magic spells and practices. 'When Tāranātha says that in the time of the Pāla dynasty of Bengal', observes Winternitz, 'that is to say, from the ninth to the eleventh century (?), *Yoga* and magic were paramount in Buddhism, his statement is probably not far from the truth.'[3] The appearance of Tāntric Buddhism in the learning and culture of Nālandā in the 'Pāla period' is attested by the images of many Tāntric deities recovered from the site.[4] The effect of this on its old cultural standards was to stunt their catholicity of intellectual interests—in fact to reduce culture to a cult.

During the 'Gupta Period', the headship of the establishment used to be reserved for scholars of liberal learning and of wide philosophical outlook, men like Dharmapāla and Śīlabhadra. But this does not seem to have been the practice under the Pālas. Scholarship of a special type was looked for.

Tāranātha (sixteenth–seventeenth century) is the author of a work in which he narrates the lives of a succession of eminent *Siddhas* or *Tantra-Gurus*, i.e. men who had won eminence in and taught the Tantra cult.[5] He professes to have written it 'on the basis of what could be perceived from the histories prepared in India and from what was given in Tibet by the believing people'. The work contains the life-story of a famous *paṇḍita* (learned man) of this category named Abhayākara-gupta who rose in the reign of Mahīpāla to be

[1] See *infra*, p. 353, for evidence of 'migrations'.

[2] Besides the *mahāvihāras* of Odantapura, Vikramaśilā, Somapura and Jagaddala, there were other monasteries, less famous, founded in the Pāla age in Bihar and Bengal, such as (i) Traikūṭaka, (ii) Devīkoṭa, (iii) Paṇḍita, (iv) Sannagara, (v) Phullahari, (vi) Pattikeraka, and (vii) Vikramapurī. See R. C. Majumdar's *History of Bengal* (pub. Dacca University, 1943), Vol. I, p. 417.

[3] Winternitz's *History of Indian Literature*, Vol. II, p. 399.

[4] See Ghosh's *Guide to Nalanda*, pp. 21 ff.

[5] This work was translated from Tibetan into German by Professor Grünwedel and published from Petrograd in 1914. An abstract of this German translation was made by Dr Bhupendranath Datta and published from Ramakrishna Vedanta Math under the title of *Mystic Tales of Lama Taranatha* in 1944 (Reprint 1957).

abbot respectively of the Mahābodhi Monastery (Vajrāsana), of Nālandā and of Vikramaśilā.[1]

He wrote a large number of works which are listed by his biographer. They seem from Tāranātha's comments to have been purely Tāntric interpretations of Mādhyamika and Yogācāra doctrines. It is said that, while writing them, Sambhara, Hevajra and Kālacakra (all Tāntric deities) showered blessings on him and glorified him.[2] 'He made some *Ṭīkās* (Commentaries): the four famous books of exorcism-methods, the *Buddhakapāla-ṭīkā,* commentaries on many *Mātrikā-Tantras* in the form of a *Sūtra* of *Abhayamārga-krama*; the *Pañcakrama-mātikā,* the *Gaṇāvatāra,* and commentaries on and explanations of Kālacakra. He wrote also many text-books and gave numerous subtle exorcism-methods.[3] In India and Tibet there are large numbers of his disciples. All the Indian teachers of the Mahāyāna who came after him openly accepted him as the standard, and so did Śubhākara-gupta. He taught Daśabala, and Daśabala taught Vikṛti-deva. Vikṛti-deva was a well-informed Bengali *paṇḍita*. He went to Nālandā and busied himself much about the *dharma* and all the *Upadeśas* (i.e. Tāntrika Cult and its literature).'[4]

During this period of Tāntric predominance at Nālandā under the Pālas, this centre of liberal learning seems to have fallen from its standard of liberal scholarship to become more and more a centre of studies in Tāntric doctrines and Tāntric magic rites.

The end of Nālandā, after a lifetime of over seven centuries, is shrouded in mystery.

In the Tibetan legends, several raids on Nālandā by the Turaṣkas are spoken of. Not all of them are historical. One raid, incredibly enough, is said to have occurred when Candrakīrti (early seventh century) was its abbot. It is said: 'Without being obstructed by pillars and ramparts of stone and riding a stone-lion, he repulsed the Turaṣka armies'.[5] However brave it may sound, to fight an army from the back of a stone-lion, the Turaṣkas were in their homes outside India and nowhere on Indian borders when Candrakīrti was at Nālandā. The sum of real historical knowledge that Tibetan historians had about Nālandā's end-period is conveyed by

[1] Abhayākaragupta is referred to in *Pag-sam-jon-zang* also (S. C. Das's Ed., p. 120) as having appeared in the forty-sixth year(?) of Rāmapāla's reign. He is said to have been the *adhyakṣa* (Head) of Buddhagaya, Nalendra (Nālānda) and Vikramaśilā. See also article on Abhayākaragupta in *Indian Culture* (ed. by Bhandarkar, Barua and Law, Vol. III—July 1936–April 1937), pp. 369–72.

[2] Datta's *Mystic Tales of Lama Taranatha*, p. 66.

[3] The works of Abhayākaragupta included in the *Tanjur* and *Kanjur* are Nos. 1,499, 1,500, 1,654, 2,484, 2,491, 3,140, 3,142, 3,266, 3,743 in the *Tohoku Imperial University Catalogue*. Those in Cordier's *Catalogue* are listed in Phanindra Nath Boe's *Indian Teachers in Buddhist Universities*, pp. 87–89.

[4] Datta's *Mystic Tales of Lama Taranatha*, pp. 66–67.

[5] S. C. Das's Ed. of *Pag-sam-jon-zang*, p. 94–9.

Tāranātha's generalized statement that 'the Turaṣkas conquered the whole of Magadha and destroyed many monasteries; at Nālandā they did much damage and the monks fled abroad.'[1]

(vi) *The Last Days*

We know on historical evidence that Odantapura Mahāvihāra was sacked and razed to the ground round 1198. Round 1234, when Dharmasvāmī visited it, Odantapura was Muslim military headquarters.[2] Nālandā, only about six miles off, may have been after the sack of Odantapura a target of attack by roving bands of Muslim soldiery. But this mahāvihāra was not demolished like Odantapura and Vikramaśilā, though, as Tāranātha says, much damage was done with the result that many monks deserted it. But the very last report about its condition after the worst had been done by the ravagers, coming from an eye-witness, the Tibetan monk Dharmasvāmī, shows that Nālandā, though doomed to death, was fated not to die, for teaching and learning was going on here over at least four after-decades.

But what a Nālandā it was!—like the strange nightmare of Hsüan-tsang six centuries back when Nālandā was in all its glory brought up by the whirligig of time.

Yet even then the ghost of past magnificence loomed darkly over the desolation. There were still to be seen 'seven great lofty pinnacles (*Śikharas*)' and out to the north, fourteen.[3] Eighty small vihāras, damaged by the Turaṣkas and deserted by monks, were still there and, beyond, as many as eight hundred. The guess could not, however, have been numerically precise. It is impossible to say when this crop of small vihāras had gone up; Dharmasvāmī says only that a Rājā and his queen had built them[4]—probably not very long before the Turaṣka threat descended. Archaeologists have discovered no trace of them: they were probably of flimsy construction.

But somewhere in this melancholy mass of decayed and deserted buildings, a lingering pulse of life feebly went on.

Somewhere here a nonogenarian monk-teacher, named Rāhula Śrībhadra,[5] had made his dwelling and taught Sanskrit grammar to

[1] Schiefner's Translation of Tāranātha's *History of Buddhism*, p. 94.

[2] Dharmasvāmī mentions Odantapura in his travel-record twice as the residence of a Turaṣka military commander (see *Biography of Dharmasvāmin*, Intro., p. xlii.)

[3] Roerich's *Biography of Dharmasvāmin* (pub. by K. P. Jayaswal Research Institute, Patna, 1959), p. 91.

[4] Dharmasvāmī's reference may be to 'Rājā Buddhasena of Magadha' who is said by him to have fled from Gayā into a jungle at the time of Turaṣka raid on Gayā and returned when the raid was over. He is said to have been a patron of the Nālandā teacher and his pupils (see *Biography of Dharmasvāmin*, p. 90).

[5] Rāhula Śrībhadra's name was probably known in Tibet through Dharmasvāmī's narrative, for Tāranātha gives precisely the same information about Śrībhadra and states the number of his pupils as seventy, as told by Dharmasvāmi (see *Biography of Dharmasvāmin*, Altekar's Intro., p. vi).

seventy students. He was in the last stage of poverty and decrepitude. He lived on a small allowance for food given by a Brāhmaṇa lay disciple named Jayadeva who lived at Odantapura. Time and again came threats of an impending raid from the military headquarters there. Jayadeva himself became a suspect. In the midst of these alarms, he was suddenly arrested and thrown into a military prison at Odantapura. While in captivity, he came to learn that a fresh raid on Nālandā was brewing and managed to transmit a message of warning to his master advising him to flee post-haste. By then everyone had left Nālandā except the old man and his Tibetan disciple. Not caring for the little remainder of his own life, the master urged his pupil to save himself by quick flight from the approaching danger. Eventually, however,—the pupil's entreaties prevailing—both decided to quit. They went—the pupil carrying the master on his back along with a small supply of rice, sugar and a few books—to the Temple of Jñānanatha at some distance and hid themselves. While they remained in hiding, 300 Muslim soldiers arrived, armed and ready for the assault. The raid came and passed over. Then the two refugees stole out of their hiding place back again to Nālandā.

Dharmasvāmī says that the Tibetan pupil could after all complete his studies and, after a brief stay, left the place with the teacher's permission. The libraries had perished long, long ago; Dharmasvāmī could not get a scrap of manuscript to copy, though some of the monks there possessed a few manuscripts.[1]

This is the last glimpse vouchsafed to us of Nālandā before its lapse into utter darkness.

[1] This thrilling account of the last days of Nālandā is taken from a Tibetan text kept in a monastery of central Tibet, of which a photostatic copy was brought by Rahula Sankrityayana and left to be edited and translated with the K. P. Jayaswal Research Institute of Patna. The text is entitled 'Biography of Chag lo-tsa-ba Chos-rje-dpal'—the Tibetan name of Dharmasvāmī. It was evidently written by a disciple under his dictation. This Tibetan monk-pilgrim visited some districts of eastern India and was in Bihar in 1234–36. He records in the work his experiences in the country. The work has been edited with an accompanying English translation by Dr G. Roerich (Moscow) and published by the Institute. Dharmasvāmī's account of Nālandā is contained in Chapter X (pp. 90 ff.).

3

The Pāla *Establishments*

NĀLANDĀ was an old establishment—functioning over two centuries as a Mahāvihāra—when Gopāla, round the middle of the eighth century, founded the Pāla royal dynasty and built Odantapura.[1]

The Pālas, as the inscriptions on their coins show, were Buddhists, but the Buddhism professed by them was not what had prevailed in the Gupta age. The religion had entered on a phase in which the Mahāyāna philosophy, of which Nālandā had hitherto been the intellectual stronghold, had slanted off to an esoteric cult known as *Vajrayāna* (Tāntric Buddhism).

The earliest exposition of this cult is in two works, *Guhyasamāja Tantra* and *Mañjuśrī-mūlakalpa*, the latter assignable to the eighth century.[2] Mahāyāna and Vajrayāna were different in orientation; the one being a system of transcendental philosophy, while the other an empirical system. Vajrayāna stemmed undoubtedly out of some of the doctrines of Mahāyānist philosophy. Its sponsors and exponents were known as *Siddhas* or *Tantra-gurus*, corresponding to the ācāryas of Mahāyāna Buddhism. But in its development in their hands it took a shape in which spells and magical rites and practices supposed capable of producing supernatural effects predominated. It enlarged the Mahāyānist pantheon with deities unknown to the older faith.[3] The discovery in the ruins of Nālandā of several Tāntric images, all of which belong to the 'Pāla period' of its history,[4] betrays the emergence at Nālandā of this new development of the faith.

Nālandā of the Pāla period is scarcely represented in Chinese records which assemble so fascinating a picture of it in its earlier, more glorious epoch. In fact there are few instances after the turn of the eighth century of Chinese monks coming to India for study and learning. Perhaps the movement which had started the exodus of Chinese monk-scholars to India was then at its ebb. But from Nālandā and other centres Indian monks did not cease to migrate to

[1] 'His (Gopāla's) accession to the throne may be placed with a tolerable degree of certainty within a decade of AD 750, and he probably ceased to rule about AD 770.'—R. C. Majumdar's *History of Bengal* (Dacca University, 1943), Vol. I, p. 103.

[2] The first of these two works has been published in Gaekwad's Oriental Series; the second (partly) in Trivandrum Sanskrit Series. They are believed to be the earliest available texts on Tāntric Buddhism. See N. Dutt on 'Schools and Sects of Buddhism' in the *Cultural Heritage of India*, Vol. I (published by the Ramakrishna Missions Institute of Culture, Calcutta, 2nd Ed., 1958), p. 487.

[3] See, in *Ibid.*, Benoytosh Bhattachayya's *Mahāyānic Pantheon*, pp. 526 ff.

[4] See Ghosh's *Guide to Nalanda* (Pala Art at Nalanda), pp. 22 ff.

China. They introduced into the country the prevailing Tāntric Buddhism of India of the period.

Thus in AD 716, Śubhākara, a monk of Nālandā, went to the Chinese capital, 'taking with him many Sanskrit texts'. Chinese translations of five of them, made by himself are listed in the Ming-dynasty *Tripiṭaka* catalogue. Vajrabodhi, a Tāntric Buddhist monk, arrived in China from South India in AD 719 and translated many Tāntric texts into Chinese. But the person who gave a fillip to the Buddhism of this school in China was Amoghavajra, a disciple of Vajrabodhi. He is said to have been held in high veneration at the courts of successive Chinese sovereigns. 'Under his influence the Tāntric doctrines . . . first gained currency in China.' He died in that country in AD 779 in his seventieth year.[1] Buddhism had a period of revival under the Sung dynasty after a temporary setback during the struggle for power in China of the 'Five Dynasties'. In the reign of Tai-tsung a number of Indian monks appeared in that country—Dānapāla, Dharmadeva, 'Tien-hsi Tsai' and others, famous in the later history of Chinese Buddhism. Of them Dharmadeva hailed from Nālandā, and, between AD 973 and 1001, he translated numerous Buddhist works into Chinese.[2]

Sino-Indian intercourse, however, was definitely petering out on the Chinese side by the middle of the eighth century. Tibet now took the place of China in cultural intercourse with India.

It had started already with Thonmi Sambhota's residence at Nālandā when Hsüan-tsang also was there.[3] The consequence, as we have noted, of Sambhota's visit to India was the proclamation of Buddhism by the Tibetan king as Tibet's 'State religion'. This set in train a long intercourse between the two countries which lasted throughout the four centuries of Pāla history.

Two outstanding landmarks of this intercourse are noted in Tibetan historiography: (*a*) the mission of Padmasambhava and his followers (eighth century) and (*b*) the mission of Dīpaṅkara Śrījñāna (eleventh century).

Padmasambhava was a saint and scholar of Kashmir, a sojourner in Tibet at the time, who was assisted in his missionary work in that country by two eminent scholars of Nālandā, Śāntārakṣita and his pupil Kamalaśīla.[4] They instituted the lamaist system in Tibet and

[1] For Śubhākara, Vajrabodhi and Amoghavajra, see Nanjio's *Catalogue*, Appendix II.

[2] See Nanjio's *Catalogue*, Appendix II, 450–51, and 453, and also Chou's *Indo-Chinese Relations*, pp. 163–68.

[3] See Part V, Sec. 2, p. 342.

[4] About these two distinguished scholars of Nālandā, whose works are preserved in Tibetan translation in the canonical collections, see S. C. Vidyabhusan's *Indian Logic: Mediaeval School*, pp. 124–30. The main work of Śāntārakṣita entitled *Tattvasaṁgraha* and Kamalaśīla's commentary on it have been discovered in the Pattana Bhandara and published in G.O. Series, Baroda. See Part IV, Sec. 1.

established the first Buddhist monastery at Sam-yas, of which Śāntarakṣita was named the first abbot.[1] But Buddhism thus established had to counter the native *Bon* cults and its final victory was achieved only through Dīpaṅkara's thirteen years' missionary labour in Tibet.[2]

The comings and goings between Tibet and eastern India of Tibetan lamas and Indian Paṇḍitas, through the windswept winding *la*'s (passes) of the eastern Himalayas, never came to a stop till the last days of the Pālas. In one of the last batches of these lamas was Dharmasvāmī who visited eastern India in 1234–36.[3]

Proofs of this intercourse appear in the history of the Pāla establishments. At Vikramaśilā, Tibetan lamas seem to have been held in great esteem. At least one Tibetan scholar is known to have been appointed a *dvāra-pāla* of Vikramaśilā.[4] The famous Tāntric saint (*siddha*) and scholar Naropa held, about the time when Dīpaṅkara left Vikramaśilā for Tibet, the office of the 'Keeper of the Northern Gate of the establishment.[5] Here Tibetan scholars, one of whom had the Indian name Dharmakīrti,[6] translated Sanskrit works into Tibetan. Indian monks of these Pāla establishments seem thus, through contacts with the lamas, to have become conversant with the Tibetan language. Later in time, in the Jagaddala monastery, two Indian monks Vibhūticandra and Dānaśīla not only wrote original works in Tibetan, but also translated a large number of Sanskrit works into that language; they are in the Tibetan canonical collection.[7] After the flight of their *guru* Śākya Śrībhadra, these two Jagaddala scholars became fugitives in Nepal and Tibet from the Muslim terror, like many other monks before them and in their time.

The Pāla dynasty had stemmed from northern Bengal (Varendra) where Gopāla, its founder, had been 'elected' king after a spell of anarchy and turmoil. The dynasty did not rule in peace; there were strong kings and weak kings. During the long regime of Gopāla's successors, the limits of their dominion expanded and shrank, varied and shifted, many times. Tibetan legends and modern researches do not agree about the names of the dynasts nor of their order of succession,[8] but outstanding names like Dharmapāla, Devapāla,

[1] See Part V, Sec. 3, footnote 1 at p. 355.
[2] See Part V, Sec. 3, for Dīpaṅkara's life and work in Tibet at pp. 363 ff.
[3] See Part V, Sec. 2, p. 359. [4] See Roerich's *Life of Dharmasvāmin*, Intro., p. xl.
[5] Naropa was the disciple of a Tibetan saint named Tilopa. Naropa's works are found in Tibetan. His life in Tibetan historiography is heavily embroidered with grotesque miraculous legends. He was perhaps not a Tibetan, but an Indian who was steeped in Tibetan Buddhist lore.
[6] See Phanindra Nath Bose's *Indian Teachers of Buddhist Universities*, pp. 94–5.
[7] See Part V, Sec. 3, under Jagaddala.
[8] A list of the Pāla kings (with dates), compiled from Tibetan sources, is given in Satish Chandra Vidyabhushan's *Indian Logic: Mediaeval School*, Appendix B. It may be compared with the account of the kings, based on modern researches, in Nihar Ranjan Ray's *Bāṅgālir Itihāsa* (in Bengali), pp. 475 ff. For the lists, see Appendix I.

Mahīpāla, Nyāyapāla, Rāmapāla, etc., are common. The Pāla kingdom lived throughout under a constant threat of Muslim invasion from the *Doab*, the bordering region of the Uttar Pradesh between the Ganges and the Jumna, where the *Turaṣkas*, Khilijis from Afghanistan, had settled themselves with expansionist aims.

The political history of the Pālas is a chequer-board of successes and failures in military enterprise. Their territories at one time embraced a part of the Uttar Pradesh and large parts of Bihar, Bengal and Orissa, but they began to shrink even in a century's duration. Near the end of the twelfth, however, some of the lost territories were regained by a great king of the dynasty, Mahīpāla. But round the same century's beginning, another dynasty which was not Buddhist but Brāhmaṇical—the Senas—had snatched away a big slice from the Pāla territories in Bengal. At last came the inevitable incoming tide of Muslim invasion and conquest from the *Doab* which relentlessly swept away both the Pālas and the Senas.

A large assortment of Pāla relics—coins, images and inscriptions—has been recovered from various sites in Bihar and Bengal. Together they bear testimony to the Pāla kings' active patronage of learning, culture and the fine arts.

Nālandā, as we have seen, lived on into this regime; it came into the possession of the Pālas as a cultural legacy from the past—from the great and spacious age of the Guptas—and the legacy was prized and cherished. Nālandā was looked upon as the *beau ideal*, the time-honoured exemplar, of what a seat of learning should be.

Some of the kings, being Buddhist themselves and keenly interested in the promotion of Buddhist learning within their territories, established Mahāvihāras at different centres on the model of Nālandā. About these Mahāvihāras (including Nālandā itself in its later period) our information is from Tibetan sources: (i) historiographical works which conserve old legends current in Tibet, and (ii) texts in the *Tanjur* and *Kanjur* recording their having been composed or copied at one or another of these Mahāvihāras.

An interesting feature of these establishments under the Pālas is the existence of a system of co-ordination among them. Evidently all of them were under State supervision.

Each seems to have been recognized as a separate corporation with a standardized official seal of its own. The seals, which belong palaeographically to the same age, have been obtained from two sites—Nālandā and Somapura (Paharpur)—*terra cotta* seals with the same device, a *Dharmacakra* flanked by a deer on each side in the upper register, and the name of the corporation in the lower, viz. *Śrī-*

23. *View of a courtyard, used for discourses and discussions, with pillars supporting a roof, at Nālandā. (Only the sockets of the pillars remain.)* (Photo: Department of Archaeology, Government of India)

Image of a Tāntric deity named Mārīcī found at Nālandā. (Photo: Department of Archaeology, Government of India)

24. *Specimens of Nālandā sculpture (a) Stucco head of a female figure.* (Photo: Department of Archaeology, Government of India)

(*b*) *Bodhisatva figure in Stucco.* (*From a Stūpa.*) (Photo: Department of Archaeology, Government of India)

Nālandā-Mahāvihārīya-Ārya-Bhikṣusaṁghasya at Nālandā and *Śrī-Dharmapāladeva-Mahāvihārīya-Ārya-Bhikṣusaṁgha* at Somapura.[1]

A monk named Vīradeva was commissioned by King Devapāla to look after Nālandā, and his activities in renovating its buildings are recorded in a lithic inscription.[2] It is said by Lama Tāranātha that the head of Vikramaśilā had control over Nālandā.[3] In the narratives of the lives of eminent Buddhist saints and scholars, interspersed in Tibetan histories, references are made to their occupancy of the headship of different centres of Buddhist learning—Vajrāsana (at Gayā), Nālandā, Odantapura and Somapura. Migration of monks from one to another is also spoken of; the great Atīśa (Dīpaṅkara Śrī-jñāna) himself is said to have received ordination at Nālandā and, having studied there for some time, gone to Odantapura for further studies and finally become the head of Vikramaśilā from where he was escorted to Tibet.[4] One Vipulaśrī, a resident of Somapura, has left an inscription at Nālandā recording his construction of a temple to Tārā at Somapura, as well as the erection of a monastery at Nālandā. The inscription, on palaeolographic grounds, is assigned to the first half of the twelfth century.[5] When Śākya Śrībhadra, coming all the way from Kashmir to Magadha in 1202 to visit all Buddhist centres of learning, found Odantapura and Vikramaśilā laid waste by the Muslims, he betook himself to Jagaddala in Bengal where he found pupils and disciples.[6]

It seems from the evidence that the different seats of Buddhist learning that functioned in eastern India under the Pālas were regarded together as forming a network, an interlinked group of institutions.

[1] Compare Plate X in Ghosh's *Guide to Nalanda*, and Plate LIX (h) in Dikshita's *Memoir on Paharpur Excavations*.
[2] See Ghosh's *Guide to Nalanda*, p. 46.
[3] Schiefner's Translation, p. 218.
[4] See *infra* under Vikramaśilā for the career of Atīśa, pp. 362 ff.
[5] See Ghosh's *Guide to Nalanda*, p. 35. The inscription with translation will be found in *Epigraphia Indica*, vol. XXI, pp. 97–101.
[6] See *infra* under Jagaddala, p. 378.

APPENDIX I

(to Part V, Sec. 3)

(on the Order of Succession and approximate Regnal Years of kings of the Pāla Dynasty)

From Tibetan sources

(See S. C. Vidyabhushana's *Indian Logic: Mediaeval School,* Calcutta University, 1909, Appendix B, pp. 148–49.)

1. Gopāla (660–705)
2. Devapāla (705–53)
3. Rasapāla (753–65)
4. Dharmapāla (765–829)
5. Masu-rakṣita (829–37)
6. Vanapāla (837–47)
7. Mahīpāla (847–99)
8. Mahāpāla (899–940)
9. Śamupāla (940–52)
10. Śreṣṭhapāla or Praiṣṭhapāla (952–55)
11. Canaka (955–83)
12. Bhayapāla (983–1015)
13. Nyāyapāla (1015–50)
14. Āmrapāla (1050–63)
15. Hastipāla (1063–78)
16. Kṣāntipāla (1078–92)
17. Rāmapāla (1092–1138)
18. Yakṣapāla (1138–39)

On the results of Modern Researches

(See Nihar Ranjan Ray's *Bāṅgālīr Itihāsa* in the Bengali language, published by Book Emporium, Calcutta, Magh, 1356, January, 1950, pp. 475–93.)

1. Gopāla (mid-eighth century)—founder of Odantapura Mahāvihāra
2. Dharmapāla (770–810)—founder of Vikramaśilā Mahāvihāra
3. Devapāla (810–50)—founder of Somapura Mahāvihāra
4. Vigrahapāla I (850–54)
5. Nārāyaṇapāla (854–908)
6. Rājyapāla (908–40)
7. Gopāla II (940–60)
8. Vigrahapāla II
9. Mahīpāla I (988–1027)
10. Jayapāla (1038–55)
11. Vigrahapāla III (1055–70)
12. Mahīpāla II (1070–75)
13. Śūrapāla (1075–77)
14. Rāmapāla (1077–1120)—founder of Jagaddala Mahāvihāra
15. Kumārapāla (1120–25)
16. Gopāla III (1125–40)
17. Madanapāla (1140–55)

a. ODANTAPURA

When Gopāla, founder of the Pāla dynasty, built the new city of Odantapura in Magadha, the thought was perhaps in his mind that it should grow to be a centre of Buddhist learning like Nālandā of the Guptas. So he founded a Mahāvihāra here within walking distance of Nālandā—only six miles off. There is a Tibetan legend that the monastery was built upon a lake that had miraculously dried up.[1]

In its complete layout and structure, it must have been in existence, newly-built, some time in the earlier half of the eighth century AD, for the first Tibetan Buddhist monastery at Sam-Yas in

[1] The story occurs in Bu-ston's work. See Obermiller's Translation, Part II, p. 157.

Tibet was built on its model in AD 749.[1] The lifetime of the Mahāvihāra must have been upwards of four and a half-centuries preceding its complete destruction by Muslim soldiers.

No full-length description of this establishment is available in the Tibetan legends so far known. But they occasionally mention it as a seat of learning visited or stayed in by some of the illustrious monks of the Pāla age whose life-stories the legends tell. If the Sam-Yas Monastery was really built on its model, some idea may be inferred of the grand and elaborate architectural plan of the original from its Tibetan replica.

The Sam-Yas Monastery itself fell into ruins centuries ago, but even in 1874 when Pandit Nain Singh, one of Waddell's collaborators in his explorations in Tibet, resided for some time in the ruins, parts of the original buildings still remained. His description of the remains is thus reproduced by Waddell:[2]

'The monastery, which contains a large temple, four large colleges, and several other buildings, is enclosed by a lofty circular wall about a mile and a half in circumference, with gates facing the cardinal points, and along the top of the wall are many votive brick *chaityas*, of which the explorer, Nain Singh, counted 1,030, and they seemed to be covered with inscriptions in ancient Indian characters. In the centre of the enclosure stands the assembly hall, with radiating cloisters leading to four chapels, facing at equal distances the four sides of the larger temple. This explorer notes that "the idols and images contained in these temples are of pure gold, richly ornamented with valuable cloths and jewels. The candlesticks and vessels are nearly all made of gold and silver". And on the temple walls are many large inscriptions in Chinese and ancient Indian characters. In the vestibule of the chief temple, to the left of the door, is a colossal copy of the pictorial Wheel of Life.'

(*Note*—This was evidently a later Tibetan addition.)

These ruins were visited again in 1912 by Alexandra David-Neel, the well-known Tibetan explorer and scholar, on her fifth journey in

[1] The following account of the building of Sam-Yas monastery is given in *Pag-sam-jon-zang*, Part II (see S. C. Das's Ed., p. 171): 'The (Tibetan king's) messengers accidentally met Padma Sambhava in Upper Tibet and brought him to the king then residing at Sam-ye. . . . In consultation with Śāntarakṣita, Padma Sambhava suggested the necessity of establishing a grand monastery at Sam-ye for introducing monasticism into Tibet. Accordingly the king founded the great monastery, ordinarily called Sam-ye (in Sanskrit *Acintya Vihara*, which is of the same significance as Ajanta of Central India). Sam-ye was built after the model of Odantapura Vihāra, then a famous monastery of Magadha. The king invited twelve ordained Buddhist monks from Magadha. These with Śāntarakṣita as the High priest constituted the earliest Buddhist congregation in Tibet' (S. C. Das's ed., Analytic List of Contents, p. xi. The passage has been slightly abbreviated and modified).

[2] Waddell's *Buddhism of Tibet* (2nd Ed., 1934), p. 267.

Tibet. It was then an abandoned site and successive fires had destroyed the original buildings, though a few temples remained in good condition.[1]

With the Odantapura Mahāvihāra, the names of some great and famous monks are associated in Tibetan legends—the most venerable and illustrious of them being Dīpaṅkara Śrījñāna (AD 980–1054) or Atīśa, as the Tibetans named him, who studied here for two years under Dharmarakṣita, a Hīnayānist teacher. From here he passed on to Vikramaśilā where he became the head of the institution and stayed until his departure for Tibet.[2]

No connected history of the establishment can be reconstructed out of the Tibetan legends; and so far they are our only source of information. One may surmise, however, that under the founder and some of his descendants it rose to fame and flourished greatly: at least one Tibetan legend puts the number of its inmates at 12,000—a token number, yet indicative of a large and prosperous establishment.[3]

But towards the end of the eleventh century AD, it must have gone far into decline. This can be inferred from a statement in a *stotra* (Hymn) composed by Atīśa's Tibetan disciple Nag-tsho and dedicated to his master's memory. It is entitled the '*Stotra* of Eighty Ślokas (verses)' in which Atīśa's life in different phases is presented. Describing his phenomenal influence and prestige in the monasteries of India where he had lived, Nag-tsho mentioned 'Odantapura with its fifty-three monks' and 'Vikramaśilā with about a hundred'.[4] But whatever the number of its last inmates, they were killed off to a man when Ikhtiyar Khiliji's soldiers swooped down upon it round 1198.

The gruesome massacre and destruction are on historical record. The setting is the same as for all the Pāla centres of learning—of Nālandā in its last years, Vikramaśilā, Somapura and Jagaddala—the Turaṣka invasion. Spreading terror and panic through all the towns and countryside of Bihar and Bengal, it came in the following sequence of historical events:[5]

'In 1175 Ghiyas-ud-din Muhammad (of the Ghaznavids) led his first expedition into India. He appointed Qutub-ud-din Aibek, the most trusty of his Turkish officers, as viceroy of all his conquests in India. An officer subordinate to Aibek had been carrying on the banner of Islam further afield. He was Ikhtiyar-ud-din Muhammad, son of

[1] See David-Neel's *My Journey to Lhasa* (Penguin Ed., 1940), pp. 275–76.
[2] It is so stated in the narrative of the life of Atīśa in Book V, vol. I of the *Blue Annals*. See *infra* (under *Vikramaśilā*) for the life and career of Atīśa.
[3] For this legend, see *Blue Annals*, Vol. II, p. 1,031.
[4] See *Blue Annals*, Vol. I, p. 243, footnote 2.
[5] *Cambridge History of India*, Vol. III (Turks and Afghans), p. 42.

Bukhtyar, of the Turkish tribe of Khalj. His mean and unprepossessing appearance and his ungainly build, which enabled him, while standing upright, to reach with his hands the calves of his legs, had long debarred him from employment commensurate with his ambition and his merits, and he had entered the service of Hijabr-ud-din Hasan Adil, an adventurous officer who had conquered Budaun . . . Ikhtiyar-ud-din received some fiefs from him between the Ganges and the Sone. From this advanced base he led raids into Bihar and Tirhut and took so much booty that a large number of his own tribe, eager to serve under so fortunate a leader, joined him. With this accession of strength, he invaded Bihar, took its capital Udantapura, put to death the Buddhist monks dwelling in its great monastery, and returned with his plunder, which included the library of the monastery, to make obeisance to Aibek, now in the summer of 1193, established at Delhi . . . (Ikhtiyar was under a cloud for some time), but he regained the favour of Aibek who sent him with fresh honours to Bihar after conferring upon him a fief for his past and future conquests.'

The whole doomed area in the east—ancient Magadha and northern Bengal, where the great Pāla monasteries still whispered the last Tāntric accents of Buddhist learning—echoed to the tramp of marauding soldiers and the fleeing feet of men and women in blind panic. It was not possible for the Afghan soldiers to distinguish a Buddhist monastery, with its enclosing wall and its tall towers rising high above, from a circumvallated fort, nor to tell Buddhist monks from Brāhmaṇa priests. A fierce assault was directed upon the Mahāvihāra at Odantapura.

The story of this assault was told long afterwards, in 1243, by an eye-witness to the Persian historian Minhaz who reported it in his work *Tabaquat-i-Nasiri*:[1]

'It is said by credible persons that he, Bukhtyar Khiliji (*Note*—This is a mistake for Ikhtiyar Khiliji who was Bukhtyar's son), went to the gate of the fort of Bihar with only two hundred horse and began the war by taking the enemy unawares. In the service of Bukhtyar (?) there were two brothers of great intelligence. One of them was named Nizamuddin and the other Samsuddin. The compiler of the book met Samsuddin at Lakhanauti (i.e. Lakṣaṇāvatī in Gaur in the district of Malda, north Bengal) in the year AD 1243 and heard the following story from him. When Bukhtyar (?) reached the gate of the fort and the fighting began, these two wise brothers were active in that army of heroes. Mahammed Bukhtyar (?) with great vigour and audacity

[1] Elliot and Dawson's *History of India as told by its own Historians* (1869), Vol. II, p. 306.

rushed in at the gate of the fort and gained possession of the place. Great plunder fell into the hands of the victors. Most of the inhabitants of the place were Brāhmaṇas with shaven heads. They were put to death. Large numbers of books were found there, and when the Mahammadans saw them, they called for some person to explain their contents. But all of the men had been killed. It was discovered that the whole fort and city was a place of study (*madrāsā*): in the Hindi language the word Bihar (i.e. *Vihāra*) means a college.'

If some of these books picked up from the wreckage of the monastic library had really been taken to Delhi and laid by the victor at the Sultan's feet, we may imagine how they must have been treated: the infidel literature was either burnt or dumped in a garbage receptacle.

b. VIKRAMAŚILĀ[1]

Hsüan-tsang speaks thus of Nālandā's high reputation in his time and the impact of its influence on the intellectuals of contemporary society:[2]

'Learned men from different cities, who desire to acquire quickly a renown in discussion, come here in multitudes to settle their doubts, and then the streams (of their wisdom) spread far and wide. For this reason some persons usurp the name (of Nālandā students), and in going to and fro receive honour in consequence.'

This old prestige of Nālandā seems to have devolved on Vikramaśilā in the Pāla age. In Tibetan legends it holds about the same position of pre-eminence as is accorded in Chinese records to Nālandā.

The site of Vikramaśilā still remains uncertain: it is said to be somewhere 'east of Magadha'[3] on the lower course of the Gangā, which may be anywhere on the river's miles-long multi-channelled course through the plains of Bengal and Bihar. In fact the only dependable clue to its topography is a casual statement in Bromton's detailed account, inset in his 'life of Atīśa',[4] of Nag-tsho's mission to Vikramaśilā to escort Dīpaṅkara Śrījñāna to Tibet.[5] It is said that the Tibetans came upon the mahāvihāra on a tall bluff hill on the river Gangā. But on the banks of that river and its channels,

[1] Both forms, *Vikramaśīlā* and *Vikramaśilā*, occur in Tibetan legends for the name of this *mahāvihāra* and there are legends in explanation of the etymology. Schiefner in his Introduction to the German translation of Tāranātha's work disparages *Vikramaśīlā* as a 'strange form' (see *Indian Historical Journal*, Vol. III, March 1927—No. I, p. 64). The other form of the name has been adopted here.

[2] Beal's *Buddhist Records*, ii, p. 170.

[3] As stated by Sumpa. See *Pag-sam-jon-zang*, p. 113.

[4] See Part IV, Sec. 1, p. 244 and footnote 1.

[5] See Appendix II.

finds of Buddhist images and other relics have been made at many a spot. Two places, however, where the finds are somewhat widespread and numerous—Pātharghātā and Colgong—have been suggested as the site of Vikramaśilā.[1] But no lithic record of the name has been discovered up to date.

Lama Dharmasvāmī came to Nālandā in 1235. His report about the Vikramaśilā Mahāvihāra, which at that time did not exist, is to this effect:[2]

'Vikramaśilā was still existing in the time of the visit of elder Dharmasvāmī (AD 1153–1216) and of the Kasmiri Paṇḍita Sākya Śrībhadra (AD 1145–1225), but when Dharmasvāmī visited the country there were no traces of it left: the Turaṣka soldiery, having razed it to the ground, had thrown the foundation stones into the Gangā.'

The report suggests that even at the time of Śākya Śrībhadra's visit to Magadha (AD 1206), the mahāvihāra had not been wholly destroyed, but it was completely effaced by 1235. Perhaps, after the destruction of Odantapura, it had been subjected to repeated raids at the hands of the Turaṣkas, which seems probable because explosive bombardment had not come into practice in warfare then. The huge masses of brick-and-stone structures that Nālandā or Vikramaśilā presented to the raiders were difficult to demolish wholesale by a single assault.

The Tibetan legends, though not completely unanimous on this point,[3] ascribe Vikramaśilā's foundation to King Dharmapāla. He was the second king in dynastic succession and by prowess and diplomacy enlarged the small kingdom inherited from his father to the extent of an empire. Even making allowance for the hyperbole of courtly poetry, it seems from an inscription of his reign that Dharmapāla stood high in the regard of his people:[4]

[1] Nundalal Dey identified Pātharghātā (anciently called *Śilāsaṁgama*) with Vikramaśilā in his article on *The Vikramasila Monastery*, in JASB (New Series), Vol. V, 1909, pp. 1 ff. This identification is accepted by S. C. Vidyabhusana (see *Indian Logic: Mediaeval School*, 1909, p. 150, footnote 5). The claim of Colgong to be the site of Vikramaśilā has been advanced in recent times. The place abounds in Buddhist ruins, but it has not yet had archaeological exploration. Cunningham's identification of Vikramaśilā with Bargaon in the *Archaeological Survey Report*, Vol. viii, p. 83, has long been rejected as untenable as it does not agree with Tibetan descriptions of the site.

[2] See *Biography of Dharmasvāmin*, p. 64.

[3] Both Tāranātha and Sumpa refer to Dharmapāla as the founder of Vikramaśilā. But it seems from the colophon of a Tibetan work ascribed to Dīpaṅkara Śrījñāna, a *Dharma*-exposition given to a disciple named Jayaśilā (see Cordier's *Catalogue*, Part III, pp. 321–22) that there was also a tradition that Vikramaśilā was founded by King Devapāla. The colophon refers to the Mahāvihāra as an establishment of Devapāla's foundation.

[4] Khalimpur Copperplate *Praśasti* (see *Epigraphia Indica*, iv, p. 252).

'Cowherds sang his praises on the borders of the empire; foresters in the forest; villagers on the outskirts of villages; children in every courtyard; comptrollers of weights and measures in every market; caged parrots in pleasure-houses; yet from all these paeans of praise, the emperor bashfully turns aside.'

Commensurate no doubt with his greatness as a king was the magnitude and grandeur of the mahāvihāra built by him.

In the absence of identifiable remains, we have to fall back for evidence on the traditions recorded in Tibetan histories. As we shall observe later, Vikramaśilā in its flourishing period was well-known to the Tibetans; it attracted scholars and visitors from Tibet; there was intercourse between Vikramaśilā and Tibetan Buddhist centres. Hence Tibetan traditions about the mahāvihāra have some claim to authenticity.

These traditions agree about its location on a hill on the bank of the Gangā. Sumpa describes it as a mahāvihāra with a surrounding wall which is said to have been built by one Buddhajñāna-pratiṣṭha; outside this circuit wall and probably set all round it were 107 temples; within the enclosure were fifty-eight '*saṁsthās*' (institutions) in which 108 *paṇḍitas* (professors) lived.[1] Tāranātha refers to its Six Gates each of which was 'kept' by an eminent *paṇḍita*.[2] The legends supply no definite information about the area or configuration of the campus, but the description available gives the idea of a grand and very extensive establishment. It is said that when, in the reign of King Rāmapāla, Abhayākaragupta was at its head, there were 160 professors and 1,000 resident monks at Vikramaśilā.[3] But, as we have it from Nag-tsho,[4] the number of monks dwindled to about a hundred, perhaps in the days when Muslim raids were going on all over this part of the country.

It appears from the legends that a functionary whose designation was 'Guardian of the Gate' acted both at Nālandā and at Vikramaśilā. The gate-keeper of Nālandā, evidently a learned monk of high status, is designated as '*men-che*' in the Chinese records, and of Vikramaśilā as '*go-srun*' in the Tibetan. The Chinese and the Tibetan expressions are synonymous. Nālandā had one gate, while Vikramaśilā had six, each 'kept' by a *Go-srun*, equivalent to Sanskrit *Dvāra-pāla* (Keeper of the Gate).

His function at Nālandā is reported in the Chinese records to have been to judge the qualifications of persons intending to join one of its 'schools of discussion'. Whether the Vikramaśilā 'gate-keeper'

[1] *Pag-sam-jon-zang* (ed. by S. C. Das), p. 113.
[2] Schiefner's Translation, pp. 234–35.
[3] *Pag-sam-jon-zang*, p. 130. [4] See p. 356.

exercised the same function is not known, but those named in the Tibetan legends as incumbents of the office of *Go-srun* or *Dvāra-pāla* were all scholars of high eminence and celebrity, holding the office on royal commission.

We have a list from Tāranātha of six such 'gate-keepers' who functioned contemporaneously in the reign of Canaka. Canaka is not known to Pāla history. Tāranātha, describing in section xxxiii of his history 'The Events in the Time of King Canaka', remarks that, 'although this king Canaka rendered great service to the doctrine, he is not counted among the "seven Pālas" because he was not of the Pāla family.'[1] According to the Tibetan chronology of Pāla kings, Canaka's reign covered AD 955–83.

The gate-keepers of Vikramaśilā in this period were: (i) Ācārya Ratnākaraśānti (of the Eastern Gate), (ii) Vāgīsvarakīrti (of the Western Gate), (iii) Naropa (of the Northern Gate), (iv) Prajñākaramati (of the Southern Gate), (v) Ratnavajra (of the first Central Gate), and (vi) Jñānaśrīmitra (of the second Central Gate).[2] They were all scholars of eminence whose works are extant in the Tibetan *Tanjur* and *Kanjur*.[3] The designation, *dvāra-paṇḍita*, is still known in Bengal, but it applies to a learned Paṇḍita of the priestly class, officiating in the house of a rājā or a landed aristocrat—an office now all but extinct.

Sumpa refers to the fifty-eight *saṁsthās* of Vikramaśilā. Ordinarily the term means an 'institution'. Whether these *saṁsthās* corresponded to or were in any way like Nālandā's 'Schools' cannot be definitely said, nor whether there were arrangements for instruction in the Vidyās. Vikramaśilā was identified with the study and cultivation of Tāntric Buddhism and it is likely that this study was divided into different branches. The legends, apart from giving the designations of the officers, do not throw much light on Vikramaśilā's internal organization.

The Head of the establishment was called *Adhyakṣa* who, as well as the *Dvāra-pālas*, held their posts by commission from the king. Of the *Adhyakṣas* of Vikramaśilā, a few names are scattered here and there in the legends—Buddhajñānapāla, who was the founder's contemporary and the first *adhyakṣa*; Jetari who was at first a *dvāra-pāla*, but rose to be *adhyakṣa*; Abhayākaragupta; Dīpaṅkara Śrījñāna; Śākya Śrībhadra and others. The custom of conferring an academic degree, of which we find no trace in the history of Nālandā, seems to have obtained here. The degree was a title of distinction: it was *Paṇḍita* (learned) or *Mahāpaṇḍita* (vastly learned) and was conferred

[1] See Schiefner's Translation, pp. 234–35.
[2] These six names occur in section xxxiii of Tāranātha's history.
[3] Nine of Ratnākaraśānti's; one of Prajñākaramati's; one of Jñānaśrimitra's. See *Catalogue-Index* (Tohoku Imperial University Publication).

by the king. A professor was called an *Ācārya*.[1] A succession list of the great Tāntric teachers (*Ācāryas*) of Vikramaśilā from Dharmapāla's reign to the Turaṣka invasion is given by Tāranātha in section xxxviii of his history. The pictures of the most eminent among the *Paṇḍitas* and *Mahāpaṇḍitas* of Vikramaśilā, it is said, decorated the walls.[2]

Vikramaśilā, as already mentioned, had considerable cultural intercourse with Tibet. Many scholars of Vikramaśilā since its foundation are named in the Tibetan legends as having visited Tibet. It seems also in its turn to have attracted scholars from Tibet: Nag-tsho and his party found accommodation on the first night of their arrival at Vikramaśilā in the Tibetan hostelry within the gates.[3] The *Tanjur* and the *Kanjur* hold a good deal of evidence of this intercourse in the number and bulk of Tibetan translations of Sanskrit works incorporated in the canons, that were prepared at Vikramaśilā, not only by Tibetan, but by Indian scholars as well. They may be traced in the *Catalogues*.[4] The great Dīpaṅkara himself translated into Tibetan at Vikramaśilā with the help of a learned monk named Vīryasiṁha a number of his own works.[5]

The Tibetan canonical collections contain a fairly large number of works, either original ones in Tibetan or Tibetan translations from Sanskrit, ascribed to some *paṇḍita* or other of Vikramaśilā. They were written either there or in Nepal or Tibet. We can trace among the authors the names of as many as thirteen scholars who belonged to Vikramaśilā—Buddhajñānapāda, Vairocanarakṣita, Jetari, Prajñākaramati, Vāgīsvarakīrti, Ratnavajra, Jñānaśrīmitra, Ratnākaraśānti, Vīryasiṁha, Dīpaṅkaraśrījñāna, Abhayākaragupta, Tathāgatarakṣita and Dharmakīrti (who was a Tibetan).[6] The most distinguished of these authors are mentioned here and there in Tibetan histories also, with casual notice of their lives and careers as tradition partially and dispersedly retained them.

Pre-eminent among them all is Dīpaṅkara Śrījñāna. He left on the mind and imagination of the people of Tibet the deepest and most abiding impression. They deified him as ATĪŚA the Venerable Lord (*Joborji Atīśa*), an incarnation of Mañjuśrī, and he still receives worship in Tibetan *gumphās* (monastic establishments).[7]

[1] 'Tāranātha speaks of Tathāgatarakṣita as the *Tantrācārya* of Vikramaśilā, along with Jñānapada, Dīpaṁkarabhadra, Sridhara, Bhavabhadra and others'—Bose's *Indian Teachers of Buddhist Universities*, p. 92.

[2] S. C. Vidyabhusan's *Indian Logic*: *Mediaeval School*, Appendix C, p. 151.

[3] S. C. Das's *Indian Pandits in the Land of Snow*, p. 58.

[4] See Cordier's *Catalogue du Fonds Tibetain de la Bibliotheca Nationale* and *A Complete Catalogue of Tibetan Buddhist Canons* (with a *Catalogue-Index*), published by Tohoku Imperial University, Sendai (Japan), 1934.

[5] See Bose's *Indian Teachers*, etc. pp. 49–81, about Vīryasimha's translations.

[6] See *Ibid*, p. 33.

[7] The author of the present work saw at Ghoom (near Darjeeling in Bengal) at the local Tibetan temple a human image of Atīśa among the monstrous images of Tāntric deities, placed in a heap on a dais at which offerings were made.

The most active and historic part of his life and career was the end-part in Tibet.

Owing to Dīpaṅkara's thirteen years of missionary work and activities, backed by the support and patronage of royalty, Buddhism was finally established as the religion of Tibet and the hierarchy of Lamaism, inaugurated by Padmasambhava, put on an organized and permanent basis. Many pages in Tibetan historiography, which is church history in the main, are given to Atīśa and his life and career in Tibet. The whole of Book V of the '*Blue Annals*' for example, composed between 1476 and 1478, a little over four centuries after Atīśa's death in Tibet, is devoted to 'Joborji Atīśa and his Spiritual Lineage'. The author Bu-ston must have drawn in this part of his work upon older materials like the account of Atīśa's life by his chief Tibetan disciple Brom-ton.[1]

The main outline of Dīpaṅkara's biography is known from these sources among which there are no major discrepancies. The following is based mainly on the version of the *Blue Annals* (Book V):

Dīpaṅkara was born in AD 982. He was a Bengali by birth, born at Vikramapura, a town in the Dacca district of Eastern Pakistan. Evidently he grew up to be a man of very attractive personality, for, though old when he arrived in Tibet, the Tibetans were attracted by the charm and graces of his person. 'His demeanour, personal beauty though sixty years old, and his pleasant appearance made him worthy of divine honour. A smile was ever present on his face and Sanskrit *mantras* were always on his lips. His voice was distinct, loud and impressive. His expression was happy;—Oh, how sweetly he talked and how noble he looked! At the end of a sentence, he often said: "Ati Bhāla, Ati Bhāla, Ati Maṅgala, Ati Bhāla hai".'[2] The words quoted are Bengali words, meaning 'very good, very good, very auspicious, very good indeed!'

Dīpaṅkara's parents were Kalyāṇa-śrī and Śrī-prabhā (or Prabhāvatī, as she is named in Nag-tsho's *Stotra* in praise of his master). His father is said to have been a man of kingly rank, dwelling in a palace, but this may be just a hyperbole for a man of wealth. Dīpaṅkara's heart was evidently set not on worldly things and he sought and received initiation in early youth at the hands of a Tāntric *yogin* at Kālaśilā, an ancient site of Rājagriha.

Urged by a dream, he became a Buddhist monk at the age of thirty-one, was ordained at Nālandā by a learned monk Śīlarakṣita, who belonged to the Mahāsāṅghika school. After his ordination he applied himself to the study of the canons of the four schools of

[1] There are other Tibetan biographies of Atīśa. See pp. 243–44.
[2] S. C. Das's *Indian Pandits*, etc. p. 74.

Buddhism—Mahāsāṅghika, Sarvāstivāda, Sāmmitīya and Sthaviravāda.

Completing two years' study at Nālandā, he went to Odantapura and studied the *Mahāvibhāṣā* with a teacher, Dharmarakṣita by name, who himself was a Hīnayānist. With other teachers, he studied the *Prajñāpāramitā* and the doctrines of Vajrayāna. In particular he studied with the famous Nālandā scholar, Ratnākaraśānti. He took lessons later with Dharmakīrti also. He thus became thoroughly read in the lore of Buddhism of all sects and schools and the reputation of his learning spread far. He was summoned to take up the office of *Adhyakṣa* of the Vikramaśilā Mahāvihāra. Here he lived and worked, and, while working, he received repeated invitations to come to Tibet to promote the cause of Buddhism in that country. He received also from time to time presents of gold from Tibet, which seems to have been at the time rich in gold mines.

Indo-Tibetan intercourse was then already two centuries old. Its urge and motive had been the same as India's earlier intercourse with China—to safeguard the purity of the religion from admixture with native cults. The intercourse with Tibet had developed largely during the reigns of the Pālas and Buddhist kings of Tibet who were anxious to maintain contact with Buddhist seats of learning in eastern India. Several missions from Tibet failed to draw Dīpaṅkara to that country. But at last a mission led by Nag-tsho succeeded.

The story of this Tibetan mission, Dīpaṅkara's adventurous journey to Tibet, his work and activities there over thirteen years and his death at a Tibetan township—are told in vivid and arresting detail in Brom-ton's 'life'. A summary of it will be found in Appendix II to this section.

Dīpaṅkara spent his first three years in Tibet in giving to disciples 'instructions in *sādhanā*' (spiritual course). Among the first batch of his Tibetan disciples was the venerable Tibetan scholar and translator of Sanskrit works, Rin-chen-san-po. Rin-chen was eighty-five years old when he first met Dīpaṅkara, and this meeting of the two most famous scholars of the two countries is described by Bu-ston at great length as an historic event.[1] Afterwards numerous translations were made by them in collaboration.

Dīpaṅkara's two foremost Tibetan disciples were Brom-ton and Nag-tsho.

About Brom-ton, Bu-ston tells the story that he had been in the employ of some traders, doing menial jobs for them and at the same time carrying on his studies secretly. In the neighbourhood lived a Tibetan scholar who had the nickname, Grammar-thorn, for his

[1] See Obermiller, ii, pp. 213–14. It is described also in the *Blue Annals*, Vol. I, p. 68.

attachment to linguistic studies. Brom-ton studied scripts with him. One day Brom-ton asked him: 'Who is the greatest scholar in India?' Grammar-thorn said in reply: 'When I was in India, the greatest was Naropa (one of Vikramaśilā's "gate-keepers"). There was also a monk named Dīpaṅkara Śrījñāna who was of a royal family. If he be still alive, he will have become great'. Brom-ton knew that Dīpaṅkara had come to Tibet. So, taking his books and other personal belongings on a donkey's back, he set forth in search of him. Brom-ton met him after many adventures on the way, stayed with him, and became in time the greatest of his disciples.

Brom-ton, as already mentioned, is the putative author of a standard Tibetan 'Life of Atiśa'. He became the first hierarch of the sect Ka-dam-pa that rose out of the reformation of Buddhism in Tibet conducted under Atiśa.[1] The sect, in the course of a couple of centuries and a half of its foundation, developed into the Ge-lug-pa which is the central sect of Tibetan Buddhism.[2] The 'spiritual lineage' of the sect is sketched in Book V of the *Blue Annals*.

Nag-tsho, who had led the mission which brought Dīpaṅkara to Tibet, was the other famous Tibetan disciple. He was his master's companion and attendant in Tibet and was a learned lama, author of many texts. After Dīpaṅkara's death at Nethan, Nag-tsho built to his memory a great monastery in that town and when he himself followed the master to the other world barely a year after, a grand and historic funeral ceremony was held by his countrymen in his honour. Nag-tsho left numerous disciples in Tibet.

Bu-ston gives cursory accounts of several other prominent Tibetan disciples of Dīpaṅkara.

On the expiry of his first three years in Tibet, Dīpaṅkara wished to return to Vikramaśilā. Nag-tsho had given to Śīlākara at Vikramaśilā, on the eve of Dīpaṅkara's departure, a promise that the master would be escorted back after three years' stay in Tibet. Remembering this, he fell in with his master's wish. But perhaps the complete success of his Tibetan mission was the dominant thought in Dīpaṅkara's mind. Anyway he shook off the thought of returning and set out on a tour of Central Tibet where he was received at every place with widespread and demonstrative enthusiasm. After this Central Tibetan tour, he was invited to Lhasa.

Lhasa with its countless sacred images and numerous monasteries struck him as an historic city. He was curious to know its annals. It is said that there existed an old copy of a history of Lhasa in the custody of a witch (*dākinī*) who was known as the 'Mad One of

[1] 'Dīpaṅkara delivered to him (Brom-ton) the precepts of *Ka-dam-pa* which thenceforth was expanded'—Obermiller, ii, p. 214.

[2] Waddell's *Buddhism in Tibet*, p. 36.

Lhasa'. With the witch's consent he was able to extract the manuscript from within a beam. But the witch custodian would not allow it to be kept out for more than a day. So his disciples shared the manuscript and prepared copies, after which it was again thrust back into concealment.

On his preaching missions in Tibet, Dīpaṅkara received much wealth as gift from devotees and admirers which he despatched on three occasions through his disciples to Vikramaśilā.[1] He preached most extensively in four cities of Tibet—Lhasa, Yar-pa, Lan-pa and Nethan.

His last visit was to Nethan. His health and physical vigour were declining at the time. Yet he was keen on going to Nepal to meet a famous Kashmirian *paṇḍita* named Jñānākara, who was then in that country. But Nag-tsho, fearing the journey would be too great a strain on the master, went there himself to deputize for him. Dīpaṅkara was sad at heart over his physical disabilities; already his body had become greatly emaciated. It was at Nethan that he breathed his last.

The exact year and date of his death are not quite certain. The author of the *Blue Annals* puts it as the 'twentieth day of the middle autumn month of AD 1054', adding: 'I have given (the date) after a thorough examination of the different dates mentioned in the "Lives".'[2]

There are many works by Dīpaṅkara in the *Tanjur* and *Kanjur* collection,[3] both original works in Tibetan and Tibetan translations from Sanskrit. The most popular with the learned in Tibet is *Bodhipatha-pradīpa* (Lamp showing the way of Bodhi or Supreme Wisdom).[4]

[1] *Blue Annals*, Vol. I, p. 259.
[2] *Blue Annals*, Vol. I, p. 261.
[3] The Tohoku *Catalogue-Index* gives 28 titles, but Waddell and S. C. Das give a list of 20 (*Buddhism of Tibet*, p. 36, footnote 2, and *Indian Pandits in the Land of Snow*, p. 76).
[4] This work has the title *Bodhimārga-pradīpa* in the *Tohoku Catalogue*, No. 3948.

APPENDIX II

(to Part V, Sec. 3)

(Tibetan cultural missions to India described in Brom-ton's 'Life of Atīśa')

THOLIN was the capital of Tibet in AD 1025. Here a Buddhist king of Tibet had built a monastery. It was a sort of training institute. Monks after a course of training here were sent out to different parts of India—to Magadha (Bihar) and Kashmir where Buddhism was best known, practised and studied. They were authorized to invite learned monks from India to Tibet.

Of twenty-one monks sent out from this monastery, nineteen, it is said, died in India of heat, fever, snake bite and other mishaps. The two survivors found their way to the great Vikramaśilā monastery on the bank of the Gangā where they heard of the fame of Dīpaṅkara Śrījñāna. They conveyed reports about him on their return to the Tibetan king, who despatched at once a mission to Vikramaśilā under a monk named Gya-tson, with a hundred attendants and a large quantity of gold. This was the first Tibetan mission to Vikramaśilā.

Its result is thus described:

'After encountering immense hardships and privations on the journey, the traveller (Gya-tson) reached Magadha. Arrived at Vikramaśilā, he presented to Dīpaṅkara the king's letter with a large piece of bar gold as a present from the sovereign and begged him to honour his country with a visit. On this Dīpaṅkara replied: "Then it seems to me that my going to Tibet would be due to two causes—first, the desire for amassing gold, and second, the wish to acquire sainthood by the loving of others. But I must say that I have no necessity for gold nor any anxiety for the second at present". At this unexpected reply, Gya-tson wept bitterly, wiping his tears with a corner of the sacerdotal robe. . . . Dīpaṅkara sympathized with him and tried to console him.'

Further attempts were made to induce him to come to Tibet. Two or three other missions were organized, but with no better success. To defray the expenses of these repeated missions, the king had to go out prospecting for gold.

While on a visit to a lately discovered gold-mine on the border of his kingdom, the king fell into the hands of the *rājā* of Gharwal who was inimical to Buddhism. He was cast into prison by the *rājā* and offered the alternative of either renouncing Buddhism or paying as ransom a block of solid gold of the size and weight of the captive king's person. His nephew made repeated attempts to collect the necessary amount of gold, but the total fell short. At last the long-suffering king summoned the nephew to the prison and expressed a desire to die a martyr. 'Do not give a grain of gold to this cruel *rājā*', he said to the nephew; 'take back the entire quantity of it that you may conduct religious service in our great monasteries and spend it in bringing an Indian *paṇḍita* to Tibet.' So the devout king expired in captivity and was succeeded by his loyal nephew.

The nephew, whose name was Chan Chub, became a monk after accession to the throne and made it his life's purpose to carry out the last wishes of his royal uncle.

He sent for a learned Tibetan monk named Nag-tsho who had already visited and studied at Vikramaśilā, having gone there on one of the previous abortive missions. He had, on return, settled down to a life of scholarly pursuits in a monastery in Tibet. To him, the king said: 'Now that you are accustomed to hot climate, Vinayadhara (learned monk), and acquainted with the way to India and can talk in and interpret the Indian language, you should go as our envoy to bring Dīpaṅkara to Tibet. Should he decline to come, you must try to bring someone who is second to him in learning and holiness'.

Nag-tsho begged to be excused, feeling that a mission so delicate and hazardous was beyond his capacity. But the king was importunate. 'Vinaya-dhara', bade the king, 'it behoves you not to disregard your sovereign's commands. If you go this time and please him, the opportunity to please you will not be allowed to be lost. Whether you study here or in India or even if you do not study at all, you shall have to serve the State. This time, under any circumstances, you should go to India.' Nag-tsho in duty bound had to obey.

The king allowed Nag-tsho one hundred attendants, but the latter wished to make a party of five only. He was provided with a large quantity of gold for the expenses of the journey and also a bar of gold, weighing sixteen ounces, to be offered to the Indian *paṇḍita* at Vikramaśilā.

The party reached the Indian frontier in safety, but on crossing it, became at once the object of unwelcome attention from robbers. One night, when they were bivouacking in a bamboo shed, a band of Indian robbers, who had shared the shelter with them, plotted to shut them in and set fire to the shed. But the Tibetans, getting wind of this plot, effected an escape through an opening in the bamboo wall. Then they travelled all night.

In the morning they met a Nepalese prince who was proceeding with a large retinue to Vikramaśilā. The Nepalese party escorted the Tibetans up to the bank of the Gangā and then crossed over in a ferry-boat. Left without guide or escort, the Tibetans were frightened and waited anxiously for the boat's return.

It was night: the surroundings were strange and robbers were abroad. They concealed their store of gold under the sands of the foreshore and stood round concentrating their minds on the Buddha, the divine protector. When night was far advanced, the *chol chol* noise of falling oars on the water was heard. The boatmen returned and ferried the Tibetan party across. Nag-tsho squatted in the boat, reciting and repeating the mystic syllables—*Om Maṇi Padme Hum* (The Jewel is in the Lotus)—and counting the beads of his rosary. Reaching the other side of the river, the Tibetan party walked by night up to the portals of the monastery, which was perched on a hilltop, and found accommodation for the night in a guest-house.

There was a detached lodging-house outside the portals which was assigned to Tibetans. An eminent Tibetan scholar, a disciple of Dīpaṅkara, whose name was Gya-tson Senge, was in residence there. To him the party presented themselves on the following morning. Nag-tsho, who had been his pupil in Tibet, was at once recognized. Gya-tson, however, advised him to keep his mission secret for fear of exciting hostility. He was asked to wait for a favourable opportunity to meet Dīpaṅkara and disclose his mind to him.

At the morning congregation Nag-tsho had his first sight of Dīpaṅkara: 'When all the rows of seats were filled up, there came at last Jovo (Lord) Atīśa, the venerable of all venerables, in all his glory, at whose sight the eyes felt no satiety. His graceful appearance and smiling face struck everyone.

From his waist hung a bundle of keys. The Indians, the Nepalese and the Tibetans all looked at him and took him for a countryman of their own. Even the gods would own him. There was brightness mixed with simplicity of expression in his face, which acted as a magic spell upon those who beheld him.'

One morning while Dīpaṅkara was supervising the daily feeding of the poor at the monastery, Nag-tsho made bold to approach him. The incident is thus described by him: 'Tears of joy flowed from my eyes. I followed him as he walked towards his place and I was about to fall from a bridge, my attention being wholly engrossed upon him. He recognized me as a Tibetan and said: "Ah, Tibetan Ayusmat (Sir), you Tibetans are earnest men. Do not shed tears. I have much regard for the Tibetan people, your king and his ministers. So it seems you have again come for me without losing heart; offer your prayers to the Three Holies".' 'As these words dropped from his lips', says Nag-tsho, 'I became hopeful and cheerful.'

After a few days' stay, Nag-tsho was conducted by Gya-tson to Dīpaṅkara's presence. The bar of gold, brought with so much anxious care all the way from Tibet, was placed on a circular tray about a foot and a half in diameter, called the *Maṇḍala* or Circle of Offerings. A quantity of gold dust also was put in a small bag and handed over to Dīpaṅkara.

Gya-tson then gave a moving narration of the chequered history of the Buddhist religion in Tibet and the heroic efforts of Lha Lama, the martyred king, and of his nephew Chan Chub to reform and revive it, winding up with a passionate appeal to Dīpaṅkara to cast a gracious look on that benighted country. Dīpaṅkara was visibly moved, but he felt that he could not leave his post at Vikramaśilā for a few years to come. He was sixty then. 'Nevertheless, in the meantime', said he, 'I shall consult my tutelary deities. For the present do take back the gold.' So saying, he returned the presents.

The oracles were duly consulted by Dīpaṅkara, but their predictions, though generally favourable, were saddled with a warning that his life, which would otherwise have lasted till the ninety-second year, would be cut short by twenty years if he proceeded to Tibet. Unheeding the warning, he made up his mind to go.

The settlement of the affairs of the monastery and the transference of charge took four years more and the Tibetans stayed on at the monastery, improving their learning and going out on short tours.

The time came when Dīpaṅkara, having relieved himself gradually of his charge, intimated his decision to the Tibetans to accompany them to their country. But he wished to leave in secret for fear of opposition. It was given out that he would be going on a visit to the Temple of Svayambhū in Nepal after a pilgrimage of the eight holy places of Buddhism in India. Nag-tsho packed sixty loads on thirty horses and the caravan crossed the Gangā at midnight. Secret word of it was at the same time sent to Dīpaṅkara's disciple Gya-tson, who was then laid up with fever at Nālandā, but he came post-haste to Vikramaśilā in a *dooly* (man-borne chaise).

The charge of the monastery was formally made over to Ratnākara and the gold presented by the Tibetans handed over for the use of the institution. To Nag-tsho, Ratnākara made a final appeal not to deprive the country of so illustrious a teacher: 'O Ayusmat (Sir), without Dīpaṅkara India will be in darkness. He holds the keys of many institutions. The looming signs prognosticate evil for India. Numerous Turaṣkas are about to invade India and I am deeply concerned at heart.'

Leaving Vikramaśilā the party proceeded to a monastery near the boundary between India and Nepal—Gya-tson with two attendants, Nag-tsho with six and Dīpaṅkara with twenty. The frontier was crossed and the party found themselves in Nepal.

The great Temple of Svayambhū, which to this day dominates Khatmandu, the Nepalese capital, was reached at last. A grand ovation was given them by the *rājā* of Nepal and an imposing religious assembly was held.

Dīpaṅkara's sojourn in the Nepalese capital, however, was darkened by a melancholy incident. Gya-tson, his favourite Tibetan disciple, who had come from Nālandā in ill health to join his master at Vikramaśilā and accompanied him all the way to Nepal, died, as it is said, through the effect of an evil charm cast upon him by a *Tīrthika* (heretic). It cast a deep gloom over the party. Dīpaṅkara himself was inconsolable. The deceased was a most accomplished *locava* (interpreter) and Dīpaṅkara had hoped to address the Tibetan people through him. 'Now that my tongue has dropped off', he lamented, 'I shall be of no service to the Tibetans.' A whole month was spent in Nepal.

Before leaving the country, Dīpaṅkara presented to the king of Nepal, who was a pious Buddhist, an elephant named 'Driṣṭa-Ouṣadhi' ('One whose sight effects a cure'—a somewhat strange name for an elephant), on condition that it was not to be used as a war-elephant, but employed only in carrying sacred objects, scriptures, symbols and images.

At the boundary between Nepal and Tibet, a spectacular reception awaited the party. A hundred horsemen were drawn up clad completely in white, and in front of them rode four Tibetan generals, each attended by sixteen lancers bearing white flags, and at the rear of the military formation waited a long procession of Tibetans carrying twenty huge umbrellas of white satin and innumerable buntings of white. A musical band kept playing all the time on reeds, bagpies, guitars and other musical instruments. At the sight of Dīpaṅkara, the entire concourse moved up, chanting in unison the sacred syllables, *Oṁ Maṇi Padme Hum.*

A ceremonial offering, consisting of five ounces of gold, a tray filled with treacle and a cup of tea decorated with figures of Chinese dragons, was held out to Dīpaṅkara. The tea was a strange drink to him and he asked its name. The Tibetan interpreter explained: 'Venerable Sir, it is called *Chā*. The monks of Tibet drink it. We do not know if the *Chā* (tea) plant is eaten, but the leaves are churned in hot water, mixed with soda, salt and butter, and the soup is drunk.' Dīpaṅkara found this Tibetan tea an excellent beverage.

The whole party then proceeded towards the capital, stopping for a month on the way at the home of Nag-tsho and passing by the shore of the famous Tibetan mountain-lake, Mānasa-sarovar, celebrated in Indian legends. Dīpaṅkara halted at the lake for a week, performing ablutions and offering oblations to the manes.

The royal monastery of Tholin, the destination of the journey, was reached in a huge triumphal procession which kept lustily singing the ancient welcome of Tibet—*Lo a lo ma lo la lo la.* This song of welcome had been composed and sung when the illustrious scholar of Nālandā, Śāntārakṣita, had been escorted three centuries earlier from the Indian borders to Tibet. It is also said that a novel musical instrument was invented and for the first time sounded to mark the occasion of Dīpaṅkara's arrival at the capital, a long brass trumpet curiously shaped, of the type known as '*ragdun*' in Tibet. The particular trumpet sounded on the occasion came to be known by the name of *Lopan Chen Denpai Dun,* meaning the 'Trumpet of inviting the Paṇḍita'.

Dīpaṅkara was established at the capital in the office of the High priest of Tibet and invested with the honorific title of 'Jovo Je' (Supreme Lord).

Besides holding religious services, addressing assemblies and administering the church, he engaged himself in writing books on the esoteric doctrines of Buddhism.

After a residence of several years at the capital, Dīpaṅkara started on a missionary tour of Central Tibet. He went from Tholin, the capital, to the city of Lhasa and, while on a journey from Lhasa to a monastery in the interior, he died at a wayside place called Nethan. He had just completed his seventy-second year.

His body was duly cremated at Nethan, but, in accordance with the Buddhist practice of relic-worship, a handful of ashes and charred bones from the funeral pyre was enshrined in a tomb. Waddell in his book, *Lhasa and its Mysteries* (1905), describes this tomb, known as Sagro-ma in the locality, as a circular building painted yellow outside and decorated with a few crude paintings. At the time of Waddell's visit, it was partly in ruins and buried among tufts of willows. Half a dozen illiterate lamas, who lived in the neighbourhood, had charge of the monument.

c. SOMAPURA

In the course of his travels eastward in northern India, Hsüan-tsang came in AD 639 to the province called Puṇḍravardhana. It was then a large State (*Bhukti*) of northern India covering the modern districts of Bogra, Dinajpur and Rajshahi, now in East Pakistan.[1]

Hsüan-tsang noticed some Buddhist establishments here, but remarks that 'the naked Nirgranthas (Jains) are the most numerous'.[2] Among the many Jaina temples and monasteries of this region was an ancient Jaina establishment at the village of Pāhārpur in the district of Rajshahi. When this part of the country came under Pāla dominion, Buddhism became the dominant religion and the site, which had been well known in this part and presumably a popular resort, was selected by a Pāla king to be the site of a mahāvihāra known as the Dharmapāla Mahāvihāra of Somapura.

This interesting early history of the establishment comes to us from a copperplate discovered in 1927 in the ruins of the great temple which dominates it. The plate is dated in AD 479 and records a grant of several plots of land by a Brāhmaṇa couple for the maintenance here of the worship of *Arhats*. The donors were Nāthasarmmā and Rāmī, and Guhanandī was the high priest of the establishment, then a Jaina one. The locality is named as Vaṭa-Gohāli (Cowherd's settlement), a name still retained by a neighbouring village called Goālpārā (the settlement of cowherds).[3]

It seems that at the time when this existing establishment was overhauled and remodelled and the Jaina temple rebuilt as a Buddhist

[1] See Nihar Ranjan Ray's *Bāṅgālīr Itihāsa*, p. 144.
[2] Beal's *Buddhist Records*, ii, p. 195.
[3] See Dikshit's *Paharpur Copper-plate Grant of the* (*Gupta*) *Year* 159 in *Epigraphia Indica*, Vol. xx, p. 59 ff.

one by a Buddhist Pāla king, a township named Somapura had sprung up here. The name, but slightly modified, is still borne by a village called Ompur about a mile off.

A Mahāvihāra centring round and dominated by a temple is a somewhat rare phenomenon among the monastery-ruins of northern India. But here a vast temple, in ruins now, stands dominating an extensive monastic site, and the temple itself is peculiar in that its architecture differs from all normal temple-architecture, Brāhmaṇical or Buddhist, of India. Perhaps in rebuilding the site, something of its ancient contour of the time when it was a Jaina shrine, was kept, though nothing definite can be said on this point.

The main gate, a huge structure judging by the remains, faces north. Outside it spread the ancient town of Somapura. Entering by this gate, one faces the temple and, going round it, enters a vast quadrangle about a mile square. It was surrounded by an encompassing wall and, along this wall, separated by a running portico, were the monks' cells, numbering 177 in all. They are usually rectangular in shape with no stone-beds in them, but several have altars and pedestals built inside rendering the living accommodation somewhat exiguous. There used to be a channel of flowing water, perhaps an inlet of the river Padmā, running along the foundation of the wall on the eastern side where, for convenience of flushing, the privies were arranged. This channel has long since dried up, though the remains of a bathing *ghat* still show. Here and there round the wall there are grouped chambers, perhaps intended as stations for guards and administrative officers. A common kitchen and dining hall, where broken pieces of cooking utensils and scattered grains of rice blackened by age have been found, is also among the remains.[1]

It is the ruined temple, however, which, towering above the ruins, forms the most outstanding feature of the ensemble. It has the pyramidal shape of a Burmese pagoda, built in terraces and topped by a shrine with a hollow underneath going right down to the temple's foundation. Three storeys still stand above ground and local archaeologists believe that two more storeys have sunk underground. One could climb from storey to storey through running corridors and each storey had chambers where, however, no ritual objects have been found. The terraces are built round a central block which has the shape of a gigantic cross. Between each arm there are rectangular projections, all embellished with friezes of decorative bricks and over two thousand terra-cotta plaques showing a bewildering variety of human and animal motifs and a large number of mythological

[1] For a sketch of the ground plan of the entire establishment, see Plate 1 in *Memoir of the Archaeological Survey of India, No.* 55 (Dikshit's *Excavations at Paharpur*).

figures, both Brāhmaṇical and Buddhist, as well as stone bas-reliefs round the basement.

The art arrests attention. It is purely decorative, contributed evidently by journeyman artists. The earlier decorations are in late Gupta style, while others show the formative beginnings of a regional (Bengali) style of art. It is not Buddhist art—in fact among the figures of common men and women and those of saints and ascetics, a Buddha-figure has to be looked for: it has no prominent enplacement.

The Paharpur temple, however, from the architectural and artistic point of view, is a most interesting monument. The realism of the terra-cotta plaques that profusely decorate it is striking in its study and rendering of contemporary and regional life and society in different types and phases. Their importance is considerable for the social history of the region. They also betray concepts of mythology and folk-lore that were current in that age, though purely Buddhist ones are surprisingly few. The *Jātaka* tales, the stock-in-trade of the ancient *stūpa* decorators, do not appear at all and seem to have been unknown to these artists. More striking is the architectural form of the temple. It has none of the characteristic features of Indian temple architecture, but is strongly reminiscent of Buddhist temples of Burma, Java and Cambodia, reproducing their cruciform basement, terraced structure with inset chambers and gradually dwindling pyramidal form. 'There can be no doubt', says Mr Dikshit, 'that this style of architecture has most profoundly influenced that of Burma, Java and Cambodia. The nearest approximation to the plan and the superstructure of the Pāhārpur temple is afforded by the temples known as Chandi Loro Jongrang and Chandi Sevu of Prambanam in Central Java.'[1]

It is a question whether the great temple of Pāhārpur was the prototype of these south-east Asian temples: such a possibility is suggested by the fact that during the age of the Pālas some sort of intercourse between eastern India and south-east Asia existed. Evidence of it is the construction of a monastery at Nālandā by a king of Sumatra in the reign of Devapāla, founder of the mahāvihāra at Somapura, of which there is a record in a copperplate inscription discovered at Nālandā.[2] But how this temple-type, represented in India by this solitary example, became the standard of Buddhist temple architecture of south-eastern Asia is not known. Perhaps the Jaina structure which had originally stood on the site of this temple influenced to some extent the plan and pattern of its later enlarged reconstruction. But this is merely speculative, as it is unknown how its architect actually proceeded.

The temple having been fixed in the ensemble, the other parts had

[1] *Ibid*, p. 7. [2] See *Epigraphia Indica*, Vol. XVII, pp. 310 ff.

to be designed in relation to it. The congregational buildings were in its extensive quadrangular court, and the monastic cells were placed along each side of the surrounding wall, nearly half a mile in length. Entering through the main gate on the north, one had to go round this temple for access to the monastic buildings.

There is no doubt that these buildings, containing as many as 177 cells for the residence of monks, constituted a unitary mahāvihāra. It bears the name of Dharmapāla. We have mentioned already that in the age of the Pālas, the mahāvihāras were under State supervision and each was recognized as a separate but co-ordinate corporation. Monastic corporation seals of the Pāla period have been discovered both at Nālandā and at Somapura, having the same device and emblem. Two terra-cotta sealings found at Somapura have the following legend in the lower register:

First line—*Śrī Somapure* (At Somapura).

Second line—*Mahāvihārīya-ārya-bhikṣusaṁghasya* (Of the community of venerable monks of the Mahāvihāra).

Intercourse in the Pāla period between this mahāvihāra and that of Nālandā is suggested by the decorative style of a stone temple at Nālandā (site No. 2) where terra-cotta plaques are arranged in rows exactly as in this temple, and in the plaques the technique as well as the themes depicted are strikingly similar.[1] A number of Somapura sealings refer to two persons Dharmasena and Siṁhasena. Their seals have been discovered also at Nālandā. It is surmised from this that they must have been two dignitaries or officers of the Pāla regime who had charge of supervision of the mahāvihāras.[2] Besides, the inscription at Nālandā of Vipulaśrīmitra of Somapura shows that he built a monastery at Nālandā, a Tārā temple at Somapura and carried out large renovations of monastic cells at the latter place.[3]

Tibetan tradition, recorded by both Tāranātha and Sumpa,[4] is that the founder of the establishment was Devapāla (AD 810–50), son and successor of Dharmapāla. Devapāla carried on the enterprise of empire-building launched by his father and it was during his reign that the dominion of the Pālas in the east had its largest extension. Both kings seem to have been keen on the spread and consolidation of Buddhist culture in the Pāla dominion which they were extending on all sides. As Dharmapāla had built the Vikramaśilā establishment, so his successor built the Somapura Mahāvihāra, both planned and designed on a strikingly large scale. But in the finds obtained so far

[1] See Ghosh's *Guide to Nalanda*, p. 12. [2] Dikshit's *Memoir*, p. 19.

[3] See *Epigraphia Indica*, Vol. XXI (N. G. Majumdar on the *Nalanda Inscription of Vipulasrimitra*), pp. 97–101.

[4] See *Indian Antiquary*, Vol. IV, p. 366, and *Pag-sam-jon-zang* (S. C. Das's Ed.), pp. 111–16, and Index, p. cxxx.

from the Pāhārpur ruins, the name of Devapāla nowhere occurs, while a lithic inscription and several clay-seals describe the establishment as 'Dharmapāla Mahāvihāra'. Perhaps the name was meant to be commemorative—the son's dutiful tribute to the memory of the father who was the founder of Vikramaśilā and whose example he followed in erecting this mahāvihāra.

The Dharmapāla Mahāvihāra, in the opinion of Dikshit, 'is easily the largest single *saṅghārāma* that was ever erected in India for Buddhist monks'.[1] It undoubtedly has a larger spread and layout than any other single monastic site so far known. The establishment seems to have been designed for the occupation of some 600 to 800 inmates. In the eleventh century, the number probably diminished to half. Several cells were renovated by placing ornamental altars and pedestals in them, thereby reducing the size inside the living room. Perhaps in the later history of the establishment, congregational meetings were largely replaced by private worship in the monks' cells. Whatever the reason for the construction of these interior altars and pedestals, it suggests a large dwindling in the number of inmates.

The Mahāvihāra must have existed and functioned over nearly four centuries—from the early ninth when it was founded by Devapāla to the late twelfth when the cataclysm of Muslim invasion overtook all Pāla Buddhist institutions. Its history, however, is almost a blank except for one lurid episode to be presently related.

Somapura undoubtedly carried on the Nālandā tradition which had passed on to Odantapura and Vikramaśilā and was inherited by it. Dīpaṅkara Śrījñāna of Vikramaśilā, according to Tibetan tradition, stayed here for some time before his departure for Tibet. It was here that he translated a work by Bhāvya, in collaboration with Vīryasiṁha and his own Tibetan disciple Nag-tsho, which is found in the Tibetan canonical collection under the title *Mādhyamika-ratna-pradīpa*.[2] Another work in the collection composed in the mahāvihāra of Somapura is *Dharmakāya-dīpa-vidhi* translated into Tibetan by one Prajñāśrījñānakīrti.[3] Other names of learned monks of Somapura are known from inscriptions and also from references in Tibetan histories. We have, for example, the story of a learned Tāntric monk of this place in the *Blue Annals* (vol. II, pp. 844–45), one named Vairocana Rakṣita who used to wander from monastery to monastery, stayed to acquire learning at Nālandā and Vikramaśilā and received instruction from one Paṇḍita Śaraṇa described as the 'head of the assembly of Yogins in the town of Somapura'. One Vīryendra, a

[1] Dikshit's *Memoir*, p. 18.
[2] Listed in Cordier III, p. 299 with the colophon that the work was composed at the *vihāra* of Somapura. It is No. 3854 in the *Tohoku Catalogue*.
[3] Cordier II, p. 166; Tohoku, No. 1953.

native of Samtata (south-east Bengal), made a donation at Boddhgayā and describes himself as belonging to Somapura in the donatory inscription.[1] It is interesting to notice that, among the monks of Somapura whose names appear in the inscriptions, lineage-names like '-garbha' and '-mitra' are found.[2] A 'Mitra' lineage among the elders of the Somapura monastery is indicated by the inscription of Vipulaśrī-mitra at Nālandā who names as his spiritual predecessors Karuṇāśrī-mitra, Maitriśrī-mitra and Asoka-mitra. The first died a martyr. His end is described in Vipulaśrīmitra's inscription assignable to the first half of the twelfth century, in the context of a gruesome episode, the only one known of the four-centuries' history of Somapura.[3]

It seems to have happened round the middle of the eleventh century—about a hundred years before the inscriptional record. At that time a family migrating perhaps from the south, with the surname *Varman*, had set up a sort of kingdom in East Bengal (*Vaṅgāl*). The first king was named Jātavarmā. He seems to have been inimical to Buddhism and tried to achieve notoriety by destroying the great monastery that was flourishing at Somapura in his time in northern Bengal. With this object, he sent troops who marched on the Dharmapāla Monastery and set fire to it.[4] Among the inmates was Karuṇāśrīmitra. While the conflagration spread around, he refused to flee, and clung to the feet of the Buddha's image till the flame with many tongues came and licked up his prostrate body.

Though the Mahāvihāra suffered grievously from the conflagration, it was not destroyed. Repair and renovation seem to have gone on by fits and starts over a century after and Vipulaśrīmitra himself, as it appears from his inscription, took a large hand in the restoration. He renovated a number of monks' cells and it is likely that the altars and pedestals found in a number of them were contributed by him. He also built a temple of considerable dimensions to Goddess Tārā, the ruins of which still stand outside the monastery-walls.

The ruins of the temple and monasteries at Pāhārpur do not bear any evident marks of large-scale destruction. The downfall of the establishment, by desertion or destruction, must have been sometime in the midst of the widespread unrest and displacement of population consequent on the Muslim invasion.

d. JAGADDALA

The last great seat of Buddhist learning founded by a Pāla king was Jagaddala. It was in northern Bengal known anciently as Varendra

[1] See *Journal of the Asiatic Society*, 1908–09, p. 158. [2] Dikshit's *Memoir*, p. 74.
[3] See *Epigraphia Indica*, Vol. xxi (N. G. Majumdar on *Nalanda Inscription of Vipulasrimitra*, pp. 97–101).
[4] See Nihar Ranjan Ray's *Bāṅgālir Itihāsa*, p. 519.

(or Varendrī). This Mahāvihāra flourished in Rāmapāla's reign (*c.* 1077–1120) and in all probability was founded by the king himself. The Pāla kingdom in his time was tottering to its fall. Torn with internal strife and whittled down by external aggressions, it was limited only to a circumscribed northern area of Bengal.

The king was fortunate in having a court-poet, named Sandhyākara Nandī, to celebrate his greatness. This poet composed an epic in four cantos, adding to it as a supplement a poetic self-eulogium (*kavi-praśasti*)—a work in the peculiar style of the kind of artificial epic known as *Rāghava-pāṇḍavīya* in Sanskrit poetics.[1] The poem is entitled *Rāmacaritam* and in each stanza it relates obversely the story of Rāma as told in the *Rāmāyaṇa* and reversely the life-story of the poet's patron, King Rāmapāla. The latter is in fact the real intended theme of the epic.

A glorified description in epic style of Varendrī, Rāmapāla's kingdom, and of its capital Rāmāvatī built by him occurs in Canto III of the poem. In recounting the glories of Varendrī, the poet mentions its great Jagaddala monastery:[2]

'(Varendrī)—which had elephants of the *mandra* type imported (into its forests)—where, in the "great monastery" (Mahāvihāra) of Jagaddala, kindly love for all was found accumulated—which country bore (in its heart) the image of (Bodhisattva) Lokeśa—and whose great glory was still more increased (or pronounced) by (the presence of) the great (heads of monasteries) and the (image of) Tārā (the Buddhist goddess).'

From the description it appears that in Rāmapāla's time Buddhism prevailed in Varendrī and had its centre at the Jagaddala monastery. It is somewhat uncertain whether the monastery itself was situated in Rāmapāla's capital Rāmāvatī or outside it,[3] though the former alternative is likelier.

[1] See Keith's *History of Sanskrit Literature*, p. 137. A *Rāghava-pāṇḍavīya* epic has for its theme the story of the *Rāmāyaṇa* and that of the *Mahābhārata* told with *double entendre* in the same words.

[2] See Canto III, verse 7, of the *Rāmacaritam* (Ed. by Dr R. C. Majumdar and others, pub. by Curator, Varendra Research Museum, Rajshahi, 1939):
'*Mandrānāṁ sthitimuḍhāṁ Jagaddala-mahāvihāra-cita-rāgaṁ; Dadhatiṁ lokeśamapi mahat-tārodiritoru-mahīmānam.*'
The editors' translation is given above.

[3] Dr Radha Kumud Mookerji says: 'According to the historical epic, *Rāmacaritam*, King Rāmapāla of Bengal and Magadha(?), who reigned between 1084 and 1130, founded a new city which he called Rāmāvatī on the banks of the rivers Gangā and Karotoā in Varendra and equipped the city with a *vihāra* called Jagaddala' (*Ancient Indian Education*, MacMillan, 2nd Ed., 1951, p. 595). This is not quite correct. The reference to Jagaddala occurs in Canto III, verse 7, in a sequence of verses describing Varendrī, *after* which the description of the capital Rāmāvatī is taken up (see *Rāmacaritam*, Varendra Research Museum, Rajshahi, 1939, Intro., p. xxi).
There is a village called Jagaddala in the district of Bogra in northern Bengal (ancient Varendrī—now in East Pakistan) where there is a mound, not excavated yet.

It became a resort of scholars of Tāntric Buddhism. It seems also to have been in lively intercourse with Tibetan centres of Buddhism—a fact of some interest suggested, as we shall observe later, by the large number of *Tanjur* and *Kanjur* texts, both original and translation from Sanskrit, said to have been made or copied in the monastery of Jagaddala.[1] The existence of Rāmāvatī can be traced down to the reign of Akbar the Great (1556–1605), but the history of Jagaddala monastery stops short near the turn of the thirteenth century.

A stray spot of light falls on its end-period from the story of Śākya Śrībhadra in the Tibetan legends.

This learned Kashmirian monk had come all the way from far-off Kashmir to visit existing Buddhist seats of learning in Magadha. But as he found both Odantapura and Vikramaśilā destroyed, he wended his way farther east until he came to Jagaddala which was till then intact.[2] Here he found asylum, but not for long—for about three years only. The ruin that had already fallen on the two older monasteries was impending also on Jagaddala. Śākya Śrībhadra, however, during his brief residence at Jagaddala, found here a *guru* (spiritual guide) named Śubhākaragupta[3] who seems to have been both a saint and a scholar. One of the texts in the *Tanjur* is Dānaśīla's Tibetan translation of a Sanskrit work, a commentary on a *tantra*, composed by him.[4] Śrībhadra also had pupils and disciples here—among them two bright scholars, Vibhūticandra and Dānaśīla. They are authors of a number of works, of which the originals are lost, but Tibetan translations exist in the *Tanjur* and *Kanjur*.

Little is known about the lives and careers of these two scholarly disciples of Śrībhadra at Jagaddala; they were bilingualists, proficient in both Sanskrit and Tibetan. In the *Tanjur* texts, both are mentioned with the appellations *Paṇḍita* (learned), *Mahāpaṇḍita* (vastly learned), *Upādhyāya* (professor) or *Ācārya* (teacher). They were Tāntric Buddhists and almost all their works relate to Buddhism of the Tāntric school. After Dīpaṅkara Śrījñāna, it was Śākya Śrībhadra and his disciples, Vibhūticandra and Dānaśīla, who kept alight the torch of Tāntric Buddhist learning in Tibet. Much of the Tāntric literature of a later stratum in the *Tanjur* and *Kanjur* was the outgrowth of this learning. The Tibetan tradition is that Vibhūti-

[1] See D. D. Kosambi's Introduction (pp. xxxvi–xxxix) to *Subhāṣita-ratna-kośa* compiled by Vidyākara, Harvard University Series, Vol. 42 (1957).

[2] See *Pag-jam-zon-zang* (S. C. Das's ed.), p. 122, and S. C. Das's *A Note on the Antiquity of Chittagong* in the *Journal of the Asiatic Society of Bengal*, 1898, p. 25. In the Tibetan legend, Jagaddala is said to be situated in Otivassa (Orissa) which is a mistake for Varendra.

[3] In the colophon of Dānaśīla's Tibetan translation of Śubhākara's work (see footnote 3 next page), Śubhākara is mentioned as the *Guru* of Śākya Śrībhadra. See Cordier's *Catalogue*, II, p. 293.

[4] It is a commentarial work, entitled 'Siddhāika-vīra-tantra-ṭīkā.' See Cordier's *Catalogue*, Part II, p. 293. It is No. 2,674 in the *Tohoku Imperial University Catalogue*.

candra was a prince who had forsaken his princedom to become a monk. His works preserved in Tibetan are of a miscellaneous sort—original productions, translations, scholia and emendations. Among them is a commentary on Śāntideva's *Bodhicaryāvatāra*[1] and also translations into Tibetan of some of the works of Abhayākaragupta.[2] The other disciple, Dānaśīla, translated about sixty texts of Tāntric Buddhism into Tibetan.[3] Among the translated works of Vibhūticandra and Dānaśīla in the Tibetan canons, it is not possible to separate those written in India from those written in Nepal or Tibet where they took refuge leaving Jagaddala to escape from the Muslim peril.

Śākya Śrībhadra, Vibhūticandra and Dānaśīla—all three of them—were in Nepal and Tibet within three years of Śrībhadra's arrival at Jagaddala. Life for the monks had become unsafe in Varendra; the Turaṣkas had penetrated into northern Bengal and were already on the rampage.

The situation that was unfolding in this region at the time is thus summarized by the Tibetan historian:[4] 'At the time of Lavang Sena (the first ruler of the Sena dynasty), some Bhikṣus were sent as emissaries to the region between the Gangā and the Jamunā (i.e. the place where the Turaṣkas were settled). The Turaṣkas combined. They destroyed Odantapura and Vikramaśilā and killed many Bhikṣus. At that time Śākya Śrībhadra fled towards Orissa (*Note*—Probably mistake for Varendra). Within three years after that, he reached Tibet and gave initiation to many Bhikṣus. Others fled to other places. (*Note*—They are named in Tibetan legends as Ārkhān, i.e. Ārācan; Munād, i.e. Burma, and Kambhoja, i.e. Cambodia[5]). Thus Buddhism came to an end in Magadha.'

Yet at Jagaddala, as probably also at other Pāla seats of learning, something of the tradition of Nālandā's liberal culture and learning seems to have lingered. The old *Vidyās* were not rooted out completely by the Tantras: there were scholars still pursuing those *Vidyās*.

One such scholar of Jagaddala was Mokṣākaragupta. He devoted himself to the study of a main branch of Mahāyānist learning—*Hetuvidyā* (Science of Logic). He appears to have been more a scholar of the old school than a follower of the Tantras, and his treatise on

[1] For this work by Śāntideva, see Part IV, sec. 5 (Lives and Works) under Śāntideva. For Vibhūticandra's commentarial work, named *Viśeṣa-dyotanī*, see Cordier's *Catalogue*, III, p. 310, and *Tohoku University Catalogue*, No. 3,880.

[2] For the works of Abhayākaragupta, see Part V, Sec. 2, p. 346.

[3] A list of translations from Sanskrit into Tibetan ascribed to Dānaśīla, which appear in Cordier's *Catalogue*, is given in Bose's *Indian Teachers of Buddhist Universities*, pp. 151–54.

[4] Only the purport is given. See *Pag-sam-jon-zang* (S. C. Das's ed.), p. 122.

[5] *Ibid*, p. 112.

logic entitled *Tarkabhāṣā* concludes with the same *pariṇāmanā* formula[1] as the old Mahāyānist scholars usually conclude their works with:

'Whatever merit I have acquired by writing this work, *Tarkabhāṣā*, with that merit let the world proceed to Buddhahood.'[2]

The work purports to elucidate the 'technicalities of Logic' for the purpose of introducing learners to the system of Dharmakīrti.[3] It is in three chapters under the heads: (i) Perception, (ii) Inference for one's own self, and (iii) Inference for others. A Tibetan translation of the work exists in the *Tanjur*, ascribed erroneously to one Jñānaśrī,[4] but its original has been discovered in the Jaina manuscript library at Pattan[5] with the following colophon:

'Finis. Ended is the third chapter on *Parārthānumāna* (Inference for Others) in the *Tarkabhāṣā* composed by the great ascetic (*Mahā-yati*) Śrīmat Bhikṣu Mokṣākaragupta belonging to Rāja-Jagaddala monastery.'[6]

The name 'Royal (*Rāja*) Jagaddala Monastery' by which Mokṣākaragupta calls the establishment was perhaps the name by which it was then known, for it occurs elsewhere in the *Tanjur*-texts.[7]

The condition to which the city of Rāmāvatī with the Mahāvihāra was reduced by Turaṣka ravages, which overtook them probably round 1207—some time after Odantapura and Vikramaśilā had been destroyed—is not known. The great monastery must have been deserted altogether, but the site of Rāmāvatī seems to have been repopulated after the Muslim conquest and continued, as its mention under the name of Rāmāutī in the *Ain-i-Akbari* shows, for at least three to four centuries more.[8]

---

[1] See Part IV, Sec. 5, p. 283 and footnote 4.
[2] '*Tarkabhāṣāmimāṁ kṛtvā puṇyamāsādi yanmayā
Tena puṇyena lokoyaṁ buddhatvamadhigacchtu.*'
(See *A Descriptive Catalogue of Mss. in the Jaina Bhandaras at Pattan*, Vol. I, p. 59. The translation is mine.)
[3] For Dharmakīrti, see Part IV, Sec. 6, p. 290.
[4] See S. C. Vidyabhushan's *Indian Logic: Mediaeval School*, pp. 138–39.
[5] See *A Descriptive Catalogue*, etc. Vol. I, p. 59.
[6] '*Iti Śrīmad-Rāja-Jagaddala-vihārīya mahā-yati bhikṣu Mokṣākaragupta-viracitāyāṁ tarkabhāṣāyāṁ parārthānumāna-paricchedaḥ samāptaḥ.*' (*Ibid*, Vol. I, p. 59.)
[7] e.g. Cordier III, p. 285, where the Tibetan author of the work is called 'Rāja-Jagaddala-vāsin' and in the colophon the name of the founder King (*nṛpati*) Rāmapāla occurs.
[8] See Jarret's *Ain-i-Akbari*, pub. by Asiatic Society of Bengal, 1891, Vol. II, p. 131. Rāmāutī was in *Sarkar* of Jannatābād or Lakhnauti, paying a revenue of 194,767 *dams*.

BIBLIOGRAPHY

NB—Particulars about the edition used are given in the footnotes in the book.

Abbreviations—Ed. (Edited), Tr. (Translated), SBE (Sacred Books of the East), PTS (Pali Text Society), SBH (Sacred Books of the Hindus, Panini Office, Allahabad).

I. LITERARY SOURCES

PALI, SANSKRIT AND GENERAL

(a) *Original Texts* (*Pali*)

1. Oldenberg's Vinayapiṭakam (Tr. SBE, Vols. 13, 17 and 20).
2. Rhys Davids and Carpenter's Dīgha Nikāya (Tr. *Dialogues of the Buddha*, Sacred Books of the Buddhists).
3. Trenckner and Chalmers' Majjhima Nikāya (Tr. *Further Dialogues*, Sacred Books of the Buddhists).
4. Morris and Hardy's Aṅguttara Nikāya (Tr. Woodward and Hare's *Gradual Sayings*).
5. Taylor's Kathāvatthu (Tr. Aung and Mrs Rhys Davids' *Points of Controversy*).
6. Therī-gāthā (Tr. Mrs Rhys Davids' *Psalms of the Sisters*).
7. Fausböll's Jātaka (Tr. by various hands under the editorship of E. B. Cowell).
8. Dhammapada (Tr. SBE, Vol. X).
9. Trenckner's Milindapañha (Tr. SBE, Vols. 35–36).
10. Buddhaghosa's Visuddhimagga (Ed. by Kosambi).
11. Buddhaghosa's Samanta-pāsādikā (Simon Hewavitarne Bequest Series, Colombo).
12. Other works of Buddhaghosa (PTS).
13. Oldenberg's Dīpavaṁso (Text and Translation).
14. Geiger's Cūḷavaṁsa (Text and Translation).
15. Geiger's Mahāvaṁso (Tr. by Turnour and by Geiger).
16. Gray's Buddhaghosuppatti (Text and Translation).

(b) *Original Texts* (*Sanskrit*)

1. Rig-veda, Atharva-veda, the Upaniṣads and the Smṛtis of Manu, Yājñvalkya and others.
2. Pāṇini's Aṣṭādhyāyī.
3. Patañjali's Mahābhāṣya.
4. Mahābhārata (Ed. Asiatic Society of Bengal and Bhandarkar Research Institute).
5. Padmapurāṇa (Anandasrama Sanskrit Series).
6. Śrīmad-bhāgavatam.
7. Divyāvadāna (Ed. by Cowell and Neil).
8. Mañjuśrī-mūlakalpa (Text and Translation in Jayaswal's *Imperial History of India*).
9. Mahāvastu (Ed. by Senart).
10. Aṣvaghoṣa's Buddhacaritam.

11. Aṣvaghoṣa's Mahāyāna-śraddhotpāda (Tr. Suzuki's *Awakening of Faith in the Mahāyāna*).
12. Nāgārjuna's Mūla-Madhyamaka-Kārikā (Tr. by Stcherbatsky).
13. Saddharma-puṇḍarīka (Tr. SBE, Vol. 21).
14. Suvarṇa-prabhāsa (Text and Tr. by Nanjio and Idzumi, Kyoto).
15. Asaṅga's Yogācāra-bhūmi-śāstra (Ed. by V. S. Bhattacarya).
16. Asaṅga's Mahāyāna-sūtrālaṅkāra (Ed. by Lévi).
17. Śāntideva's Śikṣā-samuccaya (Ed. by Bendall).
18. Śāntideva's Bodhicaryāvatāra (Ed. and Tr. by Śāntibhikṣu, Lucknow).
19. Kṣemendra's Avadāna-Kalpalatā (Ed. Bibliotheca Indica Series).
20. Daṇḍin's Daśakumāra-caritam (Ed. by Kale).
21. Somadeva's Kathā-sarit-sāgara (Ed. by Pandit).
22. Mādhavācārya's Sarva-darśana-saṁgraha (Tr. by Cowell in Trübner's Oriental Series).
23. Aṣṭa-sāhasrikā-prajñāpāramitā (Ed. Bibliotheca Indica Series).
24. Kauṭilya's Arthaśāstra (Ed. and Tr. by Sama Sastri).
25. Bhāvaviveka's Karatala ratna (Tr. from Chinese into Sanskrit in Visvabharati Studies).
26. Vasubandhu's Abhidharma-kośa (Ed. by Rahula Sankrityayana).
27. Āryadeva's Catuḥ-śataka (Ed. by V. S. Bhattacharya).
28. Vajra-cchedikā (Tr. by Gemmel in *Diamond Sūtra*).
29. Śūraṅgama Sūtra (Tr. by Goddard).
30. Śāṇḍilya's Bhakti-sūtra (SBH, Vol. VII).
31. Nārada's Bhakti-sūtra (SBH, Vol. VII).
32. Gouḍapāda's Āgama-śāstra (Ed. by V. S. Bhattacharya).
33. Bāṇa's Harṣa-caritam (Tr. by Cowell and Thomas).
34. Ānandagiri's Śaṅkara-Vijaya (Ed. by Jivānanda Vidyāsāgara).
35. Sandhyākara Nandī's Rāma-caritam (Ed. by R. C. Majumdar and others).

WORKS OF REFERENCE

1. Macdonell and Keith's *Vedic Index*.
2. Hastings' *Encyclopaedia of Religion and Ethics* (Abbr.: ERE).
3. *St. Petersburg Sanskrit Dictionary*.
4. Monier-Williams' *Sanskrit-English Dictionary*.
5. Childers' *Dictionary of the Pali Language*.
6. Rhys Davids and Stede's *Pali-English Dictionary* (PTS).
7. Trenckner's *Critical Pali Dictionary* (partly published).
8. Malalasekera's *Dictionary of Pali Proper Names*.
9. Malalasekera's (Ed.) *Encyclopaedia of Buddhism* (Volume of Specimen Articles).
10. Catalogue of Sanskrit Buddhist Manuscripts in the Bodleian Library.
11. Descriptive Catalogue of Mss in the Jaina Bhandar at Pattan (Baroda).

BOOKS CONSULTED (IN ALPHABETICAL ORDER)

1. Altekar. *Education in Ancient India*.
2. Bapat (Ed.). 2,500 *Years of Buddhism*.
3. Basak (Radha Govinda). *History of North-eastern India*.
4. Basham. *The Wonder that was India*.

5. (Bharatiya Vidyābhavan). *History and Culture of the Indian People.*
6. Bhattacharya (Binayatosh). *Mahayanic Pantheon.*
7. Bose (Phanindra Nath). *Indian Teachers in Buddhist Universities.*
8. *Cambridge History of India.*
9. Campbell. *The Mystics, Ascetics and Saints of India.*
10. Chattopadhyaya (Devi Prasad). *Lokāyata.*
11. Chattopadhyaya (Sudhakara). *Early History of Northern India.*
12. Conze. *Buddhism: its Essence and Development.*
13. Coon. *The History of Man.*
14. Cunningham. *Ancient Geography of India.*
15. Datta (Bhupendra Natha). *Hindu Law of Inheritance.*
16. Demiéville. *L'Origine des Sectes Bouddhiques.*
17. Deo. *History of Jaina Monachism.*
18. Deussen (Paul). *The Philosophy of the Upaniṣhads.*
19. Dikshit (T. R. C.). *The Sannyāsa Upaniṣads.*
20. Dutt (Nalinaksa). *Aspects of Mahāyāna Buddhism.*
21. Dutt (Nalinaksa) (Ed.). *Gilgit Mss.*
22. Dutt (Nalinaksa). *Early Monastic Buddhism.*
23. Dutt (Sukumar). *Early Buddhist Monachism.*
24. Dutt (Sukumar). *The Buddha and Five After-Centuries.*
25. Eliot. *Hinduism and Buddhism.*
26. Elliot and Dawson. *History of India as told by its Own Historians.*
27. Frauwallner. *The Earliest Vinaya and the Beginning of Vinaya Literature.*
28. Frauwallner. *On the Date of Vasubandhu.*
29. Ghurye. *Indian Sadhus.*
30. Hikato. *The Prajñāpāramitā Sūtra.*
31. Hobhouse. *Social Development.*
32. Hodiwala. *Studies in Indo-Muslim History.*
33. Hoebel. *The Law of Primitive Man.*
34. Höernle. *The Uvāsaga-dasāo.*
35. Humphreys (Chistmas). *Buddhism.*
36. James. *Myth and Ritual in the Ancient Near East.*
37. Jarret. *Ain-i-Akbari* (Asiatic Society of Bengal).
38. Jayaswal. *Manu and Yājñavalkya.*
39. Jayaswal. *Hindu Polity.*
40. Kale. *The History of the Dharmaśāstras.*
41. Keith. *Buddhist Philosophy.*
42. Keith. *History of Sanskrit Literature.*
43. Kern. *Manual of Indian Buddhism.*
44. Kimura. *An Historical Study of the terms Hīnayāna and Mahāyāna.*
45. Leff (Gordon). *Mediaeval Thought.*
46. Lal. *The History of the Khilijis.*
47. Law (B. C.). *Tribes in Ancient India.*
48. Law (B. C.). *History of Pali Literature.*
49. Law (B. C.). *Buddhaghosa.*
50. Law (B. C.) (Ed.). *Buddhistic Studies.*
51. Lin Yutang. *Wisdom of India.*
52. McCrindle. *Ancient India as described by Ptolemy.*
53. Mahadevan. *Gauḍapāda: A Study of Early Advaita.*
54. Maine (Sir Henry). *Ancient Law.*
55. Majumdar (Ramesh Chandra) (Ed.). *History of Bengal.*

56. Max Müller. *Origin of Religion.*
57. Mitra (R. C.). *Decline of Buddhism in India.*
58. Morgan. *Ancient Society.*
59. Mukherjee (Radha Kumud). *Ancient Indian Education.*
60. Pachow. *A Comparative Study of the Prātimokṣa.*
61. Panikkar. *A Survey of Indian History.*
62. Pargiter. *Dynasties of the Kali Yuga.*
63. *Periplus of the Erythrean Sea.*
64. Puri. *India in the Time of Patanjali.*
65. Radha Krishnan. *The Principal Upaniṣads.*
66. Radha Krishnan (Ed.). *History of Philosophy, Eastern and Western.*
67. Ragozin. *Vedic India* (Story of the Nations series).
68. Rahula (Walpola). *History of Buddhism in Ceylon.*
69. Ray (P. C.). *History of Chemistry in Ancient and Mediaeval India.*
70. Ray Chaudhuri (Hemchandra). *Political History of Ancient India.*
71. Rhys Davids. *Buddhist India.*
72. (Mrs) Rhys Davids. *Buddhist Psychology.*
73. Ray (Nihar Ranjan). *Theravāda Buddhism in Burma.*
74. Ray (Nihar Ranjan). *Bāṅgālīr Itihāsa* (in Bengali).
75. Sangharakshita. *Survey of Buddhism.*
76. Sarkar (K. L.). *Mīmāṁsā Rules of Interpretation.*
77. Scott (Archibald). *Buddhism and Christianity.*
78. Selbie. *Psychology of Religion.*
79. Smith (Vincent). *Early History of India.*
80. *Shorter Cambridge Mediaeval History.*
81. Stein (Aurel). *On Central Asian Tracks.*
82. Subbarao. *Personality of India.*
83. Surya Kant. *Kṣemendra Studies.*
84. Suzuki. *Studies in the Laṅkāvatāra Sūtra.*
85. Takakusu. Translation of Paramārtha's *Life of Vasubandhu in T'oung Pao.*
86. Thomas. *History of Buddhist Thought.*
87. Tucci. *On some Aspects of the Doctrines of Maitreya (nātha) and Asaṅga.*
88. Tylor. *Primitive Culture.*
89. Vriji. *Ancient History of Sourāshtra.*
90. Warren. *The Religions of the World and World Religion.*
91. Winternitz. *History of Indian Literature* (English Tr.).

CHINESE AND TIBETAN

(*Chinese*)

1. Beal's *Buddhist Records of the Western World* (Popular Edition in one volume).
2. Watters' *On Yuan Chawng.*
3. Beal's (Tr.). (Hwui-li's) *Life of Hiuen-Tsiang.*
4. Takakusu's (Tr.). *A Record of the Buddhist Religion.*
5. I-tsing's *Ta-Tang-shi-ku-fa-kao-sung-chuan.*

WORKS OF REFERENCE

1. Nanjio's *Catalogue of the Chinese Tripiṭaka.*
2. *Tables of Taisho* (Hobogirin, Tokyo, 1931).
3. *Taistro Issaikyo* (Japanese Ed. of the Chinese Tripiṭaka).

BOOKS CONSULTED (IN ALPHABETICAL ORDER)

1. Bagchi (P. C.). *Le Canon Bouddhique en Chine.*
2. Beal. *Catena of Buddhist Scriptures.*
3. Chavannes. *Memoire.*
4. Chou (Hsiang Kwang). *Indo-Chinese Relations.*
5. Chu Cha'an (Tr.). *The Sūtra of Forty-two Sections.*
6. Fitzgerald. *China: A Short Cultural History.*
7. Grousset. *In the Footsteps of the Buddha.*
8. Lo (Chia Luen). *Chinese Sources for Indian History* (published in the *Indian Archives,* 1949).
9. MacNair. *China.*
10. Suzuki. *Zen Buddhism and its Influence on Japanese Culture.*
11. Wieger. *A History of Religious Beliefs and Philosophical Opinions in China* (translated from French).

(*Tibetan*)

1. S. C. Das's Edition of Sumpa's *Pag-sam-jon-zang.*
2. Bu-ston's *History of Buddhism* (Tr. by Obermiller).
3. *The 'Blue Annals'* (Tr. by Roerich).
4. Tāranātha's *History of Buddhism* (Tr. by Schiefner).

WORKS OF REFERENCE

1. Cordier's *Catalogue du Fonds Tibetain de la Bibliotheque Nationale* (Parts II and III).
2. *A Complete Catalogue of the Tibetan Buddhist Canons* (published by Tohoku Imperial University).
3. *A Catalogue-Index of the Tibetan Buddhist Canons* (published by Tohoku Imperial University).

BOOKS CONSULTED (IN ALPHABETICAL ORDER)

1. Das (S. C.). *Indian Pandits in the Land of Snow.*
2. Datta (Bhupendranath). *Mystic Tales of Lāmā Tāranātha.*
3. David-Neel. *My Journey to Lhasa.*
4. Roerich's. *Biography of Dharmasvāmin.*
5. Vidyabhusana (S. C.). *Indian Logic: Mediaeval School.*
6. Waddell. *Buddhism in Tibet.*
7. Waddell. *Lhasa and its Mysteries.*

II. ARCHAEOLOGICAL SOURCES

INSCRIPTIONS, ARCHAEOLOGY, ART AND GENERAL

1. Marshall's *Taxila* (*and other Reports on excavations in the area*).
2. Marshall and Foucher's *Monuments of Sanchi.*
3. Hultzsch's *Inscriptions of Asoka* (Corpus Inscriptionum Indicarum).
4. A. C. Sen's *Asoka's Edicts.*
5. Lüders' *List of Brāhmī Inscriptions.*
6. Marshall's *The Bāgh Caves.*
7. Vallabhaji's *Historical Inscriptions of Gujerat.*
8. Fergusson and Burgess's *Cave-temples of India.*
9. Burgess's *Buddhist Cave-temples and their Inscriptions.*
10. Barua's *Barhut.*
11. Gray and Vincent's *Buddhist Cave-paintings at Tun-huang.*

12. Ghosh's *Guide to Nālandā.*
13. *Archaeology in India* (Ministry of Education, Government of India, 1950).
14. *Memoirs and Reports of the Archaeological Survey of India.*

JOURNALS AND PERIODICALS

1. *Journal of the Royal Asiatic Society.*
2. *Journal of the Asiatic Society of Bengal.*
3. *Indian Historical Journal.*
4. *Indian Culture* (*defunct*).
5. *Journal of Oriental Research, Madras.*
6. *Journal of the Bombay Branch of the Royal Asiatic Society.*
7. *Bulletin of the School of Oriental and African Studies*, University of London.
8. *Indian Archaeology* (periodical publication of the Archaeological Survey of India).
9. *Indian Antiquary.*
10. *East and West* (Organ of the IsMeo of Rome).

BOOKS CONSULTED (IN ALPHABETICAL ORDER)

1. Brown (Percy). *Indian Architecture.*
2. Grünwedel. *Buddhist Art in India.*
3. Kramrisch (Stella). *Indian Sculpture.*
4. Rowland (Thomas). *The Art and Architecture of India.*
5. Short (Ernest H.). *History of Religious Architecture.*

INDEX

(In Order of English Alphabet)

(Note—'ā' follows 'a'; 'ś' follows 's'; titles of books and texts in italics.)

'A'

'B'

'C'

'N'

'T'

GEORGE ALLEN & UNWIN LTD

London: 40 Museum Street, W.C.1

Auckland: 24 Wyndham Street
Bombay: 15 Graham Road, Ballard Estate, Bombay 1
Buenos Aires: Escritorio 454-459, Florida 165
Calcutta: 17 Chittaranjan Avenue, Calcutta 13
Cape Town: 109 Long Street
Hong Kong: F1/12 Mirador Mansions, Kowloon
Ibadan: P.O. Box 62
Karachi: Karachi Chambers, McLeod Road
Madras: Mohan Mansion, 38c Mount Road, Madras 6
Mexico: Villalongin 32-10, Piso, Mexico 5, D.F.
Nairobi: P.O. Box 12446
New Delhi: 13-14 Ajmeri Gate Extension, New Delhi 1
São Paulo: Avenida 9 de Julho 1138-Ap. 51
Singapore: 36c Prinsep Street, Singapore 7
Sydney, N.S.W.: Bradbury House, 55 York Street
Toronto: 91 Wellington Street West